ELECTRIC CAPITALISM

RECOLONISING AFRICA ON THE POWER GRID EDITED BY DAVID A McDONALD

Routledge
Taylor & Francis Group

LONDON AND NEW YORK

First published 2009 by Earthscan in the UK and USA

Published 2016 by Routledge
2 Park Square, Milton Park, Abingdon, Oxon OX14 4RN
711 Third Avenue, New York, NY 10017, USA

Routledge is an imprint of the Taylor & Francis Group, an informa business

First issued in paperback 2015

For a full list of publications please contact:
Earthscan

Notice:
Product or corporate names may be trademarks or registered trademarks, and are used only for identification and explanation without intent to infringe.

Earthscan publishes in association with the International Institute for Environment and Development.
A catalogue record for this book is available from the British Library.
Library of Congress Cataloging-in-Publication Data has been applied for.

The views expressed in this publication are those of the authors. They do not necessarily reflect the views or policies of the Human Sciences Research Council ('the Council') or indicate that the Council endorses the views of the authors. In quoting from this publication, readers are advised to attribute the source of the information to the individual author concerned and not to the Council.

Copyedited by Karen Press
Typeset by Christabel Hardacre
Cover by FUEL Design

ISBN 978-1-84407-714-4 (hbk)
ISBN 978-1-138-99342-6 (pbk)

Contents

List of tables and figures

Tables

Figures

Acronyms and abbreviations

ACHPR	African Charter on Human and Peoples' Rights
AEB	Atomic Energy Board (1949–1970)
AEC	Atomic Energy Corporation (1970–1999)
AES	Allied Energy Systems
AESNP	AES Nile Power
AfDB	African Development Bank
AFREC	African Energy Commission
AMEU	Association of Municipal Energy Undertakings
ANC	African National Congress
APF	Anti-Privatisation Forum
ARN	African Rivers Network
ASGISA	Accelerated and Shared Growth Initiative for South Africa
BEE	black economic empowerment
BPC	Botswana Power Corporation
BSA	British South Africa Company
CALS	Centre for Applied Legal Studies
CANSA	Campaign Against Neoliberalism in South Africa
CAPP	Central African Power Pool
CCS	carbon capture and storage
CCT	City of Cape Town
CDM	Clean Development Mechanism
CEDAW	Convention on the Elimination of All Forms of Discrimination Against Women
CEF	Central Energy Fund
CER	Certified Emissions Reduction
CESCR	United Nations Committee on Economic, Social and Cultural Rights
CHP	combined heat and power generation
COMESA	Common Market for Eastern and Southern Africa
COP	Conference of Parties
Cosatu	Congress of South African Trade Unions
CSIR	Council for Scientific and Industrial Research
DBSA	Development Bank of Southern Africa
DEAT	Department of Environmental Affairs and Tourism
DfID	Department for International Development
DG	Director-General
DME	Department of Minerals and Energy
DNA	Designated National Authority

DOE	Designated Operational Entity
DPE	Department of Public Enterprises
DPLG	Department of Provincial and Local Government
DRC	Democratic Republic of the Congo
DWAF	Department of Water Affairs and Forestry
EAC	East African Community
EAP&L	East African Power and Lighting Company
EAPP	East African Power Pool
ECB	Electricity Control Board
ECCAS	Economic Community of Central African States
ECOWAS	Economic Community of West African States
EDI	Electricity Distribution Industry
EdM	Electricidade de Moçambique
EDRC	Energy for Development Research Centre
EIA	environmental impact assessment
EIB	European Investment Bank
ENE	Empresa Naçional de Electricidade
ERA	Electricity Regulatory Authority
ERIC	Electricity Restructuring Inter-departmental Committee
ERP	Economic Recovery Programme
Escom/Eskom	Electricity Supply Commission
ESMAP	Energy Sector Management Assistance Programme
ESP	electrostatic precipitator
ET Africa	Eskom Telecommunications Africa
EU	European Union
EWG	Electricity Working Group
EWURA	Energy and Water Utilities Regulatory Authority
FBC	fluidised bed combustion
FBE	free basic electricity
FEMA	Forum for Energy Ministers of Africa
FGD	flue gas desulphurisation
GDP	gross domestic product
GE	genetically engineered
GEAR	Growth, Employment and Redistribution strategy
GECOL	General Electricity Company of Libya
GEPC	General Electric Power Company Limited
GESCO	Global Electricity Services Company
GHG	greenhouse gas
GHS	General Household Survey
GNU	Government of National Unity
GVA	Gross Value Added
HCB	Hidroelectrica de Cahora Bassa
HSRC	Human Sciences Research Council
IA	Implementation Agreement

ICA	Infrastructure Consortium for Africa
ICEM	International Federation of Chemical, Energy, Mine and General Workers' Unions
ICESCR	International Covenant on Economic, Social and Cultural Rights
ICRAF	World Agroforestry Centre
IDA	International Development Association
IDC	Industrial Development Corporation
IEA	International Energy Agency
IEP	Integrated Energy Planning
IFC	International Finance Corporation
IGCC	Integrated Gasification Combined Cycle
IGG	Inspector-General of Government
IHA	International Hydropower Association
IIEC	International Institute for Energy Conservation
IMF	International Monetary Fund
INEP	integrated national electrification programme
IPCC	Intergovernmental Panel on Climate Change
IPP	Independent power producer
IPPF	Infrastructure Project Preparation Facility
IPTL	Independent Power Tanzania Ltd
IRN	International Rivers Network
Iscor	Iron and Steel Corporation
IT	information technology
IUCN	World Conservation Union
JI	Joint Implementation
LNB	low-NO_x burners
MDG	Millennium Development Goal
MEC	minerals-energy complex
MIG	Municipal Infrastructure Grant
MIGA	Multilateral Investment Guarantee Agency
MP	Member of Parliament
MTEF	Medium Term Expenditure Framework
Naledi	National Labour and Economic Development Institute
NAPE	National Association of Professional Environmentalists
NBI	Nile Basin Initiative
NECSA	Nuclear Energy Corporation of South Africa
NELF	National Electrification Forum
NEMA	National Environmental Management Authority
NEP	national electrification programme
NEPA	National Electric Power Authority
NEPAD	New Partnership for Africa's Development
NERSA	National Energy Regulator of South Africa
NFA	National Framework Agreement
NGO	non-governmental organisation

NNR	National Nuclear Regulator
NP	National Party
NPT	Nuclear Non-Proliferation Treaty
NRM	National Resistance Movement
NUM	National Union of Mineworkers
NUMSA	National Union of Metalworkers
NWSC	National Water and Sewerage Corporation
O&M	operations and maintenance
OCGT	open cycle gas turbine
OECD	Organisation for Economic Co-operation and Development
OKM	Operation Khanyisa Movement
OPEC	Organisation of Petroleum Exporting Countries
PAC	Pan African Congress
PBMR	Pebble Bed Modular Reactor
PC	Pulverised Coal
PCF	Prototype Carbon Fund
PCRF	Phiri Concerned Residents Forum
PDD	Project Design Document
PEAC	Pool Energétique d'Afrique Centrale
PERD	public enterprise reform and divestiture
PF	Pulverised Fuel
PM	particulate matter
PPA	Power Purchase Agreement
PPIAF	Public Private Infrastructure Advisory Facility
PRG	Partial Risk Guarantee
PSRC	Parastatal Reform Commission
PV	photovoltaic
PWR	pressurised water reactor
RCEW	Rand Central Electric Works
RDP	Reconstruction and Development Programme
REA/REF	Rural Energy Agency and Fund
RED	Regional Electricity Distributor
RET	renewable energy technology
RMPSC	Rand Mines Power Supply Company
SABS	South African Bureau of Standards
SACAN	South African Climate Action Network
SACP	South African Communist Party
SADC	Southern African Development Community
Sanco	South African National Civics Organisation
SANERI	South African National Energy Research Institute
SAPM	Southern African Power Market
SAPP	Southern African Power Pool
SAR	South African Railways
SAR&H	South African Railways and Harbours

SCR	Soweto Concerned Residents
SECC	Soweto Electricity Crisis Committee
SHS	solar home system
SIDA	Swedish International Development Cooperation Agency
SNEL	Société Nationale d'Électricité
SNO	second national fixed line operator
SoeCo	State Owned Enterprises Company
Stats SA	Statistics South Africa
STS	Standard Transfer Specification
SWAPHEP	Society for Water and Public Health Protection
TANESCO	Tanzania Electricity Supply Company Limited
TAP	Trans Africa Projects
TNBS	Tanzanian National Bureau of Statistics
TNC	transnational corporation
TRC	Truth and Reconciliation Commission
TREC	tradeable renewable energy certificate
TSI	Technology Services International
UBOS	Uganda Bureau of Statistics
UCB	Uganda Commercial Bank
UCG	underground coal gasification
UDF	United Democratic Front
UEB	Uganda Electricity Board
UEDCL	Uganda Electricity Distribution Company Ltd
UEGCL	Uganda Electricity Generation Company Ltd
UETCL	Uganda Electricity Transmission Company Ltd
UN	United Nations
UNEA	UN-Energy/Africa
UNEP	United Nations Environment Programme
UNFCCC	United Nations Framework Convention on Climate Change
URC	Uranium Research Committee
US EIA	US Energy Information Administration
UWS	Uganda Wildlife Society
VFPC	Victoria Falls Power Company
VFTPC	Victoria Falls and Transvaal Power Company
WAPP	West African Power Pool
WCD	World Commission on Dams
Wesgro	Western Cape Investment and Trade Promotion Agency
Westcor	West African Power Corridor/Western Power Corridor Project
WSSD	World Summit on Sustainable Development
ZESA	Zimbabwe Electricity Supply Authority

Technical abbreviations

Ω	ohm
A	ampere
AC	alternating current
BTU	British thermal unit – a unit of energy used in the USA to describe the heat value (energy content) of fuels. A BTU is defined as the amount of heat required to raise the temperature of one pound of water by one degree Fahrenheit.
DC	direct current
GWh	gigawatt-hour
GWh(e)	gigawatt-hours of electrical output – nominally one-third the thermal output of a generator
HVAC	high-voltage AC
HVDC	high-voltage DC
J	joule
kWh	kilowatt-hour
m/s	metres per second
MW	megawatt
MW(e)	see GWh(e) above
rpm	revolutions per minute
TWh	terawatt-hour
V	volt
W	watt

Watt-hour units

1 watt-hour: one watt-hour is the amount of electricity expended by a one-watt load (e.g. a light bulb) drawing power for one hour. A 50-watt light bulb will consume 500 watt-hours of energy if left on for 10 hours.

10^3 watt-hours	= 1 kWh	(kilowatt-hour)
10^6 watt-hours	= 1 MWh	(megawatt-hour)
10^9 watt-hours	= 1 GWh	(gigawatt-hour)
10^{12} watt-hours	= 1 TWh	(terawatt-hour)

Acknowledgements

This book is a product of the Municipal Services Project, a multi-partner research, policy and educational initiative examining the restructuring of municipal services in southern Africa. The Project's central research interests are the impacts of decentralisation, privatisation, cost recovery and community participation on the delivery of basic services to the rural and urban poor, and how these reforms impact on public, industrial and mental health.

Research results are disseminated in the form of books, occasional papers, a project newsletter, academic articles, popular media, television documentaries and the internet (see www.queensu.ca/msp for a full listing of material).

Research partners include Rhodes University (South Africa), the International Labour Research and Information Group (South Africa), Queen's University (Canada), the Human Sciences Research Council (South Africa), Equinet (Zimbabwe), the South African Municipal Workers' Union, and the Canadian Union of Public Employees. The Project is funded by the International Development Research Centre of Canada.

My first thanks go to the contributors to this collection, most of whom have spent a lifetime researching and writing about these issues. It was a privilege to work with such talented and dedicated people.

I would also like to thank Garry Rosenberg of HSRC Press, who has been a supportive and professional publisher, committed to providing publicly accessible academic research. Peer review comments from anonymous referees on the original manuscript were very useful, as was input from Ben Fine and Vishnu Padayachee on some of the conceptual material.

Assistance from Karen Cocq and Derek Brine was instrumental in pulling together data for the Statistical Appendix. Thanks also to Toby Moorsom for help with literature reviews on (sub)imperialism and Mélanie Josée Davidson for technical assistance with some of the figures. Permission to reproduce various illustrations was kindly provided by FT Sparrow, Brian Bowen and Zuwei Yu of Purdue University, AV Smirnov of West Virginia University, the SASI Group (University of Sheffield) and Mark Newman (University of Michigan).

This book is dedicated to researchers and activists on the ground in (southern) Africa struggling for a more just and sustainable form of production and distribution of electricity on the continent. *A luta continua!*

INTRODUCTION

The importance of being electric

David A McDonald

This book is about the importance of electricity in Africa. Although much of the discussion focuses on South Africa (largely because that country dominates the electricity sector on the continent), there are important lessons to be learned for the continent as a whole, not least because of the aggressive expansion of South African capital and the South African state into other parts of Africa to develop and control the electricity market.

At the centre of this discussion is a paradox: Africa is the most under-supplied region in the world when it comes to electricity, but its economies are utterly dependent on it. This contradiction is explained in part by the enormous inequalities in electricity access, with mining and industry receiving abundant supplies of cheap power whilst more than 80 per cent of the continent's residents remain off the power grid (see the maps in Appendix 2 for comparisons within Africa and with other regions of the world).

Africa is not unique in this respect, but the inequities of infrastructure investments and decision-making control are particularly pronounced here – especially in South Africa – due to the inherent unevenness of what I will call 'electric capitalism'. I discuss this phrase at length in Chapter 1, outlining both its theoretical and metaphorical utility (and limitations). My central argument is that electricity has become an integral part of all capitalist activity and that we can best understand the inequities of its availability and affordability by looking at the (neo-liberal) market dynamics within which it operates. Electricity is obviously not the only factor to consider when studying capitalism on the continent, but given the electricity-intensive nature of the region's economies, and massive plans for electricity expansion, it is essential to investigate how electricity fits into the larger dynamics of capitalist accumulation and crisis in Africa.

Chapter 1 also discusses the use of the phrase 'recolonising Africa', which forms part of the subtitle of this book. An anticipated doubling of electricity needs within South Africa over the next 20 years, coupled with growing foreign direct investment on the continent by South African capital, has led to plans for a rapid expansion of electricity generation and distribution capacity on a regional, and even continental, scale. South African capital (public and private) is not the only party interested in this electricity expansion – American, European and Asian firms are also active in Africa – but South Africa is particularly dependent on this electric power capacity growth, and is well poised to direct and control this particular set of resources.

In many ways the rush to build electricity capacity today is akin to the 19th-century 'scramble for Africa', with electricity grid lines replacing the colonial railway lines of yesteryear. This is not a perfect analogy, theoretically or empirically, but it does serve to convey both the scale and the speed at which these sectoral developments are taking place and their potential long-term impacts on the continent. From concrete investments in hydro-power plants and distribution lines, to the more abstract diffusion of neo-liberal ideology and management strategies, South Africa is at the forefront of a recolonisation of the continent, from 'the bottom up'.

Not all the chapters in this book utilise these conceptual frameworks. Nor do they all discuss developments in the electricity sector outside South Africa. Collectively, however, the chapters offer an in-depth review of key electricity restructuring developments in the southern African region, shedding light on the larger social, economic, ideological and spatial dynamics shaping electricity reforms elsewhere on the continent – with relevance, it is hoped, for an understanding of developments in this sector in other parts of the world.

This is a momentous time in the electricity sector in South and southern Africa. The multi-billion dollar expenditures planned over the next 20 years constitute the most significant investments ever made in electricity on the continent, with far-reaching consequences affecting the lives of millions of people. The South African state has made the electricity sector one of its key development objectives, promising to invest R150 billion in infrastructure over the next five years alone, dwarfing all other sectoral state expenditures.

In some respects, these are welcome and long overdue investments. As the voluminous literature on electricity attests, there is a wide range of potential 'goods' associated with the expansion and upgrading of electricity services, and there are millions of people in South and southern Africa who would benefit from expanded electricity services.

Much work has been done to explore the positive relationships between human well-being and electricity consumption. Though not exhaustive, Table 1 summarises some of these benefits, as they relate to the United Nations' Millennium Development Goals (MDGs).

But so, too, is there a long list of potential 'bads' associated with electricity, with many of the items listed in Table 1 having a possible negative flip side. As many of the chapters in this book attest, 'business as usual' in the electricity sector will be an environmental catastrophe in much of Africa. From the dirty coal-fired electricity generation stations of South Africa to nuclear waste, to the flooding, siltation and loss of biodiversity associated with hydro-electric dam developments, an unaltered electricity growth path would counter many potential gains. 'Business as usual' would also mean social oppression and forced relocation for hundreds of thousands of people who find themselves in the wake of these infrastructural developments.

Table 1: Benefits of electricity as they relate to the Millennium Development Goals

Millennium Development Goal	Benefits of electricity
Eradicate extreme poverty and hunger (MDG-1)	Refrigeration Better cooking methods Easier fuel-gathering Irrigation (through pumping) Job creation
Achieve universal primary education (MDG-2)	Allows for study after dark. Attracts teachers to rural areas. Allows for use of latest media. Frees up children's time from household and other chores to attend school.
Promote gender equality and empower women (MDG-3)	'Traditional' women's tasks become easier. Lighting of streets makes travelling safer. Access to education may increase as time spent gathering fuel and water, and cooking, decreases. Reduces indoor air pollution.
Reduce child mortality (MDG-4)	Permits access to better services and improved hospitals. Reduces indoor air pollution. Frees up time for parents to spend with their children. Allows for better water and effluent treatment stations.
Improve maternal health (MDG-5)	Enables access to better services and improved hospitals, including operating theatres. Refrigeration increases the number of tests and medication/vaccines that can be stored. Allows for use of electronic equipment for pre- and post-natal care and monitoring.
Combat HIV/AIDS, malaria and other diseases (MDG-6)	Allows for better-equipped medical facilities. Local clinics can be equipped with modern treatments and vaccinations due to refrigeration.
Ensure environmental sustainability (MDG-7)	Potential renewable sources of electricity can be developed. Deforestation and soil erosion can be reduced.

Sources: This summary is drawn largely from Flavin and Hull Aeck (2006: 12) but there is a wealth of literature on the topic (see for example Barnes 1997; Barnes & Floor 1996; Ghanadan 2004; Ha & Porcaro 2005; Hulscher & Hommes 1992; Munasinghe 1989; Pasternak 2000; Rehfuess et al. 2007; Spalding-Fecher 2003; UN Energy 2005; World Bank n.d.)

But even if infrastructure is built in ways that minimise or avoid these social and environmental problems, there is a host of other operational inequities which can arise from electricity's production and distribution. Pricing and user fees can make electricity unaffordable for many, forcing people to under-consume and/or practise unsafe energy methods, once again undermining potential benefits. Management systems (such as privatisation) can also create multi-tiered delivery systems with vastly different degrees of quality. Both can serve to 'contain' people in poverty, limiting expectations and restricting access to this important resource.

We must also ask for what purpose electricity is being produced. Although electricity can undoubtedly make life easier, more interesting and more pleasurable, at what point is it simply a vehicle for promoting consumption? Light bulbs, computers and music systems are conveniences that many of us enjoy, but if electricity is simply a vehicle for promoting economic growth ('growth for growth's sake', in Marx's terms), it is also problematic.

Not all of electricity's 'goods' and 'bads' are discussed in this book. Some are taken up in detail while others are merely touched upon. Nevertheless, the chapters included here provide powerful evidence of an electricity restructuring programme in South and southern Africa gone terribly wrong – one that generates enormous 'goods' for a relative few, while perpetuating poverty, illness, social exclusion and environmental decay for many, and serving as little more than a platform for economic growth for capital.

This is not to suggest that there have not been important gains made on the electricity front, particularly in South Africa. Millions of South African households have been connected to the grid since the end of apartheid and there have been more progressive systems of pricing (including 'lifeline' tariffs) put in place.

It is the larger picture that we are after here, however – a more global theoretical and empirical review that cuts through the rhetoric of the 'development state'. Our intention is to get beyond superficial numbers to explore the nature of expenditures taking place, the rationale for electricity infrastructure investments, the types of technologies being employed and the real beneficiaries of massive public spending.

In this regard it is, indeed, largely 'business as usual' in South Africa. The mining and industry sectors remain the primary beneficiaries of state electricity expenditures, but these firms are joined by a growing (urban) services sector that has begun to dominate the South African economy. These firms, along with the transnational elites that run them, have begun to reshape the electricity sector in important ways, including demands for its liberalisation, such as various forms of privatisation. I refer to this new dynamic in Chapter 1 as the 'minerals–energy complex (MEC)-*plus*', an expansion on a MEC conceptual apparatus developed by Fine and Rustomjee (1996) in their seminal work on the subject in the 1990s.

Chapters 2 and 3 provide a detailed look at Eskom – the large, state-owned electricity generator and distributor in South Africa. One of the largest electricity utilities in the world, Eskom is the institutional giant on the continent, driving and shaping much of the restructuring currently taking place, in collaboration with the South African state and South African capital. In Chapter 2, Leonard Gentle provides an historical overview of Escom/Eskom, from its initial days as a nationalised, Keynesian entity through to its role as a state- and class-building tool during apartheid, and finally to its early stages of neo-liberal reform shortly before the dismantling of formal apartheid. What Gentle makes clear is the way in which Escom (as it was called before the Afrikaans acronym shift) facilitated capitalist growth from its very inception. He shows that, despite shifts in state ideology, it continued to play this role for decades, with as much continuity as difference in its operational mandate and ideological orientation during apartheid and after.

In Chapter 3, Stephen Greenberg looks at reforms in Eskom since 1994, with a focus on its deepening commercialisation and its forays into the rest of the continent. Although scaled back somewhat after initial failures outside South Africa with Eskom Enterprises, Eskom as a whole remains a major player in the electricity sector on the continent, offering human and capital resources that overwhelm all other players and which work to leverage open new electricity markets.

Chapter 4, by Richard Worthington, looks at the coal-fired electricity market in South Africa. With approximately 90 per cent of South Africa's current electricity production coming from (dirty) coal-fired stations – helping to make South Africa one of the worst contributors to greenhouse gas emissions in the world on a per capita basis – coal will remain a dominant feature of the South African electricity landscape for many years to come. There is also considerable potential for expansion in the region. Efforts to clean the industry are examined, but business-as-usual would appear to be the most likely trajectory.

Chapter 5 examines the potential for hydro-electric developments in the region, with a particular focus on Inga in the Democratic Republic of the Congo. Located on the Congo River, downstream from Kinshasa, current and future hydro developments at Inga represent the largest single-point source of hydro-electricity in the world (with some 100 000 megawatts of potential energy). This is the holy grail of electricity development in Africa, with the potential to more than double electricity capacity on the continent. It also serves as the pivot for a planned continental energy grid that could see electricity exported throughout Africa and as far away as Europe and the Middle East. Terri Hathaway and Lori Pottinger explore these developments.

Nuclear energy is the subject of David Fig's analysis in Chapter 6. With only one nuclear power generating plant on the continent, near Cape Town, Africa is a small global player in this subsector. But with concerns over greenhouse gas emissions, and efforts to build new, home-grown 'pebble bed' technology in South Africa, nuclear power is back on the agenda in a significant way, with the South African state investing billions of rands in research and development and with plans for a new commissioned station within the next 5–10 years. Links to the nuclear weapons industry remain, however, and Fig paints a grim picture of secrecy and lies that hark back to the bad old days of apartheid and the Cold War.

Liz McDaid explores the potential for 'alternative' sources of electricity in Chapter 7. Although significant potential for such energy sources exists in southern Africa in particular – with its abundant supplies of sun and wind – little has been done to invest in the technologies, infrastructure or management systems required to roll them out on a large scale, once again suggesting 'business as usual' for capital accumulation patterns in the region when it comes to electricity. Lip service is paid to alternative energy by the South African state, but this serves more to illustrate the attempts by the African National Congress (ANC) to portray themselves as 'progressive' and 'developmental' on the environmental front while moving ahead with a 'business as usual' agenda.

Chapter 8 moves us more directly into the realm of electricity policy, with a look at prepaid electricity meters. South Africa has become a continental and world leader in this technology, exporting millions of prepaid meters around the globe. Peter van Heusden looks specifically at the experience of the City of Cape Town, but he offers a history of prepaid meters in South Africa as a whole and highlights their role in neo-liberal cost recovery regimes and the inherently unfair and unequal nature of the way they operate, forcing low-income families to cut themselves off from electricity by terminating their consumption at the point when they can no longer afford to buy more.

Greg Ruiters examines the South African government's 'free basic electricity' programme in Chapter 9. Introduced as an ANC election promise in 2000, free basic electricity in the form of a free block of 50 kilowatt-hours (kWh) of electricity per household per month has been slowly rolled out by the state; it is designed to ensure access to a 'lifeline' supply of electricity for all. Ruiters criticises the policy for being too stingy in its allocation and uneven in its rollout. Most importantly, he argues that 'free electricity' has been used as a neo-liberal ploy to contain low-income consumption of electricity at a 'basic' level, forcing households which consume more than 50 kWh per month to pay relatively high prices for consumption above this level, and thus failing to substantively address the enormous inequalities in electricity access in the country.

Chapter 10 looks at electricity-related legislative and constitutional developments in South Africa and explores how socio-economic rights are affected by electricity commercialisation. Constitutional expert Jackie Dugard notes that there are no explicit constitutionally defined rights to electricity, as there are for water and other amenities, but argues that the state is nonetheless responsible for ensuring adequate access to and affordability of safe and reliable supplies of energy, and that local and national authorities have failed to deliver on these commitments in many respects.

In Chapter 11, Wendy Annecke looks specifically at the gendered nature of electricity inequities in South(ern) Africa, arguing that women and girls bear the brunt of unequal electricity access – an injustice made worse by the commercialisation of the sector and by hardline policies of cost recovery, making the difficult lives of poor, black women even harder.

Prishani Naidoo and Ahmed Veriava write about social movements in the electricity sector in Chapter 12, with a focus on the sector's most active organisation in South

Africa, the Soweto Electricity Crisis Committee (SECC). Once the epicentre of electricity activism in the country (and arguably on the continent), the SECC has been through difficult times of late, an indication of a weak resource base for anti-privatisation activist organisations, as well as differences of opinion on activist strategy. Whether the anti-privatisation movement in South Africa will learn and strengthen from these experiences, or remain fragmented, remains to be seen, but Naidoo and Veriava's review provides an insightful look into one of the most dynamic social movements in Africa.

Chapter 13 by Patrick Bond and Graham Erion tackles the controversial world of carbon trading. First introduced in Europe, carbon trading is being hailed by neo-liberal pundits around the world as an essential way to reduce global greenhouse gas emissions. The South African state has latched onto this policy framework as well, but Bond and Erion demonstrate its hollow conceptual and empirical foundations, arguing that carbon trading allows industry to eat its cake and have it too, doing little or nothing to address South Africa's inordinately high greenhouse gas emission level, much of it from (coal-fired) electricity production.

Chapters 14 and 15, by Christopher Gore and Rebecca Ghanadan respectively, provide detailed reviews of the electricity sectors in Uganda and Tanzania, highlighting their links to powerful South African and other international interests. In both cases we see the adoption of neo-liberal investment and management strategies, with electricity provision and pricing in these two countries being just as unequal as it is in South Africa. These two case studies are not intended as proxies for the rest of the continent, but they do provide concrete evidence of the kinds of managerial colonisation referred to above that is sweeping the electricity sector in Africa (as it is with other core public services).

The concluding chapter provides a brief discussion of possible alternative visions for electricity developments in South Africa and on the continent as a whole. It is not intended to be comprehensive in geographical scope or strategic detail but it does highlight the need (and potential) for more sustainable, democratic and equitable forms of electricity production. Here it is argued that there are two basic options for progressive activists. The first is to take a reformist approach to the sector, looking for ways to ameliorate the worst excesses of unequal pricing, investments and environmental decay, such as lobbying states to raise free basic supplies of electricity, putting an end to cut-offs to low-income households, banning prepaid meters and introducing more renewable energy technologies. None of these tasks will be easy, but gains have already been made in some areas and there is support across a wide spectrum of groups for many of these initiatives.

But it can also be argued that 'electric capitalism' is inherently unequal and unsustainable, requiring a much more radical anti-capitalist approach to reforms in the sector. The latter part of Chapter 16 explores these ideas and the potential that exists for these more fundamental changes. The epilogue briefly considers changes that have taken place in the electricity sector since the chapters of this book were first drafted.

Finally, two appendices are included in the book. Appendix 1 by Derek Brine, is called 'Electricity 101'; it provides a lay introduction to what electricity is, how it is generated and distributed, and the technical options that exist for its production. Though taken for granted by many of us, electricity is an enormously complex entity which poses unique technical challenges – all with important social, economic, spatial and environmental implications. Most important, perhaps, is the fact that electricity cannot be stored. Unlike water, which can be treated and stockpiled until it is needed, electricity must (with some exceptions) be used the instant it is generated, creating capacity challenges that do not exist with other 'commodities'.

Having said that, electricity production is a relatively straightforward technical process that has changed little in its core operating principles since the late 1800s. This technical appendix illustrates both the complexities and the simplicities of electricity, demystifying its physical properties and shedding light on the potential and limitations of this special resource.

Appendix 2 provides a visual comparative reference for the electricity sector on the African continent, illustrating differences within Africa and between Africa and the rest of the world. Note that colour versions of these maps plus an overview of key electricity and energy statistics are available for free download at http://www.hsrcpress.ac.za/product.php?productid=2243&cat=0&page=1&featured. Please click on the file 'Electronic Appendix: Statistical data'.

A note on racial terminology

Although apartheid-era racial classifications are a social construct with no objective significance, the legacies of apartheid and the heavy correlation between race and class in South(ern) Africa are such that racial classifications remain an integral part of political analysis. There are, however, many different versions of racial terminology, and a brief explanation of the use of terms in this book is in order. Following the tradition of the anti-apartheid movement, 'African', 'coloured', 'Asian' and 'white' will be used to describe the four major racial categories of apartheid South Africa, with the most common use of upper and lower case letters being adopted. The term 'black' is employed to refer to Africans, coloureds and Asians as a whole, in recognition of their common oppression under apartheid.

In conclusion, it must be noted that much is at stake in the electricity restructuring processes taking place in southern Africa at the moment. From public health to gender relations, environmental sustainability, definitions of the state, the rights of citizens, the role of social movements, African integration, and the future trajectory of capitalism on the continent, electricity restructuring represents one of the most important contemporary developments in Africa. It is hoped that this volume will contribute theoretically and practically to this critical debate.

References

Barnes DF (1997) Tackling the rural energy problem in developing countries. *Finance & Development* 34: 11–15

Barnes DF & Floor WM (1996) Rural energy in developing countries: A challenge for economic development. *Annual Review of Energy and the Environment* 21: 497–530

Fine B & Rustomjee Z (1996) *The political economy of South Africa: From minerals–energy complex to industrialisation.* London: Hurst & Company

Flavin C & Hull Aeck M (2006) *Energy for development: The potential role for renewable energy in meeting Millennium Development Goals.* Washington DC: Worldwatch Institute

Ghanadan R (2004) Electricity reform in developing and transition countries: A reappraisal. *Energy* 31(6/7): 815–844

Ha P & Porcaro J (2005) Energy and the Millennium Development Goals: The impact of rural energy services on development. *Journal of International Affairs* 58(2): 193–209

Hulscher WS & Hommes EW (1992) Energy for sustainable rural development. *Energy Policy* 20(6): 527–532

Munasinghe M (1989) Power for development: Electricity in the third world. *Institution of Electrical Engineers Review* 35(3): 101–105

Pasternak AD (2000) *Global energy futures and human development: A framework for analysis.* Washington: US Department of Energy, Lawrence Livermore National Laboratory

Rehfuess E, Mehta S & Pruss-Uston A (2007) Assessing household solid fuel use: Multiple implications for development. *Environmental Health Perspectives* 114(3): 373–378

Spalding-Fecher R (2003) Electricity and externalities in South Africa. *Energy Policy* 31(8): 721–735

UN-Energy (2005) *The energy challenge for achieving the Millennium Development Goals.* United Nations. Accessed 20 December 2007, http://esa.un.org/un-energy/pdf/UN-ENRG%20paper.pdf

World Bank (n.d.) *Rural energy and development for two billion people: Meeting the challenge for rural energy and development.* Accessed 20 December 2007, http://siteresources.worldbank.org/INTENERGY/Resources/Rural_Energy_Development_Paper_Improving_Energy_Supplies.pdf

Electric capitalism: Conceptualising electricity and capital accumulation in (South) Africa

David A McDonald

> On a global scale, the South African economy is uniquely dependent on electricity and is uniquely electricity-intensive. (Fine & Rustomjee 1996: 8)

> A short circuit on a high-voltage transmission line near Cape Town automatically tripped the reactor's single functioning generator, resulting in one of the worst crises in South Africa's post-apartheid history...
> [A] catastrophe. (Hammer 2006)

Power failures in Cape Town and elsewhere in South Africa in late 2005 and early 2006 made front-page news across the country for months. After decades of reliable, and seemingly endless, supplies of cheap electric power, white urban residents and South African industry were faced with their first real electricity 'crisis'.

Black South Africans had experienced electricity crises for most of their lives, of course, having been left off the power grid entirely or having been provided with services of such low quality, or at such high prices, as to effectively make electricity an inaccessible luxury good.

This latter situation is changing. Efforts to electrify townships and rural areas began in the 1980s and accelerated dramatically after the end of apartheid. In fact, South Africa has electrified low-income areas on a scale, and at a pace, that is unprecedented in modern history. Nevertheless, there are still major disparities in electricity access and affordability along race and class lines.

The electricity experiences of both the rich and the poor are relevant to this chapter. On the one hand, power outages in suburban and commercial South Africa reveal the dependence of the country's economy, and middle-class lifestyles, on electricity. On the other hand, ongoing inequalities in electricity access reveal just how uneven capitalist development has been in post-apartheid South Africa and how electricity provision exemplifies the inherently unequal nature of neo-liberal market economies.

I will discuss both of these points below, through the lens of what I call 'electric capitalism'. This is an odd turn of phrase, however, and one that requires some careful explanation. The first section of the chapter describes what is meant by the term and discusses how it helps us understand the electricity sector in particular, and capital accumulation in the region more generally.

It is not my intent to suggest a new theoretical framework for understanding market economies. My aim is to update and enrich a conceptual framework on the 'minerals–energy complex' (MEC) developed by Fine and Rustomjee (1996) in the 1990s, while at the same time applying what I see as a useful metaphor to the metabolism of contemporary capitalism. With this in mind, my conceptual framework is both narrower and broader than that of Fine and Rustomjee. It is *narrower* in the sense that I focus solely on the electricity sector. Though other direct energy sources (such as coal and oil) are obviously important in South Africa, and their links to mining are still critical, I will not be discussing these other energy sectors in detail – though it is worth noting that electricity was, according to the Department of Minerals and Energy (DME), only the third-largest energy carrier by demand in 2000, after liquid fuels and coal (MDE 2003a: 7). Readers are also referred to the chapter on coal-fired electricity in this volume (Chapter 4) which provides a detailed background on coal mining in South Africa.

My framework is *broader* than that of Fine and Rustomjee in that it brings new sectors to the analysis (urban producer services in particular), explores the expansion of the electricity grid to black areas of the country (still in its infancy in 1996), and looks at the commercialisation and fragmentation of the electricity sector as a result of neo-liberal restructuring in the South African economy over the past 15 years. This new analytical framework I will call the 'MEC-plus'.

Finally, I will expand the Fine and Rustomjee analysis to a more regional and continental level, with possible relevance for electricity sectors in other parts of the world. This geographic expansion is the reason for the subtitle of this book – *Recolonising Africa on the Power Grid* – and is intended to reflect the fact that increasing demand for electricity in South Africa, and the expansion of South African capital into the region, are leading to the development of electricity generation and transmission infrastructure in the rest of Africa. As the electricity giant on the continent, South Africa's appetite for electricity has created something of a 'scramble' for the continent's electricity resources, with the transmission lines of today comparable to the colonial railway lines of the late 1800s and early 1900s, physically and symbolically.

This recolonisation along the power grid also has implications for the spread of neo-liberalism in the region. The electricity sector is not solely responsible for this ideological imperialism, but the expansion of electricity is illustrative of the kinds of micro- and macro-mechanisms of neo-liberal control being imposed around the world: from the disciplinary powers of prepaid electricity meters to the private-sector conditionalities of international financial institutions in infrastructure development, the electricity sector in southern Africa exemplifies the cutting edge of neo-liberal reform.

The South African state and South African capital are responsible for many of these developments, making for a recolonisation of the continent from 'the bottom up'. But this analysis must be tempered by the fact that powerful European and North American interests are at play in the electricity (and related) sectors, and that China is an increasingly significant presence on the continent as well. The latter may prove to be the biggest factor in the future, and I close the chapter with some discussion of how this appears to be playing itself out at the moment.

These American/European/Asian forces notwithstanding, I will argue that South African capital – along with the South African state (in its various manifestations) – is positioning itself to dominate the electricity sector in southern Africa, and that cheap and reliable electricity provision is increasingly central to all forms of capitalist accumulation in the region. And although efforts to extend services to low-income households in South Africa and beyond are motivated in part by a commitment to social justice (and have some Keynesian-welfare aspects to them), these 'pro-poor' policies are undermined by the reality of aggressive cost recovery practices directed at low-income families and massive subsidies for private capital and upper-income (largely white) households.

The fact that these changes are being made within new neo-liberal ideological, discursive and institutional frameworks serves to disguise the real beneficiaries of electricity reforms while at the same time opening up new terrains and spaces of accumulation. In other words, the much lauded restructuring and expansion of the electricity sector in South Africa is largely 'business as usual', albeit with new and important twists, and with implications that extend well beyond the borders of South Africa.

Why 'electric capitalism'?

Why use the phrase 'electric capitalism'? It is not an unproblematic concept. For one thing, electricity is not 'necessary' for capitalism. Capitalism began before the advent of electricity, and it continues to operate – at least indirectly – in many parts of the world without it. The fact that fewer than 20 per cent of Africans have access to electricity – and as few as 2 per cent in many rural areas (Madamombe 2005) – and yet the vast majority of Africa's citizens are captured to some degree by local and global market economies, is illustrative of this point.

Electricity is also substitutable. Unlike water, which has no surrogate, alternative sources of energy exist and are widely used around the world: biomass, oil, natural gas, draft power, etc. Although electricity is a unique form of energy, and increasingly required for certain economic activities (a point we return to), people can and do lead productive and healthy lives without it.

Nor is electricity the only input central to the machinery of capitalism. Oil is perhaps an even more critical requirement than electricity for capitalist production. One could, therefore, write about 'oil capitalism' (as indeed many have; see for example Apter 2005; Rutledge 2006; SLM 2005). So, too, could one write of water capitalism, wood capitalism, iron capitalism or any other basic, difficult-to-substitute-for input to the market economy.

Furthermore, the use (and abuse) of electricity is not restricted to neo-liberal capitalist modes of production. It has been employed in radically different socio-economic projects, from German fascism to Soviet communism to contemporary 'state capitalism' in China, all with their own demands and (il)logics when it comes to the use of electricity.

Finally, had electricity not been invented, capitalism would simply have evolved in different ways. In this sense, electricity is a fluke of history, not an ontological category in the development of capitalist relations of production. 'Electric capitalism' has no unique conceptual claim to understanding the dynamics of capitalist production.

And yet, there is something remarkably synergistic about electricity and capitalism. Metaphorically at least, electricity symbolises the 'creative destruction' of capitalism: the rapid development and devaluation of products and productive systems that change at the speed of light, all in the name of remaining one step ahead of the competition.

The mystifying physical nature of electricity is also emblematic of capitalism. Electricity's status as both matter and non-matter (see Appendix 1 in this volume) makes it a difficult phenomenon to understand conceptually. In the same way that theoretical physics is required for comprehension of the paradoxical characteristics of electricity, so too do we need social theory to comprehend the true nature of capitalism: the 'difference between essence and appearance', as Karl Marx put it, the 'mystification' of capital (in *Grundrisse*, as cited in Cohen 1972: 188). Theory may not 'dissipate the mist' through which commodity relations are observed, but it can help us understand the capitalist world within which we live. Perhaps this is why both Marx and Engels were so fascinated by theoretical issues related to electricity (see, for example, Engels's extensive engagement with this topic in his manuscripts for 'Dialectics of Nature').[1]

Metaphors aside, there are also strong material reasons to draw links between electricity and market economies. For one, electricity has become so integrated with capitalist production that it has effectively become 'essential' to the market. Virtually all forms of contemporary industrial, manufacturing and service activity require electricity to operate. Although some firms and individuals can and do function without it, it is impossible to compete meaningfully in today's global economy without access to (cheap and reliable) electric power.

The spread of electronics into products and production systems has served to deepen this reliance. On the production side, computer-aided manufacturing and micro-electronics have transformed industrial and manufacturing practices over the past three decades. The use of electronic technologies varies from place to place –

and there are debates as to whether electronics has made production systems more or less electricity-intensive (Doms 1993; Horowitz 2004; Ross 1992; USEPA 2007) – but the rapid and widespread increase in their use, and their importance to competitiveness, is indisputable. As a result, industry is becoming increasingly reliant on electricity as a 'premium' source of energy and 'generating and delivering quality power is an integral and essential component of the silicon world' (Azar 2000: 201). The same applies to the services sector, which is even more reliant on electricity for information technology (IT) and communications and would appear to be becoming more electricity-intensive in its production systems (Collard et al. 2005).

The same applies to consumer products. From iPods to microwave ovens to home computers, electricity demand and electricity dependency have increased dramatically over the past three decades. One research report in the late 1990s in the USA suggested that 'miscellaneous' energy demands from household consumer products would increase by 50 per cent between 1996 and 2010, 'accounting for almost all forecasted growth in residential electricity use' in that country (EETD 1998). Debates rage about how much electricity is consumed by these products – especially by computers (Koomey et al. 2002) – but few would deny that the proportion of consumer products dependent on electricity has gone up significantly and will probably continue to do so for the foreseeable future, creating increased demands for electricity generation, if not electricity intensity.

Electricity may not be an *innate* feature of capitalist modes of production but it has become an essential one, providing a stable – yet dynamic – platform upon which to build new production systems and products that lend themselves to the rapid pace of change in contemporary global markets. And as the capitalist centre of gravity shifts towards the services sector (particularly finance), electricity becomes an even more indispensable input, heightening pressures for cheap and reliable supplies of electric power from the 'commanding heights' of this new global economy and the transnational elites that run it.

These are largely empirical observations, however. Theoretical weight for this position can be drawn from conceptual insights into the over-accumulation of capital (Harvey 1982). Several points are of relevance here. The first relates to the general argument about the capital intensivity of market production. One of the fundamental 'laws' of capitalist competition is that it compels all firms to invest in labour-saving technology to survive. This technology need not be electricity-related, but practice over the past century has shown an increasing reliance on electronics, effectively making electricity a structural feature of capital intensivity.

Eventually, these competitive pressures lead to over-investment in capital stock. Although flexible micro-electronics has reduced some of the rigidity of older industrial models of production, the constant introduction of new products and incessant investments in profit-seeking strategies inevitably result in a 'crisis of over-accumulation' (in the form of commodity, money or productive capital).

When combined with a growing pool of displaced labour, this over-investment creates a situation where it is no longer possible to bring all goods produced to the market profitably. This over-accumulation typically takes place in subsectors of the economy, creating bottlenecks and disruptions here and there, but slowly spreading to the broader national/international economy, eventually creating a more general accumulation crisis (with the Depression of the 1930s being the most significant and expansive thus far).

As over-accumulation begins to set in, as structural bottlenecks emerge, and as profit rates fall in the productive sectors of the economy, 'capitalists begin to shift their investable funds out of reinvestment in plant, equipment and labour power and instead seek refuge in financial assets' (Bond 1999: 11). As a result, finance capital enriches itself at the expense of other forms of capital during periods of devaluation crisis, setting in train a long-term (and accelerating) cycle of strengthening its position vis-à-vis other factions of capital *because of* the boom-and-bust process. These dynamics do not result in an automatic or uncontested rise in power for finance capital – struggles take place within and between capitals and these struggles differ temporally and spatially – but the overall trend is towards its valorisation.

The implications of these developments for the electricity sector are that finance capital becomes an increasingly dominant player in decision-making about public and private investments in infrastructure spending, in what Harvey (1982) calls the 'spatial fix' of a capitalist crisis. Here we see investments in the built environment that are, quite literally, fixed into the ground, without which renewed rounds of capital accumulation would be difficult, if not impossible, to attain. Airports, conference centres, 'smart buildings' and gated housing developments are examples of these spatial fixes – catering to new regimes of capital accumulation and the socio-spatial and economic demands of those that control them.

Electricity infrastructure is an excellent example of these spatial fixes, and one that is increasingly central to renewed capitalist production and accumulation. Electricity may not loom large in every accumulation crisis, but it often plays a critical role in the rebuilding of the productive assets required for reconfigured accumulation regimes: new power plants for increased electricity demands; updated technologies for new production systems; expanded grid lines into new geographic areas of production and consumption, etc.

These new fixed investments should not be seen as permanent solutions to crisis management, however. Over-investments in secondary and tertiary circuits of capital (including electricity infrastructure) can exacerbate periods of devaluation, putting investments in the primary circuit at additional risk of becoming obsolete or devalued. As a result, spatial fixes are necessarily temporary, unpredictable and unstable – despite the huge investments that are sometimes required for them, such as those involved in the construction of electricity-generating plants – potentially resetting the equilibrium required for another cycle of capital accumulation but then exposing capitalist firms to the same general tendencies towards a falling rate of profit in the longer run.

The spatial fix is therefore a transitory and partial solution to accumulation crises, staving off one disaster and laying the groundwork for the next (though it may take years or even decades for the cycle to run its course). The aggregate effect, as Brenner and Theodore (2002: 354) argue, is that capitalism 'continually renders obsolete the very geographical landscapes it creates and upon which its own reproduction and expansion hinge'. New technologies, changes in electricity demand and a host of other spatial, political and economic factors can make even the largest of investments in electricity infrastructure appear out of date – even obsolete – in short order.

Finally, the state usually plays a key mediating role in these accumulation cycles. Capital accumulation can happen within a weak state, as can recovery from an over-accumulation crisis, but 'the preferred condition for capitalist activity is a bourgeois state in which market institutions and rules of contract (including those of labour) are legally guaranteed, and where frameworks of regulation are constructed to contain class conflicts and to arbitrate between the claims of different factions of capital' (Harvey 2003: 91). The nature of this state – how it is appointed, its ideological character, its various scales – cannot be predetermined, but international trends point towards a state that is increasingly neo-liberal in its orientation.

This need for an interventionist state is particularly evident in the electricity sector, where production and distribution have typically been state-owned and state-operated (after having been nationalised in many parts of the world – South Africa included – in the first half of the 20th century). Private producers and contractors are an important feature of this neo-liberal electricity market, but even here the state plays a critical role in facilitating private-sector participation and regulation.

In sum, electricity has been deeply integrated into both the boom and bust cycles of capitalism. It s required for competitive profit-taking and has become an essential feature of most post-Fordist accumulation regimes. The mechanics of generating electricity may have changed little over the past 100 years, but the technology behind it, the ways in which it is incorporated into production, the products that it makes and the ways in which it is managed have changed dramatically, making electricity as subject to the cyclical forces of capitalist crises as any other resource.

Electricity and capital accumulation in South(ern) Africa

Nowhere is this link between capitalism and electricity more relevant than in South Africa. Since the introduction of electricity to the mining town of Kimberley in 1882 (electrified even before London, England), the South African economy has been heavily reliant on cheap and abundant supplies of electric power. Fine and

Rustomjee (1996: 8) make this point forcefully, arguing in the mid-1990s that 'the South African economy is uniquely dependent on electricity and is uniquely electricity-intensive'. Just how 'unique' the South African case may be is a matter of debate, but the economy's historical dependence on (cheap) electrical power is indisputable (Christie 1984; DME 1996; Gentle, Chapter 2 of this volume; MERG 1993; Winkler 2006).

Fine and Rustomjee's argument hinges on the notion of a MEC, a set of national economic activities centred on mining but vertically and horizontally integrated into a composite set of related industrial and manufacturing activities (machinery, construction, etc.), as well as services (most notably finance).

Although Fine and Rustomjee's arguments differ somewhat from the over-accumulation thesis described above, there are strong conceptual parallels. In what follows, I summarise their position, highlighting the role of electricity in the MEC, and then use this analysis to develop my MEC-plus argument, taking into account developments in the South African electricity sector since the mid-1990s.

At the heart of Fine and Rustomjee's MEC model is mineral extraction and processing – a productive nucleus that has driven the South African economy for more than 100 years and which has led to the development of a wide range of mining-related industrial and manufacturing firms. Together, these mining and mining-related sectors 'lie at the core of the South African economy', not only by virtue of their weight in economic activity, but also through their 'determining role in the rest of the economy' (Fine & Rustomjee 1996: 5).

Electricity has been key to this development because these mining and mining-related processes have been so electricity-intensive. In the mid-1990s it was estimated that mining and mineral processing accounted for 40 per cent of electricity consumption in the country, with related manufacturing and industry accounting for a major proportion after that (Fine & Rustomjee 1996: 8). Gold is particularly electricity-intensive, with electricity costs making up about 32 per cent of the intermediary costs of production (as compared to 11–17 per cent for most other minerals in the country) (Winkler 2006: 44). Production of one fine ounce of gold requires an estimated 600 kilowatt-hours (kWh) of electricity, slightly less than that used by an average suburban household in South Africa in a month.

It is also useful to compare South Africa's electricity intensivity to that of the USA. In 1999, the USA Energy Information Administration estimated that South Africa's economy was almost three times more electricity-intensive than that of the USA (at 34.462 Btu/US$1990[2] as compared to 12.638 Btu/US$1990).[3]

The demands of mining drove much of the expansion of the electricity sector in South Africa, but this productive base has been eroding over time. Though still heavily dependent on mining and its related manufacturing and industrial sectors, the conglomerates that rose to control the MEC have become increasingly integrated into, and reliant upon, the services sector, most notably finance. This process was accelerated with the crises of accumulation during the late apartheid period – from the mid-1970s onwards – with mining-related firms increasingly seeking refuge in financial markets in South Africa and abroad, contributing to the financialisation of the South African economy.

The result, Fine and Rustomjee argue, is that it is now possible to identify finance as a 'separate but related' set of economic activities at the very 'epicenter' of the MEC, creating a finance-led 'system of accumulation' – one which is still strongly associated with minerals and related sectors but in which 'corporate restructuring and financial speculation have occurred at the expense of providing funds for investment for the expansion and restructuring of production itself' (Fine & Rustomjee 1996: 10–11).

Does the same hold true today? Yes and no. Yes, in the sense that mining remains a central feature of the South African economy and is still largely oligopolistic. Mining is South Africa's largest industry in the primary economic sector and the country has the world's largest reserves of platinum-group metals (87.7 per cent of world totals), manganese (80 per cent), chromium (72.4 per cent), gold (40.1 per cent) and alumino-silicates (34.4 per cent), as well as significant reserves of titanium, vanadium, zirconium, vermiculite and fluorspar. South Africa also accounts for over 40 per cent of the world's production of ferrochromium and vanadium and is the leading world producer of chrome ore and vermiculite (DME 2006a: 6). It was ranked seventh in world mining exploration expenditure during 2005, with 'considerable potential for the discovery of new world-class deposits' (DME 2006a: 7).

With regard to the national economy, mining contributed R94.3 billion, or 7.0 per cent, to Gross Value Added (GVA) in 2005, an increase of R6.83 billion over the previous year. Over the previous 10 years, mining's contribution as a percentage of total GVA had increased from 6.8 per cent in 1998 to 8.7 per cent in 2002, followed by a decrease to 7.0 per cent in 2005, 'the latter probably reflecting the growth experienced in the secondary and tertiary sectors of the economy and the contraction of the gold-mining industry' (DME 2006a: 8). However, the addition of mineral beneficiation adds 'significantly' to this figure.

The forecast for growth in mining is also considered strong. Largely export-driven (more than 70 per cent in the case of South Africa), it is expected that 'moderate' growth in the world's major economies will provide increased mineral demands and 'significant price increases' in the period to 2010 (DME 2006a: 11). Investments of at least R55 billion in minerals-related projects in South Africa in 2006 alone suggest the scale of this anticipated growth.

Outside South Africa, there are major platinum-group metal resources in Zimbabwe, a 'world class repository' of copper-cobalt deposits and other ores in Zambia, major diamond deposits in Botswana, Angola and Namibia, possible uranium deposits in Malawi, nickel in Madagascar and gold in Tanzania. Both the

Southern African Development Community (SADC) Mining Advisory Committee and the Africa Mining Partnership see 'current world economic expansion and the increasing demand for metals augur[ing] well for the future of mining within the SADC region' (DME 2006a: 21–22).

So while it may no longer be possible to argue, as Fine and Rustomjee (1996: 9) did in the mid-1990s, that the South African economy's 'dependence on mining and energy and directly related activity has increased and not decreased', it would be an error to suggest that these activities are not still central to the national and regional economy. Little wonder, then, that the most comprehensive report to date on urban electricity use in South African cities still points to the MEC as being 'at the heart of the South African economy' and 'useful for understanding the potential for various trajectories in future energy development in our cities' (SEA 2006: vi). Combined with minerals-related industrial and manufacturing entities, it is safe to say that the MEC still represents a 'system of accumulation' in South Africa and one that will probably remain so for some time to come.

All of this mining and related activity will, of course, require massive amounts of electricity. Newer forms of deep mining have added to this electricity intensivity, as has minerals processing. South Africa has attracted mining and minerals-processing firms to the country exactly because it has 'a reliable national electricity grid [that] provides the cheapest power in the world' (DME 2006a: 3), contributing to the establishment of sizeable ferro-alloys, stainless steel and aluminium smelting industries, including an aluminium smelting plant planned for the Coega industrial zone near Port Elizabeth. Between 1992 and 2004, electricity consumption for the production of non-ferrous metals and non-metallic minerals increased threefold and twofold respectively, while electricity consumption in the iron and steel sector more than doubled (DME 2006b: 44).

The aluminium smelting plant at Coega (owned by Canadian multinational Alcan, which, at the time of writing, had recently been purchased by Rio Tinto Zinc) is expected to be one of the largest in the world when it is fully operational after 2010, consuming 675 megawatts (MW) of electricity – enough to power a small city – and increasing to over 1 300 MW (*Business Day* 22 June 2007). The South African government will spend R11 billion to get the overall Coega facility into shape – R7 billion for the development of a deep-sea port and container terminals and R4 billion on electricity power upgrades – with the Alcan smelter being the main beneficiary of the power investments. Alcan will also receive a R1.93-billion tax incentive, as one of the last beneficiaries of the government's strategic industrial projects programme (*Business Day* 25 June 2007).

These kinds of core MEC activities go a long way towards explaining the massive investments being planned by the South African government in new and upgraded electricity generation and transmission over the next 25 years – *arguably the largest sectoral investments in public infrastructure ever undertaken in South Africa.*

Although the specifics are constantly changing, the rate at which investment projections have increased over the past few years is itself of interest.

In September 2004 the Department of Public Enterprises announced plans to spend R84 billion on new electricity infrastructure between 2005 and 2009. In early 2005 this was raised to just over R100 billion (more than five times the national housing budget for 2004/05): R74 billion on generation, R11.8 billion on transmission and R15.9 billion on distribution (*Business Day* 24 February 2005). An additional R23 billion in electricity infrastructure spending was expected to come from the private sector in the form of new power plants and other investments.

These announcements were met with delight by the business community in South Africa, with the *Financial Mail* (29 October 2004) hailing the investments in electricity generation as coming '[n]ot a moment too soon'. Writers in the *Business Report* (24 October 2004) expressed 'amazement as spending turns to expectations of growth', with Public Enterprises Minister Alec Erwin having 'invited the private sector to come to the party'. All in all, 'a reason for serious excitement', according to the paper's editorial.

Imagine their excitement, then, when Eskom announced in early 2007 that it planned to raise its capital expenditure plans in the electricity sector to R150 billion between 2007 and 2012, followed by even larger capex layouts thereafter. The Eskom board had determined by that time that R100 billion would be insufficient to meet the capacity needed to power South Africa's growing economy, and was given the go-ahead to begin work on a new R110-billion nuclear plant and an R85-billion coal-fired power station – in addition to the R70-billion coal-fired power station already approved. The higher spending would also double the outlay on Eskom's transmission network to R20 billion over the next five years. In total, it has been estimated that new capital expenditure by Eskom could reach R1 trillion by 2025 – a figure that the *Financial Mail* describes as 'hitherto unknown in SA infrastructure terms' (7 December 2007).

But it is not just the traditional MEC economy that will benefit from these investments. As important as they are, the mining and mining-related sectors are not as powerful or as central to the South African economy as they once were. The services sector is growing in size and clout, and the financial epicentre of the sector is changing, with the largest of the conglomerates having moved their headquarters offshore and being less reliant on the South African economy in general and South African mining activity in particular.

Moreover, there are new political demands on electricity (some from the wealthy, some from the poor), and new institutional, technological and ideological models being deployed in the operation and expansion of the electricity sector.

We turn, therefore, to an analysis of what this MEC-plus looks like, and its implications for electricity, beginning with an exploration of the growing (and largely urban-based) services sector.

The MEC-plus

Growing urban services economy

Arguably the biggest shift in the South African economy over the past 15 years has been the growth of producer services. The financialisation of the South African economy described by Fine and Rustomjee in the 1990s (Fine & Rustomjee 1996) is part of this phenomenon, though it has expanded to include a much wider range of services and firms than was the case in the late apartheid and early post-apartheid years.

'Producer service' firms are those that service the centralisation requirements of globalised manufacturing and industrial companies (including mining). Most notable amongst these are accounting, law, advertising, corporate travel, security, public relations, management consulting, IT, real estate, storage, data processing and insurance companies. Although not entirely separate in corporate ownership terms from 'consumer services' (i.e. services intended for consumption by individuals, such as leisure travel or home insurance), producer services overwhelm even the large and growing consumer services sector (Sassen 2001, 2002).

Driven initially by the manufacturing sector, the producer services economy has now taken on a life of its own. As specialised service companies have grown and internationalised, so too have their own needs for specialised outsourcing of the same command-and-control functions as their manufacturing counterparts. A multinational advertising firm, for example, may require the services of a legal firm, a financial services company, IT specialists, and so on. In what has become a self-perpetuating cycle of producer services growth and service company expansion, there has been a transformation of the global economy from one with industry and manufacturing at its centre to one with producer services at the core. Producer services now dominate international trade, foreign direct investments and job creation (Sassen 2001).

Geographically, this growth in producer services has occurred almost entirely in cities. This is due in large part to the agglomeration economies associated with these specialised service firms, which have little choice but to locate themselves in major urban centres (or, more accurately, in certain areas within these cities) where related service firms are located. Critical to the success of this agglomeration economy, in turn, is the infrastructure required to make it all work: 'smart buildings', conference centres, transportation networks and telecommunications, as well as the less formal 'soft' infrastructure required for networking and the daily living requirements of the individuals who run these firms, such as restaurants, entertainment venues and education facilities. All are part of an agglomeration package that determines how well a city works for the service firms that inhabit it (or whether these firms choose to locate elsewhere). The most important of these so-called 'world cities' are those best provisioned with this infrastructure, hard and soft.

South Africa has been attracting more and more of these producer service firms, with Cape Town and Johannesburg having become world cities in their own right (albeit tertiary players in the larger world city network, and largely of regional significance) (McDonald 2008). Many of these producer service firms are still dependent on the MEC economy, but developments in film, telecommunications, retail, education and other corporate services outside of the traditional MEC are amongst the fastest growing areas of the South African economy, with tourism (personal and corporate) now earning several billion rands more in foreign exchange each year than gold (Koumelis 2005). Although it is difficult to disaggregate urban from rural elements in an economy as intertwined with the MEC as that of South Africa, it is worth noting that the urban proportion of national gross domestic product (GDP) has been growing steadily for two decades and now generates some 80 per cent of the country's economic output, with Johannesburg, Cape Town and Durban alone accounting for nearly 50 per cent of GDP, even though they contain only 30 per cent of the national population (SACN 2007).

Electricity is critical to this urban services growth. Though not as electricity-intensive as mining and its related industrial activity, the rapid growth of the sector has meant increasing urban demands for electric power – in terms of both quantity and reliability.

Disaggregated data on urban commercial electricity in South Africa do not exist, but the 'commerce sector' consumes approximately 15 per cent of the country's electricity (DME 2006b: 43) and cities as a whole consume as much as 50 per cent, a figure that has been growing for the past two decades. The six largest metro areas, along with nine other industrial and non-industrial towns that formed part of a survey of urban electricity in the country, consume some 41 per cent of the country's electricity (and produce about 62 per cent of South Africa's GDP) (SEA 2006: 48–53).

Much of this urban electricity use is probably still going towards manufacturing and industry – particularly in industrial towns such as Saldanha – but given the rapid growth of the producer service economy, and its increasing reliance on power-hungry telecommunications and IT, the service sector constitutes a significant (and politically powerful) share of the electricity market in South Africa.

Not surprisingly, then, infrastructure is being extended and upgraded to provide for these service-sector demands as part of the overall electricity infrastructure investments described above. As I have discussed elsewhere in greater detail (McDonald 2007: Chapter 5), massive electricity investments in South African cities constitute a large part of the new 'urban spatial fix' designed to make them more globally competitive in their quest to attract (and retain) profit-seeking producer service firms for whom electricity is a significant consideration.

The importance of cheap and reliable electricity to this competitive, world city process is illustrated by the hysterical manner in which businesses in Johannesburg and Cape Town responded to the power outages of 2005 and 2006. Electricity failures in Johannesburg were said to be 'paralysing' the economy (*Sunday Times* 6 May 2006). In Cape Town, blackouts were considered 'one of the worst crises in South Africa's post-apartheid history', according to the former Africa Bureau Chief for *Newsweek* magazine, Joshua Hammer; nothing less than 'a catastrophe' (Hammer 2006).

A survey of business attitudes in Cape Town undertaken in late 2006 by the Western Cape Investment and Trade Promotion Agency (Wesgro) underscored these corporate concerns. Some 71 per cent of firms interviewed cited 'electricity reliability' as the second-largest 'constraint' on business growth in the city (after crime), noting that unreliable electricity supply had 'a serious to debilitating impact on their business' (as cited in SALGRC 2007a: 19–24). The authors of the report used these results to argue that the city should make electricity infrastructure an investment priority, noting that 'Cape Town is increasingly competing against a wide range of global investment destinations for investment in a number of growth sectors such as tourism, manufacturing, and other services such as business process outsourcing, film, and information and communication technologies' (SALGRC 2007a: 19–24) and that electricity is critical to this growth.

The mayor of Cape Town, Helen Zille, responded quickly to the Wesgro report with a keynote address at a symposium held by the Cape Town Regional Chamber of Commerce and Industry in early 2007 where she promised to 'upgrade and expand electricity distribution networks and substations' as an 'appropriate investment in infrastructure…[for] economic growth' in the city. She also promised to invest 'half a billion rand in electricity distribution over the next three years as part of our preparations for [the FIFA World Cup in] 2010, and we will be investing more after that' (Zille 2007).

Shrill demands by capital for electricity infrastructure investments in Johannesburg have resulted in similar promises, with City Power (an arm's-length corporatised utility responsible for power distribution in the city) calling its electricity infrastructure 'technically obsolete' and 'embarrassingly primitive' in a report to a parliamentary committee. As a result, City Power plans to spend 'at least R259-million over the next four years to clear electricity backlogs, repair its equipment and ensure substations are secure'. It also plans to spend R2.2 billion of public funds to 'beef up the city's capacity to cope with rising electricity demands', much of this 'in preparation for [the 2010 World Cup]' (*Sunday Times* 9 July 2006).

The chairperson of the parliamentary committee reviewing City Power's report was 'impressed' by the presentation, noting that '[i]t is clear that city officials have the political will to ensure that Joburg is turned into a world-class city' (*Sunday Times* 9 July 2006).

Expanding domestic consumption

Not all complaints and demands for improved and expanded electricity are coming from business, however. There are also strong residential pressures that are important to our discussion of a MEC-plus. Although households make up only 15 per cent of electricity consumption nationally – a figure that has remained steady in proportional terms in South Africa since 1982 – residential demand for electricity in the country has risen in absolute terms by more than 50 per cent since the 1980s, and constitutes the third-largest market for electricity consumption after mining and manufacturing (CCT 2003: 6; DME 2003a: 7; Van Horen et al. 1998: 8).

Residential consumers also account for the overwhelming majority of electricity connections in the country – more than 95 per cent (Eskom 2006: 176) – and about 75 per cent of the national variable load (Van Horen et al. 1998: 8), making them important – if 'inefficient' from a cost recovery point of view – electricity customers.

Wealthy and middle-class suburbs are responsible for much of this residential consumption. This was certainly the case during the apartheid era, when virtually all urban white residents had access to electricity – infrastructure investments in white municipal areas in South Africa were equal to or better than those of most European and North American cities on a per capita basis from the 1960s onwards (Ahmad 1995), and this continues to be the case, despite considerable efforts to connect black townships to the grid (discussed below). Affordability is one factor here; another is widespread ownership and use of increasingly electricity-intensive household appliances in suburban areas.

Once again, reliable disaggregated data on electricity use are difficult to come by, but middle- to high-income urban households in South Africa are very high energy consumers with large carbon footprints, with the average suburban household consuming approximately 9 600 kilowatt-hours per year (kWh/year).[4] This compares favourably to average household consumption in the USA (which, at 11 200 kWh/year, has the most intensive household consumption of electricity in the world) but unfavourably to an average European household (about 4 700 kWh/year) and Japanese household (about 6 000 kWh/year) (Greenpeace 2007).

Efforts are under way to try and reduce per capita electricity use in suburban South African homes – e.g. the introduction of solar water heating, which on its own could reduce household electricity consumption significantly (SEA 2006). But a lack of political commitment and financial resources for these kinds of energy-saving alternatives (see McDaid, Chapter 7 of this volume), combined with rising per capita incomes for wealthy South Africans, no significant increase in electricity prices in real/proportional terms for middle-class South African households since the early 1990s, and a seemingly endless appetite for power-hungry electronic goods such as cell phones and computers (in line with global consumption patterns), has meant that electricity demands in the suburbs are increasing and will probably continue to do so for some time.

Most importantly, these suburban demands for electricity continue to be catered to by the local and national state. Residential electricity in South Africa is amongst the cheapest in the world and there are enormous pressures from middle-class ratepayer organisations to keep electricity prices down, as well as to minimise the cross-subsidisation of electricity in townships. There are also enormous pressures from suburban residents to keep their electricity infrastructure 'world class', with many municipalities investing much more heavily in suburban areas than they do in townships. The maintenance of these electricity distribution systems in the heavily treed and hilly suburban areas of Cape Town, for example, is a world away from the flimsy, low-amperage, poorly installed distribution systems in that city's townships, where high winds blow down clusters of live cables and where shoddy housing construction and poor network installation have resulted in dangerous domestic connections.

It is to these low-income residential areas that we now turn.

Low-income consumers

Although the apartheid state began an electrification programme in the 1980s – when they realised that extending basic services to township areas could help 'transform a discontented and threatening people into more compliant members of a mass-consumption society' (Smith 1992: 2) – serious efforts to roll out electricity infrastructure to urban and rural black areas did not begin until the early 1990s.

Since 1992, an average of about 300 000 new connections have been made each year, mostly to low-income households. Between 1994 and 2000 Eskom connected 2.5 million houses to the grid, with many more being connected by municipalities. By the end of 2006 the national grid had reached 73 per cent of the population (DME 2006b: 39–40), up from about one-third of households in the early 1990s (Winkler 2006: 46). This has been a significant investment on the part of the South African state and is unprecedented in 'developing'-country history.

Despite these new connections, low-income households account for probably no more than 5 per cent of national electricity consumption,[5] with relatively little per capita demand growth on the horizon. The biggest problem here is affordability. Millions of low-income households simply do not have enough regular income to buy (enough of) the electricity they may now have access to, forcing many to make tragic choices between buying electricity, water, food or clothing (McDonald & Pape 2002; SACN 2004). As a result, electricity is used sparingly by low-income households, while paraffin, coal and other dangerous energy sources continue to be drawn on, leading to hundreds of deaths each year from shack fires and paraffin poisonings in South African townships and rural areas (SEA 2006).

Original estimates by Eskom that low-income households would use an average of about 350 kWh/month have proven to be much too high, with typical consumption patterns being in the 50–200 kWh/month range. In 2001, the DME estimated that '56 per cent of households consume no more than 50 kWh per month' (DME 2003b).

Appliance ownership is also a factor, with limited distribution in low-income areas. Approximately 10.3 million South African adults do not have refrigerators in their homes, for example, with the overwhelming majority of these being black (SALGRC 2007b). Table 1.1 illustrates these electrical appliance inequities in the country, by race.

Table 1.1: Electrical appliance ownership in South Africa (percentages), by race, 2006

	Total	African	White	Coloured	Asian
Television	78	73	98	93	98
Fridge/freezer	67	58	98	93	100
Electric stove	62	53	97	90	92
Microwave oven	35	21	92	65	85
DVD player	32	22	73	53	76
Washing machine	25	9	91	67	64
VCR in home	19	9	67	35	57
Computer	10	2	55	14	28
Satellite television	8	2	47	8	19

Source: SALGRC 2007b

Even where electricity-intensive appliances such as refrigerators are found in low-income households, they are often turned off to save money, creating additional health and safety hazards (Fiil-Flynn 2001). It should also not be forgotten that approximately one-quarter of the country is still off-grid entirely – an estimated 2.9 million households at the end of 2006 (Hemson & O'Donovan 2006: 22–30). A significant proportion of these households are in urban areas but the vast majority are rural (Winkler 2006). Around 16 per cent of urban households do not have access to electricity – the figure is as low as 9 per cent in Cape Town but as high as 58 per cent in some rural towns (SEA 2006: vi–vii). The low rate of access in rural areas is due in part to the high per capita costs of remote rural infrastructure development, one of the reasons why the South African state has said it will focus on off-grid, solar electricity in these areas.

Nonetheless, the rollout of electricity infrastructure in low-income areas, and the potential for overall increased electricity demand, are important considerations in any analysis of the electricity sector in South Africa and must be factored into our discussion of a MEC-plus.

Neo-liberalism

It is not just new demands that have reshaped the MEC, however. Of increasing importance are the neo-liberal policies and institutions that have come to shape the ways in which electricity is provided in South Africa, transforming the managerial side of the energy landscape. Cheap electric power is still the goal, but the ways in which institutions are constructed, pricing schemas developed and payments collected have changed considerably since the heyday of the MEC. Flexibility, commercialisation and protection from cross-subsidisation are but a few of the neo-liberal tactics being employed at the national and local levels in South Africa.

Significantly, this is not an issue that Fine and Rustomjee address in their book on the MEC (1996). The omission is understandable because little had been done to commercialise electricity services at the time, and the neo-liberal thrust of the ANC was still in its infancy. Nevertheless, neo-liberal reforms at the parastatal Eskom had begun in the 1980s. As both Gentle and Van Heusden make clear in their analyses of the giant state-owned electricity provider (Chapters 2 and 8 of this volume, respectively), the post-apartheid neo-liberal changes that took effect in Eskom (and in the electricity sector more generally) had their roots in late apartheid, highlighting the oft-neglected economic and ideological continuity between these two political epochs.

Equally important is the fact that neo-liberalism itself has shifted quite dramatically during the period from the early 1990s to today. Borrowing from Brenner and Theodore (2002), one can identify two key 'moments' of neo-liberal reform: one that 'destroys' the ideological and institutional vestiges of the previous Fordist–Keynesian regimes of accumulation, and one that 'creates' new and revised modes of neo-liberalism, responding in part to the failures and contradictions of the first moment of neo-liberal reform. The first, destructive phase of neo-liberalism occurred in the 1970s and 1980s in Europe and North America when there was an aggressive assault on welfarist policies and institutions. What these authors also refer to as 'roll back' neo-liberalism involved efforts to shrink the size of the state through fiscal restraint, privatisation and the rolling back of state powers, as well as efforts to deregulate the economy and reduce the power of unions. But as the 'perverse economic consequences and pronounced social externalities' of these narrow market-driven reforms became apparent, and increasingly difficult to ignore (the failures of outright privatisation being one example), neo-liberal pundits began to change their policy prescriptions, morphing them into more 'socially interventionist and ameliorative' forms of neo-liberal planning, 'epitomized by the Third-Way contortions of the Blair and Clinton administrations' of the 1990s (Peck & Tickell 2002: 388–389).

In this second, 'creative' moment of neo-liberalisation, policy-makers and capital recognise the shortcomings and dangers of the initial phase of neo-liberal dismantling, and scramble to put in place a revised version of economic reform in an effort to secure a more stable platform for economic growth. The underlying agenda remains the same – the 'creation of new infrastructure for market-oriented economic growth, commodification, and the rule of capital' (Brenner & Theodore 2002: 362) – but the institutional methods change, with efforts to put a 'human face' on neo-liberal policy and clean up earlier, messier outcomes.

Peck and Tickell refer to this as the 'roll out' phase of neo-liberalism, a re-introduction of state institutions and corporatist planning into the social and economic spheres, without undermining the overall agenda of market liberalisation, and with the added advantage of strengthening the state's mediating role in society: 'No longer concerned narrowly with the mobilisation and extension of markets (and market logics), neoliberalism is increasingly associated with the political foregrounding of new modes of "social" and penal policy-making, concerned specifically with the aggressive reregulation, disciplining and containment of those marginalised or dispossessed by the [roll back] neoliberalism of the 1980s' (Peck & Tickell 2002: 389).

It is here that we see the shift from narrow, market policies to more mediated forms of economic change – for example, a shift from the outright divestiture of state assets to the creation of public–private partnerships; from crude forms of decreased welfare spending to more targeted and invasive forms of indigent policy; from hands-off urban planning to highly regulated urban spaces and extensive security systems.

Ironically, then, the rollout phase of neo-liberalism has seen a strengthening, not a weakening, of the state. This is not the 'bloated' and 'unaccountable' state of the previous Keynesian period (as neo-liberals tend to characterise the Keynesian state model) but a leaner, more efficient, more competent and more market-oriented set of governing bodies, better able to manage the interests of capital and the (inevitable) tensions and contradictions of the market economy, and better able to step aside to let the market deliver the services that the state used to provide.

This phased transition of neo-liberalism is not a smooth or necessarily linear process. The destructive and creative moments are 'dialectically intertwined' (Brenner & Theodore 2002: 362). There is no single, abrupt time or event at which a society switches from Keynesianism to neo-liberalism or from one neo-liberal regime to another. There are periods of stop-start, back-and-forth reform as political struggles take place over policy models, and as the economy itself shifts.

Nor is this transition to rollout neo-liberalism stable in the long run. Even the most 'progressive' forms of neo-liberalism cannot resolve the contradictions of their more aggressive predecessors or, most importantly, the inherent contradictions of capitalism itself. Rollout neo-liberalism can, at best, ameliorate the worst excesses of uneven capitalist development and help to stave off crises only in the short to medium term.

In South Africa, these 'moments' were somewhat condensed, with much of the destructive, 'roll back' phase being skipped, in part because of the fact that Keynesian-style welfarism had never been extended to the majority of the country's black population. South Africa leapfrogged over much of this intermediary stage, learning from the contradictions and failures of 1980s privatisation elsewhere, and opting instead for more palatable (and predictable) neo-liberal mechanisms such as public–private partnerships and corporatisation.

The electricity sector in South Africa has been radically transformed by these changes. While Fine and Rustomjee's (1996) warnings about the danger of over-emphasising the significance of flexible production and post-Fordism remain relevant, the traditional MEC model of 'big state' negotiating with 'big capital' is changing. The MEC-plus sees a much more fragmented and rescaled state (local, national, regional) negotiating with more globally dispersed capital, in many different sectors, with new technical demands.

There are also the voices of citizens to contend with. Though still largely marginalised, public-sector unions, ratepayer associations (particularly those in wealthy suburbs) and civic organisations and social movements – such as the Soweto Electricity Crisis Committee (SECC) – have been inserting themselves into debates over electricity provision in South Africa in ways that did not exist 15 years ago.

What are the particulars of this new neo-liberal landscape in the electricity sector in South Africa? I would argue that the two most important changes relate to privatisation (broadly defined) and pricing. In the following sections I highlight key elements of these reforms and discuss how they feed into revised (and uneven) accumulation strategies of 'electric capitalism' in the country – arguments which have relevance for the spread of South Africa's influence and control over the electricity sector in the region and beyond.

Privatisation

Privatisation, despite what the South African state and liberal analysts have to say, is still a central part of electricity restructuring. Although there is little privatisation in the narrowest sense of the term – i.e. the divestiture of state assets to private firms – the introduction of independent power producers (IPPs), the corporatisation of service providers, the contracting out of services, and the potential for future divestitures feature prominently in institutional reform models for the sector.

In the late 1990s, national government developed a strategic plan – with the assistance of multinational consultancy PricewaterhouseCoopers – to 'unbundle' the country's electricity sector (Cosatu 2005; Eberhard 2005; Odubiyi & Davidson 2004; Steyn 2006). The proposals were as follows. On the generation side, the state would divest up to 30 per cent of Eskom's existing production capacity, introduce IPPs for new production, outsource functions, and more fully corporatise Eskom. On the transmission side, the state would create a separate transmission utility (Transco) that would be owned by the state (and possibly sold off in the future), as well as outsource some functions. On the distribution side – much of which is the responsibility of municipalities, which buy bulk electricity from Eskom for resale – national government wanted to create six independent Regional Electricity Distributors (REDs). These REDs would serve as geographically defined distributors, in an effort to rationalise pricing structures and management systems across municipalities, but also compete with one another for municipal business. It was suggested by the national agency responsible for creating REDs that they might 'become world-class assets that international investors may be interested in venturing into' (EDI 2004: 4).

Steps were taken to follow through on all of these liberalisation proposals, but in 2003–2004 the ANC began to rethink this strategy. Mainstream analysts have characterised the changes as a retreat from privatisation and a strengthening of a pro-poor developmental state, with one influential analyst arguing that it represents a move 'from state to market and back again' (Eberhard 2005). But does the revised vision really offer what one newspaper headline has described as a 'bold' new strategy of electricity reform, let alone one that will 'help [the] poorest in SA' (*Daily Dispatch* 16 November 2005)?

Closer analysis suggests the opposite, with plans for private-sector involvement and increased commercialisation still central to restructuring plans, all in the name of providing cheap and reliable energy sources to MEC-plus corporations. Although Eskom no longer plans to sell 30 per cent of its existing generating capacity, it has said that 30 per cent of all *new* capacity development is 'expected to come from independent power producers' (Eskom 2006: 52–53). The first of these will be a 1 000 MW oil-fired gas turbine network to be commissioned by the end of 2009. Coal, gas and nuclear IPP options are also being considered for future years (Eskom 2006: 52–53).

Beyond 2009, Eskom notes that 'there are potential investment opportunities for independent power producers in line with government's decision for new players to provide for South Africa's generating needs'. Overall, 'independent power producers are expected to invest about R9 billion' (Eskom 2006: 37).

Eskom's revised capital expenditure estimates of R150 billion (cited earlier) would appear to cloud the matter somewhat – with the *Financial Mail* (29 October 2004) report suggesting that the new investment plans make Eskom solely 'responsible for all the new generating capacity' – but it is likely that IPPs are still part of the planning. Eskom has made no official announcement to the contrary and there are already IPP projects in the works. The establishment of offices in South Africa by large electricity multinationals such as International Power (UK), Cinergy and AES (USA), EDF (France) and Tractebel and Shell (Belgium) would suggest that these firms see significant investment potential as well (Cosatu 2005), with IPPs likely to be an important factor in medium- to long-term expansion plans as Eskom *doubles* its capacity over the next 20 years (Eskom 2007a).

Internally, Eskom itself continues to become more corporatised every year. The process began in the 1980s, accelerated in the 1990s, and was formalised with the parastatal's conversion to Eskom Holdings Ltd in 2002. Increasingly hard-nosed business principles, coupled with outsourcing and divestitures of non-core assets, have created a new ideological and institutional structure that puts its profit – and that of its priority clients – ahead of poverty alleviation and social and environmental justice (see Chapter 2 by Gentle, Chapter 3 by Greenberg and Chapter 7 by McDaid, in this volume). With the aggressive behaviour of Eskom

Enterprises on the rest of the continent, Eskom has come to be seen as a 'corporate powerhouse' in its own right (Ashe 2002).

On the transmission front, plans to create a separate unbundled utility appear to have been shelved and there is no suggestion of divesting these assets, at least for the time being. However, there has been extensive internal unbundling of transmission services within Eskom – based on the financial ringfencing of its generation, transmission and distribution activities – intended to allow for better cost recovery (Eskom 2007b). This internal unbundling is a precondition for any private equity investment or divestiture, and although neither would appear to be planned for the immediate future, it must be kept in mind that the ground has been laid for deeper privatisation in this subsector.

In terms of distribution, the plan to introduce REDs stalled in late 2006, largely due to resistance from local authorities which risked losing significant revenue sources through the buying and reselling of bulk electricity in their municipalities (as much as 10 per cent of some municipal budgets), but the issue is far from dead. Much of the rationale for REDs remains – with more than 180 municipalities selling electricity at different prices and with different management structures and policies, there are enormous inefficiencies and inequities in the system – making it likely that REDs will remain on the policy agenda for some time to come. The establishment of RED 1 in Cape Town in July 2005 is one indication of the momentum behind this, as is the ongoing corporatisation of electricity providers in large municipalities throughout the country, in preparation for some form of competitive, stand-alone unbundled distribution system. Plans are also under way for the creation of RED 2 in Ekurhuleni municipality, which is part of the larger Johannesburg metropolitan area.

Nor is there any shortage of outsourcing and petty privatisation taking place at the municipal level. Meter reading, infrastructure maintenance, fleet management, revenue collection and a host of other functions are increasingly being outsourced to private firms – some in the name of black economic empowerment – and the trend would appear to be increasing.

What, then, are we to make of this reconstituted 'public' service in South Africa? Although there has been a shift away from the explicit privatisation policies of the early 2000s, the neo-liberal undertones and some of the uncertainties of future direction give cause for concern. The ANC-allied Congress of South African Trade Unions (Cosatu) has expressed its worries, noting in an analysis of the Electricity Regulation Bill that '[t]he absence of an explicit end-state vision of the restructuring drive creates the impression that this regulatory framework is only an intermediary step along the route towards a completely liberalized [electricity sector]' (Cosatu 2005: 5). Cosatu's research department, the National Labour and Economic Development Institute, has also taken umbrage with reform plans in this sector, arguing that 'capital intensive industries will be the main winner in the process of electricity restructuring' (Naledi 2006: 3).

In the end, these revised restructuring plans are a classic illustration of the kind of rollout neo-liberalisation described above. Put simply, ruling elites in the ANC have come to recognise that the state can be more effective than the private sector in creating the kind of electricity spatial fix required to support a MEC-plus system of accumulation in South Africa and to sustain corporate profit levels. Private capital, for its part, has also recognised the risks inherent in privatising the electricity sector (California's experience resonated loudly in this regard)[6] and would appear to be happy with a predictable, state-led investment strategy – particularly one as bountiful and beneficial to private capital as the massive investments being planned for the electricity sector in the short and long term.

In the revised restructuring model, the South African state (at various levels) will hold on to the assets it deems critical to the accumulation demands of its key MEC-plus clients, pour new public resources into electricity infrastructure that it deems necessary for future accumulation requirements, and run these entities increasingly like private businesses. Meanwhile, there will be continued outsourcing and some private-sector greenfield development to reduce capital expenditure costs somewhat, and to appease the demands of private capital for direct accumulation opportunities, with the carrot of potential future divestitures and equity partnerships.

In other words, 'privatisation' in the electricity sector in South Africa will not mean a withdrawal of the state. Privatisation is not an either/or situation (*either* the state owns and runs a service *or* the private sector does). It must be seen as a continuum of public and private mixes, with varying degrees of involvement and exposure to risks by the two sectors (Starr 1988).

Nor should we limit our discussion to direct private-sector participation. The introduction of private-sector operating principles and mechanisms into the public sector in the form of corporatisation is just as crucial to our analysis – foregrounding, as this process does, surplus maximisation, cost recovery, competitive bidding, performance-targeted salaries, ringfenced decision-making and demand-driven investments in publicly owned entities, as opposed to the more traditional public-sector operating principles of integrated planning, (cross-) subsidisation, supply-driven decision-making and equity orientation (Dunsire 1999; Leys 2001; Olcay-Unver et al. 2003; Stoker 1989). So complete can this shift in public management culture be that utility systems which are fully owned and operated by the state (i.e. considered to be fully 'public') can be more commercial than their 'privatised' counterparts, with managers aggressively promoting and enforcing cost recovery and other market principles, as has already been demonstrated across a variety of public services in South Africa (Bond 1999; McDonald & Pape 2002; McDonald & Ruiters 2005; Qotole et al. 2001).

The ANC's attempts to repackage its electricity reforms as a 'return to public' must be seen in this light. Post-apartheid restructuring in the electricity sector may be illustrative of a strengthened 'developmental state', but this is a state that operates primarily in the development interests of capital – particularly those factions of capital closest to the MEC-plus economy.

One must be careful, of course, not to develop too instrumentalist a position here. Class interests 'do not translate readily and transparently into specific policies' and 'cannot be read off immediately from state policies' (Fine & Rustomjee 1996: 8). Demands from within the ANC-alliance for investments in electricity that serve low-income needs are one indication of the contested terrain in the electricity sector, as are demands from civil society for 'free electricity' and expectations from competing factions of capital. Nonetheless, the starkly neo-liberal policy trajectory of the South African state, coupled with massive investments in infrastructure geared for the MEC-plus economy, point to a very visible public hand working in the interests of private capital.

Uneven pricing structures

A second set of important neo-liberal reforms in the electricity sector relates to pricing. In this section I look specifically at tariff structures, user fees, cut-offs for non-payment and so-called free basic electricity as indicators of this ideological trend.

I alluded earlier to the difficulties that low-income households experience in paying for electricity. A concrete illustration helps to demonstrate the point. At the domestic level, there are typically two tariff rates in South Africa: one for consumption under a certain number of kilowatt-hours per month (usually between 500 and 700 kWh) and a second, higher price for monthly consumption over this amount. The price differentials tend to be minimal, however, and a lack of rising block tariffs after the second price point means there is no incentive for reduced consumption at higher levels. These tariff structures also do little to generate funds for cross-subsidising low-income households, and can even serve to make electricity cheaper for middle-class suburbanites than it is in the townships.

The tariff structures introduced by the Cape Town RED in July 2006 are an example of these structural inequalities. Households in the high-consumption category (more than 600 kWh/month) pay R0.305/kWh and a 'daily service charge' of R1.99. Low-consumption consumers are charged a flat rate of R0.4065/kWh and no daily service charge (CCT 2006). The only other difference is that low-consumption users receive their first 50 kWh/month of electricity free, as part of the 'free basic services' package the city designed to ease the cost of services for the poor.

The intention of this pricing structure is to save low-consumption users (mostly township households) the daily service charge, but in the end they actually pay more per kilowatt-hour. Using the pricing structure outlined above, a high-consumption household consuming 700 kWh of electricity would pay R263.50/month (an effective rate of R0.376/kWh) while a low-consumption household using 500 kWh of electricity would pay R182.93/month (taking into account the free 50 kWh allocation). At these rates of consumption, the poor pay about 8 per cent more per kilowatt-hour than wealthy suburbanites.

If we look at these charges in relation to household incomes, the pricing inequalities become even starker. At 700 kWh, electricity costs make up only a small percentage of a suburban household's income (which is typically in the range of R10–15 000 per month) while the R182 charge for 500 kWh in a township household would make up 23 per cent of an R800 monthly income (not uncommon in households relying on pensions and grants). As a result, many low-income households either under-consume electricity or cannot pay their electricity bills.

The introduction of user fees for installations and repairs has had an additional negative impact on the poor. According to Cape Town's 2004/05 pricing schedule, it costs R184.21 for an inspection of an electricity connection, R662.68 to have a prepaid meter installed and R1 429.83 to have a 'tariff, quality of supply or load profile investigation requiring equipment and personnel' (McDonald 2008: 237). There are also steep charges for disconnection and reconnection if a household tampers with its meter or attempts to connect illegally: R482.46 for disconnecting an illegal connection; R991.93 to have it reconnected (R1 885.97 for second-time offenders); and R57.02 for the city to 'deliver a notice of impending disconnection of supply for non-payment of account' (McDonald 2008: 237).

These charges have effectively barred many households from having their electricity systems upgraded or repaired, and have prevented some households from reconnecting to the grid. The city has recognised this problem and has introduced a system whereby costs can be paid in instalments via the prepaid metering system, but in this case a surcharge is added to every unit of electricity purchased to pay for the fixed costs, raising the kilowatt-hour charges even higher.

Industrial rates for electricity contribute further to the uneven nature of pricing in the sector. Commerce and industry make up 60 per cent of electricity consumption in Cape Town but they pay much less on average than domestic consumers, with 'large power users' paying just R0.1649/kWh and a daily service fee of R9.68 (as of July 2006). At a monthly consumption of 10 000 kWh this translates into an effective charge of R0.194/kWh, almost two-and-a-half times lower than rates paid by low-income households.

The justification for these electricity pricing schemes? They '[help] to build Cape Town's competitive advantage', according to the head of the city's RED (CCT 2004: 67). The city's Energy Strategy makes a similar point, arguing that Cape Town should be a city where the provision of electricity 'supports economic competitiveness and increases employment ... and where energy prices remain competitive' (CCT 2003: 5).

The inequities become even bigger when one looks at the large MEC-related industrial firms in the country. The aforementioned aluminium smelting project in Coega with Alcan involves a secret 25-year deal signed in November 2006 to provide that firm with cheap electricity, making it the first international company to benefit from a new 'development electricity pricing programme' intended to attract industry to the country – part of what the DME sees as the need to keep electricity prices 'as low as possible in order to continue attracting industrial development and lure foreign industries to South Africa' (DME 2006a: 50). On average, Eskom charges R0.16/kWh for industry and R0.29/kWh for residential consumers, while it is estimated that Alcan may receive its electricity for as little as R0.05/kWh in this deal (*Business Day* 25 June 2007).

The end result is a pricing scheme that subsidises industry and middle-class suburbanites, while charging low-income households higher absolute and relative prices for a service they more desperately need. As a result, low-income households either consume less electricity than they actually require, or cannot afford to pay for what they consume. If the latter, many find their electricity services cut off altogether by municipal and Eskom distributors keen to recover their own costs of production.

Electricity cut-offs reached a peak in the early 2000s, when tens of thousands of households were having their supplies cut due to non-payment each month. In Soweto alone, Eskom was cutting off a reported 20 000 households per month in 2001, while the Department of Provincial and Local Government recorded 256 325 electricity disconnections in other municipalities across the country in the last three months of that year (DPLG 2002: 30–31). Using these and other national survey data it was also estimated in 2002 that as many as 9.6 million people had been affected by electricity cut-offs at some point over the previous eight years, for varying lengths of time (McDonald 2002).

The number of electricity cut-offs appears to have slowed in South Africa, but they have not disappeared. In early 2007, for example, the City of Cape Town issued 455 000 'pink slips' threatening to cut off water and electricity supplies to households that had not paid their bills (*Mail & Guardian* 16 May 2007). Meanwhile, the largest single defaulters on electricity payments are businesses (about one-third of Cape Town's payment arrears), which are seldom threatened with cut-offs or the inconveniences, dangers and embarrassment that come with them.

One reason cut-offs may have slowed somewhat is that they are a politically explosive way to manage revenue collection. Another reason has been the introduction of prepaid electricity meters. The latter have been popular with utility managers because they avoid non-payment problems altogether, due to the fact that households are forced to pay for their electricity in advance (on a computerised system which is then entered into the household metering device). This system avoids the costly (political and financial) procedures of cut-offs while effectively downloading the act of cut-offs to households themselves, with people discontinuing their electricity consumption at the point that they no longer have the money to consume. The service provider also benefits from the fact that there is no longer any need to read meters on a monthly basis or to incur the administrative expenses of billing.

The popularity of this cost recovery technology with politicians and bureaucrats in South Africa is evidenced by the fact that Eskom installed 3.2 million of these meters between 1992 and 2003, and municipalities have installed hundreds of thousands more (Cape Town alone has installed close to half a million units). Prepaid electricity meters are now in use in most, if not all, of the 284 municipalities in the country, with one private company – Syntell – operating prepaid electricity meters in over 100 local authorities.

It should also be noted that South Africa is a leading international manufacturer of prepaid electricity meters. Durban-based Conlog is the largest producer of prepaid meters in the country and one of the largest in the world, able to boast (on its website) that it has 'the world's largest installed base of over four million electricity pre-payment meters'.[7] The company exports throughout Africa as well as to Asia and Latin America. In 2001 the company 'sold 300 000 prepaid electricity meters to Khartoum, one of the poorest cities in the world' (Ruiters 2007: 491).[8]

There is also the issue of free basic electricity. Introduced in 2001 as part of a pre-election promise by the ANC, a free 'lifeline' supply of electricity has reduced the cost burden of electricity somewhat for the poor, but the 50 kWh/month/household that is allocated is barely enough to run two 60-watt light bulbs for four hours a day. Eskom considers this 'sufficient to provide basic electricity services to a poor household' (Eskom 2006: 178), but a growing number of non-governmental organisations, civic groups and labour unions have challenged the government on this point, arguing that 50 kWh/month is an insufficient and 'miserly' allocation. Ruiters (Chapter 9 of this volume) takes the argument one step further, arguing that free electricity is in fact intended to 'contain consumption', keeping expectations low in poor areas and minimising the cross-subsidisation impact on suburban households and industry.

This is not to deny that the post-apartheid state has spent considerable amounts of money on the upgrading and extension of electricity supply in low-income areas of the country. Millions of people now have access who did not have it before, and the expansion of the grid across urban and rural areas and the introduction of a lifeline tariff have benefited many.

My argument is that the low-quality infrastructure that is often provided in low-income areas, the starkly uneven pricing schemes and aggressive cost recovery that is taking place to collect these fees, as well as the meagre supplies of free electricity being offered, all suggest an electricity sector restructuring strategy that is designed to create the image of a progressive, developmental state in South Africa while the substantive investments and subsidies are being geared towards MEC-plus industrial and service sectors and elite residential consumers. Even the mildly Keynesian goals of the original Reconstruction and Development Programme

(ANC 1994) to boost white goods sales in low-income areas with the introduction of electricity seem to have gone by the wayside, with attention firmly focused on the key export-oriented sectors of the MEC-plus economy and the elites that run it.

Neo-liberal strategies of privatisation and cost recovery have served to strengthen these biased investment patterns of electricity infrastructure in the country, creating a two-tiered delivery system that is qualitatively and quantitatively prejudiced towards the interests of MEC-plus capital.

Recolonising Africa

I turn my attention now to the implications of these reforms for the southern African region and the continent as a whole. I begin with an explanation of my use of the phrase 'recolonising Africa', and discuss how this relates to the electricity sector.

At one level, it is impossible to discuss capitalism without addressing colonisation and imperialism in some way, inherent as these dynamics have been to the profit-seeking behaviour of firms and their host countries for more than a century (Harvey 2003; Lenin 1996/1916; Luxemburg 2003/1913). Marxist theory tells us that heightened competition and new technological innovations compel capitalist firms to search for cheaper ways of producing goods and/or finding new consumers. One of the most common strategies has been to relocate (or outsource production and resource extraction) to another country where social wages are lower, environmental laws more lax and/or resources more abundant. The intensity and timing of this structural imperative differs sectorally, temporally and geographically, but the underlying structural necessity of profit-seeking competition obliges all large capitalist firms to globalise in some way or another.

South African capital is no different in this respect and has been aggressively expanding into the region/continent since political sanctions were lifted in the early 1990s (and in some cases earlier than this). Mining and mining-related firms are at the forefront of this African expansion, but there is significant growth in manufacturing and services as well (Bond 2006; Miller 2007; Southall 2007).

There is a useful debate over whether this expansion of South African capital is 'imperialist' or 'subimperialist'.[9] Proponents of the former position highlight a relatively independent role for South African capital and the South African state, arguing that 'South African multinational corporations are the social actors orchestrating the opening up of the continent implied by measures spelled out in the NEPAD [New Partnership for Africa's Development] programme. In this process, the South African state serves to facilitate this penetration of African economies...to enable capital to resolve crises of world capitalism that have been around since the early 1960s' (Lesufi 2004: 810). For Lesufi, it is 'the limits of the internal market [in South Africa]...and the large reserves of capital that this gave rise to...that explain the expansive tendencies of South African capital...The deepening economic, social and political crises meant that the ruling class could no longer sustain old methods of surplus extraction and thus had to establish a new foundation for capital accumulation [by expanding into the rest of Africa].'

The subimperialist argument differs insofar as it points to a 'USA-led capitalist Empire that uses Africa for surplus extraction and the spreading and deepening of global neo-liberalism, [one] that especially relies on South Africa for legitimacy and subimperial deputy-sheriff support' (Bond 2005: 220). In this view, the USA wants the extraction of 'ever cheaper minerals and cash crops' and South Africa acts as a regional hegemon. Imperialism is 'facilitated in Africa by the Pretoria-Johannesburg state-capitalist nexus, in part through' NEPAD and 'in part through the logic of private capital' (Bond 2005: 220).

It is beyond the scope of this chapter to engage with these debates in detail, though I would argue that in the (admittedly narrow) case of the electricity sector, South African capital – and the South African state – can be seen to be playing a more classically imperialist role. Though never operating in isolation from the larger dynamics of global capitalism, South Africa does function relatively autonomously from USA and other capital when it comes to the development of electricity infrastructure and management of the sector.

Evidence for this comes from South Africa's home-grown restructuring strategies. Though informed by the rollout neo-liberalism of Third-Way governments and international financial institutions such as the World Bank, South Africa's electricity restructuring plans are shaped primarily by the demands of its own MEC-plus economy – as is its own brand of 'developmental government', designed to put a democratic and egalitarian face on what is a largely skewed and unaccountable decision-making system.

Most importantly, this domestic restructuring strategy is being exported to the region and elsewhere on the continent. The imperative for this is once again the electricity needs of South Africa's MEC-plus economy. It stems partly from South Africa's desire to have more access to, and more control over, electricity production in the region for its own domestic use. Eskom estimated in 2006 that with electricity consumption growth rates of 2–3 per cent per annum, it could run out of excess peaking capacity in 2007 and excess base load in 2010, requiring an additional 1 200 MW of capacity per year (Eskom 2006: 36, 52). If South Africa is to meet the 6 per cent per annum GDP growth target set by national government, it will need as much as 2 000 MW per annum – approximately 47 000 MW of new capacity over the next 20 years, more than doubling existing capacity in the country.

Eskom's projected time frame for new generating capacity required to meet this anticipated domestic demand is outlined in Figure 1.1. Notably, these forecasts include approximately 5 per cent of capacity contributed by non-Eskom generators and imports from neighbouring countries, as well as a 15 per cent

Figure 1.1: Projected time frames for electricity demand and capacity development in South Africa

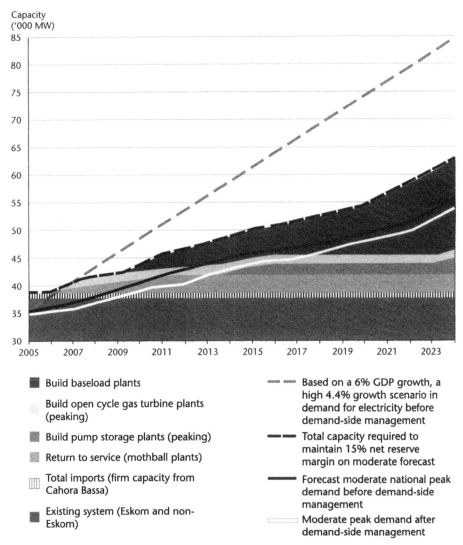

Source: Eskom 2006: 36

reserve margin which Eskom considers 'prudent' for its operation (down from as high as 30 per cent in the 1970s and 1980s).

Although much of this expansion in generating capacity will come from within South Africa, there are strong indications that significant investments in new generation will come from outside the country, to be transmitted back on a regional – even continental – power grid. Eskom says there is a limit to how much power would be imported, noting that 'for strategic reasons imports will be limited to the reserve margin of 15%' (Eskom 2006: 36), but there is no binding legislation to this effect, and pressure on the country to reduce carbon emissions from its coal-fired generators is likely to push it to look more favourably at the vast hydro-electric potential in southern and Central Africa.

The rapid expansion of South African capital into the continent is also creating pressures for new electricity capacity development in the region, critical as cheap and reliable electricity is to this MEC-plus-oriented growth trajectory. Some of this electricity may be exported from South Africa (Lesotho and Swaziland are 100 per cent dependent on South Africa for their supplies), but much will have to be produced in, or near, host countries.

The development of new generating capacity and a regional electricity transmission network capable of supporting these expansion plans is already well under way, and is being facilitated by the South African state through the creation of supranational bodies to govern electricity investments and operations. The Southern African Power Pool (SAPP) is one concrete indication of this regional energy strategy. Created in 1995 by various SADC members (see Table 1.2 for current SAPP membership), the primary aims of the SAPP have been to:

- facilitate the development of a competitive electricity market in the SADC region;
- give the end user a choice of electricity supplier;
- ensure that the southern African region is the region of choice for investment by energy-intensive users;
- ensure sustainable energy developments through sound economic, environmental and social practices;
- provide a forum for the development of a world-class, robust, safe, efficient, reliable and stable interconnected electrical system in the southern African region (SAPP 2006: 2).

Table 1.2: Southern African Power Pool membership, 2006

Name of utility	Status	Abbreviation	Country
Botswana Power Corporation	OP	BPC	Botswana
Electricidade de Moçambique	OP	EdM	Mozambique
Electricity Supply Corporation of Malawi	NP	ESCOM	Malawi
Empresa Naçional de Electricidade	NP	ENE	Angola
Eskom	OP	Eskom	South Africa
Lesotho Electricity Corporation	OP	LEC	Lesotho
NamPower	OP	NamPower	Namibia
Société Nationale d'Électricité	OP	SNEL	DRC
Swaziland Electricity Board	OP	SEB	Swaziland
Tanzania Electricity Supply Company Limited	NP	TANESCO	Tanzania
ZESCO Limited	OP	ZESCO	Zambia
Zimbabwe Electricity Supply Authority	OP	ZESA	Zimbabwe

Source: SAPP 2006
Note: OP = operating member; NP = non-operating member; DRC = Democratic Republic of the Congo

Connected by a grid of transmission lines, member states have engaged in extensive bilateral trading of power (increasing from 16 terawatt-hours (TWh) in 2004 to 19 TWh in 2005), and some limited short-term energy trading on a competitive pricing market (4 222 gigawatt-hours (GWh) in 2004) (SAPP 2006: 14). Figure 1.2 shows a map of existing and planned networks.

Figure 1.2: Southern African Power Pool transmission networks (existing and planned)

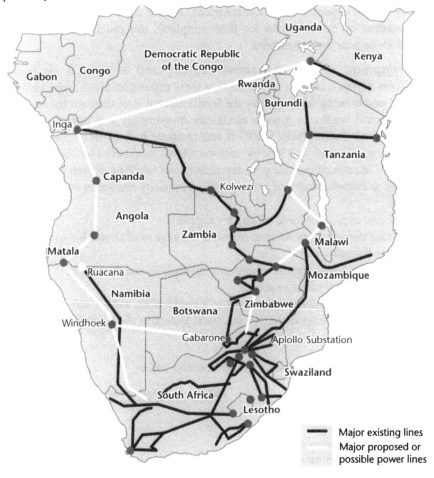

Source: Eskom 1998

However, the excess production capacity that existed for many years on the SAPP grid – approximately 8 000 MW in 2006 (SAPP 2006: 6) – is rapidly diminishing as overall electricity demand by member countries increases at about 3 per cent per annum. This has forced major infrastructure investments by member states in rehabilitation of the grid network (adding about 3 200 MW in 2007) and in new generating capacity in the short term (adding an additional 4 200 MW to the SAPP grid by 2010 at an estimated cost of US$3.8 billion) (SAPP 2006: 9).

Longer-term expansion plans would appear to be more continental in their orientation. Co-operation agreements signed between SAPP and the other power pools operating in Africa are one indication of this broadening geographic horizon, with efforts being made to integrate planning of transmission and production between SAPP, the Central African Power Pool (CAPP), COMELEC of North Africa (the Maghreb Electricity Committee, which includes Tunisia, Algeria, Libya, Mauritania and Morocco), the East African Power Pool (EAPP) and the West African Power Pool (WAPP) (see Hammons 2006; Musaba et al. 2006; Sparrow et al. 2005). Table 1.3 provides a breakdown of electricity production and consumption in the major regions of the continent, while Figure 1.3 provides a graphic illustration of the power pools and their member states (additional data are available for free download from http://www.hsrcpress.co.za/).

Table 1.3: Electricity capacity in Africa, by region, 2005

Region	Average potential (GWh)		Actual production (MW)		Actual consumption (kWh/hour)	Provisionally needed capacity (GWh)	
North Africa	41 000	(3.7%)	134 000	(33.2%)	739	209 300	(36.8%)
West Africa	100 970	(9.2%)	38 033	(9.4%)	143	50 546	(6.8%)
Central Africa	653 361	(57.7%)	10 537	(2.6%)	109	13 052	(2.4%)
Southern Africa	151 535	(13.8%)	208 458	(51.7%)	1 617	279 409	(49.0%)
East Africa	171 500	(15.6%)	12 281	(3.1%)	68	12 281	(3.0%)

Source: Hammons 2006: 675

Figure 1.3: African regional power pools – CAPP, EAPP, SAPP and WAPP

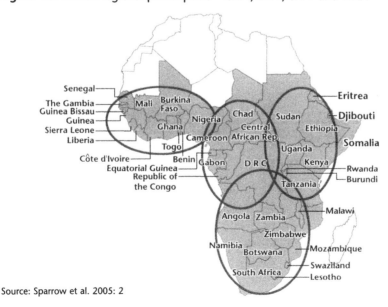

Source: Sparrow et al. 2005: 2

A concrete indication of this planned regional networking is the massive expansion plan for the Inga hydro project in the Democratic Republic of the Congo (DRC). Located 150 km upstream from the Congo River mouth and 225 km downstream from Kinshasa, the Inga site represents the biggest potential single-point source of hydro-power in the world, with networks planned to transmit this power down to South(ern) Africa and as far away as Europe and the Middle East (see Figure 1.4 for a map of how Inga fits into planned continental distribution networks).

Figure 1.4: A continental distribution network

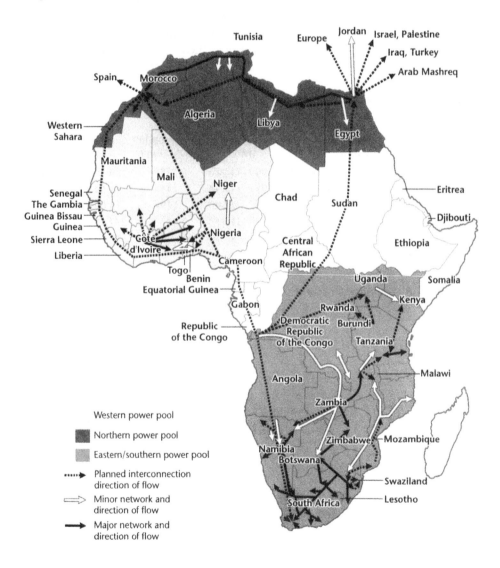

Source: Eskom 2001

The upgrading of Inga I and II (commissioned in 1972 and 1982 respectively), and the building of Inga III (at a cost, with its transmission systems, of about US$5.23 billion), are the first phases of this regional networking (*Engineering News* 4 June 2004). The much larger Grand Inga is still in the planning stages, and would increase the continent's electricity generation capacity by as much as 45 000 MW – a 50 per cent continental increase. At a cost of roughly US$50 billion to build – and as much as US$100 billion when transmission lines are factored in (Hammons 2006: 679) – it is a mammoth undertaking. Overall, the DRC is estimated to have 100 000 MW of hydro-power potential – 13 per cent of prospective global developments – boding well for longer-term electricity-dependent accumulation strategies in Africa (World Bank 2007) (for a detailed discussion of Inga see Chapter 5 in this volume by Hathaway and Pottinger).

Transmission plans are already under way for the current Inga projects, with the development of the Western Power Corridor Project (Westcor) being the most critical. This transmission line is expected to move 3 500–4 000 MW of power from Inga to southern Africa and to pick up an additional 6 500 MW of generation at Kwanza River in Angola (SAPP 2006: 9) (see Figure 1.5). The Westcor agreement was signed in October 2004 by the DRC, Namibia, Angola, South Africa and Botswana. Eskom and similar power utilities in each signatory nation will contribute funds to infrastructure development, while the remainder of the funding will probably come from the World Bank, the European Development Fund and private sources (including IPPs). The signing of a memorandum of understanding was seen as a crucial step towards attracting private-sector support.[10]

Figure 1.5: Planned Western Power Corridor Project

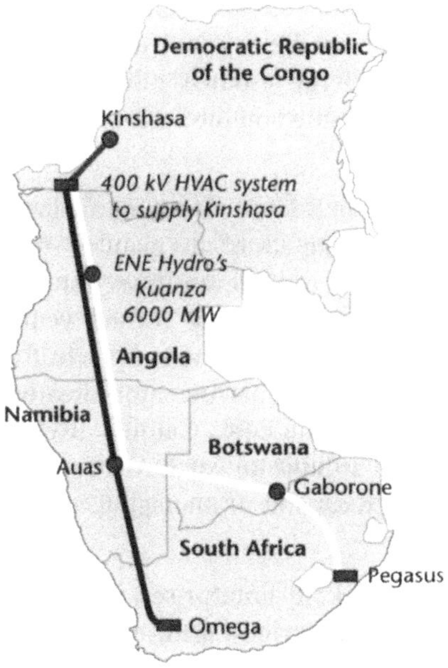

Source: SAPP 2007: 2

Who is going to benefit from these colossal infrastructure projects? The World Bank claims that Inga will provide 'cheaper and more reliable power' to the 93 per cent of DRC citizens without access to electricity, 'including over 350 000 new connections in Kinshasa' (World Bank 2007). But given the World Bank's neo-liberal emphasis on cost recovery, prepaid meters and commercialisation, it is hard to imagine how these 'pro-poor' projects would unfold any differently than they have in South Africa – if they unfold at all. According to Terri Hathaway, Africa Campaigner with International Rivers Network, 'Grand Inga is not meant to benefit Africa's poor…[P]oor people are being used to sell a prestige project that will benefit industrial enclaves and urban elites.'[11]

There is certainly no concrete evidence of low-income electricity distribution being made a priority within the Inga development plans. Westcor and SAPP documents use poverty reduction rhetoric but the investment focus is on high-voltage transmission lines along the Western Corridor that will bypass millions of low-income households in the region, feeding a grid of MEC-plus consumption in southern African cities and remote mining locations. So, too, will thousands of megawatts of power be exported half a continent away to feed Europe's electricity-hungry accumulation patterns.

Who will build and operate this new infrastructure? It is not clear where the funding is going to come from, but Westcor and SAPP literature suggest a heavy reliance on international financial institutions such as the World Bank (SADC 2006; SAPP 2006; UNECA 2006). In 2007, the World Bank contributed US$226.7 million in funding for the rehabilitation of Inga I and II (in partnership with unnamed sources), with plans to lend another US$272.3 million in another four phases of the project (to be co-financed with the African Development Bank). This is part of the World Bank's Regional and Domestic Power Markets Development Project, designed to support the 'regional networking approach', which it bases on the 'wisdom articulated by African leaders in NEPAD that the efficient use of energy resources offered by large scale power generation schemes such as Inga is best framed on the basis of the needs provided by multi-country markets' (World Bank 2007).

State-owned utilities will be involved as well, notably Eskom. As one of the largest electricity utilities in the world, and the overwhelming electricity giant in Africa, Eskom is well positioned to provide human and capital resources for these infrastructure developments. Although Westcor is an equally owned venture among the five signatory states, it is very likely that Eskom will take *de facto*, if not *de jure*, control of its operation. With joint projects and partnerships already in operation in Zambia, Botswana, Tanzania, Zanzibar, the DRC, Gambia, Rwanda, Kenya, Nigeria, Uganda and Mozambique, as well as links to North Africa, Eskom is already well integrated on a continental level and capable of managing complex, multi-country programmes.

According to Jan de Beer, Managing Director of Eskom Enterprises, interviewed for a BBC report, the building of a pan-African electricity grid, especially for exports to Europe, is 'going to happen, it's just a question of how fast we can do it. Africa's got everything – the resources, the raw materials and the energy. It's just a matter of developing it. If things go well, we'll have an African grid within four or five years. It's just a case of innovative thinking'.[12]

According to one independent analyst interviewed for the same BBC report, 'If Eskom can build the network, then the Southern European market is definitely there. Italy and Spain have some of the highest electricity prices in Europe and both are keen to import cheaper power.'

Eskom is prepared to commit up to R4 billion over the next four years. It is also likely that private South African capital from the electricity sector will become heavily involved in these infrastructure projects, either through competitive bidding for projects or through preferential access to contracts via the South African state.

There are, of course, opportunities here for large energy multinationals from North America, Europe and China – a point I return to shortly – but South African capital (including Eskom) is particularly well poised to expand its ownership and management roles in the electricity sector outside South Africa via these Inga-related projects.

In short, aggressive expansion plans for new power generation in southern and Central Africa provide enormous potential for the continued growth of an electricity-intensive MEC-plus economy out of South Africa. Once in place, this new electricity infrastructure will provide a long-term platform for stable (if unpredictable) accumulation patterns for South African capital – including opportunities for privatisation and greenfield developments in the electricity sector itself.

In the end, the power grids of today are akin to the railway lines of colonial Africa, lacing the continent with ribbons of steel that have little connection to the social, economic or demographic needs of its people. But instead of being driven solely, or even largely, by European capital, this particular 'scramble' for African resources is being determined primarily by the South African state and South African capital.

We can also see from these expansionist developments an important rescaling – and distantiation – of the South African state. Eskom is the most obvious example, active as it is throughout the continent and acting very much like a private multinational. Here we see a dramatic 'scaling up' of the South African state, as well as further distancing from public oversight and control, with Eskom's already notoriously opaque and unaccountable modes of operation (Cosatu 2005; Hallowes 2006; Steyn 2006) being exacerbated by the actions of its distant subsidiaries.

The creation of the SAPP and Westcor has served to heighten these estrangement trends, setting up powerful supranational decision-making centres that most South Africans are not even aware of, let alone able to have a sense of ownership of. Combined with NEPAD, the African Development Bank, the World Bank and other funding agencies involved in the electricity sector in the region, the electricity sector in South and southern Africa has arguably become less accountable, less democratic and less understood by the citizens that it serves than it was during the apartheid era.

The simultaneous 'scaling down' of the electricity sector to the municipal level in South Africa has only served to confuse matters. South African citizens ostensibly have the right to take part in decision-making about infrastructure investments and pricing decisions at the level of local government, but in reality these participatory mechanisms have tended to cater to the interests of residents and businesses with sufficient resources to participate effectively, or have simply been non-existent (Desai 2002; McDonald 2007; Van Heusden, Chapter 8 of this volume). In the end, developmental local government in South Africa has been little more than a ruse for undemocratic control of the electricity sector, turning these local agencies into enforcers of neo-liberal governance while obscuring the important flow of large, supranational public subsidies to private capital.

The Chinese factor

Having made an argument that a recolonisation of Africa is taking place 'from the bottom up', it is important to include a caveat. Despite its massive investment plans and its capacity and material incentives to intervene directly and indirectly in the electricity market on the continent, South Africa's initiatives will not go uncontested. There are large and powerful North American and European multinationals that have been active for many years in the electricity sector on the continent – including in South Africa itself – and these powerful firms continue to play a part in the renewed 'scramble' for African resources, competing with Eskom and private capital from South Africa for contracts and ownership opportunities in the electricity sector.

Equally important is the fact that South African capital (public and private) is not always welcome in other parts of the continent. As noted earlier, Eskom has a reputation as an aggressive multinational, as do other South African parastatals such as Rand Water and Umgeni Water (Loftus 2005; Van Rooyen & Hall 2007), and many private South African companies are seen as problematic by African governments and citizens alike. Electricity-related firms from South Africa may have important advantages over their European and North American rivals because of cultural, political, linguistic and economic ties on the continent, but their dominance of the market is not a foregone conclusion.

Another important factor is the (re-)entry of China into the electricity sector. Once very active in energy developments in Africa in the 1960s and 1970s – tied in part to Cold War politics – China has again become a major player on the resource scene. High-profile visits to African countries by senior Chinese officials, and continent-wide multilateral conferences on Africa–China relations, have served to heighten China's profile in this part of the world and have deepened its economic ties (spawning a mild panic in former colonial and current neo-colonial circles in Europe and North America).

African oil and minerals would appear to be the main objective of Chinese firms and the Chinese government, desperate as they are for key inputs to a rapidly growing economy. China is the second-largest consumer of crude oil in the world (after the USA) and now obtains more than 25 per cent of its supply from Africa – largely from Nigeria, Angola, Sudan and Equatorial Guinea. In addition to a wide range of minerals, additional African resources in demand include timber and natural gas. Another motivation for strengthened ties would appear to be the need to develop new markets for Chinese goods (CCS 2006).

Overall, bilateral trade between Africa and China increased tenfold from 1995 to 2005, from US$4 billion to almost US$40 billion, with a US$2.38 billion surplus in Africa's favour in 2005. In 2006 this trade volume doubled, with additional growth anticipated for the foreseeable future (Kirchick 2007).

Nevertheless, as the *New York Times* noted in February 2007, 'China is not yet an overwhelming presence in Africa'.[13] Of the US$29 billion in foreign direct investment that went into the continent in 2005, only US$1.2 billion (4.1 per cent) came from China. And 'except for a relatively small number of resource-rich countries such as Angola and Zambia, the majority of African economies have mounting trade deficits with China' (CCS 2006: 7).

What makes China's role important is its potential for growth as well as its willingness to provide 'favourable' trading terms and 'gifts' such as sports stadiums, hospitals, cheap financing and significant debt relief to its African trading partners, with few (if any) strings attached. China has, in fact, been remarkably uninterventionist in its African dealings, trading with any nation that has the resources it needs (including Sudan and Zimbabwe) and insisting that it will not interfere with internal politics. As one senior adviser to the Chinese government has been widely quoted as saying, 'No matter if it's rogue's oil or a friend's oil, we don't care. Human rights? We don't care. We care about oil...Anyone who helps China with energy is a friend' (as reported in the *Washington Post* 13 July 2005).

African governments appear to have met this outreach from China with cautious optimism. Alec Erwin, South Africa's Public Enterprises minister, captures this mood. When asked if he saw China as an 'opportunity or a threat', he said that 'the opportunities that China offers the SA economy are massively overwhelming ...and to think of China as a threat would be crazy' (*Sunday Times Business Times* 20 November 2006). When asked about accusations that China was operating in a neo-colonial fashion in Africa, Erwin said: 'I think we should be used to that, having dealt with the Europeans. I always find it a little bit amusing when the Europeans start telling us about neo-colonialism. I think China is like any major economy. We are big enough to look after ourselves, we don't need any advocacy from Europe warning us about China' (*Pretoria News* 30 March 2007).

With regard to the electricity sector, China's role is relatively small but growing. Its interests in the sector would appear to be twofold: firstly, ensuring electricity supplies to mining operations in which it has a direct or indirect stake; and secondly, as an investment outlet for skills and capital developed in its own electricity sector growth, most notably from the Three Gorges Dam.

China's activities in Africa in the electricity sector include the following:

- Zambia – China's Sinohydro is working to develop the 660 MW Lower Kafue Dam and has shown interest in the 120 MW Itezhi-Tezhi Dam (Bosshard 2006: 3). China Henan International Corporation won a bid from the Zambia Electricity Supply Corporation in 2006 to construct a substation as part of the power supply project for Lumwana copper mine in Zambia's Northwestern Province at a cost of US$23 million. The mine will be the biggest copper mine in Africa once completed in 2007 (CCS 2006: 68).
- Sudan – China holds the US$650 million contract to build the Merowe Dam and hydro-electricity plant north of Khartoum, as well as 1 745 kilometres of transmissions lines (*Sudan Tribune* 23 December 2003).
- Ethiopia – Chinese companies are building the 300 MW Yekeze Dam (Bosshard 2006: 3).
- Benin – China Export Import Bank is providing partial funding for the Adjarala Dam (Bosshard 2006: 3).
- Ghana – China is providing US$500 million in financing for the building of the Bui Dam (*Wall Street Journal* 15 September 2006).
- Mozambique – China Export Import Bank is providing up to US$2.3 billion in financing for the Mphanda Nkuwa Dam, with production capacity of 1 350 MW (the Cahora Bassa Dam, along the same river, has a capacity of 2 075 MW) (*Wall Street Journal* 15 September 2006). With 39 rivers flowing into the Indian Ocean, Mozambique has one of the highest electricity generation potentials in southern Africa, estimated at up to 12 000 MW of electricity (while the country consumes just 350 MW).[14]
- Zimbabwe – China is investing US$1.3 billion to manage coal mines and build three coal-fired power stations, in return for rights to chrome and other metals (*Southscan* 17 November 2006).
- Angola – China Export Import Bank provided a US$2 billion loan in 2005 for use in agriculture, energy and water, education and mass media. US$1 billion has been spent on various projects, including expansion of the electricity network in Luanda province (CCS 2006: 18–19).

In addition to these projects there are two Chinese energy companies worth highlighting. The first is Anhui Construction Engineering Group Co. Ltd, a state enterprise owned by the Anhui provincial government. The company has over 10 000 employees and focuses in part on water and electricity projects. It has worked in Tanzania, Algeria, Sri Lanka, Iraq, Kuwait, Madagascar, France, Russia, Finland, Denmark, Singapore, the USA, Pakistan, Afghanistan, Sierra Leone and Mongolia. The second is Sinohydro Ltd, also state-owned and the largest hydraulics and hydro-electricity construction company in China. The company also provides services in investment, finance, real estate and international trade. Sinohydro has built close to 100 hydro-electric stations in China, and has engaged in projects in more than 50 states in Asia, Africa, Europe and North America (CCS 2006: 92–96).

Will any of this interrupt the accumulation and recolonisation strategies of the South African state and MEC-plus capital? There can be little doubt that Chinese firms will continue to look for construction opportunities in the electricity sector on the continent, and that China will want to ensure cheap and reliable electricity supplies to its own mining and manufacturing investments in Africa, but these interests will probably be complementary to those of South Africa rather than derailing them, contributing to the overall expansion and deepening of a multinational extractive economy. Heightened competition may reduce super-profits for South African capital, and weaken Eskom's grip on the sector in the region, but neither of these possibilities threatens to undermine South Africa's current piloting of electricity expansion in the region or the overall growth trajectory of the MEC-plus economy.

The only real losers in this scenario will probably continue to be low-income urban and rural residents who cannot afford to buy their way onto the power grid or afford the cost recovery-driven prices being enforced by neo-liberal governments across the continent.

Conclusion

The phrase 'electric capitalism' may not be a perfect conceptual device, but it does help to shed light on a particularly important feature of contemporary capitalism, especially in countries such as South Africa which are so heavily reliant on cheap and abundant supplies of electric power. The 20th century has seen an entrenchment of electricity within production systems and outputs worldwide, making it an integral factor of globalisation dynamics in a 'silicon world'.

Industry and manufacturing continue to consume the lion's share of electricity production internationally, but the rise of producer services and the rapid spread of electricity-intensive consumer goods such as cell phones have begun to reshape some of the technological and managerial aspects of the electricity sector. Decisions about where electricity investments are made, how pricing schemes are designed, who builds and operates these services and who gets to make these choices are changing rapidly.

The underlying dynamics of boom-and-bust capitalism, and the valorisation of finance capital, still shape the material foundations of this globalised market economy, but the introduction of neo-liberal policies and institutional models has changed the particular ways in which these dynamics unfold.

In the case of the electricity sector in South Africa, the commercialisation and privatisation of service provision, the aggressive enforcement of cost recovery (particularly upon the poor) and the uneven ways in which capital benefits from public subsidies and investments are some of the concrete manifestations of these neo-liberal reforms. There was no preordained path to this particular outcome in South Africa – as policy blips along the way demonstrate – and there is no guarantee that the restructuring trajectory outlined above will not change again, but the material imperatives of abundant and competitively priced electricity for South African capital will continue to drive uneven patterns of investment and accumulation in the country and in the region.

In fact, revised restructuring in the electricity sector is virtually guaranteed, inscribed as it is in the very inequality of neo-liberal reform. Resistance to privatisation, cut-offs and prepaid meters has been strong in South Africa and this will continue, helping to speed up the cycle of reforms. The most notable opposition has come from social movements such as the SECC and the Anti-Privatisation Forum, but labour unions, environmental justice groups and other non-governmental organisations have also been active. This resistance was perhaps strongest during the peak of electricity cut-offs in the early 2000s, and has become more fragmented and divided than it once was, but it continues to exist, lobbying the state for a more equitable distribution of the benefits of South Africa's rich electricity supplies while at the same time arguing for 'greener' energy and a reduction of the hedonistic consumption patterns of industry and wealthy elites. There is also a growing recognition of the gendered inequalities that have been a part of the South African energy landscape, much of it pre-dating neo-liberalism (see Annecke, Chapter 11 in this volume).

Resistance to these restructuring initiatives is made all the more urgent – and all the more problematic – by the large-scale and long-term nature of electricity sector investments. With generation plants costing billions of dollars to build, and having lifespans of 30+ years (with nuclear facilities having much longer-term impacts), it is imperative that more public debate takes place concerning the nature and purpose of these investments in South Africa. Once in place, electricity can be redirected, prices can be changed and management systems and ideologies altered, but opportunities will have been lost once the 'spatial fix' of accumulation strategies in electricity has been implemented, much of which will be impossible to alter in the short to medium term.

The secrecy with which much of this planning is taking place (particularly on the nuclear side; see Fig, Chapter 6 in this volume), and the fragmented levels at which capital and the state are operating, do not bode well for critical intervention, but it is possible – a discussion I return to in the concluding chapter of this book.

An additional concern is the ways in which not only physical infrastructure but neo-liberal ideologies are inundating the larger regional and continental restructuring plans for electricity. The chapters in this volume on Uganda and

Tanzania (Chapters 14 and 15) give some indication of this creeping neo-liberal hegemony. Nor is electricity the only sector subject to these neo-liberal pressures, as work on water privatisation in Africa indicates (Bayliss & Fine 2007; McDonald & Ruiters 2005).

This is a critical moment in South and southern Africa's history. With some of the largest investments ever made in the region being directed towards the electricity sector over the next 5–10 years, there is an opportunity to make them more equitable, more democratic and more sustainable. Implementing more progressive reforms will be an uphill battle, but understanding the nature of this particular restructuring beast is at least one step along the way.

Notes

1   Engels's writing on the subject can be found online at
http://www.marxists.org/archive/marx/works/1883/don/index.htm. Chapter VI looks
specifically at electricity.

2   The British thermal unit (BTU or Btu) is a unit of energy used in the USA to describe
the heat value (energy content) of fuels. When used as a unit of power, BTU per hour
(BTU/h) is understood. A BTU is defined as the amount of heat required to raise the
temperature of one pound of water by one degree Fahrenheit.

3   Information obtained from the Sustainable Energy Policy Concepts website, accessed
28 May 2007, http://www.ises.org/sepconew/Pages/CountryCaseStudySA/1.html.

4   This figure is based on the author's readings of various city reports and municipal tariff
structures which tend to differentiate between 'low' and 'high' electricity consumption at
between 600 and 800 kWh per month. For figures on Cape Town see CCT (2003: 6).

5   This estimate is derived from data from the City of Cape Town which show that low-
income households consume about one-third of the electricity that is consumed by
domestic residences in that city (CCT 2003: 6). If this percentage is extrapolated to the
national level, low-income households consume about one-third of the 15 per cent of
electricity that is consumed by domestic residences in the country as a whole. The actual
figure could be significantly lower, however, given the dearth of electricity connections in
rural areas.

6   The California electricity crisis of 2000–2001 resulted from the manipulation of a partially
deregulated California energy system by private energy companies such as Enron. The
crisis was characterised by a combination of extremely high prices and rolling blackouts.
Due to price controls, utility companies were paying more for electricity than they were
allowed to charge customers, forcing the bankruptcy of Pacific Gas and Electric and the
public bail-out of Southern California Edison. For more information see Weare (2003).

7   http://www.conlog.co.za/aboutus/accessed 20 December 2007.

8   Conlog has since been purchased by the French multinational Schneider Electric, and
there are other international firms involved in the prepaid market in the country.

9   I am grateful to Toby Moorsom for his assistance with literature reviews for this section of the chapter.

10 Sourced from *World News* online, accessed 2 June 2007, http://archive.wn.com/2007/01/27/1400/saenergy/.

11 International Rivers Network (Cameroon), 'Grand Inga: A dam for prestige, not poverty reduction in Dem. Republic of Congo'. Press release, 15 March 2007, accessed 15 May 2007, http://www.irn.org/programs/congo/index.php?id=070316inga.html.

12 Interview with BBC News, 17 October 2007, accessed 17 October 2007, http://news.bbc.co.uk/2/hi/business/2307057.stm.

13 China's influence in Africa arouses some resistance, *New York Times*, 10 February 2007.

14 www.macauhub.com.mo, accessed 17 September 2007.

References

Ahmad J (1995) Funding the metropolitan areas of South Africa. *Finance and Development* 32: 50–53

ANC (African National Congress) (1994) *The Reconstruction and Development Programme: A policy framework*. Johannesburg: Umanyano Publications

Apter A (2005) *The pan-African nation: Oil and the spectacle of culture in Nigeria*. Chicago: University of Chicago Press

Ashe B (2002) ESKOM: Corporate powerhouse or green company?: South Africa's mammoth electric company leads the way in utility privatisation while touting sustainable development. *CorpWatch* 16 August. Accessed 12 January 2007, http://www.corpwatch.org/article.php?id=3528

Azar K (2000) Power consumption and generation in the electronics industry – a perspective. Paper presented at the Sixteenth IEEE Semi-Therm Symposium. Accessed 25 May 2007, http://ieeexplore.ieee.org/iel5/6765/18078/00837085.pdf

Bayliss K & Fine B (2007) *Privatization and alternative public sector reform in sub-Saharan Africa: Delivering on electricity and water*. Basingstoke: Palgrave MacMillan

Bond P (1999) *Elite transition: From apartheid to neoliberalism in South Africa*. Durban: University of Natal Press

Bond P (2005) US empire and South African subimperialism. In L Panitch & C Leys (eds) *The Empire reloaded: Socialist register 2005*. New York: Monthly Review Press

Bond P (2006) *Looting Africa: The economics of exploitation*. London: Zed Books

Bosshard P (2006) China conquers Africa's hydropower market: International standards on the block. *World Rivers Review* 21(4): 3

Brenner N & Theodore N (2002) Cities and the geographies of 'actually existing neoliberalism'. *Antipode* 34(3): 349–379

CCS (Centre for Chinese Studies) (2006) *China's interest and activity in Africa's construction and infrastructure sectors: A research undertaking evaluating China's involvement in Africa's construction and infrastructure sector*. Centre for Chinese Studies, Stellenbosch University.

Accessed 20 December 2007, http://www.dfid.gov.uk/pubs/files/chinese-investment-africa-full.pdf

CCT (City of Cape Town) (2003) *Cape Town energy strategy.* Draft, October. Cape Town: CCT

CCT (2004) *City of Cape Town budget, 2004–2005.* Cape Town: CCT

CCT (2006) *RED 1 (City of Cape Town supply area): Schedule of electricity tariffs effective from 1 July 2006.* Accessed 5 August 2006, www.capetown.gov.za/wcmstemplates/Electricity.aspx?clusid=458&IDPathString=5992-6182&catparent=6182#electariff

Christie R (1984) *Electricity, industry and class in South Africa.* Albany, NY: State University of New York Press

Cohen GA (1972) Karl Marx and the withering away of social science. *Philosophy and Public Affairs* 1(2): 182–203

Collard F, Feve P & Portier F (2005) Electricity consumption and ICT in the French service sector. *Energy Economics* 27: 541–550

Cosatu (2005) Cosatu, NUM, Numsa and Samwu submission on the Electricity Regulation Bill. Paper presented to the Portfolio Committee on Minerals and Energy, 28 October

Desai A (2002) *We are the poors: Community struggles in post-apartheid South Africa.* New York: Monthly Review Press

DME (Department of Minerals and Energy, South Africa) (1996) *Meeting South Africa's electricity distribution challenges.* Pretoria: DME

DME (2003a) *Integrated energy plan for the Republic of South Africa.* Pretoria: DME

DME (2003b) *Guidelines for the introduction of free basic electricity services.* Department of Minerals and Energy, May 5. Accessed December 2007, http://www.dme.gov.za/pdfs/energy/electricity/fbe_guidelines.doc

DME (2006a) *South Africa's mineral industry: 2005/2006.* Pretoria: DME

DME (2006b) *Digest of South African energy statistics.* Pretoria: DME

Doms M (1993) *Energy intensity, electricity consumption, and advanced manufacturing technology usage.* Working Paper No. 93, Center for Economic Studies, US Census Bureau

DPLG (Department of Provincial and Local Government, South Africa) (2002) Quarterly monitoring of municipal finances and related activities, summary of questionnaires for quarter ended 31 December 2001. Mimeo. Pretoria: DME

Dunsire A (1999) Then and now: Public administration, 1953–1999. *Political Studies* 47(2): 360–378

Eberhard A (2005) From state to market and back again: South Africa's power sector reforms. *Economic & Political Weekly* 50: 5309–5317

EDI (Electricity Distribution Industry) (2004) *The transformer.* EDI Holdings newsletter, October

EETD (Environmental Energy Technologies Division) (1998) *Small appliance energy use surging in U.S. homes.* US Department of Energy, Lawrence Berkeley National Laboratory, April. Accessed 15 May 2007, http://www.lbl.gov/Science-Articles/Archive/res-energy-growth.html

Eskom (1998) *Annual report 1998*. Pretoria: Eskom

Eskom (2001) *Annual report 2001*. Accessed 15 December 2007, http://www.eskom.co.za/annreport02/home.htm

Eskom (2006) *Annual report 2006*. Pretoria: Eskom

Eskom (2007a) *Handover to the new chief executive of Eskom*. Media release, April 16. Accessed 29 May 2007, http://www.eskom.co.za/live/content.php?Item_ID=3714&Revision=en/0

Eskom (2007b) *Strategic pricing directions for standard tariffs, 2007*. Pretoria: Eskom

Fiil-Flynn M (2001) *The electricity crisis in Soweto*. Occasional Papers Series No. 4. Cape Town: Municipal Services Project

Fine B & Rustomjee Z (1996) *The political economy of South Africa: From minerals-energy complex to industrialisation*. London: Hurst & Company

Greenpeace (2007) *Twelve clever ways to save lots of electricity and money (and, by the way, also the planet)*. Accessed 29 May 2007, http://www.greenpeace.org/canada/en/campaigns/climate-and-energy/solutions/energy-efficiency/12-steps

Hallowes D (2006) Sustainable energy?: Towards a civil society review of South African energy policy and implementation. Mimeo. Johannesburg: Earthlife Africa

Hammer J (2006) *South Africa's energy meltdown: Power crisis*. Accessed 20 December 2007, http://newsgarden.org/community/?q=node/234

Hammons TJ (2006) Status, plans of action, further developments, and recommendations for power pools in Africa. *IEEE Transactions on Power Systems* 21(2): 673–682

Harvey D (1982) *The limits to capital*. London: Verso

Harvey D (2003) *The new imperialism*. Oxford: Oxford University Press

Hemson D & O'Donovan M (2006) Putting numbers to the scorecard: Presidential targets and the state of delivery. In S Buhlungu, J Daniel, R Southall & J Lutchman (eds) *State of the nation: South Africa 2005–2006*. Cape Town: HSRC Press

Horowitz MJ (2004) Electricity intensity in the commercial sector: Market and public program effects. *The Energy Journal* 25(2): 115–137

Kirchick J (2007) Africa's new hegemon. *The Weekly Standard* 12(24): 17–18

Koomey JG, Calwell C, Laitner S, Thornton J, Brown RE, Eto JH, Webber C & Cullicott C (2002) Sorry, wrong number: The use and misuse of numerical facts in analysis and media reporting of energy issues. *Annual Review of Energy and the Environment* 27: 119–158

Koumelis T (2005) Tourism is South Africa's new gold. *Travel Daily News* July 6: 12–14

Lenin VI (1996/1916) *Imperialism: The highest stage of capitalism*. London: Pluto Press

Lesufi I (2004) South Africa and the rest of the continent: Towards a critique of the political economy of NEPAD. *Current Sociology* 52(5): 809–829

Leys C (2001) *Market-driven politics: Neoliberal democracy and the public interest*. London: Verso

Loftus A (2005) Free water as commodity: The paradoxes of Durban's water service transformation. In DA McDonald & G Ruiters (eds), *The age of commodity: Water privatization in southern Africa*. London: Earthscan Press

Luxemburg R (2003/1913) *The accumulation of capital*. New York: Routledge

Madamombe I (2005) Energy key to Africa's prosperity: Challenges in West Africa's quest for electricity. *Africa Renewal* 18(4): 6–7

McDonald DA (2002) The theory and practice of cost recovery in South Africa. In DA McDonald & J Pape (eds) *Cost recovery and the crisis of service delivery in South Africa*. London: Zed Books

McDonald DA (2008) *World city syndrome: Neoliberalism and inequality in Cape Town*. New York: Routledge

McDonald DA & Pape J (eds) (2002) *Cost recovery and the crisis of service delivery in South Africa*. London: Zed Books, Cape Town: HSRC

McDonald DA & Ruiters G (eds) (2005) *The age of commodity: Water privatization in southern Africa*. London: Earthscan Press

MERG (Macro-Economic Research Group) (1993) *Making democracy work: A framework for macroeconomic policy in South Africa*. Cape Town: Centre for Development Studies

Miller D (2007) South Africa as regional bully boy: African farmers protest. *South African Labour Bulletin* 30(5): 19–23

Musaba L, Naidoo P & Chikova A (2006) Southern African Power Pool plan development. Paper presented at IEEE Power Engineering Society General Meeting, June 18, Montreal

Naledi (National Labour and Economic Development Institute) (2006) *Equity and efficiency in the restructuring of South Africa's electricity sector*. Johannesburg: Naledi

Odubiyi A & Davidson IE (2004) An assessment of the proposed TSO model for South Africa's proposed new electricity industry. *Seventh AFRICON Conference in Africa* 2: 855–859

Olcay-Unver IH, Gupta RK & Kibaroglu A (eds) (2003) *Water development and poverty reduction*. London: Kluwer Academic

Peck J & Tickell A (2002) Neoliberalizing space. *Antipode* 34(3): 380–404

Qotole M, Xali M & Barchiesi F (2001) *The commercialisation of waste management in South Africa*. Occasional Papers Series, No. 3. Cape Town: Municipal Services Project

Ross M (1992) Efficient energy use in manufacturing. *Proceedings of the National Academy of Sciences of the United States of America* 89(3): 827–831

Ruiters G (2007) Contradictions in municipal services in contemporary South Africa: Disciplinary commodification and self-disconnections. *Critical Social Policy* 27(4): 487–508

Rutledge I (2006) *Addicted to oil: America's relentless drive for energy security*. London: IB Tauris & Co.

SACN (South African Cities Network) (2004) *State of the cities report*. Johannesburg: SACN

SACN (2007) *Media release: Focus on cities*. Accessed 17 May 2007, http://www.sacities.co.za/pr/2.stm

SADC (Southern African Development Community) (2006) *Directorate of infrastructure and Services Council of Ministers 2006 media brief.* Accessed 20 December 2007, http://www.sadc.int/news/news_details.php?news_id=630

SALGRC (South African Local Government Research Centre) (2007a) Crime and electricity supply the main constraints to investment in Cape Town. *SA Local Government Briefing* April: 19–24

SALGRC (2007b) Housing study by FinScope South Africa. *SA Local Government Briefing* September: 43–44

SAPP (Southern African Power Pool) (2006) *Annual report 2006.* Accessed 1 June 2007, http://www.sapp.co.zw/documents/SAPP%20AnnRep'06.pdf

SAPP (2007) *The Westcor Power Corridor Project.* Accessed 1 June 2007, http://www.sapp.co.zw/documents/The%20Westerns%20Power%20Corridor%20Project.pdf

Sassen S (2001) *The global city: New York, London, Tokyo* (2nd edition). Princeton, NJ: Princeton University Press

Sassen S (ed.) (2002) *Global networks, linked cities.* New York: Routledge

SEA (Sustainable Energy Africa) (2006) *State of energy in South African cities: Setting a baseline.* Cape Town: SEA

SLM (Socialism and Liberation Magazine) (2005) Oil, capitalism and natural disasters. *Socialism and Liberation Magazine* 2(11)

Smith DM (ed.) (1992) *The apartheid city and beyond: Urbanization and social change in South Africa.* London: Routledge

Southall R (2007) South Africa in Africa: Introduction. In S Buhlungu, J Daniel, R Southall & J Lutchman (eds) *State of the nation: South Africa 2007.* Cape Town: HSRC Press

Sparrow FT, Bowen BH & Yu Z (2005) The future of SAPP, WAPP, CAPP and EAPP. Paper presented at the IEEE Power Engineering Society General Meeting, June 15, San Francisco

Starr P (1988) The meaning of privatization. *Yale Law and Policy Review* 6: 6–41

Steyn G (2006) *Investment and uncertainty: Historical experience with power sector investment in South Africa and its implications for current challenges.* Working Paper prepared for the Management Programme in Infrastructure Reform and Regulation, University of Cape Town

Stoker G (1989) Local government for a post-Fordist society. In J Stewart & G Stoker (eds) *The future of local government.* Basingstoke, UK: Macmillan

UNECA (United Nations Economic Commission for Africa) (2006) *Report on 'Energy for sustainable development' in Africa: Extended executive summary.* Addis Ababa: UNECA

USEPA (USA Environmental Protection Agency) (2007) *Energy trends in selected manufacturing sectors: Opportunities and challenges for environmentally preferable energy outcomes, March.* Accessed 2 May 2007, http://www.epa.gov/sectors/energy/index.html

Van Horen C, Simmonds G & Parker G (1998) *Joint implementation initiatives in South Africa: A case study of two energy-efficiency projects.* Ernest Orlando Lawrence Berkeley National Laboratory, Environmental Energy Technologies Division. Prepared for the USA Environmental Protection Agency Climate Policy and Program Division

Van Rooyen C & Hall D (2007) *Public is as private does: The case of Rand Water in South Africa.* Occasional Papers Series No. 15. Cape Town: Municipal Services Project

Weare C (2003) *The California electricity crisis: Causes and policy options.* San Francisco: Public Policy Institute of California

Wegerif M (2004) *A critical appraisal of South Africa's market-based land reform policy: The case of the Land Redistribution for Agricultural Development programme in Limpopo.* Nkuzi Development Association, Research Report No. 19

Winkler H (2006) Energy policies for sustainable development in South Africa's residential and electricity sectors: Implications for mitigating climate change. DPhil thesis, University of Cape Town

World Bank (2007) *World Bank approves a grant of US$296.7 million for the development of regional and domestic power markets.* Press release No. 2007/409/AFR. Accessed 3 June 2007, http://web.worldbank.org/WBSITE/EXTERNAL/COUNTRIES/AFRICAEXT/ CONGODEMOCRATICEXTN/0,,contentMDK:21351576~menuPK:349472~pagePK:2865 066~piPK:2865079~theSitePK:349466,00.html

Zille H (2007) *Addressing the constraints to economic growth.* Keynote address given at the Cape Town Regional Chamber of Commerce and Industry symposium, April 24. Accessed 3 May 2007, http://www.capetown.org.za/clusters/viewarticle3.asp?conid=14987

CHAPTER 2

Escom to Eskom: From racial Keynesian capitalism to neo-liberalism (1910–1994)

Leonard Gentle

> The South African Electricity Supply Commission sees its task as to 'render, by the provision of power without profit, a worthy and ever-increasing contribution to the development of South Africa and the welfare of her peoples'. (Escom 1948, cited in Christie 1984: 1)

> Eskom will grow shareholder value by exceeding the needs of local and foreign customers with energy and related services. (Eskom 2006)

In 1987 the apartheid state amended the Electricity Act (No. 42 of 1922) and, amongst other things, scrapped the Electricity Supply Commission (Escom) which had been set up in 1923 as a result of the 1922 Act. In its place a parastatal called Eskom came into being. In many ways the change from Escom to Eskom (its Afrikaans translation) seemed a mere change in nomenclature. Indeed the 1987 change, as well as the Eskom Act (No. 41 of 1987) and, later, the post-apartheid Eskom Conversion Act (No. 13 of 2001) – which made Eskom subject to the Companies Act (No. 61 of 1973) and a dividend-paying, tax-paying entity – has largely been downplayed by commentators, given that Eskom remained a state-owned company.[1]

Eberhard (2003: 2), for instance, speaks of the 1987–2001 reforms that transformed Escom into Eskom as 'slow and modest', noting that 'Eskom remains in state ownership. There appears to be no political urgency to unbundle Eskom'.

But the change from Escom to Eskom marks a radical rupture in the nature of South African capitalism and its mode of accumulation. The 1987 Act scrapped section 6(4) of the 1922 Act which specified that electricity should be supplied 'in the public interest' and that the Commission's operations should be carried out 'neither at a profit nor at a loss' (see Ramokgoba 2004). It replaced this specification with the wording: 'to provide the system by which the electricity needs of the consumer may be satisfied in the most cost-effective manner, subject to resource constraints and the national interest' (Electricity Act of 1987). This corporatisation perpetrated by the apartheid state in its neo-liberal phase (circa

1987) has been carried forward under the ANC government since 1994, leading to the Eskom Conversion Act of 2001 which saw Eskom become an entity on the JSE Limited, offering shareholder value to its sole shareholder – the South African state – and paying dividends and taxes.

This is a change from a form of Keynesian racial capitalism,[2] in which the state secured the conditions necessary for accumulation for the capitalist class as a whole based on cheap black labour power, cheap energy and regulated capital, to a neo-liberal state attempting to open up new arenas for commodification. In the case of the former the state intervened to *constrain* the commodification of certain processes (electrification, rail transport) deemed essential to ensure capital accumulation; in the case of the latter, the state intervened to *expand* the terrain of commodification.

In its evolution since its establishment in 1923 Escom/Eskom has been at the centre of, and epitomised the trajectory of, the South African form of capitalism; a trajectory that saw a distant outpost of the British Empire in the 19th century transmogrify into a semi-industrialised power with a strong national bourgeoisie between the World Wars, and into a continental power with imperialist ambitions in the early 21st century. Escom/Eskom's various guises have also epitomised the various political configurations inside which accumulation took place – from segregation between the Act of Union in 1910 and 1948, to grand apartheid after 1948, to reformed apartheid in the 1980s and the neo-liberal restructuring that took place prior to and after the end of apartheid in 1994.

This chapter looks at that trajectory as a set of milestones, and locates Escom/Eskom on its path. Along the way it engages with a number of assumptions made today about South Africa's electrification needs, about the social forces which underpin the current conjuncture and about the nature of the South African state in the Mbeki period.[3] These include assumptions about the need for competition to challenge Eskom's monopoly (for much of its history, in the form of its predecessor, Escom, Eskom *was* challenged by a competitor, in the form of the Victoria Falls and Transvaal Power Company [VFTPC]); about the need for separation between generation, transmission and distribution (which did in fact exist until 1948); about the need to generate its own finances and not be a drain on the fiscus (this was how it was set up, in the first place); about the need for a developmental state (we've had that since the 1920s); about the irrationality of the apartheid system and the view that it was bad for business (it was Anglo American that paid for the nationalisation of the VFTPC); about the apparent isolationism of the apartheid regime (Escom was receiving World Bank loans and private USA bank loans from the 1950s).

A history of Escom/Eskom is therefore a welcome opportunity to re-engage with the critical questions of the nature and character of the new state, and its continuities and discontinuities with the previous century's phases of segregation (1910–1948), grand apartheid (1948–1972) and reformed apartheid (mid-

1970s–1994). This chapter is therefore not an empirical history of Escom/Eskom from its origins to 1994 but a look at the changing socio-economic character of Escom/Eskom as an index of the changing character of the state, underpinned by the changing character of the social forces – chiefly capital in its various fractions and configurations – which contested the state in the above periods.

Electrification in the period of segregation: from state regulation to state monopoly

The period of segregation I designate from the Act of Union establishing South Africa as a polity in 1910, to the victory of the National Party (NP) in 1948 and its introduction of the policy of apartheid. Apartheid's policy of racial oppression of the black majority did not initiate the disenfranchisement of black people – after all, the Act of Union had established the notion of citizenship and governance as exclusively for those of European descent and granted limited citizenship rights to black South Africans. Nor did various forms of influx control (e.g. the Native Urban Areas Act [No. 21 of 1923], subsequently amended throughout the 1920s) and the compound labour system (a product of the Kimberley diamond mines in the late 19th century) or even political repression (witness the various Hertzog Bills of the 1920s and 1930s[4]) begin under 1948-style apartheid.

Political oppression and the exclusion of black people from citizenship were features of the 1910–1948 period. In this sense there is much continuity with the post-1948 apartheid period. But the name 'segregation' is used here to distinguish the 1910–1948 period from the systematic racial engineering (in the form of legislation such as the Group Areas Act (No. 41 of 1950) and the Population Registration Act (No. 30 of 1950) of the 1950s) that occurred post-1948 and, in particular, the state-legislated notion that black people were members of different nations with separate geographies (first bantustans, then homelands and then independent/self-governing states).

The year that marked the end of the period of segregation and the rise of the era of grand apartheid, 1948, is also the year of the evolution of Escom from a state regulator of private and municipal electricity generation and distribution, a role it had fulfilled since 1923, to that of a state monopoly over electricity generation, transmission and provision.

Electrification in the period of segregation took place largely under a regime of private and municipal provision, with Escom playing the role of regulator and subordinate supplier. The electrification of the country actually started before the Act of Union in 1910; it dates from the period of activity which revolutionised social relations in South Africa, namely mining – first diamond mining in the Kimberley area and then gold mining on the Witwatersrand. Electricity was first publicly supplied in South Africa in 1882 when the diamond city of Kimberley switched on electric street lights. The discovery of gold on the Witwatersrand in 1886 led to Johannesburg installing an electricity reticulation system in 1891.

Pretoria followed suit in 1892, Cape Town and Durban in 1893, Pietermaritzburg in 1895, East London in 1899, Bloemfontein in 1900 and Port Elizabeth in 1906 (Christie 1984: 6). These city-wide installations were carried out by municipalities that established power stations, and generated and distributed electricity for the commercial city centres.

Outside of these instances of municipal installation, the history of electrification in South Africa was shaped by the energy needs of the nerve centre of industry – the gold-mining industry of the Witwatersrand. In 1948 gold mining alone consumed as much as 59 per cent of all electricity generated in the country (Christie 1984: 218); Fine and Rustomjee (1996) go so far as to say that a 'minerals-energy complex' has been fundamental to the shaping of the South African social formation.

The fortunes of South Africa's electrification march were therefore directly tied to the vicissitudes of mining. In this regard the mining revolution transformed South Africa's social relations irrevocably. Frederick Johnstone (1976), Stanley Trapido (1971) and others successfully established the link between the peculiar needs of the mining barons and the ensuing set of racial labour legislation which came to be known first as the compound labour system, then as segregation and, finally, as apartheid.

Briefly, Johnstone (1976) and others have argued that the nature of South Africa's gold mines – deep-level, low-grade ore, albeit with consistency of reefs – placed a great burden on cost reduction to ensure profitability. Unlike other commodities where these greater costs could be compensated for by higher prices, the price of gold was fixed internationally. This squeeze imposed a severe need to reduce costs – chiefly through the lowering of labour costs.

At the same time, the deep-level nature of the reefs and their distance from ports required capital expenditure on refrigeration and cooling, blasting and transportation processes – all of which raised energy costs which could not be compensated for by higher consumer prices for the final products. So, like labour, energy costs had to be reduced.

Electrification in South Africa therefore followed the demands of the mining industry. Power stations were initially sited in close proximity to the Witwatersrand mines, with steam-powered generators using high-grade available coal railed in; later, coal pithead-located power stations using low-grade coal were built which could transmit energy over power transmission lines to the mines.

As the mining industry grew in absolute terms and along specific geographical contours, so electrification expanded and followed those contours. In 1905 the nine largest power stations sold a total of only 42.6 megawatt-hours (MWh) per year. In that year the total generating capacity was only 18 MW. Within less than 10 years, the VFTPC was selling 500 MWh per annum and had generating capacity of 112 MW. Over this short period South Africa developed, for its time, one of the most sophisticated energy systems in the British Empire, generating more electricity than London, Birmingham and Sheffield combined (Christie 1984).

Initially mining houses set up their own power stations – at Randfontein, East Rand Proprietary Mines and New Kleinfontein. Some collieries also set up their own power stations. And in addition there were private power companies in existence – the Rand Central Electric Works Limited and the General Electric Power Company Limited, for instance.

But the need for economies of scale and for reliability drove mine owners to seek larger and more centralised sources of electrical energy.

> [Initially]…the use of electricity by the mining companies was restricted to illuminating work areas and driving small equipment. However, as the exploitation of gold deposits became more complicated, the power requirements of the mining companies increased. As the gold-mining industry recovered from the effects of the Anglo Boer War, an adequate supply of cheap power became essential. (Eskom 2006)

The increased demand for electrical power opened up possibilities for entrepreneurship and the Witwatersrand mines offered a major opportunity for a centralised power provision system. The building of a bridge across the Victoria Falls, long-standing imperial ambitions and the example set by the building of a hydro-electric power station at Niagara Falls in the USA, inspired Cecil John Rhodes to think of setting up a similar hydro-electric power station at the relatively distant Victoria Falls and selling the power to the Witwatersrand gold mines over transmission lines. Despite the fact that the seasonal variations in water pressure at Victoria Falls made such a project unfeasible, the idea of a centralised power system for the Witwatersrand mines did offer opportunities for profits, and the name of the original proposed energy source lived on in the final enterprise.

The Victoria Falls Power Company (VFPC) was created in 1906 by a subsidiary of Rhodes's British South Africa Company – initially as a venture capitalist enterprise backed by German money, specifically the Deutsche Bank and Dresdner Bank; the hostilities of the World War I saw this enterprise being transferred into British hands. The VFPC became viable once coal-generated steam power from the Eastern Transvaal coal mines became a more practical alternative, and the VFPC later became the Victoria Falls and Transvaal Power Company (VFTPC).

From 1906 until it was nationalised and incorporated into Escom in 1948, the VFTPC, as a private power company, was the principal supplier of electricity to the Transvaal gold mines, and for most of this period it eclipsed Escom (which, apart from generating electricity for the railways, mainly regulated municipal suppliers and private power companies and licensed electricity suppliers).

In 1939, for instance, on the verge of World War II, the breakdown of electricity undertakings and consumption in South Africa read as shown in Table 2.1.

Table 2.1: Electricity sales in South Africa, by company, 1939

Electricity undertakings	GWh sold	Percentage
Local authorities	802	15
VFTPC	3 112	57
Other private undertakings	837	15
Escom	702	13
Total	5 453	100

Source: Price papers, cited in Christie 1984: 128

The establishment of the VFTPC, and its subsidiary the Rand Mines Power Supply Company (RMPSC), though immediately beneficial to bringing down costs for the gold-mining houses, threatened the interests of a number of important capitalist groups in the Transvaal. As Christie notes,

> The formation of a monopoly for the supply of electricity to the gold mines threatened the interests of a number of important groups in the Transvaal. Yet the interests of the state were fundamentally linked to monopoly capital, and to gold-mining capital in particular. Gold mining needed the new power stations. The state therefore conducted an exercise of accommodation, whereby the new, highly necessary, electricity monopoly was fitted into the existing relations of production, in such a way as to ensure the minimum of unnecessary disruption of vested capitalist interests. (1984: 39)

Coal-mining capitalists supplied coal to the individual mining houses and municipal power stations and feared the consequences of what could become a monopsony on their profits. Colliery owners, on the other hand, were reliant on the railway network to deliver coal, and this network was both a user of coal for the steam engines – and therefore a ready market for coal – but also a source of relatively high transportation costs, which could possibly be reduced by electrification. Electricity lines from pithead power stations would also in effect be in direct competition with the railways in transporting energy.

So the need to address the contradictory requirements of gold mining (cheap power from economies of scale) and coal mining (steam-driven railways as a market for coal) as well as the preference of many buyers of coal for independent power stations, became a concern of successive governments in the period before and after the Act of Union in 1910.

Prior to the Act of Union, the Governor General of the colonial government had appointed a Commission of Inquiry into the Power Companies in 1909, to look at the desirability of establishing large electric power companies. The colonial government was interested in an integrated system of power generation and transmission which did not harm existing power arrangements in the mining industry. The Commission led to the publication of a Power Bill, subsequently the Power Act of 1910 (published three days before the Act of Union, and surviving this Act), which, amongst other things, regulated power companies by issuing licences and (what was to become critical later) allowed the authorities to expropriate power companies after a fixed period of time.

> The Power Act introduced on 28 May 1910 by the Transvaal Colonial Government, limited the future existence of the VFTPC. The Act authorised the operational expansion of the VFTPC, but provided for the state's expropriation of the company, or any other electricity undertaking, after a period of 35 years. The state viewed the provision of electricity as a public service to be placed under its authority. (Eskom 2006)

After the Act of Union, and with the increased scale and domination of gold mining after World War 1, the burning issue of reducing energy costs and tackling the contradictory interests of the different capitalist groupings led to the revisiting of the Power Act. Of particular significance was the issue of electrification of the rail network.

The development of the railways drove the next phase of electricity utilisation in South Africa. The South African Railways (SAR), in looking at the possibility of switching from steam to electricity, found that it could purchase electricity either from the private power companies or from the municipalities. The need to reduce transport costs forced it to seek state intervention. This led to the government reviewing the Power Act and appointing the Merz Commission (under Charles Merz) to 'study the general question of electric power and to find a solution to the problem of the SAR power supply in the Union of South Africa' (cited in Ramokgoba 2004: 4)

At the time when Merz began his study there were more than 58 electricity undertakings in South Africa. These included 40 municipalities and 18 private companies, of which the VFTPC and RMPSC were by far the largest. The conclusions and recommendation of the Merz Commission were that:
- An Act should be passed by Parliament providing for the regulation and unification of the supply of electricity and other forms of power throughout the Union.
- Priority should be given to the development of an electrical power supply infrastructure to meet the needs of transport.
- An Act should be passed by Parliament to provide for the establishment of a small body of commissioners with a mandate to encourage new schemes for the development of electricity supply and generally to administer the Act in accordance with the principles documented in his report (Ramokgoba 2004: 5).

During the 1922 miners' strike, a consortium consisting of Prime Minister Jan Smuts, SAR General Manager William Hoy and the mining engineers and scientific advisers Robert Kotze, H Warrington Smyth and Hendrick van der Bijl drafted an Electricity Bill, which became the Electricity Act of 1922. The Act incorporated provisions of the 1910 Transvaal Power Act, including provisions for electricity to be provided as a public service, without profit, and for the state to have the authority to expropriate private power companies.

The 1922 Electricity Act set up two institutions: the Electricity Control Board (ECB) and the Electricity Supply Commission or Escom. The ECB controlled and licensed the supply of electricity and fixed processes and enforced the sharing of surplus profits (with customers) in the case of private power companies. Escom was controlled by commissioners appointed by the Minister of Minerals and Energy Affairs and was given 'statutory powers to establish generation and distribution undertakings to supply electricity at the lowest possible cost' (Eberhard 2003: 3).

The Act allowed Escom to exercise these powers in three ways:
- through establishing its own generation capacity either through building such undertakings or through acquiring existing private undertakings;
- by entering into co-operation agreements with existing private companies so as to encourage investments in areas likely to facilitate industries' needs;
- together with the ECB, through regulating private power companies and municipalities by issuing licences with certain conditions and ensuring that surplus profits were conscribed.

In deciding whether to issue a licence, Escom could undertake the supply itself or could permit private undertakings to supply electricity, the only significant proviso being that 'the action must be in the public interest' (section 6(4) of the Electricity Act of 1922, cited in Ramokgoba 2004: 6).

This type of tight state regulation, including the capacity to decommodify a service – through expropriation – in order to assure capital accumulation, was typical of the kind of demand management associated with Keynesian[5]-regulated capitalism, whose generalised application became such a feature internationally after World War II.

Escom was created primarily out of the desire to electrify the railways (see Christie 1984) in the context of the transport needs of colliery owners, and came into operation in 1923. In this regard Escom's genesis took as a point of departure that the principal mining houses already had their own power stations and the VFTPC already had a regional monopoly, and therefore sought to complement them by serving another need – that of electrifying the rail network.

Initially this was not seen as a generalised rail network; the focus was on the rail service delivering coal from the Natal midland collieries to the ports of Durban and Lourenço Marques to create the means, at low cost, for the collieries to gain access via rail to the harbours. Escom's first act was to take over the Colenso power station from the SAR. This was followed by the construction of the Congella power station near Durban and the Witbank, Klip and Vaal power stations – all serving collieries. The result was a kind of carefully crafted synergy between Escom and the VFTPC. From the outset Escom often had such synergistic relations with the VFTPC; for example, the Witbank power station was commissioned and owned by

Escom but built and operated by the VFTPC. In general, the VFTPC generated power for the mines and Escom generated power for the collieries and the railways (whilst having a complex arrangement of regulation and partnership with the VFTPC) throughout most of the period of segregation.

Escom was legislated not to make a profit or a loss but to operate independently of government and Parliament. This latter point meant that Escom had to finance operational costs and capital expansion out of revenue generated by sales. The ECB ensured that price changes were limited,[6] and it required an Act of Parliament to make possible any contribution towards Escom out of the national fiscus.

The South African economy boomed after the shift from the gold standard in 1932 and particularly in the period 1933–1939, because of the build-up to war that was taking place. South Africa moved swiftly out of, and hardly felt the effects of, the Great Depression.

Between 1933 and 1948 the consumption of electricity generated by Escom grew fivefold. On average, a new amount equal to the entire 1933 consumption was added to Escom's sales figures every three years. Most of Escom's power was sold at cost, in bulk, to the VFTPC for distribution to the gold mines at a profit. Several very large new power stations were built for Escom, some of them being operated by the VFTPC on Escom's behalf.

Escom acquired the Port Shepstone power station in 1944. In 1947 it took over the running of the West Bank power station at the request of the East London municipality. At an Escom meeting in 1947, it was decided to take over the central power station of De Beers mines in Kimberley. Escom purchased the Alice and King William's Town municipal undertakings in 1948. All of this resulted in the establishment of the Border and Northern Cape undertakings.

In the meantime, in the last 15 years of its existence, the VFTPC's sales soared. The VFTPC was so profitable that its profits had to be hidden (it did so by constantly expanding infrastructure investment and paying minimal dividends).

But the VFTPC was essentially a foreign company making abnormally high profits, and the demand for electricity was increasing as gold mining boomed after World War II. The 1946 mineworkers' strike had suggested that labour conditions might necessitate further mechanisation and additional electrical supply. The ore-rich Orange Free State mines were on the point of being opened up. The mines had become deeper, and very hot, and refrigeration and ventilation costs escalated. Lead times on new power stations had become longer during the war and requests to the VFTPC for larger blocks of power were met with uncertainty; mine owners entered into protracted negotiations with the VFTPC: '...As a result, the Anglo American Corporation demanded that the VFTPC be expropriated early so that uncertainty could be avoided' (Christie 1984: 144).

The Power Act of 1910 provided for the option of the state nationalising power utilities by 1950. The VFTPC could therefore be nationalised by that date. But mine owners were impatient and wanted this done two years sooner, in 1948. In addition, Escom needed £14 500 000 to pay compensation; this was provided by a loan of £15 000 000 floated by Escom (agreed on in discussion with the Chamber of Mines) and this was subscribed within three hours, chiefly by the Anglo American Corporation.

From its inception as an initiative to support the collieries and electrify the railways, Escom had played a key role as a main source of cheap energy for the gold mines and as the lever for the overall industrialisation of South Africa, particularly during the pivotal inter-war years of 1918–1939. As Fine and Rustomjee (1996) have demonstrated, South Africa did not follow the path of classic import substitution during this time, whereby economies industrialised by processing 'backwards' (typically by protecting food and beverage production), but rather adopted the strategy of forward industrialisation from mining – i.e. developing capacity internally to produce capital goods for mining. This was achieved through a nexus of state development of iron and steel (via the Iron and Steel Corporation (Iscor) set up in 1928), state railways and harbours, and state provision of finance (through the Industrial Development Corporation (IDC) set up in 1940) for a market provided by and at the behest of the mining industry, and made possible by revenues accrued to the state from taxation of that same industry.

Over the period of the inter-war years we see a massive transformation of South Africa from a colonial outpost to a semi-industrialised country, with a strong independent ruling class centred on mining capital and industrialising to support mining capital; the physiognomy of that capital is, by 1948, increasingly national in the location of its profits and in its quest for an appropriate lever to ensure capital accumulation. This is the new South African state.

All these processes of transformation were underpinned by cheap labour power and cheap energy.

> Since 1905 South Africa has had perhaps the cheapest steam-generated electricity supplies in the world, for three major reasons. First, the coal seams are thick, shallow and unfaulted. Second, compounds, pass-laws and reserves provide cheap black labour both for the coal mines and for the power stations. Third, the electricity supply industry is structured by the state to provide cheap power for mining, transport and manufacture. Cheap power is crucial to most South African production. Cheap energy is one reason that South Africa is an industrial state. The share of electricity in total South African energy consumption is among the highest in the world, and so is the amount of energy consumed per unit of gross national product. South Africa's international specialisation is not only cheap mining labour; it is also cheap energy, especially cheap electricity. (Christie 1984: 1)

The location of power stations provided a snapshot of South African power relations. Initially municipal power stations and early independent power stations relied on high-grade coal being transported via rail, using steam-driven trains, to the points where the coal could produce the steam that drove the turbines of the power stations. The setting up of Escom was an attempt to lower power costs considerably and produce a win–win situation for gold-mine owners, coal-mine owners and municipalities through the following arrangements:

- Power stations could be established at pitheads and the electricity transported over long transmission lines instead of having coal transported over railways to distant power stations. This substituted cheaper electrical power transmission for expensive rail travel.
- The railways were electrified so that they did not use coal as an energy source any more.
- The greater amount of electricity generation as a result of all of these changes meant that the overall market for coal increased.
- Having pithead power stations opened up the possibility of locating these in areas where low-grade coal mining would previously have been economically unviable, for example the Eastern Transvaal (now Mpumalanga).
- Electrifying the railways may have meant a drop in coal revenues earned by coal-mine owners from the railways, but transportation costs, including the costs of coal transportation, would be lower.
- Combining pithead power stations with an electrified railway network would produce a virtuous circle of lower coal transportation costs, the viable use of low-grade coal at pitheads, the lowering of electrical energy costs and the viability of exporting the export-grade coal via a lower-cost, electrified railway network.
- After 1927 and the establishment of Congella, which operated with pulverised fuel (previously discarded as not economically viable), the Escom power stations allowed colliery owners to have a ready market for their previously discarded low-grade coal whilst having the higher-grade coals available for export.

Escom and electricity in the period of grand apartheid

Electricity is most efficiently supplied, under capitalism, by a monopoly. Even the most ardent believer in free competition will usually see that two or more large power station networks, with two or more overlaid reticulation systems, arranged so that consumers can choose between suppliers, are likely to be an uneconomic waste of resources. It rapidly becomes obvious to competing capitalists that a merger or cartel would suit all parties better: consumers might get lower prices because of increased economies of scale, and suppliers would have security of demand, so that capital would not lie idle. Power networks are so large and take so long to build that once a vested interest is established 'entry into the market' is exceedingly difficult. Nevertheless entries are made, and competition does occur at the boundaries of networks. The sheer size, however, of investments in electricity systems, means that high risks are run where systems compete. (Christie 1984: 27)

In 1948 the NP led by DF Malan came to power in the whites-only general election with an avowed programme of apartheid and a social base that united white workers, the white middle classes and Afrikaner capital. Dan O'Meara (1983) has written about the evolution of a section of the Afrikaner petit-bourgeoisie and its transformation into a rising capitalist class, from the 1920s onward. The NP itself was a core of the erstwhile Afrikaner National Party of the Afrikaner middle classes which had allied itself with the Labour Party of white workers in the 1924 Pact Government, and whose leaders wished to distance themselves from the conduct of those NP leaders who had gone into an alliance with Smuts in the Fusion Government of 1933 and adopted a pro-Allies stance during World War II. Within 10 years, much of the architecture of what came to be known as grand apartheid was put in place – the Suppression of Communism Act (No. 44 of 1950), the Population Registration Act (No. 30 of 1950), the Group Areas Act (No. 69 of 1955) and the Promotion of Bantu Self-Government Act (No. 46 of 1959).

Liberal commentators who wished to see apartheid as a kind of irrational, frontier mentality-driven, Afrikaner nationalist, anti-modernist project have emphasised these Acts, and seen links with the Nazi sympathies of leading NP figures (the later prime minister, BJ Vorster, for instance). These commentators have attempted to characterise apartheid's interventions in capitalist accumulation as signs of hostility to capital, and have bolstered their arguments with references to Nazi connections and the fact that the German National Socialist Party initially appealed to a plebeian constituency. They have therefore tended to list a plethora of state interventions in the economy to prove these similarities (as well as citing theories of convergence between German National Socialism and the communism of the Soviet Union). Thus state institutions such as the Land Bank, the Agricultural Control Boards, the huge state bureaucracies and others are frequently cited as examples from the apartheid era of state opposition to the logic of capital (see Dubow 1989).

Yet this argument fails to explain the principal institutions of state intervention in the economy founded before 1948 – Iscor in 1928, the IDC in 1947 and Escom in 1923. In this regard, a comment by then Prime Minister Jan Smuts regarding Escom buying out the VFTPC and establishing a state monopoly over electricity offers an apt perspective on the pre-apartheid era developmental state:

> [Electricity in South Africa was]...as cheap as anywhere in the world, because wasteful competition had been eliminated...There will always be a very large field for private capital to operate in, but there are certain industries which experience has taught us can be driven better by Government without loss through wasteful competition. (Smuts, cited in Eberhard 2003: 4)

The newly elected NP government was faced with an electrical power crisis soon after taking political power. Coal shortages had occurred throughout the war years, due to high demand as a result of the rapid growth in manufacturing, exacerbated by the incapacity of the railways to handle the scale of coal transport required. This situation was further aggravated by conflict between the Afrikaner capitalist coal-mine owners, who were fighting price control at the pithead, and the

English-owned collieries. Afrikaners primarily owned low-grade coal mines; they wanted to export coal directly (a monopoly exercised by high-grade coal-mine owners), and set about defying state regulation to do so.

Meanwhile, mining capitalists were gearing up to expand gold mining significantly through the newly onstream, richly deposited Orange Free State gold mines. The combination of the defiant export of low-grade coal by the Afrikaner capitalists and the need for massively increased electrical power by the large gold-mining monopolies led to severe power outages, and Escom was forced to introduce policies of load shedding over the period 1948–1953.

In response to this crisis the state sought capacity to increase the number of power stations and to finance this in a context whereby Escom was legally bound to sell electricity at cost and 'not make a profit'. The crisis thus saw Escom seek loans from the then International Bank for Reconstruction and Development (now the World Bank) of £10.75 million in 1951, and then US$30 million for equipment for the Hex River, Vierfontein, Vaal, Congella and Witbank power stations; legislation had to be enacted to make this possible.

This expansion to meet greater electricity needs, and the financial solutions sought to generate the resources necessary, were to be themes quite dominant in the Keynesian period of South Africa's history (and were later to influence key apartheid line departments to pressurise the apartheid government to seek reforms – reforms which ultimately led to the first quest for neo-liberal solutions to South Africa's economic crisis of the 1970s).

Electricity-generating capacity increased sixfold from 2 378 MW in 1948 to 14 134 MW in 1975, while the amount of current produced increased almost sevenfold from 11 045 million amperes to 74 918 million amperes in 1975 (Christie 1984: 151).

From 1960 onwards, Escom began to increasingly interlock its power stations in a national grid. This was finally achieved in 1973. Simultaneously, Escom automated its production processes so that entire power stations could be switched on and off from the grid's control room in Simmerpan, where 'five operators controlled sixteen power stations and over 1 000 substations' (Christie 1984: 163).

Throughout the 1970s Escom undertook a major programme of expansion, building very large pithead power stations on the coal fields of the Eastern Transvaal and Northern Natal. By 1975 it had commissioned Arnot, Hendrina, Camden, Grootvlei, Ingagane, Kriel, Matla and Duvha – all major power stations operated using the latest technology to burn low-grade coal. The nuclear power station Koeberg was commissioned in 1976. The growth in Escom power stations in the 1970s and 1980s is shown in Table 2.2.

Escom also became a strategic arm of the apartheid regime's geopolitical objectives – particularly in the case of the Cahora Bassa project in Mozambique. When the

Table 2.2: Electricity generation capacity growth in South Africa, 1961–1992

Power station	Date of entry into commercial service	Maximum capacity (MW)
Komati	1961	906
Camden	1966	1 520
Grootvlei	1969	1 130
Hendrina	1970	1 900
Arnot	1971	1 980
Kriel	1976	2 850
Koeberg	1976	1 840
Matla	1979	3 450
Duvha	1980	3 450
Tutuka	1985	3 510
Lethabo	1985	3 558
Matimba	1987	3 690
Kendal	1988	3 840
Majuba	1992	3 843

Source: Eskom Statistical Yearbook 1995, cited in Eberhard 2003: 7

Portuguese colonialists began a project to set up a hydro-electric power station on the Zambezi River in Mozambique, the project was conceived of within a colonial nexus. The electricity generated by Cahora Bassa would be transmitted via the new high voltage direct current (HVDC) method (as opposed to the conventional alternating current method). This made it inappropriate for transmission to Mozambican consumers, who did not have the technology to convert the HVDC to alternating current for household and industrial use there.

South Africa had the thyristors required to make this conversion,[7] however, so Cahora Bassa was set up in Mozambique, with a schema involving Escom buying electricity from the Portuguese owners at a discount price, using a percentage for its own use and then selling the rest back to Mozambique. The fact that Frelimo's war against the colonial power and rising capital costs delayed the completion of Cahora Bassa until independence did not significantly derail this schema, and the project was a factor in limiting the newly liberated Mozambique's ability to forge a development path independently of South Africa.

Nor did Cahora Bassa give the new Mozambican government the kind of clout they might have hoped for against the apartheid regime. As Christie notes,

> The [transmission] lines could not be easily tapped and used, because of the expense of converting DC to AC. Cahora Bassa power had therefore to be converted at Apollo near Pretoria and then sent back along different lines to feed Maputo in Mozambique. Cahora Bassa would also be a poor weapon against South Africa: it would never be more than the equivalent of half of the reserve of the Escom system. (1984: 167)

Escom and electricity in the period of apartheid's reforms

Between 1972 and 1976 international bank lending became the major form of foreign investment in South Africa, quadrupling in size in the period (at current prices), and largely financing state-owned corporations, especially Escom. Many banks began to feel overexposed and refused further investment, however – more perhaps to try and spread the risk than to put pressure on South Africa's apartheid regime. By 1978 South Africa was reportedly prepared to pay up to twice the going market rates of interest, and was still having difficulty raising international finance. Escom moved towards local financing as far as possible but at least one projected coal-fired power station, Ilanga, was postponed indefinitely due to inadequate finances.

By the early 1980s conditions were more favourable again as South African borrowers saw a unique opportunity to borrow, due to a record gold price and the low cost of borrowing resulting from the flush of petrodollars. Escom was a major player in this borrowing spree and by 1982 had become 'the biggest borrower of medium-term funds abroad', with that year's borrowing alone 'being close to R2 billion' (Padayachee 1991: 96).

When the price of gold collapsed and civil unrest intensified in South Africa, things turned sour. In 1983 the country received a negative International Monetary Fund (IMF) report, and in 1985 declared a moratorium on debt repayment. Parastatal debt soon became a millstone around the neck of the apartheid regime and was to be a powerful impetus for reforms at the political level.

It was at this time that the state appointed a special commission – the De Villiers Commission, established in 1983 – to examine Escom and electricity pricing throughout South Africa. Although the Commission is often credited with relatively modest prescriptions – it recommended that South Africa have nationally generated electricity tariffs, as opposed to municipalities being able to charge highly varying tariffs – its more radical recommendations can be seen with the benefit of hindsight. The recommendations of the De Villiers Commission also included that the public-interest limitation on Escom be lifted and that the parastatal operate on a more commercial basis, including paying taxes and dividends to its shareholder – i.e. the state.

These recommendations were made against the backdrop of a much larger canvas of burgeoning neo-liberal ideas internationally – specifically the view that public utilities should be privatised or operate on a commercial basis. And the work of the De Villiers Commission led directly to the landmark Electricity Act (No. 41 of 1987) and the Eskom Act (No. 40 of 1987), both reflecting this new neo-liberal approach.

What were the significant changes in the 1987 Acts? These can be summarised as follows:
- The provision of the 1922 Electricity Act had compelled Escom to supply electricity in the public interest and specifically forbade profit-making. With

this *de facto* form of price control the commodification of electricity was effectively circumscribed. The repeal of this requirement in 1987 marked an intervention on the part of the state to expand the terrain of commodification of public services – albeit in its specific South African variant, which had seen Escom as a public utility set up to benefit whites.

- The scrapping of the Electricity Control Board and its replacement by an Electricity Council – a body composed of monopoly capitalists (e.g. the Afrikaner Handelsinstituut [Trade Institute], the Chamber of Mines, the SA Chamber of Business) – marked the direct involvement of private capital in the decision-making processes of the state.
- The transfer of ministerial accountability from the Ministry of Minerals and Energy Affairs to the Ministry of Public Enterprises (whose brief was to oversee the process of privatisation of Escom/Eskom) ended the long run of the 20th-century brand of racial capitalism, whereby energy policy and mining capital were regarded as virtually synonymous.

The year 1987 was a critical time in the evolution of South African neo-liberalism. At the beginning of the year the apartheid state announced its new economic programme: deregulation, greater independence of the Reserve Bank and the privatisation of parastatals. Iscor and Escom were targeted for privatisation and the South African Railways and Harbours (SAR&H) was to be restructured into different commercialised business units (Transnet, Portnet, Spoornet, etc.). This announcement was made in the context of a lull in popular struggles after the 1983–1985 period of mass insurrection, and was combined with a series of new repressive measures: the banning of the United Democratic Front, the suppression of Congress of South African Trade Unions (Cosatu) meetings (except for bona fide collective bargaining meetings), the extension of the state of emergency and the crackdown on activists.

Of the objects intended for privatisation and commercialisation, only Iscor was actually sold off to private capital (for years the SAR&H pension debts precluded finding any buyer). Eskom, for its part, was kept in public hands but the Electricity Act of 1987 fundamentally altered its terms of reference, the most significant being that it was no longer required to operate 'without profit'.

This change indicated that important elements within the state and business had begun to perceive neo-liberal methods of managing cost structures – through greater use of market mechanisms – as the way to achieve cheap electricity.

Writing of the reforms introduced in 1987, Stephen Gelb (later to be one of the co-writers of the ANC's Growth, Employment and Redistribution (GEAR) economic policy in 1996) had this to say:

> The present government [in 1987] and big business are increasingly implanting an accumulation strategy which we call neo-liberal export-oriented growth. The De Klerk administration has introduced into government economic policy a much higher degree of internal coherence,

as well as greater consonance with the expressed concerns of much of South African big business. While many of the policies incorporated in this strategy have been long advocated in the course of the crisis, they are now being implemented, while others that do not fit have been abandoned.

The strategy focuses on restructuring and regenerating the manufacturing sector in particular by using neo-liberal policies to alter cost structures and restore profitability, and to expand markets for manufacture, above all through exports. The emphasis is on the export of beneficiated minerals (currently exported in a semi-processed form) and intermediate manufactures.

Neo-liberal policies involve the state limiting its own economic activity in relation to the provision of goods and services, for example by a process of privatisation... (Gelb 1991: 29)

Here we see a much earlier transition to neo-liberalism than many observers admit, who see the introduction of the GEAR strategy in June 1996 as the start of the neo-liberal phase of capital accumulation in South Africa.

Conclusion

In the run-up to the 1994 democratic elections (1990–1994) much of the focus of intellectuals linked with the mass movement became focused on the question: what would a new South Africa 'look like' and, particularly, how could the movement put forward concrete policies for the new state which would tilt the balance of forces in favour of the working class?

This 1990s preoccupation with strategic initiatives to shape the content of the new South Africa meant that the preoccupation on the left was with policy alternatives, in the course of which the questions of the nature of the state and the relations between capitalism and apartheid fell off the table (after all, if apartheid's demise was a certainty, why study its evolution?). Fine and Rustomjee (1996) are spot on when they identify the instrumentalism that began to take over in the absence of any analysis of the political economy of South Africa, the nature of the capitalist class and the social forces which shape the current conjuncture.

Of course, nature abhors a vacuum... And, in the absence of any continuity with the body of Marxist scholarship of the 1970s and 1980s, the space has been filled with all the liberal prescriptions and conceptual categories that the left had so successfully railed against in the 1970s and 1980s (for a review from a liberal perspective of these debates, see Lipton 1986). So apartheid has come to be seen as a relatively short-lived chapter of irrationality associated with white Afrikaners post-1948; South Africa's big business monopolies are seen to have been of solid anti-apartheid stock (witness the accolades delivered by the government, the ANC and the South African Communist Party (SACP) to the recently departed Anton Rupert). Thabo Mbeki has resurrected the 'two economies' apartheid justification for social policies[8] and, more recently, a number of commentators (see Daniel et al. 2005) have begun to append the term 'developmental state' to Mbeki's second presidential term.

In this regard, the outgoing chairman of Eskom, Reuel Khoza, in 2005 articulated a perspective on apartheid which is dominant in government and the media today:

> Naturally, the 2004 celebrations of 10 years of democracy were of great significance. Ten years earlier South Africa had been a country in isolation from the global community, an insignificant player in the global economy and excluded from multilateral institutions. In addition, South Africa had a government intent on being exclusionist, a polarised society, internal conflict, a global resistance struggle and an ailing economy.

> The political miracle of 1994 led to the first democratic elections and the thrust towards reconstruction and development. Ten years later, the country has a new political order, peace, rapid economic growth and impressive gains in areas under government control such as fiscal, monetary, trade and industrial policy. South Africa today boasts the highest level of macroeconomic stability in 40 years. There has also been great progress in addressing poverty and inequality. (Eskom 2006)

So in government circles and in the mainstream the changes from the Reconstruction and Development Programme (RDP) of the early Mandela years are contrasted with the GEAR programme of Mbeki's first term in office (1999–2004), which in turn is contrasted with the ostensibly more 'pro-poor' policies of Mbeki's second term of office now that South Africa has been successfully integrated into the world economy. One of the most significant indicators in this construction of Mbeki's new term is the move away from privatisation and the withdrawal of the state from large-scale expenditure of the kind undertaken in the GEAR years, towards the kind of increased state investment in the economy captured by the Accelerated and Shared Growth Initiative for South Africa (ASGISA) policy unveiled in 2006.

On the left there are some sentiments which operate within this discourse. The ANC's alliance partners, the SACP and Cosatu, laud ASGISA as part of the post-GEAR consensus and celebrate its commitment to increased state expenditure on the parastatals. The SACP and Cosatu veer between asserting that GEAR represented a pitch for power by a '1996 class project' (which is still being contested) and taking government at its word that GEAR was simply a neutral technical tool to achieve macroeconomic stability. Therefore ASGISA represents a new turn, a 'post-GEAR consensus', now that government has gotten the painful but necessary and irritating GEAR out of the way. These views may well not be entirely unexpected from formations within the Tripartite Alliance.

But, surprisingly, a lack of analysis of the period of reformed apartheid also lies within the periodisation of some of the anti-government left. Here we find a clear characterisation of GEAR as neo-liberal and the character of the state as monopoly capitalist. But GEAR was unveiled in 1996, and therefore there is a tendency to see its imposition as coming from 'outside', and the origins of neo-liberalism as lying in the pressure exerted by foreign forces (the IMF, the World Bank) on the ANC government.

This has spawned a range of studies that look at neo-liberalism's origins and seek to explain the shift from the radical social democracy of the ANC in the 1980s to the neo-liberalism of GEAR in the 1990s, with a focus on the RDP as an example of a redistributive programme which was abandoned after it had promised so much. Evidence is cited of the loan solicited by the Government of National Unity[9] (GNU) from the IMF in 1994, of the pressures exerted by the IMF and the World Bank and of the 're-entry' of South Africa into the international economy, all seen as signals of neo-liberalism at work. In this scenario, apartheid South Africa is characterised monolithically as all about racial exclusion, and uncritically lumped together with views that an isolationist regime, suffering under sanctions, was eventually forced to play by the global rules of neo-liberalism.

The recent history of Escom, and its transformation into Eskom, suggest at least two critical errors in this model – errors which need to be engaged with if we are to understand the current conjuncture in South Africa more critically.

Firstly, they suggest a very narrow understanding of the content of neo-liberal restructuring – largely confined to the apparently reduced role of the state and the increased role of the private sector, embodied in privatisation. From this narrow understanding, the continuity of state ownership from Escom to Eskom suggests that the neo-liberal project was not under way or not full-blown. But analyses of neo-liberalism have been enriched by an understanding of neo-liberal economic reforms as the *commodification* of state enterprises and services – which includes a whole range of *forms of ownership* (state, public–private partnerships, outsourcing), including much of what is known today as 'new public sector management'.

Secondly, there is the problem of agency. Much of the discourse on neo-liberalism in South Africa places the emphasis on some kind of external agency – the World Bank and the IMF. Within Cosatu and the SACP this is seen as a kind of unfavourable balance of forces 'out there' associated with globalisation and South Africa's 're-entry' into world markets after the end of the sanctions period. Within this discourse the apartheid apparatchiks are seen as antediluvian defenders of the old order of white privilege. But the timing of and the sources of neo-liberalism – circa 1987 – suggest not only an internal source, but a source closely aligned to the apartheid state itself, namely managers of the parastatals. In this regard the notion of the apartheid-era parastatals as bastions of conservatism, as opposed to agents of modernisation, needs to be revisited. Not only do many of them (including Escom) pre-date the period of grand apartheid, they were sometimes forces for modernising capitalist reforms and are today (in the case of Eskom and the Water Boards) lined up to play a major role in the next phase of capital accumulation –

the seizure of the global commons on the African continent and South Africa's imperial ambitions in Africa.

The evidence of a neo-liberal programme underpinning the latter-day apartheid regime – Escom/Eskom included – subverts the current assumptions of many analysts of South Africa's transition, both those made about the origins of apartheid and the social forces which drove its agenda, as well as those concerning the timing of the beginning of neo-liberalism in South Africa and the social forces which underpinned it. Instead, the evidence suggests a considerable degree of continuity between the South Africa of the reformed apartheid era and the South Africa that emerged after 1994 (the democracy era), despite the change from an exclusively white government to a government elected by the majority.

The continuity has been at the level of the identity of the social force which has presided over South Africa's evolution over the last 100 years – largely the same white monopoly capitalists, who rose from mining barons in the early 20th century to become multi-sectoral industrialists in the 1950s and 1960s, and leaders of transnational corporations and international financiers after 1994. Along the way the political shell has changed from segregation to apartheid to reformed apartheid to a neo-liberal democracy.[10] Underpinning this historically were the twin pillars of cheap labour and cheap energy, as described by Christie:

> Cheap power made mechanisation and high productivity easier to achieve. On the other hand low wages, maintained by the state's increased control of workers, meant that there was less need to mechanise. However, the flow of workers into the labour reserves could be increased by mechanisation, and pressure from the unemployed would then complete the circle by keeping wages down. 'Labour-saving' cheap electricity buttressed the whole system. (Christie 1984: 151)

To be sure, each version of this shell began to outlive its usefulness for capital accumulation, as internal political contradictions and new popular struggles began to reshape the terrain and made what was once advantageous for capital the very focus of a new crisis. Segregation eventually led to a larger, urbanised black working class which apartheid then had to divide and police; reformed neo-liberal apartheid had to respond to the depth and spread of militancy and the costs of maintaining an unpopular state.

It remains to be seen whether this transformation from Escom, with its commitment to providing electricity in the public interest and 'without profit', to Eskom, an entity structured as Eskom Holdings and including Eskom Enterprises, and the promise of growing 'shareholder value', indicates the successful extrication of South African capital from its historical roots in extractive mining, cheap, racialised labour and cheap energy, to become a global player in finance markets – or whether it will unleash new contradictions as post-apartheid neo-liberalism confronts apartheid's legacy of mass urban and rural poverty.

Notes

1   The Congress of South African Trade Unions (Cosatu), in its submissions to Parliament on the 2001 Eskom Conversion Bill, took comfort in the fact that the then forthcoming Act kept Eskom as a state entity and therefore still available for developmental and redistribution purposes. Cosatu therefore focused its reservations on the fact that the state could be preparing to privatise Eskom (a claim that the government has successfully been able to counter).

2   The concept 'racial capitalism' is associated with a body of work by what was then called 'the revisionist school' of historians and political economists in the 1970s. Analysts associated with this body of work include Frederick Johnstone (1976) and Stanley Trapido (1971). They counterposed themselves to the dominant liberal perspective, which saw apartheid as dysfunctional to capitalism and industrialisation. Instead they argued that racial segregation and apartheid were integrally linked to capitalism in South Africa.

3   Thabo Mbeki , previously one of two deputy presidents under President Nelson Mandela, became president after the second democratic elections in 1999. Whereas the Mandela years – from the first democratic elections of 1994 until 1999 – were characterised by some policy uncertainties, given that South Africa was just emerging from the period of the negotiations between the apartheid state and the liberation movement, the Mbeki presidency has come to be seen as framing a period of greater clarity as to what the future South African social formation would look like, at least in the short to medium term.

4   Prime Minister JBM Hertzog first introduced the job colour bar in 1924 and then served notice of the intention to remove Africans in the Cape from the voters' roll via the Hertzog Bills of 1935. This intention was formalised in the Native Trust and Land Act (No. 18 of 1936).

5   John Maynard Keynes himself only published his *General Theory of Employment, Interest and Money* in 1936, but these ideas of regulated capitalism were present in the 1920s, grew after the Wall Street crash of 1929 and became economic orthodoxy after World War II. After the crisis of over-accumulation in the 1960s and 1970s and the attacks on the welfare state, neo-liberalism and the Washington Consensus, carried out through institutions such as the International Monetary Fund, became the new orthodoxy.

6   With regard to electricity pricing, the 1922 Electricity Act stipulated that electricity prices charged were to cover the cost of production, the interest on money raised by way of loans, and a reserve fund for the replacement of obsolete plant and machinery. The Act provided for a schedule of standard prices as a condition of the licence granted by the Control Board. In addition, any surplus profit had to be shared between the licensee and its customers: the licensee was obliged, within six months of completion of each financial year of the undertaking, to distribute to the undertaking's customers, on a pro rata basis to their payments, 25 per cent of the surplus profit for that year. This share was increased gradually from 25 per cent to 50 per cent, and finally to 70 per cent before 1948.

7   Thyristors are solid-state semiconductors which act as switches; they continue to conduct electricity, under certain conditions, even when switched off. They are used to make possible the conversion of direct current to alternating current and vice versa, so as to make long-distance transmission possible without the relatively large-scale energy losses normally incurred.

8   In the 1960s and early 1970s liberal commentators spoke of white South Africa as a first-world country and black South Africa as a third-world country, which would catch up as black people were more integrated into a modern industrialised economy. They shared the presumption of two economies with apartheid ideologues of this period, who justified the separation of the races by arguing that it was a way to allow black people to develop in the protected environment of their own people. Liberals, however, differed from the apartheid apologists by accusing the NP government of promulgating laws that prevented black people from gaining access to the modernising influences of the 'first economy'.

9   As part of the agreement reached at the negotiations which led to the democratic dispensation after 1994, it was agreed that the new government would be a GNU, which would include two vice-presidents, and a Cabinet in which there would be guaranteed ministries drawn from the ANC's chief negotiating partner, the NP. Under this agreement FW de Klerk of the NP became one of the two deputy presidents and representatives of his party were given key portfolios – Finance and Agriculture being the most significant. The NP withdrew from the GNU in 1996.

10 Much of this chapter is concerned with demonstrating the continuities between the period of segregation and the period of grand apartheid, and between reformed neo-liberal apartheid and neo-liberalism after 1994. This is a corrective to the intellectual amnesia which dominates much of current writing on apartheid and South Africa's political economy, and is not intended to downplay the significant differences between these periods at the level of the different configurations of class forces (including race and gender) which have shaped the various state configurations since 1910.

References

Christie R (1984) *Electricity, industry and class in South Africa*. Albany, NY: State University of New York Press

Daniel J, Southall R & Lutchman J (eds) (2005) *State of the nation: South Africa 2004–2005*. Cape Town: HSRC Press

Dubow S (1989) *Racial segregation and the origins of apartheid in South Africa (1919–1936)*. London: Macmillan

Eberhard A (2003) The political economy of power sector reform in South Africa. Paper presented at the Political Economy of Power Market Reform conference, 19–20 February, Stanford University

Eskom (2006) Mission statement. *Heritage website*. Accessed 14 May 2006, http://heritage.eskom.co.za/heritage/escom

Fine B & Rustomjee Z (1996) *The political economy of South Africa: From minerals-energy complex to industrialisation*. Johannesburg: Witwatersrand University Press

Gelb S (ed.) (1991) *South Africa's economic crisis*. Cape Town: David Philip

Johnstone F (1976) *Class, race and gold: A study of class relations and racial discrimination in South Africa*. London: Routledge and Kegan Paul

Lipton M (1986) *Capitalism and apartheid: South Africa, 1910–1986.* Aldershot: Wildwood House

O'Meara D (1983) *Volkskapitalisme: Class, capital and ideology in the development of Afrikaner nationalism 1934–1948.* Cambridge: Cambridge University Press

Padayachee V (1991) The politics of South Africa's international financial relations, 1970–1990. In S Gelb (ed.) *South Africa's economic crisis.* Cape Town: David Philip

Ramokgoba B (2004) Tariff history. Unpublished report. Accessed 2 May 2007, http://www.eskom.co.za/content/TariffHistory.pdf

Trapido S (1971) South Africa in a comparative study of industrialisation. *Journal of Development Studies* 3(3): 310–320

CHAPTER 3

Market liberalisation and continental expansion: The repositioning of Eskom in post-apartheid South Africa

Stephen Greenberg

The struggle against apartheid created space for civil society to participate in discussions about how the electricity sector should be restructured to serve the interests of those who were denied services under apartheid. However, this became an increasingly technocratic process, with business consultants leading the way and grassroots formations increasingly marginalised.

More than a decade passed while proposals were put forward on the restructuring of the electricity sector, and in particular Eskom as the monopoly utility. In 2001 Eskom was converted into a company, Eskom Holdings, and its regulated activities were separated from non-regulated activities. The latter were located in Eskom Enterprises, a new company wholly owned by Eskom Holdings. These activities included Eskom's substantial holdings ranging from telecommunications, engineering and related services to property and the pebble bed nuclear project. Eskom Enterprises was given the mandate and task to push into Africa, which it did with vigour. At least part of the motivation for this was to find other markets, in anticipation of the liberalisation of South Africa's internal electricity sector. Not all these markets proved as lucrative as Eskom had hoped, and in 2004 the utility refocused on the domestic market in line with government's greater emphasis on using state-owned enterprises for development.

This chapter examines the role of Eskom after 1990, with a focus on its participation in the National Electrification Programme. The first section presents an overview of the restructuring process undertaken by Eskom that began in 1990. This is followed by a consideration of the impact of these processes on employment trends and working conditions at the utility, and on the National Electrification Programme. The chapter then discusses the activities of the newly created Eskom Enterprises, in particular its ventures into other African countries and into the telecommunications and information technology (IT) domain. The conclusion considers future directions that are being considered by Eskom, and the inherent tension between the developmental and privatisation imperatives that it faces.

Overview of Eskom since 1990

Eskom restructuring: from popular initiative to technocratic process

Under apartheid black local authorities (i.e. municipal structures responsible for the townships to which African, coloured and Indian South Africans were residentially restricted) were not given the necessary resources to meet the basic needs of the black populations under their jurisdiction. This inability of local government to deliver quality services to black households was one of the principal reasons for the intensity of resistance that was a significant contributing factor in the ultimate demise of apartheid. The illegitimate black local authorities sought to increase their revenue by sharply increasing rents and service fees. The popular response was the effective use of rent and electricity payment boycotts to further weaken the power of the imposed local authorities.

The late apartheid government attempted to depoliticise service provision by making selective concessions to demands for arrears write-offs, while generating support for a primary role for private enterprise in development. A joint National Energy Council/Eskom workshop held in 1990 called for the depoliticisation and deregulation of the supply industry. It put forward proposals to adopt a market-oriented approach to distribution and the introduction of tariffs between generation, transmission and distribution sectors of the supply chain (the seeds of ringfencing) (Charles Anderson Associates 1994). These efforts were initially unsuccessful. With the unbanning of the organisations of the liberation movement in 1990, expectations of rapid transformation and redistribution were high. In the face of the apartheid government's proposals to privatise Eskom and some of the other big state-owned enterprises, the liberation movement threatened renationalisation. This brought privatisation plans to a halt, and the apartheid government was forced into sectoral negotiating forums during the transition to democratic rule between 1990 and 1994 (Hirsch 2005; Robinson 1997).

In 1992, the African National Congress (ANC) held its own national consultative meeting on electricity in Cape Town, with a wide range of civil society representatives (Theron 1992). While the ANC at the time favoured the route of local government carrying out an electrification programme, the organisation recognised a number of technical, financial and human resources constraints that could undermine such an approach, especially in black areas where local government did not really exist as a meaningful entity capable of delivering adequate services (Veck 2000). Despite a strong distrust of Eskom expressed in the meeting by activists, the National Electrification Forum (NELF) was set up following the meeting, comprising representatives of the Development Bank of Southern Africa (DBSA), the ANC, the Department of Minerals and Energy (DME), the Association of Municipal Electricity Undertakings, the United Municipal Executive, the South African Chamber of Business, the Chamber of Mines, the South African Agricultural Union, Eskom, the National Union of Metalworkers (NUMSA) and the National Union of Mineworkers (NUM), and the national civic structure, the South African National Civics Organisation (Eberhard 2003).

The general viewpoint of the liberation movement was that Eskom should remain in public ownership (Macro-Economic Research Group 1993). There was also a strong emphasis on cross-subsidisation of services for the poor (ANC 1994). However, the ANC gradually developed a position – reflected in the Macro-Economic Research Group report and the Reconstruction and Development Programme (RDP) – that the possibility of privatisation did exist, but would be decided on a case-by-case basis (ANC 1994; Macro-Economic Research Group 1993).

Throughout the transition period (1990–1994) and in the first years of democratic government, a series of proposals concerning the restructuring of the electricity sector was jointly developed by the government, Eskom, municipalities and private consultancies. The NELF was a non-statutory negotiating forum of key stakeholders that played a role in initiating these discussions. But after the democratically elected government took power, proposals were increasingly made by a smaller group of technocrats. Following the formation of the National Electricity Regulator of South Africa (NERSA) in 1995, the NELF was dissolved. The NERSA formed the Electricity Working Group (EWG) in 1995 to further develop proposals to restructure the distribution industry. Progressive civil society was increasingly marginalised, especially after the trade unions were locked into the restructuring process as subordinate partners following the 1996 National Framework Agreement between government and the unions on restructuring of state assets (Ministry of Public Enterprises 1996). The EWG itself comprised representatives from the NERSA, government, Eskom and the municipalities, but excluded unions and civic organisations (Eberhard 2003).

In the heyday of the privatisation thrust in South Africa, around the time of the adoption of the Growth, Employment and Redistribution (GEAR) macro-economic strategy in 1996, Eskom was targeted for partial privatisation. This had a number of consequences for restructuring proposals. In order to bring in the private sector, distinct markets had to be created to permit competition within each node of the supply chain while preventing the formation of a potential monopoly across the nodes. Eskom's status was to be downgraded from a vertically integrated state monopoly supplier to just one amongst many energy companies operating in a competitive market. In 1996 the EWG made recommendations to Cabinet on rationalising the electricity distribution industry and on changing the manner in which the electricity-supply industry funded its obligations. The EWG recommendations were referred to an inter-ministerial committee that in turn formed an internal government committee. This, the Electricity Restructuring Inter-departmental Committee (ERIC), comprised directors-general, senior officials and advisers in the Departments of Minerals and Energy, Housing, Public Enterprises (DPE), Provincial Affairs and Constitutional Development, Finance, and Trade and Industry.

ERIC made three key recommendations: the consolidation of independent regional distributors; a shift to cost-reflective tariffs across all electricity industry sectors; and the opening of the generation sector to competition, encouraging private-sector participation (DME 1996).

These considerations underpinned the proposals to separate out the generation, transmission and distribution nodes into distinct industries. If the aim was to create separate markets and prevent monopolies (including a public monopoly), Eskom would have to relinquish its control over the three nodes in the supply chain. ERIC's proposals formed the basis of the 1998 White Paper on Energy (DME 1998). This was followed by an in-depth study by consultancy PricewaterhouseCoopers with recommendations, accepted by government in 2001, about how to go about separating, ringfencing and corporatising the generation, transmission and distribution sectors (Eberhard 2001; PricewaterhouseCoopers 2000).

Corporatisation of Eskom

In 1995, through amendments to the Electricity Act (No. 41 of 1987), the NERSA replaced the ineffectual Electricity Control Board (ECB) as the national regulator. It had far greater power than the ECB had had, since its regulatory jurisdiction included Eskom and local authorities. It regulated market access by licensing all producers, transmitters, distributors and sellers of electricity (greater than 5 gigawatt-hours per annum). All electricity tariffs had to be approved by the NERSA.

The Eskom Amendment Act (No. 126 of 1998) vested ownership of Eskom's equity in the state, repealed Eskom's tax-exempt status, and mandated the public enterprises minister to act to incorporate Eskom as a limited-liability company with share capital. Until this point, Eskom had not had share capital and its equity had consisted of reserves accumulated through retained earnings from the sale of electricity.

Following the passing of the Eskom Conversion Act (No. 13 of 2001), holding companies were established in the generation, transmission and distribution sectors. The Act created the conditions for Eskom's conversion into a company in terms of the Companies Act (No. 61 of 1973), with the government as the sole shareholder. The aim of the Act was to bring Eskom into line with an internationally accepted business governance model that would 'facilitate Eskom's entry into global markets' (Eskom 2002: 20). An explicit goal of the Act was to place Eskom in the legal position to be able to list on the stock exchange in the future (Eberhard 2001).

In 2002 Eskom was converted into a company which was required to pay taxes and dividends to the state as its sole shareholder. Control of the corporatised entity would be managed through the negotiation of 'shareholder compacts' between the utility's management and government as the shareholder. These compacts would be 'reassessed when outside bodies acquire equity' (DPE 2001a). The newly established board included the chief operating officer of the UK energy trader and electricity generator and retailer Innogy, and the president of telecommunications group Ericsson (Chalmers 2002b). Chaired by Reuel Khoza, the board comprised almost entirely big business representatives, with a handful of academics and a sole representative of the DPE.

Restructuring of generation, transmission and distribution

The restructuring process involved separate sets of interventions relating to the three components of Eskom's electricity supply system – generation, transmission and distribution. Each of these is discussed separately in this section.

GENERATION

Following the conversion of Eskom into a company, restructuring began in earnest. The first task necessary for restructuring the electricity supply industry was the ringfencing of Eskom's generation assets and finances from the transmission and distribution nodes. Ringfencing refers to the separation of the organisational structure and finances of each segment of the production chain, and their conversion into stand-alone business units. A two-pronged strategy followed to bring in the private sector. Eskom's generation assets were prepared for partial sale, and a competitive market structure was created in the electricity supply industry to allow for other private-sector competition.

Generation was to be opened to competition from black economic empowerment (BEE) companies and transnational corporations, with the goal of ensuring that 30 per cent of the generation market was occupied by the private sector by 2004 (Chalmers 2001i; Ministry of Public Enterprises 2001). Government anticipated that Eskom would maintain revenues by making up any capacity lost in the domestic market through the acquisition of generation capacity in Africa – hence the role of Eskom Enterprises (see below) (Chalmers 2001b). Eskom's power stations were organisationally restructured into five clusters. The Arnot, Hendrina, Kriel and Matla stations were in the first group of power stations; Duvha, Majuba and Kendal in the second; Lethabo, Matimba and Tutuka in the third; the nuclear power plant Koeberg in the fourth; and Simunye in the fifth (Chalmers 2001a). Simunye was the name given to a cluster of Eskom's three mothballed power stations – Komati, Grootvlei and Camden. The clusters were organised into Eskom's Generation Division. The companies were to operate independently of, and in competition with, one another, and be fully owned by the state (Ministry of Public Enterprises 2000). The clusters formed the basis for competing privatised companies in the future, with the state retaining a portion of generating capacity (Eberhard 2001). The DPE proposed the model for restructuring. Eskom followed suit as part of the 'shareholder compact' with government, despite underlying uneasiness. Eskom CEO Thulani Gcabashe was reported as saying that he did not believe government should introduce competition just for the sake of competition. Gcabashe said, 'Eskom has the lowest electricity price in the world, and excellent technical performance when benchmarked against the rest of the world. We need clear objectives as to why we are going this route' (Chalmers 2001a).

In 2003 government began to back off from the plan to privatise part of Eskom's generating assets. Finance Minister Trevor Manuel cited the poor global climate for privatisation and the Californian energy crisis that had been sparked off by total deregulation in the energy sector (Ensor 2003). Restructuring of the electricity generation sector was to continue, however, and government issued a tender calling for bids for consultants to assist with this at the start of 2004 (Phasiwe 2004a). Following its 2004 national election victory, the ANC announced that it would not sell the core assets of Eskom (Chalmers 2004). Then the minister of public enterprises announced that government had changed its objective from establishing a wholesale market to focusing on ensuring security of supply (Eskom 1999–2006: 2005 report). The focus of restructuring in the generation sector shifted away from the partial sale of Eskom assets and towards the introduction of private-sector power producers to build and operate new capacity.

Anticipating opportunities after 1996, a number of foreign multinationals had already positioned themselves to enter a deregulated electricity market in South Africa. These included the UK's International Power; Cinergy and Allied Energy Systems (AES) from the USA; and France's national utility, EDF (Chalmers 2002c). Direct private-sector participation was kick-started in 2000 when the NERSA granted a licence to Biomass Energy Ventures to generate and sell electricity. In July 2001, the NERSA issued a licence to AES to refurbish Kelvin power station and provide power to the Johannesburg Metropolitan Council (Chalmers 2001c). With the retreat from the disposal of core assets, the emphasis was placed on drawing in private-sector power producers to build, maintain and operate new generation infrastructure and sell electricity as demand grew. Eskom's share of the supply market would accordingly be reduced not by selling Eskom's generation assets, but by drawing in the private sector to meet new requirements (Rumney 2005; Singh 2005).

In 2005 Cabinet announced that future generating-capacity projects would be commissioned on the basis of a 70 : 30 split between Eskom and independent power producers (IPPs) (I-Net Bridge 2005). The plan was to meet short- to medium-term supply through a combination of refurbishing mothballed power stations and the construction of open gas turbine plants. But long-term supply was to be supported by the construction of new baseload plants, anticipated to start generating electricity sometime in 2009 (Lunsche 2006a). A tender was to be issued for IPPs to provide additional needed capacity by the end of 2008. Five international energy companies participated in the consortia that were shortlisted to build, own and run the first private power plants in the Nelson Mandela Metropole in the Eastern Cape and Durban in KwaZulu-Natal. The international companies participating in the shortlisted consortia were AES, Suez Energy, Tata

Power Company, HSBC Bank and YTL from Malaysia (Njobeni 2005). No decision on the successful bidder had been made at the time of writing. Eskom committed itself to signing a 15-year power purchase agreement with the winning bidder, creating a ready-made market for the new power producers (Phasiwe 2005).

Eskom planned to invest R12 billion to refurbish the three mothballed Simunye power stations (Komati, Grootvlei and Camden) and bring them onstream by 2011 (*Business Day* 2004), under Eskom's ownership and management. The first power started flowing from Camden in June 2005 (Lunsche 2006b: 6). In 2005 Eskom announced plans to construct two gas-fired peaking power plants at Atlantis and Mossel Bay in the Western Cape, with a combined capacity of 1 050 megawatts (MW), to be operational by April 2007 (Lunsche 2006a: 7).

Government approved an additional plan for Eskom to invest up to R22 billion to relieve worsening electricity shortages. The investment would involve expansion of the coal-fuelled Matimba plant by a third, or the construction of a new power station of the same size and on the same site at a cost of about R1 million/MW. Consideration was also being given to building a new combined cycle gas turbine plant in the Western Cape with a generating capacity of between 1 800 MW and 2 200 MW (*Business Day* 2006a).

These investments formed part of the R84 billion spending plan for the following five years, as part of the government's Accelerated and Shared Growth Initiative for South Africa (ASGISA) (Presidency of the Republic of South Africa 2006: 6). But instead of contributing to the revival of local manufacturing, a study by the Industrial Development Corporation (IDC) found that direct imports would account for R53 billion of Eskom's and Transnet's combined R134 billion capex programmes, with indirect imports accounting for a further R22 billion. This led Jorge Maia, the IDC's head of research and information, to charge that '[p]arastatals too often have only financial returns in mind rather than considering developmental returns as well' (Lourens 2006).

Despite the planned retention of Eskom's core assets, the planned disposal of non-core businesses and assets was set to proceed (Singh & Lunsche 2005). Eskom has not listed the divisions it wants to sell, though Public Enterprises Minister Alec Erwin stated that some 14 non-core businesses and assets valued at around R200 million would be sold (Ministry of Public Enterprises 2005). These are likely to include Rosherville Properties, Eskom's property arm, as well as Sapphire Air. The Congress of South African Trade Unions (Cosatu)-affiliated unions did not have a principled opposition to the disposal of non-core assets, but sought to ensure that this would not lead to downward variation of employment conditions for workers.[1]

TRANSMISSION

According to ERIC proposals for restructuring the transmission sector, the medium-term aim would be to separate out high-voltage from low-voltage transmission, with the possibility of privatising the latter. However, being a natural monopoly, transmission-sector privatisation was not on the immediate agenda. The sector was only to be corporatised and removed from Eskom's control in the meantime. A ringfenced Transmission Unit was established within Eskom, with the aim of eventually forming a separate company. The transmission sector was restructured to create a wires-and-system-operator business, as well as an independent system operator (Eskom 2002). The aim was to have a state-owned transmission company (not owned by Eskom), with the possibility of outsourcing sections of transmission (DME 2000). This goal has not yet been achieved, partly as a result of the reconsideration of the form of electricity sector liberalisation and restructuring, and is 'probably not a priority at the moment'.[2]

A national power exchange, or energy trading market, was to be implemented at the start of 2005. A trading market theoretically allows non-discriminatory access to the grid. Power is purchased from a number of generators and put into the pool. There is one price in the market that includes a capacity and an energy element. Generators indicate the price at which they will sell electricity, and this is then put on a schedule of use for the following day, with the cheapest scheduled first, all the way to most expensive, until demand is met. Once expected demand and reserve requirements are met, the market is closed for the day. The price paid for the last unit to be scheduled becomes the pool price. Generators are not obligated to supply, and may withhold electricity if they do not feel the price is reasonable. The system is driven by competition, and thus generators are unlikely to share information regarding costs with one another. Those who benefit the most will be those who are able to produce electricity at the lowest rate and sell at a rate closest to the 'marginal rate' (the price of the last unit scheduled) (Van Zyl et al. 1997).

Distributors purchase power from the pool, based on the marginal price plus a transmission cost. The transmission cost includes the cost of losses incurred in transporting the electricity to the distribution points of buyers. This means that buyers closer to power stations will pay less because they will incur fewer of the losses associated with long-distance transmission. In another version being contemplated, trading through the pool is voluntary rather than mandatory. In this system, bilateral contracts are concluded between individual generators and individual suppliers and/or customers (Eberhard 2001).

Eskom already had an internal power pool in operation from the mid-1990s. It was seen as a prototype for a broader South African pool in the future. By 2005 Eskom had ringfenced its Power Exchange Department (as a business unit within the Transmission Unit) in preparation for the possible establishment of a South African Power Exchange (Eskom 2005). However, faced with a looming supply crisis, the plan for a power market was put on hold until South Africa was able to maintain the security of its supply (National Treasury 2005). According to Eskom CEO Thulani Gcabashe, 'In the first phase of the rollout programme it makes sense for the transmission to remain within our stable. In five years' time, particularly if new power utilities enter the market, we will have to revisit the structure' (cited in Lunsche 2006c: 10).

A future South African exchange may be integrated into the regional Southern African Power Pool (SAPP), already operating since 1995. Utilities buy and sell power to one another through bilateral agreements – with a duration typically ranging between 5 and 10 years – negotiated within the framework of the SAPP agreement (*ESI Africa* 2004a; Singh 2003b). Eskom generates about 80 per cent of electricity produced in southern Africa, and so dominates the regional market. Nevertheless, the regional pool remains a small part of electricity trading in South Africa, with South African imports amounting to no more than 5 per cent of the total electricity pool in the country. At the same time, this has been creeping up and South Africa is expected to rely increasingly on regional imports, especially as the Grand Inga project unfolds (see Chapter 5 in this volume). South Africa, it is anticipated, will use 60 per cent of the Democratic Republic of the Congo (DRC) project's output. In 2006, more than 80 per cent of South Africa's energy imports came from the Cahora Bassa scheme in Mozambique, although more than a quarter of this was sold on to the Zimbabwe Electricity Supply Authority (ZESA) in terms of agreements between the utilities.[3] In 2001 a short-term energy market became fully functional at the regional level, with participating utilities from Botswana, Namibia, South Africa and Zimbabwe. The short-term market facilitates the sale and purchase of surplus power on the day-ahead market, and is used 'to take advantage of gaps between day-to-day demand and contracted supply' (*ESI Africa* 2004a).

DISTRIBUTION

The distribution sector usually includes supply functions. Supply refers to the provision of the services related to electricity. These include customer interfacing, billing, operations and maintenance (O&M), administration and so on. The remaining distribution activities refer to network construction (including the electrification programme). Distribution is supply to the end user, whereas transmission is bulk supply of electricity and associated infrastructure. According to the ERIC proposal, distributors would be responsible for electrification, but the programme would be funded nationally. The distribution sector was to be rationalised, with the formation of six Regional Electricity Distributors (REDs) to carry out low-voltage transmission and supply functions. This would require the merging of the infrastructure and distribution functions of Eskom and the municipalities. According to Job Motsepe, NUM's Energy Sector Co-ordinator, the original discussion on distribution restructuring at the NELF in the early 1990s was an economic and social debate, primarily about how to standardise and reduce tariffs for residents. But by 1996–1997 the debate had shifted to an ideologically driven argument in the context of plans to privatise part of Eskom. Says Motsepe, 'There never was a problem with electrification under Eskom, or service delivery in the townships once Eskom took over there. Now people are looking at making money rather than how to make the country work. How will the REDs improve the situation with regard to the collapse of the electrification programme? They cannot point to one place in the whole world where it has worked.'[4] The municipalities were not pleased with the plan, since electricity distribution had historically been a major revenue channel for them. In order to bring municipalities in line with the plan, the Electricity Distribution Industry Restructuring Bill was prepared and was awaiting the president's signature for it to become law in early 2006. The Bill sought to make it mandatory for municipalities to participate in the reform process (Phasiwe 2006c).

Despite ongoing lack of regulatory and financial clarity about how the REDs would function, Eskom proceeded with the ringfencing of its own distribution functions and infrastructure in preparation for restructuring. In 2003 the independent but state-owned EDI holding company was established to plan and implement the formation of the REDs. A presidential deadline of January 2007 was set for the establishment of all REDs. In July 2005 the assets of the Cape Town metro distributor and Eskom's Western Region were merged, with the establishment of the first RED. At the end of 2005 the RED model was simplified so that most municipalities were initially excluded. As the situation stands at the time of writing, the six REDs will be confined to the metro boundaries with a seventh, national, RED to cover all non-metro areas. Eskom will run the national distributor, which will be responsible for meeting the national electrification target of universal access by 2012 (Lunsche 2006d). This should be read as recognition of the value of an integrated national utility in carrying out electrification, at least for the areas that were not to be covered by REDs. At one stage these areas were intended to become peripheral additions of the REDs rooted in metros. This would have fragmented supply to a greater extent than if there were a national RED serving all these areas. This does not, however, imply that the separation of distribution into the REDs does not also result in a fragmentation of supply.

The distribution restructuring process was eventually to arrive at a point where low-voltage distribution (the wires leading up to and into the building) would be separated from the supply of an electricity service. It was envisaged that the retail supply would eventually be opened to market competition, allowing customers to choose the supplier from which they would buy electricity (although it would still be distributed to the building by a monopoly distributor). This would mean the physical infrastructure would remain in the hands of a single entity, although the service provided through the infrastructure would be open to competition. To illustrate, a consumer would be able to choose which company they wanted to supply their electricity. This choice might be based on cost of service or efficiency, for example. But that service provider would pay a fee to a monopoly infrastructure holder to use the existing infrastructure to get the service to their customer. The alternative would be for every service provider to set up their own power lines to their customers, a patently unworkable option. The delivery infrastructure is therefore referred to as a natural monopoly. However, this part of the privatisation process was never likely to be carried out before 2010 (Winkler &

Mavhungu 2001). There are no current plans to ringfence low-voltage distribution and service supply separately.[5]

Employment trends and working conditions

The long-term processes of restructuring Eskom had a significant negative effect on employment levels at the utility. Between 1990 and March 2005 employment dropped by 40 per cent (Figure 3.1). This reduction was partly achieved through processes of 'natural attrition' – in which workers who left were not replaced – and voluntary retrenchment (*Financial Mail* 1996). As Eskom unbundled, some workers were transferred to the separate units. For example, between 1999 and 2005 the 2 500 employees in Eskom Enterprises were not on Eskom's books. While most of the jobs lost at Eskom do still exist, they are outsourced and are no longer carried out by Eskom workers or even by permanent workers. Contract work has included 'non-core' functions such as cleaning services and security, but also core functions such as electrification. The jobs are contracted out for short periods to different groups of workers, resulting in a fragmentation of employment, with short-term contracts and job insecurity, poor working conditions and a difficult organising environment.[6]

In 2001, the South African government acknowledged that changing operational requirements resulting from restructuring could lead to significant job losses (DPE 2001b). The Ministry of Public Enterprises suggested that short-term job losses might be offset for labour 'as a group' by the 'appreciation in the value of shares acquired in the restructured enterprises' and 'improved economic conditions that permit re-absorption into the job market' (Ministry of Public Enterprises 2000: 39). In other words, retrenched workers would lose out, but those who remained might benefit from having shares in the restructured company. The retrenched workers would then be able to find new jobs if job-creating growth ever occurred, sometime in the distant future.

About three-quarters of Eskom's workforce (24–25 000 workers) are organised into three unions. The Cosatu-affiliated NUM and NUMSA organise mainly black workers. NUM is the largest union at Eskom, with 10 700 workers. NUMSA has around 5 000 workers.[7] Most of the black workers organised into these two unions are in the semi-skilled categories, although they are making some inroads into the skilled categories as more black workers are trained to perform skilled jobs. The conservative Mynwerkers Unie (Mineworkers' Union; now part of Solidarity) began organising white workers in Eskom in the 1960s, and continues to do so today. Solidarity has started recruiting black workers at Eskom and this has assisted it to increase its numbers in recent years. It has an estimated 6 000 members, mainly in the skilled categories. The main issue for Solidarity is opposition to affirmative action. Although there are tactical alliances between all the unions on most issues, Solidarity's resistance to racial transformation has hindered longer-term strategic alliances between the unions.[8]

Figure 3.1: Eskom employment, 1990–2005

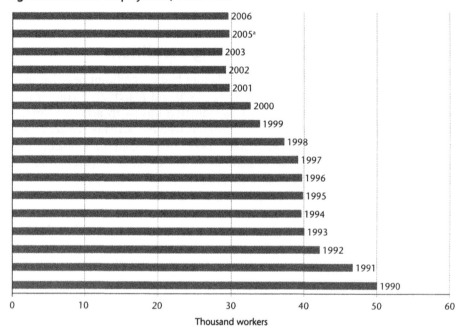

Sources: Eskom 1996, 1999–2006
Note: a 2005 covers the period 1 January 2004–31 March 2005.

The unions have lost membership as the workforce has declined. The key challenges for the progressive unions are to organise contract workers and to recruit the new intake of young professionals. The Cosatu affiliates (especially the NUM) continued to organise workers in Rotek (Eskom's engineering arm, discussed further below) and Eskom Enterprises, but these workers have no longer been able to participate in collective bargaining structures since they were outsourced. Job insecurity and the power of the contractor to fire at will have made the organising of outsourced workers extremely difficult. The re-absorption of Eskom Enterprises into Eskom Holdings has meant the redeployment of Eskom Enterprises workers back into Eskom, although excluding those from Rotek Industries and Roshcon (the electrical and civil infrastructure, as well as holding company for property and vehicle services; see below for more details). On the other hand, the young professionals in Eskom, who constitute a growing percentage of the workforce, have little interest in joining the unions, preferring to pay an agency fee than to pay union membership fees.[9] Workers who benefit from gains won by unions but are not union members pay an agency fee that is shared between the unions.

According to Osborne Galeni, a former national organiser for the NUMSA, the process of retrenchments was handled in a fairly consultative way in the late 1980s and early 1990s. For this reason, there was little overt conflict between the unions and Eskom around the retrenchments. However, the process subsequently became increasingly conflictual.[10] Galeni indicated that the goals of transformation from the 1980s on had been fundamentally about using Eskom as a publicly owned vehicle for delivery of basic services to the black population and to drive equitable economic development. However, new management sought to reverse these goals, becoming obstructionist and limiting the meaningful functioning of transformation structures of the past. Workers' benefits have declined substantially since 1996, including the loss of gratuities, housing allowances and other benefits. Relations between management and the unions soured in 1998 when management began imposing its solutions on workers. There was an incident at Eskom's head office at Megawatt Park in July 1998 in which buildings were burned down while workers were protesting. Workers were arrested and the NUM was sued for the damages, but the case is still in the high court awaiting appeal. Since then, the relationship has remained poor. Primary causes are the continual outsourcing, poor wages and working conditions and the autocratic management style. [11]

From the perspective of workers, it appears that the consolidation of the post-apartheid management in Eskom has made the utility less willing to engage openly with workers than was the case in the transition period of the late 1980s and early 1990s. It is ironic that the end of apartheid has brought to the fore a management ethos that is less responsive to workers and more responsive to the needs of big business.

According to the NUMSA, there are union programmes for assisting unions in other African countries where Eskom has projects through the International Federation of Chemical, Energy, Mine and General Workers' Unions (ICEM). However, it does not seem that the NUMSA is actively involved in organising in the region or on the continent. Job Motsepe, the NUM's Energy Sector Co-ordinator, says the ICEM has ceased functioning.[12] There are no unionised workers at all in Eskom's operations in other African countries, according to Motsepe. Workers from the energy sector in general in other countries have approached South African unions for assistance, and the NUM has provided some assistance on how to organise, but mainly in mining and construction. The union has been pushing for one set of conditions of service throughout Africa. However, support needs to be deepened and extended to energy workers, and remains a priority for the NUM. Motsepe asks how Eskom can outsource and destroy jobs in South Africa, and then think it will create jobs in other countries. He cites as an example the fact that in South Africa, each power station employs around 1 000 permanent workers. But in Swaziland, where unions are weak, there are only 50 permanent workers and the rest are subcontracted. It should be noted that the stations in Swaziland are smaller than those in South Africa. The point is that there is a higher degree of subcontracting as a result of weak unionism.

Impact of restructuring on the national electrification programme

In 1987 Eskom started a black residential electrification programme under the slogan of 'Electricity for All'. The programme started off slowly, reaching just

25 000 new connections in 1991. In 1994, the RDP set an electrification target of 2.5 million household connections by 2000 (450 000 connections per year), and the electrification of all schools and clinics as soon as possible. Eskom integrated its programme into the RDP targets, aiming for 1.75 million household connections (300 000 per year). Eskom set its targets on the assumption that municipal distributors would be responsible for the remaining RDP connections. Local councils did begin making connections, rising above 100 000 connections per year from 1993 (Figure 3.2). In 1995 Eskom's electrification programme hit its peak, with over 325 000 new connections in that year. The utility maintained a high rate of new connections over the following few years, but there was a substantial reduction as plans for corporatisation solidified. The 1998 Energy White Paper had indicated that there would be a slow-down in the number of connections from 1999 (DME 1998). Indeed, 1997 proved to be the peak year for the number of household connections made, at just under 500 000, thanks to a spike in the number of connections made by local authorities.

Figure 3.2: Eskom and local government electricity connections, 1991–2005

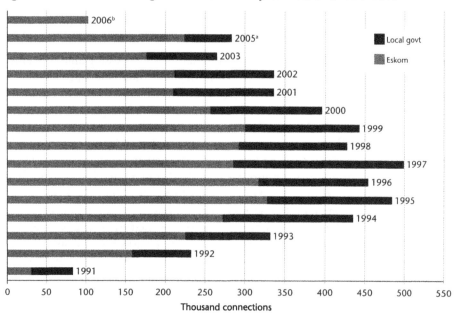

Sources: Eskom 1996, 1999–2005; NERSA 1995, 1998, 2000b, 2003b
Notes: a The Eskom figure for 2005 is a 12-month approximation based on reported figures for the
15 months January 2004–March 2005 for the sake of comparison; the local government figure for
2004 was supplied by Chris van Zyl, Senior Manager: INEP Capital Programme, DME, personal
communication, 23 March 2006.
b Local government figures for 2006 are not available.

Funds for the national electrification programme (NEP) came from Eskom's internal resources, through a combination of loans raised on the capital markets and a levy on grid consumers, estimated to be an average of 4 per cent of the cost of electricity consumption in 1997 (DME 1997: 2). Municipalities relied partly on debt financing and partly on Eskom subsidies. Until 1995 Eskom refunded municipalities R400 of the cost of each new connection, and made available bulk discounts to municipalities on the basis of their electrification programmes (Davis 1996: 475). In 1996 Eskom pledged an additional R300 million/year for five years over and above its own capital expenditure to subsidise electrification costs incurred by local governments. The NERSA administered the funds, providing an average subsidy to municipalities of R2 400 per connection. While more than R6.5 billion was spent on electrification between 1994 and 2000, expenditure in 2000 was more than 30 per cent less than in 1994, even before inflation is taken into account (DME 2002: 16).

Responsibility for the NEP was transferred from Eskom to the DME with the withdrawal of Eskom's tax-exempt status in 2001. This was in line with the Energy White Paper, which indicated that financing of the NEP would be shifted from an implicit surcharge in the electricity price to the budget. The surcharge went into the National Revenue Fund controlled by the Department of Finance and was then allocated to the National Electrification Fund. The department explicitly stated that the shift would affect neither the overall level of funding for electrification nor the level of the electricity tariff. In a programme evaluation in 2000, government acknowledged that the NEP was not commercially sustainable and had to be recognised as a long-term social investment programme. In particular the evaluators argued that 'where electrification is directed to very poor communities, subsidies are needed for both network construction and ongoing operations and maintenance' (DME 2001b: 23). The evaluation further went on to state that, despite being a marginal economic investment, the socio-economic benefits were important. These are important points that indicate that government delivery should not only be considered from the point of view of short-term and direct economic return, but also in relation to the longer-term social and economic returns that accrue more broadly than merely to the investor.

In the year following Eskom's corporatisation, the amount the utility provided for electrification declined from R1 billion to R600 million. But Eskom was approved as the business planning and implementation agent for the new integrated national electrification programme (INEP), receiving R446 million from the DME in 2001 for this purpose (Eskom 2002: 64). However, this was on condition that the function was ringfenced inside Eskom so that it could be 'moved to an appropriate home' as EDI restructuring unfolded (DME 2001a: 42). As part of the 'shareholder compact' between Eskom and government in 2000, the utility committed to undertaking a further 600 000 connections over three years.

The budget for the NEP grew rapidly in the DME. There was a 30.5 per cent increase in the budget for the national programme delivered through Eskom between 2001 – when the department took over funding of the programme – and 2005/06. This was set to rise another 35 per cent over the Medium Term Expenditure Framework (the government's three-year budgeting framework) period to 2008/09 (National Treasury 2006a: 711). In addition, the DME transferred around R200–250 million per year to local government for local-level electrification projects through the INEP (National Treasury 2003: 740). This amount was also set to rise significantly to more than R450 million in 2008/09 – a 133 per cent increase in the conditional grant to local government over four years – but concerns were raised about the capacity of local government to meet targets because of 'inability of municipalities to conclude funding agreements and service level agreements' (National Treasury 2006a: 708–709). Indeed, from 1997 onward the number of local government connections showed a constant annual decline, so that in 2004 there were 71 per cent fewer connections by local government than in 1997 (a drop from 214 000 to 61 000). Chris van Zyl at the DME suggested that part of the problem was that housing delivery was not meeting targets, and electrification in the urban areas was linked to housing construction.[13] Dispersed rural connections also began receiving greater priority once the easier to reach and cheaper to connect urban connections had been completed. These differences mean that rural connections are more expensive, resulting in a reduced number of connections for the same cost (DME 2001b). Figure 3.3 shows the rapid rise in average costs per connection after 2001.

Figure 3.3: Average cost per connection, 1992–2006

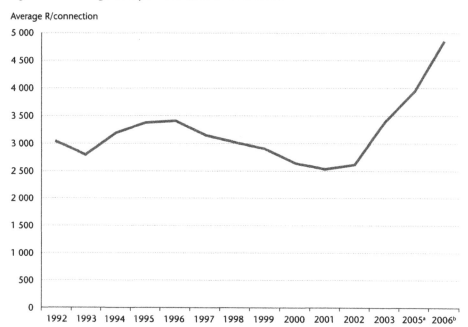

Sources: Davis 1996; Eskom 1999–2006

Notes: a The 2005 figure covers the period January 2004–March 2005.

   b This figure indicates direct and farm worker connections divided by capital expenditure on these connections.

The municipal component of the INEP fund was to be integrated into the newly consolidated Municipal Infrastructure Grant, but at the end of 2005 Cabinet made a decision to retain INEP in the DME until the completion of the restructuring of the distribution industry and the formation of the REDs.[14] In 2006 Eskom and licensed municipalities took over the co-ordination of INEP from the DBSA and the NERSA, with the DME continuing to play a planning and monitoring role.

Government argued that the conversion of Eskom into a tax-paying entity would not affect the electrification programme because the money derived from taxes would be used to continue to fund the programme. An agreement between Eskom and government allowed Eskom to report a loss until 2004, and use the surpluses – that would previously have gone into the electrification programme – to position itself for competition (Cosatu 2001). The DME acknowledged that 'if Eskom pays taxes and dividends, then there is a possibility that less funds will be available from this source for electrification. Electrification funds may then have to flow through the fiscus. Other governmental priorities may include a further reduction in electrification funding' (DME 1997: 2).

Eskom and government did meet the RDP target of 2.5 million connections by 2000. Eskom also connected 6 324 schools by 2000 (NERSA 2000a: 17). Between 1991 and 2005, Eskom made over 3.2 million new connections. Local government made an additional 1.7 million connections. Although more than 200 municipalities were licensed to carry out electrification in 2005, many of them relied on subcontractors to execute the programme.[15] The percentage of households with access to electricity infrastructure increased to 68 per cent at the end of 2002. But less than 40 per cent of rural households had electricity in the largely rural Eastern Cape and KwaZulu-Natal provinces (NERSA 2003a: 19). Despite a backlog of 32 per cent of households without electricity, the number of connections declined precipitously after 1999, as shown in Figure 3.2.

In addition to the declining number of annual new connections, access to infrastructure only unevenly translated into improvements in quality of life. Statistics South Africa's annual household survey showed a significant rise in the number of households using electricity for lighting, from 63.5 per cent in 1995 to 80.1 per cent in 2004. However, growth in the number of households using electricity for cooking only rose 3.9 per cent over the decade 1995–2004 (from 55.4 per cent of households to 59.3 per cent). The number of households using electricity for heating actually declined over the decade, from 53.8 per cent to 49.6 per cent (Stats SA 2001: 78–80, 2005: 46–48).

An evaluation of the NEP in 2000 found that average consumption was a little over 100 kilowatt-hours (kWh) per household per month, compared to the expected 350 kWh at the start of the programme, resulting in lower than expected welfare benefits (DME 2001b: vi). The primary reason for low consumption is the cost of the service. For example, in 2001 Soweto residents were paying 30 per cent more for electricity than nearby white suburbanites. Overall, domestic consumers paid 700 per cent more, at R0.25/kWh, than some large corporations that paid R0.04/kWh (Fiil-Flynn 2001: 6). Stringent cost recovery policies meant that residential consumers had to pay the full cost of the service, regardless of levels of poverty.

Data on disconnections are very hard to come by. The Department of Provincial and Local Government released detailed quarterly statistics on connections and disconnections at municipal level from 1996 to March 2002. These showed that more people were being disconnected than were receiving new connections, at least during this period (Greenberg 2002). The primary reason for disconnections was lack of payment for services. There is an ongoing debate about the causes of lack of payment. A large component of these causes related to inability to pay. Unwillingness to pay is not as clear-cut a cause as it may sound. There is certainly evidence to suggest that users will be less willing to pay if services (including billing) are poor or if there is a sense that services are not distributed evenly to all.

The response from Eskom and local councils was to implement a policy of cut-offs and to tie partial write-offs of arrears to customer willingness to pay for the remaining arrears or to the acceptance of prepaid meters (Anti-Privatisation Forum 2005; Fiil-Flynn 2001; Smith 2002). So, although the infrastructure was being rolled out, access remained limited to those who could afford the service.

Eskom Enterprises

Eskom restructuring involved the transfer of the utility's non-regulated functions into a new company, Eskom Enterprises, in 1999. Regulated functions were the domestic generation, transmission and distribution of electricity. Non-regulated areas included support services (such as telecommunications, engineering and transport) and research into nuclear technology both inside and outside South Africa, as well as any energy-related activities outside South Africa. Eskom Enterprises was created as a wholly owned subsidiary of Eskom and took the form of a company governed by the Companies Act of 1973. Therefore it was required to pay taxes and dividends like any other company. Its mission was to lead the global expansion of Eskom activities, with a focus on Africa.

The message of an Eskom Enterprises advertising campaign was that Eskom was no longer a South African-based utility focused on the generation, transmission and distribution of power, but was in the process of becoming a diversified energy group with interests in, among others, telecommunications, IT and engineering (Chalmers 2001d). The approach was in line with the export-oriented economy being built on the basis of the GEAR macroeconomic strategy and the New Partnership for Africa's Development (NEPAD). It was also based on diversification of economic activities to reduce the impact on profitability of future competition in the local electricity supply industry.

Eskom Enterprises took over significant service and support functions for Eskom, including engineering and maintenance, and internal communications. Eskom and, increasingly, other parastatals remained the biggest market for Eskom Enterprises' services. At the same time there was a concerted drive into Africa not only for energy-related services, but also for telecommunications, IT, engineering and other support services. Construction and engineering and technical consulting services formed the core of Eskom Enterprises' capacity, built around Rotek Industries and Technology Services International (TSI). Rotek and TSI were subsidiary companies wholly owned by Eskom Enterprises. The aim was for the strategic paths of Eskom and Eskom Enterprises to gradually diverge from one another (Eskom 1999–2006: 2005 report).

The emergence of Eskom Enterprises coincided with the deregulatory thrust inside South Africa. More emphasis was placed on the unregulated global side of the business in an attempt to diversify away from the internal electricity market, where Eskom expected to lose market share as competition was introduced. In 2002 Eskom's chair, Reuel Khoza, said that the utility expected that revenues coming from outside the regulated business would be equal to those emanating from within South Africa (Chalmers 2002a). A newspaper article described Eskom's trajectory as a transformation from 'an efficient South African monopoly into a diversified global company capable of competing with the most efficient producers in the world' (Chalmers 2002a).

But Eskom Enterprises did not perform according to expectations. Targeting a 12 per cent return on equity in the first years of operation, it fell well short of this goal with less than 6 per cent returns from 2000 to 2005. Eskom Enterprises' revenues constituted a small portion of Eskom's overall revenues. In 2002, when figures for both companies were available separately, Eskom Enterprises' revenues were R2.9 billion compared to Eskom Holdings' revenues of R29.8 billion – about 10 per cent of revenue derived from regulated activities. Its activities were far less profitable than the regulated activities. Eskom Enterprises made an average annual loss of R47 million loss between 2000 and 2006 (Figure 3.4), compared with Eskom's average yearly R2.96 billion after-tax profits for regulated business over the same period (Eskom 1999–2006).

High initial costs for long-term projects such as the Pebble Bed Modular Reactor (PBMR; see more details below) and telecommunications investments were partially responsible for losses in Eskom Enterprises. Delays in government licensing of the second national fixed line operator (SNO; see below) meant that Eskom Enterprises' massive investment in fibre-optic cable was not recouped and the investment began to decay, accounting for the R719 million loss in 2003. Conducting business in Africa was more difficult than anticipated. In many places, especially beyond southern Africa, Eskom was unknown and found it difficult to break into new markets. In addition, even where Eskom did succeed in getting into the market, results were worse than expected (see below for more details). In Lesotho the mobile telecoms business made a loss in the first years, and arivia.com – an IT company that was formed out of the IT units of Eskom, Transnet and Denel in 2001 and operated as a commercial entity – did not generate expected income. Amidst fears of its imminent collapse, Eskom Enterprises was increasingly criticised for a lack of focus, leading to a restructuring exercise in 2003 and recapitalisation in 2004. The plan involved focusing and consolidating African operations closer to home in the Southern African Development Community (SADC), and selling non-core assets to focus on the electricity supply industry and, to a lesser extent, telecommunications (Chalmers 2005; Phasiwe 2004c). At the same time, Eskom made a strategic shift to focusing more closely on domestic business, especially in the light of greater than expected electricity demand.

Figure 3.4: Eskom Enterprises after-tax profit/loss, 2000–2005

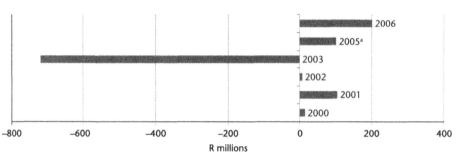

Sources: Eskom 1999–2005; Eskom Enterprises 2002
Note: a This covers the period January 2004–March 2005.

Following the Revised Business Model introduced in 2004, Eskom Enterprises was reabsorbed into Eskom Holding Company, as a wholly owned subsidiary. According to the Eskom *Annual Report* (2005: 72), 'the change in focus indicated the need for greater integration of the activities of Eskom and Eskom Enterprises'. Eskom Enterprises (Pty) Ltd's primary function from this point on was to service the line divisions within Eskom (project management and technical support), with line divisions as clients. Given Eskom Enterprises' role in executing the design and building components of Eskom's business, it would be centrally involved in Eskom's capital expansion programme. Eskom Enterprises would also house Eskom's non-core assets and businesses identified for disposal (Eskom 2005: 67). Non-core assets scheduled for disposal by mid-2007 included Eskom's five jets, seven helicopters and housing loan book, worth a combined R200 million (Phasiwe 2006b).

Energy services in Africa

Eskom Enterprises was viewed as Eskom's vehicle to expand into Africa. According to then Eskom chair Reuel Khoza, the formation of Eskom Enterprises to spearhead Eskom's involvement in Africa was the first phase of expansion into other parts of the globe (Chalmers 2000a). All acquisitions by Eskom in Africa were made through Eskom Enterprises. In 2002, Eskom Enterprises had 32 bids and projects in Africa, with another 9 in the rest of the world (Eskom Enterprises 2002: 94–95). Figure 3.5 shows some of Eskom's activities in Africa by 2003.

Figure 3.5: Eskom in Africa, 2003

Source: International Rivers Network & Earthlife Africa 2003

Eskom Enterprises used NEPAD as the basis of its forays into Africa, to the extent that its chair and Eskom CEO Thulani Gcabashe established a NEPAD unit in his office. The unit aimed to integrate all NEPAD initiatives in Africa that were in line with group strategy. According to Gcabashe, 'Eskom has a strong commitment to NEPAD. All our activities and EE's [Eskom Enterprises'] role must be seen in that context' (Singh 2003a). Eskom has seconded staff to strengthen capacity in the NEPAD secretariat, and participates in the NEPAD economic forum. The public motivation for support to NEPAD and its projects is to assist with development of infrastructure as the basis of economic and social progress. At the same time it also serves as a conduit for the expansion of capital – including but not limited to South African capital – into Africa. The necessity of modernising capitalist development in Africa is a basic underpinning of NEPAD.

In 2002 Eskom proposed the prioritisation of four energy projects under NEPAD. The first was a study into the feasibility of the Western Power Corridor Project power transmission line (covering the DRC, Angola, Namibia, Botswana and South Africa). Just before the launch of Eskom Enterprises in 1999, Eskom and Namibian Power (Namibia's state-owned power company) had completed a 600 kilometre transmission line between the two countries (Eskom 2000). In 2004 the electricity utilities from the five countries – Botswana Power Corporation, Empresa Naçional de Electricidade of Angola, Eskom, NamPower of Namibia and Société Nationale d'Électricité (SNEL) of DRC – signed a memorandum of understanding on the project. Later in the same year the five participating governments signed an intergovernmental memorandum of understanding on the Western Power Corridor Project, and a joint venture company called Westcor was set up to conduct feasibility studies (DME 2005).

Westcor's primary activities will be to construct and run a power station at Inga III, two 1 500 MW converter stations, and high-voltage transmission lines terminating in South Africa (Bakaya-Kyahurwa 2004). Another target was the construction of hydro-power stations in Angola, especially on the Kwanza River, and in Namibia (Ministry of Public Enterprises 2004). According to Peter O'Connor, Eskom Enterprises' senior general manager in charge of the capital expansion programme, 'risk issues' remained a key stumbling block to a go-ahead (Lunsche 2006b). Nevertheless, the five participating utilities each paid US$100 000 to Westcor at the end of 2005 to start the project.[16]

The second NEPAD priority was the connection of Malawi, via Mozambique, to the SAPP. The third was the connection of Tanzania and Kenya to the SAPP. In 2003 the World Bank and the Norwegian Development Agency NORAD granted funds for the first phases of these projects, to the amounts of US$87 million and US$178.6 million respectively (*ESI Africa* 2004b). The fourth priority was restoration of capacity of the Zongo and Sanga hydro-electric facilities in Kinshasa, DRC, including a dedicated supply to Brazzaville (Lennon 2002). Projects were guided by Eskom's overarching vision of the development of a pan-African grid, concentrating on the development and implementation of regional 'power highways' (Eskom 2005: 115). The plan centres on the Grand Inga Dam hydro-power project on the Congo River, estimated to have the potential to produce sufficient electricity for Africa's entire needs plus a surplus for export to Europe (Hale 2002). Eskom Enterprises helped to set up the African Energy Fund in 2002 as a vehicle for NEPAD's energy infrastructure projects (no information is readily available on total capitalisation capital set aside by Eskom for this fund).

The Eskom Enterprises Africa unit co-ordinated African activities, and included sub-sidiary Eskom Enterprises Global West Africa Ltd based in Nigeria. Eskom Enterprises Africa was tasked with the development and implementation of the key NEPAD grid connection projects between Malawi-Mozambique, Tanzania–Zambia, Kenya–Tanzania, and DRC–Angola–Namibia–South Africa. It was also tasked with the Lesotho rural electrification project. Other projects directly under Eskom

Enterprises Africa included a partnership with the DRC's SNEL and Magalloy Corporation (magnesium mining in Congo Brazzaville) to develop a transmission line for mining operations; infrastructure rehabilitation projects in Nigeria; and utility management in Zanzibar (Eskom Enterprises 2002). In Mozambique, Eskom Enterprises formed Elgas, a joint venture with a number of South African and Mozambican companies, to distribute and sell natural gas from the Pande gas field to consumers around Vilanculos, Inhassoro and Nova Mambone in Mozambique. Agreements for gas supply were also signed with exclusive holiday resorts and hotels on the Bazaruto Archipelago (*Energy Management News* 2001).

In 2002 Eskom Enterprises signed a 20-year concession to operate and maintain two hydro stations (Nalubale and Kiiri) in Uganda. These two facilities generate 95 per cent of Uganda's electricity supply, with an installed capacity of 300 MW. In 2004 Eskom Enterprises, in partnership with Commonwealth Development Corporation subsidiary Globeleq, was awarded a 20-year concession to operate the electricity distribution system in Uganda. Eskom Enterprises (44 per cent) and Globeleq (56 per cent) formed a jointly owned company, Umeme Ltd, to lease the electricity distribution network from Ugandan Electricity Distribution Company Ltd under the concession agreement (Globeleq 2005). In neighbouring Burundi, Eskom Enterprises installed a prepayment meter project and started work on a similar one for thermal power plants in Sudan (Ministry of Public Enterprises 2004).

Apart from Eskom Enterprises' direct energy-related activities in Africa, subsidiaries TSI and Rotek constituted the core of Eskom Enterprises' involvement in Africa. In turn, each of these subsidiaries had a number of companies reporting to them. TSI focused on technology and engineering, project management and O&M services. Throughout Eskom Enterprises' period of existence TSI continued to sell services to Eskom in South Africa as well as to clients in other countries, as far afield as Vietnam and Georgia. TSI (Pty) Ltd is the holding company for shares in joint ventures and subsidiaries, including Electricity Africa and Trans Africa Projects (TAP). Transmission resources were consolidated in TAP, including those for Eskom in South Africa. TAP was active in Tunisia and Nigeria, as well as in India and China in 2002 (Eskom Enterprises 2002). In a joint venture with international engineering company Fluor Daniel, TAP signed a deal in 2001 with the National Electric Power Authority (NEPA) in Nigeria to roll out a 380 kilometre transmission line between Gombe, Yola and Jaling in Nigeria's western regions (Wessels 2001).

TAP was also involved in setting up a transmission line and substation in Swaziland, a transmission grid expansion in Mauritius, a transmission line joining South Africa and Namibia and a transmission line between South Africa and Maputo (Wessels 2001). The company participated in constructing the privately owned Motraco transmission line, a joint venture between Swaziland Electricity, Eskom and EDM (Mozambique's electricity utility) to transmit power to the Mozal aluminium smelter in Mozambique.

TSI was directly involved in Eskom Energie Manantali, a 15-year concession to manage and operate the Manantali Dam hydro station in Mali, and to transmit power to the national utilities of Mali, Senegal and Mauritania from the dam. TSI works on the project together with SOGEM, a company formed by the three countries for this purpose. TSI also participates in a joint venture in Libya called Global Electricity Services Company (GESCO) that was awarded a steam power plant rehabilitation contract by the General Electricity Company of Libya (GECOL). GESCO also had other consultancies for GECOL, including a seawater intake project at Khoms Power Station east of Tripoli, and support for planning to develop IPPs in North and West Africa. Through TSI, Eskom acquired a 51 per cent share of Lunsemfwa Hydro Power Company in Zambia. The company owns two hydro-power stations at Mulungushi and Lusemfwa, with a combined capacity of 36 MW. TSI was also awarded electrification contracts in Zambia and a management contract with Escom Malawi (Eskom Enterprises 2002).

The Rotek/Roshcon Group had four divisions separated into two legal entities: Rotek Industries consisting of the Rotek engineering and property divisions; and Roshcon, owning the Roshcon and Rosherville vehicle services divisions. Rotek Industries accounted for up to half of Eskom Enterprises' turnover. Rotek was established in 1989 when the assets and operations of Eskom's central maintenance services were transferred to an independent holding company. This allowed Eskom to 'contract out' its power system maintenance. Rotek provided services that included heavy electrical and mechanical repairs and refurbishment, infrastructure development, property management and transport projects. Rotek was involved in both Eskom Enterprises and external projects in Africa, as well as in Australia and South-East Asia (Chalmers 2001e). Rotek engineering was involved in repairing and maintaining electricity generation and distribution equipment and machinery, and also had a bulk water services division that operated, repaired and maintained water schemes, including maintenance contracts with the Department of Water Affairs and Forestry in South Africa. Eskom Holdings remained its most significant customer, but it also operated in a number of other countries in Africa and further afield. The privatisation of Rotek was started with the announcement of the full disposal of Rotek vehicle services in 2002 (DPE 2002).

Roshcon operates in the electrical and civil infrastructure sectors, as well as in waste management. Electrical infrastructure activities have ranged from installation of meters in domestic homes to the construction of 132 kiloVolt transmission networks. Roshcon was involved in some of Eskom Enterprises' contracts in southern Africa, including the Lesotho electrification project. Rosherville vehicle services operated transport fleets under contract for Eskom as well as for other companies in South Africa. The Rosherville properties division managed the 240-hectare Rotek site near Johannesburg, as well as the group's residential, industrial and commercial buildings and offices. In 2003, Eskom Enterprises planned to sell the Rosherville vehicle unit as well as the non-core properties owned by the group (Eskom Enterprises 2002). According to the NUM, the privatisation of Roshcon is likely to mean the loss of 400 jobs.[17]

Telecommunications and IT

There is a technological convergence between power generation and distribution, IT and telephony. Cables and wires can be used to distribute power, data, voice and video. This resulted in a strategic focus on telecommunications by Eskom Enterprises as the non-regulated subsidiary of Eskom, both in South Africa and in the rest of the continent. It was seen as a way of more fully exploiting the infrastructure and servitudes Eskom had at its disposal, to augment income from power system sales and to diversify the revenue base. An added synergy was that 'power infrastructure tracks the same demographic targets as is desired by telecommunications systems' (Pillay 2002).

In 2001 in South Africa, the Telecommunications Amendment Bill was passed, becoming the Telecommunications Amendment Act (No. 64 of 2001); it made provision for an unspecified percentage of a SNO to be set aside for Eskom Enterprises (at that time through a company called Esi-tel) and Transnet (through Transtel) (Chalmers 2001f). Following Eskom's rebranding exercise in 2002, all Eskom's telecommunications functions were situated in Eskom Enterprises' new telecommunications division. Eskom and Transnet's 30 per cent shares in the SNO were eventually combined as SoeCo (State Owned Enterprises Company) when a licence was granted at the end of 2005. The other shareholders in the SNO consortium were three BEE companies – Nexus Connection (19 per cent), CommuniTel (12.5 per cent) and TwoConsortium (12.5 per cent) – and Tata Africa Holdings (representing Videsh Sanchar Nigam Ltd, an international telecoms operator based in India) with a 25 per cent stake. Along with the PBMR, retrofitting fibre-optic cable to its transmission network was one of Eskom Enterprises' two largest projects (Phasiwe 2002). Hem-Kom Liveline, a joint venture between Eskom Enterprises (through TSI) and Electhem South Africa, installed 10 000 kilometres of cable in preparation for the launch of the SNO in 2003.

Fitting fibre-optic cable to the overhead power cable as the power grid was established was also one of the anticipated by-products of the upgrading of transmission lines in Africa. The African component of telecommunications expansion was situated in Eskom Telecommunications Africa (ET Africa). The activities of this section included the installation of fibre-optic cable in Nigeria, a concession to develop a long-distance digital backbone in the DRC, and fibre-optic cable installation between Arnot in South Africa and Mozambique (Eskom Enterprises 2002).

Towards the end of 2000, Eskom Enterprises made its first acquisition in the telecommunications sector, buying a controlling stake in fixed-line monopoly Telkom Lesotho together with Econet Wireless International of Zimbabwe and Telkom Mauritius. Eskom Enterprises has a 35 per cent share of the consortium, valued at US$7 million. In 2002 ET Africa acquired a majority share in holding company Mountain Communications. The consortium was also granted a licence to operate a second cellular network in Lesotho, called Econet Ezi-Cel Lesotho. This was followed by a successful consortium bid in Kenya, with Eskom Enterprises as technical partner, to purchase 49 per cent of fixed-line operator Telkom Kenya (Taka 2001: 13). Consortium partners were Econet Zimbabwe and SaskTel of Canada. In 2000 Nigeria's NEPA awarded Hem-Kom a contract to install 1 300 kilometres of fibre-optic cable on the power authority's power lines (IT Web 2001). Eskom Enterprises was also involved in a joint venture with NEPA, called Nepscom Telecommunications, to build and operate telecoms infrastructure in Nigeria.

Following the Revised Business Model of 2004 the future of Eskom Enterprises' telecommunications investments is in doubt. A separate strategic plan for the SNO has been developed, but Eskom Enterprises has refused to provide details, citing sensitivity. Eskom Enterprises will retain its existing investments in telecommunications activities in Africa but is likely to review these shortly. The integration of Eskom Enterprises into the enterprises division confines the business focus to generation, transmission and distribution of electricity.

Part of the broader restructuring of state assets included the integration of similar functions within different enterprises. A new company – arivia.com – was formed in 2001 out of Eskom, Transnet and Denel's consolidated telecoms and IT networks. Shareholding was based on the value contributed by each partner, with Eskom Enterprises' telecommunications division holding 45 per cent of the shares (*ESI Africa* 2001). In 2006 Eskom Enterprises' share in arivia.com rose to 58.5 per cent, following arivia.com's buy-back of shares from Denel (Eskom 2006: 81). In its first year of operation, 75 per cent of arivia.com's income came from contracts with the three parastatals (Eskom Enterprises 2002: 46). Other South African government contracts included a virtual private network for the State Information Technology Agency, a five-year strategic partnership agreement with Spoornet (the state-run railway service), and a contract to overhaul the national Department of Transport's technology system. The stated aim was to serve the IT and telecoms needs of the shareholding companies, as well as other arms of government and the private sector. Africa was the main target of the company's ITC services, with the goal of eventually moving away from dependence on the three state-owned enterprises. Arivia.com inherited a number of projects in Africa from its parent enterprises. These included a fully computerised transport information system in Malawi; motor vehicle registration systems in Tanzania, Egypt and Zambia; national identification card systems in Botswana and Zanzibar; police IDs in Uganda and Botswana; electoral registration systems in Zanzibar and Lesotho; social welfare payment systems in Uganda and Namibia; and drivers' licence systems for Lesotho, Namibia and Uganda (Ministry of Public Enterprises 2004).

Pebble Bed Modular Reactor

Eskom began work on the PBMR in 1993. The project aimed to develop and commercialise pebble bed nuclear technology. In 1999 the entity PBMR (Pty) Ltd was set up to run the project. The South African government was a major investor – Eskom Enterprises held a 40 per cent stake and the IDC held 25 per cent – and USA company Exelon with 12.5 per cent and British Nuclear Fuels with 22.5 per cent also came on board as investors. The South African Nuclear Energy Corporation was contracted to develop the fuel manufacturing capability. In 2002 Exelon withdrew its investment, saying it wanted to concentrate on core business (US EIA 2003). With the unbundling of British Nuclear Fuels and the subsequent sale of Westinghouse, the latter took over the 15 per cent stake in PBMR formerly held by British Nuclear Fuels. Westinghouse has designed, built and maintained almost half of the world's nuclear power stations (*Business Day* 2006b). PBMR planned to build a 165 MW mini-demonstration power plant near the Koeberg power plant in the Western Cape (Phasiwe 2006a).

Eskom plans a significant reduction of its shareholding in PBMR, down to 5 per cent, with the remainder being taken over by government to prevent a conflict of interest with Eskom's role as a future customer (Ensor 2005). Government restructured its participation and mandated the IDC to oversee further developments on its behalf (National Treasury 2006b). National government had made a big investment in the project and began pressurising Eskom to commit to buying R45 billion worth of reactors. However, Eskom is distancing itself from the project, saying it would only buy the technology if it were the best-priced option (Davie 2005). Eskom is expected to be a major buyer, and the future of the project would be brought into doubt if Eskom decided not to buy in (Ensor 2005).

Co-operation or competition in Africa?

Superficially, the creation of a pan-African electricity grid and the facilitation of a telecommunications infrastructure on the back of this grid appear to be positive contributions to African development. But on closer analysis, a pattern of exporting a particular version of development becomes apparent. This development model is premised on the privatisation of state assets or the outsourcing or concessioning of public services to the private sector.

On the one hand, Eskom, through Eskom Enterprises, has been providing consultancy and management advice in assisting governments to liberalise their energy sectors. One example is feasibility studies on the introduction of IPPs in Libya. Eskom's stated strategic intervention with regard to the SAPP was to reposition the pool 'in line with global trends of liberalising and introducing competition into electricity markets' (Eskom 2002: 18). While the pool initially functioned on a co-operative basis, the introduction of the spot market introduced a competitive dynamic that was likely to eclipse the more co-operative functioning of the pool over time (Elmissiry 2000). Eskom Enterprises' Enerweb Division provided energy trading and related systems and services in anticipation of energy sector deregulation. These included online trading systems, remote metering services and specialised billing services. In 2002 Enerweb developed a Southern African Power Exchange demonstration project to facilitate the formation of a competitive market and to encourage regional power deregulation.

Despite the apparent co-operation of the SAPP, there was an underlying economic aggression. In 2000 Eskom was looking to bid for ZESA's power stations as repayment for outstanding debt owed by ZESA to Eskom. South Africa also threatened Zimbabwe with electricity cut-offs if the debts were not at least reduced. If the outstanding amount started to increase, 'supply would be interruptible again, as was the case from January 27 to April 1 2000', according to South African Public Enterprises Minister Jeff Radebe (Chalmers 2000b). Once ZESA had managed to pay off the debts, Eskom put the money into a special account to be used for feasibility studies in support of the privatisation of the Zimbabwean utility (Chalmers 2001g). In 2001, Eskom signed a contract with ZESA to manage, operate and maintain the Hwange power station (Chalmers 2001h). The possibility of taking ownership of the station was seen as an inroad into SADC countries (Singh 2002).

At the start of 2002, a disagreement broke out between Mozambique and Eskom regarding fair prices to be paid for electricity produced by the Cahora Bassa hydro-electric scheme. Power generated by the scheme is transmitted through Eskom's South African network and then resold to Mozambique at inflated prices. According to Carlos Viega Anjos, chair of the board of the Cahora Bassa Dam's operating company Hidroelectrica de Cahora Bassa (HCB), Eskom was buying electricity in rands at very low prices and then selling it back to Mozambique's electricity company, EDM, in US dollars for use in the southern provinces of Maputo and Gaza (Chalmers 2002a). However, in 2004 Eskom and HCB agreed on a new tariff regime over the next 18 years which would see Eskom paying significantly higher amounts than the tariffs set in the last agreement in 1988 (Phasiwe 2004b). Not only Eskom but also ZESA were reportedly interested in purchasing shares in HCB following the Mozambican government's purchase of Portugal's shares in the scheme in 2005.

The adoption of a liberalised, market-based energy system has permitted Eskom Enterprises to enter as a private-sector entity into management or concession agreements with utilities and governments. Eskom Enterprises' re-absorption into Eskom Holdings has been interpreted as ushering in an era of reduced trans-parency, as Eskom would no longer need to reflect the results of non-regulated business separately. This may allow the utility to cross-subsidise its unregulated activities with profits derived from its regulated activities (Yelland 2004). In essence this means subsidising private business interests on the continent with profits generated by regulated service functions inside South Africa. Eskom has also gone a step beyond management contracts to the outright purchase of African energy infrastructure, as the earlier examples indicate. This recalls Eskom's takeover of municipal infrastructure in the townships of South Africa in the early 1990s – using debt as a lever to consolidate assets under its control. According to the NUM, the SAPP is being used to impose decisions on the region on the basis of Eskom's model and needs, in particular with regard to the formation of a competitive energy market and the privatisation or outsourcing of energy infrastructure and services.[18]

Conclusion: future directions

We should use less [power] in our homes and allow industry to have more power to achieve this 6% growth [yearly GDP growth targeted in ASGISA].
(Thulani Gcabashe, Eskom CEO, cited in Philp 2006)

The launch of government's ASGISA initiative in 2005 signalled an increasing level of state investment in economic infrastructure (Presidency of the Republic of South Africa 2006). However, investment decisions are being made on the basis of financial returns rather than the real needs of the population at large. To be sure, capital needs an expanded energy infrastructure to realise economic growth. But to date the character of this growth – especially in the post-apartheid period – has been of a kind that is incapable of absorbing labour at the necessary pace to reduce unemployment. On the rest of the African continent, as much as in South Africa, a breakdown of planned investments reveals that capital, especially mining and minerals beneficiation, largely determines where investments will be made.

One clear indicator of this bias towards capital is the 'user pays' cost recovery policy that charges individual users for the 'inconvenience' to the supplier of requiring numerous distribution points, and refuses cross-subsidisation from industry to residential users (despite the fact that residential users consume just 18 per cent of total electricity output) (NERSA 2003b: 26). Another is differential pricing for industry and residents, with industry paying lower per-unit rates than domestic users of electricity, and the lowest rates in the world for electricity. In the post-apartheid period, this gap has actually widened. Between 1994 and 2005, average nominal tariffs for commercial, industrial and mining users (taken together) rose 40.5 per cent. For residential users, the related increase was 130.9 per cent (Eskom 1999–2006). In the face of a growing energy crisis, Gcabashe's response quoted above is to exhort domestic users to tighten their belts further, to allow industry to take even more of the country's available energy.

There is a tension regarding infrastructure and service delivery in Africa between much needed infrastructure and profit-making imperatives. South Africa's competitive, profit-driven business model is being exported to the rest of Africa under the guise of development. In one sense it *is* development – of capitalist methods and relations of production. Having started liberalising its own national energy sector, the South African state and Eskom have created the imperative for Eskom to look to other countries to diversify its base of operations. Energy sector liberalisation and privatisation of energy infrastructure and services are pivotal for Eskom to grow in the region.

Notwithstanding these conjunctural issues, the case for a single, integrated, publicly owned electricity utility remains strong, especially when there is a necessity to clear infrastructure backlogs in relation to the poor and to provide a sustainable and cheap service. While ringfencing and sector restructuring are supposedly designed to lower prices and remove some redundancy in the system, a decentralised, market-oriented electricity business is more vulnerable to system failure than one that is centrally co-ordinated, because it strips the system to its bare essentials and leaves little margin for error (Kay 2003). A power company that operates for profit will not want to hold a big reserve of capacity against rare emergencies because this eats into profitability. On the other hand, a parastatal can, and should, take into account the importance of reliability of supply for a national economy (Friedland 2003).

The government and Eskom seem to be acknowledging the important role of a vertically integrated utility, especially following the return of Eskom Enterprises' support functions to the heart of Eskom. The realisation that the skills that were separated out with the establishment of Eskom Enterprises in 1999 are required in a more integrated way inside Eskom offers another indication of the importance of retaining management and technical support skills as core competencies of an electricity utility. However, whether this realisation can spur the stabilisation of a production and delivery structure that serves the entire population, or only powerful sectional interests, remains to be seen. As long as ever-increasing profit is the ultimate bottom line by which success will be measured, the beneficial potential inherent in a co-ordinated and integrated electricity utility will not be fully realised.

Notes

1   Bafana Ndebele, Eskom organiser, NUMSA, personal communication, 29 March 2006

2   Willie Majola, General Manager: Grids (Operations & Maintenance), Eskom Transmission Unit, personal communication, 22 March 2006

3   Dr Lawrence Mushaba, Head of Southern African Power Pool Co-ordinating Centre, personal communication, 24 March 2006

4   Job Motsepe, Energy Sector Co-ordinator, NUM, personal communication, 31 March 2006

5   Tom Skinner, Programme Manager: Restructuring, Eskom Distribution Unit, personal communication, 16 March 2006

6   Job Motsepe, Energy Sector Co-ordinator, NUM, personal communication, 31 March 2006

7   Job Motsepe, Energy Sector Co-ordinator, NUM, personal communication, 31 March 2006

8   Bafana Ndebele, Eskom organiser, NUMSA, personal communication, 29 March 2006

9   Job Motsepe, Energy Sector Co-ordinator, NUM, personal communication, 31 March 2006

10 Osborne Galeni, former national organiser for NUMSA, personal communication, 27 September 2002

11 Job Motsepe, Energy Sector Co-ordinator, NUM, personal communication, 31 March 2006

12 Job Motsepe, Energy Sector Co-ordinator, NUM, personal communication, 31 March 2006

13 Chris van Zyl, Senior Manager: INEP Capital Programme, DME, personal communication, 23 March 2006

14 Chris van Zyl, Senior Manager: INEP Capital Programme, DME, personal communication, 16 March 2006

15 Chris van Zyl, Senior Manager: INEP Capital Programme, DME, personal communication, 23 March 2006

16 Dr Lawrence Mushaba, Head of Southern African Power Pool Co-ordinating Centre, personal communication, 24 March 2006

17 Job Motsepe, Energy Sector Co-ordinator, NUM, personal communication, 31 March 2006

18 Job Motsepe, Energy Sector Co-ordinator, NUM, personal communication, 31 March 2006

References

ANC (African National Congress) (1994) *The Reconstruction and Development Programme: A policy framework.* Johannesburg: Umanyano Publications

ANC (2005) State owned enterprises: Driving growth and development in the coming years. *ANC Today* 5(15). Accessed 17 October 2006, www.anc.org.za/ancdocs/anctoday/

Anti-Privatisation Forum (2005) Statement on Johannesburg City Council's 'indigent' arrears write-off. Press statement, May 15

Bakaya-Kyahurwa E (2004) Energy efficiency and energy awareness in Botswana. *ESI Africa* 2. Accessed 17 October 2006, www.esi-africa.com/archive/

Business Day (2004) Eskom to revive mothballed plants. *Business Day* 8 October

Business Day (2006a) Eskom gets green light for R22 bn expansion. *Business Day* 10 March

Business Day (2006b) SA mini reactor gets backing of US player. *Business Day* 3 March

Chalmers R (2000a) Eskom Enterprises buys into Telkom Lesotho. *Business Day* 10 November

Chalmers R (2000b) Eskom may take part in tender. *Business Day* 26 April

Chalmers R (2001a) Eskom's generation division gets new look. *Business Day* 3 April

Chalmers R (2001b) Capacity sale will not affect Eskom's size. *Business Day* 13 September

Chalmers R (2001c) Eskom unveils its new plan to restructure. *Business Day* 1 October

Chalmers R (2001d) Eskom heads for global arena. *Business Day* 2 February

Chalmers R (2001e) Rotek works hard to play worthwhile world role. *Business Day* 1 March

Chalmers R (2001f) Two utilities determined to be part of the new operator. *Business Day* 10 September

Chalmers R (2001g) Eskom keen on troubled ZESA. *Business Day* 27 March

Chalmers R (2001h) Eskom enters Africa, Mideast. *Business Day* 8 November

Chalmers R (2001i) SA must get it right first time. *Business Day* 17 July

Chalmers R (2002) Eskom spearheads five African ventures. *Business Day* 16 July

Chalmers R (2002a) Eskom appoints two foreign directors as it gears up. *Business Day* 27 August

Chalmers R (2002b) Top energy advisor comes to SA. *Business Day* 14 March

Chalmers R (2002c) Eskom's big dam power struggle. *Business Day* 18 January

Chalmers R (2004) ANC no to Eskom, Transnet sell-off. *Business Day* 11 May

Chalmers R (2005) Powering down in Africa. *Business Day* 27 June

Charles Anderson Associates (1994) *National electricity policy synthesis study* Vol. 1. Report submitted to the Department of Minerals and Energy

Cosatu (Congress of South African Trade Unions) (2001) COSATU submission on the electricity restructuring. Presented to Minerals and Energy Portfolio Committee, Parliament, 19 September

Davie K (2005) Mini-nukes cost a bomb. *Mail & Guardian Business* 2–8 December

Davis M (1996) South Africa's electrification programme: Progress to date and key issues. *Development Southern Africa* 13(3): 469–483

DME (Department of Minerals and Energy, South Africa) (1996) *Meeting South Africa's electricity distribution challenges.* Pretoria: DME

DME (1997) *Re-appraisal of the national electrification programme and the formulation of a national electrification strategy.* Pretoria: DME

DME (1998) *White Paper on the Energy Policy of the Republic of South Africa.* Pretoria: DME

DME (2000) Minister's address to Forum on Transformation of the Electricity Industry in South Africa, 27 June

DME (2001a) *Annual report 2000/2001.* Pretoria: DME

DME (2001b) *National Electrification Programme (NEP) 1994–1999: Summary evaluation report.* Pretoria: DME

DME (2002) *INEP planning and implementation manual Version 0.* Pretoria: DME

DME (2005) Budget vote speech, Deputy Minister of Minerals and Energy Lulu Xingwana. Parliament, Cape Town, 19 May

DPE (Department of Public Enterprises, South Africa) (2001a) Budget vote speech delivered by Minister Radebe. National Assembly, 1 June

DPE (2001b) Radebe reaffirms government's commitment to National Framework Agreement. Press release, 2 May

DPE (2002) Budget vote speech delivered by Minister Radebe. National Assembly, 16 May

Eberhard A (2001) Competition and regulation in the electricity supply industry in South Africa. Paper presented at the Trade and Industrial Policy Strategies Annual Forum, Muldersdrift

Eberhard A (2003) The political economy of power sector reform in South Africa. Paper presented at the Political Economy of Power Market Reform conference, 19–20 February, Stanford University

Elmissiry M (2000) The Southern African Power Pool and its impact on billing and metering. *ESI Africa* 4. Accessed 17 October 2006, www.esi-africa.com/archive/

Energy Management News (2001) Eskom Enterprises enters into gas project in Mozambique. *Energy Management News* 7(3): 15

Ensor L (2003) State will not be rushed into sale of assets. *Business Day* 28 February

Ensor L (2005) Talks under way with potential investors for nuclear project. *Business Day* 9 November

ESI Africa (2001) Eskom becomes major shareholder in new IT giant. *ESI Africa* 1. Accessed 17 October 2006, www.esi-africa.com/archive/

ESI Africa (2004a) Preparation for a competitive power market in Africa. *ESI Africa* 1. Accessed 17 October 2006, www.esi-africa.com/archive/

ESI Africa (2004b) The SAPP power market project. *ESI Africa*. 1 Accessed 17 October 2006, www.esi-africa.com/archive/

Eskom (1996) *Statistical yearbook.* Pretoria: Eskom

Eskom (1999–2006) *Annual reports.* Pretoria: Eskom

Eskom Enterprises (2002) *Eskom Enterprises annual report 2002.* Pretoria: Eskom Enterprises

Fiil-Flynn M (2001) *The electricity crisis in Soweto.* Municipal Services Project Occasional Paper No. 4. Cape Town: Municipal Services Project

Financial Mail (1996) Feature Company – Eskom: Walking the political and operational tightrope. *Financial Mail Top Companies Supplement* 28 June

Friedland R (2003) Eskom ain't broke, so don't fix it. *Business Day* 19 August

Globeleq (2005) Globeleq enters distribution business in Uganda. Press release, 1 March

Greenberg S (2002) *Eskom, electricity sector restructuring and service delivery in South Africa.* Cape Town: Alternative Information and Development Centre

Hale B (2002) Africa's grand power exporting plans. *BBC News* 17 October. Accessed 17 October 2006, http://news.bbc.co.uk/1/hi/business/2307057.stm

Hirsch A (2005) *Season of hope: Economic reform under Mandela and Mbeki.* Durban/Ottawa: University of KwaZulu-Natal Press/International Development Research Centre

I-Net Bridge (2005) Independent producers in line for power station contracts. *Business Day* 23 June

International Rivers Network & Earthlife Africa (eThekweni branch) (2003) Eskom's expanding empire: The social and ecological footprint of Africa's largest power utility. Accessed 17 October 2006, http://www.irn.org/programs/safrica/index.php?id=030601eskomfactsheet.html

IT Web (2001) Eskom Enterprises bullish about African prospects, prepares for second network operator. Accessed 17 October 2006, http://www.itweb.co.za/sections/telecoms/2001/0105170959.asp?A=AFN&S=All%20Africa%20News&T=Section&O=C

Kay J (2003) Positive, negative of private electricity. *Business Day* 2 October

Lennon S (2002) Concept proposal for an African Union-NEPAD energy fund for financing African energy development programmes aligned with NEPAD Priorities (Rev 1). Ref SJL/1349/gc. Pretoria: Eskom

Lourens C (2006) Local firms fear imports may squeeze them out of Eskom's Transnet's plans. *Business Day* 10 March

Lunsche S (2006a) Overview: Power drive. *Financial Mail Corporate Report on Eskom* 3 February

Lunsche S (2006b) Generation: Green issues colour plans. *Financial Mail Corporate Report on Eskom* 3 February

Lunsche S (2006c) Transmission: Catering for coastal SA. *Financial Mail Corporate Report on Eskom* 3 February

Lunsche S (2006d) Distribution: Eskom plans for new role. *Financial Mail Corporate Report on Eskom* 3 February

Macro-Economic Research Group (1993) *Making democracy work: A framework for macroeconomic policy in South Africa*. Cape Town: Centre for Development Studies

Ministry of Public Enterprises (1996) *National framework agreement on the restructuring of state assets*. Pretoria: Ministry of Public Enterprises

Ministry of Public Enterprises (2000) *An accelerated agenda towards the restructuring of state owned enterprises – Policy framework*. Pretoria: Ministry of Public Enterprises

Ministry of Public Enterprises (2001) Parliamentary media briefing by Minister of Public Enterprises, Mr Jeff Radebe, 18 September. Pretoria: Ministry of Public Enterprises

Ministry of Public Enterprises (2004) *Africa first! South African state owned enterprises in Africa*. Pretoria: Ministry of Public Enterprises

Ministry of Public Enterprises (2005) Department of Public Enterprises budget vote, Vote 9, by Minister of Public Enterprises, Mr Alec Erwin. Pretoria: Ministry of Public Enterprises

National Treasury (2003) Minerals and Energy Vote 31. Pretoria: National Treasury

National Treasury (2005) Public Enterprises Vote 9. Pretoria: National Treasury

National Treasury (2006a) Minerals and Energy Vote 30. Pretoria: National Treasury

National Treasury (2006b) Public Enterprises Vote 9. Pretoria: National Treasury

NERSA (National Electricity Regulator of South Africa) (1995) *Electricity supply statistics in South Africa, 1995*. Pretoria: NERSA

NERSA (1998) *Electricity supply statistics in South Africa, 1998*. Pretoria: NERSA

NERSA (2000a) *Lighting up South Africa 2000*. Pretoria: NERSA

NERSA (2000b) *Electricity supply statistics in South Africa, 2000*. Pretoria: NERSA

NERSA (2003a) *Annual report 2002–2003*. Pretoria: NERSA

NERSA (2003b) *Electricity supply statistics in South Africa, 2003*. Pretoria: NERSA

Njobeni S (2005) Five-horse race for new power plants. *Business Day* 24 August

Phasiwe K (2002) Eskom puts energy into regional strength. Mimeo

Phasiwe K (2004a) Tender sparks reform in power industry. *Business Day* 9 February

Phasiwe K (2004b) Eskom to pay much more for power from Cahora Bassa. *Business Day* 10 February

Phasiwe K (2004c) Eskom Enterprises spreads wings out of Africa. *Business Day* 4 April

Phasiwe K (2005) UK's Ipsa leads way for foreign power players in SA market. *Business Day* 20 September

Phasiwe K (2006a) Nuclear deal for local firm. *Business Day* 16 March

Phasiwe K (2006b) Asset sale at Eskom, Transnet 'on track'. *Business Day* 13 January

Phasiwe K (2006c) Power revamp bill ready for Mbeki to sign. *Business Day* 20 March

Philp R (2006) Ask not what Eskom can do for you. *Sunday Times* 12 March

Pillay K (2002) Synergies between electricity and telecommunications. *ESI Africa* 3. Accessed 17 October 2006, www.esi-africa.com/archive/

Presidency of the Republic of South Africa (2006) *Accelerated and Shared Growth Initiative: A summary*. Pretoria: Office of the Presidency

PricewaterhouseCoopers (2000) *Electricity distribution restructuring project*. 7 Working Papers. Johannesburg: PricewaterhouseCoopers

Robinson R (1997) *Power to the people: A case study of the use of 'forums' in conflict resolution in post-apartheid South Africa*. Harvard Business School Working Paper 97-036. Boston, Massachusetts: Harvard Business School

Rumney R (2005) *Restructuring of state assets versus privatisation in South Africa: What's in a name?* Policy Brief No. 45. Michigan: William Davidson Institute

Singh S (2002) Becoming Africa's leading light. *Financial Mail* 26 July

Singh S (2003a) Overview: Looking ahead. *Financial Mail Eskom Survey* 4 July

Singh S (2003b) Power pool: A partnership in development. *Financial Mail Eskom Survey* 4 July

Singh S (2005) Bidders keener than expected. *Financial Mail* 18 February

Singh S & Lunsche S (2005) Clearer government policy illuminates bright future. *Financial Mail* 1 July

Smith C (2002) Guerilla technicians challenge the privatization of South Africa's public resources. *In These Times* 30 August

Stats SA (Statistics South Africa) (2001) *South Africa in transition. Selected findings from the October Household Survey of 1999 and changes that occurred between 1995 and 1999*. Pretoria: Stats SA

Stats SA (2005) *General Household Survey July 2004*. Statistical release P0318. Pretoria: Stats SA

Taka M (2001) The internationalization of the South African telecommunications sector. Paper presented at the Trade and Industrial Policy Strategies Annual Forum, Muldersdrift

Theron P (ed.) (1992) Proceedings of the ANC National Meeting on Electrification. University of Cape Town, February. ANC Department of Economic Planning/Centre for Development Studies

US EIA (US Department of Energy, Energy Information Administration) (2003) *Nuclear power in South Africa.* Accessed 17 October 2006, http://www.eia.doe.gov/emeu/cabs/safr_nuke.html

Van Zyl L, Klein S & Gordon D (1997) A South African wholesale electricity market vs. the Southern African Power Pool. *ESI Southern Africa* 4: 40–43

Veck G (2000) The politics of power in an economy in transition: Eskom and the electrification of South Africa, 1980–1995. PhD thesis, Faculty of Commerce, University of the Witwatersrand, Johannesburg

Wessels V (2001) S Africa's Eskom to roll-out 380 km power line in Nigeria. I-Net Bridge, 5 February. Accessed 17 October 2006, http://my.reset.jp/~adachihayao/010206M.htm

Winkler H & Mavhungu J (2001) *Green power, public benefits and electricity industry restructuring.* Report prepared for the Sustainable Energy and Climate Change Partnership. Cape Town: Energy Development Research Centre

Yelland C (2004) Perspectives on Eskom's electricity price increases. Posting to *Electrical Engineering-News* list, December 17

CHAPTER 4

Cheap at half the cost: Coal and electricity in South Africa

Richard Worthington

Key questions facing the South African government are the extent to which coal-fired electricity generation will be increased, the technologies that will be deployed, and to what extent the full costs involved will be integrated into the market mechanisms related to electricity supply or borne by the commercial enterprises involved. This chapter explores these questions, rather than evaluating solutions, in the hope of contributing to a profound improvement in national energy planning, including information management and resource and technology assessment with full life-cycle analysis.

There are compelling reasons for reducing the share of coal in electricity production in South Africa, and converting to the best available technologies where coal is used. Introducing fiscal and regulatory reform to apply the 'polluter pays' principle would support these goals, while the policy of redistribution which mandates government to ensure that no additional costs are imposed upon the poor and negative impacts are reduced, would be more meaningfully implemented. This chapter seeks to contextualise and illustrate some of the shortcomings of current practice, including the prioritisation in macroeconomic policy of providing low-priced electricity to commercial enterprises. It does not, however, consider the regulations, market mechanisms and realignment of state spending that would most effectively deliver the potential public benefits that could be realised in the electricity supply industry.

A just transition to sustainable energy is a long-term project in which the electricity sector, so essential to commercial activity, yet significantly undervalued, must play a leading role. While 'business as usual' – i.e. more reliance on coal – may be the easiest option for meeting growing electricity demand, it is not the cheapest. In addition to externalised costs, investment in a new coal-fired plant, with a planned lifespan of 40 years or more, carries major long-term economic, environmental and social risks that are alluded to below. Weaning ourselves off our heavy reliance on coal will need to include major improvements in efficiency, in both coal use and electricity use, and massive deployment of renewable energy technologies. This in turn requires facing up to the real costs of our current system.

Why study coal and electricity?

Electricity is the cleanest form of energy at the point of use, and access to electricity is increasingly regarded as a basic human right (see Dugard, Chapter 10 in this volume). Generating electricity, on the other hand, is traditionally a very dirty business that epitomises the ability of extractive industries to externalise the true costs of their operations to society at large. The many social benefits that can be achieved with electricity – from reduced labour to refrigeration of medicines, access to information and education, security, improved gender equity and expanded business opportunities – are generally considered to justify extensive externalised social and environmental impacts in the course of generation. Energy planners are still trying to get to grips with a comprehensive cost–benefit analysis that could inform decisions about trade-offs between extending access in the short term and incurring costs over the long term.

If nuclear fission is humankind's most sophisticated and perilous way of boiling water to generate steam to drive the turbines that turn the generators to produce electricity, then burning coal to boil water to generate steam, etc., is our most basic and wasteful way of generating electricity. Electricity dispatched from South African power stations represents about 33 per cent of the energy in the coal burned, the rest being lost as waste heat. Burning liquid fuels and gas achieves higher conversion efficiencies and lower pollution levels, but fuel costs are higher and the impacts of emissions still very significant, particularly in the case of oil products.

This chapter will focus primarily on coal, since this is the energy source for about 92 per cent of South Africa's electricity; this proportion is even higher when the Koeberg nuclear power plant near Cape Town is not producing its 5–6 per cent contribution (DME 2006: 36). Other fossil-fired electricity options will be considered in this discussion – i.e. gas and liquid fuel – but their current contribution in South Africa is negligible according to Department of Minerals and Energy (DME) statistics, and there is very little information on their use, much less their impacts. Coal, offering the lowest costs to electricity suppliers, is also government and industry's first choice for increasing baseload generation capacity, not only in South Africa but in all countries with substantial coal reserves – 94 new coal-fired plants were being proposed in the USA in early 2004 (Clayton 2004). There is also increasing competition for imported coal, including from China, which, despite an ambitious renewable energy and efficiency programme and massive domestic production, is becoming a net coal importer.

But despite the importance of South Africa's coal mining, reporting on its impacts and use is far from comprehensive, and the state of energy data collection, at least in the public domain, leaves much to be desired. The state-owned electricity provider, Eskom, publishes its data in highly aggregated form and the most recent national *State of the Environment Report*, published in 1999, also deals in generalities (DEAT 1999). Most of the environmental impacts of coal combustion for electricity generation are distributed over huge areas, particularly after emitting-stack heights were increased and basic particulate capture introduced, and are thus difficult to quantify. Estimations of South Africa's coal reserves are also the subject of much uncertainty, with 55 billion tons having been the official figure for nearly 100 years; this figure is given as the 2001 figure in the *Digest of South African Energy Statistics 2005* (DME 2006), citing the BP *Statistical Review of World Energy*. More conservative reserve estimates by the Minerals Bureau in the DME are discussed below.

Coal is still the most abundant stock energy in South Africa and globally, and will be in use for a long time to come, even under the most progressive scenarios seeking to minimise fossil fuel use. It is hard to imagine that the use of coal will ever be truly clean, as it is mostly a very impure material, but advanced technologies do offer substantial improvements on the vast majority of equipment currently in operation. While many commentators, particularly geologists (e.g. Heinberg 2005), believe that production of oil, and later gas, will start to decline in the short or medium term due to resource depletion, coal use is set to accelerate in mainstream projections of energy consumption, even as its share of primary energy supply declines: 'Coal will continue to play a key role in the world energy mix, with demand projected to grow at an average annual rate of 1.4% to 2030. At that time, coal will meet 22% of global energy needs, only 1% less than it does today' (IEA 2004: 170). This would mean coal use totalling 7 029 million tons in 2030 compared to 4 791 tons in 2002. Constraints on coal use will probably be based on the costs and impacts, rather than on resource depletion.[1]

What is fossil fuel?

Coal, like oil and natural gas, is essentially fossilised biomass: millions of years' worth of deposited organic matter, transformed over hundreds of thousands more years by high pressure and temperature within the earth. These fossil fuels, or stock hydro-carbon energy sources, contain energy taken up from the sun over thousands of millennia, accumulated and transformed as the earth rebuilds itself on the geological time-scale. With the advent of industrialisation, humanity is releasing this vast stock of energy on a human time-scale.

In addition to the carbon and hydrogen in which energy is embodied, fossil fuels are impregnated with impurities, including sulphur and a wide range of minerals. Coal is found mixed to varying degrees with rock – referred to as the ash content when coal goes to market – as well as with heavy metals such as mercury and even radioactive materials. Alex Gabbard, of the Oak Ridge National Laboratory, a USA government institution, maintains that population exposure to radioactive material through coal combustion for electricity generation is greater than exposure from the operation of nuclear power plants, including the full fuel cycle particularly pertinent to local communities in the coalfields and workers serving their captive power stations. He concludes that:

naturally occurring radioactive species released by coal combustion are accumulating in the environment along with minerals such as mercury, arsenic, silicon, calcium, chlorine, and sodium, as well as metals such as aluminium, iron, lead, magnesium, titanium, boron, chromium, and others that are continually dispersed in millions of tons of coal combustion by-products. (Gabbard n.d.)

'Coal' is a term that embraces a range of products, from high-quality coal (with low ash and sulphur levels) such as anthracite, to lignite or brown coal – bituminous deposits with a low energy content or calorific value. Lignite is generally subject to high levels of processing before use, although it is still simply burned in a number of countries in Eastern Europe, where it is responsible for enormous environmental destruction and human suffering. Steam coal refers to a range of qualities of coal used to fire boilers – including those of power plants – and a variety of technologies have been developed to handle different properties of the diverse coal products. Coal-fired boilers in factories and even hospitals are generally less efficient than those in electricity generation plants, with greater environmental impacts due to low stack heights and urban locations. Higher quality coals are required for process heat, with the very high carbon content of coking coal providing the cleanest heat, e.g. for steel production.

Oil is similarly of varying quality, with 'sweet' crude fetching higher prices than 'sour' (high-sulphur) or heavy oils, and oil refineries being designed to process particular grades of oil. With sustained high oil prices, extensive resources are being reclassified as reserves, although there is no international verification system for reporting of national reserves and resources. Within the Organisation of Petroleum Exporting Countries (OPEC), the allocation of production quotas, or limitations, is based on stated reserves. Currently there is rapid development of formerly 'unconventional resources', such as Canada's extensive 'tar sands', which requires massive inputs of heat and/or chemicals to separate oil from other material and leaves vast amounts of contaminated wastes.

Natural gas, consisting primarily of methane (CH_4), is the cleanest of the fossil fuels, with the highest energy content by weight. Initially considered to be a troublesome by-product of oil wells, where it was simply flared as it is safer to burn it than to discharge it into the air, it has become the premium fossil fuel. Even Nigeria has passed a law against flaring, though this has yet to be enforced. It is also found in deposits with negligible oil content and in varying concentrations in coal deposits. Methane emissions from coal-mining operations make a significant contribution to global warming, but are very hard to quantify, particularly those from opencast mining.

Technologies for using fossil fuel, to the extent that they may be used for electricity generation, are discussed in some detail below. Coal can be converted into a gas, involving partial burning and/or high temperature and pressure and thus substantial energy loss in the process. The product can be cleaned and used as 'town gas', the gas used in the first street lights and until recently reticulated to homes in parts of Johannesburg, where it is being replaced by natural gas. Gas can be further processed to produce liquid fuels, a technology in which South Africa has become a world leader. Such liquid fuel production has only become economically competitive in the last few years and for electricity generation it is far simpler, cleaner and more efficient to burn the gas.

Coal was the main source of energy internationally well into the 20th century and may soon regain this position, as oil supplies are inadequate to meet growing energy demand. It is still the most dependable energy source for bulk electricity generation (the main reason that China has become a net importer of coal) and is the fuel of last recourse for poor communities in South Africa. Coal remains the most abundant fossil fuel on the planet, but its use threatens the viability of life-support systems.

Fossil fuels provide concentrated energy that is extremely convenient, and have been the primary driver of industrialisation, economic growth and globalisation. They also serve as feedstock for the production of a vast array of products such as fertilisers, pesticides and plastics, as well as fabrics and even food products. While we have developed increasingly sophisticated ways of utilising the planet's hydro-carbon reserves, and it is likely that future generations will develop far more efficient and less polluting ways of utilising these resources, we continue to squander them inefficiently at a future cost that we are only beginning to appreciate.

Coal and other fossil-derived energy forms are still extensively used in poor South African households, where their adverse impacts on people are far greater than those produced through electricity generation; this is why extensive efforts have been made to extend electrification. According to the Department of Environmental Affairs and Tourism (DEAT), 'The national household electrification level has increased from 36 per cent in 1996 to about 71 per cent in 2004' (DEAT 2006: 48). Access to the national grid does not, however, guarantee affordable access to electricity, and high cut-off rates have been reported, although figures vary widely. Low consumption by newly connected households also indicates that many using electricity also continue to use fuels directly.

The impacts of household fuel use include poisoning through accidental ingestion of paraffin (kerosene), and burns, deaths and extensive property damage from fires started by candles and paraffin stoves, which spread to particularly devastating effect in informal settlements. Air pollution in general, but particularly indoor air pollution, increases the risk of acute respiratory infections in children (the second highest cause of infant mortality), as well as pulmonary disease (particularly affecting women), lung cancer, tuberculosis and cataracts. A government programme intended to make a cleaner fuel – a processed form of coal – affordable to poor households has stalled, and coal used domestically is of poor quality and thus high impact (DEAT 2006).

The heat needed for much primary processing of minerals can be directly produced by coal, generally in its more refined form of coke, but some products, such as aluminium, require electrical energy on a large scale, with consumption comparable to that of a city. According to Terence Creamer, 'the Coega aluminium smelter's electricity demand will be 1 180 megawatts (MW) to produce 720 000 t/y [tons per year] from two pot lines' (Creamer 2006a). With average electricity consumption of 15.2 megawatt-hours per ton of aluminium (Moodley 2005), annual consumption will total 10 944 gigawatt-hours (GWh), or 6.2 per cent of electricity consumption for all of South Africa based on 2002 DME statistics (DME 2006).

Electricity generation

Electricity is generated by magnets moving in relation to a coil of wire, activating a current of energy within the connected network. Small magnets can spin around or within the coil of wire, or huge coils of wire can spin within a powerful magnetic field. The spinning of the generator must be driven by a source of energy, generally heat and/or pressure propelling a turbine; this heat or pressure is sourced by burning fossil fuels, impounding large bodies of water or setting off controlled nuclear reactions (see Appendix 1 in this volume for a more detailed description of coal-fired and other forms of electricity generation).

Electricity can also be generated using energy from renewable resources: harvesting dispersed energy using wind-driven turbines; concentrating solar heat to raise steam; photovoltaic conversion; drawing on the earth's geothermal heat; placing a small turbine in running water; a range of biomass technologies, including direct burning of biomass, production of liquid biofuels or bio-digested gas (including methane emissions from landfills); and using ocean power – wave, tidal and ocean current – a promising emerging option.

Electricity demand falls into three categories, which are also applied to generation plants suited to meeting such demand:
- Peak demand occurs early in the morning and in the late afternoon or evening, particularly during weekdays, and requires plants that can start up quickly and follow sharp fluctuations in demand but are unlikely to operate for more than three hours per day.
- Baseload – the level of demand that remains almost constant – requires plants that run continuously and thus efficiency is more important than flexibility or quick start-up, favouring large scale and low fuel costs.
- Mid-merit demand is more predictable and evenly distributed than peak and will optimally be met by plants that start up and shut down on a daily basis.

Any generation system needs excess capacity, both for planned outages for maintenance and to cover unexpected events. Running a baseload plant to follow fluctuations in demand will severely shorten its life expectancy.

Fossil-fired electricity generation

Fossil-fired electricity generation involves turbines driven either by steam or by hot gas. The heat from coal combustion carries so many pollutants that it must be transferred to another medium, traditionally water/steam, before entering a turbine; such a system on a large generating unit takes hours to get up to speed. Gas-driven turbines are less efficient at capturing the energy in the flow passing through them than steam turbines, as steam is more dense, but they can be started up and shut down more quickly than steam systems. The exhaust stream from a gas turbine is hot enough to produce steam, which can then be used to drive a steam turbine, in a configuration referred to as combined cycle generation. This is far more energy-efficient than a single cycle, but loses the advantage of a quick start-up. Together with nuclear power, geothermal and concentrated solar heat, these are known as thermal power options.

Gas turbines require relatively clean-burning fuel, such as gas or kerosene, but nevertheless have a shorter lifespan than steam turbines, particularly if low-grade liquid fuel is used. Steam can be produced using any kind of fuel, as the flue gases – smoke and waste heat – are kept separate from the turbines, but much heat is lost in condensing the steam back to water before it can re-enter the drive cycle. The cooling required for condensation traditionally involves evaporative cooling, and thus extensive water use. Dry cooling has been introduced at a number of coal-fired power stations, but requires driving huge fans and thus involves a reduction in overall plant efficiency.

Fuel oil is used in thermal power plants in some countries and is used to raise steam in some individual South African industries, but not in the country's electrical power plants. Diesel engines are widely used to drive generators, but in South Africa diesel is either a small-scale option, for remote areas or portable power, or a back-up power option, such as for hospitals and cold storage; however, it does include a grid-supply plant in Cape Town. Natural gas is used extensively for electricity generation in Europe and the USA because of its low pollution emissions, but is generally considered too expensive for developing countries.

There is a wide variety of coal combustion technologies, from old-fashioned moving-grate systems to emerging coal gasification options that only burn gas, while solid and gas impurities are mostly separated prior to combustion. Most coal-fired plants use pulverised fuel that is blown into the combustion chamber, to ensure complete combustion of the fuel, with electrostatic precipitators or bag filters to remove particulate matter from flue gases. Flue gas desulphurisation (FGD) is increasingly regarded as the standard method internationally, but only takes place at a few South African plants. Improvements in technologies, from coal cleaning, through the combustion stage, to treatment of exhaust gases – referred to by the industry as 'clean coal technologies' – are discussed in detail later.

As up to two-thirds of heat produced for electricity generation is usually wasted, considerable efficiency improvements can be achieved by using such heat for industrial processes or space heating, which is referred to as combined heat and power generation (CHP). This is practised by some auto-generators – industries generating their own power, e.g. sugar producers burning the waste by-product, bagasse – but there are limited opportunities in South Africa for this, as power stations are mostly far from industrial or high-density residential areas and the infrastructure costs of providing CHP for heating residential space and water are hard to justify in a mild or warm climate. Some applications of CHP are expected to be explored in future, but CHP is best suited to relatively small and clean generation units located close to demand for heat.

Fossil fuels, particularly gas, can also be used to produce hydrogen, which can either be burned as a fuel or fed into a fuel cell to produce electricity, with pure water the only 'waste' product. This is still an immature technology and as there are significant waste streams from fossil-derived hydrogen production there is considerable debate as to whether it is worth the effort, given that hydrogen can also be produced using renewable energy sources. Hydrogen is an energy carrier that is relatively easy to store and transport, at least in modest quantities, being cleaner and more efficient than chemical batteries, but currently more expensive. It has considerable potential in the transport sector and fuel cells are being used for standby (back-up) and remote area power supply, but hydrogen complements rather than competes with grid electricity supply.

Coal mining and transport

Extraction of fossil fuels is never an environmentally or socially benign activity. Concentrated energy attracts concentrated wealth – venture capital – and investors seek high rates of return, especially in developing countries. There is not scope here to contemplate the hideous legacy and ongoing destruction driven by the quest for ownership or control of fossil fuels in general, not to mention its transport and various transformations. Since the use of other fossil fuels for electricity is incidental to their general development in South Africa, the focus here will be on the impacts of coal-fired electricity generation, though here too there are significant gaps reflecting poor availability of information.

Coal mining and processing is highly polluting, dangerous for workers who still die by the dozen, and leaves mountains of waste from which heavy metals and other pollutants leach into run-off water and, through the hydrological cycle, into the broader environment, where some bioaccumulate – increase in concentration in living things as they move up the food chain. Miners are also exposed to coal dust and toxic material, resulting in many premature deaths, and many other workers are exposed to coal dust along the distribution systems. Opportunity costs are seldom considered when dealing with applications to mine. The environmental impact assessment (EIA) system may be applied to mining in future, but various attempts by non-governmental organisations to have EIA processes include rigorous consideration of alternatives have been unsuccessful (though these attempts are not well documented).

Opencast mines – over 44 per cent of South African coal mining – involve ripping up large areas of land to strip out seams of coal 60 metres or more below the surface. They can theoretically be restored to a 'natural' condition after the wealth has been extracted, but no documentation of implementation, or even demonstration in the field, of this restoration has been found for South Africa. Underground mines can lead to subsidence, damaging surface infrastructure, and direct pollution and physical disruption of aquifers, e.g. where blasting can cause groundwater to move to a lower level. Heaps of discard coal produce acidic run-off with dissolved solids that render water unfit for use, and cases of abandoned coal resources left slowly burning and spontaneous combustion of coal discards are still reported, although this does not seem to have been documented. Distribution of coal to markets is also a significant source of pollution, with trucking of coal into townships and to industries increasing dust and vehicle exhaust pollution.

The high cost of transporting coal has resulted in power plants being built as close as possible to the source of supply – the 'mine mouth' – so that conveyor belts can take coal to the plant, which also gives rise to large quantities of coal dust. The failure of the mine at the Majuba power station to deliver as expected (the coal seam is not as regular as had been assumed) has led to massive road damage as a result of the need to truck in coal from another mine – one of the more obvious examples of indirect public subsidy to fossil fuels – as well as increased travel time for other traffic and thus increased vehicle emissions. A new railway line of some 69 kilometres is proposed, at a cost of R1.8 billion, to bring coal from the next-closest mine (Tyrer 2006).

According to 1997 figures from the DEAT, 42 million cubic metres of solid waste were produced annually (DEAT 1999). According to Van Der Merwe and Vosloo (1992), in South Africa 'by far the biggest contributor to the solid waste stream is mining waste (72.3%), followed by pulverized fuel ash (6.7%), agricultural waste (6.1%), urban waste (4.5%) and sewage sludge (3.6%)'. While this refers to all types of mining, a substantial portion of this will be associated with coal mining (which has increased substantially in recent years), although it is not clear whether discard coal, some of which might be used in future, is included in these waste figures. According to Winkler (2006: 46), 'Discards – too low in heating value and too high in ash to have commercial value – amounted to 69 million tons' out of total production of 290 million tons in 2001.

Figures on the full extent of land given over to coal mining in South Africa are not accessible in the public domain. Some of the social costs, such as worker health and safety, have been quantified, as indicated in figures given below, but based on incomplete information, poor data and questionable methodologies, as acknowledged by authors. The most comprehensive information available on the impacts of the coal-to-electricity supply chain in South Africa relates to Eskom's power stations. Valuation of such externalised costs is an important part, but provides an incomplete picture, of the full social and environmental costs of delivering 'cheap' electricity.

About a third of South African saleable production, including most of the high-quality coal, is exported, mostly to Europe. Long-term contracts for lower-grade 'steam coal' supply to Eskom provide revenue security for mines, while the higher prices and energy content by weight (calorific value) of high-grade coal make better sense for long-distance transport. Most South African coal, particularly now that some rich deposits in KwaZulu-Natal have been exhausted, has low sulphur (about 1.2 per cent) but high ash content (up to 45 per cent).

The most up-to-date overview of coal sales is provided by the Directorate: Mineral Economics in the DME:

> Of the 245 Mt [mega/million tons] coal sold during 2005, approximately 29.2 percent, worth R21.4 billion, was exported at an average price of R296/ton (3.44 times higher than the average inland price). The remaining 70.8 percent sold inland – 173.4 Mt – was worth R14.9 billion. The electricity sector consumed 106 Mt but the synthetic fuels sector used only 41 Mt, as some of the coal previously used as feedstock for gasification has been replaced by natural gas from Pande, Mozambique. The industrial sector, including mining, consumed 11 Mt, the metallurgical industry used 7 Mt and merchants bought 7.5 Mt. (Prevost 2006: 4)

This suggests, assuming no significant depletion of power station stockpiles, that the electricity sector's share of domestic coal consumption in South Africa has been steady: 61.5 per cent based on 2002 statistics (DME 2006: 27) to 61.1 per cent reflected in the 2005 figures above. Coal constitutes about three-quarters of South Africa's primary energy supply and 83 per cent of production is in Mpumalanga. 'Almost 90 percent of the saleable coal production was supplied by mines controlled by the six largest mining groups, viz. Ingwe (BHP Billiton), Anglo Coal, Sasol, Eyesizwe, Kumba Resources and Xstrata' (Prevost 2006: 3). This source also gives a figure of 34 224 Mt for South Africa's coal reserves in 2005, being 4.4 per cent of world reserves and ranked as the sixth largest.

Energy use in mining in 2002 was 7.8 per cent of total energy consumption (DME 2006: 4), but total energy use for coal mining is not reported separately. In 2002 coal mines used 2 815 GWh of electricity (about 1.5 per cent of total national consumption), compared to 11 571 GWh used by oil refineries (DME 2006: 37). The impacts reported for electricity generation do not include the upstream environmental impacts arising from delivering coal to power stations. As noted below, more recent studies of externalised costs of electricity generation do attempt to include worker health and safety impacts of associated coal mining.

Electricity use in South Africa

The end use of electricity is reported in very broad categories in official statistics, and DME staff have anecdotally recognised that one should allow for a generous margin of error. For example, it is likely that significant commercial use is probably recorded under the residential sector, and data collection for electricity use on farms is poorly developed. The most recent data in the *Digest of Energy Statistics*

(DME 2006) apply to 2002. Figure 4.1 shows the breakdown of final consumption, with industry at 66 per cent, agriculture at 3 per cent and residential at 17 per cent.

Figure 4.1: Sectoral breakdown of electricity use in South Africa (GWh), 2002

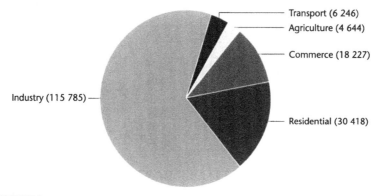

Transport (6 246)
Agriculture (4 644)
Commerce (18 227)
Industry (115 785)
Residential (30 418)

Source: DME 2006

Electricity generation in South Africa

The use of coal in South Africa has largely been driven by the exploitation of other mineral resources; the discovery of gold created concentrated demand for coal, and diamond mining in Kimberley (the second city in the world to be electrified) at the end of the 19th century in turn created demand for coal-fired electricity. Development of the coal-to-liquid fuels industry from the late 1970s was a response by the apartheid government to increasing international isolation; the need to extend local applications for coal and reduce dependence on oil imports justified massive investment in a technology not considered commercially viable elsewhere. This connection of energy provision to mining continues to provide a neat fit for extractive industries, which still benefit from the combination of minerals and energy affairs under a single government department, a situation that keeps renewable energy technologies marginalised.

Over half the electricity used in Africa is generated in South Africa, with 95 per cent of this produced by Eskom. The total capacity figure varies considerably in various reports, depending on whether all existing plants are included, or moth-balled plants – those taken out of use in the early 1990s – are excluded. The most common figure, about 40 000 MW, includes plants that are being brought back into use. The National Energy Regulator of South Africa provides details of Eskom's coal-fired stations in 2004, as referenced in Winkler (2006) and outlined in Table 4.1.

Eskom also has two gas turbine stations of 171 MW each, in Cape Town and East London, used for peaking or emergency supplies, as well as the 1 800 MW Koeberg nuclear power plant. Municipalities own 2 400 MW of generating plants, all coal-

Table 4.1: Eskom's coal-fired power stations, 2004

	Nominal capacity (MWe)	First unit commis-sioned	Thermal efficiency (%)	MegaJoules/ kg for coal	Cooling system	Operating status
Arnot	2 100	1971	33.30	22.35	Wet	Partly operating
Camden	1 600	1966	–	–	Wet	Mothballed
Duhva	3 600	1980	34.50	21.25	Wet	Operating
Grootvlei	1 200	1969	–	–	Wet	Mothballed
Hendrina	2 000	1970	32.34	21.57	Wet	Operating
Kendal	4 116	1988	34.31	19.96	Dry	Operating
Komatie	1 000	1961	–	–	Wet	Mothballed
Kriel	3 000	1976	35.02	20.04	Wet	Operating
Lethabo	3 708	1985	34.89	15.27	Wet	Operating
Matimba	3 990	1987	33.52	20.77	Dry	Operating
Majuba	4 100	1996	–	–	Wet/dry	Operating
Matla	3 600	1979	35.47	20.58	Wet	Operating
Tutuka	3 654	1985	35.32	21.09	Wet	Operating

Source: NERSA 2004

Note: MWe = megawatt electrical

fired, but few of these are run anywhere near full capacity. The Kelvin power station, now a public–private partnership with City Power (the Johannesburg distribution company) as majority owner, is being refurbished to run at its full 600 MW capacity. Some plants, such as Orlando in Soweto, have been shut down, apparently due to the heavy pollution of neighbouring communities, although anecdotal accounts suggest that poor operation and maintenance may have played a role.

Figure 4.2 provides a graphic presentation of current South African generation capacity – popularly known as the Table Mountain graph – showing the past and anticipated lifespan of existing generation plants from 1955 to 2055, with anticipated demand shown by the line going off the scale in about 2008. This shows that massive new generation capacity will be needed around the mid-2020s even without the strong growth in demand that is anticipated, although it is possible that major refurbishment will in many cases be favoured over outright replacement.

Generation capacity is expected to grow rapidly in coming years, driven primarily by economic growth and a strategy to attract foreign direct investment in energy-intensive industries, with expanding access and alleviation of poverty also adding to demand. Projections vary from 1 000 to 1 500 MW of new capacity required annually from about 2010, after the addition of about 3 600 MW by recommissioning of the 'Simunye' power stations (Camden, Komatie and Grootvlei), currently under way, and a further approximately 2 050 MW of peaking power capacity already commissioned by Eskom and the DME.

Eskom ordered seven units of open cycle gas turbines (OCGT) from Siemens, yielding a total capacity of over 1 050 MW, that were expected to be handed over to the operator in April 2007. The four units at Atlantis and three in Mossel Bay

Figure 4.2: Electrical generation capacity of existing plants in South Africa, 1995–2055

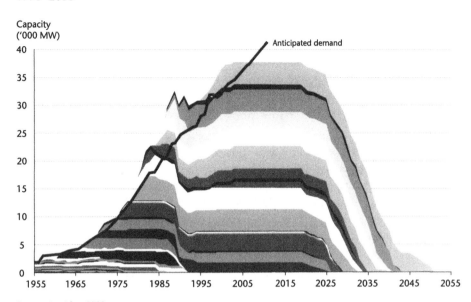

Source: Surridge 2003
Note: The shaded areas represent the lifespans of specific electricity generating stations

would be sited so as to allow for adding a second cycle (using exhaust heat from the gas turbine to generate steam), which would increase output and efficiency, but also start-up time, making retrofitted units suited to mid-merit generation (i.e. demand, or generating capacity, that is more than the baseload (continuous) but less than peak demand). The DME is commissioning a further 1 000 MW of peaking OCGT capacity for KwaZulu-Natal, as a tender to the private sector.

Most of the new capacity provided for in official plans is coal-fired, although government plans also project a role for the Pebble Bed Modular Reactor from early in the next decade, despite it's still being at the research stage. Minister of Public Enterprises Alec Erwin is quoted in the *Sunday Times* of 3 June 2006 asserting that a new conventional nuclear power plant will be brought on line within five years. Eskom's Brian Dames had anticipated that the feasibility study for such a plant (probably a pressurised water reactor), to be built on the southern, west or northern Cape coast, would be finished by the end of 2006 (Creamer 2006b), but work continued through 2007.

While an EIA for a 4 800 MW coal plant in Limpopo was in progress, 'a 2 100 MW coal-fired project for the Limpopo province [had] already been sanctioned by the board' (Creamer 2006c: 28). Plans at present provide for dry cooling, but not for FGD. Eskom is evaluating prospects for three coal-fired plants of 4 800 MW in the Waterberg/Limpopo, in Mpumalanga and in the Vereeniging area in the north of the Free State province. The first plant – Matimba B – has been granted a positive record of decision by the DEAT and EIAs were under way in 2006 for the other two.

Projects 'involving 8 391 MW are proceeding' including the 1 000 MW of peaking plant and '20 850 are at an advanced stage of planning, and projects with a potential to yield a further 17 375 MW in a less advanced prefeasibility stage of development. In addition there is a further 17 375 MW of potential locked up in blue-sky prospects, including the high-profile pebble-bed modular-reactor technology, which still has to be proved' (Creamer 2006b: 28). Also in the research category of project development is a Concentrated Solar Power plant: an EIA was initiated for a 100 MW demonstration plant in the Northern Cape and site development was expected to start in 2007.

Braamhoek pumped storage plant is under construction and expected to have a capacity of 1 332 MW. South Africa already has 1 400 MW of hydro-electric pumped storage capacity, whereby electricity generated during low demand periods is used to move water to a high reservoir from which it is released for peak-period generation. This allows for electricity generated as baseload to be converted (with losses around 12–15 per cent) to peaking power, thus offering an alternative to OCGT or allowing for renewably generated electricity to be stored for peak supply.

Underground coal gasification (UCG) is receiving growing attention as a way of exploiting deposits that are expensive to mine, e.g. because of their great depth, although this appears to be an inefficient form of utilisation that may preclude more effective future options. Coal is ignited and partially burned in situ, to deliver gas at the surface. A pilot project is under way at Majuba power station, where the coal seam at the local mine is too irregular for conventional mining techniques. The existing coal-fired plant could accept up to about 10 per cent of such gas in its fuel mix. UCG is being promoted by Kumba Resources for exploiting the Waterberg deposits, to power combined cycle (gas and steam) generation that should have lower local environmental impacts and greenhouse gas (GHG) emissions than mining and burning the coal.

The regional context: coal and electricity in southern and sub-Saharan Africa

South Africa both imports and exports electricity, by far the largest proportion of which is bought from and sold to Mozambique. It is supplied by the Cahora Bassa dam and largely serves the Mozal aluminium smelter, which needs about 1 000 MW of supply. In the winter of 2006, Eskom was expecting imports of 1 280 MW from Mozambique and 170 MW from the Democratic Republic of the Congo (DRC) (Venter 2006: 9). In the same *Engineering News* feature Venter reported that Namibia imports about 120 MW of power from South Africa, exported through the Western Cape.

The Southern African Power Pool (SAPP) is a growing venture, with 12 member countries, that seeks to link up all Southern African Development Community (SADC) countries and eventually develop a spot market for electricity trade, intended to optimise generation operations in the region and improve prospects for market entry for independent power producers. Plans include importing power from a new hydro-power development on the Congo River, which is also expected to feed into the West African Power Corridor high-voltage transmission system.

Information on electricity generation in SADC countries is generally sketchy. The Energy Information Administration (EIA) of the USA government recently released a report on southern Africa (US EIA 2006), with individual country analyses, which provides more information than has been available in the popular media, but may not be comprehensive. Synthesis of this information shows that the SADC is a net energy exporter that has, since the turn of the century, been using about three-quarters of energy produced. In 2003, SADC countries were responsible for 1.4 per cent of total world energy consumption and provided 2 per cent of world production. South Africa accounted for 83 per cent of regional consumption and 69.8 per cent of regional production (US EIA 2006).

Both Botswana and Zimbabwe have significant coal industries, but these have not been highly developed and both countries have given concerted attention to developing renewable energy technologies. Coal reserves are estimations of the existing resources that are (or are expected to be) economically viable for utilisation, and official figures are influenced not just by geological knowledge but also by opinions on technological feasibility and political and market interests. The US EIA provides an overview of southern African reserves, as illustrated in Figure 4.3.

Figure 4.3: Southern African recoverable coal reserves (million short tons), 2003

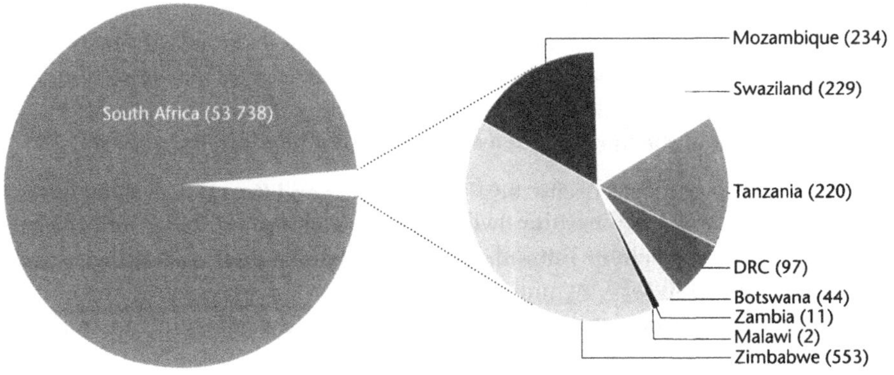

South Africa (53 738)

Mozambique (234)

Swaziland (229)

Tanzania (220)

DRC (97)
Botswana (44)
Zambia (11)
Malawi (2)
Zimbabwe (553)

Source: US EIA 2006

Further, in the US EIA report the term 'reserves' is used more loosely, as it notes that 'Moatize in northwestern Mozambique is considered to be the largest un-explored coal province in the world, with an estimated 2.4 billion tons of reserves' (an order of magnitude higher than that reflected in Figure 4.3). The report also notes that 'in September 2005 Rio Tinto Zimbabwe (RioZim) sought investments for the stalled Sengwa coal project…[in an area that] could have 2.2 billion short tons of coal reserves' (US EIA 2006: 8).

Botswana has established a consortium with Canadian and British partners to develop a new 3 600 MW coal-fired station on the Waterberg, close to the South African border, for which an EIA has been initiated. The target market for exported electricity is principally South Africa, but could include any participants in the regional power pool. Current generation capacity in Botswana is a 132 MW coal-fired station. No more than a quarter of the population has access to electricity, but government funding is planned for extending the grid into rural areas (*Engineering News* 19–25 May 2006).

Namibian generation capacity comprises the 240 MW Ruacana hydro-power plant, the 120 MW Van Eck coal-fired plant that imports coal from South Africa and the 20 MW Paratus diesel-powered plant (*Engineering News* 19–25 May 2006). The Kudu gas-to-power project proposes an 800 MW combined cycle power station near Oranjemund, with the first gas from the field expected in 2010, while the Baynes hydro project proposes 600 MW from a dam on the Kunene River in a shared project with Angola. A Caprivi link is planned to connect with the power grid to the north. With up to 50 per cent of electricity imported, and import agreements with South Africa expiring in 2006, Namibia is anticipating power shortages and planning a major upgrade for the 66 kiloVolt connection with Zambia.

Swaziland's only generation capacity is the 19 MW Maguga Dam hydro-electric plant, which came on line early in 2006. Mozambique's Cahora Bassa power station has a rated capacity of 2 075 MW and a modernisation project is planned; the government is also seeking finance for another dam downstream with up to 2 400 MW hydro-electric capacity. Zimbabwe has two hydro-electric power stations that are not functioning to capacity, and despite increasing imports from South Africa there has been load shedding – i.e. customers having their service interrupted.

Zambia, which exports electricity mostly to Tanzania and Kenya, is seeking finance for three new dams, and existing hydro-electric facilities are being refurbished. Following a 2004 drought in Tanzania a gas-powered plant was established, which had a capacity of 180 MW by mid-2005. Further work is expected on integrating the Tanzanian, Kenyan and Zambian grids, and Rwanda and Uganda are apparently interested in joining this integrated network.

Malawi – not part of the SAPP, but starting work on a connection with Mozambique – theoretically has 285 MW capacity, though some power plants have been damaged by floods and available capacity is apparently 250 MW. Venter (2005a: 74) notes that 'the Shire River, which hosts more than 95% of the country's generation capacity through aging hydropower plants, is threatened by environmental degradation and probable drought'. Venter also writes that only about 7 per cent of the population has access to electricity.

There are conflicting reports on the situation in the DRC. Venter (2005b: 17) writes that a capacity of 9 500 MW is expected once the rehabilitation of the existing 'run-of-river' hydro-power plants on the Congo River has been completed, but the USA Department of Energy notes a total installed capacity of 2 568 MW, with 600–700 MW of this operational (US EIA 2006: 9). Venter's figures probably include Inga III, a proposed plant that has not yet been commissioned. Eskom is heavily involved in future planning that envisages an eventual capacity of up to 40 000 MW at Grand Inga rapids.

Ghana has 1 180 MW hydro-power capacity and 705 MW thermal (coal or gas), and demand growth of 7–10 per cent; it is involved in both export and import of electricity and is one of the proposed customers for natural gas exports from Nigeria. Uganda has 110 MW capacity and about 10 per cent access to electricity. In East Africa there is considerable geothermal energy potential and at least two plants have been announced for Kenya, although their development status seems uncertain. Kenya has 1 092 MW installed capacity, including two geothermal plants, and expects 5 per cent growth in demand in coming years. Tanzania has 591 MW and has been experiencing demand growth of 6.5 per cent. A partial overview of the sub-Saharan region is available in the International Energy Agency's (IEA) *Key World Energy Statistics 2005*, which provides figures for 2003 (IEA 2005) (see Table 4.2).

Table 4.2: IEA energy statistics for sub-Saharan African countries, 2003

Country/region	Population (millions)	GDP (PPP)[a] ($billion, in 2000)	Electricity consumption (TWh)[b]	Total primary energy (TOE/capita)[c]	Electricity consumption (kWh/capita)
World	6 268.0	49 315.0	15 223.0	1.69	2 429
Africa	851.0	1 886.0	440.0	0.66	518
Angola	13.5	30.0	1.7	0.67	126
Cameroon	16.9	32.2	2.8	0.4	174
Congo	3.7	3.4	0.5	0.3	122
DRC	53.1	35.0	4.7	0.3	89
Côte d'Ivoire	16.8	23.5	3.0	0.4	182
Gabon	1.3	8.1	1.2	1.2	920
Ghana	20.6	43.7	5.2	0.4	254
Kenya	31.9	31.3	4.1	0.5	128
Mozambique	18.8	19.8	6.2	0.4	343
Namibia	2.0	11.8	2.5	0.6	1 259
Nigeria	136.5	135.3	13.4	0.7	99
South Africa	45.8	447.9	206.4	2.6	4 504
Zambia	10.4	8.6	6.5	0.6	625
Zimbabwe	13.1	27.6	10.5	0.7	804

Source: IEA 2005

Notes: a GDP (PPP) is 'purchasing power parity' as per the OECD/World Bank/CEPII (Paris).

b TWh = terrawatt hour (1 billion KWh).

c 'TOE' is tons of oil equivalent.

Impacts of fossil fuel use in electricity generation

The extraction and use of fossil fuels for the purpose of electricity generation have a wide range of social and environmental impacts that are not yet fully documented, or their costs understood. This section of the chapter discusses some of those impacts that have been recorded and analysed in terms of their environmental, social and financial costs.

Environmental impacts

The full extent of the environmental impacts of coal use are still emerging, as are methodologies for valuation of the full costs of such impacts. The impacts that are most widely recorded are airborne emissions, including:

* particulate matter (PM) – with increasing attention to fine matter (there is increasing evidence that PM 2.5 – particles less that 2.5 microns in diameter, which initially received far less attention than visible particles – is a major source of health impacts); generally only fly ash is accounted for, but fine particle sulphate and nitrate are formed from gaseous emissions;
* SO_x – sulphur oxides, primarily sulphur dioxide (SO_2), that cause respiratory health problems as ambient pollution and form acid rain;
* NO_x – nitrogen oxides that contribute to respiratory health problems and acid rain;
* N_2O – nitrous oxide that reacts differently to nitrogen oxides (NO_2) and is a major and potent greenhouse gas;
* CO_2 – carbon dioxide, the greenhouse gas of greatest concern; other greenhouse gasses are usually measured in CO_2-equivalents (CO_e);
* VOCs – volatile organic compounds[2] which have direct toxic effects on the respiratory and central nervous systems; many are carcinogenic. They also contribute to the formation of ozone, which also has a detrimental impact on the respiratory system; many are bioaccumulative, building up in the body and transferred up the animal food chain;
* heavy metals – mercury emissions from coal-fired power plants have become subject to regulation within the USA, and uranium and thorium emissions from coal have been highlighted by nuclear proponents.

Methane released during extraction of coal and oil is generally attributed to fuel production rather than electricity generation and is frequently flared – thus reducing the global warming impact (CO_2 having a far lower warming force than methane) but increasing local air pollution as the gas is seldom clean when burned.

Other impacts include:

* water consumption – almost two litres per kilowatt-hour (kWh) of electricity generated is evaporated for cooling in South Africa's older power stations, and some of the latest high-temperature combustion options would require more cooling than recently built plants; any water consumption for coal cleaning/processing prior to power plant delivery should also be accounted to

electricity generation; water consumption of power plant scrubber systems appears to be relatively light;

- water quality – while water can be cleaned of pollutants before discharge, it is not clear how comprehensively this is practised at coal-fired stations in South Africa or how well the resulting slurry is managed to avoid contamination of groundwater; heat discharge into bodies or flows of water may also have ecological impacts (hence the coastal location of nuclear power plants); cumulative impacts of deposition of airborne pollutants on surface water can be significant – it was the 'death' of lakes as a result of acid rain that provided major impetus to reducing sulphur emissions in industrialised countries;
- land degradation and damage to vegetation and built infrastructure – acid rain and other deposition of airborne pollutants are generally taken to be covered under consideration of air pollution, but cumulative impacts over time can be significant even when ambient concentrations of air pollution in any particular location are considered below regulatory concern.

Quantification of airborne emissions in South Africa does not provide an account of trace elements, such as mercury, arsenic and dioxins, that may be present in total suspended particulates; concentrations are also not recorded in bottom ash (which is either dumped or used in processes such as cement production) or discharge water. The extent of these pollutants will depend on the nature of the coal and the combustion process, and in South Africa is officially deemed to be negligible.

Reporting on the impacts of coal-fired power plants has improved substantially over the past 15 years, but is still far from comprehensive and does not follow a 'cradle-to-grave' approach that would factor in all impacts of the fuel chain. The Clean Air Task Force based in the USA, where coal is the fuel for more than half of generation, states that '[t]he electric power industry is the largest toxic polluter in the country' (Keating 2001: 1). They provide an overview of the health effects of the most prevalent pollutants arising from this industry, reproduced in Table 4.3.

Table 4.3: Toxic effects of selected power plant pollutants on humans

Substance	Acute	Chronic	Comments
Sulphur dioxide	Lung irritant, triggers asthma, low birth weight in infants.	Reduces lung function, associated with premature death.	Also contributes to acid rain and poor visibility.
Nitrogen oxides	Changes lung function, increases respiratory illness in children.	Increases susceptibility to respiratory illnesses and causes permanent alteration of lung.	Forms ozone smog and acid rain. Ozone is associated with asthma, reduced lung function, adverse birth outcomes and allergen sensitisation.
Particulate matter	Asthma attacks, heart rate variability, heart attacks.	Cardiovascular disease, pneumonia, chronic obstructive pulmonary disease, premature death.	Fine particle pollution from power plants is estimated to cut short the lives of 30 000 Americans each year.

→

Substance	Acute	Chronic	Comments
← Hydrogen chloride	Inhalation causes coughing, hoarseness, chest pain, and inflammation of respiratory tract.	Chronic occupational exposure is associated with gastritis, chronic bronchitis, dermatitis, photo sensitisation in workers.	
Hydrogen fluoride	Inhalation causes severe respiratory damage, severe irritation and pulmonary oedema.		Very high exposures through drinking water or air can cause skeletal fluorosis.
Arsenic	Ingestion and inhalation: affects the gastrointestinal system and central nervous system.	Known human carcinogen with high potency. Inhalation causes lung cancer; ingestion causes lung, skin, bladder and liver cancer. The kidney is affected following chronic inhalation and oral exposure.	
Cadmium	Inhalation exposure causes bronchial and pulmonary irritation. A single acute exposure to high levels of cadmium can result in long-lasting impairment of lung function.	Probably human carcinogen of medium potency. The kidney is the major target organ in humans following chronic inhalation and oral exposure.	Other effects noted from chronic inhalation exposure are bronchiolitis and emphysema.
Chromium	High exposure to chromium VI may result in renal toxicity, gastro-intestinal haemor-rhage and internal haemorrhage.	Known human carcinogen of high potency.	Chronic effects from industrial exposures are inflammation of the respiratory tract, effects on the kidneys, liver and gastrointestinal tract.
Mercury	Inhalation exposure to elemental mercury results in central nervous system effects and effects on gastrointestinal tract and respiratory system.	Methyl mercury ingestion causes developmental effects. Infants born to women who ingested methyl mercury may perform poorly on neuro-behavioural tests.	The major effects from chronic exposure are bronchiolitis and emphysema.

Source: Keating 2001: 5

Total pollutants arising from fossil-fired electricity generation in South Africa are not available, but are mostly captured in Eskom figures such as those outlined in Table 4.4 taken from the Statistical Overview in their 2005 *Annual Report*, as Eskom accounts for 93.5 per cent of total electricity production (Eskom 2005; Winkler 2006: 53); in 2002 Eskom accounted for over 97 per cent of coal use for electricity generation – (this figure is based on domestic coal consumption figures in the DME's *Digest of South African Energy Statistics* (DME 2006: 27), which records lower usage than the Eskom record, by 6.5 per cent or 6 850 kilotons (kt)).

Table 4.4: Environmental impacts of Eskom electricity generation, 2004–2005

Environmental indicators	2005 (15-month period)	2004 (12-month period)
Specific water consumption	1.28 litres/kWh sent out	1.26 litres/kWh sent out
Net raw water consumption, Mlitres	347 147	277 557
Coal burned, kt	136 437	109 508
Nitrous oxide, kt	3.552	2.924
Carbon dioxide, kt	247 000	197 700
Sulphur dioxide, kt	2 236	1 779
Nitrogen oxide (as NO_2), kt	994	797
Particulate emissions, kt	72.83	59.17
Ash produced, kt	40 800	33 100
Ash sold, kt	1 957	1 590

Source: Eskom 2005
Note: The various oxide emissions are based on coal characteristics and power station design parameters. It is not clear from the Eskom reports whether PM 2.5 emissions are included, or just emissions of the larger PM 10.

The 2005 Eskom *Annual Report* also provides factors for the environmental impacts of electricity use per unit, based on units sold (delivered) rather than those produced, which thus reflect the increase in rate of impact per unit of energy delivered that results from transmission and distribution losses – e.g. 13 820 GWh in 2002 (DME 2006: 37), or nearly 8 per cent. Own use of energy in mining and at power plants is significant, and would not be factored into such figures. Total electricity purchased for the Eskom system in the 15-month period recorded under 2005 was 12 197 GWh, about 4.5 per cent of the total produced by Eskom stations.

Coal-fired generation requires a highly centralised system with long-distance, high-voltage transmission. All energy carriers, or pathways, entail impacts, but there are few that have become as accepted or ignored as the massive power lines that radiate from South African power plants (totalling 347 204 kilometres – all voltages). There have been various studies of health impacts of transmission cables on people living close by, but results vary widely and are highly contested (much like the impacts of microwave transmission towers and actual cell phone use). With many people living in close proximity to transmission lines there are probably significant impacts that merit official investigation, but the issue will not be considered further here.

Hallowes (2006) provides a comparative overview of the major sources of air pollution (see Table 4.5); note that the figures do not reflect emissions from the *use* of petroleum products, which Hallowes calculates as adding about 57 million tons of carbon dioxide in 2000.

Table 4.5: Air emissions from South Africa's main energy producers (tons), 2004

Pollutant	Eskom	Fuel from coal (Sasol Synfuel)	Crude oil refineries
Carbon dioxide	197 700 000	52 164 000	3 570 894
Sulphur dioxide	1 779 000	189 923	18 212
Nitrogen oxide	797 000	148 300	4 790
Particulate emissions	59 170	8 000	898[a]
Volatile organic compounds	–	409 783	7 724[b]

Source: Hallowes & Munnik 2006
Notes: a Excludes Sapref.
       b Excludes Natref.

Blignaut and De Wit (2004: 293) indicate that in 2000 Eskom accounted for methane emissions of 2 267 733 kilograms[3] – 59.4 per cent of the South African total, with a further 1 per cent from non-Eskom generation; 63.9 per cent of carbon dioxide emissions, with 1 per cent from non-Eskom generation; and used 57.5 per cent of national coal consumption. DME figures for 2002 show that 61.5 per cent of national coal consumption was used for electricity generation (DME 2006: 27). These figures suggest that the proportional share of Eskom, and electricity, to total national GHG emissions has been increasing, and Spalding-Fecher and Matibe (2003: 726) note that South Africa's Initial National Communication to the United Nations Framework Convention on Climate Change (UNFCCC) shows 'Eskom contributing almost 40 per cent of total national greenhouse gas emissions in 1994'.

South Africa has a very energy-intensive economy that produces amongst the highest per capita rates of GHG emissions globally. An indication of this is given by statistics compiled by Winkler (2006), using figures supplied by the IEA (see Table 4.6). In the table, South Africa is compared to major regions (OECD refers to industrialised countries that are members of the Organisation for Economic Co-operation and Development) in terms of average carbon dioxide emissions per person (from total national fuel combustion) and emissions per unit of economic activity, first in US dollars and then adjusted to reflect the actual purchasing power parity of local currencies, rather than their dollar valuation.

This is not a calculation of a personal footprint, as it simply divides the total emissions in a country by the number of people living there, even though the bulk of emissions come from services and industries of which only a small minority enjoy the benefits. It also does not consider cumulative emissions, which are an

Table 4.6: Fuel combustion CO_2 emissions by intensity and per capita, 2000

	CO_2/capita (tons/capita)	CO_2/GDP (kg/1995 US$)	CO_2/GDP PPP (kg/1995 PPP$)
South Africa	6.91	1.73	0.79
Africa	0.86	1.16	0.43
Non-OECD	2.24	1.73	0.64
OECD	11.10	0.45	0.51
World	3.89	0.69	0.59

Source: IEA 2002
Note: PPP = purchasing power parity; GDP = gross domestic product

important indication of which countries should act first to reduce emissions, as OECD countries have been emitting at high rates for far longer than developing countries and GHG remain in the atmosphere, contributing to global warming, for a very long time. By the mid-1990s South Africa had one of the most carbon-intense economies in the world, which we have done nothing to change in the last 10 years.

An overall indication of the contribution of energy to South Africa's total GHG emissions is also provided by Winkler (2006), using figures provided in South Africa's National Communication to the UNFCCC, compiled in 2000. Since different gases have different levels of warming impact, methane and nitrous oxide emissions are converted to a common unit to allow comparison of impact with carbon dioxide emissions (see Table 4.7). Note that 'energy' covers all energy use: electricity constitutes just over a quarter of national energy consumption, but accounts for a much higher proportion of primary supply, due to the almost two-thirds energy loss in the conversion from coal to electricity supply. Detailed figures in the National Communication show electricity generation to be responsible for just over 40 per cent of total national emissions of the three main GHGs in 1994 – a proportion that is unlikely to have changed substantially.

Table 4.7: Sector emissions in South Africa, 1990 and 1994

Category	CO_2-equivalent (Mt)							
	CO_2		CH_4		N_2O		Aggregated	
	1990	1994	1990	1994	1990	1994	1990	1994
Energy	252.02	287.85	7.29	7.89	1.58	1.82	260.89	297.56
Industrial process	28.91	28.11	69.00	26.00	1.81	2.25	30.79	30.39
Agriculture			21.30	19.69	19.17	15.78	40.47	35.46
Waste			14.46	15.61	0.74	0.83	15.19	16.43
Total							347.35	379.84

Source: Winkler 2006: 98
Note: CH_4 = methane

Social impacts of fossil-fired generation

Impacts on people's health and costs associated with their treatment and with loss of productivity – such as the cost of sick days – are generally captured under valuations of environmental impacts. However, there are social impacts that are not the result of pollution, but of perpetuating heavy reliance on coal, which is premised on least-cost options for producers and requires a highly centralised electricity sector (due to high fuel transport costs and economies of scale for plants). There are also 'opportunity costs' of not directing new investment to renewable energy or energy efficiency and conservation; for example, the potential to stimulate creation of a local wind turbine industry with an order equivalent to one new coal-fired power station.

Decentralisation of electricity generation offers a range of benefits, including system stability, reduced transmission losses and compatibility with renewable energy technologies and community-based projects, whereby communities are participants in accessing or producing energy, rather than simply clients. Democratising the energy sector, or just the provision of household energy services – i.e. increasing popular participation and public benefits – is a concept that is not well developed in mainstream planning. Failure to diversify our electricity industry is increasingly recognised as a threat to energy security, but the increasing burden being transferred to future generations, as we seek to avoid capital expenditure in the present, is not quantified.

There have been very few studies looking at the social costs and benefits of potential market mechanisms to address externalised costs, achieve social goals or improve long-term security of supply. A study that deals specifically with the social impacts of competing energy technology options (as opposed to projecting benefits of a specific development proposal) is *Employment Potential of Renewable Energy in South Africa* (Agama Energy 2003). This illustrates the far greater job creation associated with harvesting renewable energy, providing a stark contrast to the legacy of maximising return from exploitation of stock energy. Employment levels in the electricity sector have halved since 1980, while electricity production has doubled (Figure 4.4).

Valuation of externalised costs

The 1998 White Paper on Energy Policy for South Africa (DME 1998) provides that the Integrated Energy Planning (IEP) process should factor in 'quantifiable externalities', which has left much room for interpretation as to what is actually taken into account. Energy planning to date has worked from the premise that in the South African context, availability of low-priced energy, or at least electricity, is such an imperative for economic growth and social welfare that benefits will outweigh any externalised costs. A study was being commissioned by the DME in 2006 to quantify externalities for input to the IEP process, but at the time of writing this had been put on hold (for a second time). While the terms of reference

Figure 4.4: Employment in coal-based electricity generation in South Africa, 1980–2000

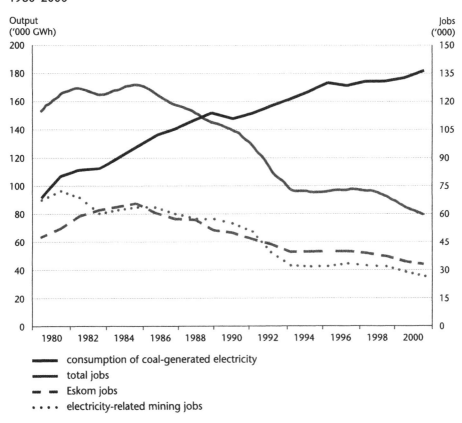

Source: Agama Energy 2003: 7

did not ensure that social costs and the potential benefits of alternative means of delivering energy services, i.e. the opportunity costs of 'business as usual', would be well covered, it would have been better than the current absence of any official quantification of externalities.

Blignaut and Lumley (2004) provide a detailed discussion of economic valuation, which is distinguished from financial analysis that works with existing market prices to focus on cash flow and profitability. Attributing a monetary value to environmental degradation, resource depletion and impacts on human health and welfare inevitably takes place within a specific context and involves a degree of uncertainty, such as the extent to which one source of pollution among many is responsible for observable effects. This means that results are usually presented as a range of values, and that values are higher in more affluent societies/countries (e.g. due to higher labour costs and standards of healthcare).

In all recent attempts to quantify the externalised environmental costs of South African electricity generation, climate change features as the major component, though this is not the case for energy services as a whole, since the polluting impacts of household fuel use are the most direct and devastating and thus offer the most immediate potential for remedial action. Efforts to attribute monetary values focus on climate change impacts, on the basis that the impacts of ambient air pollution vary greatly according to where and how the emissions take place and 'the damage caused by these pollutants depends very much on the demographic composition of the exposed population, level of exposure and dose-response functions' (Blignaut & King 2002: 12).

There is a social dimension to all environmental cost valuations, for example where healthcare costs and reduced working time arising from air pollution are reckoned alongside diminishing agricultural yields and ecosystem integrity. This is particularly true for costs attributed to climate change, where so many of the impacts relate to the viability of sustainable livelihoods, including subsistence activities (such as the viability of fisheries and low-input agriculture). The costing of loss of life or premature death is a particularly contentious area, especially since costs are generally related to the potential income of the individual, meaning that lives are valued much lower in developing and poor countries.

Blignaut and King estimate the social costs of methane and carbon dioxide emissions using figures broadly consistent with estimated global damage costs of a ton of carbon dioxide emitted, of 'a conservative $2.50/tonne to $5/tonne', using a standard conversion factor based on methane having 21 times the global warming potential of carbon dioxide (Blignaut & King 2002: 12). (Others double this estimation, and in the European emissions trading system a one-ton allowance has traded at over US$20.) Based on this valuation the 2000 'social' or global damage cost of carbon dioxide and methane emissions attributed to Eskom alone is in the range of R2.8 to 5.6 million, which is compared to a 'private cost' of R4.1 million – i.e. costs actually incurred by Eskom (Blignaut & De Wit 2004: 300–301).

Blignaut and De Wit (2004: 154) further provide 'preliminary estimates of the unmitigated damage costs of climate change in South Africa' that would pertain in 2050 or when atmospheric concentrations of carbon dioxide reach double pre-industrial levels, which may be a lot sooner. This includes damage to agriculture, biodiversity (including tourism value), human health (e.g. increased malaria) and property damage due to sea level rise; it does not contemplate the impacts of extreme weather events. It is only intended to be broadly indicative and suggests a range of 2.4 per cent to 6 per cent of GDP, with much of the burden carried by the poor.

A paper by Spalding-Fecher and Matibe (2003) appears to be the most broad-ranging recently published work focusing on externalised costs of electricity generation. It aims to update previous work by Van Horen (1996), though not covering the same scope. The authors have quantified externalised costs of Eskom generation – municipal stations were not included due to lack of information – that include costs of particulates, sulphur dioxide and nitrogen (noting that the impacts of emissions have been reduced by the use of higher smoke stacks). This does not include impacts of acidification, on the basis that recent studies by Eskom and the Council for Scientific and Industrial Research have indicated that atmospheric concentrations of sulphur oxides are lower than previously thought – 'sulphur oxides in central Mpumalanga in 1999 ranged from 5 to 15 parts per billion [ppb], well below the Department of Environmental Affairs and Tourism standard of 30 ppb' (Spalding-Fecher & Matibe 2003: 727) – and the government does not consider acidification to be a significant problem.[4]

Spalding-Fecher and Matibe also developed a value for the benefits, principally health impact changes, of electrification, as a result of avoided fuel consumption. The external costs of household fuel use were calculated, taking into account different user group and regional profiles, based on exposure to indoor air pollution, accidental paraffin poisoning, fires and burns caused by paraffin and candles, and the social costs of fuel wood scarcity. The annual avoided costs also take account of the pace of decline in fuel use post-electrification. They provide a range of costs, as outlined in Table 4.8.

Table 4.8: Summary of external costs of Eskom electricity generation, 1999

	Low (R millions)	Central (R millions)	High (R millions)
Air pollution and health	852	1 177	1 450
Electrification	173	958	2 324
Climate change	1 625	7 043	16 258
Total	2 304	7 262	15 379

Source: Spalding-Fecher & Matibe 2003: 726

It is worth noting that the range of costs related to climate change given by Spalding-Fecher and Matibe starts at a lower value than those of Blignaut and De Wit (2004), and ends considerably higher, such that the central estimate is about 68 per cent more than the upper value given by Blignaut and De Wit. While the conceptual basis for subtracting the value, or positive externality, of electrification is justified in the context of the study – looking at total external costs of Eskom operations for 1999 – this approach would presumably not be applied today, now that the electrification programme is managed and financed through the DME.

Spalding-Fecher and Matibe (2003) also report these externalised costs per unit of electricity generated, as illustrated in Table 4.9.

One can do a rough extrapolation, using these figures and coal-fired generation reported by Eskom for 2004, to estimate more recent costs, though it must be noted that there may be more severe impacts from the accumulation of pollutants or particular incidents (e.g. high-dose exposures in downwind populations) that are not reflected. The low variation in the supply mix, such as the contribution of imported hydro-power, means that this should not cause a distortion of more than

Table 4.9: Summary of external costs of Eskom electricity generation (per unit), 1999

	Per unit cost of coal-fired power produced (cents/kWh)			Per unit cost of delivered electricity (cents/kWh)		
	Low	Central	High	Low	Central	High
Air pollution and health	0.5	0.7	0.9	0.5	0.7	0.8
Electrification	0.1	0.6	1.4	0.1	0.5	1.3
Climate change	1.0	4.3	9.8	0.9	4.1	9.4
Total	1.4	4.4	9.3	1.3	4.3	8.9

Source: Spalding-Fecher & Matibe 2003: 727

1 per cent. Thus we may conclude that a central valuation of externalised costs of Eskom generation for 2004, based on Spalding-Fecher and Matibe's methodology but without subtracting electrification value (and without considering inflation), is at least R10.1 billion.

The figure of five cents per kWh used in the above extrapolation is the same as that used in a study commissioned by the National Treasury, which states: 'It is estimated that this externality cost is, at the very least, R0.05 per kWh of electricity produced by coal-fired power stations' (Conningarth Economists NBP 2004: 8). Another Treasury document, *Draft Policy Paper: A Framework for Considering Market-Based Instruments to Support Environmental Fiscal Reform in South Africa*, notes various studies attempting to estimate the costs of airborne pollution from coal-fired electricity 'suggesting a range of between R4–30 billion per year' (National Treasury 2006: 78).

As noted in the Conningarth study, local damage costs covered in Van Horen's (1996) study include the morbidity and mortality effects of coal mining, economic pricing of water consumption in power stations, morbidity and mortality effects of air pollution from power stations and damage costs from emissions of greenhouse gases (Conningarth Economists NBP 2004). The Van Horen study suggested a range of costs between R0.03 and R0.17, with an average of R0.10 per kWh.

A figure of R0.05 per kWh is thus widely recognised to be a very conservative estimate of externalised costs of electricity. Government apparently considers this to be appropriate for South Africa as a developing country. One could argue that while this may be a reasonable figure to apply to fiscal mechanisms affecting society as a whole, or to domestic electricity consumers, a higher value would be appropriate when considering the externalised costs associated with facilities supplying OECD markets, such as transnational corporations engaged in primary commodities processing. Given official recognition that South Africa has a two-tier economy, it would be consistent to apply a higher valuation of externalities, or to internalise a greater proportion of the true costs of supply, for electricity users operating primarily within the 'first', or industrialised, economy.

In practice, the opposite takes place. Firstly, with industry consuming 66 per cent of available electricity, this sector – which happens to include export-oriented extractive industries – already enjoys this proportion of the effective subsidy of upwards of an annual R10 billion in externalised costs. The more real costs are externalised, the more the 'first' economy benefits. Secondly, commercial enterprises using large amounts of electricity are treated as 'contestable customers' that can negotiate their tariffs directly with Eskom, commanding prices far lower than those paid by the majority. These bulk discounts are defended in terms of the lower transmission and distribution costs involved in such bulk supply, but as the terms of these deals are deemed confidential, there is no way to determine if there is any relationship between lower costs and lower prices. While the policy principle of 'cost-reflective pricing' (DME 1998: 8) is applied, after a fashion, to the majority of electricity users, the biggest consumers can exploit global competition for foreign direct investment to leverage further effective subsidies.

In effect, a high environmental burden – much of which translates into direct human impacts (social costs) – and rapid depletion of the finite national resource endowment are deemed acceptable in the name of development, while the benefits accrue most directly to a minority that is well developed. A more political way of expressing this would be to note that the exploitation of and particularly heavy dependence on concentrated stock energy is intrinsically linked with the concentration of wealth, while the majority hope for 'trickle-down' or 'knock-on' benefits of economic growth.

Improving coal use

Even scenarios contemplating aggressive development and deployment of a range of renewable energy technologies anticipate additional coal-fired generation over the medium term. Recent research (Banks & Schäffler 2006) shows that both energy efficiency interventions and deployment of renewable energy technologies at a rate far higher than considered in any current government planning will still leave space for new coal-fired plant development. It therefore makes sense to consider technology options for improving coal use, despite the opportunity costs and trade-offs involved in a pragmatic compromise that accommodates coal industry interests.

Electricity generation requires mechanical energy to drive turbines, and the thermal utilisation of the chemical energy in coal requires conversion first to heat, which is used to produce pressure, either with steam or gas. The energy efficiency of the overall process may be improved through more efficient combustion as well as more efficient use of the heat so produced, thus reducing the environmental and social impacts per unit of energy dispatched. The reduction of pollution from coal-fired electricity generation also requires removal of impurities, either before, during or after the production of heat (this includes sulphur, heavy metals, volatiles, etc., including ash content and particulate matter), as well as the removal of the by-products of combustion – primarily carbon dioxide and nitrogen oxides.

The term 'clean coal technologies' (CCTs) is applied to incremental as well as substantial improvements in the use of coal, either through increased efficiency of fuel use or through the capture of pollutants. Even the use of low-grade discard coal is promoted as a CCT, on the basis that specially designed combustion chambers – e.g. with a fluidised bed, where small coal particles are suspended on a bed of air – render its use economically viable within the limited constraints of local air quality regulation.

The term came into common use in the 1970s, when the focus was on the reduction of sulphur emissions and scrubbers were first introduced to power stations, driven largely by the emerging impacts of acid rain. CCT is usually divided into three categories: pre-combustion, combustion (or in situ) and post-combustion technologies. A World Bank paper classifies low-NO_x combustion and furnace sorbent injection as in situ technology, a separate category to 'advanced coal utilisation technologies', such as integrated gasification with combined cycle (IGCC) (Stratos Tavoulareas & Charpentier 1995: 19). Such coal conversion is sometimes presented as a separate category, including UCG, which involves partial combustion of coal to deliver gas at the mine head and is the subject of a pilot project at Majuba power station.

CCT generated a lot of interest and attracted considerable public funding, particularly in the USA, from the mid-1980s into the 1990s, but there was little progress in demonstration or deployment. In 2002, the Bush administration allocated US$2 billion to a programme for CCT, and companies such as Billiton and Eskom have been promoting CCT for Clean Development Mechanism projects in South Africa. An approach that has recently received much attention and increasing levels of research funding is carbon capture and storage (CCS), a concept that embraces a wide range of applications, from established practices for enhanced oil recovery to speculative proposals to inject carbon dioxide into deep ocean areas.

Pre-combustion techniques and technologies

The ash content of coal can be reduced through dry or wet processes and cleaning can also remove sulphur, with physical cleaning removing mineral sulphur and chemical or biological cleaning required for removing organically bound sulphur. Physical cleaning can remove up to 60 per cent of inert matter or ash, thus reducing particulate emissions, and 10–40 per cent of sulphur, depending on the proportion that is mineral sulphur. The resulting fuel will have lower transport costs per energy unit and reduce generation plant maintenance costs from wear and tear.

Cleaning involves an energy loss of up to 15 per cent, reducing the efficiency of the overall coal-to-electricity process, with the loss mostly from energy used for grinding, which is also required for pulverised fuel injection. Wet cleaning appears to be more effective than dry cleaning, allowing for capture of fine coal particles and up to 90 per cent of mineral sulphur, but can further reduce plant efficiency due to moisture added to the coal.

Combustion efficiency and avoidance or capture of pollutants

Optimal combustion requires an optimal combination of fuel and oxygen. The efficiency of coal combustion can be improved through increasing the available surface area of the fuel, by suspending the fuel with pressurised air or fuel pulverisation and injection into the combustion chamber, and by increasing the availability of oxygen by increasing the atmospheric pressure in the chamber.

Pulverised coal combustion

According to the IEA, pulverised coal combustion technology – also referred to as pulverised fuel (PF) or pulverised coal (PC) – accounts for well over 90 per cent of world coal-fired generation capacity. [5] PC can be used to fire a wide variety of coals and is the leading technology in South Africa, although it is regarded as less appropriate for coal with high ash content. Most of the ash passes out with the flue gases as fine particulate matter, to be collected in electrostatic precipitators (ESPs) or fabric filters before the stack.

Supercritical steam

Production of supercritical steam, i.e. steam at high temperature and pressure, improves the efficiency or energy capture of turbine operation. Eskom proposes this technology for its next coal-fired plant (originally tagged Matimba B and now going under the code-name Project Alpha) and projects an energy conversion efficiency of up to 40 per cent. Such systems involve no significant departure from the traditional design features of pulverised coal-firing systems, but would reduce costs and the rate of emissions. Even higher temperature and pressure – ultra-supercritical steam – would further improve efficiency, but requires extremely robust plant materials that are still in the research and development stage. Slagging combustion proposes high-temperature combustion to allow impurities and pollutants to be captured in a molten slag.

Fluidised bed combustion

In fluidised bed combustion (FBC) crushed coal is mixed with a sorbent, such as limestone, and supported on a strong rising current of air, with the turbulent mixture assuring efficient combustion and the sorbent removing over 90 per cent of the sulphur. Operating temperature is lower than in conventional boilers, reducing formation of nitrogen oxides (although nitrous oxide formation is increased). The resultant ash is less fine and abrasive (compared to PC), making particulate removal from flue gases easier. The system is designed for use of discard coal and use of other low-grade fuels, and allows for co-firing with waste materials. While low emissions with low-grade fuel are the main objective of FBC, efficiency of 40 per cent is expected in systems currently being deployed, with 45 per cent efficiency intended through the use of advanced systems.

Integrated gasification combined cycle

With IGCC coal is first gasified under low oxygen conditions in an enclosed, pressurised reactor to produce syngas, a mixture of carbon monoxide and hydrogen, which is used to drive a gas turbine that produces 60–70 per cent of the power output. The exhaust gases go to a heat exchanger to generate superheated steam to drive a steam turbine. While gasification can take place with a fixed bed and lump coal, for power generation either a fluidised bed and small coal particles (3–6 mm) or pulverised fuel in an entrained flow are preferred.

Major reductions in emissions of pollutants are possible because they are much more concentrated in the syngas, especially with oxygen-blown gasification, and separate by-product streams are possible, including highly concentrated carbon dioxide. The long start-up time tends to make this technology suitable only for baseload electricity supply, although a portion of the syngas could be stored for use in an OCGT to improve load-following capabilities of a more complex power plant.

Gasifiers can use lower-grade coals (with high ash and/or sulphur content), as well as other fuels such as petroleum refinery residues. The *World Energy Assessment* (UNDP 2000) provides a profile of a 400 MW plant, with total generation costs lower than a PC plant with flue gas desulphurisation. IGCC plants can achieve up to 45 per cent efficiency and the aim is to match the environmental performance of gas-fired plants, with recovery of sulphur in elemental form as the basis for marketable by-products.

Coal gasification for combined production of electricity and synthetic fuels (gas or liquid) is undergoing international development, and such technologies are expected to become competitive with oil prices over US$40–50 per barrel. IGCC is particularly suited to cogeneration, performing better than ultra-supercritical steam turbine technologies that have very similar costs and electricity generation efficiencies, and can be used for polygeneration (e.g. with hydrogen as an additional product).

Sulphur oxide control/sorbent use

Removal of sulphur can be achieved through the introduction of a fixing agent for sulphur that typically contains lime. The sorbent may be injected into the combustion chamber or downstream, and in the case of FBC is introduced in the fuel bed. The reacted sorbent contains gypsum that can be collected for sale as a by-product. The removal of sulphur oxides through sorbent injection during combustion is 30–60 per cent efficient and is relatively low-cost. It does have downstream impacts, as it changes the particulate matter in a way that reduces the effectiveness of ESPs; where these are in use it may be necessary to re-condition the exhaust gas with moisture or ammonia. Fluidised bed combustion allows for 70–95 per cent sulphur dioxide removal, with better results with high pressure, while IGCC achieves

90/99.9 per cent sulphur dioxide removal (Stratos Tavoulareas & Charpentier 1995: 52).

Nitrogen oxide control

Combustion at lower temperatures reduces the amount of nitrogen oxide (NO_x) formation, as does the staging of combustion to reduce the amount of air and thus nitrogen in the combustion reaction. Low-NO_x burners (LNB), which can be used with pulverised fuel, delay the complete combustion of coal and thus reduce NO_x formation. According to a World Bank study (Stratos Tavoulareas & Charpentier 1995: 46), FBC (atmospheric or pressurised) allows for 50–80 per cent NO_x removal, while reductions of 30–55 per cent are achieved with LNB and IGCC achieves 60–90 per cent.

Post-combustion techniques and technologies

Post-combustion technologies seek to reduce sulphur oxides (principally sulphur dioxide), nitrogen oxides and particulate emissions, either separately or in combination. ESPs are the most common technology for particulate capture, but their performance may be compromised by FGD techniques (sorbent use), while bag filters are more reliable, considered suitable for developing countries and may be more compatible with FGD interventions.

Sulphur oxide removal/FGD

Wet scrubbers are an established technology in which sulphur is reacted with calcium in a slurry after exhaust gases pass through an ESP or bag filter. Gypsum (calcium sulphate) can be recovered as a commercial by-product. Wet scrubbers can be designed for different levels of efficiency (usually 80–90 per cent) and can reach 99 per cent efficiency with the use of additives, but power requirements use 1–3 per cent of a unit's generation capacity. An additive may also be introduced for NO_x removal, but this requires precise controls and gas reheating may be required.

Spray dry scrubbers are cheaper and easier to operate and maintain than wet scrubbers. Sorbent injection, before or after an ESP, requires cooling of the flue gas before the sulphur is reacted with a calcium solution and the reaction by-products are then collected in a fabric filter. Pre-ESP injection is less efficient (30–70 per cent) but cheaper than post-ESP injection, which can achieve 80–90 per cent efficiency and is suitable for retrofitting.

Nitrogen oxide removal

Flue gas treatment specifically for NO_x control (selective reduction) involves the introduction of a nitrogen-based chemical reagent – generally ammonia or urea – to convert NO_x into oxygen and nitrogen, with or without a catalyst to accelerate chemical reactions and improve efficiency. Release of unreacted ammonia into the environment is an issue, and non-catalytic reduction also generates the greenhouse and ozone-depleting nitrous oxide.

Particulate matter control

ESPs are mainstream technology and performance is heavily dependent on optimal operation and maintenance, not just of the ESP equipment but of the whole plant, and actual performance frequently falls short of the theoretical potential, particularly in developing countries. Use of auxiliary power is significant, to the extent that power plant operators have been known to deactivate ESP equipment at night, which would also reduce waste material handling costs. Efficiency is generally given as around 95 per cent, although the means of measurement somewhat obscures higher levels of fine particulate emissions – i.e. PM 2.5 (particulates with a diameter of 2.5 microns or less) – which have been found to be the most harmful to human health (causing respiratory illness). Fabric filters, also known as baghouse technology, are highly reliable and can remove 99 per cent of particulates, including the finest particles (0.05–1 micron).

Carbon capture and storage

A somewhat controversial option for addressing the climate change impacts of fossil fuel use is CCS. Introduction of CCS is contested mostly because of the uncertainties regarding permanence, as well as the environmental impacts of some storage (also referred to as sequestration) proposals, such as deep ocean injection. The high costs also involve opportunity costs for climate change mitigation in general, making the promotion of technology to mitigate impacts of increasing coal use for electricity a potential barrier to more effective investment in end-use efficiency and conservation. However, while public funds would most effectively be used to develop alternatives to coal, if coal use increases in line with all mainstream projections, humanity will need CCS to work on a large scale if we are to avoid dangerous human interference with the climate system – i.e. to keep global warming below two degrees.

Techniques for separation of carbon dioxide that make use of membranes are undergoing research and development in various parts of the world, and chemical and physical solvents are being used commercially. The most cost-effective separation method for coal-fired generation seems to be through gasification. Using present technology, estimates of CCS costs cover a wide range: the lead DME official on this issue talks of costs of US$50–100/ton.

South Africa has also shown enthusiasm for CCS (it has been proposed at the National Climate Change Committee as a major focus for donor-funded research), sometimes in conjunction with UCG (e.g. for the deep Waterberg coal deposits). Storage options in South Africa have only been superficially investigated and are at best limited. Some geological formations may hold potential, but both capacity and potential impacts are far from being established. Dedicated infrastructure needed to transport vast volumes of carbon dioxide becomes, as distance increases, prohibitively expensive. Australia is also promoting CCS and proposing the introduction of a regulatory framework, even before resolving extensive scientific uncertainties.

Some options for South Africa

Sorbent injection for sulphur reduction would be an effective retrofit option for existing plants burning pulverised fuel, especially if bag filters are used to capture particulate matter, rather than ESPs. Baghouse filters, which deliver greater reduction of very fine particulate emissions, have been introduced at a number of Eskom plants. However, scrubbers, which can be located after ESPs and avoid compromising precipitator performance likely to result from sorbent injection, are a cheaper option and may meet sulphur standards.

Coal-cleaning is apparently (according to informal comments by industry participants) not highly cost-effective for low-sulphur South African coal, at least for generation purposes, due to its low efficacy compared to other options, and requires additional water. With South Africa being largely semi-arid and the highveld already importing substantial amounts of water from Lesotho, dry cooling is already a standard feature for proposed new coal-fired plants as it requires less than a third of the water required for evaporative cooling.

However, a strategy to support fuel exports, rather than greater local utilisation for activities that add relatively little value to the local economy, would reduce local and national impacts as well as future vulnerability to responses to climate change. There would be some vulnerability for the coal exports, but the economy as a whole would be less dependent on carbon-intensive energy use. This suggests that coal beneficiation deserves attention, since improvements in export product would also support local availability of cleaner fuels. Conversely, if the DME takes up its commitment to making 'low-smoke fuel' – treated coal – more affordable, e.g. for domestic residential use, this could potentially reduce capital requirements for applying this technology in the electricity or export markets.

Since new generation plants will require some degree of subsidisation, and plans for a competitive market in electricity generation have been put off indefinitely, the government could effectively determine which coal technology will be deployed, through targeted financing mechanisms as well as environmental regulation and fiscal reform. Many factors contribute to making a case for the use of IGCC technology in South Africa: extensive experience of coal gasification (for liquid fuel production); high levels of GHG emissions; accumulation of 'discard' coal, for which IGCC offers viable use; aspirations to be a technology pioneer; and constitutional rights to a healthy environment. The IEA notes that efficiencies greater than 60 per cent may be possible with highly integrated designs (OECD/IEA 2000, cited in UNDP 2000). According to the *World Energy Assessment* (UNDP 2000: 283), emissions from an early IGCC demonstration plant at

Buggenum in the Netherlands are such that the externalised costs, or environmental damage costs, would in the USA be less than 2 per cent of such costs for an average coal-fired plant and about 10 per cent of such costs for coal steam-electric plants that have been fitted with the best available pollution control technology. Even without credit being given for the environmental benefits of IGCC, advances in turbine technology (using steam-cooled turbine blades) could soon make IGCC more cost-effective than steam-driven plants.

Conclusion

Coal and other fossil fuels are compatible with capitalism for a number of reasons, principally that such resources are amenable to private ownership, based mostly on paying the costs of extraction, and that concentrated energy assists in concentrating wealth, particularly through enabling large-scale mechanisation to replace labour. Not that fossil fuels are incompatible with other market structures or political philosophies, but unfettered (so-called 'free') markets favour fossil fuels over all other energy resources – it is always easier to raid the storeroom than to harvest anew.

Where fossils and 'free' markets fail to add up is in providing energy security or ensuring that full costs are brought into market prices (i.e. putting an end to the practice whereby those who profit from polluting business externalise many of the real costs for others to bear). Energy security is compromised by the long lead times of exploration, extraction and utilisation projects, such that market signals regarding diminishing supply do not stimulate new projects in time to meet the growing demand. This is not a problem for the energy companies, who earn massive profits under conditions of scarcity, but it runs quite contrary to providing affordable access to energy services for the majority. The market does not register costs incurred in other sectors, such as healthcare, and ignores needs that are not expressed through spending power; the term 'suppressed demand' has been coined to try to address the latter problem and recognise the needs of the poor, at least at the planning or project level.

Interventions are being discussed in South Africa to address these shortcomings, but no measures are yet being proposed. IEP should prove useful in this regard, but focuses very strongly on security of supply and does not have a legal mandate or effective political support. Although government has ruled out any capping of national GHG emissions in a second Kyoto Protocol commitment period (i.e. before 2019), this is likely to be recognised as needing to be in place by 2020, hopefully in time to develop the necessary legislation. Recent evidence of the impacts and pace of global warming support enforceable limitation measures being introduced a lot earlier.

Recently there has been increasing focus on local energy needs, linked to international attention to energy security. Alternative paths are being entertained, at least at a theoretical level, including options whereby countless communities that need energy services could become involved in accessing sustainable energy on a human scale. Determining the full extent and cost of missed opportunities involved in pursuing a strategy of 'business as usual' will require quantification of the potential benefits of distributed generation drawing on renewable resources. Such alternatives are not being investigated with an appropriate sense of urgency (see McDaid, Chapter 7 in this volume).

Highly concentrated energy demand drives large-scale, centralised electricity supply growth, drawing on cheaply extracted stock energy, which offers more assured returns for investors and is expected to attract international capital. This ongoing trend is consistent with the postulation of 'recolonising Africa on the power grid' – the development of infrastructure, using public spending to attract and even underwrite private investment, to reticulate power around (though probably not throughout) the continent and beyond, with Europe a lucrative market prospect and localised benefits dependent on trickle-down or knock-on effects. South Africa has not critically assessed its role within such a process.

The chairman of Eskom, Mohammed Valli Moosa, in a speech at the 2005 National Climate Change Conference, reiterated a pledge initially made during the World Summit on Sustainable Development in 2002 to reduce Eskom's dependence on coal by 10 per cent within 10 years, or by 2012.[6] However, no plan has been tabled for achieving this. The major envisaged contribution is clearly through intended expansion of nuclear capacity, with plans for a new conventional plant similar to Koeberg having been confirmed in the press (*Business Day* 13 February 2007). Eskom's most advanced plans (already undergoing an EIA) for expanding baseload capacity consist of three new pulverised coal plants with a total capacity of over 14 000 MW, which would expand coal-fired generation by about 40 per cent and, according to estimations in the EIAs, result in an increase of about 25 per cent in total national GHG emissions.

Notes

1   Estimates of 'resources' indicate the amount of material that is believed to be present,
     e.g. the amount of coal within South African territory. 'Reserves' estimates relate to the
     amount of a resource that can be economically delivered to market, i.e. what is considered
     to be exploitable with available technology and under current market conditions.
     Resource estimates are extrapolated from geological data, many of which are treated as
     proprietary information. While improved information can lead to revision, the figures are
     relatively stable. Stated reserves may be subject to frequent reassessment, as technology
     improves and real prices increase. Reserve estimates are also influenced by political and
     market factors, as the prospects for a national sector or corporate market value are
     informed by reserves believed to be at their disposal. Thus, extrapolating how long a fossil
     fuel will be available, based on current rates of use and stated reserves, does not provide a
     useful prediction.

2   Methane is generally considered separately from other VOCs, so a more precise term is non-methane VOCs.

3   In the publication the unit 'tons' is given in error, as confirmed by the lead author. This also led to extrapolated costs being given in R millions rather than thousands. Corrected figures are used below.

4   However, the report of the EIA for Matimba B, a proposed new coal-fired power plant in Lephalala, Limpopo, where the original Matimba plant operates, shows that sulphur oxide levels in the area already exceed prevailing ambient standards: 'Sulphur dioxide concentrations have been measured to infrequently exceed short-term air quality limits at several of the monitoring stations...with infrequent exceedance of such limits modelled to occur at the nearby residential areas of Marapong and Onverwacht' (Bohlweki Environmental (Pty) Ltd 2006: 273). The report concludes that 'compliance with ambient air quality standards given for sulphur dioxide cannot be achieved due to the implementation of SO_2 abatement measures for the proposed power station given that non-compliance already occurs due to existing operations' (Bohlweki Environmental (Pty) Ltd 2006: 447).

5   See http://www.iea-coal.co.uk/site/database/cct%20databases/pcc.

6   Anecdotal evidence supplied to the author.

References

Agama Energy (2003) *Employment potential of renewable energy in South Africa*. Report commissioned by the Sustainable Energy and Climate Change Partnership (SECCP). Johannesburg: SECCP

Banks D & Schäffler J (2006) *The potential contribution of renewable energy in South Africa*. Johannesburg: Earthlife Africa

Blignaut JN & De Wit M (eds) (2004) *Sustainable options. Development lessons from applied environmental economics*. Cape Town: UCT Press

Blignaut JN & King N (2002) The externality cost of coal combustion in South Africa. In JN Blignaut (ed.) *Bridging the economics/environment divide*. (Published conference proceedings). Pretoria: Forum for Economics and Environment

Blignaut JN & Lumley A (2004) Economic valuation. In JN Blignaut & M de Wit (eds) *Sustainable option. Development lessons from applied environmental economics*. Cape Town: UCT Press

Bohlweki Environmental (Pty) Ltd (2006) *Environmental impact assessment report for the proposed establishment of a new coal-fired power station in the Lephalale area, Limpopo Province*. Report prepared for the Department of Environmental Affairs and Tourism, South Africa

Clayton M (2004) After 25 years on the blacklist of America's energy sources, coal is poised to make a comeback, stoked by the demand for affordable electricity and the rising price of other fuels. *Christian Science Monitor* 26 February

Conningarth Economists NBP (2004) *Economic and financial calculations and modelling for the renewable energy strategy formulation.* Final report prepared for the National Treasury, South Africa

Creamer T (2006a) Power shift. *Engineering News* 19 May

Creamer T (2006b) R2bn mini coal-corridor project on track. *Engineering News* 19–25 May

Creamer T (2006c) Power incentive extended to $2,7bn Coega aluminium project locks in market-development and pricing commitment. *Engineering News* 1 December

DEAT (Department of Environmental Affairs and Tourism, South Africa) (1999) *1999 state of the environment report.* Pretoria: DEAT

DEAT (2006) *South Africa's country report to the Fourteenth Session of the United Nations Commission on Sustainable Development* (CSD 14). First session of the second implementation cycle (2006–2007). Pretoria: DEAT

DME (Department of Minerals and Energy, South Africa) (1998) *White Paper on Energy Policy.* Pretoria: DME

DME (2006) *Digest of South African energy statistics 2005.* Pretoria: DME

Eskom (2005) *Eskom annual report 2005.* Pretoria: Eskom

Gabbard A (n.d.), *Coal combustion: Nuclear resource or danger.* Oak Ridge National Laboratory. Accessed 30 June 2006, http://www.ornl.gov/info/ornlreview/rev26-34/text/colmain.html

Hallowes D (2006) *Sustainable energy? Towards a civil society review of South African energy policy and implementation.* Johannesburg: Earthlife Africa & Heinrich Böll Foundation

Hallowes D & Munnik V (2006) *Poisoned spaces: Manufactured wealth, producing poverty.* Pietermaritzburg: groundWork

Heinberg R (2005) *The party's over: Oil, war, and the fate of industrial societies.* Gabriola, BC: New Society Publishers

IEA (International Energy Agency) (2002) *Energy balances for non-OECD countries.* Paris: IEA

IEA (2004) *World energy outlook: Energy and poverty.* Paris: IEA

IEA (2005) *Key world energy statistics 2005.* Paris: IEA

Keating (M) (2001) *Cradle to grave: The environmental impacts from coal.* Boston, MA: Clean Air Task Force

Moodley N (2005) Wonder metal continues to shine. *Engineering News* 30 September

National Treasury (South Africa) (2006) *Draft policy paper: A framework for considering market-based instruments to support environmental fiscal reform in South Africa.* Pretoria: National Treasury Tax Policy Chief Directorate

NERSA (National Electricity Regulator of South Africa) (2004) *National Integrated Resource Plan 2003/4: Reference case.* Draft 27. Compiled by ISEP – Eskom (Resources and Strategy), Energy Research Institute, University of Cape Town and the National Electricity Regulator. Pretoria: NERSA

Prevost X (2006) Coal. In I Robinson (ed.) *South Africa's mineral industry 2005–2006.* Pretoria: Directorate: Mineral Economics

Spalding-Fecher R & Matibe DK (2003) Electricity and externalities in South Africa. *Energy Policy* 31: 721–734

Stratos Tavoulareas E & Charpentier JP (1995) *Clean coal technologies for developing countries.* World Bank Technical Paper 286. Washington DC: World Bank

Surridge AD (2003) South Africa energy economy. Paper presented at the Sustainable Energy in Africa conference, 15–17 October, Somerset West

Tyrer L (2006) Tenders in for new R1,8 bn power-station coal transport project. *Engineering News* 8 December

UNDP (2000) *World energy assessment.* New York: UNDP

US EIA (US Department of Energy, Energy Information Administration) (2006) *International energy annual 2004. Southern African Development Community Country Analysis Brief (July 2005).* Posted May–July 2006, accessed 30 June 2006, http://www.eia.doe.gov/emeu/cabs/sadc.pdf

Van der Merwe AJ & Vosloo AJ (1992) Soil pollution – Action required. Proceedings of the National Veld Trust Jubilee Congress

Van Horen C (1996) *Counting the social costs: Electricity and externalities in South Africa.* Cape Town: University of Cape Town Press & Elan Press

Venter I (2005a) Neighbours mulling cross-border power option. *Engineering News* 20 May

Venter I (2005b) Power hungry. *Engineering News* 27 May

Venter I (2006) Good neighbour. *Engineering News* 19 May

Winkler H (2006) *Energy policies for sustainable development in South Africa. Options for the future.* Cape Town: Energy Research Centre, University of Cape Town

CHAPTER 5

The great hydro-rush:
The privatisation of Africa's rivers

Terri Hathaway and Lori Pottinger

'Viva Inga! Viva Inga!' chanted then South African Minister of Water Affairs Buyelwa Sonjica on the closing day of the March 2006 African Ministerial Conference on Hydropower and Sustainable Development. The room was abuzz over Inga, a 15 kilometre stretch of rapids in the lower Congo River that reportedly holds the highest hydro-power potential in the world. The minister's words were met by cheers and applause from hundreds of African government representatives, a range of impassioned believers and energy bureaucrats.[1]

A champion of the people, Sonjica knew that 500 million Africans did not have access to electric power. As she rallied the participants, she seemed to believe the hype coming from potential developers and the hydro industry: Inga could light up Africa and form the foundation of the continent's energy future.

A discussion point which seemed lost amongst the giddiness filling the conference hall was the true risks that projects such as Inga will bring, both to communities who now depend on the Congo River and to fragile economies across Africa. The continent's history of large hydro dams has been one of overlooked social costs to local communities, lost river-based livelihoods, and unmitigated impacts on human and environmental health. Rural communities in particular have sacrificed their lands and livelihoods to these projects, yet reaped few benefits.

Time and again, Africa's large hydro development schemes have falsely promised public benefits, but instead resulted in a slowed expansion of energy access for citizens, and the privatisation of the benefits provided by rivers coupled with reduction of the many free ecosystem services they provide. Building the world's largest dam in a nearly failed state as part of a grand scheme to 'light up Africa' is not only unlikely to avoid such pitfalls, it is rapidly becoming a *cause célèbre* that threatens to divert attention from the kinds of incremental projects that might actually bring light to Africans.

This chapter reviews the destructive patterns of large dams, some experiences with hydro dams in Africa, and the efforts of the World Commission on Dams (WCD) to change these. The model of African energy development based on large hydro and centralised grid schemes is analysed, including a review of important financiers and enabling processes. The Grand Inga scheme is reviewed in detail. Finally, some recommendations for Africa's energy development are given.

The problems with large dams

Large dam projects are among the most controversial and potentially destructive of all internationally financed projects. Large dams tend to transfer river resources from one set of users to another – usually, from the poorest to the richest. An estimated 40–80 million people have been displaced by large dams worldwide. Dam displacement puts communities at great risk of decreasing their standard of living and tearing apart their social structures and culture. Efforts to resettle and compensate people for their losses have been inadequate at best (McCully 2001; WCD 2000).[2]

Nearly two-thirds of the world's rivers and their associated ecosystems are suffering from the profound and often irreversible impacts of dams. Decreased and altered water flows can change the natural patterns of flooding upon which downstream ecosystems and people rely. Dams can change water temperatures, sediment levels and chemical composition. Sediment held behind dams can cause nutrient-starved rivers to erode the river banks and bed. Aquatic species have been badly affected by the world's dams, and many extinctions have resulted. Impounding rivers in reservoirs can also cause a variety of health impacts, such as creating breeding grounds for mosquitoes and parasites, reducing water quality and quantity, and harming food security for affected communities. Millions of people living downstream of dam sites have been harmed by these impacts on riverine resources.

Many sub-Saharan countries, including Cameroon, Tanzania, Uganda, Ghana, Kenya and Zambia, are all already over-dependent on hydro-power for their electricity, and all have experienced increasingly crippling droughts that have sidelined their hydro-power production and resulted in energy shortages. All but Kenya have prioritised building more large hydro-power projects over other electricity projects – a choice that will only intensify their vulnerability to climate change. The alteration of hydrological patterns and increases in extremes of drought and flooding will cause Africa's already highly variable climate and hydrology to be even more difficult to predict.[3] For example, the Inter-governmental Panel on Climate Change cites research showing a 20 per cent reduction in run-off in the Nile Basin between 1972 and 1987, corresponding to a general decrease in precipitation in the tributary basins studied and significant interruptions in hydro-power generation as a result of severe droughts (IPCC 2001).

A recent study by climate experts at the University of Cape Town reveals that even a small decrease in rainfall on the continent can cause a drastic reduction in river flows. The study predicts that a decrease in water availability could occur across about 25 per cent of the continent. For example, a 10 per cent reduction in rain over the Johannesburg area could lead to a 70 per cent drop in the Orange River's levels. A similar situation could hit Botswana, while in parts of northern Africa, river water levels would drop more than 50 per cent (De Wit & Stankiewicz 2006). 'It's like erasing large sections of the rivers from the map,' said Maarten de Wit, who headed up the study (Pottinger 2006).

According to a 2006 study by the United Nations Environment Programme (UNEP) and the World Agroforestry Centre, one-quarter of African nations are considered water-stressed or water-scarce, and the number is expected to double in less than two decades (ICRAF & UNEP 2006). Under such conditions, free-flowing, healthy rivers will become an even more valued resource than they are today.

Numerous African hydro projects have been proposed with little or no regard to whether they are the best option for meeting citizens' energy needs. Private foreign investments usually receive guarantees which protect private developers, leaving the risks to be borne by the government and citizens. Electricity from large hydro-power will not reach the majority of Africans, who live far from the power grid; expanding the grid to reach them would be prohibitively expensive. Hydro projects increase a nation's electricity supply in big increments, an inefficient way to address the gradual increases in market demands typical of African economies.

Meanwhile, the economic benefits of hydro and other large dams are often elusive. Hydro-power dams tend to underperform in relation to their targets for power generation, providing smaller revenues for paying off debts incurred to build the projects. Lengthy construction delays and large cost over-runs are routine, making numerous projects unjustified in hindsight. For local communities, project benefits, even those promised, seem to be out of reach. Time and again, transmission lines pass over the houses of villagers next to hydro dam sites, a symbol of the many benefits from dams never captured by local people. Large hydro projects can also increase national debt burdens by tens of millions of dollars.

Hydro dams are also playing a major role in spurring the development of long-distance, regional electricity grids. While regional grids and electricity trading can provide numerous benefits, regional grid systems are biased toward developing the largest supply projects, usually from big hydro and traditional fossil fuel plants. A large hydro-power dam, which a single country may not be able to justify developing on its own, can be more easily justified as part of a regional master plan. In fact, the regional planning process helps justify development of the largest hydro dams in a region, especially if planning follows a traditional least-cost planning approach, which usually does not account for the costs of externalities such as environmental damage and the full cost of social impacts. Such planning also excludes consideration of other social objectives such as renewable energy and rural electrification targets, and diversifying the energy mix. For example, the Southern African Power Pool (SAPP) anticipates that co-ordinated planning will save the region US$3 billion over individual utility expansion planning (Economic Commission for Africa 2004: 49; World Energy Council 2003: 36).

The recipients and beneficiaries of the electrons flowing over long distances in Africa are not generally Africa's un-electrified majority but large, often foreign-owned industries and urban centres. Such projects are not the most practical way to improve access for new customers, especially not for the rural areas most in need of electrification. Wider distribution of modern energy services could bring enormous benefits for the health, education and livelihoods of the majority of Africa's rural population involved in such activities as small-scale agriculture, but for now the priority is clearly industrial expansion and mega-projects.

A brief history of Africa's big hydro dams

Hydro-power accounts for two-thirds of total electricity production in sub-Saharan Africa, excluding South Africa (US EIA 2004). Below are a few examples of Africa's troubled history with large hydro dams.

Zambia, Zimbabwe: Kariba Dam

Completed in 1959, Kariba was built to bring electricity to Zambia's Copperbelt and Zimbabwe's fast-growing manufacturing sector when the countries were still under colonial rule. At 128 metres high, it was the largest dam in Africa (and in the world) for some time and its reservoir, still one of the largest worldwide, drowned 282 kilometres of the Zambezi River and an average of 16 kilometres of river banks on either side.

The project marked the debut of the World Bank's controversial role in dam financing. Additional financing came from private banks and the Commonwealth Development Fund. The project achieved its goal of sending power to the copper-mine companies where one-third of the world's copper is mined, and numerous mining companies have prospered greatly. In Zimbabwe, the power helped build up Harare, Bulawayo and other main cities.

The Kariba Dam also achieved something that project planners did not expect and to which they had barely given a passing thought beforehand: the near genocidal destruction of the Tonga people. A total of 23 000 Tonga in Zimbabwe and 34 000 in Zambia – some two-thirds of the entire Gwembe Valley Tonga population – were dislocated by the reservoir and forced by colonial authorities to move from their ancestral lands into resettlement sites on barren ground, in conditions too cramped to support the population size. It has been deemed one of the worst resettlement projects in dam history by anthropologist Ted Scudder, an expert in the field of dam resettlement in general and Kariba in particular (Leslie 2005: 127).

Little funding was allocated to the initial resettlement, and promises to supply water and electricity in the resettlement areas were never fulfilled. The reservoir physically split the Tonga community, making it difficult to maintain family ties between the two political regions. The Tonga began suffering chronic food insecurity after losing the fertile river valley lands, where they had been able to plant and harvest crops twice a year. Today, their single crop season often yields insufficient food for subsistence. In many of the resettled communities, poor yields are exacerbated by elephants invading crop fields, and a lack of government response to the problem. The effects of food insecurity, separation of Tonga families across the reservoir, and unfulfilled promises of water and electricity in the resettlement areas have led to a disintegration of many aspects of Tonga culture.

In addition to the immediate harm caused by the poorly managed resettlement process, the Tonga people have been excluded from sharing in the project's economic benefits. Much of the land lining the reservoir was turned into national parks in Zimbabwe or snatched up by colonialists and expatriates in Zambia. The fishing industry has been largely exploited by outsiders able to leverage capital to invest in fishing boats and other equipment. For Tonga fishermen, even the licences they must buy to fish are prohibitively expensive. In addition, no mechanisms were put in place to share revenues generated from tourism, commercial fisheries or sales of hydro-power.

Kariba Dam controls more than 40 per cent of the total run-off of the Zambezi River, and is operated to generate steady hydro-power production by storing peak floods and releasing a constant outflow of water. Much of the rest of the river flow is captured by Cahora Bassa and two large dams on the Kafue River, a major tributary of the Zambezi. These dams have collectively had major environmental impacts all the way downstream to the Indian Ocean, with major economic and social implications for those dependent on the ecosystem. Kariba Dam's environmental impacts were not assessed at the time of construction.

Amidst the years of kleptocratic rule, and the chaos of today's hyper-inflation and a near-bankrupt government, Zimbabwe's electricity sector has fallen into disrepair. In recent years, concerns have been raised about the dam's safety and the catastrophic risk all the way to the Zambezi Delta should the dam ever fail. The project's current status is uncertain, however: a US Army Corps of Engineers' team was not permitted to visit the dam wall during an inspection of Zambezi dams around the time of major floods in 2000. The project design also did not take into account the risk of earthquakes, although the project was built in a seismically active area.

Mozambique: Cahora Bassa Dam

In 1999, Dr Richard Beilfuss, a hydrologist with the International Crane Foundation, summarised the experience of the Cahora Bassa Dam as follows:

> While Kariba was built before the impacts of dams were well-understood, Cahora Bassa, just downstream on the Zambezi River, has no such excuse. The degree to which scientists' concerns were ignored in the planning of the Cahora Bassa project is staggering. Before the dam was completed in 1975,

South African river ecologist Dr Bryan Davies warned of the dam's severe consequences in a pre-project assessment: 'Reduced artisanal fisheries and shrimp industry productivity, reduced silt deposition and nutrient availability, severe coastal erosion, soil salinization, salt water intrusion, replacement of wetland vegetation by invasive upland species, reduction in coastal mangroves, failure of vegetation to recover from grazing, and disrupted or mistimed reproductive patterns for wildlife species.'

Just ten years later, deleterious changes to the Zambezi's riverine, wetland, deltaic and coastal ecosystems were already apparent. Fisheries ecologists G Bernacsek and S Lopez lamented in a UN document, 'It is clear that in the case of Cahora Bassa there was no serious attempt to ecologically optimize the dam prior to construction…Cahora Bassa has the dubious distinction of being the least studied and possibly least environmentally acceptable major dam project in Africa.' For decades, erratic and mistimed flooding below Cahora Bassa Dam has adversely affected the living standards of hundreds of thousands of downstream households and decimated one of the most productive and diverse wetland ecosystems in Africa, the Zambezi Delta.

The impacts predicted years ago have sadly come true. Due to the lack of the natural seasonal variations in flow, the once lucrative delta prawn fishery has declined precipitously, and only one of the main channels of the Zambezi Delta mouth supports relatively healthy mangrove. According to Davies, 'there are now large gaps in the mangrove forest along the entire northern and southern sectors that didn't exist prior to 1975, and areas of coastal erosion with dead mangroves in evidence.' Downstream residents have been further impoverished by the changes in river flow, sedimentation, and to species they depended on. Research by Mozambican ornithologist Carlos Bento suggests that the breeding cycles of many delta species have been disrupted by the irregular flooding patterns below Cahora Bassa Dam.

The devastation of the lower Zambezi seems all the more tragic in view of the fact that power lines were sabotaged shortly after the dam was completed. For more than 17 years, all but one of Cahora Bassa's turbines remained idle while Mozambique's civil war raged. Only in the past few years has power production been restored to its original capacity. (Beilfuss 1999: 8–9)

Ghana: Akosombo Dam

In 1960, Ghana embarked on its West-approved path toward prosperity. President Kwame Nkrumah had adopted a scheme that would drive the newly independent country into industrial and economic development. The scheme's cornerstone was a vertically integrated aluminium sector, the most energy-intensive industry in the world, powered by Akosombo hydro-power dam. Today, Akosombo Dam generates most of the country's power, but less than half the population has access to electricity.[4]

Fifty years on, the negotiating power of Ghana's government is proving no match for the powerful aluminium companies with whom it is dealing, and Ghana's integrated aluminium industry has not yet materialised. The long-term power purchase agreement guaranteed sales of electricity to the aluminium smelter for decades at a locked-in, ultra-low rate, while residential tariffs more than doubled, in part due to growing demand beyond the leftover supply. Benefits in terms of taxes and other revenues generated and local jobs created have been minimal. The government has at times been forced to import oil and use thermal generators to help meet its domestic electricity demand. The smelter's supply of cheap electricity means that ordinary Ghanaians increasingly subsidise the operating expenses of wealthy aluminium companies. No final products from the raw aluminium are produced in Ghana and virtually all inputs besides electricity are imported. Even though Ghana has bauxite, the mineral used in aluminium, it has no refinery to turn the mineral into alumina, the production step prior to smelting it into aluminium. The foreign companies have purposely kept their investments in Ghana away from the missing production steps in order to maintain their own vertically integrated production, which involves processing plants owned by subsidiaries in multiple countries.

Akosombo's reservoir, which displaced thousands of people in a poorly managed resettlement process, flooded 4 per cent of Ghana's land mass and represented the largest constructed lake at the time of its creation, has dropped so low that in February 2007 the aluminium smelter closed for the 11th time in its 40 years of operation, causing load shedding. While the 2007 closure left 700 employees out of work and was expected to last until 2008, it helped to boost aluminium prices on the world market, allowing foreign corporations to profit. Ghana's over-dependence on hydro-power, coupled with recent droughts, anticipated climate change, and a failed industrialisation strategy, have left Ghana's electricity sector and economy vulnerable.

South Africa: Gariep and Van der Kloof dams

The Gariep and Van der Kloof dams were part of the Orange River Development Project, a massive irrigation scheme whose roots were intimately tied to the development of South Africa's apartheid regime. As planned in the 1960s, hydro-power was one of numerous secondary functions of the project, while irrigation was the primary goal.

Gariep was commissioned in 1971 and Van der Kloof in 1978. The dams were originally planned with the option of raising each dam's height in later phases of the scheme. However, instead of waiting, both dams were built to their greatest height at the time of original construction, due in part to increasing demands for power generation. This decision increased the size of the reservoir and the number of people displaced, and was responsible for much of the project's cost increases (from US$571 million in 1962/63 to US$870 million two years later) (WCD 1998: 18).

The apartheid regime used the dams and the Orange River Development Project as a tool of development for the politically powerful white minority, and as a weapon against South Africa's black communities. The dispossession of black farm labourers during construction of the Gariep and Van der Kloof dams was done with no consultation and virtually no compensation. They were dislocated en masse to the strip of land between each dam's right of way and the road, known as the corridor. Due to policies prohibiting black people from freely moving to urban areas, many in the corridor squatted there for no less than 10 years. The squatters were forced to sell their valuables, including cattle, to buy food and other goods to meet basic needs. At a public hearing for dam-affected communities held in Cape Town in 1999, one woman recalled, 'I am even more poor than I was before, because the farmer just told us to move from the farm' (Mbalula 1999). She gave birth in the corridor shortly after being displaced.

The displaced communities suffered cultural and spiritual losses, too. Ancestral burial grounds under the dam reservoir were not properly moved and communities were not consulted about the impact on community grave sites beforehand. As of 2007, communities affected by these dams were continuing to struggle for adequate redress for the unjust impacts experienced as a result of the development of the dams.

The relevance of the World Commission on Dams for Africa

Like those communities affected by dams in Africa, numerous other communities around the world were also experiencing this reallocation of public river resources, marginalisation of their peoples, and degradation to the environment caused by dams. During the 1980s and 1990s, an intensifying chorus of voices from communities affected by dams around the globe was being echoed by their allies in civil society. With a fierce public campaign to expose World Bank and other public funding for dam projects, the global movement gained leverage in 1998 when the World Bank agreed to a review of the impact of the world's large dams. The independent WCD was born.

Between 1998 and 2000, the WCD undertook an unprecedented global process to review large dams and their development effectiveness. Twelve commissioners, representing a variety of backgrounds and a broad spectrum of interests in large dams, were appointed. A secretariat was set up in Cape Town, South Africa, and headed by former South African Minister of Water Affairs Kader Asmal. The Commission's mandate was twofold:
- to review the development effectiveness of large dams and assess alternatives for water resources and energy development; and
- to develop internationally acceptable criteria, guidelines and standards for the planning, design, appraisal, construction, operation, monitoring and decommissioning of dams (WCD 2000).

In November 1999, South African non-governmental organisations (NGOs), led by the Environmental Monitoring Group in Cape Town, organised the Southern African Hearings for Communities Affected by Large Dams, whose final report was submitted to the WCD (Environmental Monitoring Group 1999). Other important African contributions were made to the WCD Knowledge Base, including a case study on Kariba Dam, a case study on the Van der Kloof and Gariep dams in South Africa, and a regional consultation on Africa and the Middle East.[5]

In its final report, the WCD found that while 'dams have made an important and significant contribution to human development, and benefits derived from them have been considerable...in too many cases an unacceptable and often unnecessary price has been paid to secure those benefits, especially in social and environmental terms, by people displaced, by communities downstream, by taxpayers and by the natural environment' (WCD 2000: 310). The report went on to say that a 'lack of equity in the distribution of benefits has called into question the value of many dams in meeting water and energy development needs when compared with the alternatives'.

The WCD recommends transparent and participatory decision-making, and advocates for directly affected communities to be able to negotiate legally binding agreements with developers. Such an approach favours projects with low social, economic and environmental risks and high rewards for communities. Implementing the WCD recommendations would lead to energy policies which optimise existing infrastructure before building new schemes, and give preference to decentralised projects with widespread benefits over centralised mega-projects with unmanageable social and environmental impacts and benefits for limited areas.

Since the release of the WCD's final report, efforts have been made to promote its rights-based approach to water and energy planning across Africa. In South Africa, efforts were under way almost immediately to conduct a national dialogue on how to integrate the WCD recommendations into national policies and planning. The South African Multi-Stakeholder Initiative on the WCD culminated in its final substantive report in late 2004 (South African Multi-Stakeholder Initiative 2004). The Initiative's supporters now face the daunting task of implementing its recommendations in the form of tangible changes to South African governmental policy and regulation.

Impassioned NGOs in other countries have attempted to replicate the South African Initiative by educating local communities on the WCD's findings and by launching national multi-stakeholder dialogues in order to review and improve their respective nations' laws and policies relevant to energy and water planning. In Uganda, the National Association of Professional Environmentalists (NAPE) brought together various stakeholders for the Uganda Dams Dialogue. The group launched its final report in March 2007 (Muhweezi 2006). The report included the group's recommendations based on three years of work and a scoping report.

However, a major absence from the process was any discussion about the ongoing Bujagali Dam, the country's most controversial proposed dam. According to NAPE, the Dialogue experience improved communication between stakeholders, but limited political commitment and funding are hindering the steering committee from implementing the recommendations (see Gore, Chapter 14 of this volume, for a more detailed discussion of the situation in Uganda).

In Nigeria, the Society for Water and Public Health Protection (SWAPHEP), a local NGO, has spent years motivating government and community stakeholders to come together to discuss the WCD report. In 2005 and 2006, SWAPHEP undertook a series of community workshops to raise awareness of the WCD recommendations and the nation's history of dams. At the same time, the director of SWAPHEP met repeatedly with staff overseeing dams and reservoirs within the national Ministry of Water Resources. In February 2007, years of effort culminated in a national consultative conference on the WCD. But as SWAPHEP's director noted, 'Hopes to take the work forward are trying to stay afloat amongst a lack of funds.'[6] Civil society groups in Ghana, Togo and Senegal are also following suit with WCD processes, unfortunately with similar battles for funding, stakeholder interest and adequate political will.

While all of these efforts have begun to open the dams planning process to civil society, and have raised serious concerns about dams, across much of Africa it is 'business as usual'. Chinese financing is helping to drive Mambila Dam in Nigeria and Bui Dam in Ghana. In Uganda, the World Bank, European Investment Bank (EIB), African Development Bank (AfDB) and other lenders are on board to build the US$799 million Bujagali Dam on the Nile. Only in Togo has the Adjarala Dam been put on hold.

The Southern African Development Community (SADC) also made some efforts to consider the WCD's recommendations and contextualise them within the SADC's planning framework. In 2002, the SADC twice encouraged its member states to hold national consultations on the WCD recommendations, but only South Africa has done so in any comprehensive way. One-time workshops have been held in Namibia, Lesotho, and Zambia, but without substantive follow-up. The SADC reports that it has integrated the WCD into its water policy, but the policy's adequacy has not been validated through any process involving civil society and affected communities. SADC has made little effort to proactively engage civil society in dialogues and project decisions relevant to the SADC regional energy and water planning.

In 2003, the German development agency GTZ, a supporter of WCD implementation in Africa, published *Key Dam Issues in the SADC Region* (Clanahan & Hughes 2003). The report gave a brief comparative overview of SADC policies against the WCD's seven strategic priorities, as a basis for policy recommendations which would improve the decision-making framework in the SADC region. Of the 839 large dams in the SADC region, 539 are in South Africa and 213 in Zimbabwe. The report noted that many dams in southern Africa are reaching an age where maintenance and refurbishment costs will be significant.

The report also noted that there is a dearth of regulation for dam safety in the SADC region, with only South Africa having extensive safety policies.

Since the release of the WCD final report, African NGOs monitoring dam developments, promoting the WCD and advocating for communities affected by past dams have come together to build a regional network. In 2003, they announced the creation of the African Rivers Network (ARN), a semi-formal network for information exchange on the continent. Today, the network is growing and it is the most active regional civil-society network monitoring hydro-power development in Africa. ARN believes that future hydro dams can benefit Africa only after the legacy of past dams is addressed and if the WCD recommendations are followed. ARN is also committed to furthering research on the impacts of dams and alternatives to them, particularly renewable energy options.

Surprisingly, there is agreement between international development agencies and civil society that regulatory frameworks for energy planning in Africa are sorely inadequate. But Africa as a whole has been raised to a level of international crisis, and the gap in hard infrastructure is being tackled with such urgency that development financiers like the World Bank say they cannot wait for changes in the regulatory frameworks.

Sadly, the lessons of the WCD are not being streamlined into African institutions at the same rate as large-scale energy schemes are being planned and built. Those setting the infrastructure agenda are fostering a crisis-like climate about Africa's underdeveloped energy sector, allowing large-scale projects to be fast-tracked without first filling the known gap in regulatory frameworks, a measure which would help steer decision-making towards electricity and energy projects better suited to meet the needs of Africa's poor, rural majority.

The new push for dam development in Africa

In the past, big dams in Africa were promoted and financed primarily by the World Bank. Today, there are many more players and processes promoting large hydro developments, and the World Bank, which had begun to retreat from building big dams in Africa, is back. In this section we look at some of these new influences.

The plan adopted at the 2002 World Summit on Sustainable Development (WSSD) called upon the international community 'to improve access to reliable and affordable energy services for sustainable development sufficient to facilitate the achievement of the Millennium Development Goals (MDGs)...bearing in mind that access to energy facilitates the eradication of poverty' (WSSD 2002: 5). However, the New Partnership for Africa's Development (NEPAD) and the international community lining up behind it have focused a disproportionate amount of their efforts on energy projects for economic growth through industrial development, rather than on a plan for rural energy and development programmes that would directly address the MDGs.

The UK government's Commission for Africa identified the need for a US$50 billion injection into Africa's infrastructure by 2010 and a doubling of funds thereafter, intended to drive a 7 per cent growth rate in GDP. Ironically though, the Commission also said that developed countries 'should avoid funding prestige projects that have so often turned into white elephants in the past' (Commission for Africa 2005: 49).

But white elephants could again be part of Africa's future, as the golden word amongst governmental powers and development financiers wanting to spur Africa's economic growth is infrastructure, and in particular large hydro dams. A potentially massive financial commitment to Africa's infrastructure is becoming a magnet for big hydro-power schemes and their supporting long-distance grid systems envisioned by energy planners for the continent. Decision-making processes are being fast-tracked from the outset in order to keep up with the G8's promises to disburse funds through various facilities, including the creation of the Infrastructure Consortium for Africa (ICA), the EU-Africa Infrastructure Trust Fund, and the Infrastructure Project Preparation Facility (IPPF). The lack of transparent and participatory strategic planning means less oversight and accountability for the electricity sector agenda.

The ICA was born out of the G8's attempt to address Africa's infrastructure gap and provide a platform for collaboration between the private sector, financiers and African governments. Housed under the AfDB, the ICA acts as a broker, partnering projects and donors. Its emphasis is on regional priority projects shortlisted by NEPAD. The ICA's secretariat staff is provided by the AfDB and the governments of the UK and Japan, and its budget is funded by the UK, AfDB, and the Public Private Infrastructure Advisory Facility (housed in the World Bank).[7]

While in some ways the ICA is a tool to help streamline multi-agency collaboration, their agenda continues to be mega-projects, especially mega-dams and transmission lines which support centralised grid energy development. Streamlining collaboration could help support comprehensive project decision-making, but the collaboration is between agencies, not with civil society. The purpose of streamlining is not so much to improve decision-making amongst stakeholders, nor to make decision-makers more accountable, but to accelerate projects which have already received priority status through a process that has marginalised civil-society influence. Although the ICA has recognised that a large financing gap exists in the upstream area of project planning, it is not clear if they will work to make the upstream planning process more inclusive, transparent or accountable.

One year after the G8 conference at Gleneagles in Britain in 2005, the ICA surpassed its own goals by securing funding decisions on 10 regional projects totalling US$700 million, plus 13 studies (US$8 million) and 34 country-level projects (US$1.8 billion), including five NEPAD priority projects. In June 2006, the ICA noted that Africa's vast hydro-power potential was still largely untapped. In

January 2007, the ICA held its third meeting; the government of China and China Exim Bank both participated for the first time, signalling their desire to work with the ICA.

Also as a response to Gleneagles, the EU created the EU Strategy for Africa, under which the EU-Africa Infrastructure Partnership was created as one of the Strategy's pillars. The EU-Africa Infrastructure Trust Fund, launched in April 2007, is the financing instrument of the Partnership. The Fund is housed under the EIB and will channel EU commitments made at Gleneagles to support regional projects. Already the Fund has received €87 million and leveraged €260 million in loans from the EIB. The Félou hydro dam in the Senegal River basin, an identified NEPAD priority project, is receiving EU support through the Fund.

The IPPF evolved from a Canadian into a multi-donor facility after Gleneagles. Like the ICA, the IPPF is housed at the AfDB. By mid-2007, the IPPF was expected to capitalise up to US$30 million and to develop a pipeline of regional projects worth around US$600 million. The Africa Partnership Forum, tasked with monitoring implementation of Gleneagles' commitments, has called for more contributions to the IPPF and has agreed to support the building of technical capacity for project design and development.

The NEPAD strategy, fully supported by the G8's Gleneagles' commitments, continues to be kept well out of the sphere of public influence, while financial commitments line up behind it and official spin twists corporate economic growth into poverty alleviation. Formed in 2001, NEPAD was spun as the African home-grown plan for the continent's development, but was fully immersed in traditional northern views of industrial economic growth. NEPAD has included energy infrastructure at the top of its agenda, most notably via two infrastructure plans: the *Short-Term Action Plan* published in 2002 (NEPAD 2002) and the forthcoming Medium- to Long-Term Strategic Framework currently in preparation. The longer-term strategy is expected to be the primary guide for Africa's infrastructure development for the next 20 years.

Together, these two strategies propose numerous large dams and transmission interconnection projects. By June 2006 funding totalling US$764.3 million was committed for a total of 11 short-term priority projects. A further US$7.1 million was committed to studies designed to advance the implementation of short-term projects. In 2004, UN-Energy/Africa (UNEA) was set up as a UN inter-agency effort to provide streamlined support for NEPAD's energy strategy.[8] Dams prioritised under NEPAD include Mozambique's Mphanda Nkuwa on the Zambezi River, the Grand Inga project on the Congo River in the Democratic Republic of the Congo (DRC), Adjarala Dam in Benin, and the Souapiti and Kaleta dams in Guinea.

NEPAD is also aligned with the six-phase strategy of the African Economic Community (AEC) to create a continental economic bloc by 2028. The AEC was established by treaty under the African Union in 1991 and ratified in 1994. Now in its second phase, the strategy of the AEC is based on the goals of strengthening regional economic communities and energy sector integration. As part of this, the regional economic communities have been given the task of developing regional power grids and a complementary set of power pools which oversee the development of an electricity market. Power pools have been developed to conduct electricity trading, and regional master plans for each power pool have or are being prepared. All of these power pools require significant funding and technical support to become operational and effective. In January 2007, offers of further support for building the capacity of regional power pools were received from the European Commission, Japan and the USA.

The four power pools in sub-Saharan Africa are:
- the SAPP: includes the 12 countries of the SADC and was established in 1995;
- the East African Power Pool (EAPP): includes at least seven countries from the Common Market for Eastern and Southern Africa, the East African Community, and the Nile Basin Initiative (NBI) and was established in 2005;
- the Central African Power Pool or Pool Energétique d'Afrique Centrale (PEAC): includes 11 countries of the Economic Community of Central African States and was established in 2003;
- the West African Power Pool (WAPP): includes 14 countries in the Economic Community of West African States and was established in 2000.

Numerous hydro dams are being fast-tracked as priority projects under regional power master plans, but neither the process nor the criteria by which these projects were prioritised is clear. Regional power plans in Africa are further removing energy planning from public view and making it increasingly difficult for civil-society groups to monitor and engage in planning processes. These plans generally include national-level priority projects and national-level predictions of demand growth, inputs often developed without public participation or oversight. Regional economic communities are also playing an increasingly important role in project planning and decision-making, and may soon receive borrowing authority for trans-boundary energy projects. The lack of awareness about regional energy development amongst national populations and the growing authority of the regional economic communities are further minimising scrutiny at the national level. Africa is not home to a strong regional or multinational civil society, so regional projects are likely to receive less 'sunshine' than those at a national level.

In April 2002, the SAPP Executive Committee agreed to intensify its efforts to attract energy-intensive users into the SADC region 'to take advantage of low-cost, high-quality and reliable electricity' (SAPP 2002). Like an echo of this strategy, the World Bank's Southern African Power Market (SAPM) programme for the SAPP expects to 'increase the availability and reliability of low cost, environmentally friendly electric energy in the Southern African region, thereby increasing competitiveness of industry and fostering economic growth' (World Bank 2003a: 3). Project documents argue that regional integration will attract private developers and would save the region at least US$1 billion over 16 years (World Bank 2003a).

The SAPM is anticipated to be a three-phase project worth a total of nearly US$1 billion in Bank and non-Bank financing. Overall goals include: strengthening the capability of the Coordination Centre of the SAPP to promote and manage electricity trade in the region; removing transmission bottlenecks that inhibit trade; and connecting member countries that at present are not connected to the regional grid. According to the SAPP, electricity demand is growing at an average of 3 per cent per year.

The first phase, approved in November 2003, includes rehabilitating the transmission line from Inga in the DRC to the Zambian Copperbelt and a study of a transmission interconnection to Tanzania. The project also includes environmental studies for the future expansion of the DRC power sector. Project co-financing is expected from bilateral donors, including USAID and NORAD. The second phase, approved in June 2007, is support for a transmission connection between Mozambique and Malawi at a cost of US$87.4 million. Phase-three lending will be directed at the governments of Tanzania, Zambia and the DRC and will cost US$220.5 million.

While World Bank documents identified the SAPP's Integrated Regional Power Master Plan as a key document prior to the Bank's first SAPM loan, communication with the Bank concluded that this actually refers to 'a list of priority projects in generation and transmission system expansion to meet the short-, medium- and long-term needs of the growing regional power market... The priority proposed schemes/projects were based on preliminary screening taking into account estimated cost, and status of preparedness, status of financing arrangements'.[9] After using a non-existent study to help justify the World Bank loan in 2003, the Bank and the SAPP are belatedly undertaking a study on regional least-cost generation and transmission, which was expected to be completed by April 2008, which 'would serve as [the] basis of discussion with member utilities for development to meet the demand over the long term in the regional market' (see note 9).

In West Africa, the WAPP is anticipated to be fully operational by 2023. A regional master plan based on national planning and utilities was completed for the WAPP in 2004 with USAID funding, which is also supporting the institutional needs of the WAPP. The master plan projects electricity demand will grow 7.6 per cent per year, from the current 6 500 megawatt (MW) peak demand to over 22 000 MW. Nigeria is set to consume two-thirds of the electricity (Nexant 2004). Priority hydro projects include Felou in Mali, funded by the World Bank and the EIB, Kaleta in Guinea and Sambangalou in Senegal. While only about one in three West Africans has access to electricity, it is not clear whether increasing access to the grid via new connections will be a targeted goal of the WAPP.

In Central Africa, USAID is also financing a study on a regional master plan for power development, and an interconnection feasibility study has been funded by the AfDB. In East Africa, the EAPP is already developing a master plan. World Bank staff have announced several proposed interconnections cited as key projects for the EAPP: Lake Victoria Transmission Ring, Zambia–Tanzania–Kenya Interconnector, Ethiopia–Kenya Interconnector, and Rusumo Falls Hydropower Project with a backbone transmission network between Tanzania, Rwanda and Burundi. The World Bank-supported Nile Equatorial Lakes Strategic Action Plan was released in early 2007, highlighting Bujagali and Rusomo Falls dams as regional priorities.

Development banks re-engage

The World Bank and EIB, long involved in dam building in Africa, began to retreat from dam financing in the 1990s. This coincided with growing public criticism of dams, the birth of the WCD, and assumptions that the private sector would fill the funding gap. However, seeing large-scale infrastructure projects as their comparative advantage, these multilateral development banks have jumped back into dam financing in Africa, particularly through projects emerging from regional grid plans backed by the World Bank. The Bank launched its re-entry with its 2003 'high-reward/high-risk' water sector strategy (World Bank 2003b).[10] Small-scale projects, though they may better serve the populations in need and meet the Bank's stated goal of poverty reduction, are mostly left to bilateral or other, non-governmental, funders. Dams have the advantage for the banks of moving significant amounts of funding through single projects, projects which have built numerous careers within these institutions.[11] At the time of writing, the Bank was backing Bujagali Dam in Uganda and the rehabilitation of existing dams in the DRC and Nigeria, as well as Felou Dam in Mali and the dam-heavy plans of the NBI.[12]

The AfDB, too, is playing an increasingly important role in regional dam building. Besides housing the ICA secretariat and the IPPF, the AfDB is the lead agency for NEPAD's infrastructure development and houses a NEPAD unit. These multiple initiatives and the AfDB's increased orientation toward infrastructure financing make the AfDB an important institution for civil society to monitor. The AfDB is the *de facto* co-ordinator for Africa's energy priority projects and for measures taken to ensure that the first projects to receive funds will have the maximum positive impact on continental growth opportunities. Along with the World Bank, the AfDB recently approved funding for the Bujagali Dam in Uganda. At the time of writing, the inspection panels of each bank were set to conduct investigations into concerns raised by civil society; this would be the first project investigation to be conducted by the AfDB's inspection panel.

Pension funds have also recently been identified as a source of investment funds for large infrastructure. In July 2007, the AfDB and the Development Bank of Southern Africa (DBSA) launched the Pan-African Infrastructure Development Fund to invest in large-scale infrastructure. The Fund, also a NEPAD initiative, is hoping to raise US$1.2 billion and to leverage US$9–14 billion in projects by 2015.

Ghana's Social Security & National Insurance Trust and South Africa's Public Investment Corporation have both committed to investing. Four private southern African banks have also joined. Other pension funds from as far away as Singapore are considering joining. The Fund is already reviewing nearly 20 projects. The AfDB and DBSA will each have at least 10 per cent shares in the management committee (Benton 2007; Mahlangu 2007).

The Islamic Development Bank has helped finance controversial dams in Africa, including Merowe Dam (Sudan) and Manantali Dam (Mali/Senegal). The Bank recently announced a new US$10 billion Poverty Alleviation Fund for Africa to finance projects targeting the MDGs (Organisation of the Islamic Conference 2007). However, little information about the fund or its projects is publicly available.

Smaller regional development banks in Africa may also begin to play an increasingly important role. The DBSA has played a vital role, especially in protecting South Africa's interests. In addition, the Central African Development Bank is funding a feasibility study of M'emvele Dam in south-west Cameroon.

South Africa's Eskom, the single largest African utility, is arguably the most influential African voice in electricity planning (see Chapters 2 and 3 in this volume for more on Eskom). Eskom's influence is driven by its size, value, and the power-hungry country it serves. Until recently, Eskom has been in charge of all of South Africa's electricity, which accounts for roughly half of the entire continent's electricity consumption. Eskom is helping to drive SADC's energy policy and Westcor's plans to bring power from the DRC and Angola to South Africa (see below, p. 169), and is an anticipated beneficiary of the Mphanda Nkuwa Dam proposed for the Zambezi in Mozambique. Although Eskom took part in the South African WCD Initiative, nothing legally binds the utility to follow the WCD recommendations in its business activities, either in South Africa or abroad.

China dragon slays African rivers

While the World Bank and European governments continue to be important financiers of hydro dams, power pools and sector reform, they are by no means alone. China is the most important player on the African scene today.

Africa's vast bounty of oil and other raw resources has whetted China's industrial appetite, and Africa's population has become a captive consumer of China's cheap imports. Chinese corporations, financial institutions, and the Chinese government have shown a growing strategic interest in Africa, marked in 2005 by US$39 billion in China–Africa trade. One of China's only requirements is that its African partners do not recognise Taiwan. Following the November 2006 Sino-Africa summit held in Beijing, China committed to investing US$5 billion in African infrastructure over the next three years, and launched the China-Africa Development Fund in early 2007 as its vehicle to implement its promised funding. The Fund's first US$1 billion came from the state-owned China Development Bank.

Chinese companies and financiers are already involved in a number of large African dams worth billions of dollars. The controversial Merowe Dam in Sudan, currently under construction, is financed by the China Exim Bank. Tekeze Dam in Ethiopia, also under construction, is financed by China. Chinese financing is being lined up for other proposed controversial hydro dams, including Mphanda Nkuwa Dam in Mozambique, Bui Dam in Ghana, Mambila Dam in Nigeria and Souapiti Dam in Guinea.

Civil society and dam-affected peoples' movements are concerned that China's own poor record on protecting human rights and the environment could mean trouble for African rivers now targeted for Chinese-built large dams.

Rallying the troops: conferences on hydro

In March 2006, the government of South Africa, in close collaboration with the industry lobby group International Hydropower Association (IHA), hosted the African Ministerial Conference on Hydropower and Sustainable Development in Johannesburg. Organisers planned to have only a handful of pre-approved civil-society representatives attending. After months of struggling with conference planners, members of the ARN succeeded in gaining invitations and locating funds to participate in this high-level forum. Civil society managed to gain an additional foothold in the event when they received the opportunity to include a dam-affected person to make a presentation on the social impacts panel. Towards the end of the conference, civil society also had an opportunity to share its position in a statement, which read in part: 'Before new hydropower investments commence, the historical injustices must be addressed. We call upon our governments to share both the cost of breaking the eggs and benefiting from the omelettes equitably, but not to leave the burdens related to dams to the community and all the benefits to others at the cost of the community' (Dumba 2006).

The conference's final action plan included broad statements of civil society inclusion (e.g. 'Ministers commit themselves to involve civil society in all aspects of hydropower development') (African Ministerial Conference 2006: 3) but the plan is ultimately designed to smooth the way for Africa to follow a large hydro-based energy path, with few inroads along the way for civil society. As described by the WCD, by the time a decision is taken to develop a hydro-power project, critical strategic decisions on how best to meet energy needs have already been taken. The action plan in no way speaks to civil society's need to participate at these earlier stages. Given the advanced stage of the region's 'priority lists' of large-dam projects, and the close association with hydro-power interests such as the IHA, it is unlikely that this bedrock WCD strategic priority will be followed. Another key component of the action plan is the creation of an African Hydropower Symposium which would be housed within the African Energy Commission (AFREC) and work closely with the IHA. AFREC was also given secretariat responsibilities for following up the conference action plan.

Another conference relevant to Africa's hydro development was the Second Financing for Development Conference titled 'Infrastructure for Growth – The Energy Challenge', organised by the UN Economic Commission for Africa and the AfDB in May 2007.[13] The conference theme was energy, infrastructure and its contribution to economic growth. Although the conference noted the role of energy in meeting the MDGs, the conference action plan was focused on longer-term national energy planning, the importance of regional infrastructure, and the challenges of ensuring adequate financing, particularly for post-conflict countries. The conference action plan included plans to fast-track current regional initiatives, including the Inga Dam project and regional power pools, to strengthen regional economic communities and NEPAD.

Grand Inga, or Grand illusion?

Many institutions now see a regional energy integration scheme for Africa as a top development priority. At the heart of this vision is the near-mythical bend in the Congo River known as the Inga Rapids. The Inga site, located 150 kilometres upstream of the mouth of the Congo River and about 225 kilometres downstream of Kinshasa, has the greatest hydro-power potential in the world. It has attracted a variety of international partners who are touting the proposed multi-dam Inga hydro-power scheme as the cornerstone of an African power grid, and a solution to Africa's energy woes. Amongst its many supporters are SADC officials, led by Eskom, who see hydro-power from Inga as fundamental to meeting South Africa's growing electricity demand. The World Energy Council and other champions of Inga are spreading a strong media message: Grand Inga will light up Africa, and Africa will thrive.

But critics note a host of problems that make Inga more of a white elephant than a roaring lion. The Inga site is set in one of the most politically volatile and economically corrupt countries of Africa. Its enormous cost would impede trickle-up energy projects for decades to come. Like each regional power plan, Inga is being driven largely by mining and industrial interests, sectors known for their opaque dealings and exploitation of local workers and communities. A transparent framework for natural resource and power export revenues is lacking. No good-faith efforts are being made to consider options which could more effectively meet the MDGs and resolve the outstanding social and environmental issues related to the existing Inga 1 and 2 dams. The planning of the grid scheme itself lacks transparency, public participation and democratic decision-making. Current plans lack an equally well-funded distribution network, an indication of the plans' benefits to energy-intensive industry and urban centres. There are even enthusiastic, though perhaps unrealistic, discussions about power exports to Europe and the Middle East.

The Inga projects include three stages of power supply which would support existing and planned regional transmission grids: rehabilitation of the existing dams Inga 1 and 2, construction of Inga 3 (3 500 MW), and construction of Grand Inga (44 000 MW). As planned, Inga would eventually connect directly to all four sub-Saharan power grids.

Inga 1 (351 MW) was built in 1972 and Inga 2 (1 424 MW) was built in 1982, both with Italian support. Analysis of the then proposed dams found that they were not economically feasible, even taking into account the plan to attract the aluminium industry as an anchor customer. But then-president Mobutu went ahead and built the pair of white elephants anyway, disregarding the economic analysis prepared by French consultants, and consistently neglecting maintenance requirements. It is estimated that the Inga 1 and 2 dams alone are responsible for over half of the DRC's external debt.

Although the Inga 1 and 2 dams are not particularly old, they are currently undergoing a second, intensive rehabilitation effort. Poor maintenance, and significant siltation of the shared canal and reservoir, have left the two dams operating at only 30 per cent capacity. One would think that the bursting population of nearby Kinshasa would be devastated by this. But even at 30 per cent the dams still export power to mining activities in southern DRC, the Zambian Copperbelt and South Africa rather than satisfying the needs of Kinshasa's more than 5 million urban residents now without electricity.

In 2005, MagEnergy, a subsidiary of Canadian-based MagIndustries, signed its own agreement with Société Nationale d'Electricité (SNEL, the state-owned electricity utility in the DRC) to rehabilitate four of the eight turbines at Inga 2 through an undisclosed power purchase and partial privatisation agreement. The rehabilitation is anticipated to cost US$100 million. MagAlloy, also a subsidiary of MagIndustries, plans to build a potash plant and magnesium smelter at nearby towns Kouilou and Point Noire, respectively. Agreements have already been made to build a 200 kilometre transmission line from the dam to the smelter, which will receive a guaranteed 120 MW from the rehabilitated Inga 2 Dam. A Special Purpose Vehicle, of which MagEnergy owns 70 per cent and South Africa's Industrial Development Corporation 15 per cent, was created to conduct the work and sell the electricity afterwards. The EIB is supporting MagEnergy's portion with a US$16 million loan. MagIndustries has also raised US$20 million for its investment through private placement of shares.

Some of the Italian companies benefiting from contracts in Inga rehabilitation include the Tosi group, which will repair and provide maintenance for MagEnergy of one of Inga 2's eight turbines. French engineering consultants Ingerop were contracted by MagEnergy to conduct a feasibility study on its Inga rehabilitation programme. MagEnergy has also signed a contract with SNEL to build a 300 MW hydro dam at Busanga on the Lualaba River in Katanga which would provide more power to copper and cobalt mines in Kolwezi.

In May 2007, the World Bank approved the Regional and Domestic Power Markets Development Project which included rehabilitation of Inga 1 and 2, and construction of a second high-voltage line from Inga to Kinshasa in order to take pressure off the existing line which is regularly overloaded. While Bank documents identify 'enormous unmet demand' in the DRC as a primary project rationale (World Bank 2005), the loan only included an additional 50 000 connections in Kinshasa, less than 1 per cent of the city's population (only about 6 per cent of whom have electricity access). The loan also includes support for the unbundling and privatisation of SNEL, as well as efforts towards further developments at Inga.

The programme will finance rehabilitation of turbines and water supply for the Inga 1 and 2 dams worth US$200 million. The operation will enable the dams to generate 1 350 MW – their maximum capacity – compared to current production of just 700 MW. Three hydro-power plants near Katanga that feed into the Inga-Zambia transmission line will also receive US$17 million worth of rehabilitation.

Rehabilitation of Inga 1 and 2 is only a first phase of current Inga developments. Developing the 3 500 MW Inga 3 Dam is the goal of Westcor, an entity created in 2004 through an agreement signed by the utility companies of five African countries – Eskom in South Africa, Empresa Naçional de Electricidade in Angola, SNEL in the DRC, NamPower in Namibia, and Botswana Power Corporation in Botswana. Westcor, also a NEPAD priority project, is now a registered consortium company in Botswana. In order to more directly connect South Africa – the dominant market for Inga development – to Inga 3, Westcor would build two 3 000 kilometre high-voltage transmission lines through Angola. Westcor is also considering up to nine hydro-power dams in Angola's Cuanza basin (a total of 6 700 MW) as well as hydro dams on the Lower Cunene River in Namibia. These five utilities would be the direct customers of Westcor, and industrial customers would buy from the utilities.

These projects are planned to be constructed by Westcor under a Build, Own, Operate agreement. Each of the five utilities has an equal stake in the company and contributed an initial US$100 000 to fund feasibility studies. According to Westcor, the projects are geared towards fulfilling projected energy needs in the five participating countries, including newly attracted energy-intensive industries.

An initial feasibility study was conducted by Electricité de France. SNC-Lavalin was conducting an updated feasibility study and environmental and social assessment funded through the Canadian International Development Agency (CIDA). However, the study has been stalled due to 'political instability'.[14] The total cost for Inga 3, including converter stations and transmission lines, is expected to easily exceed US$5 billion.

While initial funding has come from the five utilities, Westcor is attempting to raise additional funds through the World Bank, EIB and private sources. Attempts are also being made to make Westcor a publicly traded company in order to increase financing. The Westcor project is one of NEPAD's and the SADC's highest priorities and is being promoted by Eskom and the South African government. Westcor has reportedly approached the AfDB and the DBSA to fund the $10 million feasibility studies, which are expected to be completed by 2009.

However, Westcor's Inga 3 proposal is a drop in the bucket compared to Grand Inga, also known as Inga 4. By damming the Congo River, flooding the adjacent Bundi Valley, and using a series of 52 turbines and multiple dams over the Inga Rapids, Grand Inga would produce up to 44 000 MW of electricity, over twice the capacity of the infamous Three Gorges Dam in China. While feasibility studies and financing for Grand Inga are just beginning, proponents of this mega-project are broadcasting the claim that it will 'light up Africa', even having power left over to export to Europe. With an ever-increasing price tag – its 2005 cost of US$50 billion was upgraded in 2007 to US$80 billion – concerns are growing that foreign and industrial interests will gain vast economic benefits from the project, with only cursory attention given to easing the electricity needs of Africa's poor.

In October 2006 an international forum was held to woo foreign investors for the Inga 3 and Grand Inga schemes. The AfDB, which provided financial and logistical support for the forum, refused to provide assistance to concerned civil-society groups seeking to participate. The forum was a follow-up to a similar national-level forum organised by the government of the DRC that was held in March 2006 in Kinshasa. No civil-society representatives were included in that AfDB-supported meeting either.

In March 2007, the World Energy Council held a two-day meeting in Gaborone, Botswana, to discuss the way forward for Grand Inga. Event organisers issued reluctant, but still unfunded, invitations to civil society to participate. In both cases, NGOs had to scramble to raise funds for a handful of participants, including representatives of the local community that has long suffered the social and environmental impacts believed to have resulted from Inga 1 and 2, and is now seeking recourse and rehabilitation. Upon returning to the Inga region after the meeting, one community representative was harassed by officials, an experience indicating an atmosphere of tension and suppression of local activism.

The AfDB is preparing to support a feasibility study on further development of the Inga hydro-power site. The study, which may include consideration of both Inga 3 and Grand Inga, would include an environmental and social impact assessment. A draft Terms of Reference for the study indicated that various ownership scenarios would be explored, but private development underlies all plans.[15]

In February 2006, Australian-based BHP Billiton signed a Memorandum of Understanding with the DRC's energy minister to build a US$2.5 billion aluminium smelter, dependent on additional development of Inga and nearby construction of a deep-water port. An agreement is expected to be signed with SNEL that will include construction of a transmission network specifically for BHP.

The Chinese government has also shown keen interest in the Inga projects and financing through the China Exim Bank would not be unrealistic. Chinese-based SinoHydro, which regularly benefits from China Exim Bank contracts, has had discussions with DRC authorities and has worked on the maintenance of the existing Inga dams since 2004.

Developing hydro-power at Inga will only be effective if accompanied by an equally grand scheme to link the Inga dams by high-voltage transmission lines to each regional power pool. A proposed 1 400 kilometre line to Nigeria, connecting the PEAC and the WAPP, is being proposed, as well as a 5 300 kilometre line to Egypt. In southern Africa, the 3 676 kilometre line known as the East Corridor (between the DRC and South Africa, via Zambia, Zimbabwe and Botswana) has already been partially upgraded with World Bank funding. The West Corridor is part of Westcor's plan to build a line between the DRC and South Africa, via Angola and Namibia.

These transmission lines are anticipated to connect to faraway industrial and urban centres without providing the distribution networks needed to electrify communities along the way.

A way forward

Africa clearly needs energy development. But the type and scale of energy development needed to help poor rural communities is considerably different to what is generally being planned for the continent. Generating rural incomes and reducing child mortality caused by respiratory illness are just two examples of the high rewards which can be attained through low-risk strategies to reduce poverty from improved access to modern energy services.

However, the numerous financiers and other influential actors lining up behind Africa's infrastructure are building momentum for a strategy which seems all but unstoppable. This momentum hinders the ability of civil society to question the choices being made for Africa's energy future, or to influence project decisions on issues such as compensation for affected communities, benefit sharing, ecosystem trade-offs and project operation.

The WCD came about precisely because large dams had repeatedly devastated communities and not brought the development benefits they had promised. The WCD is not meant to be mere window dressing for big dam projects. Rather, it provides the nuts and bolts for effecting positive change and sustainable outcomes in the development planning process. African governments and their development partners which turn away from the WCD, or use a piecemeal approach to choosing those of its recommendations which best suit a particular dam project, are missing a genuine opportunity for development in their countries.

Those advising on the MDGs and the WCD agree on the need to make decision-making more participatory and pro-poor. The interim report of the MDG task force lists six 'clusters' of core MDG policy priorities with important overlaps with the WCD's recommendations. The task force's priorities include 'a rights-based approach to poverty-reduction, one in which historically excluded or disempowered groups are given a greater emphasis in policy-making and a greater voice in decision-making' (Millennium Project Task Force on Poverty and

Economic Development 2004: 34). Other policy priorities include 'increased public investment in basic human needs' such as water and sanitation, promotion of rural development through raising yields on small farms on marginal lands, biodiversity preservation and watershed management (Millennium Project Task Force on Poverty and Economic Development 2004: 34).

The WCD's final report (WCD 2000) recommends a public process to thoroughly assess needs, and the best options for meeting those needs, before prioritising any single project. Unlike the approach an engineer might take, a participatory process to identify needs and choose 'best options' looks not only at technical feasibility, but also considers social impacts such as specific rural needs that need to be addressed using local resources, and stimulating the local economy by creating skilled jobs. Too many poorly planned large dams have already failed to fulfil their goals, and Africa cannot afford any more development setbacks. Without a proper planning process, such as that outlined by the WCD, new dams are likely to be built based on skewed priorities that will continue to leave Africa's majority behind.

An important key to the WCD is that *strategic planning* done upstream from project decisions must balance energy needs for industrial and human development. When large infrastructure projects make it to the top of the priority list (based on an open and participatory needs assessment and inventory-of-options process), then following the WCD'S recommendations as best practice to ensure minimal impacts, sharing of benefits, and other key elements for sustainable development is critical.

Below are some of the recommendations embedded in the WCD report that are especially important for Africa's energy development path.

1. Prioritise modern energy services to meet the MDGs and directly alleviate poverty.

Prioritising energy for the MDGs means a balance must be struck between energy development in centralised grid planning, which primarily benefits industrial development, and modern energy services for Africa's rural and urban poor. Many countries now have rural energy agencies but their budgets are relatively small in contrast to the budgets afforded to large-scale, centralised projects. International financiers in particular must shift their approach to energy financing to focus on the most low-risk strategies to achieve poverty alleviation.

In 2002, Greenpeace and the Intermediate Technology Development Group (now Practical Action) prepared a thoughtful, pro-poor energy plan for the WSSD which could electrify the homes of 1.6 billion people in 10 years at a total cost of US$90 billion, and significantly help to meet the MDGs (ITDG et al. 2002). Key recommendations included:

- International financial institutions (such as the World Bank) immediately target 20 per cent of energy sector lending and support towards renewable energy development and energy efficiency programmes.

- Subsidies to conventional energy sources are phased out within 10 years, with a transition plan and flexible time frames to avoid undue hardships for developing-country economies overly reliant upon conventional energy sources and exports.
- The necessary finance and infrastructure are made available to create systems and networks to deliver seed capital, institutional support and capacity-building, to support and facilitate the creation of sustainable energy markets of the developing world.
- Aid is targeted towards halving the number of deaths from indoor air pollution from cooking stoves by 2015, by increasing support for clean cooking strategies.

While separate processes may be appropriate for assessing rural and urban needs, those who want to bring development to Africa must work to ensure that project financing is more clearly targeted towards rural development needs and not diverted for mega-projects.

2. Support energy development that helps African nations adapt to climate change.

Diversifying away from over-dependence on hydro-power is key to increasing the resilience of African economies to climate change. Climate change models predict severe declines in the flows of several major African rivers, changes which are already devastating hydro production across the continent. The economic impacts of hydro-vulnerability will be felt both in the costs of power cuts for industrial output, and the cost of wasted investments in non-performing dams. Energy development for Africa in a changing climate will require a greater emphasis on small-scale, decentralised supply, and diversity in the type of supply. Adopting 'no-regrets' measures – strategies that move Africa towards sustainable development goals whether or not climate change proves as destructive as is predicted – would lead to improvements in water management and poverty reduction as well as reduced vulnerability to climate change.

Because climate change will also bring about new and unknown risks and possibly catastrophic shocks, improved governance and increased transparency will also be key to good decision-making. 'For climate change adaptation to be effective, empowering civil society to participate in the assessment process, including identifying and implementing adaptation activities is especially important,' according to a report by major international financial institutions (Abeygunawardena et al. 2004: 25).

In March 2007, Achim Steiner, Executive Director of UNEP, said the rush to build more large dams and fossil fuel plants in Africa would 'lock in' the rural majority to decades without power, and called for more renewables to meet local needs: 'We should not live with the dream of a trickle-down of energy supply [to villages] in 20 to 30 years time…Africa should not follow the technological path the rest of the world is willing to give it access to' (Wallace 2007).

National governments should create renewables targets. As UNEA points out, 'the potential [for renewables] is very large, but there are few African countries with comprehensive legislation to link liberalisation of national utilities with increase of renewable energy from local and national resources. In many countries, there are no national targets specifically to increase renewable energy' (UNEA 2005: 16). South Africa is the most notable exception; the government has set a target of 10 000 terawatt-hours (approximately 5 per cent) of electricity to be obtained from new renewable sources by 2013, which would include approximately 1 667 MW of new supply from renewable sources, and excludes large hydro from the definition. However, South Africa's state utility, Eskom, has included large hydro in its definition of renewables (for more on renewables see McDaid, Chapter 7 in this volume).

UNEA also notes the importance of co-ordinated policies and investments to build a sustainable renewable energy sector:

> Renewable energy policies and markets are only successful if underpinned by substantial effort in training personnel and setting technical standards. The present success of renewable energy in Europe has occurred after 25 years of sustained support in research, development, demonstration and education by the European Commission. Without such background support, countless renewable energy projects have foundered due to public misunderstanding, poor design, unsatisfactory installation, lack of maintenance, lack of spare parts and consumer misunderstanding. Only governments, working with interest groups and trade associations, can give the comprehensive support needed to initiate and maintain such new technologies. (UNEA 2005: 19)

Africans are already finding ways to bring improved energy services to their communities. Building on Africa's successes in providing decentralised energy, training a new generation of decentralised energy technicians, and listening to average African citizens to learn what their true energy needs are, will yield the best results for all concerned.

3. Strengthen the role of civil society and the protection of rights for affected communities and consumers.

Affected communities, consumers, civil society and the public in general too often bear the burden of inadequate mitigation and other negative outcomes caused by large dams. Legally binding agreements supported by a strong, independent legal system are vital to protecting the interests of those otherwise left vulnerable to project developers. When a decision is taken to construct a dam, all project sponsors' commitments to resettlement, compensation and social investment for persons and communities affected by the project should be made legally binding, and payments and relocation should be satisfactorily completed prior to project construction. An independent mechanism for handling grievances of, and providing legal recourse to, members of the affected communities should be established before construction begins and should operate for the duration of the project.

Monitoring a project's social and environmental commitments, including changes in social and environmental impacts, must continue throughout the lifespan of the dam's operation, and mechanisms should be in place for communities to be involved with evaluations and raise concerns about changing impacts which need to be mitigated.

Judicial systems in many African countries are currently too weak to provide any significant protection of the rights of affected communities or to deal with concerns raised by civil society. Emphasis on strengthening the independence and due diligence of legal institutions should continue.

The public, too, needs to be protected from decisions to develop unfavourable projects, especially closed-door deals for large hydro dams. Such non-transparent contracts foster corruption and have a history of leading to inequitable sharing of risk, with ratepayers and taxpayers too often shouldering disproportionate risk relative to the project developers. In order to reduce corruption and the building of unfavourable projects, official planning processes must open up and allow for public accountability. Affected communities and civil-society groups should be invited to play an important role in planning before choices of specific projects are made.

4. Support rural economies and local, technical sectors for sustainable economic development models.

Energy development that invests in a local energy sector and creates skilled jobs for Africans should be prioritised. Decentralised, renewable technologies such as wind, micro-hydro and solar power specifically allow for higher rates of job creation and technology transfer. For example, a 2003 report commissioned by South Africa's Sustainable Energy and Climate Change Project conservatively estimated that if South Africa set a target of generating 15 per cent of its energy from renewable sources by 2020, it would create 36 373 new jobs in the country's energy sector – more than the total employment of the national energy utility, Eskom (Agama Energy 2003).

Supporting modern energy services to meet the MDGs can also create jobs and increase productivity in rural jobs. Decentralised, renewable efforts should be accompanied by the creation of local, technical jobs to maintain systems.

Notes

1   Personal observation by Terri Hathaway, who was in attendance at the conference and witnessed the speech and response.

2   The final report of the WCD was based on arguably the most extensive body of research on the impacts of large dams yet produced, including public hearings held around the world. This documentation, known as the WCD Knowledge Base, was generated between 1998 and 2000 on behalf of the Commission and is archived at www.dams.org. Prior to the WCD, the foremost overview of the impacts of large dams was Patrick McCully's *Silenced Rivers: The Ecology and Politics of Large Dams*, originally released in 1996 and updated and republished in 2001 after the release of the WCD's final report.

3   In many places, erosion caused by deforestation and unmitigated natural erosion are exacerbating flood episodes by hindering ground absorption and causing increased run-off.

4   Ghana's major energy plants are: Akosombo Dam, 1 020 megawatts (MW); Kypong Dam, 160 MW; Takoradi Thermal plant, 550 MW; and Tana Diesel plant, 30 MW (Volta River Authority 2006). As of 2000, only 45 per cent of the Ghanaian population had access to electricity (IEA 2002).

5   All documentation for contributions to the WCD Knowledge Base is available at www.dams.org.

6   Hope Ogbeide, Director, Society for Water and Public Health Protection, personal communication, 5 February 2007

7   The AfDB is a regional development bank and was established in 1964 (operational in 1967); non-African countries were added to the membership beginning in 1982. There are currently 53 African and 24 non-African member countries. African members collectively hold 60 per cent financial control and non-African members 40 per cent.

8   UNEA includes UNIDO, UNDP, UN-Habitat, UNECA and UNEP.

9   Samuel O'Brien-Kumi, Task Team Leader for the Southern African Power Market Programme, World Bank, personal communication, 12 September 2006

10   The World Bank's 2003 *Water Resources Sector Strategy* states, 'To be a more effective partner, the World Bank will re-engage with high-reward/high-risk hydraulic infrastructure, using a more effective business model' (World Bank 2003b: viii).

11   The Bank's strategy further states, 'Task managers leading risky projects will not be "on their own", but will have consistent support from regional and corporate management, and will get recognition for this difficult work' (World Bank 2003b: 54).

12   The Bank's strategy attempts to justify the forthcoming dams of the NBI as follows: 'While the overarching goals of the NBI are conflict prevention, poverty alleviation and environmental management – not simply the construction of major water infrastructure – the mutually-agreed projects of the NBI will deliver the most apparent and immediate development impacts of this complex Initiative. Should it be difficult for the World Bank to provide this support, for example due to the reputational risks of financing major infrastructure in the Nile Basin, the resulting disengagement of the World Bank could undermine the NBI process…It is essential that when the World Bank commits to long-term, high-reward/high-risk undertakings like the NBI, it has a clear institutional mandate to fulfill the range of functions – both in terms of policy and investment support – required by such a commitment' (World Bank 2003b: 83).

13 See http://www.financingfordevelopment.org/ for details.

14 Personal communication from Grainne Ryder, Policy Director of Probe International,
referring to her communication with CIDA staff.

15 At the time of writing, the conference proceedings were not yet publicly available.

References

Abeygunawardena P, Vyas Y, Knill P, Foy T, Harrold M, Steele P, Tanner T, Hirsch D,
Oosterman M, Rooimans J, Debois M, Lamin M, Liptow H, Mausolf E, Verheyen R,
Agrawala S, Caspary G, Paris R, Kashyap A, Sharma R, Mathur A, Sharma M & Sperling F
(2004) *Poverty and climate change: Reducing the vulnerability of the poor through
adaptation.* Accessed February 2008,
http://povertymap.net/publications/doc/PovertyAndClimateChange_WorldBank.pdf

African Ministerial Conference (2006) *Action plan.* African Ministerial Conference on
Hydropower and Sustainable Development, Johannesburg. Accessed February 2008,
http://www.hydropower.org/downloads/African%20Ministerial%20Conference/Africa%20
Action%20Plan%202006.pdf

Agama Energy (2003) *Employment potential of renewable energy in South Africa.* Report
commissioned by the Sustainable Energy and Climate Change Project (SECCP).
Johannesburg: SECCP

Beilfuss R (1999) Can this river be saved? Rethinking Cahora Bassa could make a difference for
dam-battered Zambezi. *World Rivers Review* 14(1): 8–11

Benton S (2007) Singapore to invest in new African infrastructure fund. *Bua News* 5 July.
Accessed February 2008,
http://www.buanews.gov.za/view.php?ID=07070516451005&coll=buanew07

Clanahan R & Hughes J (2003) *Key dam issues in the SADC region.* Eschborn, Germany: GTZ

Commission for Africa (2005) *Our common interest.* Accessed February 2008,
http://www.commissionforafrica.org/english/report/introduction.html

De Wit M & Stankiewicz J (2006) Changes in surface water supply across Africa with predicted
climate change. *Science Express* 2 March: 1–6

Dumba L (2006) Civil society statement to the African Ministerial Conference on Hydropower
and Sustainable Development, March, Johannesburg, presented by Linda Dumba

Economic Commission for Africa (2004) *Assessment of power pooling arrangement in Africa.*
Addis Ababa, UN Economic Commission for Africa. Accessed February 2008,
http://www.uneca.org/eca_programmes/sdd/documents/POWER_POOLING_rd.pdf

Environmental Monitoring Group (1999) *Report on southern African hearings for communities
affected by large dams.* Cape Town: Environmental Monitoring Group

ICRAF & UNEP (2006) Harvesting rainfall a key climate adaptation opportunity for Africa.
Press release, 13 November. Accessed February 2008, http://www.unep.org/
Documents.Multilingual/Default.asp?ArticleID=5420&DocumentID=485&l=en.

IEA (International Energy Agency) (2002) *World energy outlook: Energy and poverty*. Paris: IEA. Accessed July 2007,
http://www.worldenergyoutlook.org/weo/pubs/weo2002/ EnergyPoverty.pdf

IPCC (Intergovernmental Panel on Climate Change) (2001) *Climate change 2001: Working Group II: Impacts, adaptation and vulnerability*. Accessed February 2008,
http://www.grida.no/climate/ipcc_tar/wg2/index.htm

ITDG, IT Consultants, IT Power & ITDG Latin America (2002) *Sustainable energy for poverty reduction: An action plan*. Accessed February 2008,
http://www.practicalaction.org/?id=energy_action_plan

Leslie J (2005) *Deep water: The epic struggle over dams, displaced people, and the environment*. New York: Farrar, Straus and Giroux

Mahlangu L (2007) NEPAD project to focus on African development projects. *Bua News* 2 July. Accessed February 2008, http://www.buanews.gov.za/rss/07/07070213151002

Mbalula (1999) South Africa: Gariep and Van der Kloof dams. We were never consulted! Submission by Mrs Mbalula to the Southern African Hearings for Communities Affected by Large Dams, 11–12 November, Cape Town, South Africa

McCully P (2001) *Silenced rivers: The ecology and politics of large dams*. London: Zed Books

Millennium Project Task Force on Poverty and Economic Development (2004) An enhanced strategy for reducing extreme poverty by the year 2015. *Interim report of the Millennium Project Task Force on Poverty and Economic Development*. United Nations Millennium Project. Accessed February 2008,
http://www.unmillenniumproject.org/documents/tfoneinterim.pdf

Muhweezi A (2006) *Decision making processes regarding dams and development in Uganda: A scoping report*. Kampala: Uganda Dams Dialogue Steering Committee

NEPAD (New Partnership for Africa's Development) (2002) *Short term action plan: Infrastructure*. Accessed February 2008, http://www.nepad.org/2005/files/actionplans.php

Nexant (2004) *West Africa regional transmission stability study*. Accessed February 2008,
http://www.ecowapp.org/Volume%202%20Master%20Plan%20-%20Final.pdf

Organisation of the Islamic Conference (2007) The 32nd annual meeting of the IDB Board of Governors launched the Poverty Alleviation Fund. Press release. Accessed February 2008,
http://www.oic-oci.org/oicnew/topic_detail.asp?t_id=134&x_key=
poverty%20alleviation%20fund

Pottinger L (2006) Africa's perfect storm? Extreme vulnerability to climate change increases pressure on rivers. *World Rivers Review* 21(4). Accessed February 2008,
http://www.internationalrivers.org/en/node/2341

SAPP (Southern African Power Pool) (2002) *SAPP annual report 2001/02*. Accessed February 2008, http://www.sapp.cozw/docs/SAPP_ANNUAL_REPORT.pdf

South African Multi-Stakeholder Initiative (2004) *Applying the World Commission on Dams report in South Africa*. Cape Town: Environmental Monitoring Group

UNEA (2005) *Energy for sustainable development: Policy options for Africa.* Prepared for CSD 15. Accessed February 2008, http://www.uneca.org/eca_resources/Publications/UNEA-Publication-toCSD15.pdf

US EIA (US Department of Energy, Energy Information Administration) (2004) Table 6.3 World net electricity generation by type, 2003. *International energy annual 2004.* Accessed February 2008, http://www.eia.doe.gov/emeu/international/electricitygeneration.html

Volta River Authority (2006) Power Activities. *Volta River Authority home page.* Accessed February 2008, http://www.vra.com/Power/power.html

Wallace D (2007) Africa must set alternative energy agenda – U.N. *Reuters* 22 March. Accessed February 2008, http://www.reuters.com/article/latestCrisis/idUSWAL232511

WCD (World Commission on Dams) (1998) *Orange River development project, South Africa.* Case study prepared as an input to the World Commission on Dams, Cape Town. Accessed February 2008, www.dams.org

WCD (2000) *Dams and development: A new framework for decision-making.* London: Earthscan. Accessed February 2008, www.dams.org

World Bank (2003a) Project appraisal document. *Southern African Power Market Program(APL1).* World Bank Report no. 26806. Accessed February 2008, http://www-wds.worldbank.org/external/default/WDSContentServer/WDSP/IB/2007/06/21/000104615_20070621115627/Rendered/PDF/SAPM0APL20post0nego3PID.pdf

World Bank (2003b) *Water resources sector strategy: Strategic directions for World Bank engagement.* Washington DC: World Bank

World Bank (2005) Project Information Document (PID). *Regional and domestic power markets development project.* 14 November. Washington DC: World Bank

World Energy Council (2003) The potential for regionally integrated energy development in Africa: A discussion document. Accessed February 2008, http://www.worldenergy.org/documents/africaint03.pdf

WSSD (World Summit on Sustainable Development) (2002) Poverty eradication. *World Summit on Sustainable Development Implementation Plan.* Accessed February 2008, http://www.un.org/jsummit/html/documents/summit_docs/2309_planfinal.htm

CHAPTER 6

A price too high: Nuclear energy in South Africa

David Fig

Nuclear energy, claims the industry, is experiencing something of a renaissance. Although the industry has for some years been rolling back, particularly in Western Europe, there is renewed interest especially in rapidly industrialising countries like India and China. The massive negative impact from the accidents at Three Mile Island in 1979 and Chernobyl in 1986 caused a halt to reactor development in the USA, with programmes in countries like Austria, Germany, Italy, the Netherlands and Sweden being reversed by popular referenda reflecting the spread of deep concerns in civil society about environmental protection, weapons proliferation and health risks.

As the memory of Chernobyl's devastation fades, the nuclear industry has been able to persuade the new generation of decision-makers – the Blairs, Howards, Bushes, Putins and Mbekis – that nuclear fission is good for national 'energy security' since it weans countries off imported fossil fuels. This was emphasised at the G8 meeting in St Petersburg in June 2006, where Russian hosts insisted that energy security, the maximisation of national energy self-reliance, be placed high on the summit's agenda (*International Herald Tribune* 2006).

Fears about global climate change as a result of carbon burning have also been invoked by the nuclear industry to make a case for switching from coal, and the industry is hoping to divert resources for this from more sustainable renewable energy solutions.

The global tailing off of oil supplies has confirmed the theory of 'peak oil' first articulated by Hubbert in 1956, that we have reached the zenith in terms of aggregate petroleum supply, and henceforth will have to adjust to a diminishing resource (Hubbert 1956). As a result, the rise in the price of all fossil fuels – including uranium, whose price rose from US$23/lb. in 2003 to US$78/lb. in October 2007 (peaking at US$138 in June 2007) – has been steep, opening the way for mining companies to search for new sources of uranium, previously too costly to uncover.

South Africa is not immune from any of these trends. Instead of using the political transition to democracy to avoid the development mistakes of the North and 'leapfrog into the solar age' (as suggested by Sachs 2002: 23), South Africa has been dragged by a small elite clustered around the nuclear industry into an inappropriate and significant public investment in an unsustainable high-technology path. None of this decision-making has been subjected to any public debate. Yet present and future generations are likely to have severe regrets that their environment, health and livelihoods were compromised by such short-sighted and misplaced technological nationalism.

Nuclear energy back on the agenda

From November 2005, the economy of the Western Cape began to be affected by a series of extensive unplanned electricity outages. Outages have been experienced periodically in other parts of the country, especially where implementation of neoliberal approaches to electricity distribution placed more emphasis on profit than on access for all, and where infrastructure had become fragile due to poor investment and maintenance. Yet the outages in the Western Cape were the result of the unravelling of the region's over-reliance on nuclear energy. Poor energy planning and a shortage of skilled reactor operators, combined with management weaknesses and a distaste for decentralised supply, have inconvenienced millions of citizens and burdened production with huge additional costs. The damage as a result of these outages included disruptions to fruit and wine harvests, food processing, clothing and other production lines, tourism and other services, and all activities reliant on information and communications technologies. There were also negative implications for seasonal labour.

For over 20 years, South Africa's electricity supply has included a component generated by nuclear energy. The two reactors which opened at the Koeberg power station, 28 kilometres north of Cape Town, in 1984 and 1985 respectively have reached about midway in their operating life, and will have to be decommissioned not later than 2034. They produce about 5 per cent of the country's electricity, but over 40 per cent of the supply to the Western Cape.

However, the eventual closure of the original plants at Koeberg will not spell the end of the national utility's commitment to the nuclear path. South Africa is one of the few countries in the world which continue to invest in this technology, despite the other available options.

This chapter will explore the way in which these investments occurred in the past and may be extended into the future. Two plans exist in South Africa for extending nuclear power generation: one for the construction of Pebble Bed Modular Reactors (PBMRs), and another for the import of a further conventional pressurised water reactor (PWR). Renewed calls are being made to revive South Africa's capacity to enrich uranium, and a recent paper delivered to the intelligence community suggests that the country may have to reconsider the nuclear weapons path (Christie cited in Schmidt 2006).

Given the global energy crisis, climate change resulting from the burning of fossil fuels, and South Africa's on-paper commitment to 'ecologically sustainable development' (*Constitution of the Republic of South Africa* art. 24), further investment in nuclear energy is seen by proponents of sustainable energy solutions as an increasingly inappropriate route to development. Yet, impelled by the current emphasis on economic growth, energy planning continues to favour large-scale, unsustainable supply options. The need to debate energy supply options, increasingly being referred to as 'energy security', is at least as significant as the debate about access to electricity. Energy security is Goal 7 of South Africa's *Energy Efficiency Strategy* (DME 2005a); this commitment needs to be unpacked to understand exactly what it implies.

Uranium: integrating South Africa into the world of nuclear weapons and energy

Nuclear weapons were first deployed at the end of World War II on the Japanese cities of Hiroshima and Nagasaki (Alperovitz 1995). They originated through the research of the secret Manhattan Project, a joint scientific–military effort between the USA, UK and Canada (Bird & Sherwin 2005). The Project perfected the fission of uranium to create the immensely destructive force of these weapons. The uranium for the Manhattan Project had been sourced from the then Belgian Congo and Canada. After the war, it was anticipated by the scientists that these weapons of mass destruction would be internationalised and handed over to the administration of the newly formed United Nations (UN). However, in the aftermath of war, growing mutual hostility between the USA and the USSR, which had been temporary allies during the war, caused the USA government to retain its control over the technology of mass destruction. The USA and the UK embarked on programmes to develop further nuclear weapons, but the constraint they faced was developing sufficient supplies of uranium in view of the limited amounts available from their wartime sources.

In a search costing US$46 million, the US and UK governments jointly sponsored a global prospecting programme for new sources of uranium. A technical paper was unearthed, authored by geologist RA Cooper in 1923, indicating that the Witwatersrand gold mines contained significant amounts of radioactive materials (Cooper 1923). Researchers were dispatched to the South African goldfields, and their report made to Professor GW Bain of Amherst College in Massachusetts, who visited the Rand during 1945 under the auspices of the Manhattan Project and undertook extensive studies of ore samples. 'Present evidence,' reported Bain's colleague from the Geological Survey of Great Britain, Dr CF Davidson, 'appears to indicate that the Rand may be one of the largest low-grade uranium fields in the world' (Taverner 1956, cited in Associated Scientific and Technical Societies of South Africa 1956: 5). By 1947, South African Prime Minister JC Smuts was able to relay to British Minister of State for the Royal Air Force Philip Noel-Baker that the Witwatersrand finds would replace the Canadian mines as the 'richest source of atomic fuel' (*Daily Express* (London) 7 February 1947).

To co-ordinate the prospecting and commercialisation of the country's uranium, Prime Minister Jan Smuts created a specialised Uranium Research Committee (URC) which met for the first time on 8 March 1946. The URC was a secretive body that included government officials, scientists and representatives of the mining industry. There was close liaison with the Atomic Energy Authority of the UK at Harwell, while Smuts in December accompanied General Leslie R Groves, head of the Manhattan Project, on a visit to the Massachusetts Institute of Technology where samples of South African ore and uranium extraction methods were being analysed.

By late 1949, the first uranium extraction plant came into operation at Blyvooruitzicht Mine, this being the start of a process which would involve 17 plants servicing 26 other Witwatersrand gold mines (Fig 1999: 78). In secret contracts with the USA and the UK, the South African mining industry agreed to supply uranium for a 10-year period on the basis of a price structure that covered extraction costs plus profits.

In May 1948, before the relevant legislation could be passed to broaden the mandate of the URC, Smuts not only lost his parliamentary seat, but his party lost control of Parliament in an all-white general election. Power fell to DF Malan, the leader of the Purified National Party, who had campaigned on the slogan of 'apartheid'. It became the task of Malan's Minister of Mines, Dr AJR van Rhijn, to steer the atomic legislation through Parliament, and the Atomic Energy Board (AEB) was constituted on 1 January 1949 with the brief of overseeing atomic research and development as well as the production of and trade in radioactive materials. It set about formalising the secret agreement with the USA and the UK to purchase all of South Africa's mined uranium. Mining company profits from uranium rose from R2.6 million in 1953 to R75.5 million in 1958; they amounted to a total of R1 billion for the years 1952–1960 (Lipton 1986: 116).

Because of South Africa's uranium the country was a key prop in the Cold War, and the growing scourge of apartheid legislation was never seriously challenged by the USA or the UK. As apartheid intensified, so too did its nuclear connections with these countries, as well as with West Germany and Israel (Adams 1984; Červenka & Rogers 1978; Fig 1999).

The UK and the USA received South African scientists into their atomic research establishments and laboratories. West Germany accepted a number of South African scientists for training on enrichment techniques, while Israel and South Africa collaborated on research and weapons testing. Israel also provided South Africa with tritium, for upgrading its nuclear weapons programme, and with Jericho missiles for weapons delivery.

As part of President Dwight D Eisenhower's 'Atoms for Peace' programme, South Africa was provided with a research reactor in 1965, which it named Safari-1.[1] The reactor was installed at Pelindaba, the new headquarters of the AEB, which had moved out of its cramped premises in downtown Pretoria to farmland west of the city. This reactor operated on weapons-grade (90 per cent enriched) uranium supplied until the late 1980s by the USA under a secret treaty. Safari-1 continues to be used to this day, especially for the production of medical isotopes.

With intensive USA collaboration, South Africa's nuclear research efforts reached critical mass. Twenty years later, the head of the AEB, Dr Ampie Roux, paid homage to this decisive support:

> We can ascribe our degree of advancement today in large measure to the training and assistance so willingly provided by the USA during the early years of our nuclear programme; [South Africa's research reactor] is of American design...[and] much of the nuclear equipment installed at Pelindaba is of American origin, while even our nuclear philosophy, although unmistakeably our own, owes much to the thinking of [American] nuclear scientists. (*Washington Post* 16 February 1977)

Reactor technology was not the only area in which the AEB had deployed scientists. Another research initiative was centred on the development of a self-sufficient enrichment process. Mined uranium cannot be used in reactors or in weapons unless the naturally occurring proportion of the fissile U_{235} isotopes in the element is raised (to over 3 per cent for most power reactors and 90 per cent for weapons).

A significant supporter of South Africa's nuclear research programme was the architect of apartheid, Prime Minister HF Verwoerd. In 1961, as the Pelindaba complex was nearing completion, Verwoerd was briefed on the research work of the AEB and became a 'staunch protagonist' of the enrichment project (Newby-Fraser 1979: 98).

Building the first civilian reactors

In the mid-1960s the Anglo-American uranium contract with South Africa came to an end and was not renewed. The bomb-makers had been able to discover uranium elsewhere, and their reliance on the South African source was no longer so acute. The local mining industry and the nuclear research establishment started to press for a local power industry to create a captive domestic market for some of the spare uranium. The Western Cape, the area furthest from South Africa's mines, was initially earmarked for the first reactors.

A commission of inquiry had been established to look into the matter at the time that the Anglo-American agreement was drawing to a close, but its report in April 1961 had concluded that no economic advantage would be served by introducing nuclear power either in the Western Cape or elsewhere in the country (South Africa 1961). The commission reasoned that existing power sources in the Cape would suffice for the duration of the 1960s. Capital and operating costs for a nuclear reactor were thought to be double those of a conventional power station (South Africa 1961). Despite these pronouncements, Dr Roux kept the reactor development programme alive at the AEB. A cadre of scientists was trained at the

Argonne national laboratory in the USA, and returned to South Africa with the idea that South Africa needed nuclear power stations.

By May 1971, the Electricity Supply Commission (Escom, now Eskom) had put aside its misgivings about going nuclear and purchased the farm Duynefontein, 28 kilometres north of Cape Town, a sign that it had plans for building a nuclear power station on this site. It was not, however, until the oil crisis broke in October 1973 that Eskom was able to justify the costs of such a plan. OPEC members had quadrupled the oil price during the Yom Kippur (Arab–Israeli) War of that year, and South Africa became subject to an oil boycott because of its support for Israel. Eskom argued that its coal reserves were therefore needed to feed the existing and future oil-from-coal plants established by the parastatal Sasol, as well as local power markets. The escalation of energy prices made nuclear power relatively competitive.

Tenders were invited from reactor companies abroad for the construction of two identical PWRs on the Duynefontein site, renamed Koeberg ('cow mountain' in Dutch) after a nearby landmark. Ultimately the tender was awarded to a French-led consortium. Its Dutch-led rival's tender had been questioned in the Netherlands Parliament, and the South Africans felt that the anti-apartheid movement in France was less effective. Thus the Koeberg contract was signed in Paris and Johannesburg in August 1976; it was followed by a bilateral agreement between France and South Africa signed that October. A further trilateral agreement involving the International Atomic Energy Agency (IAEA), aimed at assuring safeguards for the reactors, entered into force in January 1977.

South Africa felt very comfortable with the French deal. France offered good credit terms, as well as training facilities for over a hundred reactor staff, and was sympathetic to the apartheid regime's defence needs, providing submarines, Crotale missiles and Mirage fighter jets, despite UN boycotts.

Notwithstanding an explosion planted by a reactor worker who was a member of the ANC, and which set construction back by a year,[2] the two Koeberg reactors were eventually opened in 1984 and 1985. Their joint installed capacity was formally given as 1 930 megawatts (MW), but they have seldom reached the total sent-out rating of 1840 MW, and were subject to severe teething problems. Nuclear electricity output has amounted to under 6 per cent of South Africa's total electricity supply. For the initial period, nuclear electricity cost over twice as much as coal-fired power to produce (*Hansard* 26 March 1986 gave the relative prices as 5.2 cents and 1.89 cents per kilowatt-hour respectively; but in Murray 1995: 111, Eskom claimed the two had become 'very competitive in terms of rands per megawatt-hour sent out').

The cost of nuclear power raised a number of questions about whether it was masking some other process, specifically nuclear proliferation. The reactors provided South Africa with nuclear know-how, justifying the extension of the costly enrichment process, and the establishment of BEVA (Brandstofelement-vervaardigingsaanlegging [Fuel Element Manufacturing Facility]), the plant making fuel for Koeberg at uncompetitive prices. Many suspected that the enrichment process had ulterior motives.

Developing nuclear weapons capability

At the outset South Africa's nuclear establishment was keen to develop knowledge of power generation, uranium enrichment and 'non-lethal' weapons aimed at providing explosions for the mining industry. However, after the 1974 coup in Portugal, which led to independence for Angola and Mozambique under Marxist regimes, the geopolitics of the region changed. South Africa regarded the new regimes in Luanda and Maputo as hostile, and began to invade and destabilise them immediately after independence. Apartheid's problems were compounded by the youth rebellion in Soweto in June 1976, whose aftermath spread throughout the country. Calls for international sanctions against the regime intensified, and the South African state became more insecure and dangerous. The government decided at this time to embark on a programme to develop nuclear weapons.

In order for this programme to succeed, the South African nuclear establishment needed to put in place the various components of the nuclear fuel chain. Since it could obtain uranium very easily, the next problem was to convert the uranium into a gas (uranium hexafluoride) necessary for the specific jet-nozzle enrichment technology which South African nuclear scientists claimed was locally developed,[3] but which bore a great resemblance to the technology used in West Germany, a country which had received South African nuclear scientists for training. Enrichment was necessary to raise the proportion of fissile U_{235} isotopes of the metal sufficiently for the production of weapons.

From 1970, efforts were made to build conversion and enrichment facilities at Valindaba, a neighbouring property to the headquarters of the Atomic Energy Corporation (AEC), the successor body of the AEB, at Pelindaba.

The South African public was told by Prime Minister JB Vorster that the enrichment was for peaceful purposes only, and aimed at gaining economic benefit from beneficiating uranium ore (South African Parliament 1970). However it later transpired that much of the uranium enriched in Valindaba's pilot Y-plant was dedicated to the provision of weapons-grade uranium. At the time South Africa was not a signatory to the Nuclear Non-Proliferation Treaty (NPT), and therefore not subject to international inspection.

The capacity to enrich uranium, which AEC staff had the technology to achieve, is one of the weapons proliferation triggers. Unhampered by inspection, the increasingly beleaguered apartheid state began to entertain the prospect of developing its own nuclear weapons. From 1974, a sudden increase in the budget of the AEC coincided with the drive to deliver weapons-grade uranium for a bomb programme. By 1978 Prime Minister Vorster had approved the manufacturing of weapons of mass destruction.

The weapons took the form of gun-type devices, similar to the world's first nuclear weapon dropped on Hiroshima. The firing of one part of the device into another would detonate the nuclear reaction. Each device used about 55 kilograms of uranium enriched to 90 per cent. By 1989, six devices had been manufactured and a seventh one was under way.

At first the AEC remained in charge of weapons production, which occurred in Building 500 at Pelindaba. Later, however, the parastatal arms manufacturing and procurement company, Armscor, gained control of production, which was moved to secure facilities in the Magaliesberg mountains closer to Pretoria. At the Advena factory – situated within the Gerotek complex 4 kilometres outside the township of Atteridgeville, whose residents were never informed – up to 1 000 people were believed to have been involved in the bomb programme.

Would the apartheid government have launched these weapons? It is unlikely that the South African Air Force would have had the capacity to deploy them. The logic of having the weapons would have been that they would permit the obliteration of Maputo, Harare, Luanda or even Soweto, measures that would have led to unwelcome accusations of racial genocide. The bomb-makers later claimed that the devices were manufactured to keep the world guessing about South Africa's nuclear weapons capability. *In extremis*, the apartheid government would publicise a full revelation of this capacity. The programme was initiated mainly for its deterrent value.

While Advena was sheltered from observation by prying satellites, the test range built at Vastrap in the Kalahari Desert was easily detected by the superpowers. Soviet leader Brezhnev – whose satellites first noticed Vastrap – consulted US President Carter, who put pressure on Pretoria to close down the facility; as a result, the shafts which had been sunk were filled with concrete.

By the late 1980s, plans were afoot to enhance the capacity of South Africa's nuclear weapons. A new plant called Ararat, close to Advena and alongside the township of Lotus Gardens, was constructed in order to facilitate the manufacture of thermonuclear weapons.

The legacy of the bomb programme

One of South African President FW de Klerk's earliest presidential decisions after coming to power in September 1989 was to dismantle the nuclear weapons programme. The Armscor–AEC team spent part of 1990 decommissioning the Advena factory, and the uranium for the weapons was returned to safety vaults at Pelindaba. By 1991, inspectors of the IAEA had satisfied themselves that South Africa's weapons programme had closed. After years of expulsion, South Africa was re-admitted as a party to the NPT and resumed its membership of the IAEA.

South Africa was the first country in the world to voluntarily dismantle its nuclear weapons capability. Why was this done? Firstly, the dismantling of the Berlin Wall, which commenced in November 1989, was symbolic of the end of the Cold War, a development confirmed by the serial collapse of the socialist governments across Eastern Europe. No longer could the apartheid regime base its militarism on efforts to curb communism. Secondly, De Klerk recognised the high costs of a weapons programme which could almost certainly never be used in practice. Thirdly, he calculated that if there were to be a regime change, perhaps with the ANC coming to power, it would be better that they not inherit apartheid's nuclear weapons. For this third reason, he commissioned Professor Wynand Mouton of the University of the Free State to destroy all documents and records referring to the weapons programme. As a result it is extremely difficult to reconstruct all the steps in the decision-making process, and the record has to rely on memoirs of some of those involved (e.g. Steyn et al. 2003), or analysis of interview material (e.g. Liberman 2001; Purkitt & Burgess 2005). The South African Historical Archives have been making attempts to employ the Promotion of Access to Information Act (No. 2 of 2000) to obtain relevant documents where these are known and extant.

In designing the brief of the South African Truth and Reconciliation Commission to investigate the activities of the apartheid regime, responsibility for the manufacture of weapons of mass destruction was not included. None of the individuals involved in the bomb programme were required to reveal what they had done, nor to apply for amnesty against prosecution. The potentially most lethal aspect of apartheid as a crime against humanity was not regarded as worthy of pursuit.

Of the estimated 1 000 people involved in the programme, most have had to find employment outside the AEC – which, since 1999, has been known as the Nuclear Energy Corporation of South Africa (NECSA) – and Armscor. Some secured professorial posts in the Faculty of Engineering at the University of Pretoria. Others used their severance payments to open pawnbroker shops. One group went on to join an explosives firm at Keetmanshoop in southern Namibia. Another group tried to sue the AEC for larger golden handshakes in court, but withdrew their claims after the courts threatened them with breach of confidentiality agreements which they had signed on entering the programme.

In September 2004, a spate of arrests implicated some individuals in the crime of trafficking in nuclear materials. A Vanderbijlpark entrepreneur, Mr Johan Meyer, was accused under the Non-proliferation of Weapons of Mass Destruction Act (No. 87 of 1993) of importing parts for dual-use lathes from Spain for re-export to Pakistan, as part of the ring of suppliers organised by the 'father' of the Pakistani bomb, Dr AQ Khan.[4] Information about these activities had been released to the CIA as an outcome of Libya's commitment to curbing its nuclear proliferation ambitions. Dr Khan lost his seat in the Pakistani Cabinet as a result of the revelations, but was not otherwise censured. Other weapons components traffickers of Israeli, German and Swiss nationality, who were linked to the South African activities, were arrested in Germany and the USA.

Efforts to secure non-proliferation in Africa have centred around the development of the Treaty of Pelindaba, signed in Cairo in 1996. Strongly promoted by South Africa, this was an attempt to make Africa a nuclear weapons-free zone. An exception was made for the Indian Ocean island of Diego Garcia, once part of Mauritius, but separated at independence and rented by Britain to the USA as a military base. However, not enough African countries have ratified the treaty, and as a result it has never formally come into being.

The legacy of the bomb programme remains with us, as 'morbid symptoms', which Gramsci in one of his more famous observations recognised as being part of the unfinished business of political transition: 'The crisis consists precisely in the fact that the old is dying and the new cannot be born; in this interregnum a great variety of morbid symptoms appear' (Gramsci 1971: 276).

Renewed consideration is being given by the intelligence community in South Africa to the possibility of a future weapons programme. In a well-received paper presented to this community by Professor Renfrew Christie on 24 August 2006, the argument was made that China's emerging role in Africa might require the expansion of South Africa's strategic military and intelligence capabilities, including nuclear weapons 'if necessary' (Schmidt 2006: 13).

The strength of South Africa's commitment to non-proliferation may be flimsier than our general expectations lead us to assume, particularly since a new generation might argue that the abandonment of nuclear weapons was a strategy pursued by the former apartheid regime.

Nuclear policy under the ANC

The ANC government has generally endorsed the stance on non-proliferation of nuclear weapons in Africa expressed in the Treaty of Pelindaba. However, the state apparatus has promoted the expansion of the nuclear energy industry.

A few months before the first democratic elections of 1994, the ANC Science and Technology Group in the Western Cape, together with an independent NGO, the Environmental Monitoring Group, promoted a conference on the future of nuclear policy in South Africa. The conference was addressed by Trevor Manuel, then head of the ANC's Department of Economic Planning. Speakers included opponents and proponents of nuclear energy. Officially the ANC took no policy position on the question, leaving it open to future debate. However, Manuel promised that 'we shall not tolerate circumstances in which policy on issues as critical as a nuclear programme be confined to experts in dark, smoke-filled rooms. The debate must be public and the actions transparent' (EMG & ANC 1994: 5).

Two years later, the government's Department of Minerals and Energy (DME) hosted an Energy Summit, with wide attendance by a number of stakeholders, including civil-society organisations. The Energy Summit was one of the steps taken in catalysing the 1998 White Paper on Energy Policy, a document signalling the proposed direction of policy and any legislative intentions arising therefrom (DME 1998). By the time of the Summit in 1996, the state nuclear research entity, the AEC, had significantly scaled down its operations and staffing. The future of the Koeberg nuclear energy complex was also somewhat uncertain. In the White Paper on Energy Policy, it was explicitly stated that any expansion of the industry would occur within 'the context of an integrated energy policy planning process with due consideration given to all relevant legislation, and the process subject to structured participation and consultation with all stakeholders' (DME 1998: section 7.2.iv).

Other signalled intentions were that there would be restructuring of the nuclear industry 'necessary to ensure the environmental sustainability and cost-efficiency of South Africa's energy economy, while seeking maximum benefit from historical investment', done in 'a participatory fashion', and there would be a thorough investigation into Koeberg's technical and financial performance, which 'will be made available for public scrutiny and comment before a final decision is made on the future of Koeberg' (DME 1998: sections 7.2.iii, v).

In practice, none of the promised consultation or participation has materialised, and the nuclear policy continues to be crafted in Manuel's 'dark smoke-filled rooms'. The drafting of the Nuclear Energy Act (No. 46 of 1999) and the National Nuclear Regulation Act (No. 47 of 1999) was undertaken in the DME by officials whose primary consultation was with the Chamber of Mines. The period allotted for public comment on the national Radioactive Waste Management Policy and Strategy was so short that the minister was forced to extend it for an extra 90 days to accommodate public comment.[5] Very few of the concerns expressed by the public found their way into the final policy document (DME 2005b).

There has been no broad stakeholder consultation on the future of the nuclear industry, nor specifically on Koeberg, as promised in the 1998 White Paper. Most of the decisions about nuclear development have occurred within the DME and the Department of Public Enterprises, without wide consultation with other departments. Much of the decision-making has been top-down, without any stakeholder participation. What appears to be government policy has bypassed even the policy formulation processes within the ruling ANC. This became evident at a briefing conducted for ANC members of the Parliamentary Portfolio Committee on Environment and Tourism who confirmed that there had been no policy discussion on this matter.[6]

Reviving the industry in South Africa

Since the 1990s, the remnants of the old apartheid nuclear industry have been trying to find ways to survive. Many who were previously involved in working for the AEC or Armscor ended up in universities, the arms industry, the bureaucracy, the information technology and engineering sectors or Eskom. Their interests remained tied to the revival of the nuclear industry.

This has been evident from their ability to persuade government – through para-statals Eskom and the Industrial Development Corporation (IDC) – to invest in a technology which has become known as the PBMR. The PBMR is smaller than a conventional nuclear power station (generating 165 MW(e) – megawatts of electrical output – compared to the 920 MW(e) for each of the two PWRs at Koeberg) and so plans are to build it in multiples to make best use of its modular structure and to cut costs arising from regulation. Eskom has given PBMR (Pty) Ltd a letter of intent that it will purchase up to 24 units, but legal opinion is that this is not absolutely binding as it is hedged with many preconditions (including that the reactors are the lowest-cost technology at the time, which is unlikely). However, this may well be overridden by ministerial fiat. At the time of writing (2007) the Minister of Public Enterprises, Alec Erwin, was bent on seeing the project through (Joffe & Le Roux 2007).

The pebble bed reactor is based on high-temperature technology that uses helium as a coolant and graphite as a moderator. The fuel consists of minute particles of enriched uranium encased in graphite spheres the size of billiard balls (the 'pebbles'). The industry claims it is 'inherently safe' and cannot melt down. If a fault occurs, the PBMR manufacturing company believes the reactor would emit heat and not radioactivity (interview with CEO Jacobus Kriek, cited in Breitenbach 2006).

Controversy has raged about the technology. PBMRs are part of a family of reactors called high-temperature gas-cooled reactors. The techology has been tried out both in Germany (using a model close to the South African pebble bed model) and in the USA, and discontinued in both countries mainly due to technical problems (Fig 2005). The South African PBMR company is still in a race with China to commercialise the technology. Questions arise about why the research and development of these reactors is being left to emerging economies. Even so, PBMR (Pty) Ltd is obliged to pay royalties to the original patent-holders in Germany.

State financial support for the project has been mounting exponentially, while it has already seen the disinvestment of one of the USA's largest nuclear operators, Exelon (partly linked to the reorganisation of Exelon's focus, but also signalling the firm's lack of confidence in the economic and technical potential of the project). A 15 per cent stake is formally held by Westinghouse, recently sold by its British parent firm BNFL to Toshiba. Eskom's financial directors are suspected of advising the PBMR company to drop the project, but anti-nuclear activists Earthlife Africa were denied access to Eskom board meeting minutes in which this position might have been reflected by court interdict, on the grounds of violation of commercial sensitivities (*Noseweek* 2005). Eskom prefers to reduce its stake in the PBMR company, uncomfortable with its dual role as investor and potential client (Campbell 2004). Its stake is likely to be taken up not by private venture capital but by the South African state. To date, the PBMR (Pty) Ltd website notes that apart from the Westinghouse holding, the other investors are 'the South African government', Eskom and the parastatal IDC.[7]

Meanwhile the bill for construction of the demonstration model of the PBMR at the Koeberg site, and the building of the plant at Pelindaba to manufacture the pebbles, has escalated to R15.9 billion (around US$ 2.4 billion). At least R2 billion of this has already been spent. The project is about six years behind schedule, with plans to commence building the demonstration model from 2008 receding further into the future.

Under South African law, an environmental impact assessment (EIA) for the demonstration PBMR has been mandatory. The department responsible for approval is the national Department of Environmental Affairs and Tourism (DEAT). When the record of decision was issued by the DEAT's director-general, it was clear that despite lip service having been paid to public participation, he had not read comments and objections submitted by Earthlife Africa, one of the most vocal and knowledgeable opponents of the project. The final report on which the record of decision was based had never been issued to the public. Earthlife Africa appealed to the courts and in January 2005 the Cape high court ruled in its favour. The director-general was obliged to consider all stakeholder submissions before reissuing a new record of decision.

However the PBMR company decided some months later to initiate a new EIA process, given that its reactor design in the prior process had undergone significant changes. The PBMR's electrical output had been hiked from 105 MW(e) to 165 MW(e), and public demands for further containment had been taken into account. Despite the fact that the second EIA is far from completion (the first took a period of 30 months to complete), contracts worth hundred of millions of rands have been handed out to Mitsubishi Heavy Industries (turbines), IST (the helium test facility and design subsystems), SGL Carbon (graphite products), and Murray & Roberts (construction) (Business.iafrica.com 2003; Cockayne 2005; I-Net Bridge 2005; *The Herald* 2002). IST is a company comprising former apartheid-era reactor scientists who had initiated the pebble bed proposal in 1993.

The next regulatory hurdle to be faced will be the granting of a licence for the demonstration reactor and the fuel plant by the National Nuclear Regulator (NNR). One cause for concern about the NNR's impartiality was the appointment by Cabinet (on advice from the outgoing Minister of Minerals and Energy, Phumzile Mlambo-Ngcuka, now deputy president) of Maurice Magugumela as its CEO. Magugumela's former position was as safety and licensing manager of the PBMR company. This revolving-door approach has seriously dented the NNR's credibility, and it remains to be seen how rigorously it will pursue the licensing process.

In his 2007 Budget speech, the Minister of Finance, Trevor Manuel, indicated that the PBMR company had yet to present the National Treasury with a business plan. Unless the company could come up with 49 per cent of the funds to match the government's 51 per cent investment in the project, earmarked funds for the demonstration plant would not be released. Manuel's Budget review stated that '[t]he economic feasibility [of the PBMR company] is still questioned and cognisance should be taken of the socio and macroeconomic benefits' (Robinson 2007: 2–3).

The Western Cape outages

Electricity load-shedding cuts have been intermittent all over the country in the last few years, particularly in cities where the electricity utility has been placed on a commercial footing, and too little has been spent on upgrading and maintaining old equipment.

During 2005, a series of incidents, including a fire under a pylon, caused one of the two nuclear reactors at Koeberg to trip. When this happens, power to the grid is disrupted. More seriously, on Christmas Day 2005 it was discovered that the rotor of a generator linked to the second reactor had been damaged by the presence of a misplaced bolt. The plant had to be shut down for some time pending the sourcing and shipment from France of a replacement rotor in April 2006. This led to more substantial power disruptions throughout the Western Cape, affecting households, industry, services and agriculture. Large quantities of the summer harvests of fruit and wine had to be destroyed due to interruptions in cold storage and fermentation processes (Cobus Dowry, Provincial Agriculture Minister, and Albert Schuitmaker, Director of the Cape Regional Chamber of Commerce and Industry, cited in O'Connor 2006). Electric pumps operating sewerage systems failed, and sewerage leaked into wetlands and freshwater bodies important to biodiversity, ravaging their ecosystems for at least the next decade. The growing tourism industry feared that its clients would select other destinations because of the unreliability of the electricity supply in the Western Cape.

The second unit at Koeberg had to be shut down for some weeks between March and July 2006 because its nuclear fuel needed routine replacement. While both plants were shut simultaneously there were severe electricity cuts at the beginning of the local winter.

On the eve of municipal elections on 1 March 2006, Minister of Public Enterprises Alec Erwin held a press conference in the course of which he stated that the damage at Koeberg had been the result of sabotage. During the same meeting the Minister for Minerals and Energy, Lindiwe Hendricks, alleged that the actions were an attempt to affect the outcome of the elections. The ministers announced their intention to have the matter investigated by the National Intelligence Agency. The media and trade union response was one of outrage, and Minister Erwin went on to deny that he had implied sabotage, despite repeated running of the television news clip in which his accusations were audible to all. The elections in the metropolitan area of Cape Town were hung, and the opposition Democratic Alliance went on to form a coalition administration without the ANC.

The major trade union federations, the Congress of South African Trade Unions (Cosatu) and Solidarity, sharply criticised ministers Erwin and Hendricks. The regional secretary of Cosatu in the Western Cape, Tony Ehrenreich, stated: 'The sabotage accusations were clearly absurd and incorrect. After the minister was heard on radio and television making the accusation, he further discredited himself by denying it' (*Rapport* 5 March 2006).

Whilst police and intelligence operators are still expected to report on the bolt incident, the National Energy Regulator of South Africa in August 2006 issued a damning report on the outages. Its findings accused Eskom of inadequate maintenance, breaches of licensing conditions, inappropriate risk assessment, negligence, failure to conform to operating procedure, inadequate implementation of corrective measures, and complete failure to notify supervisors of abnormalities. It further declared that the six incidents resulting in shutdowns could have been avoided (NERSA 2006).

All this points to the problems having arisen as a result of gross mismanagement by Eskom, despite its awareness that electricity demand is rapidly reaching full capacity. Belated plans to add capacity to the system include recommissioning some coal-fired power stations that had been mothballed when supply exceeded demand in the 1980s, adding new coal-fired and gas-turbine power stations to the grid, and looking to the Democratic Republic of the Congo to supply hydro-power from the Inga Falls complex. Demand-side management and energy conservation measures have been stepped up.

However, despite the signals issued by the Koeberg outages, there is still too little effort being devoted to decentralising South Africa's power supply. This would not only imply the diversification of energy sources, but also the construction of a multiplicity of smaller generation units, spreading jobs and security across urban and rural communities. Decentralisation will become imperative if the move away from fossil fuels occurs.

This would include stronger commitment to renewable energy. South Africa has significant potential for solar and wind energy, but is still at the outset of a programme to harness these sources. Had the number of subsidies which were given to the nuclear industry been offered to the purveyors of renewables, there would have been far greater progress in this direction. Renewable energies would create many more jobs than the nuclear energy industry, require fewer scientific qualifications, and allow the skills of installing and maintaining these systems to be disseminated throughout urban and rural communities (Banks & Schäffler 2006).

Instead, the state prefers a highly centralised approach. It continues to invest in the pebble bed project, despite the fact that each pebble bed reactor will only deliver a small amount of energy with devastating environmental costs. In recognition of this, South Africa is currently exploring the feasibility of building a new-generation PWR. It is very interested in Westinghouse's AP1000 model, which can generate 1 157 MW(e), seven times the output of a PBMR (Cochran et al. 2005: 7; Power Group Online 2006). The EIA process for the siting of a series of PWRs has begun, with public hearings being held at the sites purchased by Eskom for this purpose in the 1980s: Bantamsklip (near Pearly Beach in the Western Cape), Brazil and Schulpfontein (on the Northern Cape coastline) and Thyspunt (close to Oyster Bay, in the Eastern Cape).

Furthermore the new head of NECSA, Rob Adam, formerly director-general in the Department of Science and Technology, is a great proponent of the idea that South Africa should enrich its own uranium. The country's enrichment capacity was closed down after its abandonment of the bomb programme. Bomb-grade uranium can be used inside the Safari-1 research reactor at Pelindaba, although there are plans to change to much lower levels of enrichment. Enrichment is expensive and highly energy-intensive. It makes economic sense only if South Africa is to add a further 10 Koeberg-sized reactors or over 50 PBMRs to its existing energy plants. Conversion and enrichment would add 90–100 per cent to the price of the mined ore (Venter 2006: 16–17). Will the drive to set up enrichment facilities spur on the expansion of the civilian nuclear programme in South Africa and the rest of the continent?

With enrichment facilities, proliferation of weapons of mass destruction would become an option. The discussions within the intelligence community, mentioned earlier, have broken through the earlier political taboo about using nuclear technology only for peaceful purposes. The genie is now out of its bottle.

These ideas for pebble beds, fuel plants, enrichment facilities and new PWRs to contribute to baseload supply have all been included in a recent nuclear policy and strategy document issued by the DME (DME 2007). The document is a form of special pleading which prioritises the nuclear industry over all other sectors of the energy industry. In terms of the strictures of the 1998 White Paper, a nuclear power policy was only supposed to be issued after a comprehensive analysis of South Africa's energy needs and after consideration had been given to all energy sources. This has not been done, and the draft document contains no scientific information on the comparative price of nuclear electricity (including externalities) in relation to other modes of supply.

The document advocates not only the reacquisition by South Africa of enrichment technology, but also the intention to put in place reprocessing technology, which is currently possessed by only a few nations and is highly subsidised. The document also proposes a security force dedicated to the industry, a nuclear police force. This feeds into the critique of the industry as placing a huge security burden on the country, something not required by renewable energy technologies.

The false logic underpinning the need for nuclear power is given as its lowering of carbon emissions; while this may be true for the reaction itself, it is not true in relation to the mining and processing of uranium, enrichment, fuel fabrication, transport of radioactive materials around the country, construction, decommissioning and decontamination of plants, as well as the disposal and reprocessing of nuclear waste products.

The document has already been challenged by Earthlife Africa, which has demanded that the DME withdraw it or face public-interest litigation (Enslin-Payne 2007).

An inappropriate development path

A middle-sized economy that is expanding like South Africa's needs to secure further energy supplies. The South African state's determination to rely heavily on coal and uranium for its bulk electricity supply makes the country a prisoner of its mineral endowments, setting it on an unsustainable path. Rather than seeking to develop a more sustainable energy model that could take great advantage of solar, wind and other renewable resources, as well as relying more on energy conservation (by far the best option), a small nexus of decision-makers is bent on steering the country down the road of high-risk, high-waste and low-job options. Ironically, one justification for pursuing nuclear options is perpetuation of the myth that the technology is relatively 'clean' and 'climate-friendly', an argument that ignores the carbon impacts and radioactive impacts of the entire fuel chain (Caldicott 2006). Nowhere on earth has the problem of disposal of highly radioactive waste been resolved, since plutonium-bearing waste emanating from spent reactor fuel has to be insulated from the environment for 244 000 years.

South Africa's development will depend on creating livelihoods for the many people currently unemployed. The renewable energy industry is one area in which jobs would be diffused more widely across society than in the nuclear industry, which requires a small number of highly skilled operators. Eskom, as a utility, clearly favours more centralised and capital-intensive options for electricity provision. Despite South Africa's push since 1996 for privatisation and the supremacy of market forces in a liberalised economy, the plans for reviving the nuclear industry cannot occur under market conditions. Instead, the industry can only be sustained through large-scale subsidisation, something that has been achieved with minimal public debate and discussion. Priorities have been set at the top, and the impacts will be borne by the current and future generations.

Conclusion

Despite a constitutional commitment to environmental protection, despite framework environmental legislation that enshrines the precautionary principle, and despite declaratory support for principles of sustainable development, the government of South Africa is pushing the country down an unsustainable energy path.

Why has this happened? In the first instance, there is a revival of technological nationalism. This is embodied in statements by nuclear officials like Rob Adam (CEO of NECSA) such as: 'Nuclear technology and expertise are essential for any country that is serious about its position in the world' (*Engineering News* 4–10 August 2006). This elides into demands for enrichment, and ultimately via the same logic for weapons proliferation.

A further driver of the nuclear energy option is an economy which values the short-term profit-taking by large corporations (especially those involved in minerals beneficiation) against competing demands for a more socially just and ecologically sustainable society. The state encourages energy-intensive minerals beneficiation processes which take advantage of South Africa's cheap electricity prices. These prices are cheap because the health and environmental costs of this energy use are externalised, or left out of the pricing, and passed on to the more vulnerable communities. A glaring example is the encouragement of aluminium smelting in South Africa, despite the fact that no bauxite is mined inside the country. The smelters do not obey the more stringent standards of their EU or Japanese counterparts, and the pollution burden is borne by local residents. In effect South Africa is thereby exporting cheap electricity, while importing a heavy pollution and health burden.

The voices of civil society, which has generally been opposed to the development of nuclear technology, are small. However, these voices are mounting, and being led by campaigns like Earthlife Africa's Nuclear Power Costs the Earth, the Koeberg Alert Alliance in the Western Cape, and a number of community organisations in Namaqualand, North West province, the southern Cape region of the Western Cape, the Pelindaba area, and elsewhere. The revival of uranium mining (due to the rapid rise in its price) in both South Africa and Namibia has resulted in expressions of public concern, including public meetings. Opposition to the nuclear industry has been given some space in local media, both print and electronic.

Nonetheless, government continues to stifle public debate, for example vetoing a public debate on the nuclear industry hosted by the Parliamentary Portfolio Committee on Environmental Affairs and Tourism which had been scheduled to take place in February 2004. While the official excuse given for its cancellation was proximity to the forthcoming April general elections, it turned out that the PBMR company had at that time sent a delegation to France in an attempt to get Areva, the French state nuclear company, to invest in its operations, and any debate back home would have destroyed the illusion of full-scale national support for the PBMR.

In April of the following year, Earthlife Africa publicised the existence of an unfenced calibration unit in the vicinity of Pelindaba, whose radioactivity was elevated above legally recognised dosages. This attracted the ire of President Mbeki and the Minister of Minerals and Energy (then Phumzile Mlambo-Ngcuka); Mbeki denounced the NGO for 'scaremongering', while the minister announced that she would pursue the introduction of legislation to curb this kind of whistle-blowing (South African Press Association 2005). The matter was dropped after the NNR confirmed that Earthlife's readings of the radioactivity levels were accurate. However, the incident revealed that the politicians were capable of knee-jerk reactions to complaints from the industry about NGOs voicing legitimate concerns.

Despite these covert threats, civil-society organisations have been resilient enough to mount challenges to poor governance in relation to these issues (such as the judicial appeal against the record of decision on the pebble bed EIA in 2004). What remains to be done is the formation of linkages with other campaigns around electricity, jobs, access to information and poor governance. These campaigns need to strengthen and broaden their expertise in areas of media, research and advocacy.

The nuclear debate is also a test of the fragility of South Africa's new democracy. As we have seen, decisions have been taken entirely from above. The culture of openness and participation, as mooted in the Energy White Paper, is no longer to be found. The nuclear industry has always been notoriously secretive and opaque, often hiding behind excuses of commercial confidentiality to avoid accountability to the public interest. Of necessity, because it involves radioactive materials capable of misuse and proliferation, it is an industry which has to operate within an intensive security apparatus. This entails a degree of legislation which enshrines the security state. Promoters of the technology seldom acknowledge how much this might compromise democratic values. In the case of South Africa, having moved away from the repressive nature of the apartheid state, it may be forced back into a similar mode as and when the nuclear industry expands.

The range of disadvantages of nuclear energy thus includes the compromising of South Africa's environment, human health, democratic values, jobs and, potentially, efforts to uphold non-proliferation of nuclear weapons. Citizens, particularly those in the Western and Eastern Cape provinces, are being told that nuclear energy is the only large-scale alternative to coal that can guarantee their power supplies. The options of safer, more renewable energy sources, or the promotion of less energy-intensive industry, are not being taken seriously enough. Future generations will wonder at how rapidly South Africans squandered their chance to build more sustainable and more democratic approaches to energy security, and lost out on the added dividend of moving toward social, economic and environmental justice.

Notes

1   Eisenhower proposed in 1953 that the USA's allies should be helped to obtain nuclear technology for peaceful purposes (see Ambrose 1984; Sterngold 2003).

2   Information supplied by one of the interviewees in the documentary film *Uranium Road*, produced by Jenny Hunter, directed by Theo Antoniou, for Teaching Screens, Johannesburg, 2007.

3   Personal communication, Atomic Energy Corporation official, Pelindaba, 30 March 1993

4   Department of Foreign Affairs (South Africa) press releases, 7 September and 10 September 2004

5   DME press release, 16 October 2003

6   The author was present at the briefing, which took place at Gordon's Bay, near Cape Town, on 16–18 September 2006.

7   Accessed on 30 October 2007, http://www.pbmr.co.za/index.asp?Content=11.

References

Adams J (1984) *The unnatural alliance: Israel and South Africa.* London: Quartet

Alperovitz G (1995) *The decision to use the atomic bomb.* New York: Alfred A Knopf

Ambrose SE (1984) *Eisenhower. Volume 2: The president.* New York: Simon & Schuster

Associated Scientific and Technical Societies of South Africa (1956) *Uranium in South Africa 1946–1956.* Joint Symposium of the Five Constituent Societies of the Associated Scientific and Technical Societies of South Africa, Johannesburg

Banks D & Schäffler J (2006) *The potential contribution of renewable energy in South Africa.* Johannesburg: Earthlife Africa

Bird K & Sherwin MJ (2005) *American Prometheus: The triumph and tragedy of J Robert Oppenheimer.* New York: Alfred A Knopf

Breitenbach D (2006) Creating energy for the future. *Professional Management Review Africa* 17(7): 35–37

Business.iafrica.com (2003) *IST nuclear gets PBMR design contract.* 18 August. Accessed 1 March 2007, http://business.iafrica.com/news/263624.htm

Caldicott H (2006) *Nuclear power is not the answer.* New York: The New Press. (Introduction in *California Literary Review.* Accessed 18 January 2007, www.calitreview.com/Essays/nuclear_5030.htm

Campbell K (2004) Eskom to seek state funding for nuclear project. *Engineering News* 7–13 May: 6

Červenka Z & Rogers B (1978) *The nuclear axis: Secret collaboration between West Germany and South Africa.* London: Julian Friedmann

Cochran TB, Paine CE, Fettus G, Norris RS & McKinzie MG (2005) *Commercial nuclear power.* Washington DC: Natural Resources Defense Council

Cockayne R (2005) SGL Carbon wins contract for pebble bed reactor plant. *Business Report* (Johannesburg) 23 November

Cooper RA (1923) Mineral constituents of Rand concentrates. *Journal of the Chemical, Metallurgical and Mining Society of South Africa* 24: 90–96. Reprinted in *Journal of the South African Institute of Mining and Metallurgy* (1994) 94(3): 47–51

DME (Department of Minerals and Energy, South Africa) (1998) *White Paper on the Energy Policy of the Republic of South Africa.* Pretoria: DME

DME (2005a) *Energy efficiency strategy for the Republic of South Africa.* Pretoria: DME

DME (2005b) *Radioactive waste management policy and strategy for the Republic of South Africa.* Pretoria: DME

DME (2007) *Nuclear energy policy and strategy for the Republic of South Africa: Draft for public comment.* June. Pretoria: DME

EMG & ANC (Environmental Monitoring Group & African National Congress) (1994) *The nuclear debate: Proceedings of a conference on nuclear policy for a democratic South Africa,* 11–13 February, Cape Town. Cape Town: Environmental Monitoring Group

Enslin-Payne S (2007) Earthlife Africa challenges nuclear thrust. *The Mercury, Business Report* 24 October

Fig D (1999) Sanctions and the nuclear industry. In A Klotz & NC Crawford (eds) *How sanctions work: Lessons from South Africa.* Basingstoke: Macmillan

Fig D (2005) *Uranium road: Questioning South Africa's nuclear direction.* Johannesburg: Jacana

Gramsci A (1971) *Selections from the prison notebooks of Antonio Gramsci.* Q Hoare & G Nowell Smith (eds). New York: International Publishers

Hubbert WK (1956) Nuclear energy and the fossil fuels. Paper presented to the American Petroleum Institute, Southern District, 7–9 March, San Antonio, Texas

I-Net Bridge (2005) *PBMR signs R100m deal with Mitsubishi.* 18 August. Accessed 1 March 2007, http://business.iafrica.com/news/663006.htm

International Herald Tribune (2006) Energy security leads G8 agenda. *International Herald Tribune* 8 June

Joffe H & Le Roux M (2007) Second nuclear plant to ease South Africa's power crisis. *Business Day* (Johannesburg) 13 February

Liberman P (2001) The rise and fall of the South African bomb. *International Security* 26(2): 45–83

Lipton M (1986) *Capitalism and apartheid.* Cape Town: David Philip

Murray S (1995) *Koeberg: Eskom's nuclear success story.* Cape Town: Churchill Murray

NERSA (National Energy Regulator of South Africa) (2006) *Investigation into the electricity outages in the Western Cape for the period November 2005 to March 2006.* Pretoria: NERSA

Newby-Fraser AR (1979) *Chain reaction: Twenty years of nuclear research and development in South Africa.* Pretoria: Atomic Energy Board

Noseweek (2005) All in the pebble bed together. *Noseweek* 66: 14–16

O'Connor M (2006) Wes-Kaap steeds in duister oor krag [Western Cape remains in the dark over energy]. *Die Burger* (Cape Town) 23 February

Power Group Online (2006) *NRC approves first generation III+ nuclear plant.* 3 January. Accessed 1 March 2007, http://pepei.pennet.com/Articles/Article_Display.cfm?ARTICLE_ID=244618&p=6

Purkitt H & Burgess S (2005) *South Africa's weapons of mass destruction.* Bloomington: Indiana University Press

Robinson V (2007) High-flying Alec is hobbled. *Mail & Guardian* (Johannesburg) *Budget 2007 supplement* 22 February–1 March

Sachs W (ed.) (2002) *The Jo'burg memo: Fairness in a fragile world: Memorandum for the World Summit on Sustainable Development.* Berlin: Heinrich Böll Foundation

Schmidt M (2006) Should South Africa re-arm with nukes? *Weekend Argus* (Cape Town) 16 September

South Africa (Union of) (1961) *Commission of inquiry into the application of nuclear power in South Africa (Forsyth Commission) report.* Pretoria: Union of South Africa

South African Parliament (1970) *Debates of Parliament (Hansard), 20 July.* Pretoria: Republic of South Africa

South African Press Association (2005) Government denounces Pelindaba 'nuclear threat'. *Mail & Guardian* 28 April–4 May

Sterngold J (2003) For 50 years, Atoms for Peace has spawned nuclear fears. *San Francisco Chronicle* 9 December

Steyn H, Van der Walt R & Van Loggerenberg J (2003) *Armament and disarmament: South Africa's nuclear weapons experience.* Pretoria: Network

Taverner L (1956) A historical review of the events and developments culminating in the construction of plants for the recovery of uranium from gold ore residues. *The South African Institute of Mining and Metallurgy* 57(4). Reproduced in Associated Scientific and Technical Societies of South Africa, *Uranium in South Africa 1946–56* 1: 1–14

The Herald (2002) New-style nuclear demonstration plant for South Africa. *The Herald* (Port Elizabeth) 15 January

Venter I (2006) South Africa considers re-entry into uranium enrichment, but for peaceful means only. *Engineering News* 4–10 August: 16–17

CHAPTER 7

Renewable energy: Harnessing the power of Africa?

Liz McDaid

This chapter aims to demonstrate that not only does South Africa have an abundance of renewable energy in the form of sun, wind, etc., but that this energy can be harnessed to meet the energy needs of the country. I argue that a commitment to moving away from polluting coal and nuclear energy and towards renewable energy would contribute to a healthy environment as well as improved socio-economic conditions for all citizens, providing a path of economic development which would grow the economy in a sustainable manner.

The chapter analyses the supposed challenges to the implementation of renewable energy, and how they can be overcome. The electricity generation and distribution monopoly now operative suits the current industrial powers, while government commitment to renewables has thus far been limited to paper statements, or pilot demonstrations.

The conclusion of the chapter is that the real challenge to implementing renewable energy is the lack of political will to transform Eskom. Civil society must therefore play a major role in lobbying government for change in the energy sector.

What differentiates renewable from non-renewable energy?

Non-renewable energy is derived from a finite source – for example, there is only a limited amount of coal, oil and uranium in the earth which can be converted into forms of energy. Renewable energy is commonly understood to be energy from ongoing, natural processes; examples would be sunshine, wind, moving water and geothermal energy. Biomass is also regarded as a renewable energy source; plants can be grown over weeks or years, the wood burned directly or plant material turned into gas or biofuels. The South African Department of Minerals and Energy (DME) has produced a White Paper on Renewable Energy which defines renewable energy sources as 'sun, wind, biomass, water (hydro), waves, tides, ocean current, geothermal, and any other natural phenomena which are cyclical and non-depletable' (DME 2003: v).

In South Africa, while we have an abundance of renewable energy in various forms, estimates differ as to how much of this is useable. Eskom estimates that there is only about 1 000 megawatts (MW) of wind power available around the coast (Eskom 2006a: 40). However, based on DME figures for 2004, Banks and Schäffler (2005: 23) provide an estimate of 50 gigawatts (GW).

Our solar resources are among the best in the world, with solar radiation levels of between 4.5 and 7 kilowatt-hours per square metre (kWh/m^2). If we look at how much solar energy would be needed to meet the energy demands of each person, it is estimated that an area of 75 m^2 per person would be sufficient (Banks & Schäffler 2005: 14).

While there are many different types of renewable energy, for the purposes of this chapter I focus largely on electricity generation options using solar photovoltaic (PV), solar thermal and wind power.

Solar photovoltaic options

Energy from the sun (solar energy) can be used to generate electricity, to heat water, and to heat, cool and light buildings. For example, PV systems capture the energy in sunlight and convert it directly into electricity. Banks and Schäffler (2006: vi) predict that up to 14 per cent of electricity supply in 2050 could come from solar PVs. The major downside for PV is that it is difficult to store, particularly if the focus is off-grid supply. However, Banks and Schäffler (2006) believe that new technologies will greatly increase the ability to store electricity at a lesser cost than is presently the case.

Solar thermal options

Solar energy can be trapped in a solar water heater and used to directly provide hot water for homes. Installation of a solar water heater could reduce the use of electricity, especially during peak times. Modern solar water heaters have a back-up electrical system for use in inclement weather (Ubushushu Bendalo 2006).

Alternatively, sunlight can be collected and focused with mirrors to create a high-intensity heat source that can be used to generate electricity by means of a steam turbine or heat engine (DME 2003).

Wind options

Wind turbines harness the energy of moving air in order to generate electricity. According to Greenpeace (2006), one-third of the world's electricity can be supplied by wind. Within South Africa, wind energy is potentially significant in the coastal regions and along the escarpment. Banks and Schäffler (2006: vii) predict that wind energy could provide up to 80 terawatt-hours (TWh).

Why renewable energy is important for South Africa

Over the last decade, there has been an enormous expansion of renewable energy use across the world. For example, in Germany installed wind capacity was 68 MW in 1990; by 2000, installed capacity was 6 095 MW and by 2004 it was 15 000 MW (Meixner 2003).

There are a number of reasons why South Africa should commit strongly to renewable energy; the most important are outlined below.

Climate change: offsetting coal-fired emissions

It is now generally accepted that the continued production of greenhouse gases such as those generated by the burning of fossil fuels has resulted in a change in the world's climate. As stated by Bond (2002: 179) in his critique of the New Partnership for Africa's Development (NEPAD), South Africa is one of the leading greenhouse gas producers in the world, if figures are corrected for population size and income (see Figure 7.1). Global initiatives such as the Kyoto Protocol and its successor are likely to put increasing pressure on South Africa to reduce its emissions.

Figure 7.1: Comparison of carbon dioxide emissions per capita, 2001

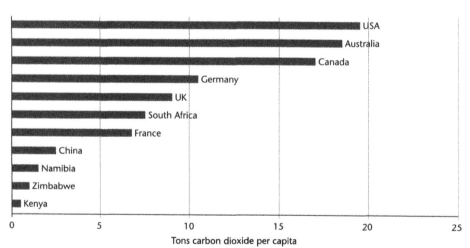

Source: DME 2005

Researchers examining the impacts of climate change predict that parts of South Africa will be at risk from projected climate change, warming and rainfall change (Midgley et al. 2005). The report produced by Midgley et al. argues that the west coast of South Africa is becoming hotter and drier, for example, with severe resultant impacts on biodiversity and sustainable livelihoods in this region.

The implementation of renewable energy technologies (RETs) provides an opportunity to address climate change. By replacing 30 000–40 000 MW of fossil fuel with renewable energy, a considerable reduction in greenhouse gases can be achieved within the relatively short time frame of 25 years, while continuing to provide a high-quality electricity supply.

Health and social benefits: reducing air pollution and creating jobs

Many poor South Africans rely on solid or liquid fuels for energy in poorly ventilated homes. This results in high levels of indoor air pollution with huge resultant health costs. Where households located close to each other are all using paraffin or wood stoves, this results in increased air pollution outside as well as inside the houses (Hallowes & Butler 2004). In her foreword to the White Paper on Renewable Energy, Deputy Minister Susan Shibanga raised the issue of children's health as part of the motivation for renewable energy: 'Research has indicated that one of the highest causes of infant mortality is from acute respiratory illness associated with the inhalation of wood smoke' (DME 2003: i).

Renewable energy at the household level could mean using the energy of the sun, rather than paraffin, to heat water. Localised affordable electricity generation by small-scale renewables leads to a reduction in dirty, coal-based electricity generation, with an associated reduction in harmful emissions.

For women – who bear the burden of fuel collection as well as cooking in a confined space – renewable energy can be a catalyst for an increased quality of life. 'Such improvements are generally part of integrated measures aimed at income generation via the pursuit of economic and agricultural development that afford women a more qualitative and productive time' (DME 2003: i).

Job creation

South Africa is a developing country experiencing rapid economic growth and high levels of unemployment. Renewable energy shows enormous potential to create jobs. If we contrast the conventional energy sector with the renewable energy sector, we see the difference in job creation potential within the two sectors (Table 7.1); the unit of measurement used is jobs per MW.

According to Agama Energy (2003: 12), if all RETs are included a total of 36 400 direct jobs alone could be created in the South African economy, with additional spin-off employment potential. Such a model assumes a government commitment to a target of 15 per cent of total electricity generation capacity in 2020 through RETs. A key finding from the Agama Energy study was that the development of large-scale RETs will sustain and substantially boost the numbers of jobs in the energy sector, particularly because of the development of manufacturing industries that would take place.

Table 7.1: Job-creation potential of renewable and non-renewable energy technologies

Renewable energy technologies	Total jobs/MW
Solar thermal	5.9
Solar PV	35.4
Wind	4.8
Biomass	1.0
Landfill	6.0
Non-renewable energy technologies	
Coal – current	1.7
Coal – future	3.0
Nuclear – pressure water reactor	0.5
Nuclear – Pebble Bed Modular Reactor	1.3
Gas	1.2

Source: Adapted from Agama Energy 2003: 6–7

It is important to note that while massive employment gains can be made quickly in the solar water heater and biofuels sectors, initially RETs would require greater investment for skills training, which needs to be planned for.

The most important conclusion arising from the study is that the South African economy needs a higher target for renewable energy than the one currently outlined in the White Paper on Renewable Energy, in order to derive the maximum employment benefit.

How much energy could we supply using renewables?

The answer to this question would help government to decide where to put its capital expenditure and how to set up its infrastructure to best meet its energy needs. The discussion in this section draws largely on the report by Banks and Schäffler, which argues that it would be possible to provide up to 70 per cent of South Africa's electricity needs by 2050 using RETs (Banks & Schäffler 2006: xii).[1] Figure 7.2 presents findings from this report.

If we accept that South Africa must grow its economy, doing so in a way that meets the goal of sustainable development, then there will be a growing need for energy throughout the country. While energy demand management, and energy efficiency measures, could reduce the overall demand for electricity, it should be accepted that South Africa will also require increased electricity generation capacity.

For South Africa, according to Eskom's own projections, economic growth of 6 per cent per annum translates into electricity demand growth of 4.4 per cent per annum, requiring generating capacity of 47 252 MW to be built between 2005 and

Figure 7.2: Renewables scenario, 2050: how electricity demand would be met

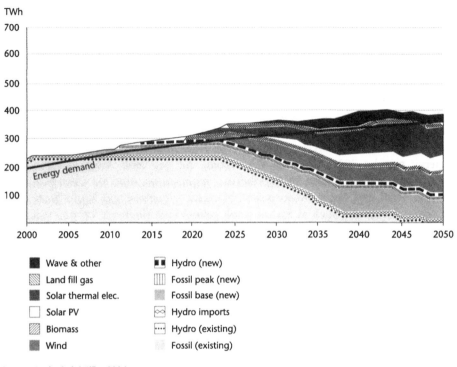

TWh

Source: Banks & Schäffler 2006

2025. Eskom's capacity planning programme is based on a 4 per cent growth in GDP, which translates into 2.3 per cent electricity demand growth (Eskom 2006b).

Learning from renewable energy projects in southern Africa

It should be remembered that Africa has always had an interest in certain forms of renewable energy. In fact, the vast majority of communities throughout the African continent are still dependent on biomass, in the form of wood stocks, to meet their energy needs.

And yet, a report produced by the US Energy Information Administration (US EIA) (US EIA 2005) on the current status of renewable energy in various Southern African Development Community countries only highlighted a bagasse plant and a solar power station.[2] While Tanzania, Swaziland and Mauritius have shown interest in a bagasse plant, it was only Mauritius which, in 2001, built a 70 MW plant. Plans for the others have either stalled or are in the feasibility stage. According to the US EIA briefing, a solar power station was established in the Namib Desert in November 2004.

Kenya has one of the fastest growing interests in solar power. More than 30 000 very small solar panels are sold in that country each year. The panels may only produce 12–30 watts, but they can be used to charge a car battery, which then provides sufficient power for a light bulb and other small power drawers. These small systems are of a type which is less efficient but more affordable than crystalline cells by a factor of four (Kammen 2006).

The new energy policy approved by the Malawian Cabinet in January 2003 governs the energy sector in that country as a whole and outlines a clear commitment from government to supporting the development of a robust renewable energy industry. The policy has set a target of a 7 per cent contribution by RETs to the national energy mix by 2020, up from the current 0.2 per cent. Areas identified for development include solar PV and thermal applications, wind for water pumping, biogas, mini and micro hydro-power, biomass briquettes, and liquid fuels from biomass processing such as fuel-ethanol, gelfuel and biodiesel. Various pieces of legislation to implement the policy are being finalised (Mimi interview).

In 2005, the Forum for Energy Ministers of Africa (FEMA) was formed. A paper commissioned by the forum focused specifically on energy and the Millennium Development Goals in Africa. The paper analyses the provision of energy, including electricity, gas and biofuels. While acknowledging that the continent is rich in renewable resources, it fails to describe any particular strategy for the development of these resources (FEMA 2006), apart from one weak example of PVs, which are merely put forward as an option in 'selected rural areas', suggesting a lack of commitment to heavy investment in this particular type of renewable energy. No other form of renewable energy is explored in any detail. Wind is mentioned only once in the Introduction.

The implication is that renewable energy does not form any large part of the FEMA priorities. In fact, the FEMA paper concludes that 'the energy initiative of FEMA is within the energy programme of NEPAD, and FEMA will therefore act as an advocate of the NEPAD's energy agenda' (FEMA 2006: 38).

NEPAD has a policy on energy which clearly states that 'Africa should strive to develop its solar energy sources which are abundantly available' (NEPAD 2001: 27). However, the list of identified actions fails to include any specific action to be undertaken in order to realise this objective. In contrast, the use of hydro-power is included as a major component of the energy objectives, and action to be taken to give expression to this commitment is identified – to establish a task force to recommend priorities and implementation strategies for regional projects (Bond 2002).

The FEMA paper also provides a number of case studies and examples of energy services provision in Africa. Two case studies, of Egypt and Zimbabwe, focus on how to provide energy in a way that would meet poverty reduction goals. However, the success of the Zimbabwean project appears mostly measured by its economic success – its 'economic viability' – rather than in terms of its 'potential for poverty reduction'. Other factors contributing to success are listed as 'efficient revenue collection, increased use of private contractors, capital subsidies for grid extension and cross-subsidies to support the poverty tariff' (FEMA 2006: 30). In the Egyptian case, the following revealing remark was made: 'Residential and commercial customers were *made to pay* economic rates for electricity used' (FEMA 2006: 29; italics added).

There is a dichotomy between energy priorities for industrialisation and those for poverty reduction (Hathaway 2005a). New growth in mining, and energy-intensive industries such as smelters, biases identified energy needs towards industry. Such large demands for energy come with a focus on grid-based electricity and large-scale generation plants. Many new grid generation plans, such as Grand Inga in the Democratic Republic of the Congo (DRC), are anchored by proposed industrial expansion and electricity exports to neighbouring countries.

Hathaway (2005b) also raises the issue that many African governments are already seeking funding for billions of dollars' worth of large hydro-power dam proposals, with little regard to whether such proposals are in the best interests of their citizens. Hathaway proposes that G8 funding should be directed to renewable energy and adaptation to climate change (see also Hathaway and Pottinger, Chapter 5 in this volume).

The Southern African Power Pool

There are 12 utilities that are part of the Southern African Power Pool (SAPP), from Botswana, Lesotho, Mozambique, Namibia, the DRC, South Africa, Swaziland, Zambia, Zimbabwe, Malawi, Angola and Tanzania (SAPP 2006: 3). The SAPP's vision includes '[ensuring] sustainable energy developments through sound economic, environmental and social practices', while its objectives include '[implementing] strategies in support of sustainable development priorities' (SAPP 2006: 2).

The 2006 SAPP *Annual Report* acknowledged that the SAPP was becoming increasingly unable to meet electricity demands and that measures needed to be put in place to address this shortfall. However, the SAPP priority list focuses on rehabilitation projects, short-term generation projects which have already obtained environmental approval (and for which feasibility studies have been undertaken), and short-term transmission projects. Medium- to longer-term investments include large-scale hydro-power in the DRC and Angola (SAPP 2006).

There is no meaningful reference in SAPP planning to the role of renewable energy. It can therefore be concluded that, like South Africa, the SAPP has not taken on board the need to invest in renewables now to meet future demand in an environmentally sustainable way, undermining its stated vision and objectives.

The current status of renewable electricity

The South African state-owned electricity utility Eskom has embarked on a number of pilot projects with various partners, as part of a research programme on renewable energy. Called the South African Bulk Renewable Energy Generation programme, it is aimed at 'large scale generation options'. These projects include:

- solar – the 'power tower', in which sunlight is concentrated onto a focal point where it is then used to produce steam and power a turbine to produce electricity;
- solar – the Dish Stirling, which has a dish reflector and a generator unit. This was found by Eskom 'not to be currently viable under South African conditions';
- wind – three turbines on the Klipheuwel site at Darling in the Western Cape. This is a research site and future installations would depend on its commercial feasibility;
- biomass – the System Johannsen Gasifier uses wood and other biomass to produce a gas which can then be used to drive a turbine. The first non-research unit is to be piloted in the Eastern Cape (Eskom 2006a).

Apart from these Eskom projects, there are a number of other renewable energy initiatives within South Africa. Individuals have purchased their own PV systems, as well as solar water heaters. There are an estimated 30 000 windmills pumping water. However, the total contribution of these initiatives is minute: installed capacity for solar and wind together is estimated to be only 283 MW, compared to an existing grid production of 39 493 MW (Banks & Schäffler 2005: 4).

Individual municipalities have also taken some action. The City of Cape Town's (CCT) *Energy and Climate Change Strategy* (CCT 2006) identifies a target of sourcing 10 per cent of its energy from renewable sources by 2020. In Darling near Cape Town, the Darling Independent Power Producer, the Central Energy Fund (CEF), the Danish government, the South African government and the Development Bank of Southern Africa, have combined forces in the Darling Wind Farm Project, which will be South Africa's first commercial wind farm; an annual 13.2 gigawatt-hours (GWh) of electricity will be generated using four turbines (each generating 1.3 MW). The CCT has agreed to buy the electricity supplied at a price agreed between the wind farm and the city on the basis of willing buyer/willing seller. The Global Environmental Facility has agreed to subsidise 50 per cent of the costs. This is necessary as this 'green electricity' is more expensive to produce than Eskom-generated electricity, for reasons highlighted later in this chapter.

CCT residents will be asked to pay extra for this wind-generated energy, and it will be a choice for customers if they wish to take up the offer. The wind farm is a start, but will make a negligible impact on the city's energy demand. Current peak demand is 700 MW while the wind farm is expected to deliver a maximum of 5.2 MW (CCT 2006). However, it is hoped that the Darling initiative will spur further renewable energy development in the city.

In the Eastern Cape, the Nelson Mandela metropole has also made a decision to obtain its bulk supply from renewables and cleaner energy. The mix includes solar water heaters, landfill gas and wind. The wind farm has an initial target of 20 MW with a total envisaged of 65 MW. This amounts to approximately 5 per cent of the metropole's electricity demand (Chown interview).

In Jeffrey's Bay (also in the Eastern Cape), a wind farm will be established with a proposed pump storage scheme attached to an already existing dam. The wind farm will have a capacity of 10 MW of wind energy with 5.5 MW of pumped storage. The total demand for the area is 15 MW. The renewables will be connected to the grid, and this combination of wind and pumped storage will provide some security of supply and answer the question of 'what to do when the wind doesn't blow'. Both projects use the financial mechanism of willing buyer/willing seller; the details are currently under negotiation. Customers are expected to pay a premium of R0.25/kWh for their green electricity (CCT 2003–2008; Chown interview).

Contribution of renewables by 2020 and 2050

The electricity demand predicted by Eskom for 2025 indicates that an extra 47 252 MW is required in addition to the current capacity (Eskom 2006b). Banks and Schäffler (2005) examine a number of different scenarios, with varying degrees of renewable energy in the mix. Their report examines the growth potential of different RETs and provides some indications of cost.

While there are a number of non-solar RETs such as biomass, landfill gas, waves and ocean currents, Banks and Schäffler (2005) identify solar thermal and solar PVs as large potential electricity producers for the future. They have found that because renewable technologies start from a very small base, even modelling a 10–20 per cent growth rate makes it difficult to reach a high renewable contribution by 2020. They developed three scenarios reflecting different amounts of renewable energy in the energy mix for South Africa (see also Table 7.2):

- 'Business as usual': This scenario envisages the current fossil and nuclear plants being replaced with more of the same; renewables would only contribute a negligible 4 per cent. The growth required would mean the equivalent of building a 3.6 GW power station every 30 months. Obviously, there would be severe environmental impacts if such a path were followed.
- The 'progressive renewable' scenario: This scenario sees about 13 per cent of total electricity coming from renewables by 2020. It is interesting to note that most renewable technologies become cost-competitive with new fossil-based generation plants before 2020. The report emphasises the use of lower-cost options (biomass, wind and landfill gas) from 2005 to 2020, although

experience gained with solar thermal is important, as by 2020 this is predicted to be the lowest-cost option. Solar PV costs remain high, but Banks and Schäffler (2005) point out that solar PV can be installed on an individual basis almost anywhere, and anticipate that solar PV will play a very important role in electricity supply.

- The 'high road' scenario: Banks and Schäffler attempt to model a scenario in which not only is a very large proportion of electricity generated from renewables, but there is a greater use of electricity to replace fossil fuels, for example in the transport sector.

Whereas these scenarios show a limited amount of renewables available by 2020, they change dramatically by 2050. Table 7.2 shows the total amount of renewable energy provided by this date (as a percentage of total demand), as well as the contributions of wind, solar PV and solar thermal electricity to this total.

Table 7.2: Comparative contribution of renewables to total energy demand (percentage), 2050

Scenario prediction for 2050	Total contribution of all renewables (%)	Solar thermal contribution (MW)	Solar PV contribution (MW)	Wind contribution (MW)
Business as usual	4	negligible	negligible	negligible
Progressive	70	27 311	21 479	25 287
High road	75	46 682	38 677	30 503

Source: Banks & Schäffler 2005

Does it make financial sense to shift to renewables?

While the costs of electricity generation from renewables are likely to decrease over time, the fossil fuel industries are likely to see increased costs. Oil scarcity, climate change concerns and increasing environmental safeguards applied to fossil fuel generation would contribute to this increase (Banks & Schäffler 2006). For example, in South Africa an environmental fiscal reform policy paper has been released by the National Treasury. Amongst some of the suggestions highlighted is an option to impose a tax on coal-derived electricity and exclude electricity derived from solar or wind from such taxes (Salgado 2006).

Banks and Schäffler (2005) have included a suite of complexities in their analysis and prediction of the costs of electricity production into the future. The 'progressive scenario' outlined above would have a unit cost of energy of about R0.28/kWh by 2050. Compared to current costs of about R0.11/kWh, this appears high, but it is important to remember that Eskom is in a unique position because of its history (all currently generating coal-fired plants have been paid off), and any new fossil baseload is predicted to cost in the order of at least R0.25/kWh (peak load is predicted to cost R0.70/kWh) (Banks & Schäffler 2005: 73).

In addition to operational costs, there are also the costs of developing new plant capacity. Significant investment will be needed to build new generation plants which use renewable energy. However, in the 'high road' renewables scenario developed by Banks and Schäffler, while the capital costs may be higher, the operational costs are much lower and the overall cost per kWh of energy produced is lower than the 'business as usual' path (Banks & Schäffler 2006).

Using solar thermal as an example, the starting costs for a large plant are estimated to be R0.40/kWh and predicted to decrease to such an extent that by 2012, the costs could be lower than new baseload fossil fuel plants (approximately R0.25/kWh). By 2022 solar thermal could be the lowest-cost option (Banks & Schäffler 2006: 19).

Wind electricity generation costs presently range from R0.27 to R0.70/kWh, depending on the wind regime, which enables it to compete internationally with conventional fossil fuels. According to the International Energy Agency (as cited by Banks and Schäffler 2006: 22), wind energy costs are predicted to decline by 40–50 per cent over the next 15–20 years, making it a very attractive option for grid contribution. According to Davin Chown of Ecogenesis Energy, the recently approved Darling wind farm will produce electricity at a cost of R0.47/kWh (Chown interview). The wind farm is predicted to start generating power from late 2008.

Energy demand management

While there could be long-term reductions in the costs of electricity generation, there are other areas where dramatic energy savings can be made. For example, focusing aggressively on energy demand management over time would enable the total energy demand to be reduced.

Solar water heaters provide an example of the implications of such an energy demand management approach. According to the CCT (2003), the heating of hot water in middle- to high-income electrified households constitutes 43 per cent of residential peak demand, and any actions which could reduce this demand would have a significant impact on the need for electricity generation. Table 7.3 shows a comparison of energy savings, financial costs and jobs created for installed solar water heaters versus the government plans for the new proposed nuclear reactor near Cape Town.

Table 7.3: Comparison of solar water heaters and the pebble bed technology nuclear reactor

	Solar water heaters	Pebble bed nuclear power plant
Energy saved/supplied	890 GWh/annum	750 GWh/annum
Cost	R2.6 billion	R10 billion
Creation of jobs	13 440 jobs	135 jobs

Source: Ubushushu Bendalo 2004

It is clear that the installation of solar water heaters would have a major impact on energy demand management while creating jobs, and that this could be done at a significantly lower cost than, for example, the construction of a nuclear power plant. If renewable energy makes environmental, social and economic sense, why is it not being implemented across the country?

According to Osman Asmal, Environment Department Head in the CCT, the reason that solar water heater technology was not implemented on a large scale throughout the city was partly the upfront financial costs involved, which are already committed towards existing infrastructure.[3] But another reason is that the city has not been convinced of the economic savings that would result from pursuing this option. It appears that the city has yet to conduct its own cost/benefit analysis which would show the savings to be made. Despite this, the CCT is drafting a by-law which would make installation of solar water heaters compulsory in all new houses.

Challenges to the implementation of renewable energy

It is clear that RETs offer significant benefits to South Africa, yet renewable energy currently makes a very small contribution to the overall energy supply. Why is this? The DME's renewable energy policy of 2003 raises a number of challenges and barriers to large-scale implementation of renewable energy, and proponents of renewable energy agree that there are some considerable hurdles to be overcome.

It is my view that many of these hurdles relate to the perception of renewable energy rather than to any practical obstacles, and this is supported by the statement in the *Energy Efficiency Strategy* of government which admits that solar water heating 'is financially viable but the barrier is lack of awareness/information about the technology' (DME 2005: 43).

Generating electricity when the sun doesn't shine or the wind stops blowing

As wind and solar power are intermittent energy sources, there is a need to ensure that at any one time there is sufficient energy available to generate electricity to meet demand. One way of doing this is to distribute generation sources throughout the country. For example, it is likely that at any one point in time, somewhere in the country the wind will be blowing.

Another option is to provide back-up storage. There are many different technical solutions available to meet short- and long-term storage needs. Solar thermal plants use the sun's energy to convert heat into electricity. In California, there are plants with a capacity of 350 MW which have operated for more than 10 years. The technology is therefore established, and solar thermal plants can be built on a large scale to meet industrial needs. Solar thermal plants can solve the problem of storage through storage systems such as molten salt, which would allow such plants to run 24 hours per day. Excess energy from the solar thermal plant is stored in the salt during the day and released to produce electricity at night (Agama Energy 2003).

Within South Africa currently there is about 1 580 MW of pumped storage capacity (Banks & Schäffler 2005: 24). During periods of excess electricity generation water is pumped into storage dams, and during times of shortfall the water is used to generate electricity. With current demand of approximately 40 000 MW this amounts to very little, and as a water-stressed country, there is probably little scope for significant increases in this method of storage.

However, other storage systems such as hydrogen are being developed. As in pumped storage systems, hydrogen is produced during periods of excess electricity. The hydrogen in liquid form is then used as fuel to produce electricity during times of shortfall. As an example of the potential for such systems, it was predicted in Argentina that the installation of a wind farm of 1 000 km^2 would yield hydrogen equivalent to the 2003 transport needs of Japan, and that it would be economically viable to do so once oil reached US\$35 a barrel (Spinadel et al. 2003).

Pilot projects

Despite the wealth of knowledge about renewables such as solar PV, solar water heaters and wind, it appears that such technologies are not accepted within Eskom. In the main, Eskom's response to the international focus on renewable energy has been to put forward projects to assess the viability of the technology for South Africa. Examples include the Klipheuwel (Darling) wind farm project in the Western Cape, the testing of solar water heaters, and the solar funnel project in the Northern Cape.

Eskom's insistence on proving the effectiveness of technologies which are already proven in other parts of the world has resulted in the stalling of the implementation of renewable energy technologies. The pilot phase of such projects then delays the full-scale implementation of the technology. Such insistence on pilot projects further creates a perception that the efficacy of the technologies is in question.

In the case of the Klipheuwel wind farm pilot, criticisms levelled against the project include that the turbines are at the wrong height, and that the project is in a sub-optimal site (Morris interview). Under such circumstances, it is unlikely that the research results will show wind energy as a viable option for South Africa. As the research results from such pilots would be used to justify Eskom's policy direction, and given Eskom's almost total control of energy generation, such pilot projects then retard the implementation of renewables in South Africa. Such doubts spread to other government departments, and little government support is then likely to be forthcoming for renewable energy technologies.

This use of pilot projects needs to be contrasted with the pebble bed nuclear technology project, which has received huge support from Eskom and large amounts of government funding despite having a financial track record which is abysmal compared to that of wind or solar technology (see Fig, Chapter 6 in this volume). While wind and solar technologies are established throughout the world, the pebble bed technology is still in the developmental phase. The cost of the pebble bed demonstration plant 'has increased by a factor of five and completion of the Demonstration Plant, expected in 1999 to be in 2003, is now still six years off' (Thomas 2005: 30). These figures also fail to reflect costs such as fuel production, as well as the nuclear regulatory regime required to ensure public safety.

Investment challenges

The solar thermal electricity plant which will be piloted in the Northern Cape will use 6 000 mirrors and span a 4 kilometre site. This solar technology is being assessed by Eskom, and a key component of this feasibility assessment is the determination of the cost (*Business Report* 20 July 2006). It is not clear how the cost comparisons will be calculated in order to factor in the benefits of renewable energy against the externalities of conventional coal and nuclear.

According to Awerbuch (2000), the investment analysis tools for energy have not changed in 100 years. This might have been appropriate if we had to compare one centrally-based fossil fuel power plant with another, but is less useful when faced with the diverse range of energy resource alternatives available today. If we use solar PVs as an example, the costs of PV are almost all upfront costs. There are almost no operating costs and no fuel costs.

However, these large initial investments are viewed as a hurdle and identified in the DME White Paper on Renewable Energy as the main barrier to implementation on a large scale (DME 2003). According to Awerbuch (2000) this shows a lack of understanding of renewable energy technologies. In a gas turbine, for example, less cash flow is tied up in the loan because there is more outlay needed for operational expenses. In the case of PV, there is very little cash needed for operational expenses. Awerbuch argues that low-risk investments can take on bigger loans and higher loan repayments, and that this is accepted practice elsewhere:

> Where the asset is nearly systematically riskless, high loan to value makes a lot of sense. Everyone seems to understand that, for example, when you put up riskless Treasury bills against your margin loan, your broker might lend you 90% of their value. But you might only get 50% or 75% of value if you put up risky stocks (Awerbuch 2000: 5).

It is worth noting, however, that a breakthrough has taken place in California. A Californian team announced that it planned to build a solar panel production facility with a capacity of 215 MW in 2007, and thereafter producing 430 MW annually. The investors included Google's two founders, and the price quoted was

US$100 million. The first panels were shipped to Germany in December 2007. The exciting impact of this technology is that it will bring the cost of PV to or below the level of 'delivered electricity' in a large part of the world (Freeman & Harding 2006).

Oil companies have also started to show an interest in renewable energy. According to Reuters (*Business Report* 4 April 2007), Royal Dutch Shell has invested US$1 billion in renewables over the past five years while BP invested US$500 million in solar between 1999 and 2005, and US$300 million in wind generation in 2005–2006.

This large-scale investment appears to signal that renewable energy is becoming a viable financial proposition, able to compete with fossil and nuclear energy, and is no longer the preserve of academic institutions and government-subsidised programmes.

Factoring in the hidden external costs of fossil fuels and nuclear energy

Awerbuch (2000) argues that the relative costs of RETs to fossil fuels can change over time due to uncertainties such as the increasing price of oil, the decreasing costs associated with improved efficiencies of evolving newer RETs, and the increasing cost of meeting constantly improving environmental standards.

The implications of Awerbuch's conclusions are that the costs of fuels from sources such as the sun, ocean currents and the wind can be factored into long-term financial equations as a fixed cost – e.g. zero – while there is huge uncertainty related to the oil price which must be factored into conventional electricity generation (e.g. to transport nuclear fuel to the reactor and convey waste to a dump site). To illustrate, the petrol price in South Africa rose from R3.81 per litre in 2003 to R7.23 per litre in December 2007, an increase of almost 100 per cent over four years.

These risks are ignored in conventional financial models, and the comparative benefits of renewables are not apparent (Awerbuch 2000).

Government policy and the challenges of renewable energy

In her foreword to the White Paper on Renewable Energy (DME 2003), Deputy Minerals and Energy Minister Susan Shibanga states that the policy document is there to give a much needed boost to renewables. She goes on to identify a government target of 10 000 GWh renewable energy by 2013, which amounts to 4 per cent of total electricity demand in South Africa (DME 2003: i).

How does government policy propose to achieve these goals? The White Paper identifies four areas of strategic intervention, each with a number of goals, objectives and deliverables:

- Financial and legal instruments: One of the deliverables under this heading is to identify barriers to renewable energy and to investigate fiscal instruments which could stimulate renewable energy development. In 2006, Treasury released a paper looking at financing mechanisms, including taxing polluting industry (Salgado 2006). In 2004/05, the CEF commissioned a study to investigate subsidies for solar water heaters. There appears to be some progress in this regard but it is dishearteningly slow.

- Legal instruments: Deliverables under this intervention include regulations which would increase access to the grid, stimulate the uptake of renewable energy and force power generators to base their tariffs on full-cost accounting, including environmental externalities. Unfortunately, there have been no regulations passed in this regard.

- Technology development: A key deliverable here is the inclusion of research and development in the scope of the South African National Energy Research Institute. This institute will be housed at the CEF and the plan appears to be to invest R100 million in its work over the period 2006–2009 (Hanekom 2006). Unfortunately, it is impossible not to contrast this with the R14.5 billion estimated allocation for the nuclear demonstration pilot (Cokayne 2006).

- Awareness-raising, capacity-building and education: Education and awareness-raising amongst all stakeholders through campaigns, a key deliverable, have yet to become visible. Although the DME political heads do speak of renewables in the press to some extent, it is also difficult for the public to understand the mixed messages from different Cabinet ministers, sometimes promoting renewables and sometimes ignoring them and supporting the nuclear industry.

The White Paper on Renewable Energy (DME 2003) admirably states that it 'will not reinvent the wheel' with regard to established technologies. It also states that the National Energy Regulator of South Africa (NERSA) will be able to determine the price at which power generators can sell their energy, and regulate electricity tariffs. It is therefore unfortunate that NERSA should find itself at the centre of a constitutional battle over whether it has the right to interfere in the local-authority mandate of providing electricity (Hamlyn 2006).

According to the DME (DME 2004), there are two strategic options available to facilitate the uptake of renewables onto the grid. The first is *direct capital subsidies*, which the DME believes are the answer for near-commercial projects. This appears to be an attempt to level the playing fields by subsidising capital investments, but the control of the price renewable energy suppliers would receive for their generated power remains unsubsidised.

However, in the longer term, the DME views the second option, *feed-in tariff*, favourably. A feed-in tariff would regulate the price that suppliers can charge for their renewable energy, in effect guaranteeing their viability. This would enable renewable energy suppliers to prepare their business case and look for investment on the basis of a known return. It is a system which has been implemented in other parts of the world, for example in Denmark and Germany.

According to Lackmann (2003), German suppliers were able to reduce the cost of wind-generated electricity by 60 per cent over just 12 years. They achieved this through the application of a feed-in tariff, which stimulated enormous advances in wind turbine technology. The results are startling, and South Africa needs to take note. In Germany, installed wind capacity was 68 MW in 1990 when the feed-in law was introduced. By 2000, installed capacity was 6 095 MW and by 2004 it was 15 000 MW (Meixner 2003). In the South African context, the feed-in tariff is regarded as the most effective system to promote the rapid uptake of renewables (Austin interview).

Another mechanism involves forcing the distributor to buy a certain percentage of power from a renewable supplier but allowing this to occur at market prices. However, the DME admits that this system raises problems in that renewable suppliers cannot survive on such arrangements and other subsidies must then be put in place (DME 2004).

The willing buyer/willing seller approach allows the renewable energy supplier to negotiate with the buyer in order to come to an arrangement for a fixed tariff. This is the approach that has been adopted for the Darling wind energy project.

Australia has taken the route of mandating renewable energy targets legally, with penalties for non-compliance (DME 2004), and has used a system of tradeable renewable energy certificates (TRECs). These certificates can be obtained for producing a certain amount of renewable energy, and can then be sold. They provide a further source of income to the renewable energy suppliers, and are one of the ways to supplement renewable energy supplier income which is dependent on subsidies. TRECs arise out of the global threat of climate change and are based on the idea that industries can continue 'business as usual' and then buy their way out of changing themselves by financing other businesses that generate renewable energy. Such 'greenwash' systems are attractive to renewable energy lobbyists as they provide a practicable means of offsetting the current initial high investment costs of renewables. But they fail to address one fundamental problem – the need for *existing* industry to switch from dirty and energy-wasting power production to clean energy in order to reduce the climate change impacts on the planet.

While it is ideologically correct to reject TRECs and carbon-trading systems that fail to address the impacts of climate change in any meaningful way, it is my view that these financial tools could play a role in ensuring that RETs hit the global spotlight, thereby contributing to the uptake of renewable energy globally. Such uptake of renewable energy should replace current polluting industries such as nuclear and coal over time, thereby contributing to overall sustainable development goals.

Institutional support for renewables

There are several state agencies tasked with the responsibility of investigating renewable forms of energy in South Africa. In this section I briefly review some of these organisations and discuss the extent to which renewable energy is championed by them (or not).

The CEF is a state-owned company, controlled by the minister of minerals and energy, which is responsible for a number of wide-ranging activities in the energy field. One of its portfolios is renewable energy. In 2004, the CEF established the Energy Development Corporation. This division pursues 'commercially viable' investments in renewable energy. According to the CEF website, the Energy Development Corporation is 'close to the policy makers, [and] able to lobby the relevant government departments and institutions for support when necessary. At the same time it operates as a fully commercial entity.'[4]

The front cover of the CEF's 2007 *Annual Review* shows a wind farm at sunset. While progress appears slow, the strategic objectives for 2007/08 include solar water heaters, the Darling wind farm and exploring landfill gas, but also include continuing focus on biofuels research and implementation. The CEF is also investigating a PV panel production plant for South Africa. CEF investment is given as approximately R7.8 million whereas PetroSA (part of the CEF group) showed a net after-tax profit of R36.4 million (CEF 2007: 6, 8–9, 63).

The CEF also established the South African National Energy Research Institute (SANERI) in 2006, as a result of a ministerial directive. The SANERI received a R2 million start-up grant from the Department of Science and Technology. At the time of writing, the CEF website contained one tender issued by SANERI, for oil and gas, not renewables. However, such a research body could play a decisive role in the exploitation of renewable resources. For example, the SANERI might research the best sites for wind farms within South Africa. Such research, conducted by the state and available to all, would help to guide investment decisions regarding the best sites for wind farms, without each potential wind farm owner having to undertake similar, costly research.

The NERSA is also an important player. It has not provided information on its stance on regulating renewables, but according to press reports it has been involved in the following activities:

- Two gas turbine power plants were to be built at a cost of R3.5 billion. These plants (with a total capacity of 1 050 MW) were scheduled to come online by 2007, at Atlantis and Mossel Bay respectively (Gosling 2005).
- In March 2006 the NERSA announced that it had called for bids to build two open cycle gas turbine power plants. These were to have a combined capacity of 1 000 MW (Faniso 2006).
- It was also reported that a private company, Independent Power Southern Africa, planned to build an 800 MW combined cycle gas turbine plant in Port Elizabeth (with a cost estimate of about R1.9 billion) as well as a 400 MW coal-fired power plant near East London (cost estimate not provided). It appeared from the reports that these power plants would apply for licences

within the next two years, and that the NERSA would look favourably on their application (Faniso 2006).

The NERSA has a policy position that stipulates that electricity prices must be based on the lowest-cost option for generating new capacity (*Business Report* 2006). While this may be good news for consumers and communities, the cheapest form of electricity may hide a number of externalities such as toxic emissions. The NERSA position also contradicts the White Paper on Renewable Energy, which states that power generators would 'base their tariffs on full cost accounting, including environmental externalities' (DME 2003: 40).

In April 2007, a press report indicated that the NERSA would be asked to approve an electricity price increase of 18 per cent despite inflation figures of 3–6 per cent (Williams 2007). In a press statement released by the NERSA in December 2007, it announced that 'given Eskom's capital financing needs' there would be a 14 per cent increase in electricity prices (NERSA 2007).

As for Eskom, its R97 billion capital expansion programme (increased to about R150 billion in early 2007) contains no significant plans for renewables. It is sobering to see that of a planned potential increase of 47 000 MW of new capacity envisaged by Eskom to meet South Africa's electricity needs over the next 20 years, less than 0.2 per cent will be in renewables.

Eskom controls almost all of the country's electricity generation, all transmission and some distribution (most of the latter is the mandate of local authorities). Its energy strategy, as presented on its official website, includes a reference to '[e]nsuring the sustainability of the business through balanced financial, social and environmental decision making'. This is translated into a number of descriptive points on how the core strategy would be achieved, from which it is clear that 'high quality, low cost' electricity is Eskom's primary aim.[5]

It could be argued that ensuring Eskom's 'sustainability' as a business is not necessarily going to ensure the most effective energy services for South Africa. Eskom's financial sustainability is linked to generating the largest income (from electricity sales) in order to generate profits for Eskom. Decisions aimed at achieving this are unlikely to take account of externality costs such as toxic emissions unless forced to do so by government. If Eskom makes decisions based purely on conventional cost comparisons, with no political incentives to change to renewables, coal-fired power stations are likely to remain the 'lowest cost option' in the short term.

Such a strategy cannot be read in any other way than as a firm commitment to the continuation of traditional capital-intensive energy generation projects such as coal-fired power stations, with the addition of further fossil fuels such as gas, and hydro developments in the region.

Challenging 'business as usual': returning power to the people?

In order for renewable energy technologies to play a major part in the future of South Africa, some radical changes are necessary. What types of systems would need to be put in place in order for South Africa to move beyond the fossil age into the solar age? This section provides some general suggestions for such systems.

Transforming the grid

As pointed out by the DME (2004), a utility such as Eskom, which controls generation, transmission and distribution, finds itself in a conflict of interest when facilitating access to the grid for renewable power. If the grid were 'smarter', it would be more decentralised, improving efficiencies by reducing the distances between the energy producer and the user – in South Africa transmission losses from Mpumalanga to Cape Town are presently about 10–20 per cent (Dobbins 2006). A decentralised system would also increase the security of power supply and be less vulnerable to power disruptions. The future scenario would see a flexible, dynamic grid that can accept power as well as push it out.

According to Guterl and Romano (2004), one of the challenges to such a system change would be the number of standards and specifications that would need to be developed. Obviously there is a cost attached to this, but it would be possible to draw on international best practice for assistance. Some perspective can be gained by considering the 2006 electricity blackouts in South Africa. Eskom was forced to pay customers with the ability to generate their own electricity to keep them from drawing power off the grid (Eskom generates electricity at R0.11/kWh but paid out approximately R1.70/kWh to these consumers) (Chown interview). It seems logical to assume, therefore, that a system which allows customers to feed back electricity into the grid, rather than paying inflated prices to keep customers off the grid, would be of benefit to all.

International experience clearly shows that where the systems are in place, renewable energy will flourish (Guterl & Romano 2004: 36–37):
- In Japan, Hitoshi Iokawa installed solar panels on his roof in 1997. It cost him the equivalent of US$33 000 of which the government subsidised a third. By 2004 he was generating an income of $460 per year selling electricity back to the grid – enough to offset his electricity bills. Japan started its programme of solar power in 1993. In 2004, 170 000 homes were feeding into the grid.
- In California in 2004, Ignacio Vella was powering the fridges in his cheese factory with 234 solar panels, and was able to sell leftover energy back to PG&E, the local power company.
- In countries like India, where, similarly to South Africa, power supply lags behind demand, local power producers have emerged. Sugar mills are producing their own electricity from bagasse. In Karnataka and Maharashtra, 500 MW of power is being produced per year, some of which is then sold back into the grid.

The role of civil society

The role of civil society within the energy sector has been mostly reactive to date. Organisations such as Earthlife Africa and the Environmental Justice Networking Forum, as well as some faith communities, have mobilised *against* the nuclear industry, but little has been done to mobilise *for* renewable technologies.

Groups such as the Civil Society Energy Caucus have been formed to lobby on energy-related issues, and some of their work has focused on renewable energy. I am aware of some discussion about founding a renewable energy caucus but such a body is not in existence yet. The South African Faith Communities Environmental Institute is a recent initiative amongst faith-based groups which focuses on environmental sustainability, including renewable energy. In the press, Bishop Davies, the chairperson of the institute, has called on Eskom to spend money on renewable energy, to open up to other power producers and to 'move resources from the control of giant and multinational corporations into the hands of the people' (Davies 2006).

One civil-society initiative, the Ubushushu Bendalo campaign, has raised the profile of solar water heating and concentrated on this technology as one solution. Ubushushu Bendalo has lobbied government leadership in the Western Cape at both city and provincial levels and has been selected by the CCT to assist with the rollout of solar water heaters in the metropole (CCT 2006).

There is some research being done on the renewables sector (e.g. the work of Agama Energy and the DME; see also Banks & Schäffler 2005). However, the level of lobbying and advocacy is poor and, in general, civil-society campaigns lack capacity to use the available information effectively.

Civil-society lobbying strategies could focus on advocating for a number of concrete institutional steps to be taken which would encourage the development of RETs. These could include:
- government passing laws making certain RETs mandatory, for example solar water heaters (such as the CCT's draft regulation which would make it mandatory for all new buildings to have solar water heaters);
- fiscal measures such as taxes on fossil fuel-derived electricity that would assist in levelling the playing fields as well as giving life to the principle of 'the polluter pays', which already exists in law;
- transformation of the grid to allow power to be fed into it as well as drawn off it;
- a government mandate to Eskom to direct 20 per cent of its current investment into RETs;
- government ensuring that the poor are protected from increased electricity tariffs.

Conclusion

There is no doubt that renewable energy has a place in the energy equation for South Africa and the rest of Africa. However, the target set for the South African renewables uptake is only 4 per cent by 2013 (DME 2003), and the underlying government assumption is that RET is relegated to use by the rural poor and for small-scale applications, while mainstream electricity generation will be via traditional grid-based technologies.

And yet, renewable technology is viable in areas of the world that are much poorer in renewable resources than South Africa. Renewables are economically viable, and it is technically possible to produce large amounts of reliable electricity using these technologies, sufficient to satisfy even the needs of the greedy captains of industry.

The real problem is not, therefore, the economic or technical issues related to RETs, but the absence of *political will* to take the lead. Former British Prime Minister Tony Blair's response to the challenge of climate change summarises the political dilemma: 'There is a mismatch in timing between the environmental and electoral impact' (Blair cited in Monbiot 2006: 22). In effect, the full horror of the harmful environmental impacts of our current dirty electricity generation path may only be felt in 25 years' time, whereas politicians only operate in terms of five-electoral cycles.

RETs are beneficial to a developing nation; they are sources of clean electricity, safe energy and an increase in jobs. The economics are sound, providing that a full cost/benefit analysis is performed. However, what is beneficial for the state may not be the best option for the parastatal company, Eskom. Eskom will continue to generate at least 70 per cent of South Africa's electricity and therefore must be transformed. The only way that renewables will become mainstream in South Africa is if Eskom is instructed by Cabinet to plough significant resources into implementation of RETs, not in the form of pilot research but as a rollout of large-scale power supply.

Eskom appears to have taken what it believes to be a low-risk route of sticking to technologies that it knows. Committing the country to a centralised grid also ensures that it maintains an income stream, either through charging for access to the grid by independent power producers, or by generating electricity directly into the grid using established technologies.

Is this the wisest strategy for a country where more than half of the children live in households with an income of less than R3 per day (*Cape Times* 6 February 2007)? Government has a responsibility to provide energy security to all citizens, irrespective of their ability to pay. Sustainable energy security will be found in a diversity of energy sources.

Energy is necessary for development and Africa stands at a crossroads. It can choose to follow the dirty, heavily polluting technologies which are being dumped on the continent by the countries of the First World, including large fossil fuel power plants, nuclear energy and large-scale hydro. Alternatively, Africa can take a visionary approach, the high road to sustainable development, leapfrogging over the dirty technology development phase that the rest of the world has experienced (which has led to the current crisis). This high road is not 'business as usual'; it puts people first. It provides the most suitable energy source to meet demand at the least cost. But in this case the calculation of least cost includes the impact on natural resources, the impact on human health, and the impact on future generations.

To choose such a path will allow African countries to take full advantage of the current climate change crisis to start down the visionary road. Such a growth trajectory cannot be held back or stifled by pollution taxes, and will not be held to ransom by declining and ever more costly fossil fuels, but will use the best available technology internationally, producing clean electricity forever. All that is needed to start on this path is a leader!

Notes

1   Banks and Schäffler do include small/micro hydro of up to 9 900 GWh per annum in their progressive scenario (Banks & Schäffler 2005: 26). These figures have been included in the arguments in this chapter. However, large hydro-power schemes face a number of social/environmental and political challenges which are discussed elsewhere, and their inclusion in the renewable energy mix is not supported by this author.

2   Bagasse is plant material waste left behind after sugar is extracted from sugar cane. It can be used as a fuel in an electricity-generating plant.

3   Osman Asmal, personal communication

4   www.cef.org.za

5   www.eskom.co.za

References

Agama Energy (2003) *Employment potential of renewable energy in South Africa*. Report commissioned by the Sustainable Energy and Climate Change Partnership (SECCP). Johannesburg: SECCP

Awerbuch S (2000) Investing in renewables: Risk accounting and the value of new technology. *Energy Policy*. Accessed March 2008, http://www.elsevier.com/wps/find/journaldescription.cws_home/30414/description

Banks D & Schäffler J (2005) *The potential contribution of renewable energy in South Africa*. Johannesburg: Earthlife Africa

Banks D & Schäffler J (2006) *The potential contribution of renewable energy in South Africa*. *Draft update report*. Johannesburg: Sustainable Energy and Climate Change Partnership

Bond P (ed.) (2002) *Fanon's warning*. Trenton, NJ: Africa World Press

Business Report (2006) Users won't fund reactor-NER. *Business Report* 12 January

CCT (City of Cape Town) (2003) *State of energy report for Cape Town 2003*. Cape Town: CCT

CCT (2003–2008) *Are you serious about sustainability? Then consider green electricity.* Accessed March 2008, http://www.capetown.gov.za/wcmstemplates/Electricity.aspx?clusid=458&catparent=6003&IDpathString=5992-6003

CCT (2006) *Energy and climate change strategy.* Cape Town: CCT

CEF (Central Energy Fund) (2007) *Annual review 2007.* Johannesburg: CEF

Cokayne R (2006) Critical time for nuclear project. *Business Report* 23 January

Davies G (2006) Put energy in the hands of the people. *Cape Times* 20 February

DME (Department of Minerals and Energy, South Africa) (1998) *White Paper on the Energy Policy of the Republic of South Africa.* Pretoria: DME

DME (2003) *White Paper on Renewable Energy.* Pretoria: DME

DME (2004) *Capacity building in energy efficiency and renewable energy.* Pretoria: DME

DME (2005) *Energy efficiency strategy of the Republic of South Africa.* Pretoria: DME

Dobbins A (2006) Energy efficiency. Paper presented at the Renewable Energy Workshop convened by Earthlife Africa, April

Eskom (2006a) Eskom & renewable energy – global solutions for future power needs. *African Wildlife* 60(2): 38–41

Eskom (2006b) Presentation of the Western Cape Integrated Recovery Plan to public meeting convened by Cosatu, March, Cape Town International Convention Centre

Faniso M (2006) NER opens up power plant licensing. *Business Report* 8 March

FEMA (Forum for Energy Ministers of Africa) (2006) Energy and the Millennium Development Goals in Africa April 2006. Paper commissioned by the Forum for Energy Ministers in Africa for the UN World Summit, September 2005, published by the World Bank in 2006. Accessed September 2006, http://www-wds.worldbank.org/external/default/main?pagePK=64193027&piPK=64187937&theSitePK=523679&menuPK=64187510&searchMenuPK=64187283&theSitePK=523679&entityID=000012009_20060501145407&searchMenuPK=64187283&theSitePK=523679

Freeman D & Harding Jim (2006) Solar cells change electricity distribution, *Seattlepi.com.* 10 August 2006. Accessed 15 January 2006, http://seattlepi.nwsource.com/opinion/280625_solarcell10.html

Gosling M (2005) Gas turbine power stations for Atlantis, Mossel Bay. *Cape Times* 23 December

Greenpeace (2006) *Global wind energy outlook for 2006.* Accessed September 2006, http://www.greenpeace.org/international/press/reports?related_item_id=160030

Guterl F & Romano A (2004) People power. *Newsweek* 13 September: 36–37

Hallowes D & Butler M (2004) *The balance of rights: The Groundwork report 2004.* South Africa: Groundwork

Hamlyn M (2006) Constitutionality of new electricity bill challenged. *Business Report* 21 September

Hanekom D (2006) Address of the Deputy Minister, Ministry of Science and Technology, in the Budget Vote in the National Assembly, 26 May

Hathaway T (2005a) *Hydropower and African grid development: A rights based perspective.* Paper 05GM0884, International Rivers Network

Hathaway T (2005b) *Dirty hydro won't bring clean development to Africa.* International Rivers Network. Accessed March 2008, http://www.irn.org/basics/alternatives/index.php?id=050705g8.html

Kammen D (2006) The rise of renewable energy. *Scientific American* September: 86–93

Lackmann J (2003) Reference revenue model in Germany's renewable energy feed law. Paper presented at the World Wind Energy Conference and Renewable Energy Exhibition, 23–26 November, Cape Town International Convention Centre

Meixner U (2003) Wind energy funds in Germany – specific requirements. Paper presented at the World Wind Energy Conference and Renewable Energy Exhibition, 23–26 November, Cape Town International Convention Centre

Midgley GF, Chapman RA, Hewitson B, Johnston P, De Wit M, Ziervogel G, Mukheibir P, Van Niekerk L, Tadross M, Van Wilgen BW, Kgope B, Morant PD, Theron A, Scholes RJ & Forsyth GG (2005) *A status quo, vulnerability and adaptation assessment of the physical and socio-economic effects of climate change in the Western Cape.* Report to the Western Cape Government, Cape Town, South Africa. CSIR Report No. ENV-S-C 2005-073, Stellenbosch

Monbiot G (2006) *Heat.* London: Penguin

NEPAD (New Partnership for Africa's Development) (2001) *The New Partnership for Africa's Development: Part 1.* October. Accessed 15 January 2006, http://www.au2002.gov.za/docs/key_oau/nepad.pd

NERSA (National Energy Regulator of South Africa) (2007) Eskom's electricity price increase for 2008/09 and municipality electricity tariff guideline and benchmarks for 2008/09. Press release, 20 December. Accessed 29 February 2008, http://www.esi-africa.com/node/8810

Salgado I (2006) State considers higher green taxes. *Business Report* 7 April

SAPP (Southern African Power Pool) (2006) *Annual report 2006.* Harare: SAPP

Spinadel E, Gil J & Gamallo F (2003) Wind-produced hydrogen exported from Patagonia. Paper presented at the World Wind Energy Conference and Renewable Energy Exhibition, 23–26 November, Cape Town International Convention Centre

Thomas S (2005) *The economic impact of the proposed demonstration plant for the pebble bed modular reactor design.* Public Service International Research Unit, University of Greenwich, UK

Ubushushu Bendalo (2004) Ubushushu Bendalo (heat from nature) Programme, prepared by ELA Cape Town, AGAMA Energy, for presentation in August 2004

Ubushushu Bendalo (2006) *Find out more about solar water heaters.* Cape Town: Sustainable Energy Africa

US EIA (United States Department of Energy, Energy Information Administration) (2005) *Southern African Development Community country analysis brief.* Accessed May 2006, http://www.eia.doe.gov/emeu/cabs/sadc.pdf

Williams F (2007) Eskom se tarief bo inflasie 'ongesond' [Eskom's tariff above inflation 'unhealthy']. *Die Burger* (Cape Town) 20 April

Interviews

Austin G, Agama Energy, Cape Town, October 2006

Chown D, Ecogenesis Energy, Cape Town, December 2006

Mimi S, Southern African Regional Secretariat, Renewable Energy and Energy Efficiency Partnership (REEEP), April 2006

Morris G, Agama Energy, Cape Town, October 2006

CHAPTER 8

Discipline and the new 'logic of delivery': Prepaid electricity in South Africa and beyond

Peter van Heusden

In November 1976, the Carlton Hotel in Johannesburg was the site of an unusual conference. Titled 'Quality of Life of Urban Communities', it brought together white business leaders and the Committee of Ten, a civic organisation from Soweto that had arisen after the student protests of June 1976. Afrikaner businessman Anton Rupert was one of the main speakers at the conference. 'We cannot survive unless we have a free market economy, a stable Black middle class with the necessary security of tenure, personal security and a feeling of hope for betterment in the heart of all our peoples,' he said. Rupert went on to outline a programme of development which, he thought, would lead the way out of the dead end of increasingly repressive apartheid policies: job creation, training, a living wage, greater commercial opportunities, extended home ownership, improved housing, and the provision of sporting and other amenities (Butler 2007: 8).

Rupert's vision was starkly at odds with the actions of the South African state. At the time, 'influx control' made most black South Africans foreigners in their own country, citizens of artificially created 'tribal homelands'. Education, health and other social services for black South Africans were systematically underfunded (Mandela 1964), and black aspirations were systematically quashed. Introducing the Bantu Education Bill in Parliament in 1953, Education Minister (and later Prime Minister) HF Verwoerd said: 'When I have control of native education, I will reform it so that natives will be taught from childhood to realise that equality with Europeans is not for them' (cited in Parsons 1982). The 1976 student protests served to illustrate that for black people, things had not changed much since 1953.

The 1976 protests shattered the apparent calm that white South African society had experienced since the apartheid state's repression of the African National Congress (ANC) and the Pan African Congress in the early 1960s. As Hjalte Tin (2001: 127) explains, 'the children [of 1976] somehow found a weak spot in the rule of apartheid and were able to attack the state so successfully that 1976 became the turning point of apartheid. The Nationalists would soldier on for almost two decades, but the polished surface of post-Rivonia apartheid was irrevocably shattered.' Anton Rupert's conference was a response to this rupture, a response which tried to map another strategy for capital, one that relied on something other than simply increasing state repression to maintain 'stability'.

A decade later, in 1988, Eskom (South Africa's state-owned electricity generation monopoly) launched its 'Electricity for All' mass electrification programme. The then CEO of Eskom, Ian McRae, explained the reasoning behind the programme as 'the best way to combat poverty [by] provid[ing] economic growth and social upliftment' (McRae 1998). In his study of electrification in southern Africa, Trevor Gaunt (2003: 25), who was involved as an engineer in the electrification process in South Africa, states: 'Political unrest in the 1970s and 1980s drew attention to the unequal living conditions of the different race groups in South Africa...The need for "corrective action" by supplying electricity to those [to] whom it had not been available was evident...a social "right of access to energy" will develop...because electricity will support an improvement in the quality of life.' Gaunt goes on to quote his 1988 paper – which was delivered to a technical meeting of the Association of Municipal Energy Undertakings (AMEU): 'It is therefore important to find ways of supplying at least some of the benefits of electricity at prices which are sub-economic by present standards' (Gaunt 2003: 24).

At the time that Gaunt was writing about the need to address a 'right of access to energy', and Eskom was launching 'Electricity for All', the vast majority of domestic electricity users were connected to the national grid via municipal electricity utilities. Apartheid-era local government was based on the combination of a patchwork of racially-based local authorities (for so-called white, coloured, Indian, and, after 1983, African areas) alongside provincial administrations. City planning focused on the separation of racial groups, with forced removals and spatial barriers (e.g. railway lines and main roads) being used to bring the philosophy of 'separate development' into the city in concrete form. With 'separate development' came separate budgeting, with the result that the systematic underdevelopment of services for black people in apartheid South Africa manifested itself as a lack of electricity for black people as well. By 1976, only 20 per cent of Soweto residents had access to electricity, for instance, compared to the near 100 per cent electrification of nearby white suburbs (Beavon 1997).

The 'right to access to energy' was eventually codified as part of the commitment to 'meeting basic needs' in the 1994 Reconstruction and Development Programme, the ANC's post-apartheid policy blueprint (ANC 1994). The comments cited above by McRae and Gaunt, both professionals within the electricity industry, show that these concepts long pre-dated the end of the apartheid state. Besides the pressure from below in the form of township protests, a surge of power station construction by Eskom in the 1970s had led to overcapacity in the mid- to late 1980s (Gaunt 2003). Thus, by the time that the 'Electricity for All' project was launched, Eskom had an electricity generation surplus to sell to newly connected black consumers.

The limited experiment in electrifying Soweto from the early 1980s onwards, however, had highlighted two problems. Firstly, a lack of funding to black local authorities (the municipal structures responsible for local government in black townships) hampered their ability to actually deliver electricity as a municipal utility. Secondly, the legitimacy crisis of the black local authorities, and the apartheid state in general, saw payment boycotts for municipal services being deployed as a weapon of struggle, with the resulting problem of inability to collect payments for services (Malzbender & Kamoto 2005).

The attempt to respond to black South Africans' demands through their integration as consumers of services, including electricity, thus faced structural problems in that it threatened to be, in Trevor Gaunt's term, 'sub-economic' by the standards of previous electrification in South Africa. As political pressure against apartheid grew – both internally in the form of renewed resistance from the black population, and externally in the form of economic sanctions and other pressures – those tasked with implementing domestic electrification started exploring new technologies to resolve the problems that early attempts had encountered. It is in this context that experiments with prepaid electricity meters developed.

Development of prepayment systems in South Africa

Despite being associated in most people's minds with the late 1980s and 1990s, prepaid technology in South Africa dates back to 1913, when the mining settlement of Jagersfontein (situated in what is now the Free State) minted 10 000 special tokens, each of which released three gallons of water from the town pump (Balson 1997).

However, notwithstanding examples such as the Jagersfontein 'water penny', the majority of electricity supplied to domestic consumers up to the 1980s was supplied using 'credit meters'; in other words, meters which record consumption, with their records being collected by meter readers and bills then being issued based on metered (or in some cases, estimated) consumption. The process of reading such meters, distributing bills, dealing with arrears and so forth proved costly in economic, and maybe even more importantly, political terms, however. Since credit meters simply record consumption, the process of disconnecting a household from electricity supply involves an obvious intervention on the part of the electricity utility, and since all domestic electricity utilities in South Africa have been state-owned, the process of electricity disconnection is an easy one to politicise.

As was noted above, electrification of black areas such as Soweto was accompanied by politicised payment boycotts, and in this context engineers working in the field of electricity supply were given an incentive to design revenue collection systems which could alleviate the need to physically manage electricity connections (and disconnections). In 1985, Don Taylor, an engineer who at the time was working for the South African Astronomical Observatory in Cape Town, was approached by the Qwa Qwa Development Corporation to solve the revenue collection problems they were experiencing in the electrification of the Qwa Qwa 'homeland' (in the eastern Free State). The development of low-cost integrated circuits from the 1970s onwards, and the resulting ability to implement complex encryption algorithms in a compact device, allowed for the development of a fully electronic prepaid meter system, based on the sale of numeric tokens (in early devices supplied on paper cards, and in later devices printed on a payment slip) from a central point. These tokens then had to be entered into the prepaid meter for electricity to be supplied.[1]

Eskom was drawn into the development process of the prepaid meter by Taylor and his colleagues at an early stage, being consulted in 1986 during product development to comment on technical issues. This involvement alerted Eskom employees to the possibilities of electronic prepayment technology, and they later expressed an interest in using prepaid technology for their 'Electricity for All' campaign. Although 'Electricity for All' was only launched in 1988, McRae speaks of the ideas for the project emerging from 1985 onwards; thus the discussions in 1986 fed into the early planning for the campaign, which, at the time, aimed to connect 5 million households to the electricity grid, on a purely business – i.e. cost recovery – basis (McRae 1998).

With a product in hand, Taylor's colleague Rudi Coetzee went on a marketing campaign, which led to small installations at Thabong Municipality (in the Free State), Witrivier Municipality (now in Mpumalanga, this installation was facilitated by the 'coloured' House of Representatives, one of three racially defined houses in the apartheid Parliament) and elsewhere during 1987. Another early prepaid entrepreneur, Larry Barnett, gave a presentation in Parliament on prepayment technology, with the result that elements in the apartheid government moved to standardise the technology as a means towards quality control. Taylor mentions that there were fears that poor-quality prepaid technology products could exacerbate anti-government feeling in the townships. The South African Bureau of Standards, the Council for Scientific and Industrial Research and Eskom were all drawn into this standardisation programme, which would take several years.

Eskom's involvement in the prepaid field shifted to an entirely new level, however, in 1989, when the decision was made to use prepayment technology for its national electrification programme. Taylor and Coetzee's venture, Angcon Technologies, received a contract to provide 6 000 prepayment meters for installation in Kwa-nobuhle (near Uitenhage, now in the Eastern Cape). This was, however, only a small part of Eskom's overall 'Electricity for All' programme, which grew to a maximum of more than 250 000 installations in 1993 (Gaunt 2003: 28).

At the same time that Angcon Technologies and others were providing prepaid meter systems to Eskom, multinational telecommunications firm Plessey-Tellumat started a programme of aggressively marketing prepayment technology to municipalities. By this time apartheid was crumbling, and white business was clearly focused on a post-apartheid future. In line with this planning, Nedbank and Old Mutual collaborated on a study in 1990 entitled 'South Africa: Prospects for a Successful Transition' (Gaunt 2003) which, amongst other things, promoted mass electrification as a mechanism for social and economic development. Engineers within local government also got involved in the debate, with Gaunt presenting a paper to the AMEU in 1991 promoting national electrification and tariff rationalisation (Gaunt 2003). The result of this policy work (which was also significantly supported by the University of Cape Town's Energy for Development Resource Centre) was an increasing number of new electricity users connected via municipal utilities, growing from 51 000 new connections in 1991 to 164 000 new connections in 1993. Already in 1989 Gaunt had proposed – in the journal of the South African Institute of Electrical Engineers – that 'conventional systems' would not allow for large-scale electrification of domestic consumers, and so when electricity was rolled out, so were prepayment systems (Gaunt 2003).

There is some disagreement in Cape Town as to when prepayment technology was actually adopted in the city. Neil Ballantyne, Manager for Revenue Protection for the Electricity Directorate of the City of Cape Town (CCT – the new name of the local authority that was formerly called the Cape Town City Council) in 2006, speaks of an initial rollout in Hanover Park (a historically coloured area of Cape Town characterised by council rental housing and the poverty of its inhabitants) in 1993 (Ballantyne interview). Yet Hans Smit, who was in charge of housing projects in Cape Town in the 1980s, recalls using the technology in earlier projects (Smit interview). Details aside, it is clear that by the early 1990s both the notion of 'Electricity for All' and the use of prepayment technology in the delivery of that electricity were established concepts in the city.

The concepts were further developed in a conference on the electrification of developing communities which was held by the South African Institute of Electrical Engineers in 1991, in the ANC's National Meeting on Electrification held in February 1992, and in the work of the National Electrification Forum (NELF), which met between 1992 and 1994. From 1990 onwards, Eskom developed the NRS009 standard, which allowed for standardisation of prepayment technology, and therefore the ability to make units sourced from different vendors inter-operate. This was initiated from 1993 onwards (Eskom 2007), eventually leading to the creation of the Standard Transfer Specification (STS) to which all South African prepaid meters comply. (The STS was later developed into an international specification by the International Electrotechnical Commission with the result that STS-compliant prepaid meters are now in use throughout the world.)

The narrative above demonstrates that, from its beginnings in a single small engineering project, prepayment technology rapidly became a tool adopted on a national scale by policy-makers and professionals in the electricity sector. The engineers involved in this development were, however, acutely aware that the technology they were developing had to be adopted by electricity users, in particular the newly electrified townships users – black and poor – if it was going to be successful. As Taylor remarks, 'prepayment had [a] connotation with being "not credit worthy" (you had to pay first) and was also seen as being used by government as a way to counter the service payment boycotts.'[2]

As a result, prepayment technology was marketed not just to Eskom, municipalities and government decision-makers, but also to its intended recipients. Taylor mentions that the early prepaid meters were called Budget Energy Controllers (BECs), and were promoted as a way to 'put the consumer in control' (of their electricity expenditure). Cosmetic approaches were also taken – BECs would not be black because 'black was associated with authority and government control (officials wore black clothing and drove black cars)'.[3] Neil Ballantyne notes that during the Cape Town City Council's prepayment pilot project in Hanover Park in 1993, township unrest was affecting the electricity department: 'that's why when we started with installation of the meters we actually branded our vehicles to support those meters completely differently. In other words…it was almost like the good guys and bad guys situation. The trucks for the disconnections, people knew what they looked like, and they were the bad guys, we were the good guys going in with cars with "energy dispenser support" written on the side, and the guys didn't really have trouble because they were seen as the guys helping them' (Ballantyne interview). In Lavender Hill, another coloured township in Cape Town, Councillor Eulalie Stott held meetings with local residents, using electrical appliances to explain the details of electricity consumption (Smit interview). Don Taylor states that 'we set up training and demonstrations in the community gathering halls with educational programmes promoting the concept of prepayment and training consumers on how to use the meters; this was of cardinal importance as the slightest sign of customer difficulty would jeopardise the entire installation.'[4]

Resistance and acceptance: prepayment in Tembisa, Soweto and Cape Town

One such installation that was 'jeopardised' was in Tembisa, in Gauteng. Barchiesi's (1998) essay, 'Delivery from below, resistance from above', chronicles the resistance to installation of prepayment technology in this East Rand township. As part of a Tembisa Council plan to upgrade dysfunctional electricity infrastructure in the township during the 1990s, electrified shacks and houses were moved from a uniform flat-rate service payment to a sliding scale of flat rates, roughly correlated to estimated consumption and then ultimately to metered consumption, implemented through a combination of remote metering (which allows electricity consumption to be monitored without a meter reader visiting a particular household) and prepaid meters. The result was a sudden sharp increase in the price of electricity, with households that were not on prepaid meters being billed for arrears of thousands of rands.

Tembisa residents responded from January 1997 by sabotaging meters, to which the council responded by deploying private security firms, and even the army, to protect meter infrastructure. While the different flat-rate pricing schemes had been negotiated by the Tembisa Residents' Association and its successor, the Tembisa branch of the South African National Civics Organisation, negotiations now broke down, with the council using metering and monitoring technology to ensure 'revenue protection' and residents using collective knowledge to bypass meters and make illegal connections. Barchiesi's account suggests that this programme of illegal connections, dubbed 'Operating Khanyisa' (meaning 'switch on' – this should not be confused with the 'Operation Khanyisa' launched by the Soweto Electricity Crisis Committee some years later), together with militant tactics like the destruction of some R13 million worth of prepaid meters by residents in August 1997 (Bond & Mayekiso 1998), led to the council retreating and suspending the new payment system.

However, the Development Bank of Southern Africa reports that the implementation of the new payment system continued, albeit in a way that made illegal connections much more difficult: '[A]s overhead cables were easy to tamper with, they were substituted with underground cabling…[T]he municipality introduced a high-tech prepayment metering system instead of conventional meters. A protective system for the meters was also provided. This constituted a heavy metal cover needing a hydraulic pump to lift, as well as an alarm linked to the municipality when there was unauthorised entry' (DBSA 2006: 134–135). A 2004 presentation from the Ekurhuleni Municipality, which incorporated the Tembisa Council in 2000, presented the need for prepayment technology in highly adversarial terms, emphasising its properties as 'deterrent for interference with a metering installation' and the fact that '[t]ampering, although commonplace, cannot be reversed unnoticed as can be done in the case of a credit meter' (Ekurhuleni Municipality 2004).

Areas under the Ekurhuleni Municipality's authority are classified into three groups, based on payment levels, with different metering technologies (from credit meters through prepaid meters to prepaid meters with remote monitoring) recommended for each group. Read together, the documents from Barchiesi and the Ekurhuleni Municipality confirm Malzbender and Kamoto's assertion that 'authorities saw it fit to forcefully introduce pre-paid meters with the aim of eradicating the culture of non-payment' (Malzbender & Kamoto 2005: 27). These authors conducted a case study of prepaid meters in Tembisa and neighbouring Ivory Park, surveying some 20 households, and assert that 'seventy-five percent of residents are happy with the pre-paid system' (Malzbender & Kamoto 2005: 29), which is somewhat surprising given the troubled history of prepayment deployment in the area.

Another area mentioned by Taylor as a 'hot spot' where 'the culture of non-payment of services is deeply entrenched' is Soweto, and because of this it is instructive to look at how prepayment technology has been received in that area. Nefale's (2004) study for the Centre for Applied Legal Studies shows that when 800 households in four suburbs of Soweto were asked whether 'a prepaid meter is the best way of providing electricity for our household', 47 per cent agreed with the statement and 42 per cent disagreed (10 per cent of respondents were neutral) (Nefale 2004: 8). When these answers are broken down by income, however, 42 per cent of those with a household income of under R800 per month felt that a prepaid meter was the best way of providing electricity, whereas 57 per cent disagreed with the statement. In households with income over R800 per month, 70 per cent responded positively to the question about prepaid meters and only 30 per cent responded negatively.

When the surveyed households were asked what the advantages of prepaid meters were, the most common answers focused on the ability to control (i.e. limit) the household's energy budget and avoid owing money for electricity. Slightly more than a third of respondents, however, saw no advantage in prepaid meters. Significant disadvantages mentioned included the inability to buy prepaid cards, the enforced limiting of use of electrical appliances and the fact that units, once purchased, were used up very quickly (Nefale 2004). All of these reasons speak to the difficulties households experienced in affording electricity – an impression reinforced by figures showing that credit-metered households on average could only pay R173 per month on electricity bills (nearly 25 per cent of the mean household income), while the average monthly charge was R306 per month. (Figures from Tembisa show that before the imposition of prepayment and monitoring technology there was also a substantial gap between electricity supplied and electricity paid for, with less than 50 per cent of electricity supplied in Tembisa West paid for in mid-1998.) Clearly, households using prepayment technology do not have the option of not paying their full bill, and are faced with the options of either reducing electricity consumption or spending an even higher proportion of their income on electricity.

The experience of the Cape Town City Council with prepayment technology stands in marked contrast to the experience in Tembisa. The Cape Town City Council first deployed prepayment technology in a pilot project in Hanover Park, an area of formal housing dominated by council rental flats. As Neil Ballantyne explains, the initial impetus for prepayment was the impact of payment boycotts in the later years of the apartheid era: 'There was always a non-payment history, but it became worse in the early 1990s and there was some mechanism needed to stem that non-payment, because it was not that people couldn't pay, they didn't want to pay and to force them to pay you had to go and disconnect them and then it's this continual cycle of manpower going out basically fetching the money from the people and reconnecting them' (Ballantyne interview).

The pilot project involved a door-to-door marketing campaign, promoting the benefits of prepaid meters. According to Ballantyne, 'we sold it as a device to control electricity, to control your expenditure, you won't be faced with bills at the end of the month, you know what to expect, you can buy as you can afford' (Ballantyne interview). In addition, the council agreed to freeze the interest on arrears of households that accepted prepaid meters (which were provided without an upfront cost, with the cost of the prepayment infrastructure being recovered through a surcharge of 'a fraction of a cent per unit' and electricity arrears being recovered through a charge of 14 per cent of the electricity purchase) (Ballantyne interview). Marketing teams were immediately followed by installation teams, whose vehicles, as was previously mentioned, were physically distinguished from other council electricity vehicles. The response was an almost immediate surge in demand for prepaid meters, with the result that the council ended its marketing campaign and simply relied on word of mouth for further spread. The demand rapidly outstripped the ability of the council to deliver, leading to a backlog of some 50 000 applications awaiting installation. Up to 250 installations per day were done by the Electricity Services division of the council.

This enthusiastic adoption of prepaid meters can no doubt be explained, at least in part, by the fact that the Cape Town City Council was doing a 'good few hundred' electricity cut-offs per week in the period preceding the introduction of prepayment technology.[5] As Ballantyne testifies, the relationship between the council and residents in poor areas had become quite combative, marked by boycotts and physical confrontation. Despite the restrictions imposed by prepaid technology on households' use of electricity, this option seems to have been the preferred one (under the circumstances) for many poor households.

The council then broadened the scope of its prepayment market, however, and offered prepaid meters to high-income households, on the basis that prepaid meters did away with the need for a house's grounds to be left open so that meter readers could read the meter; thus prepaid meters were promoted as enhancing security for high-income households. The decision to promote prepayment across all income ranges was also taken to ensure that prepayment was not stigmatised as 'a device for those who don't pay' (Ballantyne interview). Widespread adoption of prepaid meters, and their use in the electrification of informal settlements in the areas under CCT control, led to 540 000 meters being in place by 2006. In addition, since 2002 every new house has been required to have a prepaid electricity meter (of the split-meter design).

At first, prepaid credit was purchased via council cash offices, which are, however, not open all day, and in some areas, only open three times a week. The council thus formed partnerships with shops to allow vending outside of the cash offices and, from 1998, vending has been outsourced to Syntell (formerly Plessy), who 'would just give us [the council] transactions on our database and money in the bank and they would handle everything else at a 4 per cent commission' (Ballantyne interview). The implementation of prepayment technology has thus allowed the CCT to develop an 'arm's-length' relationship between itself and residents using electricity. Instead of manual meter-reading and cut-offs, residents now read their own electricity meters to monitor consumption, and are disconnected without any manual intervention if they do not pay for units. One of the results of this change has been that protests and disruption previously aimed at the CCT and its officials are now sometimes aimed at the prepaid meter itself. Taylor (2006) mentions, in this vein, that early prepaid meters were vulnerable to having sugar water syringed into them, after which ants would move in to consume the sugar water and in the process short the meter, resulting in free electricity. Ballantyne also highlights the tampering problem:

> [When] the [prepaid] meter was taken back into the house [in contrast to a credit meter located in the street], tampering rates went up. With a prepaid meter, unless you actively have a team going around...drawing off the vending system the purchase patterns and that sort of thing, and visiting people and doing sweeps through areas, you just end up with your meters bypassed. If people know that they're not going to be inspected they'll bypass the meter. (Ballantyne interview)

In addition to the manual inspection of meters, the CCT responded to the problem of people bypassing prepaid meters by installing 'split meters', where the only thing inside the house is a keypad and display, and the actual meter is located outside the house, either on a nearby utility pole or in an electricity box in the street. Wires run between the residence and the meter to ensure communication, but the point where electricity cut-off happens is no longer within the home. According to Ballantyne '[t]amper rates on split meters [are] the same as credit meters housed in the street, at about two to three per cent'.

This rate of 'non-technical losses' compares favourably with the situation in Khayelitsha, Cape Town's largest township, where 'non-technical losses' are variously reported at 6 per cent (Dyantyi & Frater 1998) and 10 per cent (EdF 2002: 4). Electricity in Khayelitsha is provided through Phambile Nombane Energy Services (PN Energy), a joint venture between Eskom, Electricité de France and East Midlands Energy that was established in 1994. PN Energy was a pilot project aimed at investigating 'a new scheme for providing electricity to a population with a track record of non-payment and theft of power from an electricity provider that was not well received [in the township] in part because its service to the area had been very poor' (USAID 2004: 20). As is the case in Tembisa, technology choices – like prepaid meters, and the distribution of electric power via tall poles (which are easily visible from main roads) – were largely influenced by the desire to prevent non-payment and illegal connections. It is estimated that some 70 per cent of Khayelitsha residents' electricity usage wasn't paid for in 1994, and this had dropped to the aforementioned 6–10 per cent by 1998 (USAID 2004: 20).

As in other areas, residents in Khayelitsha by and large came to accept prepaid meters, with Annecke (2005) citing debt cancellation, expenditure control, the desire to be legal and, finally, the fact that residents had no option besides prepaid meters as reasons for their acceptance. Annecke's survey of prepaid meter users in Khayelitsha showed that 80 per cent were 'very satisfied' or 'satisfied' with the prepayment system, with a further 17 per cent being 'a little satisfied'. The survey also noted, however, that pressure to limit electricity consumption and thus expenditure also led to '[p]ractices which may place strain on the household' (e.g. 'I limit reading to daylight hours/we heat less water and all use the same water to bathe/we don't heat the house'), which she categorised as 'energy deprivation'. Her reports document incidents of refrigerators being turned off with questionable effects on the food, and substitution of kerosene or wood for space heating. These are not healthy alternatives: 'the smoke from both exacerbates respiratory infections and damages eyes' (Annecke 2005).

Prepaid electricity in Africa

As the 20th century drew to a close, prepayment technology started to be deployed across Africa. By 2007, South African metering company Landis & Gyr could claim that 2 million of its 'Cashpower' meters were installed in 40 countries worldwide, with installation sites in Africa including Benin, Botswana, Burkina Faso, Comoros, Congo, Gabon, Ghana, Lesotho, Madagascar, Malawi, Mozambique, Namibia, Nigeria, Rwanda, South Africa, Swaziland, The Gambia, Togo, Zanzibar and Zimbabwe (Tarr 2007: 6). Conlog, another South African company, reported 4 million meters installed, supplied to 70 electricity utilities across the globe (Conlog 2007a, 2007b).

South African-based companies are therefore prominent in deploying prepayment technology in African countries, with Landis & Gyr, Actaris and Conlog playing major roles across the continent. Landis & Gyr developed from Spescom, a South African company that entered into a joint-venture partnership with the German-based multinational, Siemens, in 1995, before becoming involved in a dizzying range of deals that ended up with the company being bought by Australian-based Bayard Energy in 2004 (Kohlberg et al. 2004). Actaris, home to the founders of prepayment technology in South Africa, is currently owned by USA-based Itron (Associated Press 2007). Conlog is a partnership between French multinational Schneider and the South African 'black empowerment' venture company Malesela Group. As this summary shows, in each case the experience with prepayment technology (in the South African market at least) is combined with investment by international capital.

Qualitative research on the impact of prepaid meters on other parts of the continent is, unfortunately, generally not available. My discussion here is therefore based on internet searches, which are biased in favour of the 'voices' of corporations, donors and governments – i.e. those who are supportive of the technology and who have been responsible for implementing it. Nonetheless, it is instructive to highlight a few examples of prepaid meter rollouts.

In Mozambique, prepaid electricity is being used for residential households which historically have not been connected to the grid of Electricidade de Moçambique (EdM). As of 2005, only 6 per cent of Mozambican households were connected to EdM's grid, a figure which the government wants to increase to 20 per cent by 2015 (Masawi 2005). The country's 1997 Electricity Law sets a framework for electrification through privately operated electricity concessions combined with 'output-based' development funding (managed by the World Bank-linked

International Development Association) (Cockburn & Louw 2005). In terms of a 2004 contract between the Mozambican government and a consortium of ElectroTec (Mozambique) and Siemens (South Africa), electricity will be provided to 3 000 households in four rural towns of Vilankulo, Inhassaro, Nova Mambone and Machanga. Previously these towns generated their own power using gas and diesel generators, managed by a private contractor, but with less than 10 per cent of households connected to the local grid. Under the new scheme, the private consortium will be paid for each household connected and all residential electricity users will be switched to prepaid metering 'with the aim of significantly improving collection rates' (Cockburn & Louw 2005: 3). This pilot project will provide electricity at US$0.18 per kilowatt/hour (kWh), which is more than double EdM's price of US$0.07 per kWh, but comparable to the US$0.15–0.20 cents per kWh which diesel-generated electricity costs in the country.

In Namibia, a country where 20 per cent of households are electrified (mostly in the cities) (Mbendi 2006), prepayment technology was first implemented by Northern Electricity, a private electricity distribution utility formed in 1996. Early prepayment meters operated with disposable credit cards, coded at village level (i.e. the cards coded for a particular village could be used in any meter in that village). A vendor would be issued with a number of cards in different denominations (e.g. N$5, N$10 and N$20) and 'would literally sell these out of a shoe box' (Econ One Research 2002: 19).

One of Northern Electricity's main roles was to increase revenue collection in its concession area, as electricity distribution managed by local authorities was running at a N$10 million (US$1 million) annual loss. 'The firm discovered that less than half of all consumers of electricity had been registered as customers. While some illegal connections were found during the initial meter survey, most connections were in fact legal but had never been registered, and therefore never billed' (Econ One Research 2002: 3). According to Econ One's research, the 'company reduced losses from 49% in December 1996 to below 30% by January 1997 and 15% by April 1997, stabilizing at around 7% by the end of 1999'. During the late 1990s and early 2000s, Northern Electricity also saw a threefold increase in connected users, from 5 760 in January 1997 to 14 800 in January 2002. New customers were exclusively billed using prepaid meters, which made up 12 800 of the total connections by 2002 (Econ One Research 2002: 18).

In 2002 Northern Electricity was replaced by Nored, one of five Regional Electricity Distributors established in Namibia from 2002 onwards (Namibian Electricity Control Board 2005). Nored inherited the Cashpower prepayment system (sold by Landis & Gyr) from Northern Electricity (Landis & Gyr 1999) and in 2007 started migrating its 18 000 magnetic card meters to a system based on the STS standard (*The Namibian* 8 January 2007).

Prepayment technology was also used in a pilot project in Ovitoto and Oschakati, where 300 households were supplied with solar home systems (SHSs) provided by

German company SunTechnics. This project bears similarities to one run in South Africa between 1999 and 2004, in which a South African consortium planned to provide SHSs at R2 000 per connection in order to provide electricity to 60 000 off-grid rural households. The cost of the SHS would be recouped through monthly prepayments. The South African project was, however, a failure as only 8 000 units, not the 60 000 expected, were rolled out during the project's time period, and ultimately funding was reclaimed by the South African government (*Renewable Energy Today* 2004).

Finally, one of the largest installations of prepayment technology outside South Africa has taken place in Nigeria, Africa's most populous country, where about 40 per cent of the 131 million population has access to electricity (Imoke 2006). In 2006, the Power Holding Company of Nigeria ordered 168 000 prepaid meters (Lazarus 2006). These meters follow a 1998 pilot project in which 3 000 prepaid meters (supplied by Landis & Gyr) were installed in government apartments (Landis & Gyr 1998). The location of a pilot project within government employees' households is an interesting example of 'internal marketing', where technology is first promoted to those who will be involved in its implementation before being rolled out to the wider citizenry.

The new meters are being supplied by EMCON, a joint venture between the Nigerian government, Afribank and Siemens Metering (Bureau of Public Enterprises 2007), which is currently in line for privatisation. According to the EMCON CEO, Abubakar Atiku, 'meters will be installed for both new and old customers in line with the presidential directive to install 2.5 million prepaid meters nationwide' (Lazarus 2006).

As can be seen from these examples, prepayment technology in Africa has largely been deployed alongside public–private partnerships and other forms of privatisation. With its emphasis on 'minimising risk' (National Consumer Council 2006), prepayment technology provides an incentive to the private sector to get involved in electricity distribution. This has created a lucrative market for prepayment technology (meters, billing systems, etc.), which South African-based companies have exploited through their history in developing this technology and partnership with international capital.

Conclusion

Prepaid electricity meters in South Africa emerged alongside the mass electrification programmes of the late 1980s and 1990s, themselves a response to the collapse of apartheid (and its model of 'separate development') during that period. While the work that resulted in the first South African prepayment technology was initially done at the behest of the Qwa Qwa homeland administration, it was Eskom's 'Electricity for All' programme that first moved prepayment technology from a marginal position in the electricity distribution business to a central component of the national electrification programme.

Eskom's initial 'Electricity for All' programme was intended to run on a business basis, yet at the same time electrification of the households of the poor and black majority (who had been largely denied access to domestic electricity under apartheid) was perceived as a 'social right' by those associated with the liberation movements, an action which was necessary in order to correct past imbalances. National electrification was thus a programme born with built-in contradictions.

The political contestation of the meaning of electrification was already in progress during the 1980s, as payment boycotts arose and spread in many townships. In addition to organised boycotts, the lack of legitimacy of structures associated with the apartheid regime, poor service delivery, and grinding poverty led to a situation in which non-payment for services was rife and illegal connections were common. In other words, electricity supply was a terrain where users were in both co-operative and conflictual relations with (state or parastatal) electricity suppliers.

Prepayment technology brought the promise of reduced risk involved in the rollout of new electricity connections, as costs could be calculated with some certainty in advance. As it turned out, the cost per connection in South Africa was higher than anticipated: the NELF estimated a cost of R2 400 per connection (Gaunt 2003: 89) whereas the actual cost per connection varied from R3 400 in 1994 to R2 541 in 2000. As the Department of Minerals and Energy explained in its 2001 evaluation of the national electrification programme, 'Pressure to change the [standard methods and procedures of electrification] only increased in 1995, when it became clear that budgets…were being significantly exceeded' (Gaunt 2003: 28). The innovations needed in order to reduce costs occurred across the entire distribution process, not just in meter design, but it is important to remember this context when examining the deployment of prepayment technology.

In addition to the electrification of new households, prepayment technology was deployed in previously electrified areas as a means of 'revenue protection', that is, ensuring that electricity that was supplied was paid for. In this regard prepaid meters replaced previous punitive regimes of manual cut-offs that had proved unworkable when faced with popular resistance and widespread illegal connections. In a state where the poor were acknowledged as citizens, rather than separated (by 'racial group' mechanisms) into spaces of non-citizenship, a solution had to be found to the 'unrest' that gripped the townships in waves of struggle from 1976 onwards. Together with ideological attacks on the 'culture of non-payment', prepaid meters were part of this solution. In this regard prepayment technology facilitated the elaboration of a new logic of capital – the risks that prepaid meters were designed to manage were risks that specifically imperilled an electricity utility's return on investment, and thus its profitability. The high-technology nature of prepayment methods allowed (though not without struggle) new electricity users to be integrated into the system as 'consumers' within the logic of capital, as people whose social rights were at the same time asserted and also limited – by their ability to pay. As Raniero Panzieri notes, 'science, the gigantic natural forces, and the mass of social labour' are 'embodied in the system of machinery, which, together with those three forces, constitutes the power of the "master"', and '[t]he new "technical bases" progressively attained in production provide capitalism with the new possibilities for the consolidation of its power' (Panzieri 1980).

Beyond South Africa's borders, it is clear that the drive towards prepayment technology has gone alongside a drive to 'open up' African electricity distribution to private capital, in the form of public-private partnerships, distribution concessions and privatisation within the electricity industry. Once again, the 'meaning' of prepayment for capital is apparent.

The replacement of manual cut-offs and reconnection by prepayment technology, with its automatic operation, meant that electricity supply could easily be depoliticised as a merely 'technical' matter, and the consolidation that Panzieri describes could happen in a manner which appeared 'neutral', at least so long as the principle of 'ending the "culture of non-payment"' was accepted. Barchiesi (1998) points out that this was broadly the case, even in Tembisa, with the Tembisa Residents' Association negotiating a 1993 flat-rate arrangement as a step towards a 'culture of payment'.

The struggle over the level of payment, however, is a struggle on two fronts. On the one hand, the question of 'cost recovery' and the level of subsidy afforded to low-income households speak to the relationship between electricity users, the state, and ultimately also capital (as a higher level of subsidy, and thus a higher level of income for low-income households will mean a lower level of appropriation of social production by capital). In this regard, prepaid tariffs, when they are enforced and made non-negotiable, reflect a particular relation of power between the actors in this struggle. This brings us to the second front of this struggle: the struggle over payment as an income struggle. As Nefale (2004) points out in his research on prepayment in Soweto, payments for electricity on credit meters at the time of the research already took up about (on average) 25 per cent of household budgets, even when these payments were only about half of what was demanded. And as Annecke points out in her study of Khayelitsha, one effect of prepayment was to limit low-income households to practices which are characteristic of 'energy deprivation' (Annecke 2005). It is worth noting that both Nefale and Annecke's research took place after the introduction of free basic electricity, at the level of 50 kWh per month per household, on a national scale.

Given the hardships that low-income users of prepaid meters experience, it is somewhat surprising that the technology has been accepted to the extent that it has, albeit after significant struggles in some areas. Tebogo Phadu, a local South African Communist Party leader, anticipated this, in a way, when he remarked that '[the prepayment system would have a] profound impact on our tradition of community organization/mobilization as it promotes "everyone for him/herself" (i.e. individualizing payment)' (Bond & Mayekiso 1998). This acceptance of individual payment, of 'staying within a budget' and 'consuming what you pay for', would seem to also confirm what Ahmed Veriava calls 'the pedagogical function of prepaid meters', a function that Don Taylor also confirms: the prepaid meter exists, in part, to teach people that nothing is for free, to teach people to pay.[6]

Notes

1   Don Taylor, personal communication, 11 July 2006

2   Don Taylor, personal communication, 11 July 2006

3   Don Taylor, personal communication, 11 July 2006

4   Don Taylor, personal communication, 11 July 2006

5   Neil Ballantyne, email follow-up on interview, 6 July 2006

6   Ahmed Veriava, independent researcher, personal communication, 15 December 2006; Don Taylor, personal communication 11 July 2006

References

ANC (African National Congress) (1994) *The Reconstruction and Development Programme: A policy framework.* Johannesburg: Umanyano Publications

Annecke W (2005) Prepayment meters in Merlo, Argentina and Khayelitsha, South Africa. *ESI Africa* 2. Accessed 8 January 2007, http://www.esi-africa.com/archive/esi_2_2005/52_1.php

Associated Press (2007) Itron to pay $1 billion for Actaris. *CNN Money* 26 February. Accessed 27 March 2007, http://money.cnn.com/news/newsfeeds/articles/newstex/AFX-0013-14778664.htm

Balson S (1997) Jagersfontein three gallons. *Dallas, USA: TokenCoins.com.* Accessed 8 January 2007, http://www.tokencoins.com/gr07.htm#jagers

Barchiesi F (1998) Delivery from below, resistance from above. *Debate* 4. Accessed 8 January 2006, http://www.geocities.com/CapitolHill/3843/deliv.html

Beavon KSO (1997) Johannesburg: A city and metropolitan area in transformation. In C Rakodi (ed.) *The urban challenge in Africa: Growth and management of its large cities.* New York: United Nations University Press. Accessed 8 January 2007, http://www.unu.edu/unupress/unupbooks/uu26ue/uu26ue0g.htm#5%20johannesburg:%2 0a%20city%20and%20metropolitan%20area%20in%20transformation

Bond P & Mayekiso M (1998) Urban betrayal: The ANC in the townships. *Southern Africa Report* 13(4). Accessed 8 January 2006, http://www.africafiles.org/article.asp?ID=3789

Bureau of Public Enterprises (2007) *Companies for privatisation.* Accessed 28 March 2007, http://www.bpeng.org/en/companies/forPrivatization/default.htm

Butler A (2007) Black economic empowerment since 1994: Diverse hopes and differentially fulfilled aspirations. In *Proceedings of the colloquium After Apartheid: The Second Decade,*

27–28 April 2007, Yale University, New Haven. Accessed December 2007, http://www.yale.edu/macmillan/apartheid/

Cockburn M & Louw C (2005) Output-based aid in Mozambique. *OB Approaches.* Note No. 003. Washington: Global Partnership on Output Based Aid. Accessed 27 March 2007, http://www.gpoba.org/docs/OBApproaches_MozambiqueElectricity.pdf

Conlog (2007a) *History.* Accessed 19 March 2007, http://www.conlog.co.za/aboutus/history.html

Conlog (2007b) *Tanesco's pre-paid meters to be manufactured locally.* Accessed 19 March 2007, http://www.ippmedia.com/ipp/guardian/2007/06/26/93247.html

DBSA (Development Bank of Southern Africa) (2006) *Infrastructure barometer 2006.* Johannesburg: DBSA. Accessed 8 January 2007, http://www.dbsa.org/document/pbarometer2006/part%201.pdf

Dyantyi R & Frater W (1998) Local economic development initiatives in Khayelitsha. In Department of Constitutional Development, South Africa *Linking economic development to poverty alleviation.* Pretoria: Department of Constitutional Development. Accessed 8 January 2006, http://www.dplg.gov.za/Documents/Publications/linkingled/linkingledcasestudies/khayelitsha/khayelitshasocialeconomy.htm

Econ One Research (2002) *Northern Electricity distribution service in northern Namibia.* Los Angeles: Econ One. Accessed 27 March 2007, http://rru.worldbank.org/PapersLinks/Open.aspx?id=968

EdF (Electricité de France) (2002) *Urban electrification in South Africa: The township of Khayelitsha (Cape Town).* Paris: EdF. Accessed 8 January 2007, http://www.edf.fr/html/jhsburg/uk/pdf/dp_khayelitsha_va.pdf

Ekurhuleni Municipality (2004) An organised approach to the domestic metering of electricity. *ESI Africa* 4. Cape Town: Spintelligent. Accessed 8 January 2007, http://www.esi-africa.com/archive/esi_4_2004/22_1.php

Eskom (2007) *Prepayment history.* Pretoria: Eskom. Accessed 8 January 2007, http://www.prepayment.eskom.co.za/history.asp

Gaunt CT (2003) Electrification technology and processes to meet economic and social objectives in South Africa. PhD thesis, Department of Electrical Engineering, University of Cape Town

Imoke L (2006) *Address by the Honourable Minister of Power and Steel, Senator Liyel Imoke, at the inauguration of the Board of the Rural Electrification Agency (REA) on Thursday 16th March 2006 at Nicon Hilton Hotel Abuja.* Abuja: Federal Ministry of Power and Steel. Accessed 27 March 2007, http://www.fmps.gov.ng/news/news_rea.htm

Kohlberg Kravis Roberts & Co. (2004) *Demag Holding sells Landis+Gyr to Bayard Energy.* New York: Kohlberg Kravis Roberts & Co. Online press release. Accessed 27 March 2007, http://www.kkr.com/news/press_releases/2004/07-12-04.html

Landis & Gyr (1998) *Cashpower electricity meters for Nigeria.* Isando: Landis & Gyr. Accessed 28 March 2007, http://www.cashpower.com/za/press/1998/press_Apr98.cfm

Landis & Gyr (1999) *Cashpower penetrates Namibia.* Isando: Landis & Gyr. Accessed 27 March 2007, http://www.za.landisgyr.com/za/press/1999/press_Oct99.cfm

Lazarus S (2006) 7 000 PHCN's prepaid meters for Yola zone, *Daily Independent.* Ikeja: Independent Newspapers. Accessed 28 March 2007, http://www.independentngonline.com/?c=56&a=17342

Malzbender D & Kamoto B (2005) *Domestic electricity provision in the democratic South Africa.* Cape Town: African Centre for Water Research. Accessed 8 January 2007, http://www.acwr.co.za/pdf_files/01.pdf

Mandela N (1964) *Statement at Rivonia Trial.* Accessed 8 January 2007, http://www. thirdworldtraveler.com/Human%20Rights%20Documents/Mandela_RivoniaTrial.html

Masawi F (2005) Opportunities in the Mozambique ESI. *ESI Africa* 2. Cape Town: Spintelligent. Accessed 27 March 2007, http://www.esi-africa.com/archive/esi_2_2005/68_1.php

Mbendi (2006) *Namibia: Electrical power.* Cape Town: Mbendi. Accessed 27 March 2007, http://www.mbendi.co.za/indy/powr/af/na/p0005.htm

McRae I (1998) *Response by Dr Ian Campbell McRae on receipt of the World Energy Council 75th anniversary award.* London: World Energy Council. Accessed 6 July 2006, http://www.worldenergy.org/wec-geis/wec_info/annual_report/ar98/AR98IMcRae.asp

Namibian Electricity Control Board (Technical Services Division) (2005) *The planned Regional Electricity Distributors (REDs) for Namibia.* Accessed 19 March 2008, http://www.ecb.org.na/download.php?fl_id=11

National Consumer Council (2006) *Supply license review: Initial policy proposals.* London: National Consumer Council. Accessed 28 March 2007, http://www.ncc.org.uk/fuelandwater/supply-licence-review.pdf

Nefale M (2004) *A survey on attitudes to prepaid electricity meters in Soweto.* Johannesburg: Law & Transformation Programme, Centre for Applied Legal Studies, University of the Witwatersrand. Accessed 8 January 2007, http://www.law.wits.ac.za/cals/meters/Prepaid%20Meters%20(ultra).pdf

Panzieri R (1980) The capitalist use of machinery. In P Slater (ed.) *Outlines of a critique of technology.* London: Ink Links. Accessed 9 January 2007, http://geocities.com/cordobakaf/panzieri.html

Parsons N (1982) *A new history of South Africa.* London: Macmillan Education Ltd

Renewable Energy Today (2004) *South Africa reclaims funding from solar energy initiative.* Accessed 27 March 2007, http://www.findarticles.com/p/articles/mi_m0OXD/is_2004_Feb_19/ai_113428715

Tarr D (2007) *How to implement a prepayment system.* Isando: Landis & Gyr. PowerPoint presentation accessed 27 March 2007, http://www.cashpower.com/za/download/harold/implementing%20a%20prepayment%20system%20(05072006)

Taylor D (2006) Historical perspective on the development of the prepayment industry and technological advancement in South Africa. Unpublished report

Tin H (2001) Children in violent spaces. In A Zegeye (ed.) *Social identities in the new South Africa*. Cape Town: Kwela Books & SA History Online

USAID (US Agency for International Development) (2004) *Innovative approaches to slum electrification*. Washington: USAID. Accessed 8 January 2007, http://pdf.usaid.gov/pdf_docs/PNADB219.pdf

Interviews

Ballantyne N, Manager for Revenue Protection (Electricity), City of Cape Town, 6 July 2006

Smit H, Housing Department official, City of Cape Town, 4 July 2006

CHAPTER 9

Free basic electricity in South Africa: A strategy for helping or containing the poor?

Greg Ruiters

As part of its election manifesto in 2000, the national office of the ruling African National Congress (ANC) promised free basic services to all poor South Africans. This was later quantified as 6 000 litres of water and 50 kilowatt-hours (kWh) of monthly electricity per household for qualifying households. At the time, this package represented a monetary benefit of R30–R35 per household per month. With respect to free electricity, the state claimed that electrification was seen as 'a significant step towards realizing the basic rights and improving the quality of life of South Africans' (DoF 2004: 143). The 'free basic electricity' of 50 kWh per household per month, delivered in terms of the Free Basic Electricity (FBE) Programme which gave expression to the ANC's election commitment, was deemed 'sufficient energy to provide basic services for a poor household' ('household' was defined as a 'residential premises *customer* with an official point of supply, metered on a domestic tariff') (DME 2003a: 5).[1]

The aim of this chapter is to outline and evaluate the South African government's innovative FBE programme. I examine the content of the policy, its overt and underlying rationales and its practical implementation. I begin with discussion of the context and content of FBE: the official definitions and stated aims; what FBE enables households to do or not to do; and who has been getting FBE and who has been excluded. I then turn to the forms of FBE delivery (targeted at the 'indigent' with prepaid meters) and preconditions for receiving benefits.

The amount of FBE, it is argued, is inadequate for meeting basic needs, or for meaningful development and assistance for the poor. Yet FBE represents a very tiny proportion of the total electricity sold in South Africa and it seems unreasonable for a pro-poor government to take such a frugal approach. This situation is complicated further by the fact that a large proportion of the poor either do not have any electricity infrastructure at all, or if they do, still have great difficulty in accessing FBE. In many cases, only once households prove their condition of poverty (i.e. that they earn less than a specified amount per month), are registered as indigents and agree to a prepaid meter being installed, may they receive FBE. Rising tariffs, declining standards of infrastructure, outages, debt and disconnections have also eroded the already negligible benefit of FBE. The impact of FBE may be minimal. There are thus major contradictions between pro-poor intentions and their substance, as manifested in the content and implementation of government programmes.

FBE, at one level, is about the state caring for the people's welfare; at another level, it may be understood as a way to isolate and manage the 'problem' of mass poverty in South Africa. One key aim of the state is to fight a perceived 'culture of non-payment' for services and promote more acceptable market behaviours amongst its citizens. Administrative techniques and engineering technologies (such as prepayment smart cards) have thus been developed for demarcating users as indigents and limiting access. The poor are forced to accept sub-standard services (like the 10 ampere (amp) supply, which trips when several appliances are used simultaneously) in exchange for a small amount of FBE. Rather than uplifting the poor, the onerous means of access and the punitive, self-targeted pre-restriction (the 10 amp service) represent a cynical attempt to manage this sector of society, rather than provide genuine and adequate relief from poverty and social exclusion. To paraphrase Escobar (1995), while FBE might mean real improvements for the ultra-poor, providing this service could strengthen the state's bureaucratic power over the poor and limit their capacity for resistance.

The context of free basic electricity supply

Most of the electricity in South Africa (80 per cent) is used by commerce and industry. Residential consumers use less than 20 per cent of the country's electricity (DoF 2004: 141). Put differently, out of 240 billion kWh sold by municipalities in 2004, only 1.6 per cent (4 billion kWh) went into homes as part of basic electricity, *not* FBE, which makes up an even smaller proportion (National Treasury 2006: 27). Mining and manufacturing pay about half the tariff that ordinary households pay (i.e. an average of R0.16 per kWh compared to R0.29 for domestic users).

To the ANC's credit, whereas in 1991 only 38 per cent of households were electrified, by the end of 2002 the figure was 68 per cent. By 2005, electrification had increased further to 72 per cent of 11 million households. The backlog is most severe in KwaZulu-Natal (57 per cent), the Eastern Cape (72 per cent) and even in urban Gauteng, where 22 per cent of households have no access to electricity (National Treasury 2006: 25; figures based on 2003 National Electricity Regulator of South Africa (NERSA) statistics). Backlogs of the order of 70–80 per cent persist in the rural areas, but, crucially, new urban slums and urban informal settlements also suffer backlogs.

In the early 1990s, Eskom, the state-owned electricity generator and distributor, became the main supplier/retailer to rural areas and black townships. Historically, Eskom areas therefore had a very different racial profile compared to municipal consumers; its 3.3 million consumers (half the national consumer base) were also predominantly on prepaid electricity meters. Municipal supply areas (which are historically white areas), by comparison, are on credit meters, and use three times more electricity per capita (National Treasury 2006). It is important to distinguish between these two systems of residential electricity in South Africa.

The National Treasury (2006: 112) has calculated that on average a 'small' household can expect to pay R213 per month for electricity. Interestingly, 'small' is defined as 498 kWh per month. A 'large' household is expected to use 1 000 kWh and will pay around R414 per month (National Treasury 2006: 135). Although often celebrated as the cheapest electricity produced in the world, electricity in South Africa is expensive for working-class households. A three-person family in a three-roomed house using a refrigerator, heater, stove, colour television and hot water typically spends between R200 and R300 per month on electricity, with electricity bills making up a large percentage of disposable income – in the region of 8 per cent if income is R2 000 per month and 25 per cent if the income is a pension. Moreover, municipalities make significant surpluses from their electricity distribution and retail activities: these range from 28 per cent at the higher levels to 3 per cent, but average between 10 and 15 per cent (DoF 2003: 246).

FBE needs to be seen in context: almost 47 per cent of South Africans are poor – defined as living in households with less than R800 income per month (based on 2001 census data) – and cannot afford electricity. R38 billion in electricity arrears is owed to municipalities; millions have had their supply cut off. Johannesburg alone has over 100 000 households that are heavily indebted to the municipality. In Cape Town over 400 000 final letters of demand and threats of cut-offs were issued in early 2007 (*Independent Online* 17 May 2007).

Government motivation for FBE and definition of 'basic' supply

In 2000 the state motivated its decision to provide FBE as follows:
- to enhance the well being of the poor…[in] particular women and female children who are mainly responsible for carrying *firewood*;
- to maintain *functional households*;
- to produce positive impacts on the *health and safety* of the communities;
- to reduce the need for fossil-based energy sources (paraffin, which is used mainly for cooking and heating). (DME 2003b: 4, emphasis added)

It was also suggested that modern sources of energy would enhance the quality of life of indigent communities (DME 2003b). In a more politicised version of this motivation, the City of Cape Town (CCT) (then under ANC control) represented its rollout of FBE to township areas as a 'victory for the people'. In the words of Councillor Saleem Mowzer, Mayoral Committee Member for Trading Services:

> For these communities…this is the promise of a better life. Extending free basic electricity to these communities is a victory against poverty in our city. Over the past few years we have experienced many fires in Khayelitsha due to

the community's reliance on paraffin, drum fires and other forms of heating and lighting. Now we are creating a better life...They can now look forward to lighting and warmth in their homes, especially during the cold winter months. Children can now study with the comfort of a burning light, rather than by candlelight which is often dangerous. This demonstrates the human face of providing more electricity to those who need it most. (*Business Day* 30 December 2003)

The free amount of electricity (50 kWh per month), says the government, is 'suitable for basic lighting, TV and radio, basic ironing and basic cooking' (DME 2003b: section 3.5). This claim that 50 kWh is a 'suitable' amount is debatable. The state justifies this amount by suggesting that as it is, households that are 'poor' generally have a low demand for electricity, and argues that 'on average, 56% of households consume no more than 50 kWh per month' (DME 2003a: 8). These 'households would therefore consume the free basic electricity at no cost and pay the approved tariff for all units of electricity consumed above the free allocation' (DME 2003c). The Department of Minerals and Energy (DME) has also argued that '[t]he level of 50 kWh has been...accepted as a norm in respect of free basic electricity. This quantity has achieved widespread political and community acceptance and expectation' (DME 2003a: 9).

A developmental approach to the level of supply might take a different view of the minimalist understanding of needs. It is self-evident that low consumption is a reflection of the apartheid legacy, unemployment and a produced inability to consume. To change this pattern of unhealthy under-consumption, more than 50 kWh would have to be offered. In fact, municipalities often use 150 kWh as their cut-off for deciding whether or not households should be seen as poor.

Based on this conflation of use and need, the government proceeded with its FBE plan. It allocated an initial annual R300 million in central funds to be paid to municipalities for the provision of FBE to the poor – a relatively small amount of money for such a major programme meant to be a priority of the state (DME 2003a). The small cost of this intervention – a mere R25 per month per household – was equivalent to 3 per cent of a monthly state pension (DoF 2003: 234).

What can a household do with 50 kWh per month and how much does it add to households' quality of life? Does FBE achieve the improvements suggested in the original aims? Table 9.1 gives an indication of the energy used by various appliances.

As is evident from Table 9.1, a small refrigerator alone (used for six hours – itself an unreasonable assumption given that refrigerators generally must be on all the time) would use up the total FBE allotted. A hotplate (of 1 000 watts) for cooking used for two hours per day would also use far more than the FBE quota. The FBE amount is therefore clearly entirely inadequate for basic living needs. Even 'for basic cooking and lighting, the 50 kW/h per month are hardly sufficient, which is the reason why many people with access to grid-electricity still use firewood or

Table 9.1: Energy used, by appliance

Item	Watts	Hours used	Days used	kWh
1 x energy-saver light	11	5.0	30	1.7
1 x TV (B&W)	35	6.0	30	7.0
1 x iron	1 000	4.0	6	24.0
1 x kettle	1 000	0.5	30	15.0
1 x hotplate	1 000	1.0	25	25.0
1 x regular light	100	5.0	30	15.0
1 x refrigerator (small)	250	6.5	30	49.0

Source: DME 2003a

paraffin for cooking' (Mpako & Prasad 2005: 2). The overall effect of such a minimalist programme is to keep the poor in poverty and force them to use hazardous forms of energy.

Keeping the poor out: two approaches

In practice, there is a variety of ways in which FBE may be accessed. Targeted approaches can be contrasted with broad or blanket approaches. In the latter all residents of an area get the FBE, irrespective of income or circumstances, whereas targeted supply assumes means-testing, setting criteria and keeping a beneficiary list of some sort.

Another variant is the 'self-targeting' approach whereby a resident agrees to a very low level of supply (10 amps and frequent tripping) and in exchange gets the FBE. According to the DME (2003a: 12–13), this is 'suited to municipalities with lower capacity and a large proportion of poorer consumers'. Households consuming less than 150 kWh per month could be regarded as poor, and be given the 50 kWh per month on low-amp supply. The self-targeting (10 amp) method, says the state, 'will not be suitable for households with many members, since frequent tripping of the control systems will be experienced.' The policy also stipulates that the limitations of the 10 amp service should be clearly outlined to consumers before they apply for FBE (DME 2003a: 16). 'Customers', the preferred state terminology, therefore have to be aware of the choices available.

Let us look into a case of a city using means-testing or targeted approaches, and the qualifications needed to receive the benefit. Tshwane (Pretoria) uses an indigent list system (the state's preferred method). General preconditions are that only homes with a legal connection to the national grid at a metered point of supply would qualify for FBE. Households which have a record of non-payment and illegal connections are excluded until all bills are settled (DME 2003a).

In Tshwane, potential recipients are subjected to rigorous means-testing, and if they qualify, they receive only a 30 amp supply. Registration takes place through the Department of Social Development and can occur only if the applicant meets *all* of the following conditions:

- The municipal value of the property on which the household resides does not exceed R150 000 (typically a township or RDP house).
- The gross monthly income of all the members of the household does not exceed two old-age state pensions (R1 600 per month).
- The applicant agrees to accept the limited level of service and agrees to stay in the programme for at least six months.
- The applicant agrees that the municipality will install a prepayment-type electricity meter free of charge.
- If any consumer misinforms the authorities, all benefits which were accorded to the indigent debtor upon registration will be written back to the services account and appropriate legal action will be considered.[2]

The Tshwane Municipality, moreover, imposes an *upper* limit on prepaid electricity purchases a family is allowed to make in any one month: 'A partial blocking of vending of 150 kWh per month plus the monthly free units quota of prepay electricity [will] encourage payment of moneys for the other services.'[3]

This limit is intended to prevent the poor from illegally reselling electricity to neighbours through extension leads. The Tshwane system imposes an array of controls on recipients of the supply, and offers the poor citizen little room to manoeuvre. There is a strong moral and paternalistic undertone in this method of 'helping the poor' to limit their consumption and manage their finances. In 2007 only 47 000 indigents were registered for free basic services.[4] This figure shows a low rate of uptake and confirms fears that applying for indigent status might well be a 'voyage into a bureaucratic underworld' (Jones et al. 1978). In the CCT metropole only 5 000 people had come forward to register on its indigent register by early 2007. However, the city administration believed this figure was too low and in public announcements urged people to 'not be afraid or ashamed' to register for indigent relief where necessary (CCT 2007).

The targeted approach has been generally criticised by universalists for excluding poor people, rather than encouraging uptake of FBE (Jones et al. 1978). The economic logic here is that the state can keep control over the welfare budget by making welfare as demeaning and difficult to access as possible. By keeping only the 'deserving' poor on indigent lists the municipality hopes to send out a strong message that those who supposedly can afford to pay should do so. As a commentator in the national *Sunday Times* newspaper argued:

> [M]eans testing is touted by its proponents as a method of ensuring that only those in real need receive assistance while the 'undeserving' are kept out of the system. In fact, the contrary is true. Means testing prevents the needy from accessing social security grants. The Taylor report records what many working in the field know to be true – the means test harms the ability of the poor to access benefits, particularly the child support grant. Many applicants have

difficulties obtaining the relevant documentation and struggle to meet the costs of the numerous trips that are an inevitable part of working through the red tape. In the South African context, the tendency of incomes to fluctuate renders application of the means test a complex and often inaccurate exercise. (Martin 2002)

The 'blanket' or broad approach is used in Johannesburg, but is not without problems. This approach gives *all* households the free amount of service but has punitive stepped tariffs for usage above the FBE limit. So, while Johannesburg does not isolate the indigents as a group, it uses the tariff system and cut-offs instead to discipline consumers. The wealthy have no problem paying the higher tariff, but the poor do. But with many pensioners and sick families cut off from the supply, City Power (the utility company that supplies electricity to Johannesburg consumers) and Johannesburg Metro devised a 'special cases policy'.

According to Johannesburg Metro, the city loses R53 million a year on subsidising FBE to special-case households across the city. Yet Johannesburg's annual municipal budget is over R19 billion per year and the special cases account for only 0.2 per cent of the budget.[5] Prepaid domestic customers, who are becoming a large slice of the residential users, get their free allocations only once they have bought power from one of the City Power vending stations.

Finally, because it is such a small amount, FBE is used by the poor *only for lighting,* but not for cooking. The 2005 General Household Survey (GHS) conducted by Statistics South Africa shows that overall 33.5 per cent of South Africans use wood and paraffin for cooking, although 80 per cent are connected to the mains supply (Stats SA 2006: v). The GHS reports a slight decline in households using wood or paraffin from 2002 to 2005 – the period during which FBE was implemented.

A more general concern is the poor overall quality and reliability of power supply in South Africa, which affects residents in historically black townships and rural areas more adversely than those in historically white and urban contexts. A survey by NERSA in 2003 found that 49 per cent of municipalities had no maintenance plans for their electricity distribution networks and lacked comprehension of power quality and performance issues. Almost half the country's municipalities do not carry out routine maintenance checks and do not have contingency measures to deal with power cuts. The survey also found that about 45 per cent of electricity distributors are failing to identify areas requiring corrective action (Creamer 2005).

Research in rural KwaZulu-Natal found that rural women were still having to walk more than a kilometre to find wood (with the distance increasing as woodlots become depleted) and spent as long as 205 minutes daily on this task (Hemson 2004: 6). The policy logic of FBE (freeing up households from extra domestic burdens and in particular freeing up women's time, and the assumption that most households can live off 50 kWh) is contradicted by these facts.

Uneven progress towards FBE?

In assessing progress in implementing the FBE policy, we will first look at FBE supply in areas covered by Eskom (which serves 48 per cent of all domestic consumers or 3.3 million households in the country) and then at municipalities (which serve 52 per cent of consumers).

By 2003, Eskom had not yet provided FBE to the poor in any of its distribution areas (mostly former black townships and homelands). In 2004 it spent a paltry R46 million on FBE. By early 2005 there was some progress, with '322 000 of Eskom's 1.9 million poor qualifying customers receiving the benefit' (*Business Day* 19 January 2005). In 2006, Eskom reported that 84 per cent of its qualifying customers had had their meters reconfigured for free electricity (Eskom 2006).

By 28 February 2006, Eskom was providing FBE to 1 million households within its supply areas (National Treasury 2006: 28). A key question here is how a 'qualifying household' is defined (i.e. who gets disqualified?). What about the other 1 million 'qualifying poor' on Eskom's books who were still not receiving Eskom's FBE in February 2006, five years after the programme had been announced? And what does 60 million kWh mean as a proportion of the national electricity supply in the residential sector (i.e. 4 billion kWh)? In respect of Eskom's FBE, it represents a minuscule 1.5 per cent of national supply to households.

We now turn to the municipal sector. In the municipal supply areas progress with the FBE programme was not as slow as with Eskom: 18 months after its launch, in late 2002, 'only 12% of the poor had received the free electricity benefit, while expenditure on the initiative had ballooned to about R750 million – 2.4 times more than budgeted', according to Ompi Aphane, Chief Director in the DME responsible for its rollout (*Business Day* 19 January 2005). As of 30 June 2004, only 64.6 per cent of 4.7 million electrified households had access to FBE (Stats SA 2004; see Table 9.2); i.e. some 3 million households were receiving FBE from municipalities.

Table 9.2 shows the provincial breakdown of households benefiting from the FBE supplied by municipalities, and the rapid increase in the numbers receiving FBE between 2003 and 2004.

Significant trends in municipal provision of FBE include the following: by 2004 Gauteng had the highest percentage of implementation of FBE (91 per cent), followed by the Western Cape (89.4 per cent) and Free State (84 per cent). There is significant variation between provinces in the provision of FBE. KwaZulu-Natal stands out because of the very low level (6 per cent) of FBE supplied by Eskom. Certain provinces have experienced a high degree of growth in informal settlements (Gauteng, KwaZulu-Natal and the Western Cape), making the supply of FBE difficult.

But the municipal FBE was poorly targeted, since most who were getting the free supply were not poor (*Business Day* 19 January 2005). The Presidency has criticised

Table 9.2: Households receiving FBE services from municipalities, 2003–2004

Province	Number of households with access to electricity (2003)	Number of households with access to free electricity (2003)	% of electrified households with FBE	Number of households with access to electricity (2004)	Number of households with access to free electricity (2004)	% of electrified households with FBE
EC	442 829	198 492	44.8	513 979	250 041	48.6
FS	361 802	282 280	78.0	403 114	337 928	84.0
G	1 055 888	886 650	84.0	1 238 414	1 123 346	91.0
KZN	782 225	22 075	2.8	825 570	47 695	6.0
L	91 043	42 153	46.3	104 485	56 973	55.0
M	307 263	166 085	54.1	332 284	199 060	60.0
NC	103 727	46 221	44.6	125 843	48 221	38.0
NW	126 724	29 906	23.6	152 382	73 735	48.0
WC	956 148	517 696	54.1	1 010 620	903 063	89.4
Total	4 227 649	2 191 558	51.8	4 706 691	3 040 062	65.0

Source: Stats SA 2004

Note: EC = Eastern Cape, FS = Free State, G = Gauteng, KZN = KwaZulu-Natal, L = Limpopo, M = Mpumalanga, NC = Northern Cape, NW = North West, WC = Western Cape

the FBE programme because the wrong people are benefiting from it. In February 2006, President Mbeki decried the fact that 'the benefits of free basic electricity are accruing to those who are relatively well off', and blamed this and other deficits on what he termed 'the lack of all-round capacity in technical areas with regard to water, sanitation, and public works projects'. As a result, 'the programme to provide a basic amount of electricity free to all poor households has been slower to implement' (*ANC Today* 6(4), February 2006). In the majority of cases, municipalities cite 'lack of indigent data' for failing to provide free basic electricity (reply to written question in Parliament, no. 350, 30 June 2005, cited in DA n.d.). This shows that a number of gaps still exist between the original noble intentions of the FBE policy and its implementation.

Prepaid meters: a tool for managing the poor

A further set of problems related to the effectiveness of FBE concerns prepayment meters as a means of getting FBE to households, and cut-offs and illegal connections. It is important to look at the technologies for both providing and limiting households' consumption. Rolling out services to the poor has paradoxically spawned a new industry to address the question: how to limit the resources that the poor may use?

In many cases, use of prepaid meters has been made a condition for debt re-negotiations and receipt of free services. Johannesburg has programmes (Reathusa, for example[6]) that explicitly demand this, as does Tshwane Municipality. Eskom, however, has been the leader in the use of prepaid meters, which it has been automatically installing in first-time electrified homes since the mid-1990s.

For 3 million households, the experience of using electricity has been changed radically by the advent of the prepaid meter. As of 2003, Eskom and municipalities had installed 3.2 million such meters in almost half of South Africa's electrified homes (Tewari & Shah 2003). The target population was clearly residents in the black townships, but the prepaid meter has since been used beyond black townships. For example, from early 2004, every new domestic customer in Cape Town was required to have a 'self-disconnecting' meter installed, no matter what their income. In that city, by 2003, 73 per cent of the residential customers (380 000) had a prepaid meter installed in their homes (*ESI Africa* 2004; see also Van Heusden, Chapter 8 in this volume).

South Africa has led the field in the manufacture and installation of prepaid meters through companies such as ABB, Tellumat/Syntell and Conlog (a subsidiary of French company Schneider Electric).[7] The ANC blessed this new industry, which involved 'senior comrades' as active investors.[8] In 2002, Conlog was re-named Dynamic Cables; it operates as a wholesale distributor of exclusive tele-communications infrastructure and cabling, acquired from Alcatel in France. A senior manager at Eskom, Hugh McGibbon, explained Eskom's reasons for adopting prepayment technology for its metering system as follows:

> Eskom had a difficult time managing the conventional meters. Eskom used to hire workers whose main task was to read meters and disconnect electricity of those whose payments were overdue. This entailed ensuring the transportation from house to house and the protection of its employees in the event of conflict with customers. The conventional metering, in the absence of proper social attitudes to electricity, became a system demanding very high maintenance. Prepaid metering reduced this cost tremendously. (McGibbon 2002)

Eskom also stresses that prepaid meters are a good tool for managing consumption:

> Since the prepayment meter provides a continuous display of how much electricity you have left and also a flashing light showing how fast you are using electricity, many customers find it much easier to budget their electricity usage and to actually save power. Many customers do not understand the accounts for the billed system or how the amounts are calculated. With the prepayment system you can be sure you will get a Rand's worth of electricity for every Rand you pay. (Eskom n.d.)

The supposed advantages of prepaid meters are:
- No account posting costs;
- Up-front payment improves municipal cash flow;
- No meter readers are required;
- Recovery of other debts (every time a customer buys a prepaid card, s/he pays 15% towards redemption of old debt);
- No more disconnection and reconnection fees and administrative hassles;

- No need to access the customer's property, thus risk to its employees' lives is reduced;
- Eliminates the danger of inaccurate meter reading, nullifying the scope for such complaints;
- The customer learns to economise on their use;
- The customer learns to manage his/her budget;
- No cost for disconnection/reconnection and no waiting for reconnection;
- The customer is empowered. (Tewari & Shah 2003: 920)

When using prepaid meters, a household will receive a non-interchangeable voucher or token loaded with free basic units per month. When the free units have been used up, consumers need to buy additional units. If people do not claim their free allocations within a calendar month, they lose out (DME 2003a).

As already mentioned, prepaid meters can be very inconvenient if a household cannot buy a month's supply but has to make repeated trips to vendors to buy a few units at a time. Repeated trips result in extra transport costs, and running out of power can mean money lost as food in the fridge rots. Being able to observe the electricity running out may only add to desperate efforts on the part of households to borrow money, and add to family stress. According to analyst David McDonald, 'All prepaid meters do, is force poor households to consume less by cutting themselves off. So, rather than the city having to go in and cut off...for non-payment, the city lets the technology do it for them. They simply distance themselves from the "structural violence" of cost recovery' (*Metroburger* 2 May 2002). Prepaid meters are like remote control of households, using money as a disciplinary device. The prepaid meter system has the potential to break down community solidarity, with each atomised consumer blaming him/herself for bad housekeeping.

In Cape Town, a major issue seems to be that different vending firms with different systems have been used. The lack of uniformity across the city means that consumers can buy electricity only in their local areas (*ESI Africa* 2006). A second problem encountered is that waiting times at vending stations in townships can be very long.

In January 2004 Eskom and the CCT signed an agreement to provide FBE to Khayelitsha. But a report by Wendy Annecke (2005) on this rollout showed that:
- to get to the vending machine, customers had to walk far, sometimes in bad weather, running the risk of being mugged in these areas;
- they had to stand in long queues and the machines often went down, or the vendors went off duty;
- in either case they could not buy electricity and the household reverted to some other energy source;
- 90 per cent of customers could afford to buy only small amounts of electricity at a time and so had to purchase at least once a week.

An important finding of Annecke's research is that even with free units, the poor have to transact several times a month because they cannot afford to buy enough electricity at one time for a whole month. Khayelitsha respondents reported choosing to 'skip a week', meaning that a majority of households still use multiple fuels, thus running the risks of fire hazards. According to Annecke, households in her study spent an average of R120 (US$15–18) per month on electricity and another R60 (US$7–10) on other fuels.

Disconnections, illegal connections and protests

In this section of the chapter we look at disconnections, debt and illegality in the supply of residential electricity. Disconnections have been carried out en masse by municipalities and Eskom, and seriously vitiate the already eviscerated FBE programme. Electricity disconnections mean that households cannot get FBE unless they are first legally reconnected or unless they appropriate electricity and make it free by criminal means. In the second half of 2001, in the five large metropolitan areas of South Africa (Johannesburg, Cape Town, Nelson Mandela Bay, eThekwini, eKhuruleni) over 183 000 municipal consumers were disconnected within a period of three months. This was *after* the FBE policy had been announced. Only 79 000 were reconnected, leaving a balance of 104 000 in limbo or 'un-reconnected' (DPLG 2001: 30).

In Johannesburg (excluding Soweto), the city disconnected electricity supply from 20 per cent of households in one year, between June 2000 and June 2001. Those without official reconnections would often illegally reconnect services. 'Many residents, who were *legally* connected to the electricity grid, illegally supplied neighbours. Before our electricians are out of the township, they're already reconnected again.'[9] City Power operations manager for the Johannesburg township of Alexandra, Lerato Setshedi, indicated that only 16 000 houses were registered for electricity, but the utility's records showed that more than 80 000 houses were actually using the system. 'Those who steal belong to jail. It is not that people can't afford to pay…many inhabitants were resistant to paying for the service' (City Power, see note 9). It became apparent that with FBE, cost recovery was intensified because municipalities expected the poor to show gratitude and compliance.

In Cape Town, final letters (over 455 000 'pink slips' or final demand letters) show an accumulation of massive debt for unpaid municipal services accounts (already R38 billion in South Africa as a whole). 'In a march by over 6 000, resident concern was expressed that water at more than 46 000 houses had been cut and more than 16 800 houses were without electricity' (*Mail & Guardian* online 16 May 2007; *Independent Online* 17 May 2007).

Beyond disconnections there lies the spectre of illegal reconnections. Although accurate statistics are hard to come by, there is increasing evidence of wide-scale illegalities ranging from illegal extensions, illegal reconnections and tampering with meters to meter bypassing and tapping from street lights. These constitute risky but desperate strategies that indicate the extent of unaffordability, political alienation and social exclusion experienced by poor households.

In the period 2003–2005 Eskom spent R10 million trying to eradicate the problem of illegal connections in the Western Cape alone (*News 24* 28 November 2005). Illegal reselling and use of extensions have become means for households to supplement their income. One man took advantage of families who found themselves in desperate situations, obtaining an electrical cable and 'renting' out lines to neighbours. Police pulled about 10 illegal connections from his single cable (*Eskom News* 17 March 2005). There have been regular reports of municipal riots against council officials who try to disconnect communities (South African Press Association press release 16 July 2004; *Sunday Times* 29 May 2005).

Conclusion

Despite being trumpeted as a major pro-poor intervention, FBE uses a tiny proportion of the overall electricity produced in South Africa. The amount is fundamentally inadequate to make a difference to people's quality of life, especially given the chronic poverty of about half South Africa's population and high levels of debt and disconnection.

Since 2003, and given a slow start, progress in extending the FBE programme has been considerable. But among the problems with FBE are that it is pegged at a level too low to uplift the poor; it is distributed on a household basis (disregarding household size), thereby discriminating against larger households; the free amount sustains poverty rather than diminishing it; it is very hard to access through the indigent means-test process; and trying to economise with 50 kWh of electricity makes managing everyday life very complicated for poor households and the women who live in them. Furthermore, as this chapter has indicated, FBE often does not reach the poor because of the numerous administrative hurdles placed in their path.

It is also clear from the preceding analysis that FBE in its predominant form (the 50 kWh allocation and prepaid meter system) has not achieved its stated aims of relieving women of drudgery, providing normal access to electricity, and reducing health and safety risks.

Municipalities have a strong disciplinary–paternalistic approach to implementing pro-poor schemes. They seek to use FBE to limit the way households budget and spend and imagine their own needs, rather than expand the sense of how needs can be defined and satisfied.

Prepayment is effectively a *periodic* form of supply with self-imposed cut-offs, so poor households typically go without electricity for several days per month. Even once users have the right to access, they have to purchase prepaid units to activate the FBE, usually entailing transport to a vending point and queuing (a process that middle-class people can circumvent). Much frustration, time and money are spent on prepaid meter-related transactions with vendors.

FBE, although offering temporary relief for very poor households, re-inscribes social exclusion, and with the procedures and stigma of indigent means-testing, discourages the poor from seeking access. The government has imposed its own elitist and implicitly racist construction of what poor people need by insisting that 50 kWh suffices for their household activities. Considering the legacy of white privilege and the extreme poverty and unemployment prevalent in South Africa, it would be better to rethink the policy so that the existing FBE allotment can be considerably increased.

The state has been very concerned with creating public values such as a 'payment morality' and a work ethic among the poor (DoF 2003) and promoting a better popular understanding of the market duties of 'customers'. Services play a big role in this political socialisation/disciplinary process, while allowing the market (through the state) to reach deeper into the everyday lives of citizens. As Gupta (2001: 69) suggests:

> managing a population involves an immersion in the details and minutiae of people's lives. Here mechanisms of discipline and regulation are important not merely as repressive measures but as facilitators of new modes of accountability and enumeration.

In the case of the Free Basic Water Programme, the former director-general in the Department of Water Affairs and Forestry, Mike Muller, argued that supplying FBE was the state's cost recovery strategy (Muller 2001). This argument was repeated in the department's *Strategic Framework*:

> The adoption of free basic water policy has not negated...the principle of user pays. On the contrary, the free basic water policy strengthens the principle in that it clearly requires consumption in excess of the free water supply service to be paid for. (DWAF 2003: 29)

It is not only a question of bureaucratic power, but also one of the values that underpin state policies. The local state has been a key player in trying to reconfigure, formalise and manage the services for poor communities and in the process make these communities less politically threatening and more aware of the 'economic' or commodity value of services, as opposed to general social values and solidarity that public services might bring into being.

Any alternative should recognise both the questions of social justice and the self-evident multiple social and economic benefits of having an adequate free supply of electricity for the poor, delivered in ways that empower rather than stigmatise them. We should avoid what Offe (1983) has suggested occurs in some state concessions that require a 'submissive recognition' by claimants of the superior morality of the capitalist order which created these needs. The reluctant form of welfare belatedly initiated by the ANC-led government after 2000 and instantiated by FBE reflects the ANC's own ambivalent relationship to the 'people' and its continuing commitment to neo-liberalist welfare and capitalist development in South Africa.

However, inasmuch as concessions by the state are used to strengthen the state's power (ideological and administrative), these concessions form an important lever for social movements to use to make demands for real social justice, and to strengthen grassroots movements through which the poor may gain confidence to press for their own demands to be met, in ways that do not undermine their (own) collective power and social values.

Notes

1   Thus, multiple households sharing the service on the same property or in an informal settlement were disqualified, unless they had separate meters.

2   http://www.tshwane.gov.za/documents/finance/SocialPackagePolicy.pdf, accessed 30 October 2006.

3   http://www.tshwane.gov.za/documents/finance/SocialPackagePolicy.pdf, accessed 30 October 2006.

4   www.tshwane.gov.za/thirdqtr_2007.cfm, accessed 30 October 2006.

5   http://www.joburg.org.za/services/citypower_tariffs2.doc, accessed 5 February 2007.

6   Reathusa means 'we help'. For more details see www.joburg.org.za/content/view/615/114/.

7   According to the Conlog website (www.conlog.co.za), 300 000 prepaid electricity meters were exported from South Africa to Khartoum, Sudan, and since then this technology has also been used in Nigeria, Egypt and Saudi Arabia.

8   See *Noseweek* December 2003/January 2004: 11; *Business Times* www.btimes.co.za/99/0829/comp/comp10.htm; *Government Digest* May 2003 20(10).

9   City Power operations manager, cited in www.citypower.co.za/news_archive_2.asp, accessed 30 October 2006.

References

Annecke W (2005) Prepayment meters in Merlo, Argentina and Khayelitsha, South Africa. *ESI Africa* 2. Accessed 8 January 2007, http://www.esi-africa.com/archive/esi_2_2005/52_1.php

CCT (City of Cape Town) (2007) *Media release* No.119/2007, 25 April. Cape Town: CCT

Creamer M (2005) South Africa's electricity industry, 2005. *Creamer Media's Research Channel* April. Accessed 24 March 2007, http://www.researchchannel.co.za/

DA (Democratic Alliance) (n.d.) *The rot in ANC municipalities.* Accessed 20 January 2007, www.da.org.za/da/Site/Eng/campaigns/DOCS/SA_Awards4.doc

DME (Department of Minerals and Energy, South Africa) (2003a) *Electricity basic support services tariff (Free basic electricity) policy.* Pretoria: DME

DME (2003b) *Guidelines for free basic electricity.* Accessed 24 March 2007, http://www.dme.gov.za/pdfs/energy/electricity/fbe_guidelines.doc

DME (2003c) *Frequently asked questions.* Accessed 9 January 2007, http://www.dme.gov.za/energy/elect_fbe.stm#2

DoF (Department of Finance, South Africa) (2003) *Intergovernmental fiscal review 2003.* Pretoria: DoF

DoF (2004) *Intergovernmental fiscal review 2004*. Pretoria: DoF

DPLG (Department of Provincial and Local Government, South Africa) (2001) *Project viability quarterly monitor* 31 December. Pretoria: DPLG

DWAF (Department of Water Affairs and Forestry, South Africa) (2003) *Strategic framework for water services*. Pretoria: DWAF

Escobar A (1995) *Encountering development*. New Jersey: Princeton University Press

ESI Africa (2004) *ESI Africa* 1. Accessed February 2007, http://www.esi.co.za

ESI Africa (2006) *ESI Africa* 1. Accessed February 2007, http://www.esi.co.za

Eskom (2006) *Chairman's report*. Accessed 5 February 2007, http://www.eskom.co.za/annreport06/chairmansreport.htm

Eskom (n.d.) *Frequently asked questions. Customer related questions*. Accessed 12 February 2007, http://www.prepayment.eskom.co.za/faq.asp#save-money

Gupta A (2001) Governing population: The integrated child development services program in India. In T Blom Hansen & F Stepputat (eds) *States of imagination: Ethnographic explorations of the postcolonial state*. Durham: Duke University Press

Hemson D (2004) *Beating the backlog: Meeting targets and providing free basic services*. Pretoria: HSRC

Jones K, Brown J & Bradshaw J (1978) *Issues in social policy*. London: Routledge

Martin P (2002) Inaccessible social security system penalises the poor. *Sunday Times* 8 September

McGibbon H (2002) Prepaid vending, lessons learnt by Eskom. Presentation to Updea (Union of Producers, Transporters and Distributors of Electric Power in Africa) Conference, June. Accessed 21 June 2003, www.eskom.co.za

Mpako M & Prasad G (2005) The free basic electricity (FBE) policy and rural grid-connected households, solar home systems (SHS) users and unelectrified households. Paper presented at the International Conference on the Domestic Use of Energy, 29–31 March, Energy Research Centre, University of Cape Town

Muller M (2001) Free basic water, challenge, sustaining free basic water. *Water, Sewage and Effluent* 21(4): 14

National Treasury (2006) *Local government budgets and expenditure review, 2001–2007*. Pretoria: National Treasury

Offe C (1983) *Contradictions of the welfare state*. London: Hutchinson

Stats SA (Statistics South Africa) (2004) *Non-financial census of municipalities for the year ended 30 June 2004*. Statistical Release P9115. Pretoria: Stats SA

Stats SA (2006) *General Household Survey*. July 2005. Pretoria: Stats SA

Tewari DD & Shah T (2003) An assessment of South Africa's prepaid electricity experiment, lessons learned, and their policy implications for developing countries. *Energy Policy* 31: 911–927

CHAPTER 10

Power to the people?
A rights-based analysis of
South Africa's electricity services

Jackie Dugard

> We...adopt this Constitution as the supreme law of the Republic so as to –
> Heal the divisions of the past and establish a society based on democratic
> values, social justice and fundamental human rights; Improve the quality of
> life of all citizens and free the potential of each person...
>
> The Republic of South Africa is one, sovereign, democratic state founded on
> the following values:
> (a) Human dignity, the achievement of equality and the advancement of
> human rights and freedoms.
> (Preamble and section 1 of the Constitution of the Republic of South Africa,
> Act No. 108 of 1996)

Grace lives in a four-room 'matchbox' house[1] in Zondi, Soweto, in Johannesburg,
with her three children, her brother, Sipho, his two children, and their elderly
mother.[2] Both Grace and Sipho are unemployed. Their only income is from their
mother's pension, which in April 2006 increased from R780 to R820 per month,
and the monthly rental of R100 from the family of three living in the backyard
shack.

Having accumulated substantial electricity arrears because they could not afford to
pay the bills, at the beginning of 2001 the household benefited from a Soweto-wide
electricity debt write-off. However, with average monthly charges of R400 (per
volume of electricity used, higher in winter and lower in summer), Grace was still
unable to afford the household electricity bills following the debt write-off. Despite
paying what she could each month (usually around R100), arrears built up until,
by late 2002, the household owed the City of Johannesburg over R5 000. With no
chance of reducing the arrears, the household experienced regular service
disconnections. In November 2002 Grace, who was tired of living under the
shadow of electricity debt and disconnections, signed the consent form when
Eskom contractors arrived to install a prepaid meter with promises to write off
household debt.[3]

Grace has often regretted consenting to the installation of a prepaid meter, and it is the cause of much conflict in the household. Whereas previously Eskom disconnected the household's electricity service approximately once every two to three months (sometimes not restoring the supply for several weeks), now the household experiences automatic cut-offs at least twice a month, when the free basic electricity (FBE) amount[4] is exhausted and no additional tokens are bought to ensure continuous electricity supply. Although there are 11 people living on the premises, the house and backyard shack are considered to be one household by the municipal authorities (backyard shacks are technically illegal because no planning permission has been secured for their erection) and consequently Grace and Sipho's tenants receive no separate FBE allocation. With 11 people on the premises using electricity, the FBE amount only lasts about a week. After the exhaustion of the FBE supply, Grace, Sipho and their tenants try to take turns to buy prepaid tokens. However, there is often not enough money to buy tokens, and the household is usually without electricity for a few days at a stretch each month. On such days, if she can afford it, Grace buys paraffin or coal, but often, especially towards the end of the month, the household has to go without any energy source at all.

Grace's story is indicative of the human consequences of the commercialisation of municipal services, including electricity, in South Africa. As the chapters in this book show, electricity policy is increasingly based on the kind of cost recovery-driven principles normally reserved for commercial markets. Although, as yet, there has been little actual privatisation (Eskom and municipal electricity service providers are all 100 per cent state-owned), electricity distribution[5] is increasingly commercialised, with Eskom and many municipal distributors functioning as corporatised entities according to business plans. The problem with this commercialisation of basic services such as electricity is that 'private market mechanisms distribute goods and services based on willingness and ability to pay' (Flynn & Chirwa 2005: 59). As this chapter will argue, such a market-driven rationale is at odds with South Africa's constitutional framework, with its implied right to electricity and its explicit rights to equality of, and to justly administered, electricity services.

Taking as its starting point the discrepancies between the constitutional promise and the lived reality of electricity services as experienced by low-income households such as Grace's, this chapter examines the human rights implications of the commercialisation of electricity in South Africa. Locating its analysis within a human rights framework, the chapter seeks to provide a set of tools for policy engagement and, ultimately, for public-interest litigation, with a view to improving electricity services to poor households.

The chapter begins with an overview of the implied right to electricity, followed by an examination of the explicit rights to equality of electricity services and to just electricity-related administrative action. It then analyses the electricity distribution framework from the perspective of low-income households, highlighting five of the most problematic aspects of commercialised electricity services, as well as identifying possible constitutional and legal challenges in respect of each of the five areas of concern:

- inappropriate tariffs;
- insufficient FBE;
- disconnections due to inability to afford electricity services;
- imposition of prepaid meters;
- unequal customer services.

A human rights framework

Normatively, electricity should be viewed as an essential good because:
> [e]lectricity is a basic necessity and access to it has a wide range of positive developmental benefits for communities. Increased usage of electricity improves the level of welfare, decreases health expenditures and improves opportunities for low-income families, and women in particular. Poor communities should have access to electricity, and should be enabled to afford it without sacrificing other basic necessities. (Nefale & Roux 2003: 2)

This section develops the normative argument of electricity as an essential good within a human rights framework, analysing the implications for electricity providers of being located within a constitutional order that regulates basic services such as electricity. That is to say, notwithstanding theoretical arguments about what kind of service electricity is and who is best placed to provide it most effectively, this section sets out the constitutional and legislative conditions under which electricity provision, as a basic service, *must be* undertaken.

An implied right to electricity

Unlike the right of access to sufficient water (section 27(1)(b) of the Constitution), in South Africa there is no enumerated right to electricity (nor is there a right to energy). However, this right can be implied in the right of access to adequate housing (section 26(1) of the Constitution). The fact that the right to housing implies more than merely having a roof over one's head was confirmed by the South African Constitutional Court in its landmark socio-economic rights case, *Government of the Republic of South Africa v Grootboom* (2000) (hereafter *Grootboom*). According to the Court, the 'state's obligation to provide adequate housing depends on context, and may differ from province to province, from city to city, from rural to urban areas and from person to person' and while 'some may need access to land and no more...some may need access to services such as water, sewage, electricity and roads' (*Grootboom* para. 37). This means that, in the Court's view, one of the factors relevant to a consideration of the right to housing is electricity provision.

However, this section of the judgment, as *obiter dictum*,[6] is only persuasive (it is not legally binding). It remains to be seen how or indeed if a right to electricity would be considered justiciable by the Constitutional Court, which has thus far failed to provide much clarification of the state's positive obligations to promote the socio-economic rights of individuals (as opposed to a general right of everyone to a reasonable government programme in respect of the right).[7]

Notwithstanding the limited judicial enforcement of socio-economic rights by the Constitutional Court, this interpretation of an implied right to electricity is supported in international law[8] by the United Nations Committee on Economic, Social and Cultural Rights (CESCR), which monitors compliance with the International Covenant on Economic, Social and Cultural Rights (ICESCR).[9] The CESCR has construed the right to electricity as being inherent to the enjoyment of other socio-economic rights in a way similar to that in which it has construed the right to water (also not explicitly enumerated).

In the case of electricity, in General Comment 4 on the right to adequate housing (CESCR 1991), the CESCR has stipulated that 'all beneficiaries of the right to adequate housing should have sustainable access' to 'energy for cooking, heating and lighting' (para. 8(b)). Although General Comment 4 refers to energy rather than electricity specifically, the United Nations Special Rapporteur on adequate housing as a component of the right to an adequate living standard, Miloon Kothari, has clarified in his reports that the right to adequate housing 'includes access to essential civic services such as electricity' (Tully 2006: 524). Kothari's 2002 report states that 'the right to adequate housing – broadly defined' must be taken to 'include access to land, as well as other essential services such as water, electricity and sanitation...' (Kothari 2002: para. 49). Moreover, in specific relation to the rights of women, article 14 of the Convention on the Elimination of All Forms of Discrimination Against Women (1979),[10] which South Africa ratified in 1995, states:

> States Parties shall take all appropriate measures to eliminate discrimination against women in rural areas...to ensure...the right...to enjoy adequate living conditions, particularly in relation to housing, sanitation, electricity and water supply...

In all of its General Comments on socio-economic rights the CESCR has stressed that economic accessibility, availability and affordability are essential elements of each right. Such requirements are even more strongly affirmed regarding vulnerable groups such as women, children, elderly and disabled people. In General Comment 3 on the nature of states parties' obligations (CESCR 1990), the CESCR has underlined that 'even in times of severe resources constraints...the vulnerable members of society can and indeed must be protected by the adoption of relatively low-cost targeted programmes' (para. 12). Moreover, as Magdalena Sepúlveda has pointed out, it is clear from the CESCR's work that commercialisation (or indeed privatisation) does 'not relieve the state of its obligation to ensure that minimum essential levels of each right are enjoyed by individuals, particularly the most vulnerable and disadvantaged groups within society' (2003: 367).[11]

Despite being a signatory, South Africa has never ratified the ICESCR.[12] Nonetheless, section 39(1)(b) of the Constitution stipulates that, when interpreting the

Bill of Rights, a court 'must consider international law'. Crucially, given South Africa's failure to ratify the ICESCR, the Constitutional Court has established that, for the purposes of interpretation, 'international law would include non-binding as well as binding law' (*S v Makwanyane* 1995: para. 35). It is consequently clear that the ICESCR is relevant to the interpretation of socio-economic rights in South Africa.

Taken together, there is therefore a strongly implied right to electricity in international and South African domestic law. This thesis is strengthened by the inclusion of electricity in the government's 'free basic services' package. Arguably, the allocation of FBE to qualifying households (discussed below), alongside Free Basic Water, is an implicit acknowledgement of a right to 'sufficient' electricity along the same lines as the constitutional right of everyone to 'access to sufficient food and water' (section 27(1)(b)).

The inference of an implied right to electricity is that it is subject to the same obligations as the other socio-economic rights in the Bill of Rights, requiring the state to take 'reasonable legislative and other measures, within its available resources, to achieve the progressive realisation of the right' (section 27(2) of the Constitution). In *Grootboom*, the Constitutional Court established that, to be reasonable, 'measures cannot leave out of account the degree and extent of the denial of the right they endeavour to realise' (para. 44). Moreover, government programmes must 'respond to the needs of the most desperate' and must ensure that social and economic rights are 'made more accessible not only to a larger number of people but to a wider range of people as time progresses' (paras 44–45). Such pronouncements by the Constitutional Court in the context of an implied right to electricity suggest that the state is obliged by the Constitution to provide more electricity to more people, but especially to vulnerable groups such as the poor, over time. However, as noted above, the extent to which any socio-economic right in its constitutional-right form is enforceable as an individual right to a resource or service is debatable.

Notwithstanding the implications of an implied right to electricity, there are more powerful arguments for a rights-based analysis of electricity services. From a constitutional standpoint, Eskom, as a state-owned corporation, and munici-palities, as the local sphere of government, are bound by the Bill of Rights and must 'respect, protect, promote and fulfil the rights in the Bill of Rights' (section 7 of the Constitution). Of the rights that attach to the provision of essential public services such as electricity, the most important are the rights to equality of, and to justly administered, electricity services, which are not diminished through the corporatisation, commercialisation or even privatisation of services provision.

The right to equality of electricity services

Regardless of the commercialisation of Eskom and municipal electricity entities such as Johannesburg's City Power, electricity remains a public service that is 100 per cent state-owned.[13] As such, all policy choices by the state in relation to electricity distribution must comply with the section 9 right to equality. This right obliges the state to ensure that electricity provision is equal (meaning that everyone should receive an equal standard of service) and equitable (in the sense that there should be no *unfair* discrimination between groups on any grounds, including those listed in section 9(3)[14]). Specifically, section 9(2) requires the state to take steps to 'promote the achievement of equality'.

Against the backdrop of apartheid's legacy of unequal municipal services provision based on unfair discrimination on the grounds of race (and, concomitantly, on class), section 9(2) enjoins the state to take 'legislative and other measures designed to protect or advance persons, or categories of persons, disadvantaged by unfair discrimination'. In the case of *City Council of Pretoria v Walker* (1998) (hereafter *Walker)* the Constitutional Court clarified that positive discrimination policies aimed at correcting past inequalities between formerly advantaged and disadvantaged groups do not amount to unfair discrimination. Indeed, such essentially redistributive policies, designed to promote the achievement of socio-economic equality, are not only permitted, they are constitutionally mandated. As recognised by the Constitutional Court in *Walker,* the constitutional objective of equality 'will not be achieved if the consequences of those inequalities and disparities caused by discriminatory laws and practices in the past are not recognised and dealt with' (para. 46). In relation to electricity services, this means that the state is obliged to ensure that positive steps are taken to make electricity increasingly accessible and affordable to poor people.[15] In other words, the right to equality of electricity services incorporates the right to equitable services, i.e. the right to redistributive policies and practices that aim to redress socio-economic inequality.

There is no doubt that the post-apartheid state acknowledges the legacy and scale of the problem of unequal services provision. In the words of the White Paper on Local Government (DPLG 1998: para. 2.3):

> Under apartheid there was systematic under-investment in municipal infrastructure in black areas. This deprived millions of people of access to basic services, including water, sanitation, refuse collection and roads. Developmental local government has to address this backlog. Its central mandate is to develop service delivery capacity to meet the basic needs of communities.

The state is also aware of the constitutional obligation to extend and to maintain affordable electricity services to everyone. The Eskom Conversion Act (No. 13 of 2001), for example, provides that in the process of converting Eskom to a public company, 'the Minister must take into account...the promotion of universal access to, and the provision of, affordable electricity' (section 6(5)(b)). Similarly, the Department of Minerals and Energy (DME) Ministerial Foreword to the White Paper on the Energy Policy of the Republic of South Africa (DME: 1998) states:

> ...the state must establish a national energy policy which will ensure that the national energy resources shall be adequately tapped and developed to cater for the needs of the nation. Energy should therefore be available to all citizens

at an affordable cost. Energy production and distribution should not only be sustainable, but should also lead to an improvement of the standard of living for all the country's citizens.

To this end, the National Energy Regulator Act (No. 40 of 2004) was formulated to provide a co-ordinated platform for managing a national energy policy in line with the White Paper on Energy's directives. And the finalised Electricity Regulation Act (No. 4 of 2006) – which replaced most of the Electricity Act (No. 41 of 1987) (in terms of which electricity licensing and tariff-setting had been regulated) – aligned electricity regulation with the Constitution. Importantly for this rights-based analysis, section 16(1)(e) of the new Electricity Regulation Act allows for 'the cross-subsidy of tariffs to certain classes of customers', which clearly permits the kind of redistributive pricing policies that advance socio-economic equality.

Finally, in terms of policy, the stated aim of the DME's *Electricity Basic Services Support Tariff (Free Basic Electricity) Policy for the Republic of South Africa* is to 'alleviate the negative impacts of poverty on communities' (DME 2003: 11). And it is worth remembering the Reconstruction and Development Programme (RDP), which in 1994 urged future energy policy to 'concentrate on the provision of energy services to meet the basic needs of poor households' (ANC 1994: para. 2.7.3).

In terms of service delivery, electricity, along with the other basic services (including water, sanitation and refuse collection), is governed by the overall policy framework for municipal service delivery, which stresses the need to advance equal services to all members of the local community. Thus, the White Paper on Local Government requires municipalities 'to assume a developmental role in providing basic services' (Khumalo et al. 2003: 8) and the RDP stipulates that 'an accelerated and sustainable electrification programme' should be introduced to provide electricity to all citizens (ANC 1994: para. 2.7.7). Furthermore, the Local Government Municipal Systems Act (No. 32 of 2000), which provides the details of municipal services provision, stipulates that municipalities must 'ensure that all members of the local community have access to at least the minimum level of basic municipal services' (section 73(1)(c)) and that such access should be 'equitable' (section 4(2(f)).

On tariff policy specifically, the Local Government Municipal Systems Act requires the municipality to ensure that users are treated 'equitably in the application of tariffs' (section 74(2)(a)), ensuring that 'poor households...have access to at least basic services' through, inter alia, 'life line tariffs' and 'any other direct or indirect method of subsidisation of tariffs for poor households' (section 74(2)(c)).

As is elaborated further in the second part of the chapter, such equality-focused imperatives are directly relevant to practices related to tariff-setting, FBE and customer services. Such criteria suggest that, where they fail to advance socio-economic equality and/or to redress poverty, electricity services may be legally challenged.

The right to administratively just electricity services

The embeddedness of electricity provision within a constitutionally entrenched human rights framework is further strengthened by section 33 of the Constitution, which guarantees everyone 'the right to just administrative action that is lawful, reasonable and procedurally fair'. Moreover, the Promotion of Administrative Justice Act (No. 3 of 2000) (PAJA) clarifies various contours of the right, including defining what is procedurally fair administrative action. In the context of electricity services, the most important requirements are those for 'adequate notice of the nature and purpose of the proposed administrative action' (section 3(2)(b)(i)) and for a 'reasonable opportunity to make representations' (section 3(2)(b)(ii)).

These requirements are particularly important in the context of disconnections of electricity, which must comply with the notification and representation elements of the Act, and the imposition of the system of prepaid meters, which, arguably, does not comply with the requirement to allow representation at the point of automatic cut-off (when the FBE amount is exhausted and no tokens are purchased to ensure continuous electricity supply). These issues are dealt with in further detail later in the chapter.

Although there is a lot of outsourcing of electricity functions (including meter reading, meter installation and infrastructure installation and maintenance), electricity services per se have not yet been privatised. Nevertheless, it is worth noting, in light of possible future developments, that the application of the Bill of Rights is not limited to state action. Section 8(2) provides that 'a provision of the Bill of Rights binds a natural or a juristic person [i.e. a company] if, and to the extent that, it is applicable, taking into account the nature of the right and the nature of any duty imposed by the right'. The rights to equality and just administrative action are two such rights that attach even to commercial enterprises, in that section 9(4) stipulates: 'No person may unfairly discriminate directly or indirectly against anyone' on any ground listed in subsection 2. Similarly, over and above 'organs of the state', PAJA binds 'a natural or juristic person...when exercising a public power or performing a public function in terms of an empowering provision' (section 1(b)). Thus, neither Eskom nor any municipality may divest itself of its constitutional and legislative responsibilities through privatisation or outsourcing of the electricity distribution function.

Applying the rights model to electricity services in South Africa

Taken together, such constitutional and legislative obligations and policy commitments imply that electricity distribution is occurring within a rights-based framework that recognises both the implied right to electricity and the explicit rights to just and equal services. This section of the chapter suggests that, in the context of the commercialisation of electricity services, these rights are not being adequately safeguarded.

Access to sufficient affordable electricity of an adequate quality is intrinsically linked to positive transformative and developmental goals that underwrite South Africa's Constitution. In order to redress apartheid's legacy of socio-economic inequality as well as to continually improve the standard of living of citizens, it is essential that poor communities should have access to electricity 'and be able to pay for its use within their available resources without sacrificing other basic necessities' (CALS 2003: 4).

Whatever the sentiments about affordable energy expressed in policy documents such as the White Paper on Energy, it is clear that within the commercialised electricity industry, cost recovery and what Eskom refers to as 'cost reflectivity' – defined as 'the pricing method aimed at reflecting the full recovery of economic cost of supplying electricity to a customer' (DME 2004: 5) – undermine the redistributive potential of electricity provision. And, while significant advances have been made in terms of the absolute number of people connected to the electricity grid since 1994, many low-income households have subsequently been disconnected through the inability to afford electricity, as discussed below.

In stark contrast to the strategic role electricity played within the apartheid state, the post-apartheid government has struggled to wield leverage over essentially autonomous electricity entities. As noted by Maj Fiil-Flynn:

> The contrasts from the apartheid era could not be more glaring. White consumers and industry were heavily subsidised by the state and Eskom played a leading role in promoting (white) welfare and prosperity in the country. External funding played a key role here as well with more than half of the World Bank's $200 million in credits to the apartheid regime (from 1951 to 1966) going towards Eskom's expansion...To what end? Today, most low-income South Africans still rely for a large part of their lighting, cooking and heating energy needs on paraffin (with its burn-related health risks), coal (with high levels of domestic and localised township air pollution) and wood (with dire consequences for deforestation). (Fiil-Flynn 2001: 5–6)

Largely because of the commercialisation of electricity distribution following the democratic transition, the post-apartheid state has been unable to utilise electricity in the same developmental way for black/poor South Africans that the apartheid state was able to do vis-à-vis industry and white consumers. The commercialised distribution environment – in which distributors must operate as commercially viable entities and the primary tariff principle is to 'enable an efficient licensee to recover the full cost of its licensed activities, including a reasonable margin of return' (section 16(1)(a) of the Electricity Regulation Act) – limits the state's potential to deliver affordable, accessible electricity services to the poor.

This section delineates the lived reality of electricity services in low-income households from a rights-based perspective. The five major electricity-related problems faced by the poor are outlined and subjected to legal scrutiny in terms of the constitutional framework established earlier in the chapter, as well as other relevant legislation. The section focuses on Soweto, which is the subject of three recent research reports (Coalition Against Water Privatisation 2004; Fiil-Flynn 2001; Nefale 2004), but is relevant more generally across South Africa.

Inappropriate tariffs

Legislation and government policy make it clear that, in setting tariffs, the main principle to be followed by all entities involved in the supply of electricity is cost reflectivity. Within the commercialised and increasingly corporatised environment, electricity provision is separated into 'autonomous units, limiting the extent of cross-subsidisation' within or between services (McInnes 2005: 29). So, while the Electricity Regulation Act does 'permit the cross-subsidy of tariffs to certain classes of customers' (section 16(1)(e)), this is subject to the caveat in section 16(1)(a) that any licence condition 'must enable an efficient licensee to recover the full cost of its licensed activities, including a reasonable margin or return', and licensees are instructed to 'avoid undue discrimination between customer categories' (section 16(1)(d)). Municipalities are further constrained by the imperative to balance their budgets found in section G1.2 of the White Paper on Local Government, which clarifies that 'the Constitution effectively prohibits deficit budgeting at the local sphere' (DPLG 1998). David Hallowes points out that even the limited scope for cross-subsidisation that currently exists is likely to be undermined in the near future, as the DME's 2004 *Electricity Pricing Policy of the South African Electricity Industry* clearly aims to 'strip out all subsidies in time' (Hallowes 2006: 29).

As a consequence of the commercial limits of cross-subsidisation, state intervention to mitigate the actual cost of electricity provision to low-income households mainly occurs through complex transfers from the National Treasury, via the Department of Provincial and Local Government and the particular municipality, to the distributor (even if this is Eskom) in the form of the equitable share grant. Because the Constitution entrenches the autonomy of the local sphere of government, such transfers from the National Treasury cannot be ring-fenced and there is no guarantee that the funds are spent on free basic services for the poor. As such, the equitable share transfer is a relatively blunt tool for redistribution compared with a targeted system of cross-subsidised tariffs, reflected in a sufficient free basic amount followed by an upward curve of slowly rising price blocks, which only serve to penalise 'luxury consumption' (Bond 2004: 2).

In the absence of standardising cross-subsidisation and tariff intervention, a patchwork of some 2 000 varying tariffs persists across the country. Most tariff structures do not utilise the progressive kind of rising block tariffs that penalise luxury consumption while allowing low-level consumption (generally exhibited by poor people) to be much cheaper per unit. This means that in most cases, the FBE amount is followed by a standard expensive tariff cost. Moreover, many of the tariff systems continue to benefit empowered sectors and groups and are often based more on cost reflectivity than on socio-economic justice. While it may be difficult to mount a legal challenge against the cost recovery pricing model, inequitable tariffs that in effect discriminate against low-income users potentially violate the right to equality, and certainly violate the spirit of the Constitution.

One of the objectives of the current Electricity Distribution Industry (EDI) restructuring process which aims to establish a Regional Electricity Distributor (RED) system, is the standardisation of tariffs. With only one RED (the Cape Town RED, called RED 1 (Pty) Ltd) established, it is too soon to say whether this objective will be met. As it stands, electricity distribution still reflects the apartheid-inherited policy of discounting industrial tariffs at the expense of domestic consumers which, while perhaps making commercial sense, runs counter to principles of transformation and social justice. So, despite the RDP calling for cross-subsidies from industrial users to township users (ANC 1994), the opposite practice continues in many jurisdictions. Under this apartheid-inherited rubric, low-income households, which consume less than 3 per cent of the electricity generated, pay on average double the tariffs offered to industry (Fiil-Flynn 2001: 3). So in 2001, for example, domestic consumers as a whole paid an average price to Eskom of R0.2459 per kilowatt-hour (kWh) (Sowetans paid much higher average prices), 'while the manufacturing sector paid [R0.1283] per kWh and the mining sector paid [R0.1232] per kWh' (Bond & McInnes 2006: 4).

In addition, many of the persistent tariff discrepancies discriminate against the poor. For example, the cheapest tariff without a monthly network or service charge for Johannesburg residents served by City Power is the Lifeline tariff at R0.4041 per kWh while the cheapest energy-only tariff for Soweto residents (supplied by Eskom), the Hometake tariff, is R0.4537 per kWh.[16] The consequence for low-income households of the relatively higher cost of electricity, as attested by Fiil-Flynn's (2001) research in Soweto, is that, despite efforts to try to follow electricity-saving instructions and given the demands on big households, residents are still not able to reduce their electricity charges to affordable levels.

The objective inability of low-income households to pay for electricity is confirmed in Michael Nefale's 2004 survey on attitudes to prepaid meters in Soweto. The average total household income in Nefale's sample of 800 respondents was R1 220 per month, and the average monthly household charge for electricity was R306 (Nefale 2004: 18). Given that this amount represents almost 25 per cent of the average household monthly income, it is not surprising that most households in Soweto are unable to pay their electricity bills. Clearly, whatever the actual costs of providing the service, the cost of electricity is too high for low-income households. Nevertheless, as demonstrated by Fiil-Flynn (2001), and corroborated in Nefale's more recent (2004) study, the majority of Soweto residents do attempt to make some monthly payment. In Fiil-Flynn's study regular bill payments were the norm, with 'each of the households interviewed indicating some level of payment', usually approximately half of the amount owed (2001: 12). In Nefale's survey, the average household payment per month was R173, which also amounts to about half of the average monthly charge (R306) (2004: 18). Such data suggest strongly that unaffordability rather than a 'culture of non-payment' is responsible for non-compliance.[17] Moreover, Nefale's research also indicates that, far from reflecting a 'culture of entitlement' towards electricity services, the majority of Sowetans (77 per cent) recognise that 'electricity should be paid for once the free basic amount is exhausted', as long as it is affordable (2004: 19).

The net effect of low-income households not being able to afford electricity has been an endemic problem of arrears. According to Nefale's research, average electricity arrears in Soweto amount to over R3 000 per household, with the top end of the range at R117 632 (2004: 13). Such large arrears have the effect not only of contributing to financial stress within households who are willing to pay for services but who cannot afford the full amounts of their bills (Fiil-Flynn 2001), but also, increasingly, of leading to disconnections (discussed below).

Insufficient free basic electricity

Apart from its integrated national electrification programme (extending the electricity grid to historically disadvantaged communities),[18] the government's main mechanism for intervening in the commercialised electricity sector to mitigate the effects of cost recovery-related tariffs has been the provision of FBE to qualifying households.

In the run-up to municipal elections on 5 December 2000, the government announced its intention to provide free basic services, including electricity, to low-income households. By this time some municipalities were already providing a free allocation of electricity to targeted households, funded internally through cross-subsidisation from other consumer categories including rates. Seeking to establish a uniformly applicable policy, the DME accepted the amount of 50 kWh per household per month proposed by a study conducted for Eskom and the DME by the University of Cape Town between 2001 and 2002 (Eskom & DME 2002: 11), and the resultant FBE policy was rolled out from mid-2003 onwards.

However, despite the objective of creating a standardised system of FBE allocation, the disjointedness of the apartheid-inherited distribution system – in terms of which, in general terms, Eskom distributes to formerly black areas and municipalities distribute to formerly white areas – has meant that there have been major discrepancies in FBE implementation across the country. In areas under Eskom's distribution licence, DME policy applies, meaning that 50 kWh of FBE is provided to households that consume less than 150 kWh of electricity per month. But distributing municipalities have not uniformly implemented FBE at this threshold. For example, it was only in 2005 that the provision of FBE was equalised between residents of Soweto and residents of the rest of Johannesburg. Prior to that, households in the (historically white) suburbs of Johannesburg could qualify for 50 kWh FBE from their electricity provider (City Power) if they chose a 'tariff option B', which provided FBE if they consumed less than 1 020 kWh per month.

Soweto households, in contrast, with Eskom as the provider, could only receive the 50 kWh FBE amount if they consumed less than 150 kWh per month (almost 10 times less than the City Power qualifying threshold). Under this system, only approximately 1 000 households in Soweto qualified for FBE (Salvoldi interview). Since the equalisation (using a qualifying threshold of 802 kWh per household per month for the whole of Johannesburg, including Soweto), a further 82 000 households in Soweto now qualify for FBE (Govender interview).[19]

Over and above discrepancies in the implementation of the FBE policy, the amount of 50 kWh per household per month is also problematic. This amount is based on the research undertaken by the University of Cape Town in 2001 and 2002 (Eskom & DME 2002), which was formalised in the DME's *Electricity Basic Services Support Tariff (Free Basic Electricity) Policy*, which found that 56 per cent of households in South Africa connected to the national grid in Eskom's licensed area consume less than 50 kWh of electricity a month (DME 2003: 11). However, according to Professor Anton Eberhard of the Infrastructure Industries Reform and Regulation Management Programme (Graduate School of Business, University of Cape Town), the 50 kWh amount is probably not suitable for urban areas with big households and multiple energy demands (Eberhard interview), not least because the FBE amount does not take into account the typically large sizes of low-income urban households.

Indeed, although the 50 kWh amount arguably can make a big difference in rural areas where otherwise no electricity is afforded, studies on low-income usage of electricity in urban areas indicate that 50 kWh is not enough to make a developmental and environmental impact. Fiil-Flynn's study of Soweto indicates that low-income households (with an average combined income of around R1 000 per month) typically consume approximately 500 kWh of electricity per month (2001: 12). Eskom estimates that the average household in Soweto (including more wealthy households) consumes approximately 600 kWh per month (Salvoldi interview). Clearly, at 10 per cent or less of average total consumption, 50 kWh of FBE is insufficient to meet the needs of the typically large households in poor urban areas. By Eskom's own calculations, it takes an estimated 60 kWh per month to cover lighting needs alone in an average low-income urban household in South Africa (Eskom 1996: 13). With insufficient FBE allocations and electricity charges that are largely unaffordable for low-income households, many poor South Africans are not able to benefit appropriately from the expansion of the electricity grid.

Further research is necessary to determine appropriate pricing and/or FBE regimes that will contribute to the goal of advancing socio-economic equality in South Africa. Until more equitable regimes are implemented, the government's electrification programme will continue to be undermined by disconnections; as fast as new households are added to the grid, others will be disconnected from it for failure to pay for the electricity they need to enjoy an adequate standard of living. As currently implemented, any persisting discrepancies in the rollout and threshold for qualification of FBE could be subjected to a section 9 equality challenge with a view to achieving an equitable FBE regime such as the FBE equalisation undertaken by the City of Johannesburg in 2005.

Disconnections due to inability to afford electricity

Operating as commercialised entities, municipal service providers, along with Eskom, cannot afford to carry the financial burden of non-paying consumers without raising tariffs to unacceptably high levels. Consequently, electricity consumers who are chronically in arrears are disconnected from the grid (Bond & McInnes 2006). Despite the severity of this measure, there are no national guidelines and no requirements for additional caution regarding the disconnection of electricity services to vulnerable groups and low-income households. Eskom and other electricity service providers are not, for example, required to consult social welfare departments or to check if consumers are on any indigent register[20] before disconnecting their supply. The result has been that, 'seldom used before 1994 [and the commercialisation of electricity distribution], service cut-offs have become a major mechanism of payment enforcement and have been implemented throughout the country' (McDonald 2002: 11).

This has meant that although, as of February 2002, the electrification programme had connected 3.15 million additional homes since 1994 (South African Institute of Race Relations 2006: 422),[21] the progressiveness of the government's electrification programme has been undermined by cost recovery-related disconnections within the industry. According to Fiil-Flynn's research, disconnections due to inability to pay for electricity numbered up to 20 000 households per month in Soweto alone in early 2001 and this rate accelerated after April 2001, when Eskom invoked a decision to cut the electricity supply to households that were more than R5 000 in arrears for more than 120 days (Fiil-Flynn 2001: 14–15). In Fiil-Flynn's survey, 45 per cent of households experiencing cut-offs were disconnected for more than a month, and 'many reported cut-offs of up to nine months in length' (2001: 15). Based on a national survey, which suggests that 13 per cent of South Africans have experienced electricity cut-offs due to non-payment of arrears, David McDonald estimates that 3.25 million households across South Africa suffered electricity disconnections between 1994 and 2004, which is approximately the same number of households that were connected to the grid in the same period (2002: 12). McDonald makes the point that 3.25 million households, extrapolated to individuals – 'taking a conservative estimate of two other household members for every respondent who said they had experienced a cut-off' – means that the actual number of people affected by electricity disconnections since 1994 ranges from 5.5 million to as high as 9.7 million (McDonald 2002: 12).

People whose electricity services are cut off face a multitude of negative consequences. These include health problems related to the use of alternative sources of energy such as coal and paraffin, and increased danger of household fires due to candle or paraffin use. Clearly the increased use of wood and coal also has a detrimental environmental effect. In addition, given the gendered nature of domestic work in South Africa, many of the additional household burdens fall on women. So, when food spoils due to lack of refrigeration, or when alternative energy sources need to be secured, it is invariably women who have 'more work to do' (Fiil-Flynn 2001: 18). Fiil-Flynn's research also points to a rise in domestic violence against women as a result of household conflict related to electricity disconnections.

Households that have had their electricity cut off due to inability to pay their bills face reconnection fees that are often impossibly high given the fact that, for the service to be reconnected, electricity providers usually insist on arrears being paid in full (Fiil-Flynn 2001). As a result, many households 'live permanently without electricity, while others are forced into a vicious cycle of illegal connections/ disconnections and power interruptions' (Fiil-Flynn 2001: 16). This is particularly so for very poor households. McDonald's research indicates that it is 'the poorest of the poor who make up the largest absolute number' of those who have experienced cut-offs (2002: 13).

Notwithstanding arguments about the substantive unfairness of disconnecting electricity to low-income households, there is the possibility of mounting a legal challenge to disconnections that are not procedurally fair. In order to be lawful, disconnections of electricity services must meet the PAJA requirement for procedural fairness. This means that any distributor that plans a disconnection must provide the household with adequate notice of the proposed action (section 3(2)(b)(i)) and reasonable opportunity to make representations (section 3(2)(b)(ii)), which could include raising the issue of inability to afford the service. Thus, in instances such as are documented by Fiil-Flynn (2001), where customers were neither notified that their electricity supply would be cut off, nor given the opportunity to dispute bills or to rectify payments problems, the distributor is acting unlawfully and the decision to disconnect the electricity supply could be taken on review. The fact that very few, if any, cases have been brought on these grounds is largely due to a lack of legal assistance/aid for civil matters and the seeming complexity of electricity-related cases.

Imposition of prepaid meters

In response to the dual problems of widespread arrears and rising resistance to service cut-offs in low-income areas,[22] in recent years Eskom, along with many municipal service providers, has embarked on a campaign to install prepaid meters as a cost recovery mechanism (beyond the FBE amount, additional units of electricity must be purchased in the form of tokens to enable electricity provision). There is nothing wrong with prepaid meters per se, where they have been introduced out of genuine choice. Indeed, prepaid meters are welcomed in many residential areas as a means of bypassing inaccurate municipal billing (discussed below), as well as of managing household finances. However, as Nefale's research indicates, there is a strong correlation between positive attitudes to prepaid meters and higher income levels. Conversely, the poorer the household, the more negative is the attitude towards prepaid meters. In Nefale's survey, the majority of respondents whose household monthly income was above R800 agreed with the statement 'A prepaid meter is the best way of providing electricity for our household', whereas the majority of respondents whose household monthly income was below R800 disagreed with the same statement (Nefale 2004: 18).

There are two important factors behind the clear correlation between lower household income and negative perception of prepaid meters. First, poorer households are less able to afford electricity tokens after the 50 kWh FBE amount is used up, which, with a prepaid meter, means automatic disconnection from the grid. Research conducted by the Coalition Against Water Privatisation in one of the poorest areas of Soweto, Phiri, found that the overwhelming majority of respondents with prepaid meters regularly run out of electricity between one and three times a month and a fifth of them experience repeated automatic disconnections (sometimes referred to as 'self-disconnections' because the disconnection occurs within the house as opposed to at the source of electricity distribution)[23] of between four and six times each month (Coalition Against Water Privatisation 2004: 13). In Nefale's study, 48 per cent of respondents identified 'cut-offs brought by prepaid meters' as the reason why there is so much resistance to prepaid meters in Soweto (2004: 19).

Second, households in poorer localities commonly are not given any choice about the installation of prepaid meters, whereas in richer areas prepaid meters are only installed following customer request and a formal application procedure. In Soweto, which comprises relatively poorer households (compared with other suburbs in Johannesburg), 83.5 per cent of respondents in Nefale's survey who have a prepaid meter in their home did not apply for it (2004: 7). This contrasts with the policy of, for example, City Power, which distributes electricity to Johannesburg's predominantly higher-income residential areas, whose 'point of departure' for the installation of prepaid meters 'is choice' (Padayachee interview).

The fact that prepaid meters are imposed on low-income households, whereas they are only installed on request in richer areas, arguably amounts to unfair discrimination based on socio-economic status and is potentially a violation of the constitutional right to equality.[24] Moreover, any change in service provision from a normal metered supply to a prepaid meter that is made without proper consultation contravenes section 4(2)(e) of the Local Government Municipal Systems Act, which requires the municipality to 'consult with the local community about' (i) 'the level, quality, range and impact of municipal services' and (ii) 'the available options for service delivery'. Furthermore, although yet to be challenged in South Africa, it is possible that prepaid meters might be judged to be unlawful (as water prepaid meters were in the UK)[25] on the administrative justice grounds that at the time of automatic disconnection following exhaustion of FBE or credit in the form of prepaid tokens, they provide neither 'adequate notice' as required by PAJA section 3(2)(b)(i), nor 'reasonable opportunity to make representations' as stipulated in section 3(2)(b)(ii) of PAJA.[26]

Unequal customer services

Apart from being largely unaffordable, electricity accounts in low-income households are also often unreliable, reflecting widespread inaccurate accounting systems, chaotic billing and infrequent meter-reading. In many municipalities this is the consequence of a two-tiered revenue management system, in which the accounts of the most valuable (in terms of revenue) consumers are prioritised over those of middle- and low-income households. This is the case in the City of Johannesburg, where the accounts of the top 13 000 customers by value (what the City commonly refers to as 'key customers') are handled by customer relations managers within City Power, whereas the accounts function for everyone else (approximately 275 000 households), including low-income households within City Power's area of licence,[27] is undertaken by the City's overstretched revenue administration unit.

There are three major problems with this kind of revenue management system. First, it results in bifurcated accounting, with good services for top-end consumers and poor services for everyone else. In the City of Johannesburg, the more valuable consumers are handled efficiently and effectively by well-trained customer relations managers, who ensure accurate billing, reliable meter-reading and prompt resolution of problems. In contrast, the remainder of consumers, who are dealt with by the City's revenue management administration, experience a vastly inferior service, with systemic problems of inaccurate accounts and billing.

Second, the disconnection of the bulk of customers' accounts (handled by the City) from all other customer services issues across all customer categories (handled by City Power), creates an artificial separation between accounting services and customer services for everyone other than the top 13 000 customers. This means that, absence of customer relations managers notwithstanding, it is difficult to consolidate data and to resolve complaints because information and autonomy are split between institutions. Conversely, the top 13 000 customers are dealt with by an integrated accounts and customer services environment in which information is consolidated and problems can be speedily addressed.

Third, by removing the more difficult billing component (for everyone below the top 13 000 customers) from the equation, an inaccurate impression may be created of the overall performance of the commercialised service provider. In other words, where a service provider such as City Power is responsible for the accounts of only 13 000 key customers, it is relatively easy for it to score well on customer services-related indicators (which are an important consideration for renegotiating or renewing contracts) when, in actual fact, the overall accounts system, as managed by the City, is in a state of chaos.

The chaotic state of Johannesburg's basic services accounting system and the concomitant 'billing chaos' is acknowledged by the City. In an article on its official website celebrating the launch of a new municipal bond, the City admitted that one of the challenges it faced in issuing the bond was 'dealing with its billing chaos' (Abraham 2006). Yet, despite the City's acknowledgment of the endemic problem of inaccurate billing, and, in the absence of an integrated customer service system, low-income households are subjected to legal action, disconnection and the imposition of prepaid meters. City Power's 'key customers', on the other hand, experience 'an intimate level of customer care from City Power's top management' (Khumalo et al. 2003: 31), which includes regular meetings 'to enable the service provider and key customers to discuss areas of mutual concern' (Khumalo et al. 2003: 28).

Khumalo et al. demonstrate that, despite providing the City's 'political leadership with a semblance of concern for continued access to electricity services by low-income households' (2003: 20),[28] this bifurcated system results in poor customer care for everyone other than 'key customers'. In their survey of the impact of electricity service delivery and customer satisfaction in Johannesburg, Khumalo et al. found that, while there was great customer satisfaction among the 13 000 top consumers, the majority of users in Johannesburg (whose accounts are managed by the City) 'felt that City Power treated them unequally and gave them lower priority' (2003: 31). Indeed, this research found that, largely as a result of being relieved of the responsibility of managing the majority of electricity consumers' accounts, 'City Power has tended to concentrate its efforts to improve the quality of customer care and customer relations on a small section of its customer base, at the expense of deteriorating relations with the majority of its customers' (Khumalo et al. 2003: 35).

Such discrepancies in customer services, which result in the inferior treatment of low-income households compared with 'key customers', could be subjected to an equality-clause challenge based on unfair discrimination. Moreover, if the unfair discrimination is the result of inaccurate billing and/or inadequate customer services (for example, if a low-income household is disconnected on the basis of faulty accounting), any such challenge may be strengthened by reference to section 95 of the Local Government Municipal Systems Act, which stipulates that a municipality must:

> (d) where the consumption of services has to be measured, take reasonable steps to ensure that the consumption by individual users of services is measured through accurate and verifiable metering systems;
> (e) ensure that persons liable for payments, receive regular and accurate accounts that indicate the basis for calculating the amounts due;
> (f) provide accessible mechanisms for those persons to query or verify accounts and metered consumption, and appeal procedures which allow such persons to receive prompt redress for inaccurate accounts;
> (g) provide accessible mechanisms for dealing with complaints from such persons, together with prompt replies and corrective action by the municipality...

Conclusion

On the eve of EDI restructuring, South Africa's electricity distribution system is divided between the state-owned electricity corporation, Eskom, and some 200 distribution businesses operating within 187 municipalities across the country. Collectively, the municipalities – whether directly or through commercialised entities – serve about 60 per cent of total electricity consumers, accounting for approximately 40 per cent of electricity consumption by sales volume.

This unusual distribution set-up is a hangover from what Fine and Rustomjee (1996) have referred to as apartheid's 'minerals-energy complex' (MEC), a system of accumulation in which mining, petrochemicals, metals and related activities accounted for a quarter of economic activity, but which saw very few African households connected to the electricity grid (see McDonald, Chapter 1 of this volume, for an extended discussion of the MEC). In this racially divided system of distribution, typically, municipalities distributed electricity to white residential areas and Eskom distributed to industry and, following the collapse of the black local authority system, to black townships. More than a decade after the democratic transition and under the shadow of long-awaited EDI restructuring, the fragmented distribution system retains many of its apartheid-inherited contours. In the City of Johannesburg, for example, Eskom continues to distribute electricity to Soweto while the municipal entity, City Power, distributes to the historically (and substantively) white suburbs.

It is hoped that concomitant discrepancies, along with the problems faced by low-income households that have been raised in this chapter such as unequal FBE provision and inappropriate tariffs, will be addressed in the EDI restructuring process. However, as has been flagged by various authors in this book, it is questionable how far restructuring can redress underlying inequities if it occurs within the commercial paradigm.

The government has acknowledged the critical role electricity plays in improving the quality and potential of life for poor South Africans. However, as this chapter and others in this book have shown, severe limits have been placed on the transformative potential of electricity by the constraints of a highly commercialised sector. In particular, electricity distribution has been driven more by principles of cost reflectivity than by concerns to create sustainable basic services for poor people.

Many of the resulting inequalities and inequities can be challenged using the rights-based framework proposed in this chapter. Others, if not technically unconstitutional and/or unlawful, must certainly be regarded as immoral in a democracy committed to 'improving the quality of life of all citizens', freeing 'the potential of each person' and, ultimately, 'the achievement of equality' (preamble and section 1(a) of the Constitution).

Notes

1   A 'matchbox' is the typical council house built in Soweto between 1955 and 1968 to accommodate people relocated from informal settlements. It is approximately 40 m² in size and comprises a kitchen, a living room and two bedrooms, with an outside tap and lavatory. As in Grace's case, backyard shacks are common.

2   Grace and Sipho are not their real names. I have known them and followed their experiences with electricity and water services since July 2004.

3   Prepayment metering is a system for dispensing electricity (and water) which transfers the credit-control function from municipalities and/or water services providers to consumers because, in order to access electricity, consumers must pay for it in advance, by means of tokens. Like cell phone airtime bought on a pay-as-you-go basis, the tokens are ordinary paper slips with a numerical 20-digit code, which must be entered into the prepaid meter's keypad. If valid, the prepaid meter accepts the credit and the customer can consume electricity until the credit runs out, at which point the prepaid meter interrupts the electricity supply.

4   In terms of the government's FBE policy, discussed in further detail later, qualifying households receive a basic amount of 50 kilowatt-hours of electricity free each month.

5   In South Africa, as in many other countries in the world, electricity services are divided into generation, transmission (the power grid) and distribution (sometimes referred to as reticulation in the municipal sphere). This chapter focuses on distribution because it is the 'delivery' component of electricity services. As such it is most critical to this rights-based analysis, which views electricity as an essential service to be extended and maintained as a public good. However, issues of electricity generation are critical to issues of cost recovery, discussed later.

6   An *obiter dictum* is an opinion voiced by a judge that is not legally binding.

7   The *Grootboom* judgment established that, regarding positive obligations, the right of access to housing requires the state to formulate and to execute housing programmes that are 'reasonable' (*Grootboom* para. 41). The judgment explicitly steered away from any reference to individual rights to housing per se, and it also rejected the argument that socio-economic rights have a mandatory minimum core that must be immediately realised, as stipulated by the UN's CESCR in General Comment 3 on the nature of states parties' obligations (CESCR 1990: para. 10).

8   Regrettably, the African Charter on Human and Peoples' Rights (ACHPR) (1981), which South Africa ratified in 1994, is silent on the subject of housing or electricity rights. The only article that could possibly be interpreted to contain an implied right to electricity is article 24, the right of everyone to 'a generally satisfactory environment favourable to their development'. However, the African Commission on Human and Peoples' Rights, which is charged with the enforcement of the ACHPR, has not thus far in its communications interpreted article 24 as implying a right to electricity. None of the other human rights documents of the African Union refers to electricity specifically (see for example Pretoria University Law Press 2005). Nor do any of the individual constitutions within the Southern African Development Community region.

9   See www.unhchr.ch/html/menu3/b/a_cescr.htm.

10   See www.un.org/womenwatch/daw/cedaw.

11   Sepúlveda cites as evidence of this principle para. 35 of General Comment 14 on the right
     to the highest attainable standard of health: 'to ensure that privatisation of the health
     sector does not constitute a threat to the availability, accessibility, acceptability and quality
     of health facilities, goods and services' (CESCR 2000); Concluding Observations
     Philippines E/1996/22 para. 120; Concluding Observations Peru E/1998/22 para. 161; and
     Concluding Observations Australia E/2001/22 para. 395 (Sepúlveda 2003: 367).

12   Many, including this author, suspect that South Africa's non-ratification of the ICESCR
     relates to concerns over being held accountable to the minimum core content standard set
     out in General Comment 3 (note 7).

13   Eskom is wholly owned by the Department of Public Enterprises. City Power is wholly
     owned by the City of Johannesburg.

14   According to section 9(3) of the Constitution 'the state may not unfairly discriminate
     directly or indirectly against anyone on one or more grounds, including race, gender, sex,
     pregnancy, marital status, ethnic or social origin, colour, sexual orientation, age, disability,
     religion, conscience, belief, culture, language and birth'.

15   The connotation of the right to equality of electricity services is therefore almost the same
     as that of the implied right to electricity. The difference is that the right to equality is an
     explicit right, and one that the courts seem readily willing to accept.

16   Information obtained via telephone call to City Power customer services, 23 June 2006;
     www.eskom.co.za, accessed 24 April 2006.

17   For the conservative view, i.e. that widespread non-payment of bills is due to unwillingness
     rather than an inability to pay for electricity, see Ajam 2001 and Johnson 1999.

18   The national electrification programme was funded by Eskom until 2000, but since then it
     has been funded by the Treasury through the National Electrification Fund in the DME
     (Eberhard 2005).

19   The City of Johannesburg's FBE equalisation followed an intervention by the Centre for
     Applied Legal Studies in which the unfair discrimination against Soweto residents was
     highlighted. This intervention suggests that other equality-based interventions might also
     succeed.

20   Most municipalities have indigent registers, which serve to provide a social package for
     low-income households as a means of ensuring a basic standard of living. I suggest that
     part of any social package should include extra safeguards against electricity (and water)
     disconnection due to inability to pay for services.

21   This figure exceeds the RDP's goal of 2.5 million new homes by 1999.

22   For an examination of one of the most successful campaigns around electricity services, as
     mounted by the Soweto Electricity Crisis Committee, see McInnes 2005.

23   The term 'automatic disconnection' is used in this chapter because it accurately reflects a
     technocratic process without recourse to representation. It also does not risk the possible
     inference in the term 'self-disconnection' of disconnection being the result of choice.

24 Any adjudication of this issue would probably attempt to balance the consideration of equality of service with the need for cost recovery on the part of the service provider. There is not much indication from the courts as to which side of the balance is likely to carry more weight. But if less restrictive means of cost recovery are possible, this would weigh in heavily on the side of equality.

25 *R v Director General of Water Services, ex parte, Lancashire County Council, Liverpool City Council, Manchester City Council, Oldham Metropolitan Borough Council, Tameside Metropolitan Borough Council and Birmingham City Council* 1999 Env. L. R. 114.

26 For an outline of the administrative law aspects of the right to access to sufficient water, which includes a discussion of the legality of prepaid meters, see Flynn and Chirwa 2005.

27 This excludes the areas directly supplied by Eskom (including Soweto), which is responsible for its own customers' accounts, billing and meter-reading.

28 According to Khumalo et al., the probable reason for the City of Johannesburg retaining control of the accounts of ordinary households is to limit the 'massive electricity cut-offs for non-payment' that could result from the implementation of City Power's 'harsh cost recover measures' (2003: 19).

References

Abraham A (2006) *Joburg shares expertise with other cities.* City of Johannesburg official website. Accessed 6 April 2006, www.joburg.org.za

Ajam T (2001) Intergovernmental fiscal relations in South Africa. In N Levy & C Tapscott (eds) *Intergovernmental relations in South Africa: The challenge of cooperative government.* Cape Town: Idasa

ANC (African National Congress) (1994) *The Reconstruction and Development Programme: A policy framework.* Johannesburg: Umanyano Publications

Bond P (2004) *The battle over water in South Africa.* Accessed 13 February 2008, http://www.africafiles.org/article.asp?ID=4564

Bond P & McInnes P (2006) Decommodifying electricity in post-apartheid Johannesburg. In H Leitner, J Peck & E Sheppard (eds) *Contesting neoliberalism: The urban frontier.* New York: Guildford Press

CALS (Centre for Applied Legal Studies) (2003) Comment on the draft Electricity Distribution Industry Restructuring Bill. Johannesburg: CALS, University of the Witwatersrand

CESCR (United Nations Committee on Economic, Social and Cultural Rights) (1990) General Comment 3 on the nature of states parties' obligations (art. 2(1) of the International Covenant on Economic, Social and Cultural Rights). Accessed 13 February 2008, www.unhchr.ch/tbs/doc.nsf/(symbol)/CESCR+General+comment+3.En?OpenDocument

CESCR (1991) General Comment 4 on the right to adequate housing (art. 11(1) of the International Covenant on Economic, Social and Cultural Rights). Accessed 13 February 2008, www.unhchr.ch/tbs/doc.nsf/(symbol)/CESCR+General+comment+4.En?OpenDocument

CESCR (2000) General Comment 14 on the right to the highest attainable standard of health (art. 12 of the International Covenant on Economic, Social and Cultural Rights). Accessed 13 February 2008, www.unhchr.ch/tbs/doc.nsf/(symbol)/E.C.12.2000.4.En

Coalition Against Water Privatisation (2004) *The struggle against silent disconnections: Prepaid meters and the struggle for life in Phiri, Soweto.* Johannesburg: Coalition Against Water Privatisation & Anti-Privatisation Forum

DME (Department of Minerals and Energy, South Africa) (1998) *White Paper on the Energy Policy of the Republic of South Africa.* Pretoria: DME

DME (2003) *Electricity basic services support tariff (free basic electricity) policy for the Republic of South Africa.* Pretoria: DME

DME (2004) *The electricity pricing policy of the South African electricity industry.* Pretoria: DME

DPLG (Department of Provincial and Local Government, South Africa) (1998) *White Paper on Local Government.* Pretoria: DPLG

Eberhard A (2005) From state to market and back again: South Africa's power sector reforms. *Economic and Political Weekly* 50: 5309–5317

Eskom (1996) An analysis of the implications of supply capacity limitations in low income residential areas. Mimeo. Pretoria: Eskom

Eskom & DME (2002) *Options for a basic electricity support tariff.* Research Project 400903, University of Cape Town

Fiil-Flynn M (2001) *The electricity crisis in Soweto.* Municipal Services Project Occasional Papers Series No. 4. Cape Town: Municipal Services Project

Fine B & Rustomjee Z (1996) *The political economy of South Africa: From minerals-energy complex to industrialisation.* London: Hurst & Company

Flynn S & Chirwa DM (2005) The constitutional implications of commercializing water in South Africa. In D McDonald & G Ruiters (eds) *The age of commodity: Water privatisation in southern Africa.* London: Earthscan Publications

Hallowes D (2006) *Sustainable energy? Towards a civil society review of South African energy policy and implementation.* Discussion paper. Johannesburg: Earthlife Africa

Johnson RW (1999) *Not so close to their hearts: An investigation into the non-payment of rents, rates and service charges in South Africa's towns and cities.* Johannesburg: The Helen Suzman Foundation

Khumalo G, Ntlokonkulu L & Rapoo T (2003) *Alternative service delivery arrangements at municipal level in South Africa: Assessing the impact of electricity service delivery and customer satisfaction in Johannesburg.* Research Report 102. Johannesburg: Centre for Policy Studies

Kothari M (2002) *Report of the Special Rapporteur on adequate housing as a component of the right to an adequate standard of living.* United Nations Commission on Human Rights E/CN.4/2002/59

McDonald D (2002) *The bell tolls for thee: Cost-recovery, cut-offs and the affordability of municipal services in South Africa.* Pretoria: HSRC

McInnes P (2005) Chapter 1: The policy context. In 'Making the kettle boil: Rights talk and political mobilisation around electricity and water services in Soweto'. Unpublished MA dissertation, Department of Sociology, University of the Witwatersrand

Nefale M (2004) *A survey on attitudes to prepaid electricity meters in Soweto.* Johannesburg: Centre for Applied Legal Studies, University of the Witwatersrand. Accessed 8 January 2007, http://www.law.wits.ac.za/cals/meters/Prepaid%20Meters%20(ultra).pdf

Nefale M & Roux T (2003) Promoting access to affordable electricity: Comments on the draft Electricity Distribution Industry Restructuring Bill. *Economic & Social Rights (ESR) Review* 4(4): 19–21

Pretoria University Law Press (2005) *Compendium of key human rights documents of the African Union.* Pretoria: Pretoria University Law Press

Sepúlveda M (2003) *The nature of the obligations under the International Covenant on Economic, Social and Cultural Rights.* Oxford: Intersentia

South African Institute of Race Relations (2006) *South Africa survey 2004/2005.* Johannesburg: South African Institute of Race Relations

Tully S (2006) The contribution of human rights to universal energy access. *Northwestern University Journal of International Human Rights* 4: 518–548

Court cases

City Council of Pretoria v Walker 1998 (3) BCLR 257 (CC)

Government of the Republic of South Africa v Grootboom 2000 BCLR (11) 1169 (CC)

R v Director General of Water Services, ex parte, Lancashire County Council, Liverpool City Council, Manchester City Council, Oldham Metropolitan Borough Council, Tameside Metropolitan Borough Council and Birmingham City Council 1999 Env. L. R. 114

S v Makwanyane 1995 (3) SA 391 (CC)

Interviews

Eberhard A, Infrastructure Industries Reform and Regulation Management Programme, Graduate School of Business, University of Cape Town, 27 July 2004

Govender P, Director, Contract Management Unit, City of Johannesburg, 5 April 2006

Padayachee V, Vice-President: Customer Services, City Power, 6 April 2004

Salvoldi S, Electricity Pricing Manager, Eskom Distribution, 6 April 2004

CHAPTER 11

Still in the shadows: Women and gender relations in the electricity sector in South Africa

Wendy Annecke

The use of a reticulated electricity system to light up 16 street lights and a few public buildings in Kimberley in 1872 provides the entry point for this study of gender relations in South Africa. In this chapter I posit the difference between *electricity* as a current of moving electrons and *electrification* as a technology embedded in social processes – including that of relations between men and women.

For more than a century the dominant paradigm in South Africa has been that electrification is a neutral, technical process, devoid of political considerations. An example of this approach is provided by the first chairman of the National Electricity Regulator of South Africa, Johan du Plessis, whose Introduction to *Lighting Up South Africa*, a progress report on the accelerated electrification programme, reads as follows: 'Electrification is by its very nature a process dominated by technical and financial considerations' (Du Plessis 1996: 3). An alternative approach that recognises electrification as a social process, and is the one that is adopted in this chapter, is represented by David Nye:

> Technology is...part of a social world. Electrification is not an implacable
> force moving through history, but a social process that varies from one
> time to another and from one culture to another. In the United States
> electrification was not a 'technology' that came from the outside and had an
> impact on certain things. Rather, it was an internal development shaped by
> its social context. Put another way, each technology is an extension of
> human lives: someone makes it, someone owns it, some oppose it, many use
> it, and all interpret it. (Nye 1990: 1)

Recognising that electrification is more than the generation of an electric current means looking beyond the technology to take cognisance of the society, the men and women who *make it, own it, oppose it, use it and interpret it*. Accounting for the presence and absence of particular men and women, at particular times, during the process of electrification is at the heart of this chapter. Access to, control over, and benefits from the enormously significant and powerful energy sector in South Africa have not been equally shared by all. The narrative moves from those men who historically had the ability and facilities to supply electricity, to those men and women who historically have been the consumers of electricity, to a different set of men and a few women who have recently taken over the supply function, and the relations between them. There have been distinct race and gender biases operating in accrual of resources, wealth and essential services in South Africa and it is the purpose of this chapter to provide an overview of some of these. In the last section of the chapter the potential for changing these relations, as part of the restructuring of the power sectors in Africa, is considered.

Scrutinising relationships between men and women in South Africa is interesting but complicated. The familiar historical picture of electrification is one of men at work. In the 1870s when the lights went on in Kimberley, it was because a group of mining magnates had combined their technical expertise and financial muscle to accomplish this. There were no women involved in this seminal achievement. A cursory analysis of the modern electricity chain confirms the presence of men in command from the coal mines to the power stations, from transmission and distribution systems to technical teams and planning offices. In engineering departments and in boardrooms, those negotiating pricing and tariffs and holding influential and senior positions have all been men.

Another familiar historical image is of the race politics of South Africa which ensured that the men in powerful positions were white. Their decisions ensured that the mines, industry, commerce, agriculture and middle-class households were electrified, and that most mineworkers' hostels, black farmers' land and black households were not.

The absence of women from this process of electrification would have been a talking point if it were not so 'normal'. It was 'normal' in terms of the strongly patriarchal culture of first the colonial powers and then the National Party government and apartheid state. Building power stations and distributing electricity have traditionally been considered men's work in South Africa. For as long as this is the case, and women are not trained and appointed to run power stations, women entering the sector will do so as secretaries, administrators and other such underlings.

Power relations between the sexes come into play and may be exercised physically through violence, or the threat of violence. While the threat of gender-based violence is very real in South Africa and on the increase (Annecke 2005; Van Zyl 1991), power relations are frequently less overtly practised and are rather embedded in language, or negotiated through social norms and approval for particular behaviours. These gendered norms and behaviours are taught and enforced at home, at school, by religions and institutions and by peer groups. In this way what is known as *the gender division of labour* is entrenched and perpetuated. The process of considering the social roles and rules which prescribe men's and women's activities in the electricity sector is the first step in a gender analysis of the kind which is performed here.

What makes gender even more interesting is that the relations between members of the same sex are also gendered. When men meet men they typically have particular ways of interacting with each other according to specific social norms and expectations, ways which are generally quite different to those conventions they draw on when they meet with women. In South Africa, race mediates masculine interaction, so that black men may exercise a different set of rules in relating to each other than they do when meeting with white men and vice versa. Other factors which will affect their interaction include class, social position and age.

Although this chapter is about the gendered history of electrification, I do not allocate an equal amount of time to men and women. The focus is largely on women because their roles have been previously neglected. However, having opened up the discussion on gender as a facet of men's histories, brief consideration is given here to the social context of the relations between men in the electrification process. The chapter refers extensively to 'white men' and 'black men' in full realisation that these are not homogenous or self-evident categories, but the rapidly developing literature on masculinities (Connell 1995; Morrell 1998) is not yet of assistance in analysing the relations between white and black men in the electricity sector.

Relationships between men in the sector are assumed to be governed by race. The names of the white mining magnates and electricity owners have been recorded, but black men, the miners and workers at the power stations, remain largely anonymous. This has not been the case in all sectors: the lives of prominent black men such as RW Msimang, who led the Transvaal Native Congress, other trade unionists and later the founders of the African National Congress (ANC) in the early 1900s are documented. What does become clear as the history of electricity unfolds is that power and privilege reside in the hands of the white engineers and electricity distributors.

Christie (1984) is of the opinion that power sector engineers had a particularly pernicious world view which has had a significant impact on the transformation of labour processes, on material considerations especially of black people, and on the entrenchment of attitudes and ways of thinking that have had emotional and psychological consequences for the well-being of the society. But while he provides a useful source for making the connections between surveillance, race and power, he is not very useful when it comes to analysing gender biases and in this shortcoming he is joined by other well-known authors (Eberhard & Van Horen 1995; Fine & Rustomjee 1996) who sidestep 'the women question'.

As Christie (1984: 2) honestly, but unsatisfactorily, explains, 'This [book] examines domestic, manufacturing, transport and mining electrification. Nor is the sexual division of labour treated here: the number of black women electrical engineers in South Africa is nil or negligible, but having recorded that fact its explanation is left to others more qualified.' Men as gendered beings do not enter the analysis, and women are left to create a space to speak for themselves.

In the same way that the relations between men are gendered, so are those between women. Women relate to other women using different social norms and assumptions, according to their class, age, social status, and numerous other variables. The fact that they are all women has not been a key consideration in South Africa. Historically there has been no 'natural' or biological alliance between black and white women in South Africa, no easy sisterhood. Their relations have been fraught with the tensions of race. Despite the fact that patriarchy has been called the 'one truly non-racial institution in South Africa' (Govender 1993: 42), for the first 100 years of electrification women did not organise across the boundaries of race to fight gender oppression. Racial identities and political solidarity superseded gender as a mobilising principle in South Africa. In practice this meant, for instance, that in their struggle for the vote white women abandoned black women (and men and the notion of universal suffrage), while black women struggled against the pass laws largely on their own. There were whites who struggled for national liberation with blacks, and white women who joined the liberation movement, including Helen Joseph who was one of the leaders of the march against the pass laws in 1956 (Walker 1990), but the majority of white women were content with their relatively privileged positions.

Black South African women have suffered many layers of oppression: the 'triple oppression' of being black, poor and female, and the particular form that oppression has taken of being servants to white 'madams' (Cock 1980). The additional burden and effects of being colonised have also been explored. In the semi-autobiographical novel *Nervous Conditions*, author Tsitsi Dangarembga shows 'how colonisation alienated women physically and psychologically through lack of education, poverty and relegation to the private sphere' (Parker 2003: 1). This marginalisation is experienced by most black South Africa women, who even today remain largely invisible and, in relation to the powerful electricity sector, are inconsequential, small users of electricity. The 46 per cent of households that are not yet electrified are usually those housing poor, black women in rural areas, further marginalised as a result of their lack of access to electric power (NERSA 2006: 78).

Some men and women were, and still are, content to live within patriarchal rules and gender relations in which women are subordinate and treated like second-class citizens. However, internationally the principles of equity and human rights have risen to prominence and the oppression of women is no longer ethically acceptable. In 1979 the United Nations General Assembly promulgated the Convention on the Elimination of All Forms of Discrimination Against Women (CEDAW), which has been signed by some 179 countries. South Africa signed the Convention in 1996 after the ANC came to power. According to CEDAW, women should be able to participate on an equal footing with men and enjoy the same rights as men do in all sectors (Budlender 1996). This would clearly include women's right to participate in the energy and electricity sectors, and since 1996 there has been a small but discernible increase in women's participation, although the gender division of labour remains entrenched in all sectors of society (Annecke et al. 2006). One of the results of the intra-household gender division of labour is that women are responsible for cooking, cleaning, space heating and childcare, all of which require fuel sources or energy services. Although women are all but invisible on the supply side of electricity, they have been active suppliers (collectors) of wood and other biomass for domestic use for thousands of years, and are responsible for the acquisition of transition fuels (oil, kerosene and gas) for domestic use. Thus it is that women play a crucial role in managing household energy. This has gone largely unnoticed in developed countries where domestic energy use is a small proportion of total energy consumption, but in developing countries in Africa and Asia domestic energy consumption constitutes up to 80 per cent of total energy use (Parikh 2000: 11). It could be argued that domestic energy should receive attention proportional to its significance in the energy balance of the country. That it does not is a consequence of gender relations: significant domestic energy needs are considered less important than the demands of tiny industrial and commercial sectors in developing countries, driven, of course, by men.

The situation has not gone unnoticed by the development sector. For the past 25 years there has been a growing international literature on women, gender and energy. In the international arena, men in the 'energy for development' sector – for example Amulya Reddy (1980) – joined women feminists and economists such as Irene Tinker (1982) and Elizabeth Cecelski et al. (1979) when they began to document the amount of time and effort poor women spent on wood collection. Fuel acquisition was recognised as essential to fulfil women's domestic responsibilities, and the lengths women went to in order to complete these tasks were brought to the attention of mainstream developers. The insertion of women's roles into the international 'energy for development' debates created a new area of study and discussion. A brief review of these trends in the next section provides a window on these developments.

Targeting women in energy for development?

As a result of the attention drawn to women's energy needs, some development funders began to target women. In 1998 Margaret Skutsch analysed the primary reasons for donor organisations targeting women in energy interventions, and the ways in which these mirrored the evolution of thinking about women, gender and development (Skutsch 1998). The first she called a welfare approach; the second an efficiency consideration; the third, empowerment. In the welfare approach, women are targeted as wives and mothers and ways are sought to reduce the drudgery of, for example, collecting wood and water, so that women may be better wives and mothers. In the efficiency approach, gender is recognised as playing a role in society, and planners are advised to take the differences between women's and men's needs, desires and potential into account in order that these differences are accommodated and do not stand in the way of the project's success.

The equity or empowerment approach acknowledges that women as a group are systematically, socially and economically disadvantaged and that planned interventions should bring about greater equality between the sexes. The empowerment approach recognises the need to engage with men's and women's different needs and requirements of energy, in ways that offer women new opportunities to engage with the sector. Women may require access to energy to run their businesses for economic independence, or in order to have the time to engage in community or political structures, or they may need assistance in becoming technicians. Creating the space for women to take up new roles often requires working with men and women around economic opportunities, public space and power relations, where donor organisations may be reluctant to be involved (ECI 2000; Skutsch 1998).

Despite good intentions, experience has shown that in many energy interventions, benefits which were intended for women have been appropriated by men due to their stronger bargaining position. For example, woodlots planted by women are appropriated for timber and sold by men (ECI 2000), or electricity supplied to houses is appropriated by men to watch television rather than to assist with women's work (Barnes & Sen 2004). Such unintended consequences are usually a result of insufficient attention being given to the internal dynamics of who benefits from increased resources in the household. Men can often use their position as head of the family to command resources which belong to others. It was realised that energy projects might not benefit women unless the unequal social relationships could be changed, but how to accomplish this change remains a problem (ECI 2000).

In 1995, Elizabeth Cecelski, Joy Clancy and Margaret Skutsch established Energia, an international network of gender and sustainable energy workers, which has become the major international umbrella organisation for effecting change and promoting gender in the energy sector.[1] Positions within the network have matured and expanded over the past decade so that international women-and-energy programmes, which previously focused on improved cooking stoves, social forestry and small-scale income-generating projects, have begun to include projects to facilitate women's access to previously all-male economic sectors such as electricity and petroleum (Lele 1998; Matley 2005).

Recently a study led by Cecelski (2005) and involving 10 international researchers in a Collective Research Group in Gender and Energy produced a series of case studies which explore the flow and exchange of position, power, work and resources between men and women (Annecke 2005; Kelkar & Nathan 2005). The case studies attempt to examine reciprocity in domestic arrangements in order to understand men's, women's and children's roles in the household, and how these determine energy use patterns. There is also an attempt to understand gender blindness at the policy level and how this might operate to keep women in particular positions in the sector (Karakezi & Wangeci 2005). This collaborative study constitutes a major contribution to the understanding of complex women/gender and energy relationships.

Initially, the South African approach to women and energy followed the welfare approach of the rest of the developing world and sought to ameliorate women's domestic burdens through technologies such as improved stoves (Baldwin 1988). However, the emergence of feminist researchers in the energy sector changed this (Annecke 1991; Crawford Cousins 1998; James 1991; Makan 1994). These studies acknowledged that while relieving women's burden may be important, equality is unlikely to be achieved unless women's subordinate positions change. This was argued specifically in relation to the burden of domestic fuel management and cooking, but also with reference to women's social location in relation to men, decision-making structures and their ability to invest in and share ownership of the sector. The challenge this presented to male domination distinguished the early South African women/gender and energy literature from the international literature, which was generally reluctant to challenge power structures head-on (Pietilä & Vickers 1994).[2]

One of the reasons why South Africans were able to formulate their challenge in this way was that the political context in which the research emerged encouraged the articulation of women's issues (Khibi Mabuse, cited in Annecke 2003). In the 1980s the nature of women's emancipation was widely debated in women's organisations and in publications such as *Speak* and *Agenda*, which regularly carried articles explaining and debating the different types of feminism and the possibilities offered by each (Friedman et al. 1987; Van Zyl 1991). There was a strong belief that a different kind of society was possible, that some sort of social democratic state would emerge and that a new social and economic order could be persuaded to ensure that the demands of women as set out in the Charters of 1956 and 1994 would be met.[3]

The release of Nelson Mandela and other political prisoners as well as the unbanning of political organisations in 1990 heralded a period of enormous opportunity for change and unusual alliances, including among women. The conference on Women and Gender in Southern Africa highlighted the tensions between black and white feminists (Bonnin et al. 1991; Letlaka-Rennert 1991), but from 1992 black and white women of different political persuasions came together in the Women's National Coalition to draw up the Women's Charter for Effective Equality, finalised in 1994 (see note 3). It was of great concern to women activists that the roles played by women during the struggle, and the gains made, should not be lost when the new government came to power (Beall et al. 1990; Hassim 1991).

As a result of the constitutional negotiations and the efforts of the Women's National Coalition, it is now illegal to discriminate against any person or group on the grounds of gender. Chapter 9(3) of the Constitution of the Republic of South Africa (Act No. 108 of 1996) spells out South Africa's commitment to eradicating all forms of discrimination, including discrimination on the basis of sex or gender. In addition, the signing of the CEDAW agreement and a range of other inter-national agreements and national obligations could be read as a signal of government's intention to change the social construction of race and gender relations. It has been a long and arduous struggle, and this overview has highlighted some of the historical processes which, despite the equality legislation, have not fulfilled the demands of the Women's Charters and continue to exclude the majority of women.

Returning to the history of electrification and the absence of women from the electricity industry in 1872 and for more than 100 years thereafter, we can apply a gendered lens to account for this absence and to better explain the changes that followed.

Women and the history of electricity in South Africa

The electric lights in Kimberley heralded a transition in the history of South Africa as one segment of the population moved from wood and oil use to electricity, and the other did not. Energy is necessary for everyday life, and biomass – mostly wood but also crop waste and dung – had been burned through the ages in southern Africa. When the Dutch landed at the Cape in 1652 they precipitated profound changes in the natural resource base, as the settlers' demand for wood for heating and lighting, building and furniture, rapidly depleted the forests of Hout Bay and the Cederberg. This continued despite the regulations of Simon van der Stel in 1683 against tree chopping (Gandar 1988).

This is interesting because traditionally women collecting fuel wood have been held responsible for deforestation. The reality is that women prefer old, dead wood for their fires, and that the clearing of land for building materials and agriculture is responsible for the large-scale deforestation (Klunne & Mugisha 2001). Women also prefer a long-burning fuel for light, so in the Cape Colony they added sheep's fat to their energy mix as soon as they were able to do so, pouring it over maize cobs and burning them as lamps or making candles. Oil was imported, and when sales increased an international oil company was an early investor in the Cape in 1897 (Trollip 1996). Women were largely excluded from commercial enterprises, with the result that men had control of this market.

The most rapid changes in the energy mix came with the discovery of diamonds from 1860 onwards. The concentration of prospectors denuded the farm Vooruitzig (where diamonds were found) of all its trees, necessitating the bringing in of wood and oil from other areas. This was done primarily by black men, who had the ability to move around and engage in commercial enterprises more easily than black women (Roberts 1976). Wood, charcoal and oil may do for domestic purposes, but there were limits to their usefulness for mining, and the discovery of diamonds stimulated the development of the electricity industry so that from 1872 South Africa became one of the first countries to use electricity on a commercial basis (Eskom 1995). The combination of mining and energy that lies at the core of the economy, and that heralded the industrialisation of South Africa, began in Kimberley when the white-owned mining groups who had both the technical knowledge and the finances required, co-operated to build the first power station to supply their needs (see Gentle, Chapter 2 in this volume). From the beginning these needs were double-edged. Electrification was embedded in the power relations and struggles of an all-male endeavour: electricity was used on the one hand to lengthen the working day and for surveillance of miners, and on the other to ensure the comfort and safety of the white diggers by lighting the 'dark, often dangerous streets' of central Kimberley (Roberts 1976: 190). The compounds where black people lived were not lit, setting a precedent of exclusion for the future.

The question arises as to what activities occupied women while men opened up mines and lit up streets. Initially there were very few women in the frontier mining towns and diamond diggings, and the majority provided the nurturing and support expected of women, carrying out the daily reproductive tasks required to service a workforce. A Mrs Jardine, who ran the hotel at Pniel and later at Kimberley, was one of the few businesswomen already established in the hinterland. She was called 'mother' by many (Roberts 1976: 24) and provided a well-frequented meeting place for men. Roberts (1976: 66) records that white women arriving at the diggings in the 1870s were seldom seen at bars and canteens, and that they found camp life particularly tough: 'Most of them spent their days sweating over the sorting-tables and then, dead beat, had to return to the tents and attend [to] the needs of their families. Unlike the men, respectable women were unable to escape to the canteen after a hard day's work.'

The prevailing gender relations ensured that archetypal notions of womanhood were fulfilled in mining towns too. There was a lonely life for the 'respectable' women who served men's needs by carrying a double burden of working at the sorting tables and performing the domestic chores. And there were also women who served men in other ways, catering for their leisure and entertainment. A number of black and white prostitutes moved to Kimberley, and it is a reflection of patterns of racial privilege and interest that the names of white prostitutes, including 'Blonde Venus', are recorded (Roberts 1976: 85) while the names of the black prostitutes are not as well known. Friendships or alliances between black and white women seemed unlikely even among these women, who fell into a different social category to women working at the sorting tables.

There were considerable racial tensions among the men at the digs which affected women too. Conditions for poor whites on the diamond diggings and in the gold mines were harsh, but they were paid better and not subjected to the same surveillance and violence as black workers. Racial solidarity determined allegiances, and women identified with 'their men' – black or white – entrenching divisions between women which remain difficult to bridge. An illustration of white women's allegiances was to be found in the pass laws and in the attitude to body searches. When daily bodily searches were introduced at the diamond mines there was an outcry that white men should not be reduced to stripping bare as black men had to, and white women were crude and fierce in the protection of 'their' men. Worger (1987: 160) quotes a letter from 'A Sympathising Wife of Once a

Claimholder' to the *Daily Independent*, 16 July 1880: 'It is more than I can bear (and I know I have fellow sympathy in this respect), to think my husband – once a claimholder – should have to submit to such indignity…Only put it to yourself, the ill effects it would have on our children to see their father, who has always been an example of honesty, to have him placed on a level with the natives, who as a rule, do not consider stealing a sin – in fact their only sin in this respect is being found out. Then why place a white man on a level with a black?'

While women did not get involved in electrification, white women benefited from their association with the men in power. All but the poorest women gradually withdrew from the diggings and sorting tables, relinquishing mining as an occupation to the men.

The ability to engage in the development of the electricity sector required at least three things: a technical education, access to capital, and networks to facilitate and align business and political strategies and goals. Few white women or black people had any of these. Gender relations include assumptions about who gets educated and in what ways: middle-class white boys were educated in science and mathematics which enabled them to pursue careers in engineering in the minerals-energy complex and gave them the power to make decisions about who gets access to electricity and at what price. During the last two centuries middle-class white girls' schooling was limited by the expectation that they would be homemakers, and their education seldom included mathematics or science. Poor white women (and men) received little schooling of any kind in South Africa, and poor black people even less. Thus an entire group of South Africans was excluded from technical careers by a lack of educational opportunities. Furthermore, since women were largely confined to the private (domestic) sphere, unless they had private (inherited) money there was little opportunity for them to make money in business ventures; thus they could not invest in capital-intensive sectors such as mining and electricity. Since women and black men did not have the vote, they were excluded from the political networks where decisions were made. Some 130 years after the electrification of Kimberley, some of these conditions have begun to change.

One of the roles of women is to create and maintain social and community ties. Once Kimberley was an established town, a class of white women emerged who fell 'naturally' into the role of hostess and organised cultural events and celebrations, such as a grand welcoming party for the railway when it arrived in Kimberley (Roberts 1976). Not all women were satisfied with ornamental domesticity, however, and occasionally white women broke the mould and became active in the public sphere.

Olive Schreiner was one of the women who was sufficiently well educated and determined to enter the public realm of politics, but her protests against the Masters and Servants Act (first promulgated in 1841, repealed in 1856 and the scope of offences widened) (Roberts 1976) put her on the margins of politics rather than within the networks of power. Other women who became public figures in the early days of Kimberley included Sister Henrietta Stockdale, who has been credited with starting nursing at the Carnarvon Hospital in Kimberley, and Marie Bocciarelli, South Africa's first woman pilot (Roberts 1976). Bocciarelli and women like her may have had the technical capabilities required to understand the electricity sector, but no one would have thought to invite them into the male-dominated club of suppliers.

There is little recorded about black women's activities in Kimberley and, apart from those (black and white) women involved in illicit diamond-buying scams (Roberts 1976), there is little to connect women with the development of the minerals-energy complex. Their gender excluded them, just as men's gender allowed for their inclusion.

After 1890 and the Jameson Raid, Kimberley's importance faded.[4] With the discovery of gold on the Witwatersrand the locus of growth shifted rapidly to the gold mines, where the demand for electricity grew quickly and was supplied following the patterns of race, class and gender that had been established in Kimberley. In this way the links between power, mining and electricity were entrenched (Christie 1984; Fine & Rustomjee 1996; Roberts 1976; Worger 1987). Social processes, including gender relations, were in flux, both reflecting and resisting the rapidly changing landscape of the reef mining towns.

While women remained invisible in the electricity supply sector, it is useful to assess gender roles and the conditions which shaped women's current location. Successive governments, including that of General Louis Botha after 1910, attempted to control the movement of black people. The introduction of the pass laws for black women sought to deny black people the rights of family and provoked a series of protests which began in the Orange Free State in 1913 and continued intermittently. Efforts to keep black women out of urban areas were partially successful, in that the census of 1903 in Johannesburg counted 1 131 women and 1 280 children out of 5 125 people living in the African 'locations' (Callinicos 1987: 41).

This meant that there were twice as many men as women on the Witwatersrand, and there were not sufficient women to perform the reproductive tasks of washing, cooking and cleaning to maintain the workforce. Black men stepped into the gap and became domestic servants, or started businesses such as the Amawasha laundry service (Callinicos 1987). The Amawasha, a group of predominantly Zulu-speaking men, followed the example of the Indian 'dhobis' who earned their living doing washing in the Umgeni River in Durban. By 1896 there were over a thousand Amawasha, only about 10 per cent of whom were women, living in settlements some 5–12 kilometres from the mining town (Callinicos 1987: 55).

This is an example of men being able to commercialise what is usually unpaid work when women do it, much as men have commercialised large-scale wood collection and sales as they did in Vooruitzig (Prathoumvan 2000; Roberts 1976). Washing became an income-generating occupation for men as a result of the social control of women, rather than through sharing the tasks in the domestic sphere. When a new, modern, capital- and energy-intensive steam laundry was established in 1895, it began to take over the manual washing in an early example of electricity being used for mechanisation outside of the mining industry. Legislation made it impossible for the riverside washing businesses to survive, and by 1914 many of these workers were forced to join the rapidly increasing market for both black and white domestic servants in Johannesburg (Callinicos 1987).

Conditions were difficult for labourers in the coal mines and power sector, too. From 1914 a wave of strikes that protested against the wages and conditions of power workers were put down forcibly, and electricity was used to assist the mechanisation of jobs. Social relations shifted as Afrikaans speakers replaced English-speaking workers and 45 000 black workers lost their jobs (Christie 1984: 67). Both black and white workers suffered as a consequence, and the hardships experienced encompassed women and children (Callinicos 1981, 1987). These hardships did not bring black and white women together but led to the deepening of disparities between women, as white women benefited from the assistance offered to whites in the form of job reservation, housing and services, whereas black women were further marginalised.

In the early 19th century white women in South Africa did not receive educational opportunities or social sanction which would allow them to become doctors and engineers, but some women entered the labour market and politics and began to be involved in trade union activities – not in the power sector, notably, but in those sectors associated with 'women's work' such as the garment workers' union. An Irish immigrant, Mary Fitzgerald, also known as Pickhandle Mary, was particularly active in labour and public organisations and in the early 1920s became the first woman on the Johannesburg Town Council and first female deputy mayor (Callinicos 1987). In 1930 white women acquired the right to vote, and with it some right to a public voice. They also began to be noticed by the electricity sector and the subsector that manufactured appliances as a significant potential market for 'white' appliances.

The electricity sector was changing. In the early 1920s it was decided that there should be a national power system that could meet the demands of the entire country. The Electricity Act (No. 42 of 1922) established the Electricity Supply Commission (Escom) in 1923 and the first chairperson, Dr JH van der Bijl, a scientist of international repute, was appointed (Eskom 1995). (Escom changed its name to Eskom in 1987, and the latter is the form used throughout this chapter; for a history of this name change see Gentle, Chapter 2 in this volume.) It was, of course, inconceivable in terms of the gender and race relations of the time that the chairperson of Eskom could be anything other than a white male.

The electrification of white areas had continued apace. In 1925 Eskom undertook a major rural electrification programme in the Western Cape, supplying villages and wine farms as far north as Paarl, Wellington and Malmesbury (Christie 1984). White women on the farms benefited in much the same way as urban women had, being relieved of some of the arduousness of domestic tasks by electrification and mechanisation.

Further opportunities for mechanising domestic work were becoming evident, and from the early 1920s appliance manufacturers turned their attention to those responsible for doing the work: women. In 1923 Siemens (South Africa) (Pty) Ltd was one of the first companies to sell imported domestic electric goods, but by 1929 local manufacturers had begun to emerge, as the robust economy demanded electricity and appliances.

Over the next 60 years the fluctuating state of the economy and the demand for electrical appliances were reflected in the fortunes of Carl Fuchs and his company, Fuchs (Pty) Ltd. Fuchs was a young artisan who started manufacturing shades for street lights in 1929 but soon diversified into water heaters (geysers) which found a growing market in middle-class households (Christie 1984). In the 1931 Depression he had to lay off staff, but in 1932, when the government left the gold standard, business improved again. From 1940 Fuchs turned his attention to supplying the war effort and soon employed up to 1 500 workers (Callinicos 1987: 137). The end of World War 2 marked the end of the contracts and the laying off of workers. Fuchs used his wartime profits to re-gear his production to domestic needs: water heaters and kitchenware, stoves, refrigerators and washing machines. By 1963 the company's capital base had grown to R5.5 million, and its profits were well over R1 million per year. In the 1980s Fuchs was absorbed into the Barlow-Rand group of companies with assets of more than R2 billion (Callinicos 1987: 138).

With the growth of Eskom, increasing numbers of middle-class people were encouraged to use electricity in their homes. Domestic labour in South Africa in the 1930s was cheap, and initially electrical appliances were an addition to, rather than a substitute for, domestic workers (Christie 1984). However, over the years electrification of homes has had the same effect as in the mines and power stations – that of reducing paid labour.

In 1936 Eskom produced a newsletter, the first of numerous brochures and pamphlets which have been issued over the years. The purpose was to advertise 'the immeasurable benefits to be derived from the extensive use of electricity', and to publish 'instructive articles relative to the efficient economical and labour-saving aspects of electricity in the home'. The newsletter also had political undertones, suggesting that it was possible to maintain a good standard of living in an electrically equipped home with a much smaller staff than previously required to do the work manually. This, the newsletter pointed out, would mean substantial savings not only in terms of wages but also in terms of servant maintenance and accommodation. Furthermore, the newsletter proposed that the savings achieved by using 'low-wage motor-operated home-servants' could be spent on luxury goods (Christie 1984: 116–117).

While it is true that domestic labour-saving devices improved the quality of life and eased tedious tasks, it was not true that 'electricity is everyone's servant' as the newsletter claimed (Christie 1984: 117). Black men and women who were domestic servants may have used a range of electrical appliances in their employers' houses, but they would go back to un-electrified quarters or townships at night, using candles and lamps for light, and coal, wood or paraffin for heating (as many still do). (As a contribution to the understanding of gender and domestic electrification, it would be interesting to explore whether notions of masculinity changed when men ('houseboys') undertook washing and housework, but this has yet to be done from an energy and electricity perspective.)

Generally the electrification of homes freed up white women to enter paid employment, and made possible a much wider participation by women in the war effort than would otherwise have been the case. While some women returned to domesticity after the war, others clustered in factories, or worked as secretaries, administrators, nurses and teachers. By 1952 domestic work in the homes of white South Africans had been transformed so that the Board of Trade and Industry could report that year that 'hardly any domestic task remains for which an electrical aid does not exist' (Christie 1984: 116).

By 1958 the Benoni plant of the English Electric Company of South Africa was producing masses of domestic appliances. Early on, electric lights had become most commonly used, followed by irons, kettles, stoves, water heaters, refrigerators and washing machines. Christie (1984: 160) records that by the mid-1970s South Africa was producing 250 000 small-scale battery radios, together with 100 000 larger battery radios, 100 000 cookers, 130 000 refrigerators and 100 000 water heaters each year.

Domestic routines significantly altered the Johannesburg municipal power system's load curve. Washing was done on Mondays and ironing on Tuesdays, and the use of some 10 000 electric irons resulted in a load curve 6 000 kilowatt-hours (kWh) greater on that day than on other weekdays, which had to be accommodated by the system. Electric heaters on winter evenings and stoves for Sunday lunches also created peak loads (Christie 1984). Thus domestic routines and 'women's work' became visible in the system and important to suppliers and manufacturers, representing 16–19 per cent of electricity consumption over the years (deduced from DME 2002: 38).

In contrast to the conditions for white women, which gradually improved over the course of the 20th century, there was little respite for black women. Not only was their right to live in urban areas constrained, but the overwhelming majority were denied access to decent schooling and economic opportunities. Christie (1984: 106) claims that the power utility played an active role in undermining the interests of black people through 'hiding' the extraordinary profits it made after 1932, so that 'wages could be kept low and tariffs could be kept up'. White supervisors were housed on estates with many facilities, deepening the material schisms and resentment between black and white South Africans and their families (Christie 1984).

Despite legal restrictions and harsh punishments, no government has been able to prevent the movement of black people to urban areas in South Africa and by 1920 there were some 147 000 black women living on the Rand with their men and children (Callinicos 1987: 82). The permanent presence of women and children meant that there was a substantial non-migratory, urban black population who required basic facilities. Townships such as Sophiatown, Martindale and Newclare were freehold areas where families lived and paid rates but, again compared with white areas, very few services were supplied. In 1930 the Johannesburg Council began to build houses on the old Klipspruit farm, and established a black township, Orlando. The Orlando power station was built between 1939 and 1943 but it was not used to electrify the township around it. Images of huge pylons and power lines dwarfing the smoky shack settlements which they pass over but do not electrify have become symbolic of skewed electricity provision in South Africa.

In the 1950s semi-skilled black labourers in manufacturing enterprises began to be accommodated in houses (rather than hostels) in townships. In this way the state acknowledged some sort of family life for black people, including women and children, but this was short-lived and they were never allowed to become too comfortable. Christie (1984) presents the dilemma of the state in deciding whether to electrify the new townships which offered a huge potential market, or to keep wages low and urban areas not too attractive in order to discourage the inevitable further movement of black people from farms to urban areas. The political decision to electrify only a few black urban areas was made, and comfort was limited so that when coal was rationed in 1951 black households that used coal for cooking and keeping warm were unable to cope.

The world's preoccupation with the oil crisis in the 1970s had mixed effects on South Africa. The prices of oil, coal and gold soared, and during a wave of strikes from 1972 to 1976 workers, including Eskom workers in 1972, demanded and received wage increases (Maré & Fisher 1974). In the 1970s Eskom recognised that with inflationary conditions it was important to electrify rapidly, and pushed ahead with rural electrification so that by 1977 some 38 000 white farms, some in remote areas, were electrified (Escom 1975: 11–14) although many farm workers are still without electricity.

There was surplus generation capacity, but Eskom was not able to see beyond the race barrier and mothballed excess capacity at Camden, Grootvlei and Komati power stations in the mid-1970s (Ruffini 1999). The further electrification of white-owned farms continued to boost mechanisation and made the lives of some women on farms much easier, perhaps serving the purpose of building further bonds of race allegiance on the one hand and distance or distrust on the other. In any case, the 1970s saw racial tensions escalate. After the 1976 riots young black women left the country alongside young men. These young women took debates about gender equality into the liberation movement, insisting on discussions about and engagement with the place of women's emancipation within national liberation (Annecke 2003). Rita Mfenyane, the founder of the Women's Energy Group in South Africa, argues that the persistence of women in the ANC culminated in acceptance by the ANC president, Oliver Tambo, of the need for women's equality in 1984, and laid the groundwork for the ANC's commitment to gender equality in the 1990s.[5]

The 1980s saw the site of the liberation struggle shift from the national to the local level, where emerging civic organisations formed street committees and residents' associations to act against the already discredited local authorities and poor service delivery (Taylor 1997). Despite difficulties, several black women emerged as leaders and added their voices to the demands for access to clean water and electricity (Seekings 1991). It would take another 20 years before substantial delivery of services began. The Electricity Petition Committee in Mitchell's Plain in Cape Town organised against the deadline by which electricity accounts had to be paid. The issue evolved into a much bigger campaign, out of which the Cape Areas Housing Action Committee emerged and spread to other areas (Taylor 1997).

The Candlelight Campaigns in Cape Town and Durban were also organised around issues such as rental and electricity price increases (Taylor 1997), and women, both black and some white, played prominent parts in these struggles (Fester 1997). Along with local councillors, Eskom was seen to be in cahoots with the national government and responsible for exclusions and poor service delivery.

The unbanning of political organisations and the release of political prisoners, including Nelson Mandela, in 1990, which were followed by negotiations for a new government, provided the space for the development of the ANC's Reconstruction and Development Programme (RDP) which asserted access to electricity as a basic right and set a target of 2.5 million households to be electrified by 2000 (ANC 1994: 33). 'Electricity for all' rapidly became a rallying cry and an important slogan of the ANC (1994). Because electrification is relatively easily supplied and provides 'an instant improvement in living conditions of 15–20%', it is politically important (Annecke et al. 2005: 2). For the first century of electrification most of those selected to receive this 'instant improvement in living conditions' were white; the following section of the chapter elaborates the changes that began to take place as black households were included on a large scale in the electrification process.

Changes since the end of apartheid

From 1991 Eskom embarked on a national electrification programme which, after 1994, was accelerated to meet the aforementioned target of 2.5 million connections by 2000. This target was achieved by 1998, after which the programme decelerated.

However, this was an opportunity lost. The electrification programme should have continued at the same rate while there was momentum to do so. Eskom had gained considerable experience in low-cost electrification, was focused on meeting targets, and was saturating areas into which it moved with highly subsidised connections.

Since Eskom's licence areas were located largely in rural parts of the country, the connections brought welcome relief and the 'politics of hope' to many rural communities (Crawford Cousins 1998: 28). Women, many of whom were heads of households, were particularly appreciative of good lighting, particularly for children's schoolwork, watching television where this could be afforded, and an improved feeling of safety, especially where outside lights were installed (Annecke 1998). Women reported a general improvement in the quality of life brought by electrification, and optimism for the future. They believed that if Eskom could 'remember' them, then others would too. Even if the cost of appliances was an initial barrier, it would not be so forever. As one woman noted, 'Electricity makes my life much easier because we no longer buy candles for lighting and one day I will have a stove and I won't have to fetch wood ever again' (cited in Annecke 1998: 35).

Despite imperfections in the process – Eskom was criticised for its non-developmental, technicist approach (James 1998) – a vast number of people benefited from connections: 3 210 557 homes have been electrified by Eskom alone since 1991 (Eskom 2006: 114), while municipalities have added another three-quarters of a million connections to houses in urban areas.

Electrification and housing are closely linked, since the dwelling is the point of connectivity and electricity subsidies are provided per house connected. Houses need not be formal structures to be electrified, however. Shacks are electrified where tenure and safety issues can be agreed on, and where it is clear that the shacks are at least semi-permanent, as they tend to be throughout the country.

Provision of low-income housing was always inadequate, so that by the time the ANC government came to power in 1994 estimates of the backlog in urban formal housing for black people varied from 1 to 5 million units. The RDP (ANC 1994) committed the government to building 300 000 units per year, which was later raised to 350 000 units. By 2005 the Department of Housing had approved 1 698 788 beneficiaries of housing subsidies, with 1 614 000 units complete and more than 6 million people assisted in acquiring their own homes (Sisulu 2005: 268). But despite these efforts, the backlog, which is now estimated to be between 2 and 3 million units, is still growing by at least 204 000 per year (Sisulu 2005: 268; *Sunday Times* 24 February 2008). The backlog in housing provides an indication of the rate of electrification which would have to be maintained to provide 'electricity for all' in formal houses by 2012, which was promised by President Thabo Mbeki in 2005 (Hemson 2004; Mbeki 2005).

A survey conducted in 1999 showed that, once the apartheid restrictions on women were lifted, women migrated more rapidly to urban areas than did men, and there are now as many women as men in urban areas (Pick & Obermeyer 1999: 1). The study also found that the longer women stayed in an urban area, the more likely they were to head their own households. The Department of Housing has done well in developing a policy of targeting women as the main beneficiaries of housing delivery projects, but the provinces have been unevenly successful in implementing the policy. Analysed by province, between 28 per cent and 54 per cent of all subsidies approved have been given to women-headed households (UNDP 2003: 33). Notwithstanding substantial difficulties, for the first time in South Africa's history significant numbers of black women hold title deeds to their houses, though parity is still some way off.

The quality of housing provided is of major concern, however. While each new unit (known as an 'RDP house') provides secure tenure, and most have running water, sanitation and electricity, many of the new houses are judged to be sub-standard and very small, known locally as 'unos' or 'hen-coops'. In addition, the government has perpetuated apartheid spatial divides and urban sprawl by building numerous identical houses in areas with no social or economic infrastructure. This is particularly isolating for women at home with small children all day.

Despite several large projects, including the Sustainable Homes Initiative, a variety of training materials and the joint report of the Department of Minerals and Energy (DME) and the International Institute for Energy Conservation Africa (DME & IIEC 1997) to the Department of Housing, elementary principles of thermal efficiency such as a northward orientation, an adequate roof overhang and ceiling insulation have not been incorporated into the design and RDP houses are notoriously thermally inefficient.

As a result, space heating, which is expensive and often unhealthy, is necessary in the winter. Few owners of RDP houses can afford electric or gas heaters, so the majority resort to paraffin, coal or wood for heating. International studies show that women and children bear the brunt of cold houses or inadequate or polluting space heating (Von Schirnding 2000). This is because women and children tend to spend more time at home whereas men leave the house for work, or those who are unemployed tend to congregate in heated bars or restaurants (Annecke et al. 2004). Where women are responsible for seeing that there is sufficient energy they suffer emotional distress if they are not able to fulfil their responsibilities, as well as sometimes being sanctioned by the household (Annecke et al. 2005).

Women are also the caregivers to those who are ill and they bear the brunt of the additional labour and cost of nursing (Legido-Quigley 2003). Paraffin fumes and wood smoke exacerbate the condition of those who are prone to acute respiratory infections or have compromised immune systems (Van Horen 1996) and at times like the present when the incidence of tuberculosis and/or HIV/AIDS is high, all suffer through lack of access to clean water and electricity. Free basic electricity

(FBE), a component of the government's programme of free basic services provision (see below), is an imperative contribution to alleviating some of the burden of caring for those with HIV/AIDS (see Ruiters, Chapter 9 in this volume, for a fuller discussion of FBE). Further reflection is required on the impact that the HIV/AIDS pandemic is likely to have on energy planning, and recommendations are required on how policy should be strengthened to adequately reflect the government's commitment to gender equality and resource interventions.

Most new connections have been installed using prepayment meters, with more acceptance and success in some areas than others (for a lengthier discussion on prepaid meters see Van Heusden, Chapter 8 in this volume). Some see metering as an instrument of social control and revenue collection for the utility; others perceive it as assistance with budgeting and using electricity efficiently. Those who receive monthly bills and are unable to pay may be cut off by the utility, whereas with a prepayment meter the onus is on the individual to buy credits or go without electricity. Utilities are reluctant to release figures on cut-offs, but a study in Khayelitsha reports a 12–15 per cent rate of non-technical losses (i.e. self-connections or theft) (Annecke et al. 2005: 2).

Few poor households are able to use electricity for all their needs, so that multiple fuel use persists up to 10 years after electrification, with cooking being one of the last elements to change completely (Annecke et al. 2005). The cost of electric appliances constitutes a barrier to some, but until recently the main reason women did not use electricity is because they believed it to be more expensive to cook with than paraffin or gas. Recent tests show that at current prices, it is actually cheaper to cook with electricity than with gas or paraffin (Cowan 2005). Increases in the price of paraffin and gas have seen women revert to wood collection in several areas, with the concomitant health hazards (*Energia News* April 2002) or, in urban areas, begin switching to greater electricity use (Annecke et al. 2005). This transition was interrupted in the winter of 2006 in Cape Town when Eskom was unable to meet its licensing obligations to supply sufficient electricity to the metropole and, in a cynical move, swapped hotplates for gas cookers and coupons on the Cape Flats (Gaba 2006).

The introduction of FBE has brought some relief to those who receive it. Soon after her appointment, and just weeks before the local government elections were held in December 2000, the Minister of Minerals and Energy announced that Value Added Tax (VAT) would no longer be payable on paraffin, and that the national Electricity Basic Services Support tariff (known as FBE), which allows qualifying households to receive up to 50 kWh of electricity free per month, would be introduced. This was the kind of redistributive measure the women's movement had imagined and expected from women in government, and it was widely welcomed (Annecke 2003).

However, the allocation has been unevenly implemented with hundreds of thousands of eligible households not receiving FBE (for more information see

Ruiters, Chapter 9 in this volume). Eskom itself refused to supply its customers until January 2004 (the general elections were held in March 2004) and to date Eskom notes that only 57 per cent of eligible customers have received the free electricity allocation due to them (Eskom 2006: 114). Although it is not enough to support lighting, cooking and heating, FBE allows households to run one or two lights for two or three hours a night, thereby improving the feeling of safety and comfort vital to crime-ridden areas (Annecke et al. 2005).

About 30 kWh is required for minimal lighting (University of Cape Town 2002: 104), leaving about 20 kWh for television or ironing or boiling the kettle occasionally. Impact studies in Khayelitsha, Cape Town, have shown different benefits of FBE for different levels of households. Some of the poorer households, usually headed by women, are able to eke out their 50 kWh over the whole month, using it primarily for lighting. In 2004 these households spent on average R45 per month on paraffin for cooking (Annecke et al. 2005: 30) and would have been hard-hit by the price hikes over the past two years. Other households find life a little easier when FBE enables them to have a few more hours of lighting and television per month or an increase in their cooking time (Annecke et al. 2005; Cowan & Mehlakoana 2004).

A survey of electricity recipients distinguished between those who *benefit* most from having electricity and those who *use* it most. The most frequent response was that everyone benefits from electricity but especially the children, who can study and watch television (Annecke et al. 2005). Those who use electricity most were invariably women, because they do the cooking, ironing and other energy-intensive tasks. Women were unanimous in saying how much easier electricity has made their lives: it saves them time and effort in that the walls and pots no longer get dirty from fumes and smoke, ironing is easier and can be done more quickly, there are no lamps to clean or candles to buy. There is an element of social inclusion, too, with women feeling their clothes no longer smell of paraffin and that they are part of the 'civilised world'.

It is true that men are frequently the ones to make decisions about what appliances should be bought first, and that they choose televisions to watch soccer and refrigerators to keep their beer cold (Annecke et al. 2005). Women, on the other hand, tend to use refrigerators for income generation, for example by making ice lollies and keeping food for sale. Women also want televisions in their own homes, albeit in order to keep their children off the dangerous streets rather than for their own leisure. But women do watch television – often late at night – and 90 per cent of 250 households interviewed in Khayelitsha own televisions, as opposed to 86 per cent who own electric hotplates (Annecke et al. 2005: 35, Appendix 1). Electricity has also made it easier for men to share domestic tasks. A recent study has shown increased numbers of men heating water for shaving and cooking for themselves 'without having to worry our wives', because electricity makes it quick and easy to do so (Annecke et al. 2005).

In rural areas where electricity connections reach, on average, only 46 per cent of households (NERSA 2002: 25), some 18 300 solar home systems (SHSs)[6] have been installed by concessionaires (NERSA 2006: 79). A capital subsidy similar to the grid connection subsidy has been extended to SHSs in rural areas, but administration of the operational (monthly) subsidy has been problematic, with some households receiving no subsidy and paying R64 per month for their SHS and others, in the same ward, receiving a subsidy worth R45 per month and having to pay only R19. This is creating substantial conflict among neighbours (Annecke & Mehlakoana 2006). Those with SHSs do benefit from better lighting, black and white television and cell phone chargers. But in addition to paying for the solar system, women and children still have to collect wood and/or buy paraffin, since the 50 kWh SHSs do not allow for cooking or heating.

Worst off are households without grid connections or SHSs and which receive no service or subsidy. These are likely to be the poorest of the poor in rural areas (again, women- or even child-headed households), or newcomers to urban areas settling where no services are available. Some municipalities are experimenting with rolling out gas and biogel for cooking in an effort to meet poor women's cooking needs, but at current electricity prices this hardly makes sense (Cowan 2005).

Black women should receive the benefits that white women and men have received from electrification for more than 80 years, in urban and rural areas. FBE should be extended to all without delay, but it is not, on its own, sufficient to alleviate poverty. A multi-pronged strategy which includes job creation, access to health and education, better services and roads is required (University of Cape Town 2002). Indeed, these are the demands of the Women's Charters, and fulfilment of them would contribute to poverty alleviation and a more equitable society.

Changes in employment patterns

The beginning of the chapter raised the issue of an absence of women from ownership of, and contributions to, the supply side of electrification. It is noteworthy that until the 1990s there were no women in senior decision-making positions in Eskom, the National Energy Council or the DME (Viljoen, cited in Annecke 2003; Ruiters 1995). There was no overt policy of not employing women, and a few white women had begun to slip through the system into the 'masculine' professions of medicine, engineering, architecture and construction, but this was by chance, not by design (Lessing 1994).

When the ANC came to power in 1994 there were comparatively few women qualified to work in the electricity sector and, as Christie (1984) and Ruiters (1995) note, there had been practically no black women engineers working in South Africa in the 1980s. The overwhelming majority of black girl-children had systematically been denied access to technical education, but those who left the country and were offered opportunities elsewhere proved their worth. When the exiles came home in 1991 they included a substantial number of black women engineers who had trained in Budapest, Moscow and Havana, proving that given the opportunity, black women could become engineers. These women were quickly absorbed into private and public institutions and were called upon to represent black women in forums such as the newly convened National Electrification Forum (NELF) in 1993 (Annecke 2003).

The NELF was an important forum constituted to resolve electrification policy under a new government. Rita Mfenyana was responsible for drawing women with technical expertise into the forum, which she did with ease. 'The ANC had trained many women technicians (engineers),' Mfenyana said, 'and there was no reason for them not to be there' (cited in Annecke 2003: 186). This was the largest gathering of black women engineers many of the men had ever seen and it created quite a stir, although many men remained dismissive of them.[7]

That gender relations are socially constructed, and can and do change, became evident as the new government began to wield its power and black men took ascendancy over white men in the DME and in Eskom. However, women were not as easily accepted, and under ministers Pik Botha (1994–1996) and Penuell Maduna (1996–1998) the DME remained stubbornly male-dominated (James & Simmonds 1997).

Traditional relations between men and black women were rapidly inverted, though, when President Mandela appointed a black woman, Phumzile Mlambo-Ngcuka, as Minister in the Department of Minerals and Energy in 1999. Men and women immediately had to review their relationship to this powerful, able, young black woman, even if they did not extend the adjustment to their domestic servants.

The appointment of Mlambo-Ngcuka to the energy sector heralded a breakthrough. She came from a women's activist background, brought a well-known woman activist, Gertrude Fester, with her as transformation officer, and together with her deputy minister, who had a trade union background, represented the hopes and principles of the women's movement.

Mlambo-Ngcuka proceeded to promote women and gender interests within the department. By the end of 1999 all men at the DME had signed a Gender Pledge, a unique document crafted by Fester. The Pledge begins with the personal: a commitment not to perpetrate gender violence and to raise children who respect women and men equally. It continues with the public undertaking not to discriminate against women at work, to support women to further their careers and to accept leadership irrespective of gender (Annecke 2003).

However, there were no mechanisms through which this Pledge could be followed up and supported. Fester was deployed to Cape Town to assist with the municipal elections[8] and a year later the official in charge of gender transformation at the DME confessed that she found the process 'too much, too exhausting' (Annecke

2003: 280). Nonetheless, the Pledge represented an interesting experiment in making the personal political, and was an indication of what might be achieved if there were sufficient monitoring of and support for transformation.

As mentioned earlier, the minister announced the removal of VAT from paraffin and the introduction of FBE, bringing further hope of a new order in the energy sector – that of equitable access and attention to the poor. This, however, has not been the case. A study commissioned by the National Treasury found that the lower price of paraffin was not passed on to customers (PDC 2003), FBE has not been widely available (Eskom 2006) and other initiatives to address poverty and women's energy needs have been limited to small pilot projects such as low-smoke methods of lighting a fire, wider distribution of solar cookers (Wentzel 2003), and gas (IIEC-Africa 2005). In addition, the much-touted Integrated Energy Centres have had limited success in addressing rural energy needs (Maake 2006).

The minister was, however, more successful in promoting a different type of women's interests. Scanning the political landscape, she realised that she was in command of significant political power and had considerable state resources at her command (Annecke et al. 2006). She proceeded to offer other women the opportunity to move into positions of power and control by providing education and securing institutional space previously denied women. Her actions were backed by the Employment Equity Act (No. 42 of 1998). The DME established bursaries and scholarships for women, a support group, Women in Nuclear Energy in South Africa, and another, Women in Oil and Energy in South Africa, and hosted the Women in Energy workshop on the first two days of the African Energy Ministers' Conference in Durban in December 2000 (ESMAP 2001). The minister rapidly appointed women to decision-making positions within the DME so that in 2005, 25 per cent of senior positions were held by women (Annecke et al. 2006: 39).

Under Minister Mlambo-Ngcuka's watchful eye, Eskom rapidly became a national leader in promoting women's interests. As a state-owned enterprise Eskom is committed to employment and gender equality, and from 1994 steps were taken to implement these policies.[9] It was not until 2000, however, with Mlambo-Ngcuka's appointment, that these changes really came into effect. Whether this was because it took some years for women to qualify and become noticed, or whether the changes were at the new woman minister's behest, is not clear, but in 2000 Eskom appointed a number of women to the Executive Management Committee, including Mpho Letlape to the Human Resource Division and Dolly Mokgatle as managing director of the Transmissions Division. Letlape, along with several others, has been responsible for driving gender equality through a number of programmes. These have resulted in the employment of 21 women engineers in a variety of positions (Johnson & Fedorsky 2000).

Since 2000, more than 90 women have completed MSc degrees in Engineering Business Management under the bursary programme and are employed by Eskom

(Mashabela 2004/05: 341). From 2001 Eskom announced the appointment of more women to senior positions – including the first woman power station manager and the first woman general manager of Systems Operations. Leadership support and mentoring programmes have been established so that women in senior positions do not feel isolated, and a childcare programme and flexible working hours are being introduced, providing the kinds of conditions and networks that are required for corporate success (Mashabela 2004/05).

Enabling women to compete with men, fit into men's workplaces and achieve parity with men reflects a liberal feminist agenda, of course – a diluted form of the transformation sought by the women's movements in the 1980s. It may also be that Eskom's commitment to gender equality is simply pragmatic. Eskom needs all the human resources it can muster – some 400 engineers (Faniso 2006) and 5 000 technicians (Ntsokolo 2005) – and it may not be able to source these skills from men only. It may also be that women are traditionally less mobile than men, and therefore more likely to be loyal to the firm.

Whatever the rationale, the appointment of women has made a marked difference to the profile of the leadership at Eskom. In 1994, 10 per cent of senior positions were held by women, and by 2005 this had risen to 18 per cent for senior management and 27 per cent in middle management (Eskom 2006: 88). Top management, where the remuneration runs into millions of rand per year, has seen a change from predominantly white to black men, but only 1 of the 12 Executive Management Committee members is a woman, and only 4 of the 15 members of the Eskom Holdings Limited Board are women. Parity at this level has not yet been achieved.

The goal is to reach a target of 50 per cent women employed overall by 2010, but Turner (2005) believes this will be difficult and that the number of women will stabilise at around 45 per cent.[10] Both Turner (2005) and Midgley (2003) have considered the differences that women's management might make to the organisation, but it would appear that there is not yet a critical mass of women and that any changes in leadership style which might occur under women's direction are not yet evident to or measurable in the organisation as a whole.

Municipal electricity departments have had less success in attracting and keeping women engineers, and the number of women in senior positions remains very low at around 2 per cent (Annecke et al. 2006). This is partly because there are still not enough women, particularly black women, being trained as engineers in South Africa (Annecke et al. 2006). Despite various initiatives there are still far too few women taking science subjects at school, or graduating from universities (Mabandla 2002). Apart from a lack of schools where science and mathematics are taught, girls are harassed and unsafe at school and cannot be expected to do well under these circumstances. In the late 1990s, Member of Parliament, subsequently Minister of Education, Naledi Pandor, reported that the Education Ministry's Gender Equity Task Team provided 'horrifying evidence' that the disempowerment of women had taken hold in schools, where sexual harassment goes largely unchallenged and prevents girl students from attaining their goals (*Cape Times* 16 March 1999). Seven years later a South African Human Rights Commission report revealed ongoing sexual abuse of girls at schools (Mchunu 2006).

Trends in ownership

At the beginning of the chapter, three preconditions for women's equal participation on the supply side of electricity were suggested: educational qualifications, the financial ability to invest, and networks which align business and government strategies. Albeit slowly, some black women are beginning to receive educational opportunities and to establish the networks necessary to have power and influence in the electricity supply industry. The situation is still fragile and no critical mass has yet been reached. Despite black economic empowerment legislation designed to ensure the transfer of assets to black middle-class men and women, South African women's ability to invest substantially in the power sector as independent power producers (for example) is minimal.

The number of small, women-owned companies is increasing, though: over the past five years 185 women-owned companies have registered with Women in Oil and Energy. Most of these companies offer services to the energy sector, but a few are active in energy efficiency projects (audits and refitting), and one wants to invest in a mini-hydro plant (Annecke et al. 2006). This is the aspirant class, and Jacqueline Williams, National Co-ordinator of Women in Oil and Energy, points to a severe lack of resources for their training and insertion into the mainstream economy (Annecke et al. 2006). Eskom contributes to the development of small-scale women's enterprises through their corporate social investment programme (Eskom 2005).

Eskom's proactive gender equality programme runs parallel to the restructuring process which is in place, and it is not yet clear what the longer-term impacts of the latter will be on women and gender relations in the utility, or on poor women as customers. Power sector reform usually occurs as a consequence of outside pressures, and could influence the position and promotion of women in utilities. In Eskom's case the pressure was political, but there is no guarantee that the political agenda of transformation will be carried through into Eskom's potential successors, the Regional Electricity Distributors (REDs). To date neither gender equity targets in employment of staff nor targets for access to electricity for the poor have been written into contracts for the REDs.

International experience holds little reassurance for women employees. A report for the European Commission on the impact of restructuring on women in the electricity industry found that throughout England and Europe, the further countries had gone down the road of privatisation the more negative was the impact on women (Ecotec 1999).

Changes elsewhere in Africa

South Africa is only one of more than 18 countries in Africa that have undertaken power sector reform but, unlike South Africa, in most African countries restructuring has been driven by power crises, poor technical and financial performances and their inability to mobilise investment capital. Karakezi and Kimani (2002) conclude from their study of the status of power sector reform in Africa that very little consideration has been given to the differential impact of reform on men and women, and very little attention has been paid to the needs of the poor. They conclude that if the needs of the poor and women are not written into contracts, they are unlikely to be met.

Karakezi and Wangeci (2005) studied power sector policy documents in Botswana, Kenya, Tanzania and Zimbabwe and found them to be vague and narrow in their notion of gender. They found that gender equality in the power sector is unlikely to be guided by policy in the three latter countries, and unlikely to happen unless women mobilise to insist on inclusion.

Generally, electricity utilities in Africa are underdeveloped, and the possibilities for extension of services to rural facilities or legalising the poor in urban areas are limited. Wamukonya (2003), in her study of power sector reform in 18 African countries, points out that occasionally, such as in Côte d'Ivoire, restructuring has been successful in improving the quality of service to those already connected, but this would generally exclude the poor. After due consideration Wamukonya (2003) concludes that reforms have not addressed the needs of the poor, nor extended the number of connections, and that numbers of disconnections have risen as subsidies are withdrawn and profits are wrung from the customers.

In an Energy Sector Management Assistance Programme/World Bank project to track the impact of power sector reform on the poor in Botswana, Ghana, Senegal and Honduras, Prasad (2006) moves quickly from power sector reform (which she says has accomplished very little in terms of improving access for the poor) to examining the impact of the liberalisation of paraffin and gas markets on the poor. Income quintiles and urban and rural differences are used to explore differential access – gender is not a variable in the study – but the conclusion is that low-level rather than high-level energy reforms assist the poor. The emphasis for poor women in these countries is on securing an affordable and safe energy supply, through improved cook-stoves, tree planting, renewables and transitions to commercial fuels such as kerosene and LPGas. Since this situation is likely to continue, this is the level that reforms should address.

According to this study, the factors that affect the poor disproportionately (because they have no alternatives) are price, access, quality of supply, social services, and financial and economic well-being (Prasad 2006). If the needs of the poor are addressed, as they should be according to the country Poverty Reduction Strategies,[11] and if gender equality is taken seriously, as it should be according to CEDAW and Millennium Development Goal 3, power sector structures would have to formally include women's organisations in planning, implementation and evaluation; there would have to be networks established to facilitate the integration of gender into the power sector, and the links between the power sector and women's organisations would have to be structured and formalised so that women's concerns would be acted upon (Karakezi & Wangeci 2005). That is, in order to be taken seriously, gender issues and commitment to meeting the energy and electricity requirements of poor women have to be signed into agreements and stipulated in contracts. Among other actions, education for girls has to be improved, targets for electrifying schools, clinics and community facilities have to be set and met, and attitudes to men's and women's capabilities have to change, otherwise women's stake in the electricity sector will remain negligible, and the services women receive are likely to remain inadequate.

After more than a hundred years of development, women in South Africa have begun to emerge as a constituency in the electricity sector, but the majority of women in other parts of the continent are still largely invisible and on the periphery of electrification efforts. Enabling all women to turn on lights in their homes, and understand how they work, must be a goal of electrification in the future so that all may share the benefits of the electricity sector.

Notes

1   Energia has ensured that gender issues are represented at all major international forums such as the World Bank Energy Week, the World Renewable Energy Council, Beijing +10, the Women's Platforms for Action and at the annual Commission for Sustainable Development meetings from 2001 onwards.

2   Exceptions to this were Tinker (1982) and Joy Morgenstern, who made a suggestion at the international Village Power Conference held in 1998 in Vienna, Austria, that the way to alleviate women's burden would be to put men in the kitchen for an hour or two every day. Her call went unheeded.

3   For details of the 1956 charter see http://www.sahistory.org.za/pages/governance-projects/womens-struggle6.html. For details of the 1994 charter see http://www.anc.org.za/wl/docs/50years.html.

4   At the end of 1895 Dr Jameson led an abortive attempt to overthrow the government of Paul Kruger in order to gain control of the lucrative goldfields in the Transvaal. The raid was planned in collaboration with Cecil John Rhodes and its failure led to Rhodes's resignation as prime minister of the Cape in early 1896.

5   Rita Mfenyana, personal communication, 10 September 1999

6   SHSs provide power for 3–4 light bulbs, a black and white television for three hours per night and, for R25 extra, a cellular phone charger, but there is not enough power for cooking.

7   Rita Mfenyane, personal communication, 10 September 1999

8   Gertrude Fester, personal communication, November 2002

9   I thank Reetsang Setou, Senior Information Officer, and Leonard Turner, Talent Manager,
    Eskom, for guiding me in the search for this information. Ms Nerina Boshoff and
    Ms Tumi Moloto are credited with assisting Ms Mpho Letlape in implementing the gender
    equality programme.

10 Leonard Turner, Talent Manager, Eskom, personal communication, 7 July 2006

11 The Poverty Reduction Strategies formed part of the Paris Declaration on Aid
    Effectiveness in 2005; see www.sarpn.org.za/documents/d0002443/index/php and
    http://www.southernafricatrust.org/Poverty_Reduction_Strategies.html.

References

ANC (African National Congress) (1994) *The Reconstruction and Development Programme:
A policy framework.* Johannesburg: Umanyano Publications

Annecke W (1991) Out of the fire to find new fetters: The violence of poverty in a shack
settlement. Paper presented at the Conference on Women and Gender in Southern Africa,
31 January–2 February

Annecke W (1998) Benefits of electrification to rural households: Real or potential? *Journal of
Energy in Southern Africa* 9(4): 34–35

Annecke W (2003) One man one megawatt, one woman one candle: Women, gender, energy in
South Africa with a focus on research. Unpublished PhD thesis, University of KwaZulu-
Natal, Durban

Annecke W (2005) Whose turn is it to cook tonight? Changing gender relations in a South
African township. *Energia News* 8(2): 20–22

Annecke W, Banda K, Makhabane T, Mehlakoana N & Williams J (2006) *An audit of women in
the energy sector in South Africa: 10 years on.* Report for the Department of Science and
Technology, Pretoria

Annecke W, Gillespie B, Dobbins A & Sebitosi B (2005) *An assessment of PNES customer
satisfaction and the contribution of electricity to the quality of life in households in
Khayelitsha, South Africa.* Report for EdF-Access Programme. Paris: Electricité de France

Annecke W, Marialba E & Carpio C (2004) *Report on the acceptability of pre-payment meters in
Merlo, Argentina.* Report for EdF-Access Programme. Paris: Electricité de France

Annecke W & Mehlakoana N (2006) *The socio-economic impact of solar home systems in
Maphumulo and Msinga.* Report for EdF-Access Programme and KwaZulu Energy Services
Company, Cape Town

Baldwin S (1988) The design of fuel-efficient woodstoves appropriate for underdeveloped areas
of South Africa. In A Eberhard & A Williams (eds) *Renewable energy resources and
technology development in southern Africa.* Cape Town: Elan

Barnes D & Sen M (2004) The impact of rural electrification on women's lives in rural India.
Energia News 7(1): 13–14

Beall J, Bozzoli B, Ginwala F, Gwagwa L & Marks S (1990) 'Picking up the gauntlet': Women
discuss the ANC statement. *Agenda* 8: 5–23

Bonnin D, Hassim S, Posel R & Walker (1991) *Report on the conference on Women and Gender in Southern Africa*. Gender Research Group, University of Natal, Durban

Budlender D (ed.) (1996) *The women's budget*. Cape Town: Idasa

Callinicos L (1981) *A people's history of South Africa: Gold and workers 1886–1924*. Johannesburg: Ravan Press

Callinicos L (1987) *A people's history of South Africa: Working life 1886–1940. Factories, townships and popular culture on the Rand*. Johannesburg: Ravan Press

Cecelski E (2005) *From the Millennium Development Goals towards a gender-sensitive energy policy research and practice: Empirical evidence and case studies*. Draft Synthesis Report to DFID KaR on Research Project R8346, UK

Cecelski E, Dunkerley J & Ramsay W (1979) *Household energy and the poor in the third world*. Research paper R-15, Resources for the Future, Washington DC

Christie R (1984) *Electricity, industry and class in South Africa*. London: MacMillan

Cock J (1980) *Maids and madams: A study in the politics of exploitation*. Johannesburg: Ravan Press

Connell RW (1995) *Masculinities*. Cambridge: Polity Press

Cowan B (2005) An assessment of electricity for cooking in low-income households. Paper presented at the Central Energy Fund workshop on Meeting Low-income Household Cooking Needs, 23–25 November, Pretoria

Cowan B & Mehlakoana N (2004) *Barriers to energy services in low-income urban communities: Khayelitsha energy survey, 2004*. Energy and Development Research Centre, University of Cape Town

Crawford Cousins C (1998) *A question of power: The electrification of rural households*. Energy and Development Research Centre, University of Cape Town

DME (Department of Minerals and Energy, South Africa) (2002) *Digest of South African energy statistics 2002*. DME: Pretoria

DME & IIEC-Africa(International Institute for Energy Conservation-Africa) (1997) Briefing document on energy efficient low-cost housing in South Africa, prepared for Minister Penuell Maduna, Minister of Minerals and Energy and Dr Gordon Sibiya, Deputy-Director General: Energy Branch, Department of Minerals and Energy on the occasion of the Fourth Meeting of the United States–South Africa Binational Commission, 27–30 July, Washington DC

Du Plessis J (1996) Introduction. In *Lighting up South Africa: National Electricity Regulator progress report*. Johannesburg: NERSA

Eberhard A & Van Horen C (1995) *Poverty and power: Energy and the South African state*. London: Pluto

ECI (Empowerment and Creative Integration) (2000) *Changing views on development, gender and energy. Gender integration at programmatic level*. Reference material No. 3. Karachi: Pakistan Environment Programme

Ecotec Research & Consulting (1999) *The impact of restructuring on women in the electricity industry.* Ecotec: Birmingham

Escom (1975) *Escom annual report 1975.* Pretoria: Escom

Eskom (1995) *Eskom: Statistical yearbook 1995.* Pretoria: Eskom

Eskom (2002) *Annual report.* Pretoria: Eskom

Eskom (2005) *Annual report 2004.* Pretoria: Eskom

Eskom (2006) *Annual report 2005.* Pretoria: Eskom

ESMAP (Energy Sector Management Assistance Programme) (2001) *Proceedings of the US–Africa Energy Initiative including the Women in Energy Ministers' Conference,* 11–12 December, Durban

Faniso M (2006) Eskom need 400 engineers. *Business Report* 2 December

Fester G (1997) Women's organisations in the Western Cape: Vehicles for gender struggle or instruments of subordination? *Agenda* 34: 13–22

Fine B & Rustomjee Z (1996) *The political economy of South Africa: From minerals-energy complex to industrialisation.* London: Hurst & Company

Friedman M, Metelerkamp J & Posel R (1987) What is feminism and what kind of feminist am I? *Agenda* 1: 1–10

Gaba M (2006) LPGas: What's happening in the Western Cape? *Cape Times* 15 August

Gandar M (1988) The history and experience of woodlot development for fuel wood production in southern Africa. In A Eberhard & A Williams (eds) *Renewable energy resources and technology development in southern Africa.* Cape Town: Elan

Govender P (1993) Breaking the silence: Women's National Coalition. *Agenda* 16: 42–43

Hassim S (1991) Putting women on the agenda: Some issues and debates. *Agenda* 9: 10–13

Hemson D (2004) *Beating the backlog: Meeting targets and providing free basic services.* Pretoria: HSRC

IIEC-Africa (International Institute for Energy Conservation-Africa) (2005) Report on the LPGas Imbizo, Orange Farm, Johannesburg Region 11, 27 October

James B (1991) *The Mabibi community: A socio-economic study.* Report for the National Energy Council, Pretoria

James B (1998) *Community participation in rural electrification: Building human capacity through the delivery of electricity to rural areas.* Energy and Development Research Centre, University of Cape Town

James B & Simmonds G (1997) Energy. In D Budlender (ed.) *The second women's budget.* Cape Town: Idasa

Johnson E & Fedorsky C (2000) Opportunities for women in business. Paper presented at the Women in Energy Ministers' Conference, 11–12 December, Durban

Karakezi S & Kimani J (2002) Status of power sector reform in Africa: Impact on the poor. *Energy Policy Special Issue – Africa: Improving Modern Energy Services for the Poor* 30(11–12): 923–945

Karakezi S & Wangeci J (2005) The role of gender research in influencing power sector policy in eastern and southern Africa. *Energia News* 8(2): 15–17

Kelkar G & Nathan D (2005) Gender relations and energy transitions in rural Asia. *Energia News* 8(2): 22–23

Klunne W & Mugisha C (2001) Responses of rural households to the decline of woodfuel collecting areas: Case study in an expanding sugarcane area of Misinda district of Uganda. *Energia News* 4(2): 7–9

Legido-Quigley H (2003) The South African old age pension: Exploring the role of poverty alleviation in households affected by HIV/AIDS. Paper presented at the 4th International Research Conference on Social Security, 5–7 May, Antwerp

Lele D (1998) Gender equity in international petroleum projects: Women in the oil and gas sector. *Energia News* 2 (3)

Lessing M (ed.) (1994) *South African women today.* Cape Town: Maskew Miller Longman

Letlaka-Rennert K (1991) Impressions: Conference on 'Women and Gender in Southern Africa'. *Agenda* 9: 22–23

Maake R (2006) Integrated energy Centers (IeCs) as a vehicle to deliver affordable energy sources and information to rural communities in South Africa. Paper presented at the International Energy Workshop: Energy Economy and Environment, 27–29 June, Cape Town

Mabandla B (2002) Opening address at the Forum on Science, Technology and Innovation for Sustainable Development at TWOWS (Third World Organisation for Women in Science) Forum at Ubuntu Village, World Summit on Sustainable Development (WSSD), 26 August, Johannesburg

Makan A (1994) *A gendered perspective of the development context for energy planning in South Africa.* EPRET Paper No. 3, Energy and Development Research Centre, University of Cape Town

Maré G & Fisher F (1974) *The Durban strikes.* Durban: IEE

Mashabela P (ed.) (2004/05) *Enterprising women in South Africa: 10 years on: A survey on the empowerment of women in the private sector.* Cape Town: Inyathelo

Matley M (2005) Women's electrification. *Energia News* 8(2): 24–25

Mbeki T (2005) State of the Nation address by the President of South Africa, Thabo Mbeki. Joint sitting of the Houses of Parliament, 11 February, Cape Town. Accessed 29 February 2008, www.info.gov/speeaches/htm

Mchunu N (2006) Abuse of girl pupils revealed in national report on SA schools. *Cape Times* 27 June

Midgley I (2003) *The role of women leading transformation in Eskom, a large electricity utility.* Margaret College, Henley-on-Thames

Morrell R (1998) The new man? *Agenda* 37: 7–12

NERSA (National Electricity Regulator of South Africa) (2002) *Electricity supply statistics for South Africa.* Pretoria: NERSA

NERSA (2006) *A decade of effective and efficient electricity regulation in South Africa.* Pretoria: NERSA

Ntsokolo M (2005) Panel discussion at the workshop on Electricity Distribution Industry Restructuring for Developmental Local Government, Development Bank of Southern Africa, 8 October, Midrand

Nye D (1990) *Electrifying America: Social meanings of a new technology, 1880–1940.* London: MIT

Parikh J (2000) Gender and health considerations for petroleum product policy in India. *Energia News* 3(2): 11–13

Parker M (2003) 'The British are coming! The British are coming!' The effects of British colonization on Zimbabwean women. Paper presented at the Fourth Annual Composition and Cultural Studies Conference for student writers at the George Washington University, 24–26 April, Washington DC

PDC (Palmer Development Consulting) (2003) *Review of effectiveness of energy subsidies and related taxation policies in South Africa.* PDC in co-operation with Science Consultancy Enterprises.

Pick WM & Obermeyer CM (1999) Urbanisation, household composition and the reproductive health of women in a South African city. University of the Witwatersrand, Department of Community Health, Medical School, Parktown, Johannesburg

Pietilä H & Vickers J (1994) *Making women matter: The role of the United Nations.* London: Zed Books

Prasad G (2006) The impact of power sector reform on poor households in Africa. In *Proceedings of the conference on domestic uses of energy,* 4–6 April, Cape Town

Prathoumvan B (2000) Gender and wood energy in Lao PDR. *Energia News* 3(1): 12–13

Reddy A (1980) *Rural energy consumption patterns: A field study.* ASTRA, Indian Institute of Science, Bangalore

Roberts B (1976) *Kimberley: Turbulent city.* Cape Town: David Philip

Ruffini A (1999) Where will Eskom's future generation capacity come from? *African Energy* 1(1): 1–2

Ruiters W (1995) *Affirmative action in the energy sector.* EPRET Paper No. 21, Energy and Development Research Centre, University of Cape Town

Seekings J (1991) Gender ideology and township politics in the 1980s. *Agenda* 10: 77–88

Sisulu L (2005) Breaking new ground in housing delivery. In P Mashabela (ed.) *Enterprising women in South Africa: 10 years on: A survey on the empowerment of women in the private sector.* Cape Town: Inyathelo

Skutsch M (1998) Gender issue in energy project planning: Welfare, empowerment or equity? *Energy Policy* 26(12): 945–955

Taylor V (1997) *Social mobilization: Lessons from the mass democratic movement.* University of the Western Cape, Cape Town

Tinker I (1982) *Women, energy and development.* Washington DC: Equity Policy Centre

Trollip H (1996) *Overview of the South African energy sector.* Energy and Development Research Centre, University of Cape Town

Turner L (2005) Balanced leadership 50/50: Women at work. The gender equity decade in South Africa (2000 to 2010). Active perspectives from Transmission Division of Eskom Holdings Company. Unpublished master's thesis, University of KwaZulu-Natal, Durban

UNDP (United Nations Development Programme) (2003) *Development progress in South Africa 2003.* New York: UNDP

University of Cape Town (2002) *Options for a basic electricity support tariff.* University of Cape Town Research Project 400903

Van Horen C (1996) *Counting the social costs. Electricity and externalities in South Africa.* Industrial Strategy Project. Cape Town: Elan Press & UCT Press

Van Zyl M (1991) Invitation to debate: Towards an explanation of violence against women. *Agenda* 11: 66–77

Von Schirnding Y (2000) Household energy use, health and development. Background paper prepared for the USAID/WHO Global Consultation on Indoor Air Pollution and Household Energy in Developing Countries, 3–4 April, Washington DC. *Energia News 2001. Special issue on women and health* 4(4): 8–11

Walker C (ed.) (1990) *Women and gender in southern Africa to 1945.* Cape Town: David Philip

Wamukonya N (2003) African power sector reforms: Some emerging lessons. *Energy for Sustainable Development* 7(1): 7–15

Wentzel M (2003) A gender profile of solar stove buyers and users: Findings from the second phase of the GTZ/DME solar cooker field test programme. *Energia News* 6(1): 17–19

Worger W (1987) *South Africa's city of diamonds: Mine workers and monopoly capitalism in Kimberley. 1867–1895.* Johannesburg: AD Donker

From local to global (and back again?): Anti-commodification struggles of the Soweto Electricity Crisis Committee

Prishani Naidoo and Ahmed Veriava

> I remember a time when in the SECC [Soweto Electricity Crisis Committee] meetings people who were illegally connected would be asked to raise their hands, and almost everyone's hands would go up. There'd be this sense of relief as almost everyone would be illegally connected. The only thing was that they were doing it as a criminal act individually. So, it was a question of turning what was a criminal act into a collective act of defiance. (Activist Trevor Ngwane, cited in Naidoo & Veriava 2005: 50)

> Key to the success of any further struggles in Phiri and Soweto against the installation of prepaid water meters will have to be an acknowledgement that the reality of the majority of residents is that they have accepted the logic of prepayment for water, and that any attempts at collective resistance will have to begin with a challenge of this logic and language of corporate 'saving' and 'waste'. (Coalition Against Water Privatisation & Anti-Privatisation Forum 2006: 17)

These quotations represent two moments in the life of the SECC as it has sought to contest the state and private companies' attempts at imposing the logic of payment for basic services in Soweto, Johannesburg. Significant to both quotations is their representation of the central tension around which struggles against neo-liberalism have been shaped: that between collective action and individual solutions to problems. What the quotations highlight is the fact that the making of resistance and collective action is itself a contested process, often influenced by the very policies and processes that are being opposed.

As new social movements have emerged in South Africa to resist the effects of neo-liberal policies, the ways in which they have been narrated in academia, the mainstream media and civil society have often come under criticism for being over-celebratory and lacking rigour in their analyses. In the words of one proponent of this view, Ferial Haffajee, the editor of a respected South African weekly newspaper:

In trying to make South Africa a node on the map of anti-globalisation resistance, the new social movements may be trying to fit a square peg into a round hole. As somebody who believes in the importance of social movements and the radical intellectuals who support them, I must admit to be tiring quite quickly of their habit of magnifying their import, impact and size – on the basis of predictable arguments and sketchy research...It is too easy a way out of our interminable interregnum – because it doesn't require grappling with the difficulties of transition; with the nuts and bolts of local government finance; with the technicalities and policies required to extend a water connection and keep it running. (Haffajee 2004: 1)

The following analysis of the SECC runs against this grain of analysis, showing that the SECC has, through the bringing together of individual struggles against electricity cut-offs, been able to offer (albeit on a small scale) an alternative voice and logic to that of commodification, and an alternative imagination for the delivery of basic services amongst a collective of residents in Soweto. As the drive to enforce neo-liberal policies has grown stronger, with increasing resistance from social and civic movements on the ground, the strategies and tactics employed by the state and private companies have begun to try to circumvent and/or attack collective processes and practices, attempting to individualise the relationship of people to basic services. In particular, prepaid technology has marked the advent of such individualising strategies. Struggles by new social movements have not, therefore, been static or homogeneous, but represent a changing and contested field of engagement through which new strategies and tactics have emerged.

What commentators like Haffajee miss is the fact that the struggles of new social movements, such as the SECC, represent the constant struggle inherent in capitalist societies between the market and people attempting to protect themselves from its cruelties. Within new social movements, and amongst their interlocutors, have emerged various contestations over the different potential trajectories for struggle and organisation in this period, highlighting the reality that struggle against the market is itself a contested process.

In his theorisation of neo-liberalism as part of the continuous process of primitive accumulation, De Angelis (1998: 13), building on the work of Polanyi (1944), argues that capitalism is characterised by a double movement of the market and struggle: 'On the one side there is the historical movement of the market, a movement that has no inherent limits and therefore threatens society's very existence. On the other, there is society's natural propensity to defend itself, and therefore to create institutions for its protection.' For De Angelis, the second movement often involves processes of 'commoning', which may be characterised as the creation of 'social spheres of life' aimed at providing 'various degrees of protection from the market'.

It is in this struggle of people for protection from the market that new social movements emerge, in South Africa and elsewhere, sometimes rejecting the logic of the commodification of those resources necessary for survival and life. The

SECC represents one attempt at building a movement around an overt refusal to pay for electricity. Emerging out of the everyday struggles for survival of ordinary residents of Soweto, the SECC will, in this chapter, be explored through its changing experiences and forms, in particular through its attempts to give collective meaning and voice to the struggles of individual residents and households, and its encounters with the individualising tendencies of capital and the capitalist state.

From the individual to the collective

Under apartheid, the majority of Soweto residents, together with other township dwellers, boycotted paying for basic services in a collective strategy of resistance against the provision of poor and unequal services, as well as against the recognition of black local authorities and the tricameral system of governance.[1] As the African National Congress (ANC) prepared to govern after the democratic transition of 1994, its Reconstruction and Development Programme promised 'free basic services' for all, instilling in communities the expectation that a new and democratic South Africa would bring access to better quality services and some form of free services for the poor (ANC 1994). However, already by 1995 the ANC was preparing communities for the introduction of payment for all levels of basic services, evident in its campaign entitled Masakhane ('We Are Building'), aimed at encouraging residents to pay for their services as 'responsible citizens', and undoing 'the culture of non-payment' that was deemed to have resulted from the payment boycotts of the 1980s.

When, in 1996, the ANC government adopted a neo-liberal macroeconomic framework in the form of the Growth, Employment and Redistribution strategy, communities were being re-taught the 'principles of democracy' – that individual citizens would have to become 'partners' in the delivery of basic services, and that this would mean payment for services previously boycotted or thought of as something to be freely provided by a democratic state. In the 1990s, therefore, 'cost recovery'[2] and degrees of privatisation came to define the policy framework for the delivery of basic services. However, in the context of widespread job losses, the growth of precarious forms of work, and the introduction of the logic of cost recovery in all spheres of life, payment for basic services became simply impossible for large sectors of the population, for whom non-payment became a necessity in order to survive in the context of unemployment and low incomes.

In Soweto, this was to manifest itself initially as an ongoing struggle around electricity provision. As local political structures (such as ANC and South African National Civics Organisation [Sanco][3] branches) began to buy into the logic of payment for electricity, with some individuals even benefiting materially from the process, a political vacuum emerged that presented residents with a dilemma when trying to resist the hardships inflicted on their lives as a result of the introduction of the duty to pay for electricity. While Sanco and the ANC would have been expected to protect the interests of poor residents, instead they used their positions to argue for the payment boycott to be called off and led the calls for residents to begin paying for services. Sadly, they would not be able to back up these calls with measures by which residents would be able to earn enough income to pay for these services.

The interlocking hegemony of this new cost recovery mandate is evident in the ways in which ANC-aligned organisations came together to enforce payment for services. As Ngwane and Veriava (2004: 132) note, the initial calling-off of the payment boycott in Soweto in the early 1990s:

> had been effected partly through high-level negotiations between the ANC, Sanco and Eskom[4] management. The resulting deal saw local Sanco officials being given tenders to install mini-sub-stations in Soweto. Local branches of Sanco also seconded many of their members to Eskom, where they were employed as 'block representatives', basically helping to make sure that every house got its bills on time and responding to any problems that might arise. Local civic leaders were also employed by Eskom in local depots as clerical staff or other suitable low-level positions.'

In Soweto, a combination of arrears and inability to pay led to widespread electricity cut-offs from 2000 on. In 2001, a survey conducted by the Municipal Services Project and the SECC showed that up to 20 000 households in Soweto were being cut off each month for non-payment of services (Fiil-Flynn 2001: 2). According to the same study, 61 per cent of the 200 households surveyed had had their electricity cut off in the previous 12 months, with some households going as long as 9 months without power. In addition, 10 per cent of households had had their electricity cables confiscated by Eskom, for illegal grid connections.

> In response to these cut-offs Sowetans required urgent and appropriate forms of political action that would both provide immediate relief in terms of reconnecting disconnected households to the grid, wiping off unpayable electricity account arrears and, over the longer term, mitigating or transforming the policies that led to the cut-offs. These more immediate concerns also inevitably [led] to broader questions surrounding the social and economic order which precipitated the crisis. (McInnes 2006: 1)

The SECC was able to provide an alternative in the context of the political vacuum described above, linking residents across the 50 smaller townships that make up Soweto. Unlike Sanco and Eskom, the SECC actively promoted collective action and alternatives to the individualising logic of the market.

Trevor Ngwane, founding member and ongoing organiser of the SECC, tells how the organisation began by assisting people (especially older women) to negotiate for reconnection when they had been cut off:

> The idea of the SECC had also arisen in workshops being held in Soweto by the Campaign Against Neoliberalism in South Africa (CANSA)...We had a Johannesburg workshop on CANSA looking at how to spread ideas

against neo-liberalism...We met for three months, but we just couldn't find a way forward...Then one day we decided 'look, let's find an issue.' (At that time it was not just Pimvillians, [but] people from Tladi, Zola...and SACC [South African Council of Churches] types)...So, we discussed, and electricity was an issue. So, we found money for a workshop, through CANSA, from AIDC [Alternative Information Development Centre]...and we decided we were going to form an organisation, so we called another workshop, which was addressed by Patrick Bond [and] Dennis Brutus...and afterwards we had our own discussion, and we had to find a name, so we decided to call it the Soweto Electricity Crisis Committee. (Ngwane, cited in McInnes 2006: 18)

While the 'we' referred to by Ngwane (comrades considered more politically conscious and overtly 'socialist' in orientation) may have had the political theories with which to analyse what was happening in Soweto, they had to rely on their interactions with community members through meetings in order to develop any meaningful programme as a new organisation. Ngwane recalls how the majority of people were already reconnecting themselves illegally as a means of avoiding payment for electricity when the SECC was formed and began to hold meetings: 'It [reconnection] had to be announced as a political act for it to be that. People were already doing it when we got there' (Ngwane interview).

The very localised act of reconnection, therefore, provided a means by which a movement could be built. In a campaign named Operation Khanyisa ('Operation Switch On'), thousands of Soweto households were reconnected in spite of non-payment by trained members of the SECC. Within six months of its birth, Operation Khanyisa had reconnected over 3 000 households (Egan & Wafer 2004: 10). Through community meetings, door-to-door campaigns and pamphleteering, the SECC brought together thousands of Soweto residents – in particular, pensioners and the unemployed – in marches and demonstrations against Eskom and its logic of payment for electricity, as well as against ANC city councillors in Johannesburg who had been leading the implementation of these policies. In the words of Ngwane and Veriava (2004: 133):

Khanyisa had struck at the core of the social relations which enmeshed the provision of electricity: it was an act of defiance, which shifted power relations between residents and the government-owned electricity company. The power to cut off and switch on was no longer Eskom's alone. The wave of illegal reconnections posed a serious threat to the much broader project of cost recovery. Through Khanyisa, reconnections were transformed from a criminal act into a political intervention. Eskom and the bosses looked on helplessly as Khanyisa whispered through other areas.

While the ANC government and Eskom were initially adamant that people would be made to pay for electricity, with the growth of the SECC and the power of the collective action of Soweto's residents, they have been forced to try different strategies for the implementation of cost recovery. Communities have continued to find ways of resisting payment for services, and organisations like the SECC have attempted to mobilise against the logic of commodification within this context.

In October 2001, Eskom announced a moratorium on cut-offs in Soweto. In November 2001, Minister of Public Enterprises Jeff Radebe, addressing a gathering at which the mayor of Johannesburg, councillors and officials of Eskom were present, attacked the SECC for engendering a 'criminal culture' and being antagonistic to the ANC, and proposed a series of changes to electricity delivery systems in the interests of the 'twin responsibilities' of protecting 'the interests of both the community and Eskom' (Radebe, cited in Egan & Wafer 2004: 11). These included the writing off of 50 per cent of residents' arrears, reform of the billing process, and 'amnesty' for those who reported illegal reconnections.

> When Radebe made his offer to Soweto in December 2001 it was turned down. The SECC made its demands clear: electricity for everyone, including urban settlements and rural areas that still had to be electrified; scrapping all arrears; free basic supply of electricity and water the ANC had promised during the 2000 municipal elections campaign and a return to the flat-rate monthly pricing system that the community had managed to wrest from the apartheid regime in the 1980s. (Egan & Wafer 2004: 11)

The SECC would continue to mobilise in the interests of residents. In May 2003, Eskom announced the scrapping of arrears in townships of Johannesburg, including Soweto, to the tune of R1.4 billion. With the SECC having refused the initial deal to partially scrap arrears in 2001, Radebe and the ANC were able to portray the agreement as a 'deal' that was brokered between Sanco and Eskom. However, there is no doubt that the work of the SECC, and Operation Khanyisa, had a direct effect on this policy change by Eskom, a change that was to affect not only Soweto but other townships in Johannesburg as well.

But the scrapping of arrears was to be followed by the introduction of prepaid meters, ushering in a new form of payment rule, one in which individualised, commodified systems of service delivery are naturalised through techniques of self-government and individual saving and restraint. With the introduction of the prepaid meter, responsibility for access to electricity has become the individual's, with limited interaction between the recipient ('client') and the service provider, and limited responsibility on the part of the state. With the prepaid meter, there is no possibility for the accumulation of debt, removing the debt burden shouldered by private companies, and no possibility for individual access to a service (over and above the 'lifeline'[5] provisions made by the state) without money. The state and private companies have been teaching the poor how to 'budget properly' so as to be able to afford to pay for the services that they need, and the logic of individualism and the market is spreading its roots in the lives of people as they struggle to survive under neo-liberalism. In spite of this, the SECC has come out against the introduction of prepaid electricity, ripping meter boxes out and delivering them in marches to police stations, in order to reinforce the collective dimension of their opposition to the system. Most striking about this campaign of the SECC is its reassertion of collective commitments to the delivery of decommodified electricity in the face of the individualising strategies and discourse of Eskom and the municipality.

As cost recovery came to define the nature of delivery in other sectors, the SECC's focus would grow to include the problem of access to water, its name becoming a limiting factor in the manner in which it would be understood and portrayed by outsiders. As its own members began to experience water cut-offs, the SECC's Operation Khanyisa was expanded to take on Operation Vula 'Manzi ('Operation Open The Water'), reconnecting households to free water supplies. As water cut-offs, in a similar vein to electricity cut-offs, did not work successfully as a punitive measure in Soweto, prepaid water meters also became a strategy used by the authorities to enforce payment for water. While the imposition of prepaid electricity met widespread resistance and led to collective reconnection in Soweto, the prepaid water meter would prove more difficult to resist and to use as a focus for strengthening collective action.

The struggle over water

In 2003, quoting the 'success' of a pilot project in Stretford, Extension 4, Orange Farm,[6] Johannesburg Water[7] and the municipality launched Operation Gcina 'Manzi ('Operation Save Water'), through which prepaid water meters would be installed in all households in Soweto, beginning with Phiri. The discourse of 'conservation', 'saving', 'careful budgeting', and 'efficient management' of water accompanied these efforts at getting residents to 'take control' of their access to water. It has been in this struggle that the SECC has fought its most bruising battles (in the streets of Soweto, in residents' yards and homes) and learned its hardest lessons as it has had to deal with the effects of the individualisation of people's relationship to water, manifested in the difficulties experienced in trying to organise collectively in an increasingly individualised context.

In the early days of this struggle, the SECC, together with the Phiri Concerned Residents Forum (PCRF) which later became an SECC affiliate, assisted and supported residents to physically oppose and prevent the laying of pipes for the installation of the prepaid water system by Johannesburg Water. By toyi-toying in the streets of Phiri,[8] and by physically blocking access to workers from Johannesburg Water, residents, supported by the SECC, made first attempts at the installation of the prepaid water system almost impossible. This resulted in Johannesburg Water enlisting the support of the police, the notorious 'Red Ants' (employees of Wozani Security, a private security firm noted for wearing red overalls and previously employed for other local authority purposes, such as eviction of people from inner-city buildings and informal settlements), and eventually securing a court interdict which prevented any person from coming within 50 metres of a Johannesburg Water work site (sometimes encompassing people's own gardens). In spite of this, Johannesburg Water is known to have lost hundreds of thousands of rands over the first few months of Operation Gcina 'Manzi in Phiri, as residents engaged in a campaign of digging up the pipes laid by the company (Ngwane & Veriava 2004).

Over time, resistance has been met with harsher responses – arrests, fines, and cut-offs from any water supply.[9] Johannesburg Water and the municipality have also embarked on campaigns to teach residents the values of the prepaid water system and to demonstrate how this system can assist individual households with their budgeting. In addition, residents have been given little choice but to sign on to the system. The only alternative to a prepaid water meter currently is a standpipe outside an individual's yard (as opposed to a prepaid system that runs inside the house). With a standpipe, individuals are unable to have flush toilets, and are threatened with heavy fines for connecting their households to the standpipes. Individuals who have chosen the standpipe over the prepaid system complain of terrible sanitation problems; when they seek assistance from the local council in dealing with these problems, they are told to sign on for the indigent management policy. This policy, however, requires residents to sign on to prepaid systems of water and electricity. While some low-income residents argue that they will not be able to pay for their water if they sign on to the prepaid system, and therefore choose not to sign up for the indigent policy, others are finding it difficult to resist the other promise that has come with signing on to the indigent register: the scrapping of all or part of one's service-related debts. This highlights the fact that residents are given very little choice in deciding whether to obtain a prepaid water meter or not, making collective resistance against the prepaid water system all the more difficult. A research report by the Coalition Against Water Privatisation and the Anti-Privatisation Forum (APF) on the effects of the prepaid water meters on life and resistance in Phiri states the following:

> Three years since the launch of Operation Gcina 'Manzi, and the start of resistance against the installation of prepaid water meters in Phiri, our findings suggest that residents have had no choice but to accept the prepaid system, and have begun internalizing the logic of payment for water. For the few who have chosen not to sign onto the prepaid system, life has become more difficult, with access to water made possible only by walking to standpipes outside one's yard, and living without flush toilets. For the majority, life has come to mean finding ways of accessing water through the prepaid system. While the PCRF argues that a majority of Phiri residents are by-passing their water meters, our findings suggest that residents have begun to speak the language of 'saving water' and 'budgeting efficiently' in order to meet their basic water requirements within the prepaid system. In our survey, 83 per cent of respondents said that they were paying for water every month. Where by-passing is happening, individuals have paid for this reconnection and live with the constant threat of punishment if they are found out by Johannesburg Water or council officials and workers. In most cases, where

resistance is occurring, it is taking place at a very individualised level, and tactics are emerging on this plane to evade discovery and prosecution. (Coalition Against Water Privatisation & Anti-Privatisation Forum 2006)

The emergence of the SECC as part of the movement of people trying to protect themselves from the cruelties of the market has meant that it has evolved and been shaped by this constant interplay, represented perhaps best in the constant struggle between collectivist and individualist approaches to the delivery of water and electricity in Soweto.

From local to global

The First Political Prisoners Of Neoliberalism: On 15 August, Soweto Electricity Crisis Committee activists jailed for non-violent protest against the denial of electricity, water, housing and basic human rights will appear at Jeppe Court in Johannesburg. They are asking for your solidarity. (Globalise Resistance 2002)

In April 2002, a group of SECC members boarded a bus and visited the house of the Mayor of Johannesburg, Amos Masondo, in Kensington (central Johannes-burg), to protest and deliver a memorandum demanding an end to water and electricity cut-offs. The mayor's bodyguard opened fire on the protesters, and 87 members of the SECC were arrested. They were held at the notorious 'Sun City' (Johannesburg Central Prison) for two weeks without being formally charged, while 'their addresses were being verified' by the police. In a trial that was to extend over a period of a year, the SECC was to gain much exposure, both nationally and internationally, as the Kensington 87 became celebrated heroes of the international struggle against neo-liberalism.

Frustrated by the slow rate of response by local authorities to resistance in Soweto, the SECC decided to adopt more radical and far-reaching tactics. In the relations established through the events relating to the arrest of the Kensington 87, the SECC not only built its public profile as a movement, but also extended its networks of solidarity and partnership with other activists, movements and organisations, both locally and globally. While the SECC had enjoyed support from a few outside organisations and individuals from its inception, the Kensington 87 experience marked a more consciously outward-looking approach by the SECC to questions of its growth and orientation as a movement.

The very nature of the struggle for free basic services has also lent itself to easy interpretation through the lens of broader struggles against privatisation and neo-liberalism, allowing for links to be made between the SECC and other struggles and movements organising against the introduction of neo-liberal policies. Nationally, these have included the Concerned Citizens Forum in Durban, the Anti-Eviction Campaign in Cape Town, the Freedom of Expression Institute and Jubilee South Africa. In Johannesburg, the SECC has both gained support from and helped to build the APF, an umbrella body of over 20 groups fighting neo-liberalism in its various forms that emerged in 2000, in struggles against attempts at privatisation at the University of the Witwatersrand and in the City of Johannesburg. The APF consists mainly of community groups, and has two political groupings that are formally affiliated to it – the Socialist Group and Keep Left (both Trotskyist in their orientation). There are also a number of individual activists (students, academics, NGO workers) who belong to the APF. In addition to providing support for community programmes of action, the APF brings communities and activists together in common campaigns and joint actions against illegitimate actions of the state and private companies. The SECC has been an affiliate of the APF since its birth.

Through its participation in the APF, the SECC has been able to broaden the struggle for free basic services beyond the borders of Soweto, by building joint campaigns with other community affiliates of the APF at a regional and provincial level, and offering support and advice to other communities beginning to engage in struggles against the introduction of neo-liberal policies. It has also received support in the form of material and human resources for its campaigns and, in particular, when faced with legal challenges.

It has also, through the APF, as well as through the personal connections of individual SECC activists and the profile built for the SECC through activist networks such as Indymedia and the Debate list-serve, been able to participate in a global network of activists. At home, large numbers of SECC members came together with activists from around the world to protest the promotion of the neo-liberal agenda at the World Conference Against Racism in Durban in 2001 and the World Summit on Sustainable Development in Johannesburg in 2002. A few SECC members have also had the opportunity to participate in global forums, such as the World Social Forum and other gatherings of the anti-globalisation movement. Beginning as a movement organising people around a 'local' issue, the SECC has become a movement that resonates with other movements struggling against neo-liberalism around the world, and has found comradeship and solidarity in a global movement linking local struggles against manifestations of a global system.

Often this resonance has been immediate, as the enemies at the local level (e.g. Johannesburg Water) have been recognisable as the same enemies at a global level (e.g. Suez Lyonnaise) through the networks of activists around the globe that have been built over the past few years in and through common but diverse struggles against neo-liberalism. These networks of support have assisted tremendously in collectivising the struggle against privatisation and commodification in Soweto.

While the case of the Kensington 87 is certainly striking in terms of the kinds of solidarity and support that it raised for the SECC, both nationally and internationally, there have been other instances when similar networks of support have been mobilised in the interests of the SECC's struggles. The creation of the Coalition Against Water Privatisation stands out as an example of the extent of the reach of struggles in Soweto. By September 2003, when Johannesburg Water started installing prepaid water meters in Phiri, the SECC had learned from its struggles for free electricity and had built its networks through this struggle. In giving support to residents of Phiri, the SECC was therefore able to mobilise a far-reaching network of support and solidarity. In Johannesburg, through the APF, a coalition was formed bringing together academics, activists, NGOs, and community groups and movements to campaign against the installation of prepaid water meters in Phiri, and the privatisation of water more generally. Through the Coalition Against Water Privatisation, funds were raised, participatory research was conducted, mass meetings and marches were held, and legal advice was sought for a Constitutional Court case against prepaid water meters. Today, while Johannesburg Water proceeds with its installation of the meters in Phiri and the rest of Soweto, and the fiery street battles of 2003 seem a distant memory as residents claim that they are now just 'by-passing' the meters (Molobela interview; Mokwena interview), the Coalition continues to meet and provide support for the changing struggles in Soweto.

In August 2006, the Coalition embarked on a Constitutional Court case against the introduction of prepaid water meters. After a long process of research and consultation, the case was heard in court in December 2007, and at the time of writing the Coalition was awaiting the result. A second participatory research project, looking at the ways in which prepaid water meters had affected people and struggle in Phiri, was also completed in August 2006, and its findings have assisted both with the work in preparation of the court case and with more general campaign work (Coalition Against Water Privatisation & Anti-Privatisation Forum 2006). The Coalition has also allowed for international solidarity and networks of struggle to be built. Significantly, links have been made with struggles against water privatisation in Ghana. Just this cursory look at the SECC would support the view of Desai (2001) that:

> [t]he neoliberal transition has squeezed and spewed out the poor but
> galvanized them at the same time. The 'poors', as they have come to be known
> in the South African vernacular, have opposed the water and electricity cut-offs
> and evictions (consequences of the privatisation of public services), and have
> begun making connections between their situation and that of people, first in
> Soweto and Tafelsig [in Cape Town], but then also in Bolivia, South Korea,
> America's prisons, Zimbabwe, and Chiapas. But they have done this without
> any grand ideology. They are actors on a local stage, squaring off against
> homegrown villains like Operation Masakhane, which supposedly aims to
> normalize local governance and the provision of local services by convincing
> people with no money that they must pay for these services.

As the SECC faces some of its biggest challenges in a context of increasingly individualised responses to the effects of neo-liberalism, it is hoped that the organisation will be able to draw on these networks of support and solidarity in rethinking and reshaping its programmes and approaches to struggle.

Shaping a movement from within

From its inception, the SECC has been composed of individuals with rich histories in other organisations, including the ANC, the Inkatha Freedom Party and different elements of the Black Consciousness tradition (Ngwane interview). In the early days of the SECC, there was a conscious attempt by its leaders and 'propagandists' to subvert nationalist ideology and symbols by deliberately exposing the contradictions in the ANC's promises and actions. Opportunities for this presented themselves readily, and the lived experiences of the majority of SECC members spoke directly to these contradictions.

While the struggle for free electricity, and later for free water, would bring together ordinary residents in trying to forge common solutions to the problems that the state was trying to individualise, it would also provide an opportunity for a small group of Trotskyists, organised in the Socialist Group, to pursue its agenda for socialism. In Ngwane's words, 'At first we were taking grannies one by one and negotiating for a lesser price. But it became clear that this is not the way to go. We needed a stronger demand or a bigger solution – a more structural one. For that you need greater ideas' (Ngwane interview).

With the existence of the Socialist Group, and its need for 'a bigger solution', the influence of theories of socialism and grander narratives of globalisation and neo-liberalism has also been significant in the ways in which the SECC has evolved. While in its early days this manifested itself in how the SECC was represented by its Socialist Group interlocutors, more recently it has directly influenced the political orientation of the SECC and those whose support it enjoys. Believing strongly in the need for a 'mass workers' party' through which state power can be seized in the interests of the working class and a socialist future, the Socialist Group and the SECC (through its influence) have consistently argued for the APF and other social movements to orientate themselves towards contesting local and national elections. Losing this argument, in February 2006, in the broader APF network, and in the run-up to local government elections, the SECC, together with several affiliates of the Johannesburg region of the APF, nevertheless launched the Operation Khanyisa Movement (OKM), which it registered as a political party and used to field candidates in the local elections in Johannesburg that year. While the OKM was successful in getting one of its members elected as a councillor in the Johannesburg municipality in 2006, it has subsequently had to deal with her defecting to the Democratic Alliance, the liberal official opposition in Parliament. This first councillor elected by the OKM has, therefore, already been replaced by another 'more accountable' and 'more reliable' leader.

While many activists fear the use of the SECC and the OKM to legitimise unjust policy decisions by the municipality through the participation of its councillor, members of the Socialist Group believe that, through the building of local community support for its programme in the council, its participation in the municipality will reap gains for the broader struggle against commodification.

But the attempted moulding of the SECC to suit a 'bigger vision' has not been the only result of the positive growth of the organisation. In spite of the Socialist Group's attempts to infuse local struggles with a more global understanding of capitalism and the need for socialism, in 2004 Egan and Wafer (2004: 11) spoke of the 'seeming gap between the politically organised and articulate members like Ngwane who form the leadership core, and the "survivalist" members in Soweto who make up the membership at the local branch level. To suggest that this is a fundamental and deep seated cleavage would be an over-statement, but it does generate tensions within the organisation'. In fact, over time, these tensions would generate such 'deep seated cleavages'. While the profile of the SECC grew at a national and international level, at home differences with regard to leadership style, organisational processes and structuring, and overall political orientation, would lead to growing tensions and conflict within the SECC, with a significant portion of the membership eventually breaking away to form the Soweto Concerned Residents (SCR) in 2005. Activists interviewed for this chapter (Jabu Molobela, Ishmael Mokwena and Virginia Magwaza) highlighted what they saw as the controlling nature of the Socialist Group and its members as one of the reasons leading to the split. Virginia Magwaza, a former member of the Socialist Group, had the following to say about her experience while serving as the deputy chairperson of the SECC:

> The first time I went to a Socialist Group [SG] meeting, I got the sense that the SG should be controlling the SECC, even the APF. So, you will find that if there is an Annual General Meeting [AGM], it must be discussed in the SG – how the AGM should go and who do we want in the executive...same with the APF. There was also this thing of discussing comrades – you know, we don't like this one 'because he has this background'...this is one of the problems I had with the SG...They looked at themselves as having the best politics in the APF as a whole. (Magwaza interview)

Members of the SCR point to failed attempts at trying to address problems within the SECC resulting from the role played by the Socialist Group as the ultimate cause of the split. They claim that the outcome of an election process at an AGM of the SECC was rigged by the Socialist Group, and that the Socialist Group was protecting individual members from accusations of financial mismanagement, thus preventing any real efforts to deal with problems in the organisation. The Socialist Group-led faction, on the other hand, accused members of the splinter group of charging residents for reconnections and embezzling funds. Over time conflict escalated, with personal attacks and the need for outside mediation arising. When mediation failed, the SCR's battle for recognition turned to the space of the APF.

The SCR, having formed a significant number of branches and proclaimed itself socialist in orientation, approached the APF to affiliate as a member. The SECC vehemently opposed this, arguing that the SCR should try to resolve its problems with the SECC and return to the organisation. In July 2006, after a period of delayed discussions and debate, the APF resolved to accept the SCR as a separate affiliate. This was not accepted easily by members of the SECC, and relations within the APF were characterised by tensions related to the 'sides' taken by individuals in this debate for a very long time. Even today, while the SCR and SECC exist side by side within the APF, relations between them are still somewhat strained – both in the APF and in Soweto. Nevertheless, members of both organisations have been able to come together in the development of much needed campaigns in parts of Soweto, such as Kliptown, in 2007.

With regard to the SECC, the split has most definitely reduced its membership base, and negatively affected relationships between different branches and members of the organisation depending on their position on the conflict with the SCR. The role of the Socialist Group in this period, in either helping to resolve or fuelling lingering tensions, will be significant in determining how the SECC grows and develops in the future.

Since the election of an OKM councillor, the SECC seems to have been preoccupied with the work of the council, with community mass meetings, door-to-door visits, and the general direction of the organisation geared towards enhancing support for this councillor in the community. With regard to the struggle against prepaid water meters, little is being done to collectivise the strategy of bypassing the meter, with the recent research conducted by the Coalition Against Water Privatisation and the APF showing how bypassing of the prepaid water meter has become individualised in Phiri (Coalition Against Water Privatisation & Anti-Privatisation Forum 2006). Since 2006, it would seem that very few branches of the SECC have been proactively encouraging the act of bypassing in a collective manner. Members of branches who do so use each act of bypassing to teach residents about the need for a collective strategy of refusing to pay for water, and the reasons behind the installation of prepaid water meters in Phiri. In this manner, they are able to provide an alternative to the teachings of Johannesburg Water and the municipality and, in a very real and immediate way, institute an act of resistance as part of a generalised strategy of resistance amongst a collective of residents.

It is hoped that, in trying to rebuild the SECC, not too much attention will be given to the 'nuts and bolts of delivery' as they play themselves out in the corridors of state power, and that the focus will be rather on the ways in which they manifest themselves in the lived realities of residents fighting for decent lives in which they do not have to struggle to access basic services such as water and electricity. With an orientation towards the struggles of ordinary people, the SECC should be bringing together its own members from different branches to share experiences and ideas of the state's changing strategies and tactics for imposing 'cost recovery' on the poor. In this way, perhaps Phiri could learn from the experiments under way in White City, Jabavu, and greater knowledge could be produced about the struggle against prepaid water meters through activists speaking to and engaging with each other. Over time, perhaps the SECC and SCR will be able to overcome their differences and both contribute to the development of effective strategies of resistance and alternatives to the logic of the market as it continues to take root in the lives of Soweto residents. What remains certain is that there will always be a need for struggle against this market logic, as people seek protection from its cruelties.

Conclusion

It would seem that the SECC has enjoyed its greatest strength and influence when it has listened to the voices of ordinary Sowetans. Initial attempts to begin building a movement against neo-liberalism in Soweto only began to succeed once the community started being heard. Through interaction and engagement between and amongst a growing community of seasoned activists and residents, united in their action against the municipality and Eskom, a movement was built that captured the imaginations of Sowetans and activists fighting neo-liberalism around the world. It is perhaps through attempts by groups of activists to predetermine the programmes of the SECC according to their own political or other aims, rather than by listening to the needs of the people of Soweto, that the problems have arisen. Returning to the people, in a real attempt to listen rather than to tell, is probably the only way for the SECC to begin rebuilding itself.

Notes

1   From 1984 to 1994 the South African Parliament was divided into three houses, each with separate powers, for whites, Indians and coloureds. Africans were given 'representation' in a separate system called the 'bantustans' or 'homelands'. While this system suggested that each race group was able to 'rule' or 'govern' itself and take responsibility for its 'own affairs', in reality it entrenched inequality and placed the reins of power firmly in the hands of whites.

2   The term 'cost recovery' is used by the state and private companies to refer to the process of collection of the fees charged by providers of basic services to the users, implying that users are allowing the providers to recuperate the costs incurred in providing the services. In discussions and debates within the Anti-Privatisation Forum and the Coalition Against Water Privatisation, several activists have argued that the use of the term is disingenuous, as it tries to hide the fact that payment for basic services generates a profit for the individual private company by suggesting that user fees cover only the costs of delivery. We therefore choose to place the phrase in inverted commas to highlight this blurring of the truth.

3   Sanco was a national structure with branches in various townships. It was the main civic structure organising in township communities under the banner of the United Democratic Front in the 1980s and 1990s. With the unbanning of political parties and the rebirth of the ANC as a political party seeking to govern, Sanco came under the sway of the Congress tradition, and began to take its direction from the ANC. As Sanco transformed and positioned itself for corporatist governance in the 1990s, local branches and members suffered as the eyes and minds of leadership turned away from local needs to the interests of big business and the mandate to transform service delivery along

business principles. While Sanco continues to exist at a national level, there are very few functional local branches, and the organisation and its leadership have been involved in several scandals exposed in the media over the years.

4   Eskom is the Electricity Supply Commission, South Africa's national energy utility and the largest provider of energy on the African continent. For more details see Gentle, Chapter 2 and Greenberg, Chapter 3 in this volume.

5   With regard to the provision of free basic water and electricity, the government has committed itself to the provision of a basic 6 kilolitres of water and 50 kilowatts of electricity per household per month. These basic amounts have been referred to as 'lifelines' as they claim to provide for the basic survival needs of an individual. However, activists have argued that these basic amounts do not live up to their name as they do not meet the basic minimum requirements for individual survival. A few studies (Coalition Against Water Privatisation & Anti-Privatisation Forum 2003, 2004; Diaz & Meth 2004) have shown how the introduction of 'lifeline' provisions has entrenched inequality as a defining feature of service delivery in South Africa, and has been used by the government to prove its 'commitment' to free basic services for the poor without any acknowledgement of how minimal these provisions are. These studies have gone to great lengths to prove how much lower than the actual needs of households these 'lifelines' are, pointing to large household sizes and the existence of tenants or backyard dwellers in many township communities. In addition, in areas like Phiri, Soweto, the prepaid system is being sold as a more efficient means to deliver free water.

6   For a critical investigation into the effects of prepaid water meters on the lives of residents of Stretford, Extension 4, Orange Farm, see Coalition Against Water Privatisation and Anti-Privatisation Forum 2003.

7   Johannesburg Water is the private entity responsible for water provision in Johannesburg. It is owned by the Johannesburg City Council, but its management is contracted out to Suez Lyonnaise Des Eaux.

8   The 'toyi-toyi' is the name given to the popular form of protest song and dance that emerged in the South African liberation struggle and that continues to colour protest actions today.

9   For a thorough description of the initial experiences in Phiri with regard to the installation of the prepaid water meters and resistance against it, see Coalition Against Water Privatisation and Anti-Privatisation Forum 2004.

References

ANC (African National Congress) (1994) *The Reconstruction and Development Programme: A policy framework.* Johannesburg: Umanyano Publications

Coalition Against Water Privatisation & Anti-Privatisation Forum (2003) *Nothing for mahala: The forced installation of prepaid water meters in Stretford, Extension 4, Orange Farm, Johannesburg.* Johannesburg: Coalition Against Water Privatisation

Coalition Against Water Privatisation & Anti-Privatisation Forum (2004) *The struggle against silent disconnections: Prepaid meters and the struggle for life in Phiri, Soweto, Johannesburg.* Johannesburg: Coalition Against Water Privatisation

Coalition Against Water Privatisation & Anti-Privatisation Forum (2006) *Lessons from the war against prepaid water meters: The struggle against silent disconnections continues, Johannesburg.* Johannesburg: Coalition Against Water Privatisation

De Angelis M (1998) Marx and primitive accumulation. *The Commoner* 2. Accessed 15 March 2006, http://www.commoner.org.uk

Desai A (2001) Neoliberalism & resistance in South Africa. *Monthly Review* 54(8). Accessed 16 March 2006, http://www.monthlyreview.org/0103desai.htm

Diaz R & Meth C (2004) Increases in poverty in South Africa, 1999–2002. *Development Southern Africa* 21(1): 59–85

Egan A & Wafer A (2004) *The Soweto Electricity Crisis Committee.* Durban: Centre For Civil Society

Fiil-Flynn M (2001) *The electricity crisis in Soweto.* Municipal Services Project Occasional Papers Series No. 4. Cape Town: Municipal Services Project

Globalise Resistance (2002) *The first political prisoners of neoliberalism.* Accessed 16 March 2006, http://www.resist.org.uk/reports/background/soweto.html

Haffajee F (2004) Fact, fiction & the New Left. *Mail & Guardian* 11–17 June

McInnes P (2006) Making the kettle boil: Rights talk and political mobilisation around electricity and water services in Soweto. Unpublished master's dissertation, Department of Sociology, University of the Witwatersrand, Johannesburg

Naidoo P & Veriava A (2005) Re-membering movements: Trade unions and new social movements in neoliberal South Africa. In Centre for Civil Society *From local processes to global forces.* Centre for Civil Society Research Reports Vol. 1. Durban: University of KwaZulu-Natal

Ngwane T & Veriava A (2004) Strategies and tactics: Movements in the neoliberal transition. In D McKinley & P Naidoo (eds) *Development update: Mobilizing for change. The rise of the new social movements in South Africa.* Johannesburg: Interfund

Polanyi K (1944) *The great transformation.* Boston: Beacon Press

Interviews

Magwaza V, former deputy-chairperson of SECC, member of SECC, member of APF, Chairperson of Coalition Against Water Privatisation, staff member of the Freedom of Expression Institute, August 2006

Mokwena I, chairperson of PCRF, PCRF representative to the SECC, co-ordinator of the APF Research Subcommittee, June 2006

Molobela J, member of the PCRF and SECC, member of the APF Research Subcommittee, June 2006

Ngwane T, former organiser of the APF, organiser of the SECC, June 2006

CHAPTER 13

South African carbon trading: A counterproductive climate change strategy

Patrick Bond and Graham Erion

If in coming decades floods periodically inundate the eastern third of South Africa and droughts are unbearable in the western two-thirds, and if the main ports of eThekwini, Cape Town, Richard's Bay, Buffalo City and Mandela Metropole (including the new Coega complex) are gradually submerged – perhaps four metres below present sea levels in a century – once sufficiently large sections of Antarctica, the Arctic Circle and Greenland melt, where might South Africans turn to hurl the blame?

Mainly to Gauteng politicians and capitalists, that's where. State policy-makers and allied corporations active in the last two decades of the 20th century and the first of the 21st have driven the country's energy systems into unprecedented contradictions and crises. Perhaps none is more threatening than Eskom's contribution to climate change, amplified by the African National Congress (ANC) government's 2004 policy which aims to commodify the air as a mitigating strategy.

For those concerned about global warming, there are two approaches that can be taken, both of which will be considered in this chapter: a radical approach (i.e., going to the problem's *roots*) which would entail a genuine transformation of energy, industry and transport; or the prevailing neo-liberal strategy which entails the status quo plus gimmicks such as the Kyoto Protocol's Clean Development Mechanism (CDM). The latter is far more likely, so it is to the critique of current trends that we turn first, starting with a flashback to mid-2006.[1]

Even then, as global awareness about climate change emerged, central government in Pretoria sent ever stronger signals that it would back the status quo:

- 11 September 2006, Somerset West (Western Cape): Speaking to the UN Intergovernmental Panel on Climate Change, South African Minister of Environmental Affairs and Tourism Marthinus van Schalkwyk rates CDM promotion second in his three priorities for the upcoming Nairobi Conference of Parties meeting (between more adaptation funding and tougher targets for Kyoto): 'The 17 CDM projects in the pipeline in Sub-Saharan Africa account for only 1.7 per cent of the total of 990 projects worldwide. To build faith in the carbon market and to ensure that everyone shares in its benefits, we must address the obstacles that African countries face' (Van Schalkwyk 2006).

- 5 October 2006, Monterey: In the wake of the July 2006 G8 summit in St Petersburg, which ignored climate change, the group's energy ministers plus 12 other major polluters meet in Mexico. Again there are no results, and as the BBC reports, hopes that the USA Department of Energy would consider mandatory carbon dioxide (CO_2) caps for businesses were dashed because 'the White House Council on Environmental Quality [a hard-line group of advisers with close links to the US oil industry] have ruled that out' (Harrabin 2006). Russia does not bother attending.
- 30 October 2006, London: The British government releases *The Stern Review: The Economics of Climate Change*, which estimates climate change costs of 5–20 per cent of global GDP at current warming rates. Stern calls for demand reduction of emissions-intensive products, energy efficiency, avoiding deforestation and new low-carbon technology, and insists that carbon trading has a key role (HM Treasury UK 2006).
- 15 November 2006, New York: The Oxford American Dictionary announces the term 'carbon neutral' (first used in 1991) is the 'word of the year' for 2006, even though some offsets such as tree plantations cause enormous ecological damage and many other offsets are being unveiled as illegitimate.
- 17 November 2006, Nairobi: The 12th UN climate change Conference of Parties (COP) ends. After 11 days of work there is still no timetable for post-Kyoto Protocol negotiations or reductions. Nairobi delegates and even many NGOs such as Oxfam adopt an uncritical perspective on carbon trading, and a new Adaptation Fund is established but with resources reliant upon CDM revenues. Activists from the Gaia Foundation, Global Forest Coalition, Global Justice Ecology Project, Large Scale Biofuels Action Group, the STOP GE Trees Campaign and World Rainforest Movement condemn the COP's move to biofuels and genetically engineered timber technology, which are being promoted through the CDM.
- 22 November 2006, Johannesburg: Van Schalkwyk writes in *Business Day* newspaper that South Africa achieved its key Nairobi objectives, including kick-starting the CDM in Africa, and welcomes UN support for more 'equitable distribution of CDM projects' given that only 1.5 per cent of projects are planned for sub-Saharan Africa. He concludes that this work 'sends a clear signal to carbon markets of our common resolve to secure the future of the Kyoto regime' (*Business Day* 22 November 2006).
- 24 November 2006, Pretoria: The largest industrial subsidies in African history are confirmed at the Coega export processing zone near Port Elizabeth. Alcan will build a US$2.7 billion aluminium smelter thanks to vast electricity subsidies from Eskom. The following week, the University of Cape Town's environmental studies professor, Richard Fuggle, attacks the CO_2 emissions associated with the Coega deal in his retirement speech, describing

> Van Schalkwyk as a 'political lightweight' who is 'unable to press for environmental considerations to take precedence over "development"' (Fuggle 2006).
> * 6 December 2006, Pretoria and Canberra: Van Schalkwyk and his Australian Conservative-government counterpart, Ian Campbell, sign a co-operation agreement to 'identify, develop and implement a program of joint activities designed to deliver practical outcomes of mutual benefit' (DEAT 2006) – which has the effect of lining South Africa up as an ally with one of the regimes most opposed to climate change action.
> * 15 December 2006, Washington, DC: The Asian Development Bank proudly announces that, aided by its Prototype Carbon Fund, the carbon trading market 'rose from about 13 million tons of CO_2-equivalent in 2001 to 704 million tons in 2005, when its value totaled $11 billion. The value of the market continues to rise – it was $7.5 billion in the first quarter of 2006 alone' (Kapadia 2006).

With climate change posing perhaps the gravest threat to humanity in coming years, and with free market economics still the global ruling elite's most powerful ethos, it is little wonder so much effort has gone into making the latter a solution to the former, no matter how much evidence has recently emerged to the contrary. As Daniel Becker of the Sierra Club's Global Warming and Energy Program explains, 'It's sort of the moral equivalent of hiring a domestic. We will pay you to clean our mess. For a long time here in America we have believed in the polluter pays principle. This could become a pay to pollute principle.'[2]

The idea of paying to pollute immediately reminds us that South Africa has amongst the world's most extreme distributions of income. The low wages and awful conditions faced by domestic workers, for example, reflect a historical legacy of injustice and apartheid, subsequently cemented by market-oriented labour relations – in a post-1994 context in which reparations have been rejected by the corporate-friendly ANC government, and the unemployment rate has doubled. In the same way that apartheid represented a gift to white people, according to Larry Lohmann from the British NGO Cornerhouse and the Durban Group network which formed in 2004 against carbon trading, '[t]he distribution of carbon allowances [the prerequisite for trading] constitutes one of the largest, if not the largest, projects for creation and regressive distribution of property rights in human history' (Wamasti 2007). What President Mbeki calls 'global apartheid' is hence reinforced by carbon trading based on historical allocations of pollution rights. To borrow Becker's metaphor, this occurs in the same way that pre-existing wage and social relations – evident especially in inexpensive domestic labour – are cemented by strengthened property rights in contemporary South Africa, in the wake of what the UN rightly termed a crime against humanity.

It works like this. Rather than forcing countries or firms to reduce their own greenhouse gas emissions, Kyoto Protocol designers created – from thin air – a 'carbon market' and gave countries a minimal reduction target (5 per cent from 1990 emissions levels, to be achieved by 2012). They can either meet that target through their own reductions or by purchasing emissions credits from countries/firms that reduce their own greenhouse gases below their target level. Carbon trading has become the key response of the international community to the climate crisis, most prominently through the Kyoto Protocol's CDM.[3]

This market does not lack for controversy, particularly because fatuous 'carbon offset' public relations fibs have persuaded politicians and celebrities that they can make their global conferences, rock concerts and other extravaganzas 'carbon neutral'. Contemplating what might be called 'carbon colonialism', *The Guardian* columnist George Monbiot considered a *Nature* report (Schiermeier 2006) on worsening global warming attributable to increased methane emissions from plants, which were formerly thought to be solely a 'sink' for CO_2 emissions:

> It should shake our confidence in one of our favourite means of tackling [climate change]: paying other people to clear up the mess we've made. Both through the unofficial carbon market and by means of a provision of the Kyoto Protocol called the Clean Development Mechanism, people, companies and states can claim to reduce their emissions by investing in carbon-friendly projects in poorer countries. Among other schemes, you can earn carbon credits by paying people to plant trees. As the trees grow, they are supposed to absorb the carbon we release by burning fossil fuels.

> Despite the new findings, it still seems fair to say that forests are a net carbon sink, taking in more greenhouse gases than they release. If they are felled, the carbon in both the trees and the soil they grow on is likely to enter the atmosphere. So preserving them remains a good idea, for this and other reasons. But what the new study provides is yet more evidence that the accountancy behind many of the 'carbon offset' schemes is flawed.

> While they have a pretty good idea of how much carbon our factories and planes and cars are releasing, scientists are much less certain about the amount of carbon tree planting will absorb. When you drain or clear the soil to plant trees, for example, you are likely to release some carbon, but it is hard to tell how much. Planting trees in one place might stunt trees elsewhere, as they could dry up a river which was feeding a forest downstream. Or by protecting your forest against loggers, you might be driving them into another forest.

> As global temperatures rise, trees in many places will begin to die back, releasing the carbon they contain. Forest fires could wipe them out completely. The timing is also critical: emissions saved today are far more valuable, in terms of reducing climate change, than emissions saved in ten years' time, yet the trees you plant start absorbing carbon long after your factories released it. All this made the figures speculative, but the new findings, with their massive uncertainty range (plants, the researchers say,

produce somewhere between ten and thirty per cent of the planet's methane) make an honest sum impossible. In other words, you cannot reasonably claim to have swapped the carbon stored in oil or coal for carbon absorbed by trees. Mineral carbon, while it remains in the ground, is stable and quantifiable. Biological carbon is labile and uncertain.

To add to the confusion, in order to show that you are really reducing atmospheric carbon by planting or protecting a forest, you must demonstrate that if you hadn't done it something else would have happened. Not only is this very difficult, it is also an invitation for a country or a company to threaten an increase in emissions. It can then present the alternative (doing what it would have done anyway) as an improvement on its destructive plans, and claim the difference as a carbon reduction...

But perhaps the most destructive effect of the carbon offset trade is that it allows us to believe we can carry on polluting. The government can keep building roads and airports and we can keep flying to Thailand for our holidays, as long as we purchase absolution by giving a few quid to a tree planting company. How do you quantify complacency? (Monbiot 2006)

In economic terms, would this system work as designed, regardless of its ethical and ecological shortcomings? There are very serious theoretical problems with the carbon market, which economists would recognise if they gave it serious thought. As Gar Lipow explains:

Neither emissions trading nor green taxes are the most efficient way to reduce carbon emissions, compared to an alternative combination of regulations, public works, and, secondarily, green taxes in the form of a green capital tax. Both emissions trading and green taxes are an inefficient way of reducing carbon emissions because they are largely driven by fossil fuel consumption and fossil fuel demand is extremely price inelastic [no matter how high the price goes, you are dependent and will find it hard to cut consumption].

In the short run, some savings may be achieved by simple behaviour changes. But past a certain point you are giving up the ability to heat your home, get to work and in general experience other things vital to a decent life – so in the face of higher energy prices you will give up something else and simply pay for more energy.

In the longer run, better capital investments can reduce such consumption without giving up vital things. But a combination of unequal access to capital, split incentives (where the person who makes the investment is not the one who would obtain the savings), transaction costs of energy savings vs. other investments, and other factors, mean[s] capital investment does not occur as you would expect in the face of rising energy prices. (Lipow 2006)

The remainder of this chapter explores the roots of the controversies around carbon trading, as well as the adverse effects of this market in South Africa.

South Africa's contribution to climate change

The international debate over climate change is heating up, as we see more and more irrefutable evidence of global warming and climate turbulence emerging. The overarching problem is well known to South Africans who follow the news; less understood – if it is understood at all – is the extent of this country's responsibility for the world's overdose of greenhouse gases. Like filthy laundry, it sometimes seems like a national secret that the economy we inherited from apartheid is so addicted to fossil fuel, and moreover that the post-apartheid government has made the situation *much much worse.*

South Africa is not included in the Kyoto Protocol's Annex 1 list of countries that should make emissions reductions, and hence the economy as a whole is not subject to targets at this stage. But we will be in future and, looking ahead, officials and corporations – and even a few NGOs which should know better – are promoting the Protocol's CDM as a way to continue South Africa's hedonistic output of greenhouse gases, and earn profits in the process. Pretoria's own climate change strategy argues that the 'CDM primarily presents a range of commercial opportunities' and indeed 'could be a very important source of foreign direct investment' (DEAT 2004: 2).

But do we deserve to earn such 'investment' given South African industry's indefensible contribution to global warming? On the contrary, from his base at the University of Zululand, Professor Mark Jury has gathered the following damning facts about South Africa's *debt* to the planet:

- South Africa contributes 1.8 per cent of total greenhouse gases, making it one of the top contributing countries in the world;
- the energy sector is responsible for 87 per cent of CO_2, 96 per cent of sulphur dioxide and 94 per cent of nitrous oxide emissions;
- 90 per cent of energy is generated from the combustion of coal that contains greater than 1 per cent sulphur and greater than 30 per cent ash;
- with a domestic economy powered by coal, South Africa has experienced a fivefold increase in CO_2 emissions since 1950;
- South Africa is a signatory to the United Nations Framework Convention on Climate Change (UNFCCC) and the Montreal Protocol, yet CO_2 emissions increased 18 per cent between 1990 and 2000;
- South Africa only enacted legally binding air pollution regulations in 2004 via the National Environmental Management Air Quality Act (No. 39 of 2004), but energy efficiency is low;
- in rural areas of South Africa, approximately 3 million households burn fuelwood for their energy needs, causing deforestation, reduction of CO_2 sinks, and indoor health problems;
- the industrial sector consumes 2.6 quads of energy (57 per cent of total primary energy consumption) and emits 66.8 metric tons of carbon (65 per cent of total carbon emissions from fossil fuels), though industry's contribution to GDP is 29 per cent;

- since 1970, South Africa consistently has consumed the most energy and emitted the most carbon per dollar of GDP among major countries. South African energy intensity measured at 33.5 K BTU per US$ unit is nearly at China's level;
- South Africa's carbon intensity is far higher than in most other countries due to its dependence on coal; and
- household and industrial energy consumption across the continent is predicted to increase by over 300 per cent in the next 50 years with significant growth in sulphur and nitrogen emissions. (Jury 2004)

Coal is by far the biggest single South African contributor to global warming, representing between 80 and 95 per cent of CO_2 emissions since the 1950s. But liquid CO_2 emissions, mainly from transport, have risen to the level of more than 10 000 metric tons per year since the early 1990s. It is regrettable but true, just as in Eastern Europe (whose CO_2 emissions are well below 1990 levels), that the long recession of the early 1990s was the only point in South Africa's history since the economic crisis of the early 1930s when CO_2 emissions stabilised and dropped slightly. Needless to say, South Africa is by far the primary global warming villain in Africa, responsible for 42 per cent of the continent's CO_2 emissions – more than Egypt, Nigeria, Algeria and Libya combined.

Given the vast CO_2 emissions increases by South Africa, especially during the 1980s, added to similar increases in global greenhouse gas emissions, it is only logical to find an average one degree Celcius increase in our region's temperature, over historic norms. This is merely the surface-level statistical information about the climate change crisis, as it emerges. Much more could be said about the various other indicators, ranging from droughts/floods in South Africa and Africa as a whole, to the hurricanes which belted George W Bush's oil-producing and refining belt in Texas/Louisiana in September 2005.

As noted, the Kyoto Protocol came into effect in February 2005, but South Africa is not subject to its emissions reduction targets at this stage. However, since we will be part of the Protocol in future, some state officials, international financiers and local corporations – and even a few NGOs – are promoting a gimmick, the Protocol's CDM, which substitutes investments in carbon-reducing projects for genuine emissions reductions.

To critics, including dozens of environmental justice networks which signed the October 2004 'Durban Declaration on Climate Justice',[4] the CDM and especially the new carbon market that permits trade in pollution rights represent misleading 'greenwash'. Carbon trading justifies letting the USA, the European Union and Japan continue their emissions, in exchange for a small profit pay-out to dubious South African firms and municipalities for reductions in local carbon. Those reductions are ones we should be making in any event.

For example, methane that escapes from Africa's largest landfill, at Bisasar Road in the Durban residential suburb of Clare Estate, should be captured, cleaned and safely turned into energy. eThekwini officials instead aim to burn the methane on-site, which entails keeping the toxic dump open for at least another seven years – though the ANC had promised its closure in 1996 due to community opposition to its presence. The officials' goal is to sell carbon credits via the World Bank to big corporations and northern governments. But a famous community activist, Sajida Khan, appears to have frightened the World Bank off for now. Although Khan died in July 2007, her environmental impact assessment filing in August 2005 was a crucial intervention. At the time of writing, there had been no subsequent effort to market Bisasar Road to carbon credit investors.

Unfortunately, the Department of Environmental Affairs and Tourism (DEAT) supports this form of carbon colonialism. In September 2004 the DEAT issued the *National Climate Change Response Strategy*, insisting that South Africa must understand 'up-front' how the 'CDM primarily presents a range of commercial opportunities, both big and small. This could be a very important source of foreign direct investment' (DEAT 2004: 2). In October 2005, a gathering of environmental activists at the University of KwaZulu-Natal rejected the CDM policy outright.

Indeed, the economy's fivefold increase in CO_2 emissions since 1950, and 20 per cent increase during the 1990s, can largely be blamed upon the attempt by Eskom, the mining houses and metals smelters to brag of having the world's cheapest electricity. Given that industry emits 20 times more carbon tonnage per unit of economic output per person than even the USA, South African capital's reliance upon fossil fuels is scandalous. Not only are vast carbon-based profits fleeing to the mining houses' offshore financial headquarters – there are also very few jobs in these smelters, including the proposed US$2.5 billion Coega aluminium project for which the notorious Canadian firm Alcan has been promised lucrative sweetheart deals from Eskom, the Department of Trade and Industry and the Industrial Development Corporation (IDC). Fewer than 1 000 jobs will be created in the smelter, though it will consume more electricity than the entire nearby city of Port Elizabeth.

Aside from carbon trading, the main answer to the climate question provided by Public Enterprises Minister Alec Erwin is fast-tracking the dangerous, outmoded Pebble Bed Modular Reactor technology rejected by German nuclear energy producers some years ago (for more details see Fig, Chapter 6 in this volume). As noted below, that reckless strategy will continue to be fought by Earthlife Africa, the environmental lobby group that has won two important preliminary court battles against Erwin's special advisor on energy matters, former DEAT Director-general Chippy Olver.

Instead, renewable sources like wind, solar, wave, tidal and biomass technology are the only logical way forward for this century's energy system, but still get only a tiny pittance of government support (see McDaid, Chapter 7 in this volume), a fraction of the hundreds of millions of rands wasted on nuclear research and development. In the meantime, because of alleged 'resource constraints', communities like Kennedy Road in Durban, bordering the Bisasar landfill – where impoverished people rely upon dump scavenging for income – are still denied basic services like electricity. While Kennedy Road activists are promised a few jobs and bursaries, the plan to burn the landfill's methane gas on-site could release a cocktail of new toxins into the already poisoned air. Gas flaring would increase 15-fold under the scheme Durban has tried selling to the World Bank. The generator's filters would never entirely contain the aromatic hydro-carbons, nitrous oxides, volatile organic compounds, dioxins and furans released in the process.

Aside from the World Bank, the cash-rich companies which most need to cut these deals to protect their future rights to pollute are the oil majors, beneficiaries of windfall profits as the price per barrel soared from US$11 in 1998 to more than US$70 in 2006 and stood at approximately US$100 in early 2008. The Bank itself admits in a recent study that these and other extractive firms' depletion of Africa's natural resources drain the national wealth by hundreds of dollars per person each year in Gabon (whose citizens lost US$2 241 each in 2000), the Republic of the Congo (–US$727), Nigeria (–US$210), Cameroon (–US$152), Mauritania (–US$147) and Côte d'Ivoire (–US$100) (World Bank 2005).

In the process, the oil fields are attracting a new generation of USA troops to bases being developed in the Gulf of Guinea. Once again, Pretoria is amplifying the worst trends, as Human Sciences Research Council researchers John Daniel and Jessica Lutchman concluded in their analysis of sleazy oil deals – not only by Imvume (a corrupt oil transaction company which was used as a front operation to funnel millions of dollars to the ANC) in Saddam's Iraq, replete with transfers to ruling party coffers, but also encompassing the Sudanese and Equatorial Guinean dictatorships: 'In its scramble to acquire a share of this market, the ANC government has abandoned any regard to those ethical and human rights principles which it once proclaimed would form the basis of its foreign policy' (Daniel & Lutchman 2005).

President Thabo Mbeki himself downplayed Sudan's Darfur crisis, even when sending peacekeeping troops to the region because, as he said after a meeting with President Bush in mid-2005, 'If you denounce Sudan as genocidal, what next? Don't you have to arrest the president? The solution doesn't lie in making radical solutions – not for us in Africa' (Becker & Sanger 2005). Pretoria's national oil company, PetroSA, had five months earlier signed a deal to share its technicians with Sudan's Sudapet, so as to conduct explorations in Block 14 in that country, where it enjoyed exclusive oil concession rights (Fabricius 2005).

Those ethical principles should be urgently revisited now, since our future generations' very survival is at stake. Since the DEAT's October 2005 National Climate Change Conference (DEAT 2005) did not engage seriously with these critiques, its attendees will be regarded as a large part of the problem. The irony is that while generating enormous carbon emissions, energy is utilised in an extremely irrational way. The unjust system leaves too many without access, while a few large corporations benefit disproportionately, as discussed below.

In sum, our purpose is to dig deeper in order to uncover an emerging form of environmental injustice, the carbon market, and to highlight cutting-edge attempts to mitigate that injustice through civil-society activism and advocacy that stretches from retail household reconnections to international environmental negotiations. This is not an entirely celebratory account, for notwithstanding successful civic resistance to South Africa's largest proposed project, at Bisasar Road, one of the concerns our research has uncovered is the failure of the environmental justice critique to penetrate the realm of policy. In that sphere, Big Oil and the South African minerals-energy complex (Fine & Rustomjee 1996) appear to have the upper hand.

A brief history of carbon trading

The intellectual origins of carbon trading can be traced back to a small publication in 1968 entitled *Pollution, Property, and Prices* by Canadian economist John Dales (Dales 1968). Like Garrett Hardin – who penned his famous essay 'The Tragedy of the Commons' that same year – Dales believed that natural resources in their unrestricted common property form would face tragic over-exploitation by people acting in their rational self-interest (Dales 1968; Hardin 1968).

Yet Dales went much further than Hardin in his solution to this problem. Dales proposed to control water pollution by setting a total quota of allowable waste for each waterway and then created a 'market' in equivalent 'pollution rights' for firms to discharge pollutants up to this level (Dales 1968: 81). These rights, referred to as 'transferable property rights...for the disposal of wastes', would be sold to firms which could then trade them amongst themselves (Dales 1968: 85). The more efficient firms would make the largest pollution reductions and sell their credits to less efficient firms, thereby guaranteeing a reduction of pollution at the lowest social cost.

Though Dales's proposal took a back seat to the command-and-control approach that characterised environmental policy during the 1970s, his idea would resurface in the following decades. Proponents of pollution trading – typically a mix of industry groups and self-described 'free market environmentalists' – echoed Dales's logic about greater efficiency, and added claims of lower administrative costs and greater incentives for innovation. After a series of proposals and pilot projects by the Environmental Protection Agency, the USA Congress amended the Clean Air Act in 1990 to create a national emissions trading scheme in sulphur dioxide, the main pollutant behind acid rain. Until 1997, the USA was the only country in the world with any significant pollution trading scheme. This would change following the Kyoto Protocol.

Though carbon trading was initially met with hostility from some European countries and environmental NGOs during the third Conference of the Parties to the UNFCCC in Kyoto, it was eventually adopted and appears in three separate articles of the final text of the Protocol.

Article 17 of the Protocol establishes a system of 'Emissions Trading' whereby Annex 1 countries (e.g. developed countries that have accepted binding emissions reduction targets) can trade emissions credits amongst themselves if they overshoot their targets. This aspect of trading can be controversial, especially when applied to former East Bloc countries such as Russia and the Ukraine. The collapse of the Soviet economy during the 1990s meant that these countries today have a 'free pass' for reducing emissions. Their contracted economies have already reduced gross emissions by nearly 40 per cent.[5]

For this reason the unfavourable label 'hot air' has been widely applied to this form of trading, since it has nothing to do with deliberate efforts to reduce emissions and everything to do with economic collapse. However, Europe's larger considerations about energy security and access to natural gas may still benefit Russia and the Ukraine in this market and increase the likelihood of future trading under Article 17 (PCF 2005).

The second type of carbon trading is Joint Implementation (JI) – Article 4 of the Protocol – whereby Annex 1 countries can invest in projects in other Annex 1 countries, with the investing country receiving credit for the host country's reductions. Like emissions trading, JI has thus far not played a significant role in the international carbon market.[6] According to the World Bank's Prototype Carbon Fund (PCF), this is due to a lack of investor confidence and institutional set-up in JI countries (PCF 2005).

With emissions trading and JI playing minimal roles, the global carbon market is at present almost entirely made up of transactions under Article 12 of Kyoto, the CDM. The CDM provides an opportunity for Annex 1 countries to receive emission reductions credits to use against their own targets by investing in projects to reduce or sequester greenhouse gas emissions in non-Annex 1 countries (i.e. developing countries).

One of the most controversial aspects of Article 12 is that it requires projects to show '[r]eductions in emissions that are additional to any that would occur in the absence of the certified project activity'.[7] This requirement has become known as 'additionality' and is intended to ensure that there is a net emissions reduction.[8] This is what Sasol fell foul of in its fake 2005 CDM proposal. Sasol tried to market its natural gas pipeline from Mozambique as a case of 'additionality' (in which the firm only did something above and beyond what it would have otherwise done in order to acquire carbon credits), even though the pipeline was already completed. In discussion (with Graham Erion and others), an official admitted it was a false case of additionality.

Another controversial aspect of the CDM is the requirement that projects must help developing countries in 'achieving sustainable development'.[9] The sustainable development requirement represented a hard-won victory for many of the countries and environmental NGOs that were initially opposed to the CDM. However, in meetings of the COP subsequent to the UNFCCC, countries have been allowed to set their own definition of sustainable development and judge whether a project meets these criteria, rather than adopt a universal definition that could better ensure the accountability of those authorities overseeing project approval.

A variety of domestic and international governance structures have been set up to oversee CDM projects. There are three key institutions governing CDM projects through their validation powers. The first of these is each host country's Designated National Authority (DNA). The DNA is the first institution to review a project's documentation, in the form of the Project Design Document (PDD) that lays out all the relevant information about the project.[10]

Assuming that everything is in order, the DNA will write a letter of approval saying that all participants are voluntary and that the sustainable development criteria have been met. As to the actual composition of the DNAs, they will often be housed in government departments and staffed by public-sector employees, such as in South Africa where the DNA is in the Department of Minerals and Energy. However, in other cases, such as Cambodia, the DNA function is contracted out to private consultancies.

Once the letter of approval has been issued by the DNA, the PDD is then assessed by a Designated Operational Entity (DOE). Unlike the DNAs, the DOEs are all private-sector entities. To date, 12 companies have been accredited as DOEs, though not all of them can accredit every single methodology. To validate a project the DOE will review the PDD to consider whether the project's methodology is in line with approved methodologies, the claimed emissions reductions and baseline scenarios are accurate, and the project is 'additional'. In making its determination, the DOE will also post the PDD on the internet for a 30-day public comment period.

With the approval of the DOE and the DNA, the final stage in project validation is the CDM Executive Board (EB/CDM) where the findings of the DOE and DNA are reviewed and a final decision is made whether or not to allow the project to start generating Certified Emissions Reductions (CERs).[11] There is also a final 30-day public comment period while the project is at the EB/CDM stage.

With only 12 members on the EB/CDM, they do not have the resources to closely scrutinise every project that comes across their desks. As such, they rely heavily on decisions of DOEs. According to Eric Haites, a private-sector consultant in the carbon market, 'the vast majority of validation and certification decisions by DOEs are expected to be final; the Executive Board only deals with the problem cases' (Haites 2006).

Carbon market trends

With the process of validation now established and some of the relevant institutions explained, let us turn our attention to how the global carbon market has developed since Kyoto. The first thing to note is the large role played by northern firms and consultants – such as Ecosecurities – who are able to provide a certain level of capacity and expertise that might not be as readily accessible in southern countries. Another example of this has been the prominence of the World Bank's PCF. In partnership with 6 governments and 17 companies, plus a budget of US$180 million, the PCF describes itself as 'a leader in the creation of a carbon market to help deal with the threat posed by climate change' (PCF 2004: 7). As the single largest purchaser of CERs (as of September 2006) the PCF had 32 projects in development with a total CER value potential of US$165 million (PCF 2004: 7).

A second noteworthy trend is that the market is heavily concentrated in large middle-income countries led by India, China and Brazil. The PCF admits that 'this concentration of CDM flows towards large middle-income countries is consistent with the current direction of Foreign Direct Investment' (PCF 2004: 5). By contrast, poorer countries, especially in Africa, have been almost entirely left behind. By September 2006, South Africa and Morocco were the only countries on the continent to have validated a CDM project. According to the PCF, '[t]his under-representation of Africa raises deep concerns about the overall equity of the distribution of the CDM market, as the vast majority of African countries have not, for the moment, been able to pick up even one first deal' (PCF 2005: 25). Early evidence hence contradicts the notion that the CDM will uplift the world's poorest countries to a cleaner path of development.

The other major trend in the carbon market has been the enormous profitability of non-carbon-related projects. While renewable energy projects (which offset CO_2 emissions) make up nearly 58 per cent of the total number of projects, they account for only 15 per cent of the total number of CERs that have been issued (Fenhann 2006). By contrast, projects abating nitrogen and hydrofluorocarbons (HFC_{23}) comprise fewer than 2 per cent of the overall *number* of projects, yet make up 74 per cent of the CERs issued to date by project sector (PCF 2005).

These projects are known as 'low-hanging fruit' since their high returns mean they are the first to be picked by investors. The reason is that HFC_{23} has 11 700 times the potency of CO_2, and since credits are in CO_2-equivalent a relatively small capture of HFC_{23} can bring an enormous windfall of credits. According to the PCF, the large amount of non-CO_2 projects in the carbon market has meant that 'traditional energy efficiency or fuel switching projects, which were initially expected to represent the bulk of the CDM, account for less than 5 per cent [of it now]' (PCF 2005: 5).

How these trends affect the legitimacy of the carbon market, and for whose benefit, are crucial questions for South Africa that we turn to now.

Corporate CO_2 beneficiaries

All South Africans must face up to their responsibility for permitting the country's ruthless power brokers – mining/smelting magnates such as the late Brett Kebble, the Oppenheimer family, Lakshmi Mittal, and newly enriched Patrice Matsepe, Tokyo Sexwale and Mzi Khumalo – to befriend the ANC government. The result is that the state provides them with electricity prices at the world's lowest levels, largely for the benefit of *externally-located* mining/smelting empires, whose profits and dividends now flow mainly from South Africa to Britain, the USA and Australia. The recent upsurge in earnings by mining/smelting firms is a good indicator of the extent to which South African public policy and greed are threatening our descendants' very lives.

Even though industrial users do provide a small cross-subsidy to household consumers, Eskom supplies the large firms with the cheapest industrial electricity in the world. While in other countries domestic consumers are charged twice as much as large industry, Eskom charges industry prices that are as little as one-seventh the domestic price (Leslie 2000). As a result, the University of Cape Town's Energy for Development Research Centre (EDRC) confirms that generation of cheap electricity in South Africa still relies on the extremely wasteful burning of low-grade coal, which has a worsening impact on the environment not just through emissions but also in requiring vast amounts of coolant water. Indeed, Eskom is the single largest consumer of raw water in South Africa. While industry benefits from cheap electricity as a competitive advantage, the negative social and environmental effects of electricity production have never been internalised into the cost.

One EDRC study concedes that South Africa:
*   is 'the most vulnerable fossil fuel exporting country in the world' if the Kyoto Protocol is adopted, according to an International Energy Agency report;
*   scores extremely poorly 'on the indicators for carbon emissions per capita and energy intensity';
*   has a 'heavy reliance' on energy-intensive industries;
*   suffers a 'high dependence on coal for primary energy';
*   offers 'low energy prices' which in part are responsible for 'poor energy efficiency of individual sectors'; and
*   risks developing a 'competitive disadvantage' by virtue of 'continued high energy intensity' which in the event of energy price rises 'can increase the cost of production' (Spalding-Fecher 2000).

In short, the existing levels of environmental degradation caused by coal mining, electricity generation, lack of access by the majority of low-income people, hydro-power and nuclear energy are formidable. Not including net exports of greenhouse gas pollutants – since South Africa is the world's second-largest exporter of coal after Australia – the energy sector contributed 78 per cent to South Africa's share of global warming and more than 90 per cent of all CO_2 emissions in 1994. These ratios have probably increased since then.

By 1998, South Africa emitted 354 million metric tons of CO_2, equivalent to 2 291 kilograms of carbon per person (a 4 per cent increase from 1990 levels). As indicated earlier in this chapter, South Africa is amongst the worst emitters of CO_2 in the world when corrected for both income and population size, worse than even the USA *by a factor of 20*. South Africa took no action to reduce emissions over the period 1990–1998, and indeed allowed them to increase from 2 205 to 2 291 kilograms of carbon per person (see Table 13.1 for global comparisons) (International Energy Agency 2000a, 2000b).

Table 13.1: Energy sector carbon emissions, 1999

Area	Population (millions)	CO_2/person	GDP (US\$ billions)	CO_2/GDP (kg/US\$ billions)	CO_2 (kg)/GDP population
South Africa	42	8.22	164	2.11	0.0501
Africa	775	1.49	569	1.28	0.0016
USA	273	20.46	8 588	0.65	0.0023
OECD	1 116	10.96	26 446	0.46	0.0004
World	5 921	3.88	32 445	0.71	0.0001

Sources: International Energy Agency 2000a, 2000b; final column calculated by authors
Notes: 1 The CO_2 emissions are those measurable through fuel combustion.
2 Because Purchasing Power Parity estimates by the International Energy Agency (2000a, 2000b) are dubious (e.g. Zimbabwe's GDP is given as US\$32.7 billion), the actual GDP figures are used. However, South Africa's GDP is far less than US\$164 billion, so the ratios indicating South Africa's high carbon/GDP emissions are actually quite conservative.

Finally, in 2005, the deals which gave Billiton, Anglo American and other huge corporations the world's lowest electricity prices came under attack by Alec Erwin, the Minister of Public Enterprises. It seemed like progress, at last, because the package Eskom had given Billiton for the Alusaf smelters at Richard's Bay Hillside and Mozal in Maputo, during the period of Eskom's worst overcapacity, had resulted in ridiculously cheap electricity – often below R0.06/kilowatt-hour – when world aluminium prices fell. *Creamer's Engineering News* (2005) reported in June 2005 that 'following the introduction of new global accounting standards, which insist on "fair value" adjustments for all so-called embedded derivatives …Eskom admits that the sensitivities are substantial and that the volatility it could create is cause for concern'. In the same article, Public Enterprises Minister Erwin reportedly insisted on lower 'financial-reporting volatility' – every time the rand changed value by 10 per cent, Eskom won or lost R2 billion – and he gave 'guidance that the utility should no longer enter into commodity-linked contracts and that management should attempt to extricate the business from the existing contracts'. Xolani Mkhwanazi – at the time CEO of the National Energy Regulator of South Africa, and subsequently appointed to a senior management position in Billiton's aluminium business in the region – replied that any change to the current contracts could be 'a bit tricky for us…We would adopt a pragmatic approach and, who knows, perhaps there will even be some sweeteners in it for us' (*Creamer's Engineering News* 2005).

How did that new approach play out in terms of the vast subsidies promised at Coega, where Erwin as trade and industry minister from 1996–2004 had led negotiations for a new aluminium or zinc smelter? The answer was clear within two weeks, as a long-awaited US$2.5 billion (R16.3 billion) deal with Canada's Alcan came closer to completion. According to the chief executive of the parastatal IDC, Geoffrey Qhena, '[t]he main issue was the electricity price and that has been resolved. Alcan has put a lot of resources into this, which is why we are confident it will go ahead' (Bailey 2005). Meanwhile, however, to operate a new smelter at Coega, lubricated by at least 15 per cent IDC financing, Alcan and other large aluminium firms were in the process of shutting down European plants that would produce 600 000 metric tons over the period 2006–2009, simply 'in search of cheaper power', according to industry analysts (MEI Online 2006).

A Coega plant would generate an estimated 660 000 tons of CO_2 per year. For the purpose of complying with Kyoto Protocol obligations, Europe will be able to show reductions in CO_2 associated with the vast energy intake needed – representing a third of a typical smelter's production costs – while South Africa's CO_2 will increase proportionately. Indeed, as a result of the sweeteners offered to Alcan, Eskom will more rapidly run out of its excess electricity capacity, resulting in raised prices, more coal generation, and a more rapid turn to objectionable power sources such as nuclear reactors and two proposed Zambezi River mega-dams (Bailey 2005).[12] According to University of Cape Town Professor Richard Fuggle (2006: 3):

> It is rather pathetic that our current environment minister Marthinus van Schalkwyk has expounded the virtues of South Africa's 13 small projects to garner carbon credits under the Kyoto Protocol's Clean Development Mechanism, but has not expressed dismay at Eskom selling 1 360 megawatts a year of coal-derived electricity to a foreign aluminium company. We already have one of the world's highest rates of carbon emissions per dollar of GDP. Adding the carbon that will be emitted to supply power to this single factory will take us close to number one on this dubious league table.

Climate activists divided

In this context, our first priority is to find consensus with what might be considered the 'reform' wing of the climate activist community who, through networks like the Climate Action Network and the South African Climate Action Network (SACAN), have since 1997 accepted carbon trading as a necessary evil. In October 2005, at the National Climate Change Conference in Johannesburg, SACAN did at least resolve to:

> [r]aise awareness of the limitations of the Clean Development Mechanism, the undue emphasis placed on carbon trading in strategies for renewable energy and efficiency and the need for rigorous application of the sustainable development criteria by the designated national authority to ensure that negative local impacts are not offset against global benefits. (DEAT 2005: 5)

Indeed, whether there are genuine 'global benefits' remains to be seen, for at best CDMs represent a shifting of the deckchairs on the Titanic. A better example for SACAN would be the struggle over the CDM proposal at Durban's Bisasar Road, where more critical climate justice activists led by Sajida Khan have halted the potential US$15 million carbon trading project (Bond & Dada 2007).

To be fair, however, it is also true that reform-minded environmental NGOs – including leadership at SACAN – have been far more effective in pointing out the problems in the strategy, even as they seek to improve it. Nevertheless, there are far too many staff and members of the large, corporate-funded international NGOs such as the World Conservation Union, Sierra, the World Wildlife Federation, the Environmental Defense Fund and even Greenpeace who have bought into carbon trading – although exceptional individuals do struggle against the current of market environmentalism.

Consider a fairly typical comment from the market-friendly camp (former Sierra Club Canada director Elizabeth May, now leader of that country's Green Party): 'I would have preferred a carbon tax, but that is not the agreement we have. The reality is that Kyoto is the only legally binding agreement to reduce greenhouse gasses. When you're drowning and someone throws you a lifeboat, you can't wait for another one to come along' (Athanasiu 2005: 1). Our rebuttal is that carbon trading is simply not a seaworthy lifeboat, and as temperatures (and sea levels) rise, we are discovering, to our peril, the numerous leaks.

To illustrate the importance of education (of the type undertaken by our colleagues in Carbon Trade Watch), here is a paragraph written by Andrew Leonard, whose 'How the World Works' column is familiar to readers of the popular *Salon* e-zine:

> The activists behind Carbon Trade Watch are smart, and their critique of the carbon trading system is brutal and effective. How the World Works has long been attracted to market mechanisms that would create financial incentives for reducing pollution, but after pondering the arguments marshaled by Carbon Trade Watch, we feel our optimism melting away like Greenland's glaciers.
>
> Some environmental advocacy defeats its own purposes by transparently manipulating facts to fit its own agenda, a strategy that raises hackles even when you agree with the overall cause. But Carbon Trade Watch, although clearly in pursuit of an agenda, doesn't make that mistake. In particular, the connections drawn between the root causes of climate change and the forces propelling globalisation are compelling – for example, a vast proportion of the investment capital pouring into middle-income emerging nations like Brazil, India, China and South Africa is going directly to nonrenewable energy development, with consequences for global warming that dwarf any reductions in emissions the Kyoto Protocol may accomplish, even if it works as planned. (Leonard 2006)

The implications of our findings are also clear for broader South African society and for those government officials who will probably continue to act as irresponsibly as USA officials, from the National Climate Change Conference in Johannesburg in October 2005 to the Kyoto Protocol negotiations in Montreal in December 2005 to Nairobi in November 2006, the Bali Conference of Parties to the Kyoto Protocol in December 2007, and beyond.

Conclusion

In sum, several important factors converge when we consider the nature of South African energy:

*   South Africa, already amongst the most unequal countries in the world in 1994, became more unequal during the late 1990s as a million jobs were lost due largely to the stagnant economy, the flood of imports and capital/energy-intensive investment – and these trends had enormously negative implications for the ability of low-income citizens to afford electricity;
*   billions of rands in state subsidies are spent on capital-intensive energy-related investments such as new smelters, where profit and dividend outflows continue to adversely affect the currency;
*   the price of electricity charged to mining and smelter operations is the lowest in the world;
*   a pittance is being spent on renewable energy research and development, especially when compared to investment in a dubious nuclear programme;
*   greenhouse gas emissions per person, corrected for income, are amongst the most damaging anywhere, and have grown worse since liberation;
*   electricity coverage is uneven, and notwithstanding a significant expansion of coverage, millions of people have had their electricity supplies cut as the state provider moves towards commercialisation and privatisation; and
*   there are other important environmental, segregation-related and economic benefits that flow from clean electricity as a replacement for traditional fuels, which are at present not incorporated into social and financial decision-making, especially when it comes to pricing electricity.

All of these problems can be countered by critiques from civil society. However, most challenging is the lack of synthesis among the three major citizens' networks that have challenged government policy and corporate practices: environmentalists, community groups and trade unions.

Notes

1   This chapter is expanded upon in Bond et al. 2007.

2   Cited in World Bank Press Clips, 29 November 2005.

3   For the full text of the Kyoto Protocol see www.unfccc.int.

4   See http://www.carbontradewatch.org.

5   BBC News, 'Q & A on the Kyoto Protocol',
     http://news.bbc.co.uk/1/hi/sci/tech/4269921.stm.

6   As of September 2006 there were only 126 JI projects in various stages of validation,
     compared with 1 150 projects in the CDM pipeline; for more information see
     www.cd4cdm.org.

7   Kyoto Protocol, Article 12, paragraph 5(2).

8   Since at its root, carbon trading is about northern countries 'offsetting' their pollution by
     means of reductions in southern countries, if these reductions were to occur without the
     intervention of the carbon market – and thus not additional to the status quo – there
     would be no net benefit for the climate.

9   Kyoto Protocol, Article 12, paragraph 2.

10   In addition to the PDD, in some countries project developers can submit a Project
     Identification Note (PIN). A PIN tells the DNA what the project plans to do but need not
     include all the details required in a formal PDD. The purpose of this stage is to allow a
     project developer to get a sense of how the project will be viewed by the DNA. If the DNA
     has some initial concerns, these can be addressed prior to the submission of the PDD to
     save both time and money. If the DNA has no concerns about the PIN, then the project
     developer can ask for a letter of no objection that will expedite the process later on. While
     this is the case in South Africa, it is important to remember that every DNA can establish
     its own procedures related to reviewing PINs, and what is applicable in one jurisdiction
     may not be the case in another.

11   CERs are the currency of the carbon market: once a project starts reducing emissions that
     are verified by a DOE, they pass on certificates for the reductions in CO_2-equivalent to the
     country investing in the project, which is then used against the Annex 1 country's Kyoto
     targets.

12   For a full critique of Coega, especially Erwin's role, see Bond 2002. As of September 2006,
     there were still plans in place to offer vast subsidies, very cheap (and reliable) electricity
     and other investment incentives to the Canadian firm Alcan to pursue a massive smelter at
     Coega.

References

Athanasiu A (2005) Greens divided over dissing Feds: Would keeping criticism quiet help?
     Now 1 December. Accessed 15 March 2008,
     http://www.nowtoronto.com/issues/2005-12-01/news_story.php

Bailey S (2005) Alcan will probably build $2.5 bln smelter, IDC says. *Bloomberg News*
     13 July. Accessed 15 March 2008,
     www.advfn.com/stocks/corus-left-shoulder-or-the-foothills_9431770.html

Becker E & Sanger D (2005) Opposition to doubling aid for Africa. *GreenLeft Weekly* 2 June

Bond P (ed.) (2002) *Unsustainable South Africa: Environment, development and social protest.*
     Pietermaritzburg & London: UKZN Press & Merlin Press

Bond P & Dada R (2007) A death in Durban: Capitalist patriarchy, global warming gimmickry and our responsibility for rubbish. *Agenda* 73: 46–55

Bond P, Erion G & Dada R (eds.) (2007) *Climate change, carbon trading and civil society.* Amsterdam & Pietermaritzburg: Rozenberg & University of KwaZulu-Natal Press

Creamer's Engineering News (2005) Eskom will seek to cancel commodity-linked tariff deals. *Creamer's Engineering News* 29 June

Dales J (1968) *Pollution, property and prices: An essay in policy-making and economics.* Toronto: University of Toronto Press

Daniel J & Lutchman J (2005) South Africa in Africa. Presentation to the South African Association of Political Studies Colloquium, 22 September, Pietermaritzburg

DEAT (Department of Environmental Affairs and Tourism, South Africa) (2004) *National climate change response strategy.* Pretoria: DEAT

DEAT (2005) *Bojanala special issue on the National Climate Change Conference.* 20 October. Pretoria: DEAT

DEAT (2006) *South Africa and Australia boost international co-operation on climate change.* 6 December. Accessed 15 March 2008, www.environment.gov.za/NewsMedia/MedStat/2006Dec6/06122006.htm

Fabricius P (2005) PetroSA to send technicians to explore oil possibilities in the Sudan. *The Star* 5 January

Fenhann J (2006) *CDM project pipeline.* UNEP Risø Centre. Accessed 14 September 2006, www.cd4cdm.org

Fine B & Rustomjee Z (1996) *The political economy of South Africa: From minerals-energy complex to industrialisation.* London: Hurst & Company

Fuggle R (2006) Retirement address, Richard F Fuggle, Shell Professor of Environmental Studies, University of Cape Town, 29 November. Accessed 15 March 2008, www.fosaf.co.za/word%20doc/30%20Years%20of%20%20Studies.doc

Gosling M (2006) Top academic slams SA environmental policies. *Independent Online* 4 December. Accessed 15 March 2008, www.iol.co.za/index.php?set_id=1&click_id=13&art_id=vn20061204042211461C109626

Haites E (2006) Presentation to York University's Colloquium on the Global South, 25 January, Toronto, Margaree Consulting

Hardin G (1968) The Tragedy of the Commons. *Science* 162: 1243–1248

Harrabin R (2006) *Mixed outcomes at climate talks.* news.bbc.co.uk, 5 October. Accessed 15 March 2008, news.bbc.co.uk/2/hi/science/nature/5408798.stm

HM Treasury UK (2006) *The Stern Review: The economics of climate change.* Accessed 16 January 2008, http://www.hm-treasury.gov.uk/independent_reviews/stern_review_economics_climate_change/stern_review_report.cfm

International Energy Agency (2000a) *CO_2 emissions from fuel combustion, 1971–1998.* Paris: International Energy Agency

International Energy Agency (2000b) *Key world energy statistics from the IEA*. Paris: International Energy Agency

Jury M (2004) Presentation to Durban Declaration Group. 9 October, Richards Bay

Kapadia MS (2006) Carbon fund for upfront finance. *Project Monitor* 27 November. Accessed 15 March 2008, www.projectsmonitor.com/detailnews.asp?newsid=12620

Leonard A (2006) Free market environmentalism. *Salon* 7. Accessed 15 March 2008, www.salon.com/tech/htww/2006/03/07/carbontradewatch

Leslie G (2000) Social pricing of electricity in Johannesburg. Master's research report in Public and Development Management submitted to the Faculty of Management, University of the Witswatersrand, Johannesburg

Lipow G (2006) Carbon trading. PEN-L listserve, 19 January

Lohmann L (ed.) (2006) Carbon trading: A critical conversation on climate change, privatisation and power. Special issue of *Development Dialogue* 48 (entire issue)

MEI Online (2006) *Alcan to build state-of-the-art smelter in Quebec*. 21 December. Accessed 15 March 2008, http://www.min-eng.com/commodities/metallic/aluminium/news/47.html

Monbiot G (2006) The trade in 'carbon offsets' is based on bogus accounting. *The Guardian* 17 January

PCF (Prototype Carbon Fund) (2004) *PCF annual report*. Washington: World Bank Group

PCF (2005) *Carbon market trends 2006*. Washington: World Bank Group

Schiermeier Q (2006) Methane finding baffles scientists. *Nature* 439: 128

Spalding-Fecher A (2000) *The sustainable energy watch indicators 2001*. Cape Town: Energy for Development Research Centre, University of Cape Town

Van Schalkwyk M (2006) Speech by the Minister of Environmental Affairs and Tourism, Marthinus van Schalkwyk, on the occasion of the opening of the final lead authors meeting of Working Group 2 of the Intergovernmental Panel on Climate Change's Fourth Assessment Report (AR4), 11 September, Lord Charles Hotel, Somerset West

Wamasti EN (2007) *Carbon trading faces mixed reaction at climate conference*. Accessed 12 December 2007, http://www.climatemediapartnership.org/spip.php?article249

World Bank (2005) *Where is the wealth of nations? Measuring capital for the 21st century*. Conference edition, 15 July. Washington: World Bank

CHAPTER 14

Electricity and privatisation in Uganda: The origins of the crisis and problems with the response

Christopher Gore

In July 2006, Uganda's Minister of Energy, Daudi Migereko, openly acknowledged that his country was experiencing a power supply crisis. At the same time he also suggested that the crisis would end soon (Nampala 2006). Later that year, President Museveni echoed Migereko's optimism while speaking at an international trade fair in Uganda: 'This is the last energy crisis we shall have in Uganda, even for the future. This issue of electricity in the next three years shall be history. We have learnt enough lessons' (Kasyate & Kamau Lugogo 2006). Museveni's optimism rested on the belief that two hydro-electric dams, Bujagali and Karuma (Figure 14.1), both to be privately built, would be completed by 2010, thus reducing the country's electricity supply shortfall in the medium term.

But despite these optimistic statements, Ugandan citizens could be forgiven for having low confidence in the government's projections and indeed for wondering what 'crisis' truly meant. Media reports during this same period argued that the electricity crisis would be likely to worsen or deepen in the coming years (Among 2006; *Business in Africa* 2006; Ilakut 2006; Izama 2006; *Monitor* 2006; Wakabi 2006).

Putting the problem of electricity supply in a regional context, during the same period Jamal Saghir, the director of Energy and Water at the World Bank, noted that average electricity access in most sub-Saharan African countries was 25 per cent and getting worse: 'Not only is Africa lagging behind other regions but, in recent years, the access gap has been widening' (*Business in Africa* 2006). If one compares average electricity access on the subcontinent to access in Uganda, one starts to appreciate the scale of Uganda's 'crisis'.

Calculations based on various data indicate that, of the 27 million people in Uganda in 2005, only 4–5 per cent had access to electricity.[1] Of this percentage, only 1 per cent of the rural population had electricity. These figures have changed little since 2002. Of the total population with electricity in Uganda, just over half are concentrated in the capital city, Kampala. But access to electricity in the capital is still comparatively weak. Using Uganda Bureau of Statistics 2002 census data for the mean household size in Kampala (3.8), and the number of domestic consumers

Figure 14.1: Existing and proposed large hydro-electric facilities in Uganda

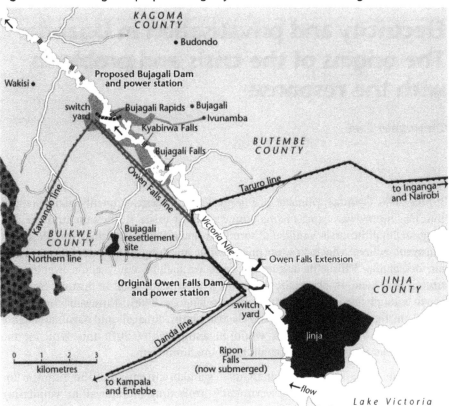

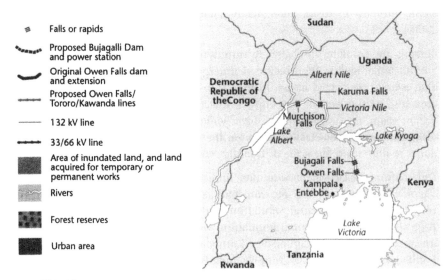

Source: World Bank[2]

in Kampala, in 2002 only 32 per cent of city residents had access to electricity (UBOS 2002). In comparison, results from the World Bank's Living Standards Measurement Study in 15 countries and for more than 55 000 households in Asia, the Americas, Eastern Europe, Central Asia and sub-Saharan Africa, showed that 89 per cent of urban households and 46 per cent of rural households had electricity (Komives et al. 2003: 83). Thus, Uganda's 32 per cent access level in the capital city and 1 per cent access level in rural areas shows the country to be an important global anomaly with respect to electricity access, and on a par with several other African countries with national electrification levels at roughly 10 per cent or below, such as the Democratic Republic of the Congo, Angola, Lesotho, Madagascar, Malawi, Mozambique, Kenya, Tanzania and Ethiopia (see Davidson & Mwakasonda 2004; Karekezi & Kimani 2004).

Unfortunately, the story does not end there. In 2002 the total average system losses in Uganda – including technical and non-technical (usually theft) – were an astonishing 41.5 per cent: generation accounted for 0.4 per cent of system losses; transmission 4.4 per cent; and distribution 36.7 per cent (MEMD 2002). The international target for total system losses is 10–12 per cent (Karekezi & Kimani 2002: 928). In relation to 12 other countries in sub-Saharan Africa (Sudan, Angola, Ethiopia, Kenya, Eritrea, Malawi, Tanzania, Zimbabwe, Zambia, Lesotho, Botswana, South Africa), in 2002 Uganda's system losses were highest (Karekezi & Kimani 2002). According to revised figures, in 2005 Uganda's commissioner for energy and minerals development explained that the sector was still losing 28 per cent of the total hydro-power generated through non-technical losses (theft) each month (Luggya 2005). This translated into a loss of 45 megawatts (MW) of electricity, which, if billed, would have provided an additional USh 3 billion per month (US$1.75 million in exchange rates at the time).

Adding to these recent statistics, due to low water levels in Lake Victoria variously attributed to drought, excessive irrigation, and overuse for electricity generation, in 2006 Uganda's capacity to generate electricity dropped from an estimated 300 MW to just 135 MW. Meanwhile, effective demand for electricity – what consumers can and will pay for – has been growing by 30 MW per year, rolling blackouts have been ongoing, and demand for biomass (firewood and charcoal), already the primary source of energy for 95 per cent of Ugandans, continues to rise. The situation in 2006 was so serious that projections of 6.5 per cent economic growth were reduced to 4.6 per cent largely due to electricity power shortages (Wakabi 2006).

When examining Uganda's electricity sector as a whole, most would be hard-pressed to script the simultaneous convergence of so many detrimental events:
- extremely low levels of household access;
- demand dramatically outpacing supply;
- supply dependent on water resources;
- the availability of water resources often limited;

- new generation sources repeatedly being delayed;
- expensive emergency generation sources;
- continual increases in the unit price of electricity to pay for emergency supply and new generation sources, despite the above factors.

In short, if ever one could imagine a 'perfect storm' for a power sector, Uganda was suffering through it in 2006. Given this information, along with a recognition that access to and availability of electrical energy supplies is centrally connected to improved human well-being and industrial development (see UNCHS 2001; World Bank 2000), it would come as little surprise that the government of Uganda and numerous multilateral and bilateral agencies have been actively engaged in efforts to improve and reform the country's electricity power sector. And of all the agencies involved, the World Bank has played the lead role.

The Bank has been the central international actor in Uganda's energy sector since the early 1960s; its very first project in the country, in 1961, Power I, was for electricity. Since that time, the Bank has provided loans for a host of projects directly and indirectly related to the sector. But owing to ongoing problems in improvement, and the Bank's admitted frustration with the lack of progress in reform and corruption charges against senior Uganda Electricity Board (UEB) personnel, by the mid-1990s the Bank was pushing firmly for the commercialisation and privatisation of the electricity sector.

This fact is not debated. Interviews by the author with the World Bank, other donor representatives, senior government officials and NGOs alike confirm the Bank's role in requiring privatisation. In the opinion of former World Bank Country Programme Manager for Uganda, Robert Blake, the 'UEB was unreformable' (Blake interview). In turn, in 1999, a new Electricity Act was passed, paving the way for the unbundling of the UEB into separate distribution, transmission and generation companies, and the entry of independent private companies to generate and distribute electricity. In theory, these actions, along with the presumed construction of a new large (250 MW) hydro-electric dam called Bujagali, were supposed to mark the beginning of improvement. Hence, in April 2001, the former monopoly UEB was unbundled, creating the Uganda Electricity Distribution Company Ltd (UEDCL), the Uganda Electricity Transmission Company Ltd (UETCL), and the Uganda Electricity Generation Company Ltd (UEGCL).

In January 2003, Eskom Enterprises – the entrepreneurial wing of the state-owned South African electricity company Eskom – assumed control over UEGCL's holdings – the Owen Falls Dam (now named Nalubaale) and Owen Falls Extension (now named Kiira Power Station) – under a 20-year concession, and under the name Eskom Uganda.

In 2005 Eskom Enterprises deepened its presence in Uganda. Under the company name Umeme, UK-based Globeleq (owned by the CDC Group) and Eskom Enterprises assumed joint control over UEDCL under a 20-year concession. In the original arrangement, Globeleq owned 56 per cent of the new company and Eskom Enterprises 44 per cent. It has, however, been recently reported that in 2006 Globeleq assumed 100 per cent of Umeme's shares, with Eskom pulling out of Uganda's distribution service (*East African* 2007). In February 2007, the *East African* also reported that Globeleq would be selling its interests in 20 electric power projects in Africa, including Umeme, adding further confusion to the concession. Paul Mare, previously an employee of Eskom South Africa, is now the general manager of Umeme.[3] UETCL remains government-owned and -operated.

In the midst of these changes, however, significant improvements in electricity supply and significant increases in the number of consumers have not been realised. The poor supply in 2007 was a result of a host of factors, including delays in the construction of the new generation sources and the low water levels needed for electricity generation at the two existing hydro facilities. As a result, in the country's ongoing efforts to address its electricity supply shortfall, the national government commissioned the addition of several privately-owned and -operated 50 MW thermal generators to the national grid. Two 50 MW generators are now operated by Dubai-based Aggreko International, and became fully operational in late 2006 and early 2007. Owing to the generators' reliance on diesel fuel, the price of the electricity has been estimated to be US$0.25 per kilowatt-hour (kWh). But as of March 2007, other procurements for temporary generators had still to be completed. In 2006, the Electricity Regulatory Authority (ERA) awarded another tender to the Norwegian firm Jacobsen AS Elektro. Generation was supposed to commence in March 2007. But, citing irregularities in the bidding process, the Inspector-General of Government (IGG) intervened and ordered the award overturned. President Museveni then ordered a re-evaluation of the bids. The evaluation team again selected Jacobsen, but the IGG has continued to raise concerns about the procurement process. Meanwhile, the finance minister denies allegations that the procurement process was mishandled, the Attorney-General argues that the IGG's report and concerns are not binding, and Ugandans have continued to suffer through routine load shedding. It is not surprising, then, that the accumulated impact of a poor electricity network needing expansion and refurbishment, the failure of the UEB to adjust the price of electricity historically, and the need for emergency electricity supplies in the form of costly fossil fuel generators have also pushed the unit price of electricity to an unprecedented high.

In late 2006, electricity in Uganda was the most expensive in the region. Domestic consumers were paying US$0.24/kWh. This price, however, did not reflect the 'real' cost in the parlance of privatisation literature. The UETCL, owned and operated by the government, subsidised the price of electricity by US$126 million in 2006 (*Monitor* 2006). Without the subsidy, at the end of 2006 domestic consumers would have been paying just over US$0.30/kWh.

While some recent analyses suggest that on the whole those who previously had access to electricity have been able to adjust to the price increases,[4] for those not yet connected to the grid there is little relief in sight. As the head of the ERA explained in an interview, the issue is not how to maintain customers but how to connect new ones when the cost of connecting is so high: 'The real prohibitive cost is not electricity, it is the connection cost – we don't need lifelines, we need connections' (Sebbowa interview).[5]

Together, this complex set of debilitating events and the state of Uganda's electricity sector raise many significant questions about the path of reform in Uganda, and the factors that are impeding the improvement of the sector. Was the convergence of events predictable? What inspired the move from public- to private-led electricity provision? Was privatisation the best option for Uganda's electricity sector? How do political and historical events factor into the state of electricity?

In this chapter, I reflect on these questions by tracing the emergence of privatisation as a dominant path, or narrative, of reform. In doing this, I confirm suspicions that the privatisation of Uganda's electricity sector was in large part a result of World Bank demands. By itself, this is not a surprising fact and taken alone it does not explain privatisation as the preferred reform choice. Privatisation is intimately connected to two other factors: firstly, the prominence of the Bujagali dam as *the* preferred response to Uganda's electricity supply problems; and secondly, the process by which other reforms in the country have taken place and the assumptions embedded in those reforms – assumptions about the speed of reform and the capacity of the private sector to make quick improvements. Hence, I approach the story of electricity reform and privatisation in Uganda from a historical and procedural perspective.

Using this approach I wish to highlight three central things. First, the chapter will explain how historical and procedural events inform both the character and content of service delivery debates in Uganda. Second, for those interested in challenging the dominant privatisation paradigm in Uganda, this chapter will provide an appreciation of the weight of history working against efforts to construct an alternative narrative or path of reform. Third, whether for or against the role of the private sector in electricity provision, readers will gain a better sense of how the process of reform has shaped and directed policy choices in Uganda's electricity sector.

Absent from this analysis is comprehensive information on the social and environmental impacts of electricity privatisation. Anecdotal evidence does suggest a correlation between privatisation and increased reliance on biomass for energy needs, increased degradation of forest resources, and electricity cut-offs, but no comprehensive ground-level analysis has yet been done to confirm that citizens are increasing their reliance on biomass or how households are adapting post-privatisation. Therefore, in the years ahead more comprehensive socio-economic and environmental analyses of privatisation impacts will be needed.

In the next section, the historical context of electricity in Uganda is presented, highlighting early debates about public-versus-private provision, and the relationship between this debate and contemporary dam construction and electricity access. In the third section these historical events and debates are connected to contemporary Uganda. At the core of this third section is an analysis of the process that led to the emergence of privatisation in Uganda. The chapter concludes by discussing the implications of the material presented, focusing specifically on the prospects for improvements in electricity provision and access, particularly for the poor, under the new private-sector-led regime.

Electricity provision: public versus private in historical context

In 1905, Winston Churchill toured the Ugandan Protectorate as the Parliamentary Under-Secretary of State for Colonies. In his 1908 book, *My African Journey*, he discussed the challenge and role of hydro-electric development in the country. What is remarkable about his deliberations is the prominence of two factors which continue to be debated today: firstly, whether private or public development of Uganda's hydro-electric resources is most appropriate; and secondly, whether private firms, if involved in generation or distribution of electricity, would reinvest in the country:

> As one watches the surging waters of the Ripon Falls and endeavours to compute the mighty energies now running to waste, but all within the reach of modern science, the problem of Uganda rises in a new form on the mind. *All this waterpower belongs to the State. Ought it ever to be surrendered to private persons? How long, on the other hand, is a Government, if not prepared to act itself, entitled to bar the way to others?* This question is raised in a multitude of diverse forms in almost all the great dependencies of the Crown. But in Uganda the arguments for the State ownership and employment of the natural resources of the country seem to present themselves in the strongest and most formidable array…In such circumstances there cannot be much opening for the push and drive of ordinary commercial enterprise. The hustling business man – admirably suited to the rough-and-tumble of competitive production in Europe or America – becomes an incongruous and even a dangerous figure when introduced into the smooth and leisurely development of a native State…When a man is working only for the profits of his company and is judged by the financial results alone, he does not often under the sun of Central Africa acquire the best method of dealing with natives; and all sorts of difficulties and troubles will follow any sudden incursion of business enterprise in the forests and gardens of Uganda. *And even if the country is more rapidly developed by these agencies, the profits will not go to the Government and people of Uganda, to be used in fostering new industries, but to diverse persons across the sea, who have no concern, other than purely commercial, in its fortunes. This is not to advocate the arbitrary exclusion of private capital and enterprise from Uganda. Carefully directed and narrowly controlled opportunities for their activities will no doubt occur. But the natural resources of the country should, as*

far as possible, be developed by Government itself, even though that may involve the assumption of many new functions...Nowhere are the powers of the Government to regulate and direct the activities of the people more overwhelming or more comprehensive. (Churchill 1989/1908: 75–77, emphasis added)

Despite Churchill's prescient concerns about private-led hydro-electric development, it was private companies that laid the foundation for electricity infrastructure in the region. The East African Power and Lighting Company (EAP&L), based in Kenya, had in fact eyed Uganda's hydro potential prior to Churchill's arrival in the country. The EAP&L was, however, denied generating and distribution licences in Uganda for some 30 years until 1936, when Harold Odam, the head of the EAP&L, met with Ugandan Governor Philip Mitchell to discuss generation and distribution opportunities in the Ugandan Protectorate.

Odam proposed constructing three thermal generating stations at Jinja, Kampala and Entebbe in order to immediately service each of the areas, with an option to later develop the Nile's hydro-electric potential near Jinja. Hence, the EAP&L's first preference was not a large hydro-electric facility. The Ugandan governor, however, thought the initial proposal for several small distributed generation sources was impractical, given that the development of one hydro-power source on the Nile could satisfy all electricity needs. What is more, the hydro-power source the governor had in mind was none other than Bujagali Falls (Hayes 1983).

The EAP&L's reluctance to embark on the construction of a large hydro-electric facility was in large part due to a concern still debated today in Uganda – whether the market of existing or potential paying customers was large enough, particularly given the absence of large industrial consumers (Hayes 1983). These concerns were also consistent with the findings of a 1935 survey of the hydro-electric development potential of the Nile conducted by the future chairman of the UEB, CR Westlake. Westlake argued that while technically feasible, a large hydro-electricity project on the Nile 'would not pay, as electricity consumption both actual and potential, was too low' (Wilson 1967: 2). Therefore, despite Governor Mitchell's ambitions for a large project, he conceded to the EAP&L's original proposal and granted the company licences for thermal generation and distribution in each of the largest settlements in Uganda. Commercial service became available in Kampala and Entebbe by 1938, and shortly after in Jinja. But the EAP&L's monopoly would last less than 10 years, during which time Britain's desire for a much grander hydro-electric project grew.

In 1945 Sir John Hall became governor of Uganda. Following the end of World War II, Hall took up his position at a time of tremendous change in Uganda and globally. Hall's goal was to see Uganda develop a vibrant export sector based on agriculture, with as much industry as possible (Wilson 1967). His vision was formally articulated in the 1946 Uganda Development Plan. And while the Plan did articulate the need for electricity, this did not feature significantly. The explanation for this lack of attention would come a year later with CR Westlake's publication of the Uganda Electricity Survey, which Gail Wilson noted 'was as much a marketing survey as a technical report' (Wilson 1967: 2). 'Westlake's recommendations, very much in line with the beliefs of the Uganda Governor, Sir John Hall, were presented to and adopted by Uganda's Legislative Council in July 1947. The prospect was awesome – nothing less than a £22 million plan for harnessing the Nile at its outflow from Lake Victoria Nyanza and the creation of a new authority, the Uganda Electricity Board' (Hayes 1983: 331). The desire for a large hydro-electric facility seemed just too difficult to resist and the government wasted little time in implementing its vision.

On January 18, 1948, the UEB was formally created as a quasi-independent, vertically integrated monopoly to generate, transmit, distribute and supply electricity within Uganda, with a vision to also eventually supply the wider East African region. Westlake was appointed the UEB's first chairman and he quickly took over the EAP&L's operations due to it encountering ongoing service delivery problems. Hence, in just over 10 years, control of national electricity development in Uganda had moved from a private firm to the state, and together the governor of Uganda and the head of the newly created UEB produced a vision for the future development of Uganda that rested on a large-scale, government-led plan to develop its hydro-electric resources: a vision that would start with the construction of a dam at Owen Falls and a plan to eventually 'tame the river Nile for the whole of its 3 850 mile-journey' (Hayes 1983: 331).

But not everyone felt this comfortable or confident with the proposed plan. When 'moving the adoption of the Ordinance setting up the Uganda Electricity Board, the Financial Secretary referred to the scheme as an "act of faith"' (Wilson 1967: 2). Nonetheless, in moving forward with the establishment of the UEB and the promotion of the Owen Falls Dam, two significant precedents had been set: the future of Uganda's electricity network was intimately tied to the development of large hydro-electric stations on the Nile, and success was deemed to be dependent on a state-led monopoly.

Initiating the vision: large electricity infrastructure in Uganda

The decision to build Owen Falls Dam rested on an emerging belief that the provision of electricity was a service to be undertaken by the government and not merely a commercial enterprise. This vision also rested on a set of contradictory factors. The condition for financial success of the new dam was quite simple: the electricity produced had to be consumed in order to recover the costs of construction. At the same time, and running in potential conflict to this principle, was the view that new power schemes should be developed that could supply foreseeable potential demand in lieu of merely meeting existing demand (Uganda Electricity Survey 1947, cited in Wilson 1967). In short, the financial success of a large generation project would depend on an accurate assessment and prediction of future consumer demand, and a complementary ability to extend a physical transmission and distribution network to match projected demand. Albert

Hirschman described this as the 'building-ahead-of-demand strategy' (Hirschman 1967: 68). Hirschman studied 11 development projects between 1964 and 1965, one of which was Owen Falls.

In East Africa, this government-led approach to electricity development was a significant departure from the previous private, small-scale, distributed electricity systems. But globally this approach was in keeping with emerging trends: the 1930s marked the beginning of a period of global large-dam construction, escalating after World War II, as well as a period of advocacy for large-dam construction led by a professional association, the International Commission on Large Dams, still ongoing today. McCully (2001: 18) writes that 'British colonialists were the most ardent dam builders outside Europe and North America in the late nineteenth and early twentieth centuries, leaving the mark most firmly on the basins of the Indus, Ganges and Nile'. Hence, the decision to move ahead with a large dam in Uganda was consistent with Britain's experience and vision, and well before construction had begun the colonial government was already planning heavy and secondary industry for the country (Hayes 1983).

Owen Falls became Britain's first choice for a large dam in Uganda. As a result of its accessibility, its potential electricity production, its ability to best control Lake Victoria's water levels, and a sound geological base, it was deemed superior to two other locations which had previously been promoted – Bujagali Falls (which was identified as a first choice in the 1920s) and Ripon Falls (which had been considered in the early 1900s) (Wilson 1967). But despite Owen Falls' technical feasibility there remained much concern over the financial viability and cost of the project, particularly given the rising prices of capital goods and the devaluation of the sterling currency in 1949 (Wilson 1967). Nonetheless, four years later, the Owen Falls Dam was complete and in the optimistic words of the future head of the UEB, CR Westlake, 'Power from this scheme [Owen Falls] will make possible the liberation of the latent riches of Uganda. The industrial development will help to provide funds for education, training, housing and medical services' (Wilson 1967: 3).

The first turbine of the Owen Falls Dam began turning for tests in December 1953, with the official inauguration of the dam occurring the following year on 29 April 1954. It was a grand event. Queen Elizabeth II, only two years into her reign, was in Uganda to inaugurate the new dam. The *East African Standard* reported on the events of the day with full journalistic colour and intrigue, noting how the 'concrete gleamed in the sun'.[6] Another editorial began by expressing the same enthusiasm that the colonial government had used to initiate the project:

> The Owen Falls scheme is a triumph of engineering achievement and of faith. It will be to East Africa a great power house, a symbol of inner light which Western Christian civilisation and the British people have lit in the minds of millions of Africans. It will give their lives a new direction and purpose for many generations.[7]

But as the commentary continued, the author went on to raise important cautionary remarks, which painted an ominous warning for the country:

> The scheme is based on the assumption that it will stimulate a great and prosperous change in the economy of Uganda, and in a measure of East Africa as a whole by making possible the development of the natural resources of the Protectorate and the industrial undertakings based upon the modern power which it will place in the hands of the civilized men. It has already been a more costly undertaking than was estimated and there is evidence that the conception of progress [that] brought it into being was more optimistic than has yet been realised, or seems likely to be achieved in the early future. The success of the enterprises which it is intended to serve depends on the availability of cheap power, on security of invested capital, on an adequate qualified force of workers, especially Africans, and on stable political policies and objectives which provide a guarantee of long-continuing conditions suitable and necessary for the evolution of an industrial revolution in a continent only yet emerging from its past into the light of the present day...If the Owen Falls scheme is to give its full value to Uganda and all its peoples, and if industry is to be attracted in adequate measure to justify it, these basic conditions of success must be a policy. The provision of the new source of power is only the beginning. Much hard-thinking...will have to be devoted to the implications of the policy of which the Owen Falls undertaking is the symbol if this great engineering feat is to contribute its full value to Uganda and its peoples and justify its existence and its cost.

Hayes (1983: 333) points out that the queen's remarks at the inauguration paralleled, with more reserve, the *Standard's* enthusiasm and concern:

> ...let us not forget that economic development and the building up of industries are not ends in themselves. Their object is the raising of the people's standards of living. We welcome this great work because, by increasing the wealth of this country, it enables people – and above all, the African people – to advance...I confidently believe that your children and grandchildren will look upon this scheme as one of the greatest landmarks in the forward march of their land.

Today, even someone poorly acquainted with the political history of Uganda will know that many of the conditions that were deemed necessary for the success of the scheme would not be realised, and that the concerns were well founded. Shortly after Uganda's independence in 1962 the stability of the country and its policies quickly unravelled, with a terrible long-term impact on the state's electricity infrastructure. The political tenure of Milton Obote, Idi Amin and then five subsequent regimes between 1980 and 1986 proved disastrous for infrastructure and electricity. Even in the more immediate years following Owen Falls' completion, when economic growth and electricity expansion were increasing, the expected economic and social transformation that was envisioned and espoused did not materialise, in large measure because the vision for electricity expansion in the country was inconsistent with the technical and financial capacity of the UEB.

After Owen Falls was initiated, the number of electricity customers increased rapidly. But in a short time the number of customers peaked and plateaued. Most of the wealthy and powerful, along with select businesses in large urban centres, were connected, but the dispersed settlement pattern of Uganda's rural areas presented the UEB with an enormous technical and financial challenge in connecting more customers. Despite this dilemma (one which still exists today owing to the country having a very high rural population – only 13 per cent of the national population in the 2002 census was designated 'urban'), the UEB felt strongly that if prosperity was to be achieved, more generation capacity would be needed imminently – the build-ahead-of-demand strategy – thus further fuelling the expansionist vision. The UEB was able to sustain this vision, even in the midst of concern, because the evidence showing a decrease in consumer connections lagged behind commissioned reports supporting more hydro-electric development. Hence, in a 1957 consultant's report, not only was a new second dam at Bujagali Falls recommended, but two additional dams downstream from Bujagali were called for as well (Economist Intelligence Unit 1957).

From a political perspective, what stands out about the real and planned expansion of the electricity network prior to 1960 was that it evolved in general isolation from national, pre-independence politics. Reports linking electricity and economic development in Uganda prior to 1960 do not consider the role that national, let alone local, politics would play in facilitating or negating the UEB's vision. Indeed, despite pre-independence political events that would have a lasting legacy in post-independent Uganda – e.g. the emergence of and competition between formal political parties, ethnic and religious conflict accentuated by colonial policies, the expulsion of the King of the Buganda (Kabaka), and constitutional negotiations – when reading historical documents and reports relating to electricity during this time one would be forgiven for thinking that the British were going to carry on administering a docile Ugandan population in perpetuity, as little reflection on national politics or the transfer of colonial administration is mentioned.

On the eve of independence in Uganda (1962), however, the separation between the UEB's vision and national politics would start to vanish. This was also the period when the World Bank became directly involved in electricity development in East Africa. The World Bank in fact denied Kenya a loan to develop its own hydro-electric resources, as it believed the future development of hydro-electric resources in Uganda would sufficiently supply the East African region – a decision that has proven problematic for Kenya and Tanzania today, owing to each country's anticipation of increased supply from Uganda.

In turn, in 1965, the UEB again recommended a new large dam at Bujagali Falls for development. The government of Uganda would approve this proposal the following year, leading the UEB to begin looking for funds overseas. One of the main sources of funding that the UEB turned to was once again the World Bank. The Bank's confidence in the UEB was growing weak, however. As a result, the Bank initially suggested a joint scheme between Kenya and Uganda instead of an independent project. While these negotiations did not produce a mutually acceptable arrangement, in a short time the discussions were moot as mounting civil unrest in Uganda eclipsed most hydro-electric development potential – joint or independent. Indeed, it was not until President Yoweri Museveni came to power in 1986 that past hydro-electric and electricity expansion studies would be revisited. In short, 'between 1971 and 1986 there was no major development in the power sector' (Engorait 2005: 1).

The role of history in contemporary Uganda

This historical account hints at several important issues relating to the provision of electricity in Uganda today. First, the rationale that political authorities used for dam construction is significant. The argument for expanding electricity was not based on a social development goal, but on financial and economic need. As a 1957 Economist Intelligence Unit report noted, 'the African' desired electricity but subsidising connection fees or access was not considered (Economist Intelligence Unit 1957). Extending electricity access was dependent on a consumer's 'willingness to pay' and on the presence of large-scale industrial users. What is striking about these historical arguments about 'willingness to pay' and electricity for industrialisation is that they are framed within a broader argument about the relationship between electricity and development; that is, they rest on a trickle-down theory of economic development that assumed that industrialisation, wage labour and increased domestic savings would provide citizens with the financial capital needed to afford the 'goods' – electricity – which would eventually improve their quality of life. Of course, this line of thinking is not surprising given that the high period of dam construction and electricity network expansion in Uganda coincided with the golden age of economic modernisation theory.

However, what is significant is the extent to which this historical vision of electricity – i.e. as primarily a tool for macroeconomic development – remains in existence in contemporary Uganda, as well as how it has been carried forward and by whom. Today, the rationale for large-scale infrastructure development is largely based on the same principles espoused historically: an assumption that more electricity for economic growth will eventually trickle down to citizens.

These observations point to a second issue – the prominence of a dominant energy narrative in Uganda. A development narrative, according to Emery Roe (1991: 288), has a beginning, middle and end, or a premise and conclusion: it 'revolves around a sequence of events or positions in which something happens or from which something follows...development narratives tell scenarios not so much about what should happen as about what will happen – according to their tellers – if the events or positions are carried out as described.'

Accordingly, it seems reasonable to assert that a dominant energy narrative in Uganda emerged in the 1960s which remains in place today. This narrative was first firmly articulated by Winston Churchill in the early 1900s and then reasserted and carried forward by the UEB. What would happen was quite simple: make electricity available for industry and economic development and more demand will follow. As the dominant 'teller' of the story, the UEB thus presented a convincing rationale for constructing the Owen Falls Dam and subsequent dams. Supporting this narrative was research from international consultants and the World Bank, as well as financial support from the World Bank and the UK's Colonial Office. What is more, as an indicator of the power of the narrative and the absence of any counter-narratives, even in the midst of technical and financial problems and mounting civil and political instability in the country, the UEB was able to continue its commitment to these goals. As Hirschman (1967: 63) explained in his 1967 study, the central problem the UEB confronted was that it needed more consumers, yet it could not afford to expand the network to reach them, so that electricity continued to be available only for those already wealthy or in positions of authority:

> The UEB stood ready to bring power to the villages in the vicinity of
> the towns it supplied, provided the villagers made an adequate capital
> contribution to the cost of the transmission, step-down transformers, and
> distribution. But since power was brought to the towns (and therefore to
> the East Indians) wholly at UEB's expense, this policy was resented as rank
> discrimination against Africans.

Thus, the cornerstone of this emergent energy narrative was the link between electricity and economic modernisation – a belief that electricity provision for industrial activity was to take place before that for individual access, and that individual provision, particularly to Africans, was to be done only out of economic necessity for the company or if the consumer could afford it.

Interviews I conducted between 2001 and 2003 show that this remained the dominant view of senior civil servants and energy regulators. This view raises many concerns, particularly with respect to the potential for low-income, unconnected households to benefit from electricity in the short to medium term, but equally because citizens are given contradictory messages from elected officials who publicly suggest that electricity should and will be available to low-income residents. In short, promises of access to electricity again conflict with the technical and financial reality in Uganda. As one former manager in the UEB explained, 'people feel that as a middle class with good jobs and an education that they should be entitled to power [electricity]'; however, electricity 'is not for the poor; people in power have tried to tell people that they deserve it and MPs tell them that they'll get it for them'. The question, he said, is whether 'government is prepared to talk about reality; the debate is between realism and fiction. If the issue is feasibility, then we are not talking about power to poor' (Karekaho interview).

In the light of this contemporary and historical data, it would be prudent for Ugandan citizens to be conscious of the historical rationale used for expanding electricity access to low-income citizens, and to consider how and whether it is presented differently today. Historically, indigenous Ugandans were only prioritised as electricity consumers insofar as they facilitated the UEB's desire to expand the network, and then only if they could afford to pay the full, or indeed a higher, price for the service. There are, therefore, some very important similarities between the UEB's approach to electricity provision in the late 1950s and early 1960s and the government of Uganda's current approach and ability to expand the electricity network, as I will explain below.

One further area of similarity between pre- and post-colonial electricity development in Uganda centres on the central agents or actors driving electricity expansion and development. Reading Churchill's early 20th-century observations about private-versus-public electricity provision in Uganda does not simply provide interesting colonial context. His remarks highlight an important moment in the pendulum-like debate between private and public electricity provision in Uganda that began, as has been common, with private firms, moving to government, and now has moved back to private firms. At the same time, what makes this back-and-forth movement equally fascinating is the role that domestic and non-domestic institutions have played in mediating and driving the debate. International organisations, particularly the World Bank, the British Colonial Office, and international consulting firms, played central roles in the emergence of Uganda's original electricity aspirations and network development. Today, the international community is again playing a significant role in driving reform in Uganda. What is different now is the way in which these organisations function in Uganda, what role they have played in advocating for the private sector, and their rationale for doing so. With this context in mind, let us move ahead to consider electricity in contemporary Uganda, focusing specifically on how the rationale for privatisation came to dominate, and what outcomes this has produced in the context of service provision and future reform.

Electricity in contemporary Uganda

In 1968, the Owen Falls Dam was operating at full capacity, producing 150 MW of electricity (Engorait 2005: 1). By 1986 the generating capacity of the power station had degraded to 60 MW. In terms of consumers, Uganda's civil conflict also had a dramatic effect. In 1971, the year Idi Amin took power, the total number of customers in Uganda was 69 500. And although the number of consumers temporarily increased during his reign, in 1979, the year the war with Tanzania ended, there were only 60 918 consumers in the country (UEB 1996, 1999). The numbers of consumers recovered from 1979 to 1986, but the successive battles with Obote and the Okellos during the armed struggle of the National Resistance Movement (NRM) not only crippled the electricity system but also produced a formidable national economic and social challenge when Museveni and the NRM took control of the country in 1986 (see Nabaguzi 1995). Thus, in 1986, the number of electricity consumers in Uganda stood at 106 450, but two years later the number of consumers had dropped again, to 80 795 – a number reminiscent of the 1970s (UEB 1996).

The essential problem that Museveni and the NRM were confronting was that they had inherited an infrastructure network that was in a dismal state. But owing to new stability in the country, demand for electricity was rapidly outstripping available supply. This produced the now oft-repeated cycle of power rationing/ load shedding that continues to plague Uganda, as the country endeavours to improve service quality and increase supply.

Two things are particularly notable in this early post-1986 period. First, the World Bank, starting in 1985, remained prominently involved in Uganda's energy sector by supporting several new energy-related projects and programmes. Second, and perhaps most surprisingly given the Bank's prominent involvement and government commitment to the privatisation of public enterprises in the early 1990s, the UEB was not formally unbundled in preparation for privatisation until 1999. In fact, until the early to mid-1990s the Bank accepted 'the prevalent view that public enterprises were the appropriate providers of power' (World Bank 2001: 35). This support or acceptance of the public-sector role in electricity manifested itself directly in the Bank's energy-specific projects and public-sector reform initiatives in the early 1990s.

In 1983, the year of its creation, the Energy Sector Management Assistance Programme (ESMAP) studied Uganda's energy sector.[8] The ESMAP advanced five electricity-specific recommendations (ESMAP 1984):

1   Owing to the poor quality of infrastructure, immediately prepare and conduct a feasibility study for the repair of the Owen Falls Dam and existing transmission and distribution networks.
2   Develop a least-cost, long-term sector development programme to respond to the anticipated shortfall in supply that was expected in 1988 and 1989, examine long-term demand potential in Uganda, and revisit and review hydro-electric development schemes for the Nile.
3   Owing to the role of electricity in economic growth, and in keeping with historic trends, extend Uganda's transmission and distribution network to all major towns and replace diesel generating stations.
4   Develop a second hydro-power station for the purposes of exporting power, but only if commitments from purchasers can be guaranteed, and adjust current export power rates to Kenya.
5   Increase tariffs as soon as possible but also introduce a 'lifeline' tariff.[9]

While this list would provide a foundation for the Bank's future energy projects in Uganda, owing to global attention to climate change, oil dependency, and renewable energies, it is worth noting that the ESMAP report also highlighted the existing and potential role of fuelwood, renewable energy, and energy efficiency in Uganda (ESMAP 1984). But much to the dismay of long-time renewable energy advocates in Uganda, throughout the 1980s and 1990s the Bank and national government's energy initiatives focused almost exclusively on electricity generation and supply initiatives. This is despite the fact that 95 per cent or more of Ugandans depend on biomass for their energy needs.[10]

Given the significant role of electricity in human development and the poor state of the sector, few would question the emphasis on electricity from a macro-economic perspective. Two central reasons explain why biomass, up until recently, has played such a small role in Uganda's energy supply strategy: firstly, there was a clearly communicated prioritisation in the sequence of energy-related reforms: first power sector reforms, then the launch of the Energy for Rural Transformation Project,[11] then a new Petroleum Bill, and then biomass – in other words, 'electricity first, biomass second'; and secondly, it was assumed that the power sector reforms would be quick and successful, thus producing improvements in distribution and transmission, increased generation, and ultimately increased access. But owing to the ongoing problems with improvements in electricity generation and distribution, the minimal focus on biomass has become a painful reminder of the problems and complexities associated with the electricity reform process. Moreover, despite recent moves to formally improve biomass energy supplies, it is clear that '[w]oodfuel will continue to be the dominant source of energy in Uganda for the foreseeable future. Even if the entire hydro-electric potential in Uganda was fully utilised...wood would still supply more than 75% of the total energy consumption in 2015' (MWLE 2002: 97).

Following the ESMAP's 1983 study, the World Bank sponsored three multi-million-dollar sector-specific reform and improvement projects: Power II was approved in 1985 for US$28.8 million; Power III was approved in 1991 for US$125 million; and Power IV was approved in 2001 for US$62 million.[12] To varying degrees Power II and Power III each focused on pricing, sector co-ordination, management, planning, rehabilitation, expansion and upgrading, while also accepting the role of the state in electricity provision (World Bank 2001).[13]

This commitment to public electricity provision was reaffirmed in 1993 when the government of Uganda, under the auspices of its policy for public enterprise reform and divestiture (PERD) programme, released a list of 40 public enterprises to be divested, including large parastatals relating to banking, insurance, railways and telecommunications (Tangri & Mwenda 2001: 118). All parastatals were classified in five categories – retain, majority share, minority share, fully divest, liquidate. The UEB was classified as a Class 1 enterprise, to be retained, though this classification would be short-lived.

Six years later, a new Electricity Act would be passed paving the way for the unbundling of the UEB and showing a reverse in support for the state-run company. What happened during this period to provoke this change? How did the decision to turn to privatisation and the construction of the Bujagali Dam emerge in these deliberations? And, ultimately, are these reforms tied to the current sector problems?

To answer these questions two things need to be discussed: firstly, trends in the privatisation of public enterprises; and secondly, the relationship between these trends and the process of reforming the electricity sector, which importantly includes efforts to construct the Bujagali Dam. By analysing these two elements, an appreciation is gained of how historical, ideological, political and procedural factors converged to impede a quick and 'clean' reform process. More specifically, what is revealed is that while World Bank documents largely attribute the problems with the electricity sector to public management concerns and technical and financial problems, the reality is that this assessment is incomplete. The desire to construct the Bujagali Dam quickly in order to address Uganda's power supply problems meant that alternative reform options were not seriously debated, historical rationales for building Bujagali were relied on as justifications for the project, and the success of reform became dependent on the quick execution of the dam project.

Privatising Uganda: laying the foundation

The UEB's designation as a public enterprise 'to be retained' in 1993 is significant when put in the context of other reforms taking place in the country at that time, and given donor pressure to privatise public enterprises. Up until 1992 the relationship between Uganda and donors had remained uneasy; macroeconomic stabilisation had proven elusive despite increased and leniently provided aid. During the period 1987–1992, donor demands for the privatisation of parastatals and further currency devaluations were debated but continued to be resisted (Dijkstra & Van Donge 2001). By 1991 donor frustration was escalating, and came to a head when Uganda refused to address concerns surrounding foreign currency and exchange rate controls. Dijkstra and Van Donge (2001) note that this culminated in some donors severing aid. Despite this reduced income, the Ministry of Finance did not cut expenditures, producing a budget deficit and an upsurge in inflation. Making matters worse, the IMF suspended programme aid to Uganda and other donors demanded firm control of government expenditure and full liberalisation of the exchange rate.

According to Twaddle and Hansen (1998), at this point only two realistic options were open to Uganda: accept donor advice quickly, or accept it less quickly. Museveni chose to do so quickly. He reshuffled his Cabinet, 'removing a hostile finance minister under advice from the IMF' (Harrison 2001: 663) and appointed a proponent of fiscal discipline, Emmanuel Tumusiime-Mutebile, as permanent secretary (Dijkstra & Van Donge 2001). Under the new permanent secretary, a cash budget was introduced so that expenditures did not exceed the sum of revenues and foreign grants and loans, and the relationship between donors and the government grew more cordial. From 1992 until the late 1990s the 'Ugandan economic miracle' started to take shape, with gross poverty levels decreasing and economic growth being one of the highest on the continent (Tripp 2004: 20), averaging 6.5 per cent per year since 1991/1992 (MFPED 2004: xvi).

Recent analyses of Uganda's economic growth in the 1990s, however, take away some of the economic optimism associated with this decade. Hickey (2005), for example, has argued that the growth that took place largely benefited urban residents and the wealthy, and questions whether the economic growth model used can be sustained. Equally, between 2000 and 2003, the government acknowledged that poverty levels had increased, while recently suggesting that they have once again decreased. Despite this mixed evidence, it is still held that Uganda's future economic success remains dependent on two things: ongoing donor support in the form of programme aid, which has helped to balance the budget and support growth (Dijkstra & Van Donge 2001), and domestic ownership of reforms.[14]

President Museveni publicly expressed commitment to macroeconomic stabilisation, public-sector and economic reform, and the privatisation of parastatals in the early 1990s following the appointment of a Public Service Review and Reorganisation Commission in 1989. Anne Mette Kjaer (2004: 397) recounts that one of the members of this Commission said that Museveni 'personally made it clear that he desired far-reaching suggestions rather than merely proposals for minor adjustments'. After meeting initial resistance within the Ministry of Public Service, as with the Ministry of Finance, Museveni took personal control and reduced the number of ministries from 32 to 21 in 1992, as well as appointing a new minister of public service and an Implementation and Monitoring Board.[15]

Initially, public-sector reform progressed quickly with 150 000 retrenchments, large-scale pay reform and major financial and functional decentralisation measures: 'The civil service reform programme was clearly perceived as part of a wider rebuilding project which the NRM government had undertaken, consisting of structural adjustment, decentralisation, constitutional and electoral reform...a rebuilding project which was the whole *raison d'être* of the NRM regime' (Kjaer 2004: 397). Coupled with civil service reform was the desire to divest from public enterprises. In the late 1980s, Uganda had 156 public enterprises, many operating at a loss with low productivity – characteristic of many public enterprises in developing countries (Nellis & Kikeri 1989; Tukahebwa 1998).[16] Privatisation, therefore, was viewed as an important component of structural adjustment.

The formal commitment to privatisation was made in the early 1990s. But critics of the early process suggest that once the decision was made, 'little was done to educate the public about the policy of privatisation and its potential benefits' (Tangri & Mwenda 2001: 118). Tukahebwa (1998) suggests that the lack of a proper communication strategy and citizen participation in the privatisation policy led Parliament to suspend the sale of public enterprises in early 1993 and that it was only after a closed session of Parliament that the law was passed. Tangri and Mwenda (2001: 119) further note that MPs 'expressed concern that state companies were being undervalued and sold at low prices; that deals were being conducted hurriedly and less than transparently; and that issues relating to the indigenisation of the economy were not being heeded'. These authors give examples of parastatals sold to MPs and confidants of the president at prices below expected value, and then sold again at higher prices.[17]

Tukahebwa (1998: 65) notes that following these initial difficulties the national government belatedly 'embarked on a propaganda campaign through advertisements in the newspapers, radio and a drama group' to persuade the public that privatisation had been and would be beneficial, producing better jobs, education and health. Nonetheless, despite the initial push, privatisation of state-owned enterprises was hardly implemented until 1995, and was then carried out slowly (Dijkstra & Van Donge 2001). As a result of concerns with delays in the privatisation process and corruption, at a 1998 Consultative Group meeting in Kampala donors asked President Museveni to take personal charge of privatisation (Dijkstra & Van Donge 2001). Writing during the same period, other observers reassert that Uganda's early experience with privatisation showed a need for transparency and better communication of policy to Ugandan citizens (see Tukahebwa 1998). What is noteworthy about these observations about process, transparency and communication is that five years after Tukahebwa's observations, interviews with civil servants engaged in public-sector reform and privatisation suggested that these issues remained prominent.

In 2002, Emmanuel Nyirinkindi was director of the Utility Reform Unit, Ministry of Finance, Planning and Economic Development. In our conversations, he acknowledged that MPs were not, and have not been, very good at communicating the rationale for privatisation in Uganda. Furthermore, those most knowledgeable about reforms, public servants, are restricted from speaking out publicly (Nyirinkindi interview). Nyirinkindi further explained that in Uganda the public perception of privatisation of state-owned utilities is that government has got a raw deal, corruption is rife, proceeds from sales cannot be found, and government does not receive enough money for the enterprises – observations consistent with other national experiences with privatisation (see Birdsall & Nellis 2003).

On the question of revenue from the sale of public firms, Nyirinkindi emphasised that part of the problem is that the value of corporations in Uganda is understood differently than in the West. In Uganda, the physical assets of corporations are valued more than the perceived market value. The Ugandan public, therefore, 'has very high but very unrealistic expectations of what's achievable when selling public enterprises'. Moreover, he explained, 90 per cent of Uganda's public enterprises were carrying massive debts that undermined their value. As a result, Nyirinkindi suggested that the government incurred strong criticism when the public did not understand the chief purpose of selling – relieving the government of the financial burden of the enterprise. Hence, from the perspective of the Ministry of Finance, while the privatisation process has experienced difficulties, the central issue confounding privatisation is not its legacy or outcome, but how the rationale for privatisation is communicated – a problem exacerbated by the unwillingness of elected officials to communicate publicly the real rationale for reform, as well as by the World Bank, the architect of reforms, not being accountable to the domestic population for the reforms it promotes and requires. These observations are not intended to serve as justification for privatisation. Rather, they highlight the general character of the privatisation process in Uganda, and the manner in which privatisation has been approached and communicated publicly.

Privatisation and public-sector reform remain priorities in Uganda. As of late 2006, 122 government enterprises had been privatised with 30 still publicly owned. Remaining public enterprises included the National Housing and Construction Corporation and the National Water and Sewerage Corporation (NWSC). In December 2006, the Uganda Railways Corporation was privatised under a 25-year concession to Rift Valley Railways, a consortium led by Sheltam Rail Company, a South African rail and marine services firm.

With respect to the NWSC, it is interesting to note that in a January 2003 interview with the team leader for the Utility Reform Unit in the Privatisation Unit, I was told that it was then being prepared for privatisation. It was explained that the Reform Unit was closely monitoring the experience with the electricity sector and being 'very cautious' as a result of the challenges faced in electricity (Ssebabi interview). Yet, in late 2007, the NWSC had still not been privatised.

Another recent event will probably complicate or delay future divestitures. In 2006 the World Bank announced that it would no longer finance the Privatisation Unit's activities, which it had been supporting since 2001. The Bank publicly stated that its withdrawal was due to a lapse in programme funding. Media reports, however, suggest that political interference, lack of transparency and the slow pace of divestiture were key reasons for the Bank's decision (*East African* 2006).

Taken together, this description of the trends in privatisation in Uganda provides some important context when considering the privatisation of the UEB. In particular, it should be noted that unlike popular examples such as Nigeria or South Africa, no nationwide or urban-based popular protests against privatisation have occurred. While a handful of public protests have taken place over electricity price increases, and newspaper editorials have taken issue with privatisation, the exercise has generally not been disrupted by public action.

The explanation for the absence of protest seems to be threefold. First, the majority of citizens have not been directly affected by the privatisations. With the exception of electricity, no highly contentious privatisations have occurred where a large number of citizens are individually affected, as would be the case with water and sanitation services. In fact, so few people are connected to the formal electricity network that there have been no mass demonstrations against price increases either. The result is that the strongest protest often comes from industry groups, such as the Uganda Manufacturers' Association, but here the issue is price increases and not the actual or potential social impact that the act of privatising might produce.

Second, while President Museveni regularly blames MPs for delays in electricity reform and other privatisations, on the whole a critical mass of MPs has not come together in Parliament to challenge the government's public-sector reform agenda. Parliamentary debates show that many key figures have supported it, while importantly taking issue with the process of reform rather than the impending outcome. Time will tell whether the recent change in the law, allowing formal political parties to be represented in Parliament, will change how MPs respond to the ruling party's policies and rules.[18]

Third, civil-society groups in Uganda remain comparatively weak; they are not focused on public enterprises, and for historical and practical reasons the vast majority have worked with donors and the government as opposed to challenging them. As a result, NGO agendas have been largely donor-driven (Brock 2004; De Coninck 2004; Dicklitch 2001; Tripp 2000) and those that have opposed government programmes have been called 'anti-government', 'anti-development' or 'economic saboteurs'. Given that most are highly dependent on international and government financial support (Barr et al. 2005) the result is that with a few exceptions, civil-society organisations do not openly challenge government for fear of compromising the limited opportunities they are afforded to participate in policy discussions or to continue with their programme work.

In sum, Uganda's general experience with privatisation demonstrates a donor- and national government-driven process that has largely been closed to public scrutiny or debate. The outcome has been a set of significant, yet problematic, precedents with important bearing on electricity. Here, three can be highlighted: reform processes are generally predetermined by donors and the national government; the real or potential outcomes from privatisations are not publicly communicated and the political process associated with privatisation is given little attention as compared to achieving the desired outcome; and the desire for privatisation has proceeded with a chief goal of producing short-term technical and financial returns, while the social and political consequences have been overlooked or ignored. In the last section of this discussion, I explain how the electricity reform process evolved and how and why privatisation emerged as the dominant response to the country's electricity challenges.

From public to private: the rationale for change

We can recall that in 1993, under the auspices of the PERD programme, the UEB was designated a Class 1 enterprise – an enterprise to be retained. Thus, despite the trends in structural adjustment programmes in the 1980s and early 1990s, in Uganda the World Bank was still willing (for a very short time, it would turn out) to support the government's role as a provider of electricity. Soon after this 1993 designation, however, the Bank's view of the UEB would change. While some suggest that the turn towards privatisation was a response to the inability or unwillingness of senior UEB managers and the board of directors to enforce internal change, there is another complementary reason for the turn to privatisation – the desire to construct a new hydro-electric dam at Bujagali Falls. In turn, to understand the decision to move from public to private electricity provision in a few short years, one must understand the connection between the rationale and method for reforming the UEB and constructing the Bujagali Dam.

There is little question that in the mid-1990s the UEB was performing poorly. The total number of new consumers between 1993 and 1999 was less than 50 000 (UEB 1999), and in 1994 and 1995 the number of consumers dropped below 1993 levels, demonstrating the inconsistency of electricity supply and consumer provision. Several government ministries and institutions were also notorious for not paying their electricity bills, most notably the Ministry of Defence and the NWSC. Furthermore, it was well known that several MPs had not paid their electricity bills in years. One former UEB employee explained that prior to 1999, there was a dangerous trend in government and the civil service: the higher individuals rose in public office, the more they felt that they were entitled to a higher level or amount of free services. Thus, I was told: '…staff in UEB are not the most efficient, but the external environment is worse than the internal' (anonymous informant).[19] Adding to this, the UEB suffered from a problematic billing system and many managers approached the need for improvement inconsistently or were hostile to internal improvements.

As a result, just two years after being designated a Class 1 enterprise to be retained, several senior civil servants confirmed that 'a dialogue' took place in 1995 where reform and restructuring were agreed. This dialogue was formalised first with an internal UEB report in 1996 which recommended restructuring and divestment, then with the creation of a Committee on Divestiture, and eventually with a 1997 Strategic Plan. In 1998 the Strategic Plan was finalised, laying out the formal plan for divestment and restructuring of the UEB and the eventual passage of the 1999 Electricity Act. During this period (1995–1998) and in keeping with overall trends in Uganda's privatisation experience, a senior reform leader acknowledged to me that 'there wasn't a lot of external participation in producing the Strategic Plan' (Nyirinkindi interview).

With respect to the UEB's internal performance, increasingly donors had been asking for quantitative indices of financial and service delivery improvements, which the UEB was unable to provide. The most glaring illustration of these performance problems comes from the ratio of electricity produced to revenue collected in the mid-1990s – at times the figure was just 50 per cent. Beginning in 1996, the UEB (and later the UEDCL) also tried multiple 'operations' or 'task forces' to disconnect illegal consumers. Variously titled 'Operation Thunder', 'Omega', then 'Sigma', these programmes were launched because of high systems losses, poor revenue collection, and theft. And while they proved effective at disconnecting many illegal consumers, in the words of one senior manager,

Operation Sigma was 'a propaganda thing for them' (anonymous informant). Weekly newspaper updates on Operation Sigma's progress emphasise this point. Moreover, it was rumoured that the UEDCL manager was financially rewarded for each illegal cut-off that Operation Sigma performed. In the words of the World Bank Country Programme Manager at the time, Robert Blake, the UEB was 'dysfunctional' and 'unreformable'; its operational efficiency was almost the worst in the world. 'It was amazing; the UEB was not even able to satisfy 5 per cent of the population using electricity' (Blake interview).

Blake further noted that the government could not mobilise new funds, the UEB could not do anything about unpaid bills from other ministries, and ultimately, donors were unwilling to provide more funding for the sector unless dramatic change came about. Divestiture was the antidote deemed most appropriate by the Bank, but in the early stages the government was still entertaining partial ownership. This designation was short-lived, however, owing to problems with previous privatisation efforts in which the government had tried to maintain partial ownership and, more tellingly, because when the government solicited interest in the distribution and generation components of electricity under partial government ownership, no companies were interested (Nyirinkindi interview).

In addition to the UEB's clear performance problems, the other central reason to cede the distribution and generation companies to private firms was related to the Bujagali Dam. Confirming this, Emmanuel Nyirinkindi stated: 'The traditional lender [the World Bank] and Bujagali were the drivers of this process.' Hence, the future of the electricity sector did not simply rest on a desire to clean up and improve the operational efficiency of the service provider. Public-sector reform was part of a much more complex and ambitious vision for sector change reminiscent of the colonial period and the construction of the Owen Falls Dam. This time, instead of *creating* a state enterprise to build a large dam and develop a national electricity network, the state enterprise would be *dismantled* to facilitate the private construction of the nation's electricity distribution network and generation facilities.

The logic of simultaneously combining restructuring, privatisation and dam construction rested on three observations. First, the UEB, due to a combination of internal and external problems, could not perform its electricity distribution functions. Second, the UEB was unable to significantly reduce system losses. Third, few private companies would invest in the construction and operation of a large infrastructure project unless its profitability could be guaranteed. For electricity generation projects, this guarantee often takes the form of a 'take or pay arrangement' whereby a government must agree, usually under the auspices of a Power Purchase Agreement (PPA), to pay for a set volume of electricity, at a set rate, over a set period of time, whether it can use the electricity generated or not. Given this arrangement, the UEB's record, and donor scepticism about the UEB's ability to change, advocates suggested that privatisation of the distribution company would follow naturally. In the words of World Bank Country Manager

Robert Blake, '[I]f you accept this then restructuring falls out naturally' and the need to create the domestic conditions necessary to attract independent power producers to the generation and distribution components of electricity is revealed (Blake interview).

Thus, the Bank and Museveni moved forward with a vision that required a bold set of 'meta-undertakings' to occur simultaneously: the restructuring and unbundling of the UEB; the development and implementation of a new Electricity Act and regulatory framework; and the construction of the Bujagali Dam. I use the notion of a 'meta-undertaking' to highlight the fact that under each of these undertakings there were several individual processes, such as multiple environmental impact assessments in the case of the dam.

In a country with a very small market of existing electricity consumers, very poor infrastructure quality, and weak organisational and regulatory capacity, this agenda was very ambitious, and its success highly dependent on the careful, consecutive and successful execution of each reform action. Most critical of all was the guarantee that there would be sufficient electricity supply. For if the supply of electricity cannot be guaranteed, is uncertain or unstable, negotiations with a private firm to take over the distribution system will be extremely difficult. Acknowledging this challenge, Robert Blake noted, 'After [these reforms are] decided, then it becomes much more complicated and timing and sequence is important – you need to figure out how the pieces fit together' (Blake interview).

Putting it in a more specific context, with respect to the Bujagali Dam, one Northern European donor representative noted that while the construction of Bujagali was not dependent on privatisation, successful privatisation in Uganda had become dependent on Bujagali. Indeed, he said, 'Bujagali is instrumental to privatisation…without [it] the whole restructuring of the sector would collapse' (Venvick interview).

Bujagali and privatisation: too much, too fast?

Bujagali was identified as a prime site for the construction of a hydro-electric dam in the early 1900s. In fact, in the 1920s it was deemed the best location for a dam in Uganda but because the Owen Falls site was easier to access, Bujagali was downgraded to a second- or possibly third-best choice. A consultant's report suggested Bujagali again in 1957, but it was never initiated. The site's priority re-emerged in a new study in 1986, at the same time that Museveni came to power. It is noteworthy that several of the same consultants who produced the 1957 study recommending Bujagali also prepared the 1986 study. Four years later, Acres International Ltd (a Canadian company) suggested that Uganda first expand Owen Falls and then build at Bujagali. A follow-up study by Acres in 1991, titled the 'Bujagali Hydro-Electric Project Pre-Investment Study', reinforced the prominence of the project.[20] Hence, in the context of contemporary debates surrounding the appropriateness of Bujagali as a site for a hydro-electric dam in Uganda, given that the development of the site has been discussed for almost 100 years, it is important to recognise the historical weight and legacy of this locale in the institutional memory of the government and its plans for electricity development.[21]

Moreover, any effort to challenge the merits of the Bujagali site would have to be exceptionally strong and go beyond just pointing out potential problems. Counter-arguments or indeed counter-narratives would have to demonstrate that the cost – typically, yet problematically, considered in terms of time and money – of developing a new site would be *less than* the cost of abandoning Bujagali, taking into account the time and money already invested. When put this way, and pre-empting the details to come, opponents of the Bujagali project faced an enormous challenge. As Pierson (2000: 253) explains, 'Each step along a particular path produces consequences which make that path more attractive for the next round. As such effects begin to accumulate, they generate a powerful virtuous (or vicious) cycle of self-reinforcing activity.' Hence, 'the probability of further steps along the same path increases with each move down that path. This is because the *relative* benefits of the current activity compared with other possible options increase over time. To put it a different way, the costs of exit – of switching to some previously plausible alternative – rise.'[22]

The first formal steps to initiate construction at Bujagali began in 1994, when the South African-based Madhvani Group of companies approached USA-based AES International about building the dam. That same year, President Museveni signed a Memorandum of Understanding with AES and Madhvani, giving them first right of refusal to build. Together, AES and Madhvani established the company AES Nile Power (AESNP). It is noteworthy that neither company had ever constructed a dam before.

But AES was not the only company in Uganda considering electricity generation sites. A Norwegian company, Norpak Ltd, a subsidiary of Norwegian-based utility company Adger Energi AS, was granted the right to develop a dam at another favoured site in northern Uganda, Karuma Falls. (For a short time in the mid-1990s, Enron was also active in Uganda.) In each case, no competitive bidding process was undertaken. Museveni's word and strength of character solidified the agreements with AESNP and Norpak. According to one source, 'Museveni took a brave stance' (Maré interview). He took the reports on the hydro-electric capacity of the Nile and 'hawked them around the world', ultimately receiving commitments from AES and Norpak. In contrast, a member of one of the domestic NGOs most critical of Bujagali, the National Association of Professional Environmentalists (NAPE), described this process as the 'silent Scramble for the Nile' (personal communication). What makes this story all the more interesting is how the World Bank Group factors into the decision to pursue Bujagali. Formally, the International Finance Corporation (IFC), the private-sector arm of the World Bank Group, was the first to become involved with the project in 1998. But according to individuals within the National Environmental Management Authority (NEMA), the independent authority co-ordinating environmental and social assessments in Uganda, the IFC began reviewing the project without their knowledge. Prior to that, AESNP was putting pressure on the NEMA to move quickly in their reviews. Adding to this, the World Bank/International Development Association (IDA) also became formally involved in the Bujagali project, requiring that its resettlement plans be adopted, as they were more stringent than those in Uganda. From the beginning of their involvement, and still today, both the IDA and the IFC are making financial commitments in support of the project. The IDA is providing a partial risk guarantee, which insures commercial lending for the project. The IFC will be providing financing in the form of long-term loans, and the Multilateral Investment Guarantee Agency (MIGA) is providing equity political risk insurance.

Here it is important to formally distinguish between the World Bank's involvement in the Bujagali project beginning in 1998/1999, and its involvement in prior dam construction efforts and the electricity sector reform process generally. In 1991, the Bank's third power project in Uganda, Power III, was approved. Owing to poor electricity supply and poor infrastructure quality, one of the central components of this project was to add an extension to the Owen Falls Dam in order to add upwards of 200 MW.

The extension, Kiira, was complete in 2000, but with additional generation units being added well after this date owing to the fact that the extension added just 100 MW to the grid initially. This delay in completing Kiira, along with the small amount of electricity it was adding to the national grid, spurred the government of Uganda's turn to the Bujagali site in 1994, and its guarantee to AES that same year. Some time shortly after this, AES asked the IFC to provide direct financing for the project and to help with additional financing. Around this same time (1995–1996) we can recall that the dialogue over the unbundling of the UEB was also under way. Subsequently, in 1997, the government of Uganda requested a Partial Risk Guarantee (PRG) from the IDA to support the development of Bujagali. Bearing in mind the earlier discussion of the timeline associated with the unbundling of the UEB, there is clearly strong evidence to suggest that the World Bank was formally involved or at minimum had direct knowledge of the development of the Bujagali site prior to, or at the same time that, it began requiring the UEB to be unbundled. Events and documents show that the government, and most directly the president, were taking a prominent lead in the development of Bujagali. Furthermore, an unprompted remark by AES's public relations representative in a 2002 conversation reconfirmed the general feeling that Bujagali was as much a World Bank project as it was a Ugandan government project. The representative said, '[t]he World Bank is really the proponent of the project' and that it was taking the lead in negotiations with export credit agencies to co-ordinate the project's financing.[23] Hence, when considering *why* privatisation became the dominant approach and *how* privatisation became embedded in sector reforms, this information reveals the Bank's central role in blending public-sector reform goals with private-sector advocacy and infrastructure construction.

Domestic NGO concerns with the Bujagali project emerged formally in 1998. Several NGOs, particularly the NAPE and the Uganda Wildlife Society, began asking for details about the financial and socio-economic viability of the project and its environmental impacts. Central concerns rested with the cost of the project and the future price of the electricity, along with the environmental impacts of a series of dams in close succession on the Nile. Important questions were also raised over how Bujagali was to directly improve access to electricity, why the economic analysis of the project that had been done was not publicly available, and whether a thorough analysis of the project had been done in comparison to alternatives.

On this point, NGOs pointed to an analysis done in the late 1990s which suggested that geothermal power was also a viable option in Uganda. But reinforcing earlier remarks made about increasing returns, Robert Blake explained that the project proposal for Bujagali was already complete after having been researched for some time, so the cost of geothermal had to be weighed against the research involved in assessing its potential, and then the cost of preparing a project proposal for the geothermal option (Blake interview).

Unsatisfied with the rationale being provided for Bujagali, and frustrated with difficulties experienced in accessing many project details, several NGOs led by the NAPE and Save the Bujagali Crusade took their concerns to the World Bank's Inspection Panel, with advice and technical support from the USA-based NGO International Rivers Network. The Panel recognised the legitimacy of the NGOs' request for inspection, and the World Bank accepted the Inspection Panel's recommendation to review the project in mid-2001, just five months prior to the date on which the World Bank Board was supposed to vote on support for the project. In December 2001, the Board approved the Bank's role in financing Bujagali – a decision made prior to the Inspection Panel publishing their findings.

It followed that in January 2002 a ground-breaking ceremony was held to mark – it was thought – the beginning of construction on the dam. However, one year later, estimating a loss of US$75 million, and amidst allegations of corruption involving project subcontractors, AES withdrew from Uganda and the Bujagali project temporarily collapsed.

World Bank documents suggest three central reasons for the original project failing to take off: export credit agency withdrawal due to high political and business risk; investigations and allegations of corruption; and the deterioration of the global financial situation of the private sponsor (AESNP), following in the wake of Enron's collapse and a loss of confidence in higher-risk global energy undertakings. These financial problems were clearly instrumental in the project's initial failure. But pointing to the problems with Bujagali as largely technical and financial, as the World Bank has done, or critiquing the Ugandan Parliament or domestic or international NGOs for undermining Bujagali (see Mallaby 2004) pays insufficient attention to the process, risk and complexity associated with the reforms being pursued in Uganda.

In the Inspection Panel's 2002 report on Bujagali, many of the central concerns raised by Ugandan NGOs were confirmed, particularly in relation to the economic analysis of the project, disclosure of information, cumulative environmental impacts, assessment of alternatives, and public participation (see Inspection Panel 2002; World Bank 2003). But given this chapter's attention to privatisation, what is even more revealing is what the Panel said about the distribution concession in relation to Bujagali. The Panel writes that another area of concern 'relates to the privatisation and performance of the distribution concession':

> It is clear that the performance of the distribution sector is likely to play a significant role in the ability of the Bujagali project to deliver sustainable benefits...The distribution sector is key to the connection of new consumers (and so to providing the benefits of access to electricity) and to collecting revenue (and hence to the ability of the power sector to finance its service provision, and to restrain tariff growth to compensate for non-payment). Because of this, the status and performance of the privatised distribution sector is an important element in risk associated with the Project. Correspondingly, therefore, there are some difficult issues: tariffs have to be low enough to be affordable but sufficiently high and sustained to make it worthwhile for a profit-making entity to commit to collecting them. In the Panel's view, an indication of a thorough examination of the institutional risk of a delayed or underperforming privatisation of the distribution system, and its impact on the robustness of the Project's affordability is missing from the [Bank's] economic appraisal...although this was needed for full compliance with [Operational Policy 10.04: Economic Analysis of Projects]. (Inspection Panel 2002: xviii)

Adding to this assessment, in 2002 India-based Prayas Energy Group published an independent assessment of the PPA between AESNP and the government of Uganda. Amongst many other findings, Prayas highlighted the fact that the original Implementation Agreement (IA) for Bujagali formally stated that the government of Uganda had to prepare and complete an implementation plan for either the privatisation or the commercialisation of the UEB (Prayas Energy Group 2002). Furthermore, the UEB could not enter into any new PPAs or IAs until AESNP attained financial closure or the UEB could demonstrate that new projects would be financially sustainable and would not affect the UEB's ability to sustain the Bujagali project (Prayas Energy Group 2002).

Given these assessments, it is not surprising that in 2001, when financing for Bujagali became questionable, 'the concessions were thrown into a loop' (Mare interview), further delaying the privatisations, investments in the entire infrastructure network, and any hopes for improved and increased access to affordable electricity. In a November 2006 story in the *Monitor* newspaper, the impact of the power supply problems on the distribution concession was elaborated (*Monitor* 2006).

Monitor reported that on 1 March 2005, Umeme had officially taken over the UEDCL, with the government set to receive over US$350 million – the highest return on any privatisation concession in the country to date. Other financial details of the agreement included a US$1.4 million transaction fee, an annual rental fee of US$18 million for use of the UEDCL's assets, and an obligation to invest a minimum of US$65 million in the distribution system over the next five years to upgrade the physical infrastructure, billing system and customer support services. Umeme was also expected to make a minimum of 20 000 annual connections each for the next five years. Owing to the ongoing uncertainty in Uganda's electricity sector, Umeme's commitments were made possible by the first ever application of a World Bank PRG to a utility regulatory system. The PRG 'provides support for potential loss of regulated revenues resulting from a "guaranteed event"…These include non-compliance by the regulator of the pre-agreed tariff framework, full pass-through of the bulk electricity tariff supply from UETCL…and timely adjustments of tariffs' (Eberhard 2005: 33).

The PRG also addresses non-payment of government agency electricity bills and ensures provisional payments pending dispute resolution during a period of 'contract stress'. According to Eberhard (2005: 33), in a presentation made at the World Bank's 2005 Energy Week, the CEO of Globeleq (initially the majority partner in Umeme) said that the provisional payment feature of the PRG was 'deal-clinching'. Despite the role of the PRG in promoting desperately needed investment, the ongoing power supply problem in Uganda has led Umeme to review and reconsider its capacity to achieve the goals originally laid out in its investment, and in November 2006 it applied for a review of its operating licence and a restructuring of its concession agreement. Quite simply, the lack of supply inhibited Umeme's potential to achieve the goals it had established, confounded the reform exercise and, more critically, repressed any hope that citizens would gain access to affordable electricity in the near future.

In a demonstration of the government's commitment to construct Bujagali, in early 2004 a call for tenders to construct the dam was issued. One year later, in May 2005, the government announced that the firm Industrial Promotion Services, a member of the Aga Khan Fund for Economic Development – the economic development arm of the Aga Khan Development Network – along with its partner company, USA-based Sithe Global, had successfully outbid five other companies to win the new contract to construct the dam. The new company they created is named Bujagali Energy Ltd (BEL).

The World Bank's commitment to the Bujagali project has not waned. In April 2007, the World Bank Group approved US$360 million in loans and guarantees for the project (Bujagali II) – US$130 million in loans to BEL from the IFC; a PRG of up to US$115 million from the IDA; and an investment guarantee of up to US$115 million from the MIGA. Financial support for the project is also coming from the African Development Bank, the European Investment Bank and the German Bank for Development. The new total estimated cost of the project is US$799 million, up almost US$300 million from the original project cost. Ministry of Energy sources report that the increased cost is a result of higher prices for oil, cement, steel, iron and consultancy services (Mugirya 2007). At the same time, Norpak's plans to construct a 150 MW dam at Karuma Falls are well under way, with estimates that it will be completed in 2009.

The evolution of the second Bujagali project has not gone without renewed controversy. The NAPE continued to voice its concern over the cost of the project, the potential rise in future electricity tariffs as a result of the cost of the project, and hydrological concerns surrounding drought and climate, fisheries and protected land. Moreover, the NAPE has continued to take its concerns to the World Bank and other project financiers. Senior Bank officials have responded to these concerns openly and directly.

In July 2007, Michel Wormser, the Bank's Sector Director for Sustainable Development, Africa Region, stated: 'The World Bank Management remains committed to the successful implementation of this project including the appropriate application of relevant environmental and social safeguards...The project is critical to Uganda's economic development and we will continue to work with the Government to ensure that this project meets high standards' (Kasita 2007). In the same interview with Ugandan media, Wormser stated: 'The project's approval reflected a shared view by management and the board of the critical importance of providing a new source of electricity expeditiously to Uganda and confidence that thorough economic, environmental and social due diligence has been undertaken to identify and realise that source.' As one indicator that the Bank has learned from some of the transparency problems encountered in its original dam construction effort, a comprehensive website exists that is dedicated solely to the Bujagali project.[24] On this site all current project documents or statements about where documents can be found are provided. BEL, the private project sponsor, has also established its own comprehensive website.[25] It is noteworthy that within the 'About Us' section of the website it states: 'Bujagali Energy Ltd is not associated with AES Nile Power Ltd (AESNP), the previous sponsor of a similar proposed project in Uganda.' As of early September 2007, the physical construction of the dam had begun. The World Bank and BEL both state the project will be commissioned in 2011.

Conclusion

In the light of Uganda's electricity supply crisis in late 2006, the aim of this chapter has been to explain from a historical and a procedural perspective how the private sector came to be regarded as the best option for electricity service provision in the country today. Tracing the origins of both electricity service delivery and infrastructure development has demonstrated that the role and debate over private- versus public-led provision has been prominent for over 100 years. What is also shown is how similar some of the concerns about electricity supply and access have been through time, how prominent various infrastructure development projects have been historically, particularly the Bujagali Dam, and the role of this prominence in producing the turn to the private sector. In explaining this backdrop to Uganda's current energy crisis, what is also revealed is the role that external actors have played in guiding infrastructure investment decisions and the structure of the sector. And while the prominence of external actors in Uganda has remained relatively consistent since independence, what has changed most recently is *how* these external actors, particularly the World Bank, have guided reforms and decision-making.

Based on the evidence presented, it can be argued that Uganda is at the centre of a very ambitious reform experiment. The experiment is driven by a strong belief that the public sector – with the exception of transmission – no longer has a role to play in electricity service delivery, and that the private sector's ability to produce more positive electricity service delivery outcomes is dependent on the successful and simultaneous achievement of a host of other reforms.

It is too early to tell whether, in the long term, the electricity privatisation experiment in Uganda will produce the positive outcomes anticipated. In the short and medium term, however, clearly this experiment has not yet borne the benefits anticipated, and in fact seems to have undermined the sector's performance significantly. Yes, technical and financial factors have been instrumental to the problems encountered in dam construction. But focusing on these factors to explain Uganda's energy crisis leaves out many pressing questions about whether these interventions are the best options for poverty alleviation, and whether the chosen mode of implementing reforms was too ambitious.

In many corners of the World Bank it is clear that these questions are being debated and that faith in the private sector does not reign supreme. For example, in 2000 the World Bank and the ESMAP asked how pro-growth, pro-efficiency reforms should be weighed against those of direct interventions aimed at improving the access of the poor to modern energy for consumption and productive uses (World Bank & ESMAP 2000). In a 2001 Operations Evaluation Department report on Uganda, entitled *Policy, Participation, People*, it is noted that 'against the framework of [an] impressive list of achievements and strengths' the Bank also has weaknesses 'switching from macroeconomic to sector and thematic reform'. Most crucially, the report notes that 'IDA's project implementation suffers from poor design and sequencing, rigid and confusing procedures (particularly for procurement and disbursement), frequent changes in task managers, injudicious reliance on project implementation units, and poor monitoring and evaluation…The resident mission lacks the requisite procurement and sectoral expertise and decisionmaking power because task managers in Washington generally make decisions' (World Bank 2001: 40).

Of equal concern are the cautionary remarks about privatisation offered by the Bank in 2004, which may seem more nuanced than critics expect. It wrote:

There is no universally appropriate model for restructuring network utilities. And the fact that state ownership is flawed does not mean that privatisation is appropriate for all infrastructure activities and all countries. Before state ownership is supplanted by another institutional setup, it is essential to assess the properties and requirements of the proposed alternative – taking into account the sector's features (its underlying economic attributes and the technological conditions of its production) and the country's economic, institutional, social, and political characteristics... In electricity, wholesale competition has worked well in industrial countries because of excess capacity, moderate demand growth, and the availability of natural gas...In contrast, electricity markets in many developing countries face capacity shortages, enormous excess demand, and periodic blackouts. Thus electricity restructuring and privatisation are more problematic and dependent on administrative ability. (World Bank 2004: 8–9)

On the surface, these passages suggest that the Bank is less committed to privatisation than is usually understood to be the case, and that there is room for debate and reflection on the models most appropriate for service provision. Nonetheless, in Uganda, as with other electricity reform experiences in sub-Saharan Africa, it seems that the Bank has demonstrated a 'blind trust in privatisation' (Pineau 2002: 1011). Equally, while the Ugandan government seemed to endorse or accept this approach in the early stages, owing to the problems now being experienced, government leaders have since been openly critical of the Bank and its approach in Uganda. The tension between Washington-generated research and analysis and on-the-ground experience, is an area needing much more attention by researchers. Emphasising this point, in 2006 former Minister of Energy and Minerals Development Syda Bbumba presented a keynote address to the plenary session of the World Bank's Energy Week which was highly critical of the Bank's approach in Uganda (Bbumba 2006).

Bbumba suggested that in implementing reforms, there must be a recognised transition process, and that resources should be allocated to both market-oriented reforms and public-sector delivery efforts. Moreover, based on Uganda's experience of trying to establish new distribution concessions in areas of high and low demand, she emphasised that there was no private-sector interest in areas of low demand, and therefore the public sector must play a role. Hence, in her view, public and private provision of electricity are not mutually exclusive. In perhaps her most critical remarks about the reform process promoted by the Bank, Bbumba states:

As we went about implementing the reforms, it was assumed that we could break away from the traditional public sector delivery and go straight into private delivery models...Our experience to date has proved this assumption wrong...The only conclusion that can be drawn is, therefore, that there is a need to re-examine and redesign the strategies and the programmes that we have put in place with the help of our development partners, basing them on the realities of each reforming country rather than the 'one-size-fits-all' prescription, which, apparently, is now being applied. (Bbumba 2006)

This material is not presented to vilify the Bank. Change within the UEB was desperately needed, as was a shift in the role played by elected officials who had been involved in undermining the UEB's capacity to provide services. But in the light of the Bank's own evaluations of its performance, the outcome of reforms to date, and the character of Uganda's electricity sector, a careful and critical re-examination of the approach to reform and the role of private and public actors in the sector is urgently needed if the current crisis is to be overcome.[26]

Notes

1 With respect to the total number of individuals and households with access to grid-based electricity, and using the most complete national statistics available, in 1999 the total number of Uganda Electricity Board customers was 163 295. Of this number 144 507 were domestic tariffs or households – approximately 89 per cent of all consumers. On the basis of Uganda Bureau of Statistics census data, this information leads to the conclusion that in 1999 only 3 per cent of all Ugandan citizens had access to electricity. Assuming that the ratio between domestic, commercial, institutional and industrial consumers in 2001 was the same as in 1999, the total number of households with electricity would have increased to 177 185 by 2001 or approximately 3.5 per cent of the total population (23 875 655). By January 2002, the Uganda Electricity Distribution Company Ltd had added 20 394 new consumers to the grid, of which approximately 18 150 would have been households. Using the national average of 4.7 individuals per household, these figures translate into 85 305 new individuals gaining access to electricity in 2001. In August 2004, there were reportedly 240 000 total electricity customers (Wakabi 2004). This figure, however, is hard to verify given the absence of regularly published and updated data by the sub-region. But assuming the ratio of domestic to commercial to industrial users has not changed over time, and using the national average of 4.7 people per household, in early 2004 it could be estimated that about 960 000 citizens, or about 4 per cent of the 25 million citizens in the country, had access to electricity. As of June 2006, the number of domestic customers totalled 267 675. Assuming 4.7 people per household, and a country population of 27 million in 2006, the gross percentage of the population connected to electricity has not risen above 5 per cent since 2002.

2 http://siteresources.worldbank.org/EXTINSPECTIONPANEL/Resources/Map1.pdf. Accessed December 2007.

3 Mare was seconded from Eskom South Africa to be the managing director of the UEB in 1999. In the two years prior to his appointment, the UEB recorded a loss of US$23 million. In the two years following, the UEB recorded a profit of US$6.5 million. Following his tenure at the UEB, he became the chief executive of Eskom Uganda before becoming general manager of Umeme.

4 ERA press release, 21 December 2004

5 For domestic consumers wanting to be connected to the electricity grid, prices are also prohibitive. It costs a household US$108 to be connected, in addition to a US$55 security deposit. If a household requires a pole to connect to the network, the connection price increases to US$178. With respect to the unit price of electricity for other non-domestic consumers, at the end of 2006 the tariffs were as follows: commercial = US$0.22; medium industrial = US$0.20; large industrial = US$0.10.

6 A varied programme for the queen in Uganda, *East African Standard* 1954

7 Uganda's royal occasion, *East African Standard* 1954

8 The ESMAP was created in 1983 under the joint sponsorship of the UNDP and the World Bank, in response to the global energy challenges that were emerging. The ESMAP is a technical assistance programme which provides policy advice on sustainable energy development to governments in developing and transition economies. It also strives to facilitate the transfer of technology and knowledge. It is supported by its two co-sponsors and by development agencies in industrialised countries (see www.esmap.org).

9 A lifeline tariff is also known as a 'social tariff' or 'increasing block tariff'. In this system, the first volume (block) of a service used (usually water or electricity) is provided at a lower, subsidised price, or sometimes for free. As the volume of consumption increases and passes a specific level, the price of the good increases. Therefore, poorer consumers or households that consume a small volume of a service are supposed to benefit.

10 The Forestry Department conducted a National Biomass Study in 1989, and recent reforms to the forestry sector have also highlighted the role of biomass in Uganda. Uganda's 2001 Energy Policy also recognised the importance of biomass energy supplies, and in the same year the Ministry of Energy and Minerals Development produced a draft biomass energy strategy. Germany's GTZ is now taking the lead in supporting work on biomass energy under the auspices of the Energy Advisory Project launched in 2003. The turn to biomass energy is long overdue, particularly given the ongoing problems with electricity supply and distribution. GTZ proposed a focus on biomass in 1999, while individuals within the Uganda Renewable Energy Association have been advocating for a biomass strategy since the 1970s.

11 The Energy for Rural Transformation Project was approved in December 2001. The project aims to increase electricity access in rural areas, by establishing an environment conducive to grid-based and/or rural/renewable electricity, which will include independent and small systems.

12 These projects have been complemented by other energy-related and institutional capacity-building initiatives. Examples of other projects include: power project supplements, financial guarantees and technical assistance for the Bujagali Dam, a privatisation and utility sector reform project, poverty reduction strategy papers, poverty reduction support credits, an environmental management and capacity-building project, the Energy for Rural Transformation Project, institutional capacity-building projects, a forestry rehabilitation project and, most recently, a thermal power generation project (to respond to the current crisis).

13 Power I, launched in 1961, was the World Bank's first project in Uganda. The US$8.4 million project focused on expanding Uganda's existing electricity network.

14 Tripp (2004: 20) writes that '[m]uch of [Uganda's] growth has been underwritten by donors, whose transfers have multiplied more than eightfold in the decade following the NRM takeover, reaching $819.5 million annually in 2000. The majority of foreign transfers after 1997 were private ones, which increased dramatically after 1995, reflecting a growing confidence in Uganda's economy'.

15 Explaining Museveni's role in reforms, Kjaer quotes a member of the reform commission: 'In a surprising and swift stroke of the pen, President Museveni reduced the numbers of ministries from 32 to 21 in 1992…This action by the president was a strong message to the conservative mainstream of the civil service. If ministers could be removed from office to promote efficiency and economy, then similar retrenchment had to be carried out at all lower levels of the government. It opened the gate. 11 out of 32 permanent secretaries were removed' (Katorobo 1996, cited in Kjaer 2004: 397).

16 This is a broad generalisation and there are gradations of performance historically. Nellis and Kikeri (1989: 659) note that evidence from the early 1980s shows that public enterprise sectors in 13 African countries accounted on average for 17 per cent of GDP. In Latin America and Asia, where evidence is sketchy, GDP contribution was sometimes at 17 per cent or below. Meanwhile, in some African countries, in the 1980s public enterprises accounted for upwards of 40–60 per cent of GDP. Examples here include Algeria, Egypt and Zambia. Nonetheless, the authors characterised the performance of public enterprises in the 1980s in the following manner: 'too many [public enterprises] cost rather than make money; and too many operate at low levels of efficiency' (1989: 660). Asian countries showed fewer problems than Latin America, which in turn performed better than public enterprises in sub-Saharan Africa.

17 This example relates to the attempted sale of the Uganda Commercial Bank (UCB). The UCB was originally privatised in 1998. However, shortly afterwards it was discovered that there were several suspicious arrangements in the sale, including one company acting as a front for another, with which Salim Saleh, the brother of Uganda's president, was associated. By 1999, the Ugandan government was taking steps to repossess the UCB, following further discoveries that the newly privatised bank was giving unsecured loans to companies associated with the new owner of the bank, Greenland Investments (see Tangri & Mwenda 2001).

18 In early 2006, the Constitution was amended to allow parties to function as political organisations and candidates to campaign on party platforms.

19 Some informants have been kept anonymous at their own request.

20 In 2002 Acres International was charged with bribery in relation to the Lesotho Highlands Water Project. Acres was found to have made over US$2 million in payments to project officials, and was subsequently sanctioned by the World Bank in 2004, halting its ability to bid on World Bank-related contracts for three years. Other engineering firms have also been found guilty of bribery, including Lahmeyer International. Acres is the first international company to be found guilty of bribery charges.

21 Further information on the Bujagali project can be found in the following informational and critical sources: Bujagali Energy Limited (http://www.bujagali-energy.com/default.htm); Esty & Sesia 2004; Gore 2008; International Finance Corporation

(http://www.ifc.org/bujagali); International Rivers Network (www.irn.org); Mallaby 2004; National Association of Professional Environmentalists (http://www.nape.or.ug/); World Bank archives (www.worldbank.org).

22   Hirschman, who was studying projects in developing countries, offered an alternative view of path dependency in his notion of the 'Hiding Hand'. He recognised that often an underestimate of costs was in fact necessary to have a project go ahead: '…underestimates of costs resulting from miscalculation or sheer ignorance were, in a number of great and ultimately successful economic undertakings…crucial to getting an enterprise launched at all' (Hirschman 1967: 16). This is required, he says, 'so that perfectly feasible and productive projects will actually be undertaken' (1967: 17).

23   Sarah Birungi, personal communication, 21 March 2002

24   www.worldbank.org/bujagali

25   www.bujagali-energy.com

26   This research was carried out with the aid of a Doctoral Research Award from the International Development Research Centre, Ottawa, Canada. Additional funding for this research was provided by: the CB Macpherson Dissertation Fellowship, Department of Political Science, University of Toronto; the Labatt Fellowship, Centre for Environment, University of Toronto; and the School of Graduate Studies Travel Grant, University of Toronto.

References

Among B (2006) Power crisis likely to worsen. *East African* 19 September

Barr A, Fafchamps M & Owens T (2005) The governance of non-governmental organizations in Uganda. *World Development* 33(4): 657–679

Bbumba S (2006) *Challenges faced in increasing modern energy access: The case of Uganda.* Keynote address, World Bank Energy Week, 6 March, World Bank, Washington DC. Video presentation. Accessed 22 January 2007, http://info.worldbank.org/etools/BSPAN/PresentationView.asp?PID=1724&EID=836#

Birdsall N & Nellis J (2003) Winners and losers: Assessing the distributional impact of privatization. *World Development* 31(10): 1617–1633

Brock K (2004) Ugandan civil society in the policy process: Challenging orthodox narratives. In K Brock, R McGee & J Gaventa (eds) *Unpacking policy. Knowledge, actors and spaces in poverty reduction in Uganda and Nigeria.* Kampala: Fountain Publishers

Business in Africa (2006) No power for 60 percent of sub-Sahara by 2020. *Business in Africa* 21 November

Churchill W (1989/1908) *My African Journey.* New York: WW Norton & Co.

Davidson O & Mwakasonda SA (2004) Electricity access for the poor: A study of South Africa and Zimbabwe. *Energy for Sustainable Development* 8(4): 26–40

De Coninck J (2004) The state, civil society and development policy in Uganda: Where are we coming from? In K Brock, R McGee & J Gaventa (eds) *Unpacking policy. Knowledge, actors and spaces in poverty reduction in Uganda and Nigeria.* Kampala: Fountain Publishers

Dicklitch S (2001) NGOs and democratization in transitional societies: Lessons from Uganda. *International Politics* 38: 27–46

Dijkstra AG & Van Donge JK (2001) What does the 'Show Case' show? Evidence of and lessons from adjustment in Uganda. *World Development* 29(5): 841–863

East African (2006) WB pulls out of Uganda's privatisation. *East African* 14 March

East African (2007) 'Secret' plan to sell off Umeme. *East African* 20 February

Eberhard A (2005) *Regulation of electricity services in Africa: An assessment of current challenges and an exploration of new regulatory models.* Paper prepared for the World Bank conference, Toward Growth and Poverty Reduction: Lessons from Private Participation in Infrastructure in Sub-Saharan Africa, June 6–7, Cape Town. Accessed 20 January 2007, http://www.gsb.uct.ac.za/gsbwebb/mir/documents/InfrastructureRegulationinAfrica.pdf

Economist Intelligence Unit (1957) *Power in Uganda. 1957–1970. A study of economic growth prospects for Uganda with special reference to the potential demand for electricity.* London: Economist Intelligence Unit Ltd

Engorait SP (2005) Power sector reforms in Uganda: Meeting the challenge of increased private sector investments and increased electricity access among the poor. In E Marandu & D Kayo (eds) *The regulation of the power sector in Africa.* London: Zed Books

ESMAP (Energy Sector Management Assistance Programme) (1984) *Uganda energy assessment.* Report No. 193/96. Washington DC: World Bank

Esty BC & Sesia A (2004) *International rivers network and Bujagali Dam Project* (A). N9-204-083. Massachusetts: Harvard Business School

Gore C (2008) Environment and development in Uganda: Understanding the global influence on domestic policy. In J Díez & OP Dwivedi (eds) *Environmental management in global context: Perspectives from the South.* Peterborough: Broadview Press

Harrison G (2001) Post-conditionality politics and administrative reform: Reflections on the cases of Uganda and Tanzania. *Development and Change* (32): 657–679

Hayes C (1983) *Stima: An informal history of the East African Power & Lighting Company.* Revised and edited by MO Macgoye. Nairobi: East African Power and Lighting Company

Hickey S (2005) The politics of staying poor: Exploring the political space for poverty reduction in Uganda. *World Development* 33(6): 995–1009

Hirschman AO (1967) *Development projects observed.* Washington DC: Brookings Institution

Ilakut BM (2006) $37 million for power. *East African Business Week* 19 June

Inspection Panel (2002) *The Inspection Panel investigation report.* Report No. 23998. Washington DC: World Bank

Izama A (2006) Sack electricity boss, IGG tells Museveni. *The Monitor* 13 July

Karekezi S & Kimani J (2002) Status of power sector reform in Africa: Impact on the poor. *Energy Policy* 30: 923–945

Karekezi S & Kimani J (2004) Have power sector reforms increased access to electricity among the poor in East Africa? *Energy for Sustainable Development* 8(4): 10–25

Kasita I (2007) World Bank snubs environmentalists' call to delay Bujagali power project. *Allafrica.com* 31 July. Accessed 12 September 2007, http://allafrica.com/stories/printable/200708010029.html

Kasyate S & Kamau Lugogo M (2006) There won't be another power crisis – president. *Monitor* 7 October. Accessed September 2007, http://allafrica.com/stories/200610060844.html

Kjaer AM (2004) 'Old brooms can sweep too!' An overview of rulers and public sector reforms in Uganda, Tanzania and Kenya. *Journal of Modern African Studies* 42(3): 389–413

Komives K, Whittington D & Wu X (2003) Infrastructure coverage and the poor: A global perspective. In PJ Brook & TC Irwin (eds) *Infrastructure for poor people. Public policy for private provision.* Washington DC: World Bank

Luggya J (2005) Electricity thefts cripple Uganda's power sector. *Monitor* 8 February

Mallaby S (2004) NGOs: Fighting poverty, hurting the poor. *Foreign Policy* September/October: 50–58

McCully P (2001) *Silenced rivers. The ecology and politics of large dams.* London & New York: Zed Books

MEMD (Ministry of Energy and Minerals Development) (2002) *Indicators on the energy policy's successful implementation.* Kampala, Uganda. Accessed 14 July 2007, www.energyandminerals.go.ug

MFPED (Ministry of Finance, Planning and Economic Development) (2004) *Poverty eradication action plan (2004/5–2007/8).* Kampala: MFPED. Accessed 15 July 2007, www.finance.go.ug

Monitor (2006) Power crisis deepens as Umeme seeks new contract. *Monitor* 21 November. Accessed September 2007, http://allafrica.com/stories/200611201714.html

Mugirya PW (2007) A dam that activists simply can't make peace with. *Inter Press Service (Johannesburg)* 31 July. Accessed 12 September 2007, http://allafrica.com/stories/printable/20070810434.html

MWLE (Ministry of Water, Lands and Environment) (2002) *The national forest plan.* Kampala: MWLE

Nabaguzi E (1995) Popular initiatives in service provision in Uganda. In J Semboja & O Therkildsen (eds) *Service provision under stress in East Africa.* London: James Currey

Nampala M (2006) Power crisis to end – Migereko. *New Vision* 9 July

Nellis J & Kikeri S (1989) Public enterprise reform: Privatization and the World Bank. *World Development* 17(5): 659–672

Obore C (2006) Power crisis deepens as Umeme seeks new contract. *Monitor* 21 November

Pierson P (2000) Increasing returns, path dependence, and the study of politics. *American Political Science Review* 94(2): 251–267

Pineau P-O (2002) Electricity sector reform in Cameroon: Is privatization the solution? *Energy Policy* 30(11–12): 999–1012

Prayas Energy Group (2002) *The Bujagali Power Purchase Agreement – an independent review. a study of techno-economic aspects of the Power Purchase Agreement of the Bujagali hydroelectric project in Uganda.* Report prepared for International Rivers Network

Roe E (1991) Development narratives, or making the best of blueprint development. *World Development* 19(5): 287–300

Tangri R & Mwenda A (2001) Corruption and cronyism in Uganda's privatization in the 1990s. *African Affairs* 100(398): 117–133

Tripp AM (2000) *Women and politics in Uganda.* Madison, Wisconsin: University of Wisconsin Press

Tripp AM (2004) The changing face of authoritarianism in Africa: The case of Uganda. *Africa Today* 50(3): 3–26

Tukahebwa GB (1998) Privatization as a development policy. In HB Hansen & M Twaddle (eds) *Developing Uganda.* Oxford: James Currey

Twaddle M & Hansen HB (1998) The changing state of Uganda. In HB Hansen & M Twaddle (eds) *Developing Uganda.* Oxford: James Currey

UBOS (Uganda Bureau of Statistics) (2002) *2002 Uganda population and housing census – main report.* Accessed September 2007, http://www.ubos.org

UEB (Uganda Electricity Board) (1996) *The thirty-third report and accounts of Uganda Electricity Board.* Kampala: Uganda Electricity Board

UEB (1999) *Report and accounts of 1999.* Kampala: Uganda Electricity Board

UNCHS (UN Centre for Human Settlements) (2001) *Cities in a Globalizing World. Global Report on Human Settlements 2001.* London: Earthscan

Wakabi W (2004) Umeme to manage Uganda's power supply. *East African* 2 August. Accessed September 2007, http://allafrica.com/stories/200408030882.htm

Wakabi W (2006) Crisis a conspiracy of nature and poor financial planning. *East African* 10 October

Wilson G (1967) *Owen Falls. Electricity in a developing country.* Nairobi: East African Publishing House

World Bank (2000) *Fuel for thought. An environmental strategy for the energy sector.* Washington DC: World Bank

World Bank (2001) *Uganda: Policy, participation, people.* Operations Evaluation Department. Washington DC: World Bank

World Bank (2003) *Accountability at the World Bank. The Inspection Panel 10 years on.* Washington DC: World Bank

World Bank (2004) *Reforming infrastructure. Privatization, regulation and competition.* Washington DC: World Bank

World Bank & ESMAP (Energy Sector Management Assistance Programme) (2000) *Energy services for the world's poor.* Washington DC: World Bank

Interviews

Blake R, World Bank Country Programme Manager, 5 May 2002, Kampala

Karekaho T, former manager at the Uganda Electricity Board, 27 May 2002, Kampala

Mare P, former Managing Director, Uganda Electricity Board, now Managing Director, Eskom Enterprises Uganda, 17 January 2003, Kampala

Nyirinkindi E, Director, Utility Reform Unit, 14 May 2002, Kampala

Sebbowa F, head of Ugandan ERA, 17 January 2003, Kampala

Ssebabi D, team leader for the Utility Reform Unit in the Privatisation Unit, National Water and Sewerage Corporation, 8 January 2003, Kampala

Venvick H, First Secretary Development, NORAD, 29 May 2002, Kampala

Connected geographies and struggles over access: Electricity commercialisation in Tanzania

Rebecca Ghanadan

> Electricity to light our homes. Safe water for our families to drink. Telephones to our loved ones far away. Ports and railways to bring us wonderful things, and to bring our goods to the world. We need these things. Our children need these things. Privatization will provide them.[1]

In the course of the last decade, electricity service provision in Africa has been rewritten along market lines. New private-sector players are being invited into historically public electricity sectors, market-based approaches are being adopted in service provision, and reform models are being developed in the name of improving service and access.

The electricity sector is not unique in this respect. Commercialisation and reform have become a driving force across infrastructure sectors throughout Africa, including telecommunications, transport and water (Estache 2005). Yet these changes are also eliciting extensive anxieties. Grassroots protests, civil society campaigns, and policy critiques are raising concerns about equity and the impact of service changes on the poor, participation in and legitimacy of the reform processes, and effectiveness of market-based approaches (Bayliss & Hall 2000; Dubash 2002; Veriava & Ngwane 2004; Wamukonya 2003b). These concerns highlight the extent of what is at stake in electricity commercialisation on the continent.

Researchers and activists concerned with Africa are looking to the process of commodification to understand the changes taking place (Agbemabiese & Byrne 2005; Bond 2002; McDonald & Ruiters 2005; Page 2005). Commodity-based conceptions of electricity are integral to market approaches and reflect a shift away from treating electricity as a public service. However, while commodity-like service provision may be an intention of reforms, reforms are negotiated processes and the changes under way are often partial, contested and varied from country to country. What is needed is a better understanding of the different interests and workings of commercialisation and reform 'on the ground' in Africa.

Tanzania has had one of the most extensive reform programmes on the continent. Changes in electricity provision are situated within a two-decade-long liberalisation process that has seen dramatic shifts toward market-based approaches across the country's economy and society. The country is often praised by the international community as one of Africa's 'bright spots' and most successful reformers (*Economist* 2006; World Bank 2006), but these reforms are also connected to numerous on-the-ground anxieties over who will share the benefits of these changes.

The stakes of reforms in Tanzania are particularly pronounced against the backdrop of the country's historical legacy of pursing African socialism under the charismatic leadership of Julius Nyerere. Tanzania's post-independence project articulated a strong ethic and philosophy of public service and a developmental state as a component of national identity and equitable economic development. This historical backdrop situates electricity reforms in Tanzania within shifting understandings of development, as well as shifts in the actual practices around electricity services.

This chapter explores the changes being implemented by Tanzania's electricity reform process from two perspectives. First, it highlights the multiple arenas in which reforms are being negotiated in Tanzania to emphasise the wide-reaching nature of the reforms. Second, it considers the relationship between Tanzania's experience and the broader process of electricity commercialisation and reform under way in Africa.

The chapter is organised in four parts. The first part describes the paradigm shift taking place in the electricity sector. The second identifies key forces that are shaping the process of reforms. The third part elaborates extensive changes under way in commercially-driven service provision and the fourth traces the reverberations of these changes for conditions of resource access and use within households and local communities.

The chapter argues that electricity reforms in Tanzania have been narrowly revenue-focused, with little emphasis on customer service. Residential customers are asked to pay more or face disciplinary enforcement, they receive poor services, and for many, new connections remain a distant hope. Under these conditions, many Tanzanians find it increasingly difficult to access and use electricity services. Visible contestations have emerged in response to some of the most tangible changes. Yet top-down government–donor relations and the narrow scope of technical reform models mean many concerns are marginalised in the reform process. Ordinary Tanzanians find themselves far removed from the technical and decision-making processes governing service changes.

Instead, pressures arising from these concerns are translating into less visible reverberations on the local level, beyond the formal gaze of the system of reform implementation. Household- and community-level research by the author shows pressures shifting through neighbourly relations, household budgeting, gender and power dynamics, and natural resources. These are less visible than more overt forms of protest around services in other parts of Africa, but they are linked to a common process of commercialisation and struggles over access.

Looking at Tanzania in a wider African context, the chapter argues that common driving forces, underlying reform models and policy relations are making commercialisation a more regional process in Africa. One important aspect is the role that donors are playing in these programmes, showing reforms to be configured by connections extending beyond national borders and beyond the electricity sector itself. Tanzania also reveals new regional connections, particularly with South African businesses providing technologies and services to support electricity commercialisation. These connections demonstrate converging technologies and approaches to commercialisation on the continent, and the expansion of South African-style service provision.

Commodification is a negotiated and often partial and contested process that takes diverse forms in different settings. However, connections between the more and less visible workings of commercialisation in Africa also reveal a broader geography. These connections highlight shared driving forces and shared anxieties, as reforms are not only a technical intervention but one having social and political consequences for the process of development, including resource access, participation in governance, and inclusion in the benefits of development. The future of reforms lies in places like Johannesburg and Dar es Salaam as much as in Washington DC, and this chapter speaks to possibilities and connections related to electricity, access and development in Africa.

Paradigm shift: from public service to commodity goods

> Whereas market failure justified intervention by the government in the past, now it is government failure justifying the role of markets. (Marandu 2002: 980)

The commercialisation of basic services such as electricity is situated within a broader paradigm of development policy reform focused on market liberalisation. This shift has been justified as a solution to the widespread deterioration of services and national economic crises experienced in many African countries in the 1980s and early 1990s (Jhirad 1990). The rationale behind reforms in services like electricity is that efficiency, commercial pricing and greater involvement by the private sector will reduce pressure on national and local government budgets and create a profitable sector, which in turn will finance necessary investments for improvements in service and access (Bacon & Besant-Jones 2001; Dunkerly 1995; Kessides 2004; World Bank 1993).

Market-oriented approaches in Africa emerged out of the conditions of the 1980s and 1990s, and were fuelled by the shifting approaches of international financial institutions like the World Bank toward policies of fiscal discipline, financial and trade liberalisation, and privatisation under the Washington Consensus and neo-liberal counter-revolution of the 1980s and 1990s (Gore 2000; Mosley et al. 1991; Williamson 1993). The two-decade process of reforms is ongoing and continues to unfold today.

In many countries in Africa, including Tanzania, this marketised vision of electricity provision represents a dramatic shift in policies that had guided the sector previously, serving to unravel public-service models of state-led development, in which electricity policy was subject to the broader goals of national development projects and explicit policy mechanisms for redistribution. These changes also involve subjective shifts in the vision and promises of development, influencing people's expectations, relations with the state, and understanding of national identity and citizenship.

The multiple dimensions of reforms cutting across local, national and international arenas situate these reforms in the context of extensive changes in the workings of international development policy in relation to Africa, as well as changes in the approach and vision of national development in Tanzania. Table 15.1 provides a breakdown of the most significant differences between the former state-led models of electricity provision and the emerging market-led models, based on Tanzania's experience. While many elements hold across African countries, specific policies and the extent to which policy ideals have matched actual conditions vary extensively from country to country.

Driving forces in an African context

A number of forces are shaping commercialisation in Africa. They include international power sector reforms, extensive donor involvement, wider liberalisation programmes and new regional connections. These forces are making electricity commercialisation in many ways a wider regional process on the continent. Together these forces reveal a commercialisation process taking place in Africa that is increasingly underpinned by common policy models, converging on similar technologies and ideologies, and shaped by relations extending beyond national borders and the electricity sector itself.

The international power sector reform model

An international model of power sector reform has directed much of the technical approach to African energy policy since the mid-1990s, and is based on the idea that private-sector involvement and competitive markets can introduce efficiency gains that can be used to benefit the sector (Bacon 1995; Hunt 2002).

This approach was built largely on the experiences of electricity privatisation and deregulation in the UK and USA that were later expanded via consultants, policy-makers and donors to developing countries (Bacon 1995; Bacon & Besant-Jones 2001). However, while reforms in the USA and the UK generally involved changes

Table 15.1: Shifts from state-led development to market-led provision in electricity

	State-led development model	Liberal market development model
Sector vision	• catalyse development and effective redistribution of benefits	• implement financial cost recovery • provide infrastructure • attract investment
Provision ethos	• public service, social contract • economic development	• commodity good • economic efficiency
Utility	• employment – civil service • organ of state-led development	• corporation • collect revenue • provide commercial services
Pricing	• equity and redistribution aims: • cross-subsidy to residential and small businesses from industry • universal lifeline tariffs	• economy efficiency and investment aims: • marginal cost pricing • minimise subsidies • unravel cross-subsidy to reduce tariff to industry • small 'targeted' subsidies
Access	• sector development mandate	• subordinate to commercial goals
Finances	• dependent on national budget • extensively donor-funded	• private investment with commercial returns • often public bears extensive risk and donors mediate publicly-borne guarantees
Areas of concern in practice	• poor service • donor-dependent • top-down, little participation of public • subject to macroeconomic crisis • subsidies benefit small fraction with service expansion falling short of goals	• narrow scope • social concerns marginalised • access low priority and little improvement • small customers face large price increases • loss of parastatal jobs • revenue emphasised over service • high returns to private sector
Debates	• modernisation and dependency	• globalisation: neo-liberal and counter-hegemonic

within the electricity sector itself, by contrast, African power sectors are often dependent on donor support, private capital and technical expertise from outside the country, over which governments have only partial control (Williams & Ghanadan 2006). This situates the workings of reforms within a wider apparatus of donor–government relations.

Much of the 1990s agenda is embodied within a set of reform steps that were formalised in the 1999 World Bank report issuing a 'scorecard' of developing countries' progress with reforms (ESMAP 1999). As in most countries in Africa, the government of Tanzania adopted this standard menu as its formal approach to electricity reforms. The implementation status of the standard elements of reform in Tanzania is provided in Table 15.2.

Commercialisation of service provision and introduction of private electricity generation have been the most concrete areas of change in Tanzania's ongoing reform programme. These efforts began in the early to mid-1990s and continue today. More recently, new institutions such as the Rural Energy Agency and Fund (REA/REF) and the Energy and Water Utilities Regulatory Authority (EWURA) have been created, but explicit institutions for access and regulation were absent during the earlier stages of reform.

Table 15.2: Key elements of Tanzania's electricity reforms, as of December 2006

Reform elements	Status	Policy elements	Year
Corporatise	Implemented	Formally corporatised 1931. Private South African company NETGroup Solutions Ltd managing utility with autonomy over operations under management contract.	1931 2002–2006 (management contract)
Commercialise operations and service provision	Extensive	Extensive commercialisation initiated in 1990s under World Bank Power VI Project. Commercialisation accelerated under management contract.	1992 initiated 2002–2006 (management contract)
	Legislation only, not operational (as of end 2006)	Non-commercial electrification (mainly rural) separated from utility mandate. REA/REF being created.	2005 legislation
Revise electricity law	General policy framework, but law not amended	National Energy Policy frameworks in 1992 and 2003 include reform intentions. Revised Electricity Act not amended.	1992 framework 2003 framework
Establish regulator	Operational as of mid-2006	Legislation in place, board and committees appointed for energy and water regulator EWURA, operational as of mid-2006.	2001 legislation 2006 board appointed
Introduce private generation (IPPs)	Implemented	Monopoly in generation lifted in 1992. Two larger IPPs: Independent Power Tanzania Ltd (IPTL)[2] (100 MW diesel), Songas[3] (180 MW natural gas), several small operators.	1992 legislation 2002 IPTL online 2004 Songas online
Restructure and unbundle utility for privatisation	Modified plan	Unbundling of national utility into separate generation, transmission and distribution companies to facilitate privatisation, revised into plan to ringfence separate business areas, while remaining state-owned.	modified plan under way
Privatisation (private-sector participation)	In flux and highly uncertain	Privatisation plans for utilities announced 1997. Management contract toward privatisation 2002. Tanesco de-specified 2005. Next steps uncertain, but increasing emphasis on private-sector participation over outright privatisation.	1997 specified 2005 de-specified

Sources: See Davies 2004; ESMAP 1999; Ghanadan & Eberhard 2007; Gratwick et al. 2006; Karekezi & Kimani 2002; Katyega 2004; Marandu 1999, 2002; MEM 1992, 2003a, 2003b; PSRC 2002; World Bank 1992
Note: IPP = independent power producer; MW = megawatt

Other elements have been affected by critiques and changing views. Most notably, the government of Tanzania at an early stage committed itself to privatising the electricity utility, Tanesco (Tanzania Electricity Supply Company Ltd) in 1997. However, this commitment was reversed in 2005 and Tanesco was taken off the list of companies specified for privatisation. Reasons for backing off on privatisation are explained later in the chapter; the future structure and management of the utility are highly uncertain.

Launching reforms: donor involvement and wider liberalisation programmes

Conditions in the 1980s and early 1990s led to the introduction of government programmes focused on reforms. While the international power sector reform model provided a technical basis for change, wider national liberalisation and reform programmes in the 1980s created the institutional apparatus and driving forces that brought these changes into the electricity sector.

In the early 1980s, Tanzania's project of state-led development was unravelled, as a crippling economic crisis spread across Africa and much of the developing world. Tanzania's crisis was brought on by external and internal factors that included world oil shocks, falling commodity prices, a costly war with Uganda (that ousted Idi Amin), periods of drought, and unsuccessful collective agriculture policies in the 1970s (Wangwe et al. 1998; Yeager 1982).

With a national development budget of which 70 per cent came from foreign aid, and facing little alternative, Tanzania sought international assistance from the IMF in 1979 (Yeager 1982). However, Tanzania's charismatic post-independence leader, moral philosopher and architect of the developmental state, Nyerere, resisted policies proposed by the IMF bail-out package. Negotiations broke down, with Nyerere famously asking the IMF: 'Who elected the IMF to be finance ministry for every country in the world?' – signalling one of the first voices in the debate over the role of the IMF in Africa (Helleiner 2002).

However, after Tanzania's two attempts at national recovery programmes proved unsuccessful, the government faced little alternative but to implement wider reforms. In 1985 Nyerere stepped down, ending 23 years as president and signalling Tanzania's submission to the structural adjustment agenda. In 1986 the government adopted a World Bank- and IMF-supported Economic Recovery Programme (ERP), which initiated the process of reorganising the economy along market lines under Tanzania's second president, Ali Hassan Mwinyi (GoT 1986; Kaiser 1996; Kjaer 2004).

The ERP followed a standard structural adjustment prescription designed to address a macroeconomic balance of payments crisis. However, with policy changes and government–donor relations put in place with structural adjustment, reforms were expanded over the next decade into nearly every sector of the economy, from banking to social services to infrastructure, including electricity (Wangwe et al. 1998).

A number of conditions contributed to the expansion of reforms into the electricity sector. First, many structural adjustment policies created a worsened situation for electricity sector finances. Prescribed currency devaluations eroded the real value of tariffs and utility revenues. Inflation eroded the utility rate base and valuation of its assets. The government was reluctant to raise rates, as Tanzanians faced an extensive loss of purchasing power and were feeling the impacts of austerity policies from many directions (Wangwe et al. 1998). Under these conditions, Tanesco went from being seen as a utility in a 'strong financial situation' in the 1960s and 1970s (Collier 1984) to one seen as in need of reform.

Another key factor was shifting donor priorities, which made reforms imperative to access electricity sector finance. Throughout the 1960s–1980s, donors were the primary financiers of electricity supply and technical assistance in Tanzania, yet by the 1990s the terms of lending had changed. Donors became unwilling to finance infrastructure; reforms rather than direct infrastructure finance became the thrust of donor support (Mosley et al. 1991). Beginning in 1993, the World Bank formally required power sector reforms as a condition for electricity loans (World Bank 1993). Within a few years, requirements were rationalised amongst other electricity donors, notably the Swedish International Development Cooperation Agency (SIDA), Tanzania's other main electricity donor.

Under combined conditions of national economic crisis, shifting donor priorities and structural adjustment, electricity sector conditions deteriorated and became the justification for further reforms. Without funds for maintenance and new investments, electricity services deteriorated. New supply development dropped off.

Tanzania launched its electricity reform initiatives in 1992. In doing so, the government regained the support and resources of donors. A World Bank Power VI Project was launched in 1993 to support the recommercialisation of electricity services. Basically all of Tanzania's formal electricity reform commitments, including plans to privatise Tanesco, have been made in relation to World Bank and donor projects and loan agreements. Donor support has been involved in all of the key reforms outlined in Table 15.2. Electricity reforms are situated squarely within relations of aid.

South Africa's growing role in electricity commercialisation in Africa

Tanzania is part of a growing trend of regional interconnections in electricity. These interconnections are taking many forms, including regional grid connections and cross-border power generation investments. But Tanzania shows another form of interconnection. South African private firms are increasingly providing services and technologies for electricity commercialisation in Tanzania and other countries in Africa, and this is playing a role in creating new links and expanding South African-style service provision elsewhere on the continent.

South Africa's involvement in electricity commercialisation in Africa has not been an intended outcome of reforms. Instead, it has emerged from conditions created by electricity reforms, in which South African firms have found themselves well-situated. As the expansion of its own electricity sector slowed in the 1990s – due in part to overcapacity – South African electricity businesses began looking outward, at the same time that power sector reform programmes were taking off on the African continent.

With one of the largest and most extensively commercialised service provision programmes in the developing world, South Africa's electricity industry had an interest in expansion, and also has the technologies and familiarity with commercialised service provision in Africa to fill a gap in providing implementation techniques.

In Tanzania, South African firms are playing a role in providing management and consulting services. The private South African company NETGroup Solutions Ltd began managing the national electric utility, Tanesco, under a management contract that came into effect in 2002. Its two-year contract was extended in 2004, and expired at the end of 2006.

Eskom – the state-owned electricity giant in South Africa – has also been influential, if only by example. Eskom's involvement in neighbouring Uganda originally sparked government interest in a management contract, and was followed up by a visit to Uganda and South Africa in 2001 by Tanzanian government officials. Eskom was also a bidder for Tanesco's management contract.

Tanzania is also one of the earliest and largest sites for deployment of South African prepayment meters. Once nationally focused, South Africa's prepayment meter industry is gaining international attention and finding its growth opportunities outside South Africa. The prepayment industry in South Africa first developed as a billing and enforcement technology for townships and rural areas in South Africa's post-apartheid electrification drive (see Van Heusden, Chapter 8 in this volume). However, South African prepayment meters are now deployed in more than 26 African countries, as well as in Latin America and, increasingly, Asia (see Table 15.3).

South Africa is not the only source of businesses operating in African power sectors, and many of its techniques are not entirely unique to South Africa. However, they are filling an important gap in providing technologies and services, and creating new convergences in commercialised service provision in Africa.

Changes and anxieties in negotiating reforms

Reforms represent changes in policy, but they also represent changes, and often threats, to resources and understandings of development. In Tanzania, resistance has emerged at key moments as specific groups have been threatened by some of the most visible and tangible aspects of reform. Their resistance has shown what is at stake, but they have also voiced wider anxieties over the vision of national development in a context of 'globalisation'. Complex struggles over legitimacy,

Table 15.3: South African electricity prepayment meters in Africa, 2005

Region	Number of prepayment meters installed
South Africa	6 300 000 (estimated)
Rest of Africa	2 000 000

Countries with South African prepayment meters

Algeria	Côte d'Ivoire	Malawi	Swaziland
Angola	Gabon	Mozambique	Tanzania[a]
Benin	Gambia	Namibia	Zambia
Botswana	Ghana	Nigeria	Zimbabwe
Burkina Faso	Guinea Conakry	Rwanda	
Burundi	Lesotho	Senegal	
Cameroon	Madagascar	Sudan[a]	

Source: Compiled by the author from unpublished company marketing data, 2005
Note: a largest installations. Approximately 80 000 prepayment meters had been deployed in Tanzania
as of the end of 2005; Sudan has the largest deployment outside South Africa with 1–2 million
prepayment meters.

sovereignty and the meanings of national development are a key part of the negotiated workings of reform, expressed in the electricity sector.

Privatisation commitments and concerns

During the 1990s, more than 400 state-owned industries were privatised in Tanzania under the newly created Parastatal Reform Commission (PSRC). In 1997 the programme expanded to include utilities, and Tanesco was specified for eventual privatisation. Yet utility privatisations have proceeded more slowly than anticipated, being more complex and more contentious than other sectors in the country. Services such as electricity and water represent some of the last frontiers of state-led development and embody resources, as well as promises, for redistribution and social development – such as jobs, subsidies and low-cost services.

Uncertainties over the meanings of these changes resonate strongly in the context of Tanzania's history of state-led development and African socialism. Public ownership and nationalised industry had been clearly articulated tenets of national development codified in the 1967 Arusha Declaration (TANU 1967), the central document in former president Julius Nyerere's vision of development. Public ownership represented not only an economic model but also a strong set of moral claims, made more meaningful against the backdrop of colonialism. Public ownership embodied promises, realised or not, to provide services for the majority. Despite the economic crises of the 1980s and 1990s, this vision has continued to shape national identity and to inform the basis on which people understand reforms.

Engaging with the subjective aspects of public understandings of these changes, the PSRC mounted an extensive public relations campaign to accompany its privatisation efforts. The PSRC worked with the British public relations firm Adam Smith International to develop posters, videos and songs to disseminate a pro-privatisation message. They were financed by the World Bank and by Britain's Department for International Development.

One highly publicised song was 'Privatisation: We Need Money' (*Ubinafsishaji, Tunahitaji pesa* in Swahili) sung by Maasai rap artist Mr Ebbo (see World Bank 2002). His lyrics asserted that privatisation was consistent with the public interest. His persona also conveyed a message of tradition, youth and progressive change, being most famous for his song 'Mi Maasai' which asserts traditional identity and pride while embracing Tanzania's youth culture and home-grown rap music. Mr Ebbo's message was that if *he* supported privatisation, you should too. But while his song was widely publicised, its message was only one aspect of the conditions influencing public perspectives.

Many Tanzanians are also concerned about who will be included in (and left out of) these changes. Anxieties have been heightened by extensive profiteering and the corruption of public services in the process of implementing reforms, on small and large scales, which have created new socio-economic divisions, particularly relating to land reforms, privatisations, service provision and real estate booms during the early liberalisation period (Doriye 1992; Kelsall 2002).

Those linked to the state have often been in the best position to benefit from these changes, creating a sense amongst the public that reforms involve manoeuvrings for personal gain. These perceptions have, as a result, created an undercurrent of concern over the legitimacy and accountability of marketised reforms.

Tanzania's first IPP, Independent Power Tanzania Ltd, has been one of the most controversial private-sector investments, and a key example of these concerns. A joint investment between Tanzanian and Malaysian investors, signed in 1995, IPTL was taken to international arbitration over construction charges and claims of bribery in 1998. In 2001 construction costs were reduced by 20 per cent, and bribery charges were dropped because of insufficient evidence; yet IPTL remains one of the most expensive projects of its kind in the developing world (Gratwick et al. 2006). IPTL provides much needed power, but at a very high cost in financial terms as well as in terms of its perceived legitimacy.

The cartoon in Figure 15.1 portrays IPTL as the young girlfriend of an infatuated (already married) government husband, who is presented disapprovingly to the traditional wife and matron of the home, Tanesco. Correctly or not, IPTL is widely seen by the public (and many donors and officials) as an icon of unaccountable investment, questionable legitimacy and epitomises the kinds of uncertain outcomes that can result from reforms.

Reforms create paradoxical conditions for many Tanzanians – who are caught between, on the one hand, a desire for change and participation in market

Figure 15.1: Political cartoon critiquing legitimacy of private electricity generators

Power struggle?

Source: *The Guardian* 2004a

opportunities and, on the other, anxieties over the erosion of a clear moral and developmental vision for national policy – that are made more pronounced against Tanzania's backdrop of developmental promises.

While many do not see it as possible or desirable to return to former economic policies, a reform- and market-based vision represents extensive uncertainties about national identity and inclusion within a vision of development. For many, the shift towards market policies means higher expectations, but it also means a widening gap between immediate realities and hopes of what markets may bring.

Contested steps toward electricity commercialisation

Commercialisation of the electricity sector began in earnest in the early 1990s. The World Bank Power VI Project that started in 1993 launched the commercialisation efforts. It aimed to re-capacitate Tanesco after structural adjustment and economic crisis had starved maintenance programmes and investments and eroded the quality of operations. Efforts focused on technical and administrative steps to reduce losses, improve billing and improve procedures. Tariffs were raised to compensate for earlier currency devaluations under structural adjustment, which had eroded tariffs in dollar terms.

Prepayment meters were introduced under Power VI to support revenue collection. Between 1995 and 1997, more than 40 000 South African-made prepayment meters were installed in selected middle- and upper-income neighbourhoods in the capital city, Dar es Salaam. The operation was mandatory, and met with fierce resistance from residents who resented the enforced policy and feared higher rates. Nonetheless, the operation continued with government and donor support (*African Energy* 1999). Prepayment meters now number over 80 000 on the mainland, with additional meters on Zanzibar.[4]

Commercialisation and management efforts were significantly accelerated and expanded in 2002 when the government of Tanzania entered into a management contract with the South African company NETGroup Solutions. The contract was highly contentious, and protests ensued over what was correctly seen as an intended step toward eventual privatisation. Tanesco workers demanded an agreement to secure the rights and intentions of employment prior to entry of the private managers. Some members of the public and the press also launched allegations of a lack of transparency and influence of personal interests of government officials involved in the deal (*BBC News* 2002). The contractors were delayed by five months in entering the utility premises.

By late April/May 2002 protests had culminated in workers barricading entrances to the Tanesco buildings. Workers waved framed pictures of Nyerere and placards stating 'Tanesco, its dams, and electricity are the hard efforts of Nyerere and Tanzanian citizens' (*Wananchi* 2002). The figure of Nyerere was used by protestors to link their immediate concerns over jobs to wider moral and intellectual claims over national interest, development and sovereignty.

To strengthen their claims workers also named the threat as South African, invoking historical memories of apartheid and Tanzania's strong role in supporting anti-apartheid resistance as a member of the Frontline States and as a safe haven for freedom fighters and intellectuals in pan-African struggles. They carried placards and sang, 'There is no entry for Boers. We do not fear the Boers, as we are energetic youths' (*The African* 2002a). The government launched its Field Force Unit of armed riot police to contain the volatile situation.

At the height of protests, Tanzania's third president, Benjamin Mkapa, gave successive speeches appealing to the public for calm (*Daily News* 2002; Mkapa 2002). He asserted that Tanzanians had borne poor services and poor management for too long and that the management contract was in the best interest of the nation. He argued that Tanzania was inexperienced in management due to its socialist history, but that by learning from foreigners the country could continue to develop and be more competitive in the future in an era of globalisation. He used evidence of utility accounting irregularities found in an international financial audit to make the case that the utility and its managers had not been serving the public interest, and promised that greater

Table 15.4: A summary of Tanzania's electricity sector development, 1908–2005

Year	Electricity sector events
1908	First public electricity supply, railway generator, under German rule
1931	Private operation of electricity supply begins
1961	Independence of Tanganyika
1964	Union of Tanzania (Tanganyika and Zanzibar)
1964	Nationalisation of power supply, Tanesco, British managers remain
1967	First World Bank power–sector loan awarded
1973	Africanisation of Tanesco, first Tanzanian General Manager
1986	Structural adjustment (economic recovery programme)
1993	World Bank policy mandates reform as condition for power–sector lending
1997	Tanesco specified for privatisation, privatisation expanded to utilities
2002	Tanesco placed under two-year management contract
2004	Tanesco management contract extended for two years
2005	Tanesco de-specified for privatisation

Sources: Collier 1984; Ghanadan & Eberhard 2007; Moffett 1955; Wangwe et al. 1998; World Bank 1993

efficiency would improve services and that these benefits would be shared among the people.

As president of a nation with a strong history of party leadership and presidential moral–political authority, his voice carried significant weight. Public opposition eased, and NETGroup was able to enter utility offices in mid-May 2002, under conditions that were tense but without incident (*The African* 2002b). A voluntary labour agreement was developed by Tanesco and accepted by the unions later that year. With the government financing the severance benefits, this led the voluntary and amicable retrenchment of more than 1 200 workers in 2003. NET Group Solutions management firm continued to cultivate union support, and the Master Workers Council of Tanesco even advocated the extension of the contract when it came up for renewal in 2004 (Davies 2004).

Overall, resistance was short-lived, then, and the crisis was resolved by the intervention of the president and the subsequent employment agreement. But these protests revealed wider concerns amongst the public about the deeper moral and philosophical meanings of market reforms, as well as their more immediate material implications.

Evolving reforms and the drive for commercialisation

Market-led reforms in Tanzania are ongoing and continue to evolve. Over the past decade there has been a quiet backing-off from privatisation as the necessary end-goal of reforms. The reversal of the government's commitments to privatising Tanesco reflects shifting national and international conditions that have destabilised earlier drivers of privatisation in Africa.

The reform agenda of the World Bank in recent years has moved from a strict focus on privatisation as the end-goal of reforms to more flexible concepts of private-sector participation and public–private partnerships (World Bank 2004). In practical terms, the donor imperative to privatise has lessened, as the World Bank has resumed direct lending for infrastructure in recognition that private investment is unlikely to meet investment needs in developing countries, and the public sector will continue to play a role in the provision of electricity (World Bank 2003).

Also significant is the fact that international investment in developing-country power sectors has dropped off significantly since the late 1990s, following the Asian financial crisis, Californian energy crisis, Enron débâcle and other pivotal events (ESMAP 2001; Lamech & Saeed 2003; Williams & Ghanadan 2006). For many countries, like Tanzania, privatisation is less realistic, even if it were desired, as it is unlikely that there would be sufficient investor interest (*Africa Power* 2006). Private-sector participation and public–private partnership arrangements are likely to be more attractive than privatisation as many risks and ownership responsibilities remain in public hands.

Tanzania's government now faces less pressure to privatise under shifting external conditions. Looking elsewhere on the continent, national policy-makers do not see successful examples of electricity privatisation. Electricity privatisation has never been widely popular in Tanzania; although Tanesco's privatisation was championed by former president Mkapa and donors, opposition remains extensive among many government officials and members of Parliament and it is also unpopular with the public (*The Guardian* 2004b, 2004c).

The end result is that many of the conditions that drove earlier privatisation efforts have now weakened, while political opposition, practical constraints and technical concerns remain. This combination has resulted in a backing-off from privatisation commitments, and Tanesco's de-specification in 2005 as discussed earlier in this chapter. The utility's ownership and management future are currently uncertain, but will depend on the continually evolving donor–government relations that drive the reform agenda.

But despite this retreat from privatisation, a more general drive towards commercialisation and private-sector participation remains, including the setting up of management contracts and concessions and the contracting out of services – almost entirely under the umbrella of formal public ownership.

It is the running of public-sector services on private-sector principles – with private-sector partners – that appears to be the future thrust of electricity reforms in Tanzania, leading to extensive changes in service provision and influencing the ability of ordinary Tanzanians to access and use electricity. Listed below are the basic premises of this commercialisation drive, with its focus on revenue generation, cost recovery and punishment for non-payment (spanning public offices and residential customers), all serving to unravel historical redistributive mechanisms such as cross-subsidies and lifeline tariffs for residential customers. Subsequent sections discuss these points in more detail:

- *Utility* priorities focus first on revenue generation and collection (other goals subject to this priority).
- *Tariff restructuring* reduces lifeline/poverty tariffs, unravels cross-subsidies and puts emphasis on cost-reflective pricing.
- *Enforcement technologies and techniques* collect arrears and discipline commercial service provision, i.e. service disconnections and prepayment meters.
- *Public relations* define 'responsible' consumers and justify policy changes, often reinforcing top-down utility–customer relations.
- *Private sector* becomes involved in providing management services, contracting out of utility functions, and providing private generation and technologies for commercialisation.
- *Public sector* maintains ownership of the utility and bears most financial and external risks.
- *Donors* support policy and institutional changes and structure private-sector guarantees.

Revenue generation and collection

The electricity management contract signed with NETGroup Solutions in 2002 had the immediate objective of increasing Tanesco's revenues (PSRC 2002). South African managers assumed five top executive positions, overseeing operations in the corporate offices. They directed the priorities of the utility's 22 regional offices, and catalysed extensive service changes, including changing tariffs and enforcement policies.

During the first two years of the electricity management contract, the formal incentives of the contractor's performance-based fees were based on revenue increases, power loss reductions, and improved quality of supply and service. These mandates were expanded to include new connections and improved reliability when the contract was extended in 2004 (Davies 2004; PSRC 2002). But in practice, more than 99 per cent of the performance fees were based on revenue alone. Overall, revenues more than doubled from US$11 million to over US$22 million per month between 2002 and 2005 (Ghanadan & Eberhard 2007) (see Figure 15.2). The revenue collection performance was seen as a major success by donors and policy-makers. An internal World Bank memo cited Tanesco as the best utility in Africa in revenue collection terms, after Eskom.[5]

But the utility did not perform in other areas. New connections and improved reliability have been slight. Customer service remains poor and has not been emphasised in contract incentives. Many of these dimensions were outside the contractor's direct control, but resulted from the narrow scope of reforms and growing costs of generation, with reliance on more costly IPP-derived power. Total contractor remuneration amounted to about US$25 million for the 56-month contract (2002–2006), equivalent to about 5 per cent of the revenue gains (Ghanadan & Eberhard 2007). Contract remuneration has been financed about 50:50 through Swedish (SIDA) donor funds and utility revenues.

Figure 15.2: Tanesco revenue collections, 2002–2005

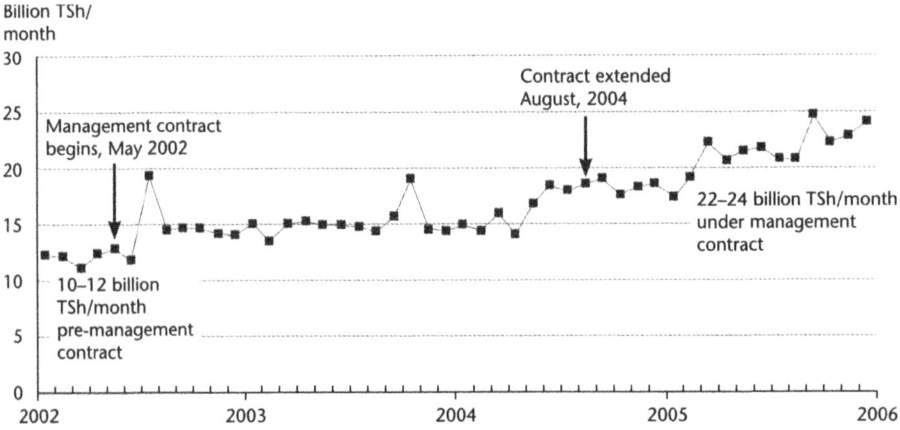

Source: Author calculations using unpublished Tanesco data, 2005
Note: TSh = Tanzanian shillings

Cut-offs of public offices

Intentions to improve revenue collection were signalled by threats of disconnection for non-payment of electricity bills. Public agency arrears accounted for the largest of these debts and were thus a priority for the new management team. Immediately upon assuming new management in 2002, Tanesco began carrying out disconnections of such high-profile consumers as the post office, the national police force and the entire island of Zanzibar.

Visible stand-offs ensued with some of the most sensitive offices and officers who ran them. But the president's office backed the Tanesco managers, and the government negotiated lump-sum back-payments of public debts. These lump-sum payments are visible as revenue spikes in Figure 15.2.

The cut-offs were seen as a victory by the new management and advocates of reform – a step toward meeting revenue targets and a message that Tanesco was serious about commercialisation. Government backing, namely by the president, was essential to implementation of these cut-offs and payments, but the contractors played a key role in carrying out controversial changes that government found difficult to effect on its own.

Residential service disconnections

Enforcement efforts were quickly extended to residential customers, with service cut-offs reaching levels of 15–20 000 per month.[6] This is equivalent to an average of about 3 per cent of the utility customer base per month. In fact, cumulative disconnections during the management contract period exceeded the total number of customers. More than 700 000 disconnections were carried out in the first three years of the management contract, compared to a total customer base of only about 570 000. Of course, disconnections may be multiple, and not every customer has been disconnected, but the figures do provide an indication of the massive scale of service disconnections (see Figure 15.3). In 2005, Tanesco also began pursuing legal proceedings, contracting local law firms to pursue cases of large outstanding arrears in court.

Notably, these disconnections took place with conventional meters (i.e. customers paying standard monthly bills at the end of each month), which means that they were disproportionately directed at low-income customers, as prepayment is primarily limited to middle- and upper-income customers (accounting for approximately 15 per cent of Tanesco's customer base at the end of 2005).

Figure 15.3: Electricity disconnections, 2002–2005

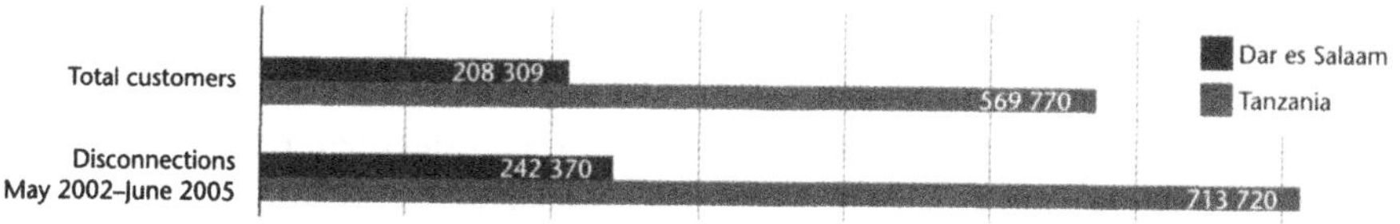

Source: Author calculations based on unpublished Tanesco data, 2005

Expansion of prepayment

Plans are under way to expand prepayment from just Dar es Salaam to higher-revenue areas of regional towns. Prepayment remains a largely middle- and upper-income technology, in part because of the additional upfront charges customers must pay to have it installed. Prepayment meters are now also being installed on a request-only basis and, as a result, do not have the same stigma and anti-poor connotations as they have had in other places (see for example Chapter 8 in this volume, on prepaid electricity meters in South Africa).

For those who can afford it, prepayment is generally preferred by customers over conventional meters, as it offers the advantages of avoiding permanent disconnections, minimising interactions with the utility's bureaucracy, and allowing customers to make smaller incremental payments which mesh better with their budgets.[7] Most low-income customers also desire prepayment meters, but these customers are considered, in the words of one utility manager, 'not worth the costs of the meter'.[8] As a result, low-income customers bear the brunt of service disconnections, poor service in utility offices, and lump-sum billing, which can be poorly suited to informal income streams.

While prepayment offers certain benefits and does not bear the stigma of being only for the poor in Tanzania, it does not offer protection against higher rates. Rate increases are being faced equally by both types of meter customers, though customers with conventional meters have less immediate feedback on or control over their expenses.

Tariff restructuring and the unravelling of redistributive mechanisms

Metering aside, residential (and light commercial) electricity users face increasing charges for electricity. While average tariffs increased by 8.5 per cent from US$0.070 to US$0.076 per kilowatt-hour (kWh) between 2002 and 2005, average residential tariffs increased by 19 per cent, while industrial tariffs *decreased* by 32 per cent, eliminating the cross-subsidy between industry and residential customers.[9] Once seen as an efficient way to harness the productive benefits of industry to fuel social development, cross-subsidies are considered inefficient in terms of the rationale of Tanzanian reforms and marginal cost pricing (Munasinghe & Warford 1982; Turvey & Anderson 1977). Lower industrial tariffs also support a foreign investment-oriented development model. Tanesco now closely monitors industrial tariffs relative to neighbouring Kenya and Uganda, in an effort to stay regionally competitive for prospective investors.

Tariff restructuring also dramatically scaled back residential lifeline tariffs. Lifeline tariffs are an initial increment of power that is given to customers at a low, subsidised rate, after which rates climb to commercial levels. Originally intended to promote modern fuel use, redistribute development benefits, and reduce deforestation, lifeline tariffs were a key aspect of state-led development policy (Wamukonya 2003a). Unlike the Free Basic Electricity Support Service Tariff in South Africa, the lifeline tariff in Tanzania is not free. However, they are similar in that the redistributive policies aim for 'targeted' rather than universal subsidies. While universal targets allocate benefits regardless of level of need, targeted subsidies on the other hand are difficult to design in ways that do not miss deserving customers. Non-universal benefits must be examined in practice, to ensure that they actually work.

Tariff restructuring between 1990 and 1995 scaled back the lifelines from 1 000 to 500 kWh per meter per month for residential and light commercial customers.[10] During the term of the management contract, the lifeline was further reduced to 50 kWh and shifted from a universal to a 'targeted' subsidy, available only to meters using less than 275 kWh per month.

The earlier 1 000 kWh lifeline tariff certainly exceeded basic needs, but current targeting also misses many customers, particularly low-income customers who rent and share meters. The loss of lifeline benefits compounds the growing costs of services, with tariff restructuring and rebalancing being major contributors to the large numbers of service disconnections among these low-income customers.

All but the lowest category of residential customers (<50 kWh/month) have seen their bills triple between 2002 and 2005.[11] Electricity charges have increased much faster than incomes, and have been more than double Tanzania's consumer price index as calculated by the Tanzanian National Bureau of Statistics in the period 2002–2005. On the ground, households must devote a greater share of their household budgets to electricity purchases to maintain the same level of service (see the case study of Manzese below).

Utility public relations

Extensive public relations efforts have accompanied utility service changes. Using various media, including newspaper advertisements, a radio show, press releases and billboards, government public relations efforts have sought to reframe key aspects of customer concerns about and interpretations of service provision. Figure 15.4 provides examples of utility public relations announcements from 2005. The advertisement on the left serves as a notice for disconnections, reminding people to budget accordingly and to pay bills on time. The advertisement on the right reads: 'The cost of stealing electricity is higher than you think', and goes on to explain the fines associated with disconnections for illegal power use.

The campaigns attempt to define what is fair and responsible consumer behaviour in the context of market-oriented service provision. While previously one became a good 'citizen' by supporting state-led development, one now

Figure 15.4: Utility public relations announcements, 2005

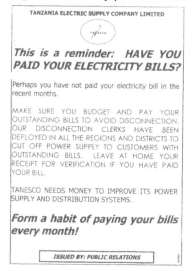

Source: Newspaper advertisements prepared by Tanesco public relations, 2005

becomes a responsible 'consumer' by paying bills on time. The campaign adds conceptual justification for the utility's disciplinary policies, particularly disconnections, as fair and in the public interest. But these relations are also largely top-down, one-way, and presented as non-negotiable. What are considered legitimate concerns is controlled by the utility and reflects its revenue focus. Within these relations there is little space for customer concerns or wider aspects of service quality or equality.

The backdrop to poor customer service

Constraints faced by customers are not only a result of growing costs and disconnections. Customers also face extensive burdens and barriers of poor customer service, which is in some cases even exploitative, with extensive hassles and delays in obtaining the services they need, particularly in regional offices. Customers routinely wait six months or more for requested new meters or connections, and can experience long delays after reporting equipment failures or downed lines in their neighbourhoods. Billing mistakes are also frequent.

In addition, some utility employees exploit and exacerbate service problems for private gain, profiteering because of shortages, delays and bureaucratic procedures. Some of them demand payments to facilitate or speed up service provisions. Third-party agents called 'vishoka' work outside, and even within, utility offices, taking payments from customers and liaising with utility employees to expedite services. Many of these vishoka are themselves part-time or former technicians, not currently employed.[12]

These dynamics between participating employees and vishoka are reinforced by reform-related employment policies that minimise new hires and promote outsourcing to temporary and short-term workers. The informal arrangements around many utility services are widespread and well known at almost all levels, including among regional managers and resident consultant managers.[13] Nonetheless, attention remains focused on realising short-term revenue goals.

The service barriers that customers face are linked in part to shortages of materials in regional offices, but they are also linked to the narrow scope of the management contract and its lack of attention to wider dimensions of service. There is, for example, no reporting on customer service required in the contract. In the words of one manager interviewed, 'We don't have a non-payment problem, we have a bad administration problem.'[14] Thus, poor customer service is a result of the fixation on revenue, and exploits the narrow scope of the reforms.

Little improvement in electrification

Tangible improvements in new connections have been minimal. Electrification stands at only 24 per cent of households overall in Africa, and only 10 per cent in Tanzania (IEA 2004). The percentage is significantly higher in the capital city,

Dar es Salaam (at 59 per cent), but only 2 per cent of the rural population has an electricity connection (TNBS 2002). Overall, electrification has increased by less than 2 per cent since 1992 (from 8.5 per cent to 10 per cent), undermined by limited capital financing and a focus on revenue collection from existing connections.

Another concern is that the creation of the REA/REF formally separated non-commercial electrification from the utility's purview. REA/REF's aim is to co-ordinate rural energy projects and to involve the private sector (Tanesco is also able to be a bidder). Its effectiveness will depend on the capacity improvements it can generate, as well as its ability to procure funding and continued donor support.

Commercial electrification and new connections remain the utility's direct responsibility. Hopes were high, at the beginning of the management contract extension in 2004, that revenue gains could be turned into service improvements. More than 100 000 new connections were promised for 2005 and 2006 as part of efforts dubbed by utility managers *Umeme kwa Wote* (Electricity for All). The aim was to make connections in peri-urban areas and regional towns, where the distribution network exists, but many remain unconnected. However, few of these new connections have been realised.

Surpluses expected to generate new reliability of service and electrification investments were instead redirected to growing generation costs, as the utility was forced to rely on more and more costly private power sources (IPPs) under drought conditions. The private management contractors and utility have had little control over these conditions as the negotiations have been done between the government, donors and private-sector companies involved, often prior to their assuming the management contract. In addition, many of the costs associated with IPP power are highly contentious.[15] The end result is that levels of new connections remain stagnant at about 2 500 per month (far fewer than the 17 000 disconnections taking place each month), and backlogs are growing rapidly (see Table 15.5).

A partial market bargain for Tanzanians

Overall, Tanzanians are only getting part of the gains promised by commercialisation, with few service or access improvements to show for the pressures and constraints they face. Residential customers are asked to pay more or face disciplinary enforcement; they receive poor services that may even be exploitative; and for many, new connections remain a distant hope. Under these conditions, many Tanzanians find it increasingly difficult to use and access electricity services.

Yet, while many of these issues are known to policy-makers, utility managers and donor agencies, they are discounted in policy-making and implementation processes. Pressures and constraints faced by customers are considered either temporary necessities or casualties of 'poor governance'. De-emphasised in this

Table 15.5: Service connections, 2002–2005

Number of customers (2005)	Total (n)	Notes
Total customers (meters)	550 000	Utility only 'sees' meters; many users share
Conventional meters	470 000 (85%)	meters (particularly renters); they may not
Prepayment meters	80 000 (15%)	receive lifeline subsidies and are invisible to
		targeting strategies.

New service lines	Average, 2002–2005	Notes
Requests for service lines	17 000/month	Service line requests exceed new
New connections made	2 500/month	connections; utility backlogs mean that
Waiting time for new connection	3–6 months	customers wait 3–6 months for new
Reported wait, via informal	1–3 weeks	connections; many report much shorter
payment & vishoka		waiting periods when using vishoka to
		facilitate side payments to utility
		employees.

Cost of new connection	US$	Notes
Conventional meter	175	Upfront customer charges are higher for
Prepayment meter	220	prepayment meters, but preferred;
Typical vishoka charges	50–150	informal payments increase the cost to
		consumers, and represent payments to
		vishoka and participating employees.

Sources: Tanesco Tariffs and Service Charges 2005 (costs of new connections and reconnections); unpublished Tanesco data 2005 (numbers of customers, disconnections, waits for connections); research interviews and focus groups with customers, employees, and vishoka, 2005 (information on vishoka charges and waits) (see note 12)
Note: Cost of new connections includes the application fee, new service line, and any deposits.

way, on-the-ground concerns find little voice within the scope of reforms. This de-legitimation and marginalisation of grassroots voices is a central tension in electricity commercialisation in the country, and throughout the continent. It explains how commercialisation programmes can be seen as a success and a failure at the same time by different groups, creating a context for a divergent and often contentious process.

Commercialisation: reactions and reverberations

Commercialisation of electricity has led to protests and resistance in Tanzania and elsewhere in Africa. Reactions have taken diverse forms, including grassroots frustrations over the slow expansion of services, organised movements resisting cost recovery policies, groups challenging the legitimacy of the reform process, and international campaigns against globalisation and privatisation. But to understand reactions, one must look to the spaces available within specific social and political contexts. Organised protest is only one of many potential manifestations of growing pressures, and it is certainly not a guaranteed outcome of commercialisation or reform. Instead, actions and resistance involve varied and often overlapping processes of everyday survival, livelihood and resource strategies which create pressures and which may be more or less visible in different contexts.

In Tanzania, most people are far removed from the policy processes that govern reforms. Commercialisation, meanwhile, is guided by a strong set of institutional relations and conceptual models that narrow the scope of what is included in these reforms. In this space people have little ability to influence the process or articulate their concerns. And with Tanzania's strong state history and national identity, many residents see protest as destabilising. Also, there are few public-interest or advocacy organisations to raise alternative perspectives on energy issues by alternative means. Few NGOs take a critical watchdog role over development relations, and the few that do have not focused on the electricity sector, which is largely out of public view.

Manifestations of pressures are numerous, as people make demands for a good life within the conditions and context of their immediate surroundings. Household- and community-level research conducted by the author in Dar es Salaam shows pressures shifting through neighbourly relations, household budgeting, gender and power dynamics, and natural resources. Pressures are borne most extensively by those with the least ability to command resources at the local level. These outcomes in Tanzania are some of the more silent reverberations of commercialisation, but they are critical arenas of struggle over access to electricity.

Techniques and strategies for coping

The most immediate impacts of commercialisation are experienced by urban residents who rely on purchased fuels. They also make up the majority of electricity customers in the country. Electricity costs are increasing at the same time as kerosene and oil prices have increased (with the liberalisation of the petroleum sector and recent increases in the price of oil, notably since 2002). Trade liberalisation has also widened consumption possibilities and created new, highly desired goods and services. These have expanded expectations and stimulated new demands, and are creating a more difficult context for household decision-making, budgeting and trade-offs.

Research in low- and middle-income neighbourhoods in Dar es Salaam in 2004–2005 shows households employing varying strategies to deal with increasing energy costs.[16] While electricity users are a privileged group by virtue of having services, overall residential electricity use is modest. Middle-income households typically have basic electrical equipment such as lights, a radio, fan, iron and, in some cases, a television, small refrigerator or mobile phone – modest accoutrements of modern urban life. Only a small minority have more elaborate appliances. With growing energy costs, middle-income households are able to do some 'budgeting' to cut back on non-essential uses, but still have very modest demands. They may also shift priorities within budgets or cut back in other areas to continue the same level of service.

In contrast, many low-income households have few ways of reducing energy use or shifting budgets without cutting back on essentials or precluding services entirely. Low-income urban households commonly have only a single light and a radio; in some cases an iron or television. For these households, even meeting basic needs often exceeds the means of their income. Increasing costs means cutting into essential uses; many residents emphasised that this was not 'budgeting'. In the words of one urban interviewee, 'What is budgeting when you don't have enough to eat? Budgeting is for those with money, those who can make decisions and make strategies. We have none.' In this context, growing energy costs can mean deep-cutting trade-offs relating to basic needs.

Table 15.6: Household strategies for dealing with increasing energy costs

Very low income: no strategies	Low income: highly invasive strategies	Middle income: moderately invasive strategies
'We cannot reduce use without hurting ourselves.' 'All our needs are basic, I cannot reduce further.' 'I am too poor to have strategies.'	Self-rationing electricity to minimum, evening hours Not using light in order to afford fuel for cooking Cooking only one kind of food to save fuel Switching to charcoal or sawdust for cooking Borrowing money	Not leaving the television on; using energy-saver light bulbs Ironing only once a week; turning off unused appliances Buying small-increment prepayment cards to promote conservation
Energy sources		
Sawdust, charcoal (cooking); candles and kerosene (light – electric lights are rare)	Charcoal, kerosene (cooking); kerosene and electricity (light, radio, iron, fan, TV)	Charcoal, kerosene, electricity in a few cases (cooking); electricity (light, radio, iron, fan, TV, small refrigerator, mobile phone)

Source: In-depth interviews with 50 households and focus group discussions with 9 different population segments in Dar es Salaam conducted by the author in 2004 (see note 16)

(Intra-)household budgeting dynamics

Many low-income urban households employ what is called *kodi ya meza*, or 'fee of the table', as a household resource and budgeting strategy. Husbands or male heads of household commonly leave 1 000–3 000 TSh (approximately US$1–3) on the table for their wife (or other female member of the household responsible for the domestic economy) each day, to use for daily household consumption expenses. She is expected to prepare meals and meet other household needs from these funds. Nearly all consumables are purchased in small, daily quantities, including kerosene, charcoal, food, salt, cooking oil and soap. Almost all households admit that this is insufficient for household needs, but the woman responsible is expected to stretch the funds or to supplement them with her own activities. Husbands keep the remaining income for private consumption; the size of this amount is commonly kept secret from the other household members.

These budgeting dynamics create conditions in which pressures reverberate unevenly through the household. With growing costs and a fixed budget, those most connected to the domestic economy must make limited resources stretch even further. For many, this results in deep and often difficult trade-offs, which are felt most strongly by those most dependent on the domestic sphere. Often, these are women without additional private income to supplement daily budgets, and children and other dependents who may rely exclusively on domestic resources to meet their needs.

These dynamics can also create tensions between the private consumption of male members with income and the collective domestic budget. As costs increase, there are greater pressures to limit contributions to the household budget in order to maintain private consumption, especially as cell phones and other technologies and consumer possibilities become more widely available. Increasing costs of services as part of the reform process and growing consumption desires work together to reinforce these gender and power dynamics, rather than to reduce them.

Shifting pressures to natural resources

Pressures are also shifting to natural resources and informal energy fuels. Over the last decade, particularly in the last few years, the prices of formal energy fuels have dramatically increased as a result of liberalisation and commercialisation. Figure 15.5 compares estimated monthly costs of cooking with different fuels in 1990 and 2005, based on a fixed amount of useful energy (that is, comparing the same amount of energy delivered to the pot). In contrast to the situation in the 1990s, charcoal was the lowest-cost urban cooking option in 2005, while cooking with electricity, kerosene and bottled gas had become significantly more expensive. These conditions reinforce the growth in charcoal use, expansion of the informal energy economy, and pressures on rural forestry resources. These pressures are witnessed in the massive trade in charcoal coming from rural to urban areas, and ubiquitous charcoal stoves and smoke rising from behind nearly every house in Dar es Salaam.

Many simply can only afford to use charcoal. But, interestingly, charcoal use is not limited to the poor. Surveys in Dar es Salaam showed that nearly every home had at least one charcoal stove (households often have multiple stoves), and many middle- and upper-income households choose to use charcoal for a major part of their cooking needs (author surveys 2004–2005; TNBS 2002).

Why is this so? For many, charcoal helps to extend limited household budgets. Middle- and even upper-income households also find growing gaps between their consumption expectations and their incomes. Cutting back on electricity consumption in a low-value area such as cooking makes it possible to expand purchasing power to other, more highly valued areas.

This is greatly reinforced by gendered labour dynamics within many middle- and upper-income homes. Reliance on the work of 'house girls' or other subordinate women for cooking means that the burdens of cooking are borne by those with the least decision-making power. Other benefits, such as reduced smoke exposure, improved convenience, or reduced time burdens – that might convince one to pay more to cook using a cleaner, more convenient fuel – rarely enter into decision-making, as those who bear these burdens are generally not in control of the resources to make the choice.

Figure 15.5: Household cooking cost comparisons[a] using various fuels, 1990 versus 2005

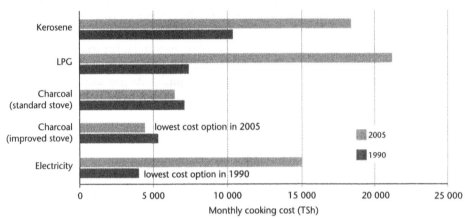

Sources: Hosier & Kipondya (1993, 1990 data); street-level retail survey by the author (2003–2005 appliance prices); Tanesco Electricity Tariff and Connections Schedules (1987–2005); TNBS (kerosene and charcoal retail prices, consumer price index, 1990–2005)

Note: a   Monthly cost estimates include fuel costs, stove efficiencies and simple amortisation of appliances, and connection costs based on 320 megajoules per month delivered to the pot. Costs are compared in constant 2000 TSh to afford direct comparison.

Massive disconnections: the case of Manzese

As noted earlier, commercialisation is also leading to large numbers of service disconnections, particularly for low-income electricity customers. Many of those disconnected are renters, who face additional barriers because they share meters. Illustrative of these conditions is Manzese, one of the largest high-density informal settlements in Dar es Salaam, where electricity bills are often the largest and most difficult household expense for many low-income households to manage.

Typical household budgets in Manzese range from 1 000–3 000 TSh per day (US$0.90–2.70), and almost all income is derived in daily increments from informal-sector activities. Prepayment meters, which allow smaller increment payments, are rare in low-income areas; more than 97 per cent of meters in Manzese were conventional meters. Renting is also extensive (82 per cent of electrified households). For many, electricity bills in 2005 had grown to equal or exceed their rent.

It is common for each room in a house to be rented out to a different family. The result is shared monthly bills and extensive meter sharing. The number of households sharing one meter ranges between 2 and 12 (or 4–38 people). Those who share meters also do not receive lifeline tariff benefits, as they are missed by the utility's targeting mechanism for allocating meters. As a best-case scenario, renters could gain 50 kWh per month of low-priced lifeline power; more often, they consume together more than the minimum cut-off for the lifeline tariff and must pay full rates. They must make collective payments, and non-payment by one member can mean disconnection of the group.

Given daily incomes, increasing charges, use of conventional meters and meter-sharing, many find it difficult to save and budget for electricity. These conditions lead to extensive disconnections and disputes. In Manzese, more than 63 per cent of electrified households had been disconnected between June 2004 and July 2005, and 90 per cent of these disconnections involved renters (see Table 15.7). Many of the disconnections were long term. Typical lengths of disconnections ranged from a few days to more than a year, with an average of 2–4 months. Nearly all these homes reported growing disputes internally. Local government officials also reported that fights over bills and disconnection by renters were increasingly entering their offices.

Even outside Manzese, interviews and surveys with more than 200 households in Dar es Salaam found only one group of renters fully satisfied with meter-sharing.

Table 15.7: Local electricity conditions in Manzese, Dar es Salaam, 2005

Budgeting		
Typical domestic daily budget	1 000–3 000 TSh/day	US$0.90–2.70
Typical rent (single room)	7 000 TSh/month	US$6.20
Typical electricity bill (often shared)	24 000 TSh/month	US$21.40
Conventional meters (vs. prepaid)	97% of households	
Meter-sharing		
Percentage of households sharing meters	82%	
Number of households sharing one meter	2–12 (mean of 4.5)	
Estimated loss of lifeline benefits, for 4 households sharing one meter	11 500–13 100 TSh/month	US$10.20–11.70/month
Disconnections		
Households experiencing disconnection, June 2004–July 2005	63%	
Typical length of disconnection	2–4 months (average); 25% of households experiencing cut-offs of more than 6 months	
Disconnections involving renters	90%	

Source: Data based on surveys by the author of 102 households in Manzese, Dar es Salaam, June–July 2005

To successfully manage their monthly bill, these four households organised a formal committee, designed an internal tariff with fixed fees for different appliances, and set up pre-arranged payment dates and terms for borrowing from each other. This example demonstrates the elaborate efforts needed to make these conditions work; the more common outcome is disputes, and often disconnections.

Conclusion: ways forward?

Electricity reforms as implemented in Tanzania are emblematic of neo-liberal change in Africa: macro-focused, finance-driven and guided by narrow reform models. Many of the changes in electricity provision have operated largely without public participation and have involved only ad hoc regulation and oversight (at best). In many ways, these reforms are a continuation of structural adjustment-initiated donor relations and a top-down state apparatus that together show little concrete evidence of emphasising sustainable development or participation-oriented approaches to electricity services.

Nevertheless, these outcomes reflect a negotiated process of reforms on a continent that is active, diverse and relevant. The commercialisation of services is not determined simply by policies insisted upon by donors, nor by African governments acting in isolation. Rather, the possibilities for improving access and services in Africa lie within internal and external relations of development that are neither unbounded nor fully predetermined.

Such an understanding illuminates connections between multiple experiences in Africa and provides a starting point for developing solutions and alternatives for social action from below as well as from above. Paying attention to the connected geographies of electricity commercialisation in Africa is critical for making reforms more accountable. Tanzania's experience reveals a number of these issues.

While not exhaustive, the following list provides thoughts on conditions necessary for a more effective and honest dialogue on the development of electricity service models that are more appropriate in an African context:

*   *Make service a priority:* High-quality services that are affordable and available to the majority need to be reasserted as the goal and benchmark for successful electricity policy. Finance and revenue are only as effective as the improvements in service and access they are able to generate. A 'commercial' sector or utility that does not provide quality services cannot be considered successful. Service needs to be made a priority, with clear goals and delivery mechanisms, rather than being left as a residual element of utility finances as it currently is in Tanzania.
*   *Incorporate avenues for expression and recognition of customer (and would-be customer) interests:* Consumer advocacy needs to be included in the formal reform process. This means more effective regulatory bodies as well as other avenues for citizens to interact with the utility and the policy process. Explicit

consumer advocacy groups are needed within public institutions as well as NGO, university and other civil-society arenas to assess changes and propose alternatives. This is also an opportunity for regional organisations to raise issues related to electricity commercialisation in Africa. A critical aspect of 'governance' is that discipline is balanced across the sector, and that there are adequate means of participation and oversight to create checks and balances between financial and development goals. The marginalisation of customer concerns emerges from the relations that guide current electricity policy.

- *African interconnections to improve access, not just commercialisation:* Prospects for improving electrification in Africa are in many ways a question of where finance will come from, and how willing donors and the international community are to support access in Africa. Electrification, even in the developed world, has been largely a publicly funded process. The private sector can play a role, but is unlikely to serve access goals without a clear policy vision and explicit mechanisms for oversight. Improving access requires an honest dialogue, combining clear policy goals and financial commitments. When will improvements come, and where from? What innovations and approaches can be used? Who is going to finance these priorities? Needs are wide-reaching, but some priorities are revealed in Tanzania. South African connections could be harnessed to disseminate low-cost electrification techniques, and not just commercialisation and enforcement technologies, given the appropriate policy vision. With much of rural electrification separated from mainstream utility activities, continued financial and institutional support of the REA/REF (and agencies like it) is necessary if these new mechanisms are to build the capacity to be effective. African utilities must also improve their ability to carry out new connections and eliminate extensive bottlenecks and backlogs in the process. This will require additional resources, but it will also require greater attention to customer service.

- *Incorporate sustainable charcoal use into the energy reform agenda:* Electricity commercialisation, petroleum liberalisation and urbanisation are drivers for increased charcoal use in Africa. Charcoal is a 'modern' energy fuel, at least in terms of its practical use in African cities. Charcoal use needs to be recognised as a critical part of emerging conditions produced by reforms, and resource management needs to enter into policy discussions. Sustainable charcoal production, improved charcoal stove dissemination, and incentives to assist in fuel-switching are critical activities for sustainable energy policy and need to be recognised within the scope of reforms. Improving charcoal conditions also requires attention to forestry resources and rural livelihoods, as the issue of charcoal connects livelihoods across rural and urban divides. An integrated policy is needed to address these related aspects of resource use, reforms and rural–urban livelihoods; its absence from reform discussions is short-sighted.

Tanzania reveals distinctive features of electricity commercialisation in an African context. Many programmes are converging on common techniques, service models and guiding rationales. It is also a process driven by wider national reform programmes that are, in many countries, situated within a wider apparatus of donor relations. The process involves new regional connections within Africa, with Tanzania showing how South African businesses are playing an increasingly important role in providing services and technologies in support of commercialisation on the continent.

Commercialisation is also marked by diverse struggles over access in a reform environment. These struggles relate to questions of legitimacy, participation and accountability of reforms. They also concern everyday experiences and strategies to seek a decent life. These concerns may be more or less visible, and their manifestations may range from protest to more silent reverberations, but they are linked.

Attention to commercialisation of services in a broader African context reveals not only shared anxieties, but also new possibilities. Within Africa lie possibilities to develop a vision for energy and development policy based on the continent's actual conditions, concerns and capabilities. The future will be determined by policy and daily life in places like Johannesburg and Dar es Salaam, as much as in Washington DC. It is time that our attention reflects this geography of possibilities on the continent.[17]

Notes

1 Captain John Komba Jr, singing a government- and donor-sponsored privatisation song; see World Bank 2001.

2 IPTL, Tanzania's first IPP, is jointly owned by Malaysian investors and a local Tanzanian investment firm, and was negotiated independently with the government of Tanzania. IPTL began selling power to the utility in 2002 (its power purchase agreement was first negotiated in 1995); however, the project is costly and remains contentious.

3 Songas, Tanzania's second IPP, has involved numerous private-sector companies and more than 20 contracts. Songas began selling power to Tanzania Electricity Supply Company Limited (Tanesco) in 2004 (the initial tender for the project was in 1993). Currently, Globeleq is the lead shareholder of Songas (56 per cent). Globeleq is a company spun off from Britain's Commonwealth Development Corporation (CDC) in 2002 as the holder of CDC's portfolio of power sector assets. Other shareholders include the Dutch Development Company (24 per cent), the Tanzania Development Finance Company Ltd, Tanzania Petroleum Development Corporation, and Tanesco. Songas is part of a larger project that has involved refurbishment and development of offshore gas wells; installation of a gas processing facility; construction of a 232 kilometre pipeline; and conversion and expansion of an existing power station. The project has involved extensive donor support from the World Bank International Development Association, the European Investment Bank, and the Swedish International Development Cooperation Agency.

4   Calculated from Tanesco billing data 2005.

5   Unpublished World Bank document, 2004.

6   Unpublished Tanesco data, 2002–2005.

7   Information gathered in focus groups with Dar es Salaam residents, 2004.

8   Interview with NETGroup-Tanesco manager of Customer Service, conducted at Tanesco corporate offices, Dar es Salaam, August 2005; consent agreement to report professional titles.

9   Author calculations based on unpublished Tanesco data, 2005.

10   I refer to meters because the utility only 'sees' meters, which may actually be shared by multiple households, as is the case with multiple renters sharing a single home, a common practice among low-income households in urban Dar es Salaam.

11   Author calculations based on Tanesco tariff schedules, 2002–2005. Calculations were done by comparing electricity charges immediately prior to the April 2002 rate increase and rates after the January 2005 rate increase. Much of the dramatic increase in bills is due to scaling back of the lifeline tariff and unravelling of the cross-subsidy between industrial and residential customers (calculated from Tanesco tariff schedules, 2002–2005).

12   Focus group discussions with vishoka operating in proximity to Magomeni and Mikocheni regional Tanesco offices, Dar es Salaam, August 2005; consent agreement for participants to remain anonymous.

13   Based on more than 25 interviews with NETGroup and Tanesco managers and staff, including corporate headquarters and Magomeni and Mikocheni regional offices, Dar es Salaam, August, September, October 2004; July, August 2005.

14   Interviews with the Human Resource Manager, Magomeni regional Tanesco office, Dar es Salaam, August 2005 and Public Relations Manager, Tanesco corporate offices, Dar es Salaam, August 2004, August 2005; consent agreements with interviewees to report professional titles.

15   Investments to improve reliability and expand services have not materialised as expected; instead, revenue gains achieved during the period of the management contract have gone to pay for more costly IPP-derived power. Private power has been more costly than expected to the utility, and thus to consumers, in terms of both construction and use costs. Many of these costs are highly contentious. In the case of Songas, a natural gas power plant and Tanzania's second IPP, private investors have earned a 22 per cent return on equity, even throughout costly construction delays. The project has received extensive risk guarantees from the government and support from a large, multi-year World Bank gas-to-electricity project. The other IPP, IPTL, has had some of the highest construction charges for a plant of its kind in the world compared to 17 other similar projects in developing countries, even after a 20 per cent reduction in construction costs after international arbitration. Use costs have also been higher than expected, as the utility has been forced to rely more heavily on IPP-derived generation, and below-average rainfall which has eroded hydro-power capacity. Recently, IPP supplies have been insufficient to fill supply gaps created by the loss of hydro-power, and Tanesco resorted to load shedding

of up to 12 hours per day throughout much of 2006. For a detailed analysis of the complex and contentious IPPs, see Gratwick et al. 2006.

16 I carried out household- and community-level research on energy and service conditions, as part of my dissertation research, in the capital city of Dar es Salaam in 2004 and 2005. The research included a survey of service conditions in seven areas of the city; in-depth focus groups and interviews; and surveys in two wards of the city – Sinza, a planned area known as a middle-income, working-class neighbourhood, and Manzese, one of Dar es Salaam's largest urban informal settlements, housing many low-income urban residents and having extensive informal commercial activities.

17 This chapter is based on my PhD dissertation research in conjunction with the Energy and Resources Group of the University of California Berkeley, conducted between 2003 and 2006. I would like to thank the Tanzania Traditional Energy and Development Organisation and the Sociology Department at the University of Dar es Salaam, and acknowledge the hard work and numerous insights of my research assistants: Doris Uhagile, Huruma Chaulla, Adrophina Salvatore, Prisca Msongo and Kamugisha Gosbert. I would also like to thank the numerous residents of Dar es Salaam who shared their experiences and perspectives on energy and service issues, and acknowledge the support of the Link Energy Foundation, Rocca Endowment for African Studies, Energy Foundation and University of California Berkeley Class of 1935.

References

Africa Power (2006) Tanesco not for privatisation. *Africa Power* 20 January

African Energy (1999) Roshcon's Tanzania pre-payment metering success. *African Energy* 1(3)

Agbemabiese L & Byrne J (2005) Commodification of Ghana's Volta River: An example of Ellul's autonomy of technique. *Bulletin of Science, Technology & Society* 25(1): 17–25

Bacon R (1995) Privatization and reform in the global electricity supply industry. *Annual Review of Energy and the Environment* 20: 119–143

Bacon RW & Besant-Jones J (2001) Global electric power reform, privatization and liberalization of the electric power industry in developing countries. *Annual Review of Energy and the Environment* 26: 331–359

Bayliss K & Hall D (2000) *Privatisation of water and energy in Africa*. London: Public Services International (PSI) Research Unit, University of Greenwich

BBC News (2002) Tanzanians unhappy at electricity award. *BBC News World Edition Online* 30 January

Bond P (ed.) (2002) *Unsustainable South Africa: Environment, development and social protest.* Pietermaritzburg & London: UKZN Press & Merlin Press

Collier H (1984) *Developing electric power: Thirty years of world bank experience.* Published for the World Bank. Baltimore: Johns Hopkins University Press

Daily News (2002) Change, workers told by Mkapa. *Daily News* (Dar es Salaam) 2 May

Davies I (2004) *Management contracts in the electricity sector. A case study, Tanzania.* Campbell Davies Consulting Report

Doriye J (1992) Public office and private gain: An interpretation of the Tanzanian experience. In M Wuyts, M Mackintosh & T Hewitt (eds) *Development policy and public action.* Oxford: Oxford University Press

Dubash NK (2002) *Power politics: Equity and environment in electricity reform.* Washington DC: World Resources Institute

Dunkerly J (1995) Financing the energy sector in developing countries: Context and overview. *Energy Policy* 23(11): 929–939

Economist (2006) Bye-bye poverty. An African country that deserves the money it gets. *The Economist* 28 September

ESMAP (Energy Sector Management Assistance Programme) (1999) *Global energy sector reform in developing countries: A scorecard.* Washington DC: ESMAP, World Bank

ESMAP (2001) *California energy crisis: Lessons for developing countries.* Washington DC: ESMAP, World Bank

Estache A (2005) *What do we know about sub-Saharan Africa's infrastructure and the impact of its 1990 reforms?* Washington DC & Brussels: World Bank & ECARES, Université Libre de Bruxelles

Ghanadan R & Eberhard A (2007) *Electricity utility management contracts in Africa: Lessons and experience from the Tanesco-NETGroup management contract in Tanzania, 2002/2006.* Cape Town: Management Programme in Infrastructure Reform (MIR), Graduate School of Business, University of Cape Town

Gore C (2000) The rise and fall of Washington Consensus as a paradigm for developing countries. *World Development* 28(5): 789–804

GoT (Government of Tanzania) (1986) *Tanzania government programme for economic recovery.* Dar es Salaam: Government of Tanzania

Gratwick K, Ghanadan R & Eberhard A (2006) *Generating power and controversy: Understanding Tanzania's independent power projects.* Cape Town: Management Programme in Infrastructure Reform (MIR), Graduate School of Business, University of Cape Town

Helleiner G (2002) An economist's reflections on the legacies of Julius Nyerere. In DA McDonald & S Njeri (eds) *The legacies of Julius Nyerere: Influences on development discourse and practice in Africa.* Trenton, NJ & Asmara: Africa World Press

Hosier RH & Kipondya W (1993) Urban household energy use in Tanzania. *Energy Policy* 21(5): 454–473

Hunt S (2002) *Making competition work in electricity.* New York: Wiley

IEA (International Energy Agency) (2004) *World energy outlook 2004.* Paris: IEA

Jhirad D (1990) Power sector innovation in developing countries: Implementing multifaceted solutions. *Annual Review of Energy and the Environment* 15: 365–398

Kaiser P (1996) Structural adjustment and the fragile nation: The demise of social unity in Tanzania. *Journal of Modern African Studies* 34(2): 227–237

Karekezi S & Kimani J (2002) Status of power sector reform in Africa: Impact on the poor. *Energy Policy* 30: 923–945

Katyega M (2004) *Outsourcing opportunities for small and medium enterprises in the ongoing utility reforms in Tanzania.* ESMAP/AFREPREN Report. Washington DC: Energy Sector Management Assistance Program, World Bank

Kelsall T (2002) Shop windows and smoke-filled rooms: Governance and the re-politicisation of Tanzania. *Journal of Modern African Studies* 40(4): 597–619

Kessides I (2004) *Reforming infrastructure: Privatization, regulation, and competition.* Washington DC & Oxford: World Bank & Oxford University Press

Kjaer AM (2004) 'Old brooms can sweep too!' An overview of rules and public sector reforms in Uganda, Tanzania and Kenya. *Journal of Modern African Studies* 42(3): 389–413

Lamech R & Saeed K (2003) *What international investors look for when investing in developing countries: Results from a survey of international investors in the power sector.* Washington DC: World Bank

Marandu EE (1999) Tanzania's power sector and reforms. In MR Bhagavan (ed.) *Reforming the power sector in Africa.* London: Zed Books

Marandu EE (2002) The prospects for local private investment in Tanzania's rural electrification. *Energy Policy* 30: 977–985

McDonald D & Ruiters G (eds) (2005) *The age of commodity: Water privatization in southern Africa.* London: Earthscan Press

MEM (Ministry of Energy and Minerals) (1992) *The energy policy of Tanzania.* Dar es Salaam: MEM

MEM (2003a) *National energy policy.* Dar es Salaam: MEM

MEM (2003b) *Proposal for establishment of a Rural Energy Agency (REA) and a Rural Energy Fund (REF).* Dar es Salaam: MEM

Mkapa B (2002) Hotuba ya Rais wa Jamhuri ya Muungao wa Tanzania, Mhesimwa Benjamin William Mkapa kwa Wananchi (Presidential speech to the people of Tanzania by Honourable Benjamin William Mkapa) 29 April. Accessed 18 September 2003, http://www.tanzania.go.tz/020429hotuba

Moffett JP (1955) *Tanganyika: A review of its resources and their development.* Prepared under JFR Hill, Member for Communications, Works and Development Planning, Government of Tanganyika. Norwich: Jarrold and Sons Ltd

Mosley S, Harrigan J & Toye J (1991) *Aid and Power: The World Bank and policy-based lending.* London & New York: Routledge

Munasinghe M & Warford J (1982) *Electricity pricing: Theory and case studies.* Baltimore & London: Johns Hopkins University Press

Page B (2005) Paying for water and the geography of commodities. *Transactions of the Institute of British Geographers* 30(3): 293–306

PSRC (Parastatal Reform Commission) (2002) Management support services contract for technical and financial operations between the presidential Parastatal Reform

Commission (PSRC) and Tanzania Electric Supply Company Limited (Tanesco) and NETGroup Solutions (Pty) Ltd. Dar es Salaam: PSRC

TANU (Tanganyika African National Union) (1967) *The Arusha Declaration and TANU's policy on socialism and self-reliance.* Written by Julius Nyerere for the Tanganyika African National Union, 5 February, revised English translation

The African (2002a) In a move to stop entry of new Tanesco management, workers barricade headquarters entrance. *The African* (Dar es Salaam) 3 May

The African (2002b) Tanesco workers give in, NETGroup officials finally get into head offices. *The African* (Dar es Salaam) 18 May

The Guardian (2004a) Political cartoon, IPTL, government, Tanesco power struggle? *The Guardian* (Dar es Salaam) 15 June

The Guardian (2004b) MPs want NetGroup Solutions to pack up and go. *The Guardian* (Dar es Salaam) 26 June

The Guardian (2004c) Why have investments that do not accommodate capacity building? *The Guardian* (Dar es Salaam) 9 September

TNBS (Tanzania National Bureau of Statistics) (2002) *2000/01 Tanzanian household budget survey final report.* Dar es Salaam: TNBS

Turvey R & Anderson D (1977) *Electricity economics: Essays and case studies.* Baltimore & London: Johns Hopkins University Press

Veriava A & Ngwane T (2004) Strategies and tactics: Movements in the neo-liberal transition. In D McKinley & P Naidoo (eds) *Development update 5: Mobilizing for change. The rise of the new social movements in South Africa.* Johannesburg: Interfund.

Wamukonya N (2003a) Power sector reform in developing countries: Mismatched agendas. *Energy Policy* 31(12): 1273–1289

Wamukonya N (ed.) (2003b) *Electricity reform: Social and environmental challenges.* Roskilde, Denmark: United Nations Environment Programme

Wananchi (2002) May Day and Tanesco workers yesterday. *Wananchi* (Dar es Salaam) 2 May

Wangwe S, Semboja H & Tibandebage P (1998) *Transitional economic policy and policy options in Tanzania.* Dar es Salaam: Economic and Social Research Foundation

Williams JH & Ghanadan R (2006) Electricity reform in developing and transition countries: A reappraisal. *Energy* 31(6/7): 815–844

Williamson J (1993) Democracy and the 'Washington Consensus'. *World Development* 21(8): 1329–1336

World Bank (1992) *Staff appraisal report: Tanzania Power VI Project.* Washington DC: World Bank

World Bank (1993) *The World Bank's role in the electric power sector.* Washington DC: World Bank

World Bank (2001) *Singing for the privatization hit parade, Tanzania's Captain John Komba promoting reform, winning strategies.* Accessed 12 June 2005, http://rru.worldbank.org/Themes/PromotingReform/Communications/TanzaniaSinging/

World Bank (2002) *Rapping for the privatization hit parade, Tanzania's Mr. Ebbo, promoting reform, winning strategies.* Accessed 12 June 2005, http://rru.worldbank.org/Themes/PromotingReform/Communications/TanzaniaRapping/

World Bank (2003) Infrastructure is once again part of the World Bank's mainstream business – interview with World Bank Executive Director Carole Brookins. *Transition Newsletter* 14/15(10/1): 1–3

World Bank (2004) *Public and private sector roles in the supply of electricity services.* Washington DC: World Bank

World Bank (2006) *Doing business 2007: How to reform.* Washington DC: World Bank

Yeager R (1982) *Tanzania. An African experiment.* Boulder: West View Press

CONCLUSION

Alternative electricity paths for southern Africa

David A McDonald

The chapters in this book describe a situation in which large corporations and policy-making elites are intent on expanding electricity capacity in South and southern Africa on terms which are beneficial to international capital, at the expense of those who need electricity the most: the poor. Is there any hope for a more sustainable and equitable electricity future in the region?

In short, yes. As the chapters in this book also attest, there is no want of alternative strategies. From solar power to decentralised electricity committees to better demand management, there are a myriad policies and practices that could be introduced relatively quickly, and with significant effect on sustainability and equity. There are also lessons from other parts of the world that could be adapted to the needs of southern African countries and municipalities.

South Africa in particular, with its remarkable generation capacity and distribution infrastructure, skilled personnel and financial resources, could make considerable gains in equity and sustainability in a relatively short period of time. The country could also contribute substantially to electricity justice in other countries in the region, many of which will need assistance in rolling out (more progressive) electricity services.

This is not to suggest that disrupting the current electricity trajectory in the region will be easy. Far from it. The inertia of planned investments, the enormous benefits to be gained by multinational capital, and the hard-nosed commitment on the part of South African policy-makers to an expansionist, supply-side policy agenda will make it difficult to create even the smallest of diversions from this electrical juggernaut. Witness, for example, the pathetically small commitments being made by the South African state and Eskom to investments in solar power, their vitriolic denunciations of the anti-nuclear lobby, and their willingness to cut off electricity supplies to the poorest of the poor for the slightest of infractions.

Nevertheless, change there must be, and this chapter explores – in very general terms – what some of these alternatives might be. The objective here is not to be exhaustive or prescriptive in the discussion of alternatives but to indicate the kinds of changes that are possible and to suggest ways in which they might be approached.

I have divided my discussion into two sections: one on 'reforming' the electricity sector and the other on 'transforming' it. As these section titles imply, the first looks at relatively modest strategies for change – ideas, policies and technologies that reform rather that radically alter the policies of the day; changes that could significantly improve access and affordability for the poor and build towards more environmentally sustainable practices while still being potentially acceptable to mainstream policy-makers and big business. These reforms are largely Keynesian in their orientation: (re)introducing a more welfarist approach to electricity delivery, tightening up regulatory frameworks, and meeting demands for public consultation and ownership. There is nothing particularly new in what I have to say here, but given how far South(ern) Africa has travelled down its neo-liberal policy path, none of them will be easily accepted or implemented by the region's policy elite.

The second section looks at more radical, transformative change. These arguments are more conceptual in nature, in part because there has never been a sustained effort at radical electricity transformation in the region (preliminary efforts by the socialist governments of Mozambique and Angola were undermined by civil wars and sabotage of electricity infrastructures), and in part because radical transformation appears only a pipe dream at the moment, given the hegemonic climate of market ideologies.

And yet, radical change is what is required. If, as I argued in Chapter 1 of this volume, capitalism in the southern African region depends on a minerals-energy complex (MEC) that provides multinational capital with heavily subsidised electricity at the expense of social and environmental sustainability, then the material basis of this extractive economy must change. Tinkering around at the edges may alleviate some of the worst excesses of the system, but it will not alter its general course.

Reforming the electricity sector

Much has been written about reforming the electricity sector in South and southern Africa. Hundreds of useful contributions have been made – particularly in South Africa – by unions (e.g. the Congress of South African Trade Unions), NGOs (e.g. Earthlife Africa), social movements (e.g. the Soweto Electricity Crisis Committee [SECC]), consulting firms (e.g. Palmer Development Group), academics (e.g. the Energy Research Centre at the University of Cape Town), governments and electricity producers themselves about ways in which electricity could be delivered in a more equitable and sustainable manner.

Many of these recommendations have already been discussed in this book. From incorporating more women and community members into decision-making structures to providing larger amounts of 'free basic electricity' to low-income households, the range of policy options is as impressive as it is overwhelming.

What follows is a synopsis of what I consider to be some of the most important – and most feasible – options for reformist policy change. The sections are brief, either because they have been discussed elsewhere in this volume at greater length and/or because there is a larger literature on the subject that readers can explore. There are two sections, however, that I delve into in slightly more detail, in an effort to make a more original contribution. The first looks at the issue of democratising electricity institutions; the second examines the question of public ownership of electricity utilities.

The focus of my discussion is once again South Africa, although there are elements of each section that could be considered relevant to other counties in the region and beyond.

Better demand management

By better demand management I am referring largely to the practice of creating disincentives for excessive consumption, both through pricing mechanisms (i.e. more progressive block-tariff structures that penalise consumption at the top end in the hopes of promoting more efficient use of electricity) as well as through legislated limits to consumption.

The former strategy is already being practised to some extent in South Africa, with block tariffs for electricity having been introduced in most municipalities in the country – though these tariffs tend to be composed of only two price blocks (high consumption and low consumption) and would appear to have little or no impact on the relatively hedonistic electricity consumption patterns of suburban South African households, with domestic electricity prices in South Africa still being amongst the lowest in the world, especially relative to household incomes for the middle class. Indeed, keeping domestic prices low is one of the key demands of manufacturers and other firms in the country anxious to sell electricity-dependent appliances and services.

There is considerable potential, therefore, to introduce more progressive block tariffs for domestic consumption in South Africa. Surplus revenue from these tariffs could be used to cross-subsidise a larger block of free electricity for low-income families (more on this below) while at the same time encouraging less wasteful electricity behaviour in the suburbs, all without fundamentally altering people's lifestyles. Much more progressive block tariffs have been introduced in the water sector in South Africa over the past 10 years for these very reasons, and although water tariffs could also still go further, they do indicate the political and economic potential for more progressive tariffs in electricity.

But it is industry that is by far the largest consumer of electricity in the country, and it is here that pricing reform is most needed. Rather than being progressive, electricity pricing for MEC-related firms is remarkably regressive, with large multinationals often receiving electricity at a fraction of the cost that households pay. The political and economic scope for price reforms is more constricted here, however, due to the entrenched and very powerful industrial lobby that exists in South Africa, and the footloose nature of global capital, always looking for the cheapest place to be based. Nevertheless, the potential for rising block tariffs in electricity exists, particularly if it is coupled with efforts by the state to assist firms with efficiency measures. Exactly what a new pricing scheme might look like, and how it would be phased in, would require considerable thought and negotiation, but the technical and economic potential is there if the political will exists.

The state could also introduce more aggressive efficiency legislation on the manufacturing and importation of electrical appliances and production systems, as well as the construction of homes and commercial buildings in terms of their energy use. South African firms and retailers have been notoriously lax in this regard and legislation has done little to shake them into action.

Finally, additional legislation to cap electricity consumption, regardless of price, could be used as an additional incentive to create efficiencies and reduce wasteful consumption. In the same way that aggressive water restrictions have been employed in the country during times of low rainfall or drought, so too might Eskom and municipalities consider tighter policing of consumption of electricity in the interest of a better distribution of existing electricity capacity, delaying the need for investments in new generating facilities.

Investment in alternative energies

A second, and perhaps more broadly acceptable, strategy for reform is to invest much more heavily in alternative, sustainable forms of energy. As Liz McDaid argues in her chapter in this volume, the potential for wind, solar and wave power is particularly high in South and southern Africa, and there are a variety of other possibilities that could be explored, including 'cleaner' forms of thermal and hydro production, all of which are receiving little more than lip service at the moment.

These investments must be made carefully, of course. 'Alternative' energy systems cannot be assumed to be benign or progressive, as the controversy over biofuels has demonstrated. There are also questions about ownership, with much of development of wind power, for example, being done by private firms in South Africa – often with state subsidies – contributing to a *de facto* privatisation of this subsector. Management practices, pricing and transmission questions must also be considered in any investment, making alternative electricity strategies anything but simple.

What is straightforward is the enormous potential for electricity in South(ern) Africa to be generated and transmitted from sources other than low-grade coal, large dams and nuclear power plants. The monies and energies being invested in substitutes are nowhere near what is required, constituting a proverbial drop in the investment bucket when compared to spending that is taking place on conventional electricity production facilities in the region.

(Re)directing investments to people and areas most in need

The post-apartheid rollout of electricity services to low-income areas has been impressive in many ways, with substantial direct and indirect resources being spent on bringing electricity to millions of South Africans for the first time – approximately 3.2 million homes were connected between 1991 and 2005 at a cost of approximately R9.4 billion (WBCSD 2006: 2). But millions are still without electricity – particularly in rural areas – and millions more have poor-quality services and/or cannot afford to pay for the services they receive. As per capita costs of connecting households to the grid become higher – as more remote communities are brought online – and as neo-liberal pricing and cost recovery strategies become more entrenched, the much vaunted electrification programme in South Africa has slowed dramatically in the past few years – from approximately 300 000 new household connections per year in the 1990s to just over 56 000 in the 2006/07 fiscal year (SALGRC 2007: 48).

Additional resources should be made available from national and municipal authorities for the capital and operating costs of electricity services in areas not yet serviced and/or with poor-quality services. Funds can come from a redirection of existing capital and operating expenditures in the sector, as well as injections of new funds to revitalise the electrification campaign.

Announcements by the cities of Johannesburg and Cape Town that they plan to spend hundreds of millions of rands upgrading their respective electricity services in preparation for the FIFA World Cup in 2010 are examples of the kinds of spatially (and racially) biased investments that need to be re-examined and publicly debated. Other infrastructure investments, such as the estimated R20 billion high-speed Gautrain designed to whisk corporate clients to and from the Johannesburg airport, can also be examined in terms of spending priorities at the national and municipal level vis-à-vis electrification in low-income areas.

Fairer pricing and less aggressive cost recovery

Implicit in my discussion above regarding rising block tariffs is the need to make electricity more affordable for the poor. As documented throughout this book, low-income households often pay higher nominal prices than suburban households serviced by the same supplier, and always pay more than commercial users. These differences become even starker when one considers the *relative* cost of electricity for low-income households, sometimes consuming more than 15 per cent of monthly household expenditure.

As a result, many low-income households restrict their electricity consumption to what they think they can manage to pay each month, forcing them to make life-and-death decisions over whether to buy electricity, food or clothing. Some households simply opt to go into payment arrears, facing the threat of electricity cut-offs, rather than limit their consumption below what is required to meet essential needs.

The introduction of 50 kWh of free basic electricity per household per month has done little to alleviate these problems, as Greg Ruiters pointed out in Chapter 9 in this volume. As a result, there have been calls by social movements, NGOs, unions and academics to increase the allotment of free electricity, and to introduce more progressive tariff pricing to make smaller amounts of electricity more affordable after the block of free consumption.

There are also calls to abolish prepaid electricity meters. Although resistance to prepaid electricity is not as widespread as it has been to prepaid water meters in South Africa, similar concerns have been raised about access and adequate supplies of electricity as a result of their introduction. I support this call to ban prepaid electricity meters on the basis that they discriminate against the poor.

I also support calls for an end to electricity cut-offs for non-payment of bills. Poor-quality service delivery in black residential areas of the country, combined with unequal capital investments and pricing schemes, makes a moral and constitutional mockery of cut-offs as a legitimate management tool, serving only to discipline and cajole potential low-income defaulters into payment in the interests of minimising rates and tariff increases for the middle class and industry.

Moreover, commercial consumers of services typically account for a third to a half of service payment defaults in South African municipalities, and yet private companies are seldom threatened with cut-offs – in stark contrast to the millions of low-income black South Africans who have suffered this indignity since the end of apartheid (Desai 2002; Hemson & O'Donovan 2006; McDonald & Pape 2002).

A fairer, more uniformly applied cost recovery regime that allows easy access to sufficient and reliable quantities of electricity for the poor could go a long way towards spreading the benefits of electricity while at the same time minimising its negative impacts.

Democratising electricity institutions

The democratisation of electricity institutions could also be of significant benefit. Eskom in particular is notorious for its behind-closed-doors negotiations with big business about pricing and investments, while at the same time failing to consult with the communities it serves. Although most South Africans know that Eskom is the national electricity supplier, few have any sense of how it really operates or how decisions are made, despite the fact that it is a publicly owned and operated utility.

Similar complaints have been made of municipal electricity distributors, despite the fact that they are physically closer to those they serve and are therefore expected to be more accessible and accountable. Some improvements have been made since the end of apartheid in this regard, but most municipal electricity decision-making still takes place in boardrooms and council chambers far removed from the average citizen.

Having said that, municipal-level utilities provide perhaps the best democratising potential in South Africa. Face-to-face meetings with residents can take place, and electricity users can articulate local needs to local suppliers. But to make such democratisation possible there needs to be much more public information provided by municipal electricity distributors about electricity services, and more opportunities for public participation. The latter must take into account logistical questions such as transportation, language and explanation of technical matters. With most municipal electricity departments dominated by white male engineers, significant efforts will need to be made to bridge these technical and cultural gaps.

Unfortunately, the ongoing corporatisation of electricity utilities in the country has made this democratisation process difficult at the municipal level, creating additional distance between the local utility and the public they serve. The introduction of Regional Electricity Distributors (REDs) will make the problem even more acute, creating another layer of political and geographic distance between the distributor and the public. The fact that REDs are being formed (and reformed) with virtually no public input or debate in South Africa is an indication of this anti-democratic trend and does not bode well for electricity democratisation in the future.

Democratising Eskom will be equally difficult, but has the advantage of addressing a large and very visible target (as opposed to the mostly small- and medium-sized municipal suppliers scattered around the country). The same basic calls for more public input, accountability and transparency apply to Eskom as well, and the same could be said of its parent ministry, the Department of Minerals and Energy, which is the most removed electricity decision-maker of all in the country. Eskom has proven to be susceptible to public pressure for reform, though it has been a slow and painful process for those involved, and its overall *modus operandi* of corporate favouritism and back-room deal-making remains largely intact (see Greenberg, Chapter 3 in this volume).

As we move up the regional scale to the Southern African Power Pool (SAPP) the challenges become even more difficult. This is the electricity institution people know least about in the region, and yet it is arguably one of the most important, with decisions being made by the SAPP that will affect generation, transmission and distribution for decades to come.

The logistical and cultural challenges of democratisation at this level are enormous, with large variations across countries in terms of capacities to engage, language differences, investment expectations and different norms of engagement and resistance.

What are the prospects for democratising electricity utilities in the region? Both good and bad. Good in the sense that there are constitutional and legislative mechanisms in place for participatory democracy – particularly in South Africa. At the municipal level there are requirements for ward committees, for example, which can influence decisions on all municipal matters, and there have been calls for special 'electricity committees' in some municipalities in South Africa to address the needs of this particular service.

The challenge, of course, is in operationalising such committees, providing them with sufficient resources, ensuring that they are broadly representative of the people they are intended to serve, and giving them the decision-making clout they need to balance out the inertia of corporate influence that currently dominates the electricity sector.

Another challenge is scalar. Given that electricity production and distribution operate at a regional – even continental – level in southern Africa, there needs to be effective communication and negotiation at community, province, national and regional scales if there is to be a more truly democratic process of decision-making. To illustrate with an example, demands for lower-priced electricity by low-income households in Durban might be made possible by a more democratic decision-making process at the municipal level, but could be undermined by decisions made at a national or regional level. Alternatively, demands for better pricing in Durban could occur at the expense of poor households elsewhere, with the expansion of a new hydro-electric facility in Mozambique, for example, and the displacement of thousands of people in that country against their will. In both scenarios democratisation is truncated and would require more multi-scalar reform.

The electricity sector is not unique in this respect, of course. There are few activities in the world today that are truly 'local' and we cannot expect to democratise every link of the commodity chain immediately. However, in the electricity sector this democratisation process may be a little easier, given the relative bulkiness of infrastructure investments and the ease with which one can track the connections between production, distribution and consumption. Creating national and international institutions and mechanisms for making these connections will not be easy, but electricity lends itself better than many other services and commodities to a democratisation of its production pathways for these reasons.

It should be noted, in this regard, that similar calls have been made in South Africa and elsewhere for 'water democracies', whereby local communities have more control over the uses and management of local and regional water resources (see Bakker 2007; Barlow 2003; Shiva 2002). These kinds of institutions are still in their infancy, however, and face the same scalar challenges associated with inter-jurisdictional resources.

A different, though complementary, approach to democratising electricity is the development of off-grid, decentralised production, particularly for remote locations. As discussed by both McDaid and Worthington in their chapters in this volume, localised off-grid production can avoid the problems of scalar consultation and negative externalities, while at the same time giving communities direct control over the production and provision of electricity.

One must be careful, though, not to allow such initiatives to entrench and justify second-rate electricity services in lower-income and/or remote communities without the skills and economies of scale associated with being on a more centralised power grid.

Which brings me back to the question of power-pooling. Though problematic because it is difficult to democratise production pathways, power-pooling in southern Africa does offer some enormous advantages. For one, there is already existing production surplus in the region that could be better distributed. There are also investment efficiencies associated with better cross-border power sharing (US$4 billion over 20 years according to Graeber et al. 2005) and an associated potential reduction of regional carbon emissions.

Combined with more aggressive forms of demand management, these regional power sources could reduce the need for new generation capacity in South Africa in the short to medium term, particularly from coal-fired and nuclear electricity stations that appear to dominate generation planning in the country.

In some respects this call for scaling up runs counter to a democratic narrative of more local control and oversight. And yet, power pools can be seen as a positive contribution to a more socially – and potentially environmentally – just system of electricity production and distribution. Keeping in mind that national borders are false physical and cultural divides in southern Africa, we must not allow ourselves to be trapped in a colonial electrical geography. The key is creating economies of scale which benefit everyone in the region, not just a corporate elite. At the moment only corporate players have the resources to take advantage of these regional benefits.

Keeping electricity public?

One of the arguments made throughout this book is that private-sector participation in electricity services tends to make utilities less accountable, less transparent and less equity-oriented. In this regard, any effort to democratise electricity institutions and involve the broader public in decision-making will be compromised by private-sector ownership and/or management.

While I agree with this position, it is important not to fetishise the public sector or public ownership. As has also been demonstrated at length in this volume, publicly owned and operated national and municipal electricity utilities in South Africa have been anything but democratic or equitable.

Much of the blame for this can be levelled at the corporatisation of electricity institutions – i.e. the creation of arm's-length, ringfenced 'business units' that are publicly owned (and typically publicly managed) but distanced from public control and oversight and run on the same basic commodified principles as a private company. These are not the kinds of 'public' entities that I have in mind when suggesting that electricity should be kept in public hands.

What, then, do we mean by 'public'? One relatively new contribution to this debate has been the development of public–public partnerships. As Hall et al. (2005) point out in their comprehensive review of the literature, there is no single concept of public–public partnerships. Although the notion has clearly been developed in contrast to the concept of public–private partnerships, the ways in which public–public initiatives have been developed and the contexts in which they have been deployed make any single definition impossible. Nevertheless, it is possible to categorise public–public partnerships along two main axes: types of partners, and types of objectives.

'Partners' in these cases refer to two or more public authorities in the same country, usually inter-municipal consortia, or collaboration between different types/levels of public authorities. A wider use of the concept includes partnerships between public authorities and any part of the public, including NGOs, trade unions and community organisations. There are also initiatives with an international dimension, involving the partnering of public authorities in different countries. Table 16.1 provides a typology of different partnership possibilities.

Table 16.1: Typology of public–public partnerships

Type of partnership	Sub-type
Public authority–public authority	Inter-municipal
	State/provincial government–municipality
Public authority–community	Public authority–community
	Public authority–NGO
	Public authority—trade union
Development partnerships	High-income country public authority–low-income country public authority
International partnerships	Public authorities from different countries
	Public authorities from neighbouring countries

Source: Hall et al. 2005: 6

The most common rationale for public–public partnerships given is that they help to achieve greater public-sector efficiency, improve service coverage and access, and develop public-sector capacity. Increasingly, proponents also argue that they are introducing them to 'defend public services from privatisation'.

This latter rationale has been used in a number of cases in the South African context, most notably in the water sector, such as those with Rand Water and the municipalities of Odi and Harrismith (Hall et al. 2005; Pape 2001; Smith 2005; Van Rooyen & Hall 2007). Rand Water, along with the Durban-based parastatal Umgeni Water, has also used the concept as a justification for expansion into other parts of the continent, citing their desire to help other African countries avoid water privatisation (Amenga-Etego & Grusky 2005; Loftus 2005).

Eskom has been less overt in this regard, but it does define its relationships with Electricity Distribution Industry Holdings and individual municipalities as public–public partnerships, and uses similar language in its expansion into other parts of the continent (e.g. via Eskom Enterprises).

While it may be that some policy-makers and bureaucrats in Eskom and other public utilities in South Africa genuinely see these partnerships as a way to strengthen the public sector and resist privatisation, there is also growing evidence from South Africa and elsewhere that public–public partnerships may be little more than just another way to 'break municipal services into discrete management units with reduc[ed] political influence' (Hall et al. 2005: 8).

In other words, there is growing concern that public–public initiatives may be just another mechanism for corporatising and commodifying service delivery, in the name of being 'public'. As Hall et al. (2005: 8, 2) conclude in their study, many public-sector managers now see public–public partnerships 'as an opportunity to practise commercial operations while expanding into privatisation opportunities elsewhere', 'paving the way for privatisation' in the services sector by creating a rhetoric of 'publicness' that distracts us from the real objectives of stand-alone business units that can be commercialised and possibly even sold off to the private sector. This is the conclusion that Greenberg (Chapter 3 in this volume) also comes to with regard to Eskom's so-called 'public' activities in South Africa and on the rest of the continent.

This is not to suggest that these initiatives are always designed with commercialisation in mind or that they should be abandoned as a short- to medium-term strategy for improving public services and resisting privatisation. They can, and have, worked for positive change in South Africa and other parts of the world (for a global survey see Balanyál et al. 2005). Faced with the choice of a public–public or a public–private partnership, the former is certainly preferred.

The problem is, this choice is seldom given in the South African context, and when it is there is little in the way of financial or other support for public–public initiatives. Billions of rand are made available in South Africa and elsewhere in the world for public–private partnerships – from national governments and international financial institutions such as the World Bank's Public–Private Infrastructure Advisory Facility. There is no comparable financial or institutional support for public–public initiatives in South Africa, beyond occasional funding by the Development Bank of Southern Africa or a large parastatal such as Eskom or Rand Water, with questionable motivations. Rumoured plans by the Department of Provincial and Local Government to establish a Support Unit for Public Provision of Services to address this imbalance have yet to materialise.

At the root of this problem, I would argue, are the underlying pressures of commodification associated with managing public entities in a market economy. Publicly owned and operated though they may be, demands on electricity utilities by private firms and transnational elites for 'competitive' pricing, cost recovery, Taylorised management systems and macroeconomic planning that promotes outward-oriented trade regimes compel these public entities to behave like private enterprises, forcing them to provide the kinds of multi-tiered services needed to attract multinational capital while at the same time keeping a lid on subsidies for the poor (see McDonald and Ruiters (2005) for a longer discussion of these commodification pressures).

In some cases these marketisation trends are simply survival responses from utility managers trying to resist privatisation, introducing market-based pricing and management strategies to maintain and justify their public existence.

All of which raises the question of whether public electricity institutions can ever be adequately reformed in a capitalist economy. Is more radical change needed?

Transforming the electricity sector

The short answer, once again, is yes. But what might radical, 'transformative' change in the electricity sector look like? This is a more difficult question to answer, given that it necessarily involves a much larger rupture of social relations and productive systems than that of 'reform', and requires changes that must reach well beyond the electricity sector. A radical transformation of electricity cannot take place in a sectoral bubble, particularly given its interlocking connections with virtually every facet of contemporary life.

Nevertheless, one can imagine transformative options such as nationalising energy-related firms (including large consumers of electricity), cancelling nuclear development programmes, implementing stringent demand-management measures to better redistribute resources, and halting or slowing the production of non-essential electricity-intensive goods and services.

These kinds of transformative actions have been taken by socialist countries in the past – with varying degrees of success and failure – and some countries are still exploring these 'revolutionary' options today.[1] In Venezuela, for example, energy companies have been nationalised by Hugo Chavez's government, and although private electricity companies continue to operate alongside public utilities, the country's minister of energy and petroleum has made it clear that he intends to banish 'the ghost of privatization' in electricity definitively.[2]

There are also rumblings of more transformative changes in countries such as Bolivia and Argentina, where extensive marketisation and privatisation reforms in the electricity sector in the 1990s resulted in widespread public discontent (Murillo 2001; Rudnick 1996; Williams & Ghanadan 2006). Some firms in the energy sector have been (re)nationalised as a result – most notably natural gas and other energy and mining firms under President Evo Morales in Bolivia – but it remains to be seen how far this nationalisation agenda will go in the electricity sector itself.

More transformative changes in the water sector may be an indicator here, where parallel privatisation programmes around the world in the 1990s led to even more pronounced protests, violence and policy reversal. Bolivia grabbed international news headlines with protests against water privatisation in Cochabamba in 2000–2001, followed by the return of water provision in that city to the public sector. In Argentina, private water companies cancelled their contracts and fled the country, while the government of Uruguay has made water privatisation unconstitutional. Similar de-privatisation initiatives and public protests have taken place in Africa, Asia, Europe and North America.

Just how transferable these experiences in the water sector are to electricity is unclear. There are different histories to the sectors and very different technical demands and developments, with water provision being a relatively simple service to manage, including at the very local, community level. Nor has there been as much public mobilisation against electricity privatisation and marketisation around the world as there has been in the water sector, in part because there are energy substitutes for electricity.

It is also unclear how truly 'transformative' changes in the water sector have been, with much of the change taking place in that sector being reformist in nature, such as with the introduction of public–public partnerships and more progressive tariffs. As Bakker (2007) notes in her review of anti-privatisation water struggles, there has not been enough critical thinking about the kinds of demands being made by anti-privatisation activists – particularly in the area of 'rights' discourse – resulting in reforms which may look transformative at one level but can actually fit neatly within a neo-liberal model of reform.

Real decommodification, after all, requires not just the removal or lowering of a price for a good or service but a transformation of the entire social process of commodified labour value that lies behind it. The call for decommodification is in fact a very radical one, and one that few organisations in the water sector are consciously working towards, despite their use of the word.

Nonetheless, developments in the water sector suggest both a potentiality and a public appetite for significant alterations to the way in which essential services are owned and managed, with possible spillover to the electricity sector. There are calls to renationalise electricity in Bolivia, for example, in part because of the political awareness arising from the renationalisation of water in that country.

How likely are these kinds of transformative changes in the near future in South and southern Africa? They are certainly not imminent, but nor are they unimaginable. There is growing discontent with neo-liberal reforms in South Africa in general – especially in the area of basic services – and there is a long and storied history of socialist thought, organisation and resistance in the country. There are also strong links in South Africa between groups resisting commercialisation in the water and electricity sectors, with groups such as the SECC working closely with the broad-based Anti-Privatisation Forum (APF) and the sectorally-focused Coalition Against Water Privatisation. Alliances are also being built between NGOs, organised labour, civic groups and others working on these issues.

It is important to remember as well that the nationalisation of MEC-related firms was central to the ANC's political manifesto during the anti-apartheid struggle (as enshrined in the organisation's Freedom Charter), and although it was abandoned shortly after the unbanning of the ANC in 1990, as part of the party's overall drift towards neo-liberalism, there remains a strong current of 1950s Freedom Charter thinking in the country, particularly within community-based social movements.

But my intention is not to be predictive or prescriptive here. Any anti-capitalism path that may emerge on the electricity front in South and southern Africa will have to be organic, arising out of the historical possibilities at the time and the material and ideological forces at play.

That some kind of transformative change will take place in the future I have little doubt. The social and environmental inequities of the MEC are simply too great to be sustained. And with the planning of a grand network of electricity production and transmission designed to pump yet another African resource out of the continent, public recognition of, and resistance to, these inequities can only deepen.

I will conclude, therefore, with some brief thoughts on how the reformist options cited earlier might be tied to longer-term transformative objectives, providing possible concrete strategies for deeper, counter-hegemonic movements. In considering these possibilities it is critical not to lose sight of longer-term objectives. Demands for an increase in the amount of free basic electricity, for example, cannot be left at that. 'Free' electricity should be tied to longer-term political goals of decommodification, with debates and education taking place on how the current free basic electricity programme serves to contain the demands of the poor and intensify commodification (see Ruiters, Chapter 9 in this volume). In this way there can be short-term improvements in the lives of low-income households, while at the same time a disruption of neo-liberal narratives and practice.

Similarly, one could legally challenge the constitutionality of prepaid electricity meters and electricity cut-offs, while at the same time using this process to ask much more radical questions about the very act of measuring and pricing consumption and how decisions are made about the allocation of resources. The SECC, the APF and other social movements have been trying to do exactly this. Unfortunately, political and tactical splits within and across these organisations have been problematic, as have serious resource constraints. There is also the ideological juggernaut of a pro-neoliberal media to contend with (particularly when it comes to the commercialisation of basic services), hostile bureaucracies and an ANC-allied labour movement and communist party which has largely abandoned any attempts to tie short-term reform in to longer-term radical change (Bond 1999; Mayher & McDonald 2007; Thomas 2007).

Ultimately, truly transformative change in the electricity sector is not going to be easy, or very pretty, in South(ern) Africa. Nor is there any guarantee that strategic short-term reforms can lead to longer-term transformation. Nevertheless, reform 'is not meaningless or irrelevant...for it can affect the shape of the field of battle' (Saul & Gelb 1981: 4). One can push for moderate reforms, therefore, without being a traitor to more radical political goals and theoretical frameworks. Radical history is replete with these kinds of strategic compromise politics, particularly as the contradictions of capitalism create the conditions and spaces for these reformist interventions.

Less evident, perhaps, is the extent to which there may be an appetite for debates about the negative effects of electricity irrespective of its ownership or degree of commodification. As the abysmal environmental record of decommodified electricity production in the Soviet bloc has amply illustrated, sustainable and equitable electricity management is not just a problem for capitalism. Socialist countries have long utilised productivist rhetoric to justify the rapid expansion of the electricity sector, and there is remarkably little debate in contemporary (or potentially) socialist countries on how much electricity consumption is 'enough' and how we might know this.

One must be careful here not to adopt a reactionary, 'eco-fascist' line which denies countries in the South increased electricity consumption in the interest of global environmental sustainability. With some 2 billion people in the world without access to electricity, growth will be needed to address widespread and desperate levels of *under*-consumption in this important sector, at least in the medium term, and I am generally supportive of expanding electricity capacity for this reason.

My point is that the objectives of sustainability and equity are not mutually exclusive. Radical changes to ownership and management can be accompanied by equally radical changes to (over-)consumption and (over-)production, at least on a disaggregated basis. In simplistic terms, this can mean a dramatic redistribution of the electricity pie and its constituent ingredients, as opposed to simply making the pie bigger.

Whether struggling social movements, NGOs and others working towards a more equitable electricity future in South(ern) Africa are ready or able to take on this expanded version of radical reform is difficult to say, but it does raise additional questions about strategy and capacity in this important struggle.

Notes

1   Ironically, Cuba formed a joint venture with a private multinational firm to operate its state-owned electricity utility in the 1990s – as it did with some of its water utilities – but in many ways the situation in that country is reversed, given that electricity remains largely non-commodified and production systems overall remain largely socialist. The rationale given by the Cuban state for these joint ventures is one of pragmatism and necessity as a result of the collapse of the Soviet Union and its access to technology and resources (see Cocq 2006).

2   Quote obtained from Global Insight, accessed 10 September 2007, http://www.globalinsight.com/SDA/SDADetail6028.htm.

References

Amenga-Etego RN & Grusky S (2005) The new face of conditionalities: The World Bank and water privatisation in Ghana. In DA McDonald & G Ruiters (eds) *The age of commodity: Water privatization in southern Africa.* London: Earthscan Press

Bakker K (2007) The 'commons' versus the 'commodity': Alter-globalization, anti-privatization and the human right to water in the global South. *Antipode* 39(3): 430–455

Balanyál B, Brennan B, Hoedeman O, Kishimoto S & Terhorst P (eds) (2005) *Reclaiming public water: Achievements, struggles and visions from around the world.* Amsterdam: TNI Press

Barlow M (2003) Water democracy: Who should control the world's water? *Resurgence* 129: 225–231

Bond P (1999) *Elite transition: From apartheid to neoliberalism in South Africa.* Durban: University of Natal Press

Cocq K (2006) Change, continuity and contradiction in the Cuban waterscape: 'Privatization' and the case of Aguas de la Habana. Unpublished master's thesis, Department of Geography, Queen's University, Kingston, Canada

Desai A (2002) *We are the poors: Community struggles in post-apartheid South Africa.* New York: Monthly Review Press

Graeber B, Spalding-Fecher R & Gonah B (2005) Optimising trans-national power generation and transmission investments: A southern African example. *Energy Policy* 33(18): 2337–2349

Hall D, Lethbridge J & Lobina E (2005) *Public-public partnerships in health and essential services.* Occasional Paper No. 9, Municipal Services Project, Cape Town

Hemson D & O'Donovan M (2006) Putting numbers to the scorecard: Presidential targets and the state of delivery. In S Buhlungu, J Daniel, R Southall & J Lutchman (eds) *State of the nation: South Africa 2005–2006.* Cape Town: HSRC Press

Loftus A (2005) Free water as commodity: The paradoxes of Durban's water service transformation. In DA McDonald & G Ruiters (eds) *The age of commodity: Water privatization in southern Africa.* London: Earthscan Press

Mayher A & McDonald DA (2007) The print media in South Africa: Paving the way for 'privatization'. *Review of African Political Economy* 34(113): 443–460

McDonald DA & Pape J (eds) (2002) *Cost recovery and the crisis of service delivery in South Africa.* Cape Town & London: HSRC Press & Zed Books

McDonald DA & Ruiters G (2005) Theorizing water privatization in southern Africa. In DA McDonald & G Ruiters (eds) *The age of commodity: Water privatization in southern Africa.* London: Earthscan Press

Murillo MV (2001) Conviction versus necessity: Public utility privatization in Argentina, Chile and Mexico. Paper prepared for the 97th Annual Meeting of the American Political Science Association, 30 August–2 September, San Francisco

Pape J (2001) *Poised to succeed or set up to fail? A case study of South Africa's first public-public partnership in water delivery.* Occasional Paper No. 1, Municipal Services Project, Cape Town

Rudnick H (1996) Pioneering electricity reform in South America. *Spectrum* 33(8): 38–44

SALGRC (South African Local Government Research Centre) (2007) National electrification programme hampered by housing delivery weaknesses. In *The SA Local Government Briefing* October. Johannesburg: SALGRC

Saul JS & Gelb S (1981) *The crisis in South Africa: Class defence, class revolution.* New York: Monthly Review Press

Shiva V (2002) *Water wars: Privatization, pollution, and profit.* Boston: South End Press

Smith L (2005) South Africa: Testing the waters of public-public partnerships. In Balanyál B, Brennan B, Hoedeman O, Kishimoto S & Terhorst P (eds) *Reclaiming public water: achievements, struggles and visions from around the world.* Amsterdam: TNI Press

Thomas DP (2007) The South African Communist Party (SACP) in the post-apartheid period. *Review of African Political Economy* 34(111): 123–138

Van Rooyen C & Hall D (2007) *Public is as private does: The case of Rand Water in South Africa.* Occasional Papers Series No. 15. Cape Town: Municipal Services Project,

WBCSD (World Business Council for Sustainable Development) (2006) *Case study: Eskom electrifying South Africa.* Accessed 10 October 2007, http://www.wbcsd.org/web/publications/case/electrification_full_case_web.pdf

Williams JH & Ghanadan R (2006) Electricity reform in developing and transition countries: A reappraisal. *Energy* 31(6/7): 815–844

Epilogue

Former British Prime Minster Harold Wilson once said 'a week is a long time in politics'. Nowhere is this truer than in South Africa, and the electricity sector has been particularly dynamic in this regard.

Significant developments have taken place in electricity since the chapters for this book were submitted for publication in mid-2007. Increased blackouts, threats of capital flight, and massive proposed price hikes are just a few examples. In light of these changes, the first part of this epilogue discusses their (potential) significance for the electricity sector in the region in the future.

But there is another maxim which holds that 'the more things change the more they stay the same'. This applies equally well to South Africa. Despite the frenzy in the mainstream media about 'dramatic' changes in the electricity sector, the neo-liberal impulses driving the reforms described in this book remain essentially intact. The era of dirt cheap electricity may very well be over in the region, but electricity prices are increasing everywhere, and southern Africa remains a relatively attractive place for the minerals-energy complex (MEC). Most importantly, there continues to be a scramble for Africa's electricity wealth.

It is this lack of change that makes a book like this so relevant. As slow as peer-reviewed academic publishing can be, it is the historical perspective, the methodological detail and the conceptual insights that give academic writing its significance to public debate, and its shelf life.

This is not to suggest that the daily media coverage of the topic has been unimportant; quite the opposite. Not only has the media provided useful and up-to-date information about changes in the sector, it has provided further evidence of the central thesis of this book – that MEC-related capital is determined to secure a stable and expanded platform of electricity production into the future through massive public and private investments with a 'business as usual' production and distribution strategy. The role of the neo-liberal press in creating a sense of 'crisis' serves to advance this MEC agenda, and blinkers the general public to alternative viewpoints and policy options.

It is therefore important to outline what has and has not changed in the electricity sector since the chapters for this book were first written, and the second part of this epilogue does just that, spelling out why a 'business as usual' thesis remains the most useful way to understand what is (and isn't) happening in the electricity sector in southern Africa.

What has changed in the electricity sector?

Perhaps the most significant change to have taken place is the application by Eskom to increase electricity prices in South Africa by 53 per cent, to meet its rising costs and investment plans. After much public outcry – from all sectors – government appears to have rejected the request, arguing instead for a cash injection for the utility to permit smaller, incremental hikes over several years. While government's response still indicates their willingness to increase user fees to finance an expansion programme, it is also an indication of the state's unwillingness to risk capital flight, or to further damage their political standing with low-income households already unable to afford electricity prices.

In doing so, the state has weakened Eskom's authority, challenging its hitherto autocratic style. Coupled with other technical and managerial errors, Eskom has been dealt what is probably an irreversible blow to its credibility and power. These may result in high-level personnel changes and perhaps even new governance structures (with the 'Zuma faction' of the ANC hinting that it is not happy with the neo-liberal 'new public management' philosophy of government to date).

Another important development was the decision in April 2008 by the Johannesburg High Court (*Mazibuko & Others v City of Johannesburg & Others*) to force the removal of prepaid water meters in low-income areas of Johannesburg, where they had been installed by the City without residents' consent. The judge also ordered the City to increase the amount of free basic water offered to low-income households. Although dealing with water rather than electricity, the judgment has potential applicability to electricity services, especially regarding the installation of prepayment meters. In the *Mazibuko* case, the decision to introduce prepayment meters was found to violate procedural requirements because, inter alia, people were not properly consulted and were not given all the water supply options available to other residents.

The judgment suggests that if any municipality wishes to introduce prepayment meters, the affected residents should be properly consulted, given all available choices, and meters cannot be rolled out in a way that unfairly discriminates against any one group of residents. Most critically, the judge found that prepayment meters are *inherently* unlawful and unconstitutional because they violate the provisions of Section 33 of the Constitution, which provides everyone with the right to lawful, reasonable and procedurally fair administrative action. However, despite the possible application of these principles to electricity meters, these arguments are much more strongly made in the context of water, which is an entrenched right in the Constitution, than with electricity, which is only an inferred right.

A third development to highlight is the progress made on the massive Inga dam in the Democratic Republic of the Congo (DRC). Also in April 2008, the World Energy Council's two-day financing workshop on Grand Inga, Inga 3, and the rehabilitation of Inga 1 and 2, made it clear that powerful actors are seeking to privatise the publicly-held assets of the Congo River's Inga rapids. Discussion of Inga 3 and Grand Inga focused on each project being set up as an independent power producer (IPP), which would ultimately be constructed and operated in private hands, minimising the participation and influence of the Congolese government.

Project development will likely require long-term contracts of bulk sales to industrial consumers and utilities, but give little attention to distribution or to increasing access rates for communities and households. At the same time, concerns were raised at the workshop that the costs of inputs for transmission lines are skyrocketing, which could increase the costs of both projects. Transmission tariffs will likely be imposed, increasing the price of electricity the further it must travel. The workshop also noted delays in the World Bank-led rehabilitation of Inga 1 and 2, MagEnergy's private rehabilitation of a portion of Inga 2, and the World Bank-financed rehabilitation of the 1 800 kilometre Inga-Kolwezi transmission line which has resulted in a US$140 million cost increase and funding gap.

Civil society in Bas Congo Province (where Inga is located) remains concerned by the government initiative to use Inga 3 and Grand Inga to attract private industrial development to the province, which may harm local communities and bypass those not yet connected to the grid. Nonetheless, the project has been elevated to 'Presidential priority' status in both the DRC and South Africa, and BHP Billiton, the world's largest mining company, has already signed an agreement with the DRC government for a 2 000 megawatt aluminium smelter.

What hasn't changed?

In some respects, developments at Eskom and on the Inga projects are also examples of what has not changed in the electricity sector since this book was written, insofar as they represent massive investments in electricity production and distribution to feed MEC in the region (and beyond). With Eskom now planning to invest as much as R1 trillion in capital expenditure over the next two decades, and with Inga requiring some US$40 billion to bring it to completion, investments in electricity show just how important the MEC remains for capitalism on the continent.

And as mentioned earlier, the sense of 'crisis' created in the South African media around electricity has only served to reinforce an accelerated, 'business as usual' model. With popular perceptions that South Africa is desperately in need of additional electricity capacity, Eskom and the state have been given a relatively free hand to fast-track IPPs and to forge ahead with controversial nuclear technologies and new coal burning power plants. The rejection of the 53 per cent price hike may have saved the poor from immediate price increases, but aggressive cost recovery remains the order of the day, prepaid meters continue to be rolled out to households in the tens of thousands, and progressive block tariffs seem a very distant possibility (with MEC-related industry continuing to receive large power subsidies).

The discrediting of Eskom – though valid on many levels – has also served to undermine affirmative action at the utility, and reinforce old-order discipline, with barely disguised racist remarks commonly in the press about the loss of 'real talent' (read white males) since the end of apartheid. While capacity may well be a problem at Eskom, the real challenges are the neo-liberal reforms that have distanced the utility even further from democratic political oversight and have it operating ever more closely with the metabolic demands of local and international capital.

While it is impossible to say for sure what the future will bring for the electricity sector in the region – and it always remains possible that the social and environmental contradictions of the global market will rear their ugly heads sooner rather than later – it should be recognised that MEC-related capital maintains a firm grip on South Africa's power switch (and that of the region), and electricity developments in the foreseeable future will likely remain as unequal as they have been for the past century.

Electricity 101

Derek Brine

This brief technical appendix serves as a primer for those interested in understanding the basic principles of current electricity, processes by which electricity is generated and the means by which it is transported. It is by no means a comprehensive review but does cover major technical issues, in terms which are intended to be accessible. The reference list at the end of the chapter includes publications, many of which are available online, that offer more detailed discussion of these issues for those who would like to learn more.

Electricity basics

The atom

To understand how electricity works one must first understand the structure of matter, the very stuff that makes up the physical world. All matter is made up of tiny 'building blocks' called atoms. These atoms can be further broken up into smaller subatomic particles called protons, neutrons and electrons. Protons and neutrons are found at the core, or nucleus, of an atom and are responsible for defining many of its chemical and physical characteristics.

There are many different types of atoms, each defined by the number of protons it possesses, and each called an element. For example, any atom with only 2 protons in its nucleus is called helium, while any atom with 92 protons is called uranium.

Neutrons are also found in the nucleus of an atom. Along with protons they help to determine the weight of atoms. For example, helium has a molecular weight of four since it consists of two protons and two neutrons. In addition, neutrons are responsible for creating isotopes – forms of the same atom with different masses and radioactivity. These latter points are central to nuclear power.

Electrons, however, are the subatomic particles that are responsible for current electricity. They are found orbiting the nuclei of atoms and are the main reason for chemical bonding between atoms. In addition, they possess an affinity to protons, a characteristic called 'charge'. The name given to this charge, however, is strictly conventional. We say that an electron's charge is 'negative' while a proton's charge is 'positive' only because scientists chose these names, not due to any physical determinant.

Most importantly, each atom generally has the same number of electrons as it does protons, a condition called electric neutrality. When an atom gains or loses an electron it becomes a negatively charged or positively charged ion, respectively. It is this ability to lose and gain electrons that creates the conditions for the phenomenon we call current electricity.

Current electricity: physics

Electricity has come to mean several things at once. It can mean static electricity (a build-up of electrons on a surface due to friction), electric charge (the affinity of positively charged particles to negatively charged particles), or current electricity (the stuff that powers our home appliances). It is the third phenomenon that we are interested in here – current electricity: the flow of electrons through a conductive electrical circuit due to a difference in electric potential.

Electricity, therefore, is an *interaction*, not a substance that can be physically manipulated. It is analogous to the *flow* of water in a pipe, *not* the water itself. In this analogy the water would instead represent the electrons that interact to create electricity.

There are several conventional methods used to produce electricity. Batteries are one method. When a battery is being used, a chemical reaction takes place that produces electrons at the negative terminal of the battery. These electrons travel through the circuit to the positive terminal, where they are used to complete another chemical reaction. This constant flow of electrons is a type of electric current called direct current (DC). Alternatively, an electric generator, or alternator, is capable of producing alternating current (AC), the most widely used form of commercial electricity. Generators and AC are described in detail later in this appendix.

Moreover, just as it is difficult to store the flow of water in a river, it is difficult to store the flow of electrons. In addition to their ability to produce DC, batteries are used to accomplish this feat. They store electrical potential as chemical energy. When connected to an electrical circuit, the above-mentioned chemical reactions, called cell reactions, take place, inducing a potential. However, when not connected, electrons do not flow and the chemical reactions do not take place. When a battery 'dies' these chemical reactions have run to completion, meaning they cannot occur any longer.

Current electricity: measurement

Above we mentioned AC and DC as types of current. What is a current and how is it produced? What makes a current more or less likely to flow through a substance? What are conductors and insulators? These questions and more are answered in this section.

As described earlier, electricity is the flow of electrons through an electrical circuit comprising conductors and powered devices, the latter of which are commonly called 'loads'. Current is the name we give to this flow. The unit that is used to describe current is the ampere, or amp, which measures the quantity of electrons moving past a point in an electric circuit each second. Each amp is the equivalent of $6.241\,509\,629\,152\,65 \times 10^{18}$ electrons moving past the point of measurement each second.

Why do electrons flow in the first place? Electrons flow because a difference in electric potential exists between two places in an electric circuit (with the measure of electric potential being the volt [V]). Electric current naturally flows from a high to a low voltage point; thus there is more incentive for a current to flow from a 10 000 V wire to 'ground', where the voltage measures 0 V, than to a 5 000 V wire. Batteries, solar cells and, most commonly, generators are capable of producing the voltage that leads to this electric current.

Voltage, however, is not the only circuit characteristic that influences the flow of electricity. Resistance, measured in ohms (Ω), is a feature of the conductor that gauges how easily electricity will flow through it. Several physical characteristics give rise to resistance, all of which affect the ease of movement of electrons through a material. These include length, cross-sectional area, imperfections in atomic and physical construction, and the relative sizes of atoms or molecules that make up the conductor. In addition, the physical expression of resistance is energy loss through heating and light emission. This phenomenon has been taken advantage of in several kinds of everyday appliance, including light bulbs, toasters and electric resistance space heaters.

The latter two causes of resistance are properties of the material that do not vary with length or cross-sectional area. The term used to describe these two features is 'resistivity', a property that must be measured experimentally. The resistivities of some common materials are found in Table A1.1.

Table A1.1: Resistivity of some materials at 20 °C

Material	Resistivity	Material	Resistivity
Conductors		Semiconductors	
Aluminium	2.82×10^{-8}	Carbon (graphite)	1.5×10^{-5}
Copper	1.72×10^{-8}	Germanium (pure)	4.6×10^{-1}
Gold	2.24×10^{-8}	Silicon (pure)	2.5×10^{2}
Iron	9.71×10^{-8}		
Platinum	10.6×10^{-8}	Insulators	
Silver	1.59×10^{-8}	Glass	10^{10}–10^{14}
Tungsten	5.65×10^{-8}	Rubber	10^{13}–10^{16}
Nickel	7.80×10^{-8}	Wood	10^{10}

Source: Vawter 2005

Materials through which electricity moves easily are termed 'conductors', whereas those through which electricity does not easily move are called 'insulators'. In construction, different types of conducting wires are surrounded by an insulator in order to provide safety. The insulation makes it difficult for electricity to run from the wire to anyone who touches it.

Moreover, current naturally takes the path of least resistance. Therefore if a 10 000 V line were connected to the ground by means of both a copper and a silver wire of the same length and cross-sectional area, more current would flow through the silver wire, since its resistivity value is less. Resistance is one of the most carefully observed parameters in the design of electric systems and the routing of electric power. The reduction of resistance minimises losses in power transmission. Electricity producers therefore select materials to use partially based on each material's resistivity, and design wires to decrease length and increase cross-sectional area if possible.

There are, however, other economic and technical considerations when choosing materials to construct transmission and distribution lines. For example, though the losses using a gold wire may be less than those using a copper wire, the cost involved in securing the material and constructing a gold wire far outweighs the benefits.

To summarise, consider the following analogy. Electricity is similar to the flow of water through a pipe. The water symbolises the electrons and the rate at which it flows represents the electric current. The difference in pressure at either end of the pipe can be considered the voltage present in the electric circuit. If the pressure on both sides of the pipe is equal, no water will flow. Similarly, if two points in an electric circuit are at the same voltage, no electrons will flow between those two points. Resistance in the pipe is related to the cross-sectional area through which water can flow, friction on the walls of the pipe, blockages and imperfections. These are analogous to the factors that create resistance in a wire: respectively, the gauge of the wire, and collisions between electrons and the atoms that compose the conductor. If one were to insert a powered device, such as a heater or turbine, into the system, it would be analogous to inserting an electric motor or other load into the electric circuit.

Finally, current, voltage and resistance are related by what is called Ohm's Law: Voltage = (Current) × (Resistance) (or V = IR). This expression is useful in determining the characteristics of an electrical circuit in order to gauge wires, determine component parameters, and define current flow directions.

Energy and power

More useful for consumers to understand, however, are units of energy and power: the joule (J), watt (W), and kilowatt-hour (kWh). These units determine the size of a consumer's electricity bill.

The joule is a unit of energy. One joule is the amount of energy needed to produce a force of one newton over a distance of one metre. In electrical terms, this is equal to the amount of energy needed to move 1 coulomb of charge (or 6.241 509 629 152 65 × 10^18 electrons) through a potential difference of 1 volt. A joule, however, is a very small measure of energy. One joule is enough energy to run a 60 W light bulb at full power for 0.016 seconds.

The watt is a measure of power defined as one joule per second. Thus, if a 60 W light bulb runs at full power it consumes 60 J of energy every second. If a dimmer switch is used and the same light bulb runs at half-power, it consumes only 30 W, or 30 J/s.

The unit that shows up on electricity bills, however, is the kilowatt-hour (kWh). This is also a measure of energy, like the joule, except that its magnitude makes it more convenient to use. One kWh is the energy equivalent of 1 000 W running for one hour (or 3 600 000 J). To illustrate, 1 kWh is the equivalent of running a 60 W light bulb at full power for 16.67 hours. The same light bulb running at half-power would take 33.33 hours to consume 1 kWh of energy.

To more fully grasp the scale of energy consumption, consider the following. Electricity use for the South African province of KwaZulu-Natal – population 9 904 698 – in the month of August 2006 was 3 563 000 000 kWh, giving an average daily per capita usage of 11.6 kWh (Stats SA 2006a, 2006b). This consumption varies dramatically between households and individuals as well as between residential and industrial users, of course, but the scale of consumption provides a reference point.

The power grid

The system over which this electric power is sent is dubbed the 'power grid' or 'network'. A country's national grid consists of an interconnected system of generating stations, substations, dispatch centres, power lines, and end users, operated as a single functioning unit. In some cases there is a single national grid with a single operator, but in some countries there are several regional networks run by utility operators that buy and sell power from each other as they see fit. These can be further subdivided into power pools – smaller local grids that manage power distribution in their respective areas. There can also be larger power pools operating *across* national boundaries, such as the Southern African Power Pool discussed elsewhere in this book.

Traditionally, power plants are operated in such a way that output equals demand. This is due to the fact that energy storage technologies are not developed enough to efficiently hold energy for later use. As battery technology improves, however, power producers are beginning to incorporate storage devices into their networks so that at times of low demand energy can be stored for a future period of high need. For the most part, though, power plants around the world run as just-in-time operations when it comes to production: the amount of energy used is exactly the amount of energy produced. This situation is maintained by a system of real-time automatic controllers that constantly and actively measure demand and attempt to match supply.

In order to manage this type of system there must be control centres located on the grid. These 'dispatch stations' are in charge of routing energy over the larger grid to the areas of largest demand. This process of sending bulk power over long distances to regional substations is called 'transmission', while the process of sending power from a substation to the surrounding local area is called 'distribution'. Accordingly, transmission lines are generally high-voltage, heavy-duty lines, whereas distribution lines are well-insulated, lower-voltage lines that are more numerous and terminate at the place of use.

Power loss is a major problem to overcome when designing a transmission system. Transformers are the foremost devices used to solve this problem and are therefore an integral part of the overall electricity system, serving to manipulate the voltage characteristics of the transmission lines. This is an efficient way to reduce resistive transmission losses in power lines.

The equation that defines power loss during transmission is $P = I^2R$. As we saw previously, Ohm's Law relates the voltage, current and resistance in an electrical circuit. Using these two principles, the effect of transforming voltage on the loss of power during transmission is evident.

Consider the following example. If we step up the voltage produced at a power station by a factor of 10, the current will be reduced by a factor of 10 to satisfy Ohm's Law. This ultimately results in a reduction in transmission losses by a factor of 100 (Kiameh 2003). It is therefore desirable to transmit power at high voltage to reduce resistive losses. Transformers are devices used to accomplish this. They convert the power produced at power plants for transmission, and then back to end-use specifications at the final destination.

The physical structure of a transformer consists of a series of two conductive coil windings wrapped around a ferromagnetic core. The coils are physically separated and only interact by means of an electromagnetic field. The input winding is connected to the power source, in this case the generator line. When current flows through it, a magnetic field is established, simultaneously inducing an electric field in the output winding. The output winding is then connected to the power transmission lines.

Transformers that are used at the power station, called unit transformers, typically step up the voltage to about 110 000 V, although voltage levels of up to 735 000 V are used for large distances and high power levels. In South Africa, typical transmission lines operate at either 400 000 or 275 000 V, at less than 4 per cent loss. The power is then sent through the grid to a substation near to its end use. The voltage is then 'stepped down' to between 2 300 and 34 500 V by a substation transformer prior to being distributed over the local network. In South Africa, this distribution voltage varies between 11 000 and 22 000 V. Finally, each end user employs a pole transformer to supply household outlets with the local voltage standard. Table A1.2 lists the standard voltage and frequency values in selected countries.

Table A1.2: Voltage and frequency standards in selected countries

Country	Voltage standard (V)	Frequency standard (Hz)
Australia	230	50
Brazil	110/220	60
Canada	120	60
China	220	50
Democratic Republic of the Congo	220	50
France	230	50
Ghana	230	50
Kenya	240	50
Lesotho	220	50
Mexico	127	60
Mozambique	220	50
Namibia	220	50
South Africa	220/230	50
Swaziland	230	50
United Kingdom	230	50
United States of America	120	60
Zambia	230	50
Zimbabwe	220	50

Source: Power Stream 2007

AC versus DC

Because of its ability to be easily transformed and sent over long distances, AC power is the standard form of electricity provided today. These characteristics make it more flexible and less costly than DC transmission and distribution.

Yet this was not always the case. The first power plants actually operated on the DC principles identified by Thomas Edison. DC power, however, has been historically difficult to transmit over long distances. As seen earlier, transmission over long distances requires the transformation of voltage to reduce losses. Transformers, however, rely on alternating voltage levels to induce a second current in their output winding and perform that transformation. This is a characteristic the DC lacks. This limitation made it necessary for consumers to be very close to generating stations, typically less than a mile, in order to be electrified. Otherwise resistive losses in the low-voltage wires would be too great to provide any meaningful electricity to users. Due to its drawbacks, and the ease with which AC power can be produced, transmitted and distributed, DC power networks eventually disappeared. Recently, however, the improved capability of modern high-voltage DC generation has made it a cost-effective competitor to traditional high-voltage AC generation. These networks, however, have not gained the prominence of high-voltage AC systems.

Electric generator or alternator

The component of almost every power plant that is responsible for the electric output is the electric generator or alternator. A generator is a device that converts mechanical motion into electricity. It does this by making use of Faraday's principle of electromagnetic induction, which states that a voltage will be produced in a conductive wire when it is moved through a magnetic field.

In its simplest form, an alternator is a coil of conductive wire rotated between the poles of a permanent magnet, as shown in Figure A1.1.

Figure A1.1: Fundamental electric generator

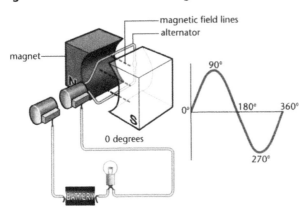

Source: Siemens Corp n.d.

Here the maximum voltage is produced when the coil velocity is perpendicular to the gap through which the magnetic flux (field) lines – shown on the diagram as parallel grey lines connecting the two magnets – pass and the minimum is produced when these two quantities are parallel. The voltage is therefore produced sinusoidally, resulting in alternating current, AC. The magnitude of the induced voltage in Figure A1.1 is depicted as a function of time, marked on the graph at the points at which the coil is 0°, 90°, 180° and 270° from its starting position.

In construction, the rotating component of any generator system is referred to as the rotor and the stationary part is referred to as the stator. In Figure A1.1, the rotor is the coil in which the electric current is produced and the stator is the magnet, which produces the magnetic field through which it rotates. In industrial applications, however, generators take different form. Figure A1.2 shows a diagram of a typical power-station generator.

Figure A1.2: Typical commercial electric generator structure

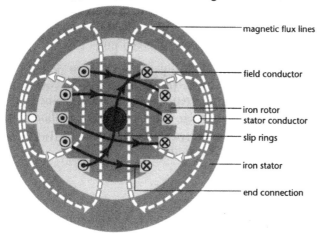

magnetic flux lines

field conductor

iron rotor
stator conductor

slip rings

iron stator

end connection

Source: Encyclopaedia Britannica n.d.

Here the components that compose the rotor and stator have been interchanged. The rotor is now a spinning electromagnet attached to the input shaft and the stator is a series of coil windings surrounding the rotor. In this case, instead of the physical coils revolving, the rotation of the electromagnet causes the magnetic field to rotate through the coils. It is analogous to a pottery wheel. Instead of the artist spinning the clay being worked, the table spins, thus rotating the clay for the artist.

This design is used for several reasons. Firstly, in order to produce electricity on a scale that is meaningful for commercial use, many coils must be used. This set of large, heavy, rotating coils is difficult and expensive to construct and cannot survive large centrifugal effects produced at high rotations. Secondly, since this structure is so heavy, it takes more energy to rotate the input shaft of the generator. This means higher fuel/energy costs and consumption rates. Lastly, a large rotating set of coils would imply a set of rotating electrical contacts that carry a large current at high voltage. From a safety point of view, it is much more desirable to let the electromagnet rotate, since this requires less current and lower voltage (Weisman & Eckhart 1985).

This same electromagnet, which comprises the rotor, may have more than two north/south poles. The most common generators have either two or four poles on the rotor. The resulting effect is to change the frequency with which the induced voltage in the stator armature windings rises and falls. If n_p is the number of poles that are present on the rotor and $!_r$ is the rotational speed of the rotor in revolutions per minute (rpm), then the generator frequency, f_g, will be:

$$f_g = \frac{n_p !_r}{120}$$

Here we see that the frequency is dependent on both the number of poles and the speed with which the rotor rotates. Thus if one power station has a generator with four poles rotating at 1 800 rpm, it will produce the same frequency as another power station running a generator with two poles at 3 600 rpm.

The generator frequency is one key factor in the integration of a new power plant with the existing power grid. In southern Africa the standard is 50 Hz. Generators must be brought and maintained to within ±0.5 Hz of the rest of the grid. A generator that leads or lags behind the system must be brought offline. If the remaining generators on the grid cannot cover demand, the network can destabilise, causing power shortages and blackouts.

Steam generation plants

Most modern power generation methods employ a generator to convert mechanical to electrical energy. This section is concerned with how power plants produce the mechanical capability to turn the generator shaft. Nuclear, fossil fuel, biofuel and geothermal plants do this through the Rankine thermodynamic cycle. Natural gas- and oil-fired plants can also use the Brayton thermodynamic cycle. Finally, wind, tidal and hydro-electric plants use low rpm generators and harness naturally occurring forces to produce electricity.

The Rankine cycle

Coal, oil, biofuel, geothermal and nuclear plants function through the use of a steam-operated turbine operating on what is called the Rankine cycle. These power stations account for more than 79 per cent of electricity generation worldwide (Woodruff et al. 2005). In South Africa, coal accounts for approximately 80 per cent of commercial power production (Eskom 2006). Such widespread use highlights the fundamental nature and historical importance of this cycle and its development.

A schematic diagram for the Rankine cycle is shown in Figure A1.3. Water is pumped into the boiler and heated by means of a furnace, reactor or geothermal fluid. This creates steam at a very high temperature and pressure, which is fed through piping to a turbine. The steam is expanded (its pressure released) over the blades of the turbine, causing the turbine to rotate at high speed, typically 1 800 or 3 600 rpm for a fossil fuel or nuclear plant. The turbine shaft is connected to the input shaft of a generator and produces the necessary mechanical input for operation. Spent steam is brought to a condenser and then pumped back into the boiler for reuse.

The thermal efficiency of such a cycle is defined as the net mechanical energy (work) produced over the net energy input. For a simple Rankine cycle like the one described above, the thermal efficiency is quite low. Typically 20–30 per cent of the heat added is actually converted to useful mechanical energy. The remaining input

Figure A1.3: The Rankine cycle

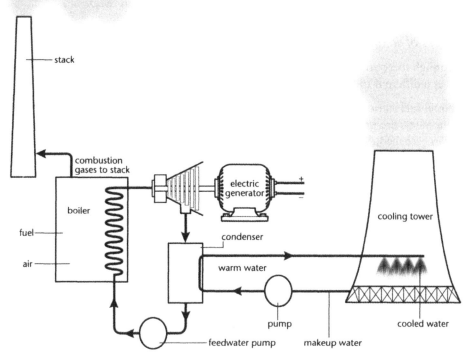

Source: Moran & Shapiro 2004

energy is a loss: a situation in which heat is not converted into mechanical work. This loss can come in many forms, including loss of heat to the environment, unused process heat, friction between steam and the walls of the piping, friction on the turbine rotational bearings, or even noise created by flowing steam.

Power engineers have come up with many ways to reduce these thermal and mechanical losses, including insulation and low-friction bearings. However, it is hard to avoid their combined effect. Nevertheless, there are still ways to increase efficiency, lower fuel costs and consumption rates and reduce the price of production and purchase of energy. In most cases, making the two following modifications can vastly improve thermal efficiency: preheating boiler feedwater with spent steam through a heat exchanger; reheating partially spent steam in the boiler and passing it through intermediate and low-pressure turbines.

These alterations are used to capture energy that would otherwise be lost to the environment. Instead of ejecting steam that is relatively hot, this steam can be used to heat the feedwater entering the boiler. This reduces the amount of fuel that must be burned to create steam, since the water will be closer to its boiling point before entering the boiler. In addition, by reheating partially spent steam, some process heat in the boiler that would otherwise be ejected into the environment can be utilised. This adds heat energy to the steam that can be converted into mechanical energy by the turbine. These changes are also shown in Figure A1.3.

Types of steam generation plant

Though there are several types of power station that run on the Rankine cycle, each uses a different method to power the boiler.

Fossil fuel stations use oil or coal as source fuels to heat the steam. In a coal plant, shipments are unloaded off large railcars or barges, separated into use and reserve piles, crushed, weighed, measured, controlled for dust, pulverised and, finally, burned as tiny particles (Woodruff et al. 2005). Large quantities of coal are burned in modern power plants. A 600 megawatt (MW) power station at full capacity burns about 300 tons of coal per hour (Weisman & Eckart 1985). Similarly, oil plants can receive shipments of petroleum by tanker, though many are directly connected to pipelines. The oil they receive and use is typically heavy or unrefined oil. Though it takes more energy than refined petroleum to burn, it is generally less expensive to prepare heavy oil to be burned by preheating and atomising it than it is to refine heavy oil before use.

After the preparation process the fuel is ready to be burned in the boiler's furnace. The furnace is a boiler subsystem that efficiently directs the hot products of fuel combustion to the heating surface(s) of the boiler to produce the maximum rate of heat transfer (Woodruff et al. 2005). After contacting the heating and reheating surfaces, those gases, called flue gases, are then ejected into the environment through smokestacks. These stacks may or may not contain subsystems to 'scrub', or treat, the outgoing products, reducing their polluting potential. Whether or not scrubbers are present is generally determined by governmental rules and regulations. In South Africa, for instance, no such regulations exist, and flue gases are generally left untreated (USA DoE 2004).

A **nuclear plant** employs a reactor instead of a furnace. This is a device for allowing a controlled nuclear reaction to take place. The preferred fuel for a nuclear plant is fissile Uranium-235. The primary deposits of uranium lie in only a few countries worldwide: Australia, Canada, Russia, the USA and South Africa. The ores that contain these deposits, however, are low-yield ores, the typical concentration of uranium being only 0.1–4 per cent. In addition, natural uranium only contains about 0.7 percent of the fissile isotope Uranium-235 (World Nuclear Association 2005). The remainder is the non-fissile isotope, Uranium-238.

In order to produce reactor-grade uranium, mined uranium must first be enriched. This is a process by which the content of Uranium-235 is increased, generally to 3–5 per cent for a nuclear power station. After it is enriched, the uranium is shaped into what are called fuel pellets, cylindrical uranium rods from 0.81–1.07 centimetres in diameter and 0.9525–1.397 centimetres long (Weisman &

Eckart 1985). Once the pellets are inserted into the reactor core, slow-moving neutrons are introduced to the fuel pellets that cause their atoms to split apart, producing two nucleus particles.

These reactions are exothermic – i.e. they produce heat. It is the heat of this process around which nuclear power stations are designed. A typical reactor has a coolant loop that passes by its core, or centre, the location at which the reaction takes place. The coolant, which is normally water but can be helium or even molten sodium, absorbs the heat of the nuclear reaction and is pumped to the boiler, where it transfers that heat to the working fluid, which runs on the typical Rankine cycle described earlier. The coolant is then pumped back to the core to be reheated and reused.

These pellets can be used for 12–24 months before being considered 'spent' (World Nuclear Association 2005). Even then, some countries do not directly dispose of their nuclear waste. Most of it can be efficiently reprocessed and turned back into fuel. This is what is called a 'closed cycle' nuclear waste management plan. In contrast, some countries directly dispose of nuclear waste after one use, generally in a geologically stable dumping site well below the earth's surface. This is an 'open cycle' nuclear waste management plan.

A **geothermal plant** makes use of naturally occurring hot fluids under the earth's surface. These can come in several forms including steam, superheated water and magma. Most plants that operate today make use of superheated water, since it is the most abundant type of geothermal fluid. 'Superheated' is a term used to describe water that is at a higher temperature than its boiling point, the point at which it vaporises, at atmospheric pressure.

In order to tap into the fluid, a well is drilled to the reservoir, which can sometimes be deeper than 300 metres below the surface. It is then brought to the surface and 'flashed'. The flashing process entails lowering the pressure to which the water is exposed in quick discrete steps, causing it to evaporate. This steam is then used to run a turbine using the Rankine cycle.

Gas turbine plants

A gas turbine is a device that directly uses the hot products and the power of combustion to turn a shaft. Such turbines are used in many applications, including both industrial power plants and jet engines. Large-scale power-generating gas turbines have been in use for many years and are used if either natural gas or oil is to be the source fuel.

Although gas turbine manufacturers state that any fuel can be used with their product if the correct changes are made to the turbine, using coal powder can cause excessive turbine blade wear and is not economically feasible. All gas turbines, however, operate off the Brayton thermodynamic cycle. A simplified schematic of this cycle is shown in Figure A1.4.

Figure A1.4: The Brayton cycle

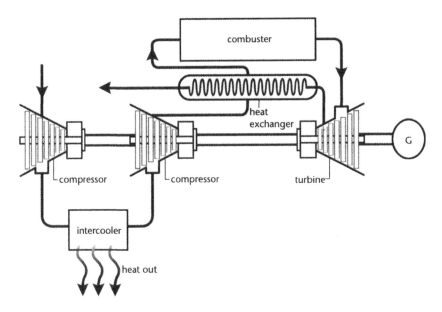

Source: Author's diagram

In the Brayton cycle a compressor pressurises the working fluid, in this case air, and passes it to a combustor where a mist of natural gas or oil is added. The air–fuel mixture is burned and passed through a turbine that spins the compressor and the generator shaft simultaneously. After the gas has passed through the turbine it is either released to the atmosphere or passed through a heat exchanger and re-injected into the compressor.

As with the Rankine cycle, the thermal efficiency of the Brayton cycle is quite low, around 40–44 per cent (Kiameh 2003). In order to improve the performance the following steps can be taken: introduce multiple-stage compression with what is called intercooling; introduce a heat exchanger immediately before the combustor. This device is typically called a regenerator.

Gases are generally easier to compress when they are cooler. At the same time compressing a gas tends to make its temperature rise. By compressing the gas over several stages and extracting the heat from it after each stage, the work required to compress it fully is considerably less than the work that would be required if only one stage were used.

The addition of a heat exchanger directly before the combustor reduces the amount of fuel required to heat the gas to the requisite temperature. This device is used to transfer heat from the hot gas that would otherwise be ejected to the gas entering the combustor. A regenerator is analogous to the feedwater heater discussed in the context of steam generation plants.

As a final note, many plants today are employing what is called a combined cycle. A plant of this construction makes use of both a generator operated by a steam turbine and a generator operated by a gas turbine, as shown in Figure A1.5.

Figure A1.5: Combined cycle gas-turbine

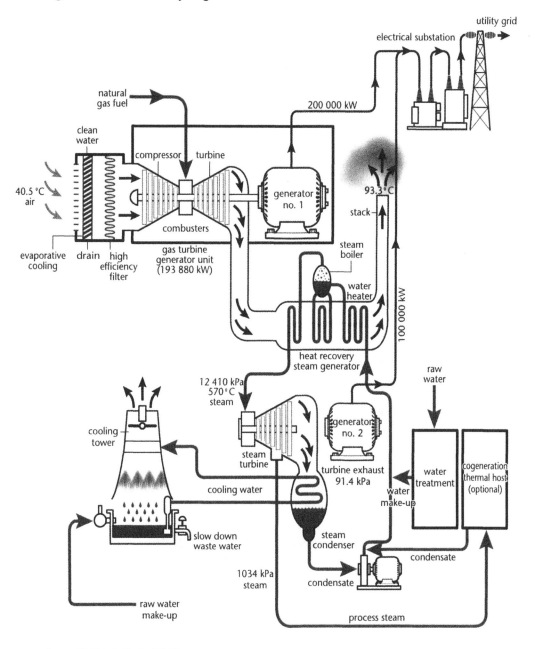

Source: SPG Media Limited 2007

Hydro-electric and wind power

As with steam-powered and gas turbine power plants, hydro-electric and wind power use a generator to produce energy. The difference is that the speed with which the generator shaft turns is much slower in a wind or hydro-electric power station. This has prompted engineers and designers to include more poles on the generator rotor in order to increase the AC frequency and harmonise with the existing power grid.

Hydro-electric power stations involve a naturally occurring waterfall, or one that is artificially created or enhanced through the damming of a body of water such as a river. In the case of tidal power, a large dam, called a barrage, is built at a river estuary and used to control the flow of the river into the sea. In either case, an intake is placed at the bottom of the dam and a generator turbine and shaft are inserted behind it. An outflow is present behind the turbine. Thus as water passes through the turbine it rotates the generator shaft, producing electricity. Figure A1.6 shows a typical hydro-electric power plant construction.

Figure A1.6: Hydro-electric power plant schematic

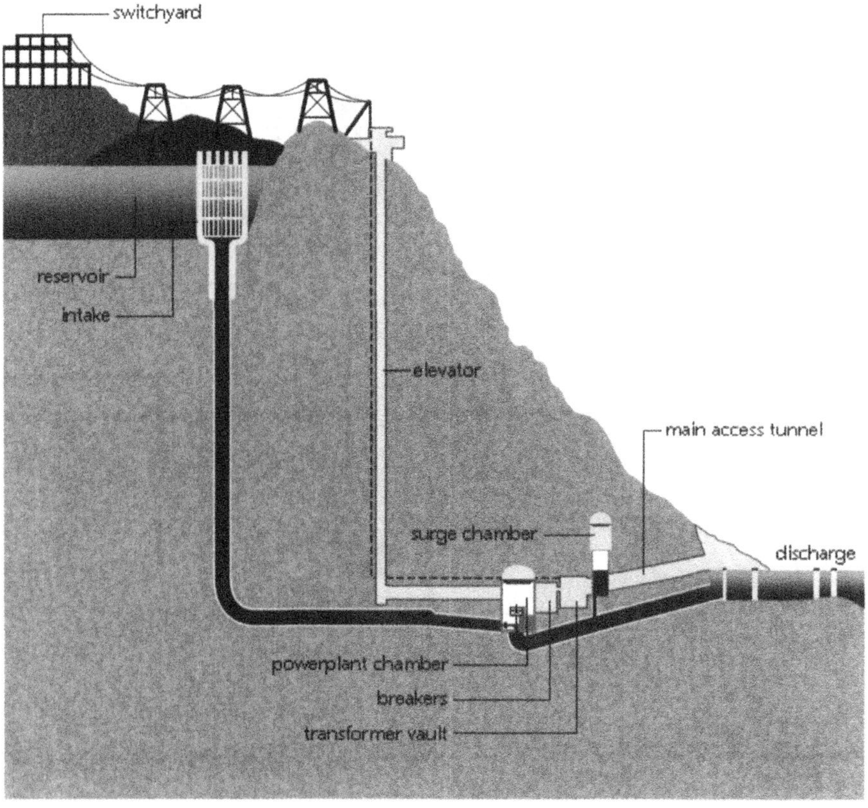

Source: Tennessee Valley Authority n.d.

A **wind farm** consists of a number of wind generators erected on a parcel of land. Each generator is capable of producing its own energy output. However, all of them are connected together to form a wind power station. Wind generation is much like hydro-electric generation when it comes to generator construction, due to the relatively slow rotation of the generator shaft by the wind.

Wind generators are generally active 75–80 per cent of the time, with generation being initiated at wind speeds of 3–4 metres per second (m/s). At this speed, however, only a few kilowatts are produced. At the other extreme, wind turbines generally employ an automatic shutdown feature used to prevent damage during storms. Between these two operational boundaries, rated power is obtained at speeds around 15–25 m/s based on performance specifications. Rated power for today's commercial wind turbines ranges in capacity from 400 kW to 4 MW, making them a viable alternative when grouped together in wind farm fashion (BWEA 2005).

Another interesting aspect of wind farm generation is its ability to be located offshore. Wind farm opponents have typically cited the large amount of land needed for construction of commercially viable wind farms as a major concern. Now, however, wind farms are being located offshore to reduce their land-intensive characteristics. Large-scale offshore wind farms are currently proposed or operating in Nantuckett Sound in the USA and offshore of Copenhagen in Denmark.

Solar power

Much of the energy we consume is from secondary sources created by the sun. Oil and coal are simply the metamorphosed remains of prehistoric plants and animals that absorbed sunlight to survive. It is logical, then, to pursue technology that directly harnesses the power of the sun. In fact, the sun is so powerful that if we could convert the energy falling over 1 per cent of the Sahara Desert – about 90 650 square kilometres – to electricity, it would be enough to meet the entire world's current energy requirements (Quaschning & Muriel 2001).

Solar energy is harnessed using two different methods. Solar thermal power uses the sun's energy to heat a coolant that is used to run a steam turbine-generator operating on the Rankine cycle. Large mirrors are employed to focus the sun's rays on a small tube at the focal point of the mirror. That tube carries water or a special water–oil mixture that reaches temperatures upwards of 400 °C.

Photovoltaic cells can also be used to harness the sun's energy. These devices make use of the fact that some semiconductor materials release electrons when struck by sunlight, the most commonly used material being silicon.

A solar cell consists of two layers of specially treated silicon that lie in direct contact, one of which is infused with boron, the other with phosphorus. The former is dubbed the 'p-type semiconductor' and the latter the 'n-type semi-conductor' because they tend to have positive and negative charges respectively. Boron bonds with silicon in such a way that it contains an electron that is easy to free by adding energy. Phosphorus, on the other hand, bonds with silicon in such a way that it is missing an electron and can easily accept one into its molecular structure. In particular, when high-energy incoming light from the sun strikes the cell, it raises the energy level of the electrons present in the silicon-dopant molecules (impurities added to a semiconductor to alter its electrical and optical properties) causing some of them to become freed. In photovoltaics this results in a free electron and a 'hole', or place where an electron can be accepted. Figure A1.7 shows the stages of this process.

Figure A1.7: Electrons and current flow in solar cells

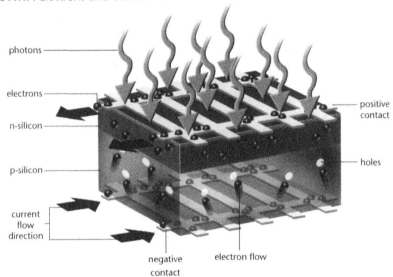

Source: Parry-Hill et al. n.d.

After being freed, these electrons migrate from the n-type terminal to the p-type terminal through an electric circuit. Meanwhile, the 'holes' migrate to the p-type terminal to be reunited with the electrons. Present at the p-type terminal are molecules that, because of the infusion of atoms of phosphorus, lack an electron and have a net positive charge. Along the way they can be used to power an electric device.

References and further reading

BWEA (British Wind Energy Association) (2005) *BWEA briefing sheet wind turbine technology.* Accessed 5 October 2006, http://www.bwea.com/pdf/briefings/technology05_small.pdf

California Energy Commission (2006) What is electricity? In *The energy story.* Accessed 31 August 2006, http://www.energyquest.ca/gov/story/chapter02.html

Encyclopaedia Britannica (n.d.) Synchronous generator. In *Encyclopaedia Britannica Online.* Accessed 7 September 2006, http://www.britannica.com/eb/art-1393/Elementary-synchronous-generator?articleTypeId=1

Eskom (2006) *How electricity is made.* Accessed 5 September 2006, http://www.eskom.co.za/live/content.php?Category_ID=96

Johnson GL (1985) *Wind energy systems.* Englewood Cliffs, NJ: Prentice-Hall

Kiameh P (2003) *Power generation handbook: Selection, applications, operation, and maintenance.* New York: McGraw-Hill

Milora SL & Tester JW (1976) *Geothermal energy as a source of electric power: Thermodynamic and economic design criteria.* Cambridge, MA: The MIT Press

Moran MJ & Shapiro HN (2004) *Fundamentals of engineering thermodynamics.* Fifth edition. UK: John Wiley and Sons

Parry-Hill MJ, Sutter RT & Davidson MW (n.d.) Solar cell operation. In *Optical microscopy primer: Physics of light and color.* Accessed 31 August 2006, http://micro.magnet.fsu.edu/primer/java/solarcell/javasolarcellfigure1.jpg

Power Stream (2007) *Country voltages and plug styles.* Accessed 1 August 2006, http://www.powerstream.com/cv.htm

Quaschning V & Muriel MB (2001) *Solar power – photovoltaics or solar thermal power plants?* Accessed 8 March 2008, http://www.volker-quaschning.de/downloads/VGB2001.pdf

Schnapp R (n.d.) *Electric power industry overview.* Accessed 10 August 2006, http://www.eia.doe.gov/cneaf/electricity/page/prim2/toc2.html

Schott North America (n.d.) *Solar thermal receiver.* Accessed 15 August 2006, http://www.schott.com/solar/images/solarthermal_receiver_270.jpg

Siemens Corp (n.d.) AC generator operation. In *basics of motor control centers.* Accessed 31 August 2006, www.sea.siemens.com/step/templates/lesson.mason?mcc:2:1:1

SPG Media Limited (2007) Combined-Cycle Gas Turbine (CCGT). In *Power-technology.com.* Accessed 8 September 2006, http://www.power-technology.com/projects/san_joaquin/san_joaquin3.html

Stats SA (Statistics South Africa) (2006a) *Electricity generated and available for distribution (preliminary).* Accessed 11 October 2006, http://www.statssa.gov.za/Publications/P4141/P4141July2006.pdf

Stats SA (2006b) *Mid-year population estimates, South Africa 2006 (preliminary).* Accessed 11 October 2006, http://www.statssa.gov.za/publications/P0302/P03022006.pdf

Tennessee Valley Authority (n.d.) Pumped-storage plant. In *Hydroelectric power.* Accessed 15 August 2006, http://www.tva.gov/power/pumpstorart.htm

USA DoE (Department of Energy, USA) (2004) *South Africa: Energy and environmental issues.* Accessed 11 October 2006, http://www.eia.doe.gov/cabs/safrenv.html

Vawter R (2005) Resistivity: Intrinsic resistance. In *Physics to the net power.* Accessed 7 August 2006, www.ac.wwu.edu/~vawter/PhysicsNet/Topics/DC-Current/IntrinsicResist.html

Weisman J & Eckart LE (1985) *Modern power plant engineering.* Englewood Cliffs, NJ: Prentice-Hall

Woodruff EB, Lammers HB & Lammers TF (2005) *Steam plant operation.* Eighth edition. New York: McGraw-Hill

World Nuclear Association (2005) *The nuclear fuel cycle.* Accessed 20 August 2006, http://www.world-nuclear.org/info/inf03.htm

Absolute and relative electricity profiles

The purpose of this appendix is to provide readers with a visual overview of electricity production and consumption in Africa and around the world, allowing for comparisons between individual countries and regions, as well as placing Africa in a global perspective. The maps that follow are available (along with all the chapters from this book) for free download, in colour and with a set of relevant statistical data, from http://www.hsrcpress.ac.za/product.php?productid=2243 &cat=0&page=1&featured. The statistics do not provide a comprehensive database but do provide a general sense of absolute and relative electricity profiles.

Mapping electricity use and production

The followings maps are scalar representations of electricity production and consumption around the world, using equal-area cartograms, otherwise known as density-equalising maps. The cartogram resizes each territory according to the variable being mapped (e.g. production of nuclear power).

To make it easier to see what a cartogram is showing, the general shapes of individual territories have been preserved and kept adjacent to other territories and seas. If a particular country is larger on one map than on another, it follows that it has a higher proportion of the world total of the variable being assessed. Data are drawn from sources ranging from 2002 to 2006 and are intended to be indicative rather than exact.

What is perhaps most remarkable about these maps is the size of South Africa relative to other parts of the continent in terms of its production and consumption capacity. Another notable feature is how small Africa is as a whole compared to other parts of the world. In this respect, Africa truly is the 'dark continent', having the lowest per capita electricity usage of any region of the world – a fact amply illustrated by night-time satellite images of the continent.

These cartograms and the methods used to develop them are the copyright (© 2006) of the SASI Group (University of Sheffield) and Mark Newman (University of Michigan) who have kindly provided permission to reproduce them. These and other maps can also be viewed on their website at www.worldmapper.org.

Figure A2.1: Access to electricity

The relative proportion of people in each country with some form of direct electricity access, including that sourced from a power grid as well as self-generated electricity (from solar, wind or hydro-electric sources). The map shows access, not the quantities of electricity used.

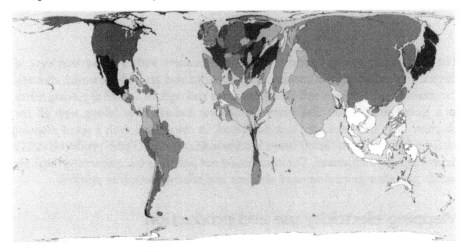

Source: SASI Group & Newman 2006

Figure A2.2: Electricity production (all types)

A proportional representation of all forms of electricity produced, by country.

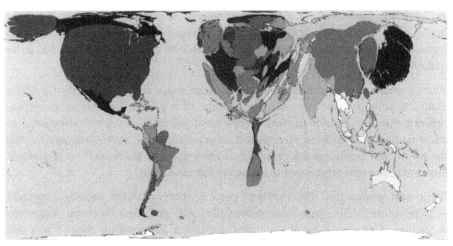

Source: SASI Group & Newman 2006

Figure A2.3: Electricity production (hydro)

A proportional representation of hydro-electricity produced, by country.

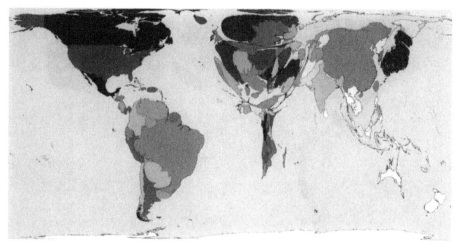

Source: SASI Group & Newman 2006

Figure A2.4: Electricity production (oil)

A proportional representation of electricity produced by oil, by country.

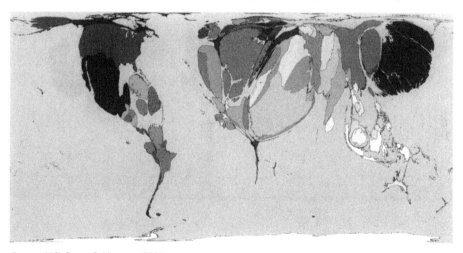

Source: SASI Group & Newman 2006

Figure A2.5: Electricity production (gas)

A proportional representation of electricity produced by natural gas, by country.

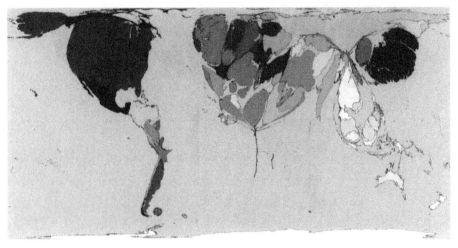

Source: SASI Group & Newman 2006

Figure A2.6: Electricity production (coal)

A proportional representation of electricity produced by coal, by country.

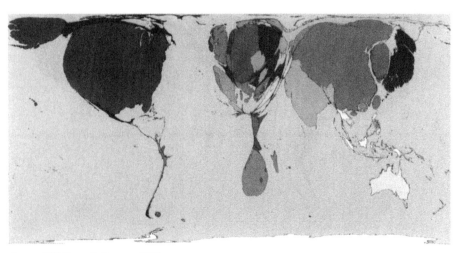

Source: SASI Group & Newman 2006

Figure A2.7: Electricity production (nuclear)

A proportional representation of electricity produced by nuclear power plants, by country.

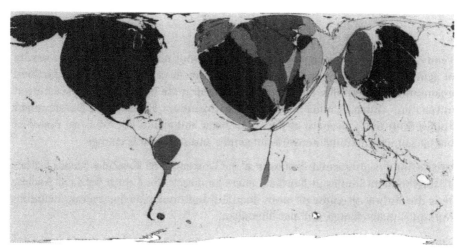

Source: SASI Group & Newman 2006

References

CIA (Central Intelligence Agency, USA) (2007) *World fact book 2007*. Accessed 17 May 2007, http://www.cia.gov/cia/publications/factbook/

International Energy Agency (n.d.) *Statistical database. Electricity/heat*. Accessed 17 May 2007, http://www.iea.org/textbase/stats/prodresult.asp?PRODUCT=Electricity/Heat

NASA (National Aeronautics and Space Administration) (n.d.) *Visible Earth*. Accessed 7 November 2007, http://visibleearth.nasa.gov/view_rec.php?id=13874

SAPP (Southern African Power Pool) (2006) SAPP *annual review 2005–06*. Accessed 17 May 2007, http://www.sapp.co.zw/documents/STATISTICS%202005.pdf

SASI Group & Newman M (2006) *www.worldmapper.org*. Accessed 15 September 2007, http://www.worldmapper.org/textindex/text_fuel.html

UN (United Nations) (n.d.) *Common database*. UN Statistics Division. Accessed 17 May 2007, http://unstats.un.org/unsd/cdb

US EIA (USA Department of Energy, Energy Information Administration) (2005) *International energy annual 2005*. Washington DC: USA EIA

US EIA (2006) *International energy annual 2006*. Washington DC: USA EIA

US EIA (2007) *Electricity prices for households*. Posted 7 June 2007. Accessed 15 December 2007, http://www.eia.doe.gov/emeu/international/elecprih.html

Notes on contributors

Wendy Annecke is an independent researcher who inadvertently started working in gender and energy studies as an activist in a women's anti-apartheid organisation in the 1980s. She has been involved in the field ever since, teaching at universities. Annecke holds a doctorate in Economic History and Development Studies from the University of KwaZulu-Natal and chairs the Advisory Board of Energia, an international network on gender and sustainable energy.

Patrick Bond is a Research Professor at the University of KwaZulu-Natal's School of Development Studies in Durban, where he directs the Centre for Civil Society. He is the author or editor of more than a dozen books on the region, including work on climate change and neo-liberalism.

Derek Brine is completing a dual Master's degree in City Planning and in Civil Engineering at the Massachusetts Institute of Technology, where he is looking at appropriate technology for international development. He has worked on development projects in Kenya, Guyana and China.

Jackie Dugard is a human rights activist and senior researcher at the Centre for Applied Legal Studies (CALS) at the University of the Witwatersrand in Johannesburg, where she works on socio-economic rights with a focus on basic services and access to justice for the poor. Prior to joining CALS, Dugard worked in the Political Affairs Division of the Commonwealth Secretariat in London. She has a PhD in Social and Political Sciences from the University of Cambridge and an LLM in International Human Rights Law from the University of Essex.

Graham Erion is a climate change activist and researcher who works on climate issues around the world. He has a Master's degree in Environmental Studies, and a law degree, from York University in Toronto. In 2005 he conducted the first-ever survey of South Africa's carbon market and works closely with the Durban Group for Climate Justice.

David Fig is a Research Fellow at Southern Africa Resource Watch, Johannesburg, where he monitors extractive industries and climate impacts across the sub-region. He has written extensively on energy, biodiversity, trade, corporate behaviour and the responses of social movements, and has been an environmental justice activist for the past 25 years.

Leonard Gentle is Director of the International Labour Research and Information Group, a South African NGO which provides popular education resources and information on international political economy issues to the trade unions and social movements. He has been an organiser for the South African Commercial Catering and Allied Workers Union as well as for the National Union of Metalworkers of South Africa.

Rebecca Ghanadan is a PhD candidate in the Energy and Resources Group at the University of California, Berkeley, where she is completing her dissertation on the social and political changes emerging in service provision with electricity reforms in Tanzania.

Christopher Gore is an Assistant Professor in the Department of Politics and Public Administration, Ryerson University, Toronto, Canada.

Stephen Greenberg is currently Research Manager at Khanya-African Institute for Community Driven Development. He has written on electricity sector restructuring in South Africa since 2002 and also has an interest in land reform and agricultural restructuring.

Terri Hathaway has been with the International Rivers' Africa programme since 2004, and has visited and worked with dam-affected communities and civil-society groups across Africa. She holds a Masters in Public Administration from the University of Washington and now lives in Cameroon.

Liz McDaid is a scientist and educator with more than 20 years of research and activist experience on environmental justice issues in South Africa. She is a member of The Green Connection.

David A McDonald is Director and Associate Professor in the Department of Global Development Studies at Queen's University in Canada. He is also Co-Director of the Municipal Services Project.

Prishani Naidoo and **Ahmed Veriava** are researchers and activists living and working in Johannesburg. They work in a collective called Research & Education in Development.

Lori Pottinger is the Africa Program Director for International Rivers in Berkeley, California. She has worked on African energy issues for over a decade.

Greg Ruiters is the Director of the Institute of Social and Economic Research's Matthew Goniwe Chair of Development and Society at Rhodes University in South Africa. He is also Co-Director of the Municipal Services Project.

Peter van Heusden is a community activist and researcher based in Cape Town.

Richard Worthington is Coordinator of the Sustainable Energy and Climate Change Project of Earthlife Africa, Johannesburg. He also represents the South African NGO Coalition and the SA Climate Action Network on energy planning and climate policy processes.

Index

For Product Safety Concerns and Information please contact our EU
representative GPSR@taylorandfrancis.com Taylor & Francis Verlag GmbH,
Kaufingerstraße 24, 80331 München, Germany

Printed and bound by CPI Group (UK) Ltd, Croydon, CR0 4YY

08/05/2025
01864520-0001